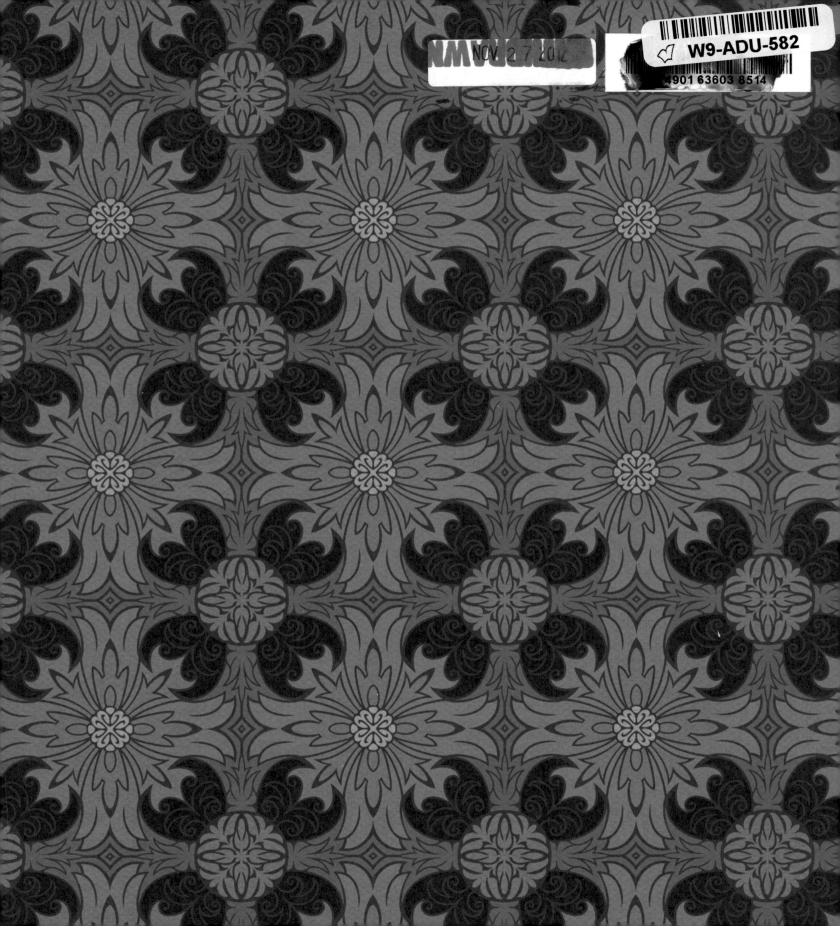

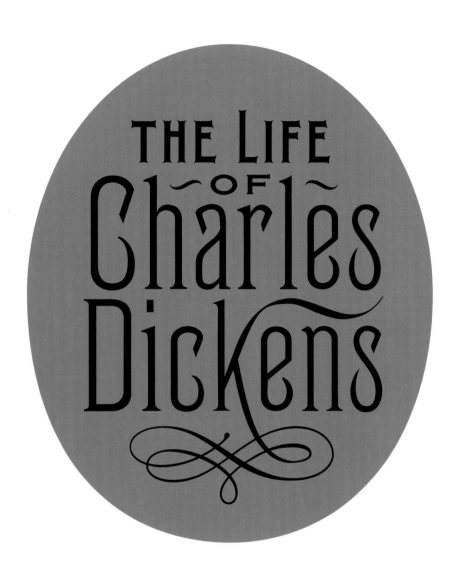

THE LIFE
~OF~
Charles
Dickens

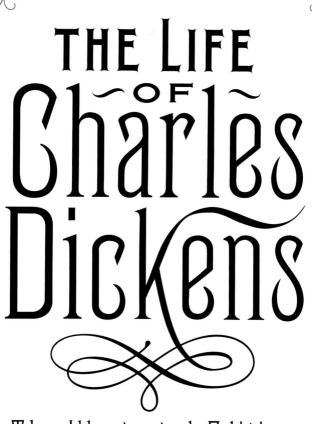

THE LIFE
~ OF ~
Charles Dickens

The Illustrated Edition

John Forster

Holly Furneaux, PhD
GENERAL EDITOR

WITH A FOREWORD BY
Jane Smiley

Sterling Signature
NEW YORK

Sterling Signature
NEW YORK

An Imprint of Sterling Publishing
387 Park Avenue South
New York, NY 10016

This is an abridged version of the original *The Life of Charles Dickens* by John Forster.
We have added images throughout to complement the text.

Cover design by Roberto de Vicq de Cumptich (roberto@devicq.com)
Jacket image: Charles Dickens and His Creations (detail), Mary Evans Picture Library
Interior design by Oxygen Design/Sherry Williams and Igor Satanovsky
Photo research by Susan Oyama and Edward C. Goodman
Special thanks to The Charles Dickens Museum, London, Dr. Florian Schweizer, Director, and Fiona Jenkins,
Curator, and to Researchers Rebecca Dobson, Philip Risley, and Tom Rodger, and Photographer Steven Rendon
for their invaluable assistance in providing images for this book.
Additional text research by Edward C. Goodman

ISBN 978-1-4027-7285-6

Library of Congress Cataloging-in-Publication Data Available

Distributed in Canada by Sterling Publishing
c/o Canadian Manda Group, 165 Dufferin Street
Toronto, Ontario, Canada M6K 3H6
Distributed in the United Kingdom by GMC Distribution Services
Castle Place, 166 High Street, Lewes, East Sussex, England BN7 1XU
Distributed in Australia by Capricorn Link (Australia) Pty. Ltd.
P.O. Box 704, Windsor, NSW 2756, Australia

For information about custom editions, special sales, premium and corporate purchases, please contact
Sterling Special Sales Department at 800-805-5489 or specialsales@sterlingpublishing.com.

Printed in China

2 4 6 8 10 9 7 5 3 1

www.sterlingpublishing.com

TO THE DAUGHTERS OF CHARLES DICKENS,
MY GOD-DAUGHTER MARY
and HER SISTER KATE,
THIS BOOK IS DEDICATED BY THEIR FRIEND,
AND THEIR FATHER'S FRIEND AND EXECUTOR,

JOHN FORSTER

John Forster and Charles Dickens, sketch by Richard Doyle, 1840

Contents

Volume II

he was abroad, he loved exploring (he went with a party of eleven, including his wife, Kate, and his sister-in-law Georgina, on mules, to the Convent of St. Bernard, ". . .the highest inhabited spot but one in the world" (p. 230) and he also loved rushing back to England for a few weeks. When he could not, for whatever reason, engage in his daily exercise, he endured a restless inability to concentrate on his writing. He prowled around London almost every night. One man later recalled seeing him "in the oddest places and most inclement weather, in Ratcliffe-highway, on Haverstock-hill, on Camberwell-green, in Gray's-inn-lane, in the Wandsworth-road, at Hammersmith Broadway, in Norton Folgate, and at Kensal New town." (p. 474) Dickens walked for hours, and kept his eyes and ears open the whole time. Even as he was getting older, and his worsening circulation problems were causing him intense pain in his left leg and foot, he got out of the house—on June 6th, 1870, after several years of ill-health, he walked four miles from his house at Gadshill into Rochester to mail some letters. On June 8th, he suffered a stroke. On June 9th, he died.

Dickens was a prickly man of sharp emotions, which occasionally proved painful to his relatives and friends. He was cruel to his wife, who gave him nine children and was continuously forced to deal with his insistence upon her accompanying him on many of his travels (including his first lengthy trip to the United States, when they left the children, one of whom was less than a year old). She was also never allowed to forget that the great love of his life was her sister Mary, who lived with the Dickenses for a while after they were first married and then died suddenly, and that the woman he came to depend upon most was another of her sisters, Georgina. When he finally left Kate in 1858, he reviled and humiliated her, both in front of his children and publically. Not a few of his friends got fed up with him, and he got fed up with not a few of them. But Forster is clear about his allure—he was uniquely charismatic, both to readers and to listeners. Even while we are being invited to judge him, he is drawing us in with his sense of fun, his energy, his inimitable style, his unprecedented inventiveness. Over the years, critics, too, have grumbled, as they did in his own day.

They have found him too sentimental, too coarse, too disorganized, too unsubtle. His female characters are flat; the moral of the story is too obvious—objections to Dickens's artfulness abound. And yet, just to take a few small examples, is there anywhere else in literature a character like Bradley Headstone, in *Our Mutual Friend*, whose obsessive jealousy and prickly self-consciousness are as painful to himself as they are to the reader? Or one like Edith Dombey, in *Dombey and Son*, who so hates her role in society that she eventually destroys herself and those around her without really losing the reader's sympathy? On the open-hearted side, we have David Copperfield's aunt, Betsey Trotwood, who is full of sharp opinions, but just can't help being generous and forgiving. Dickens enters into their minds in an uncanny way, forestalling his own judgements, and ours.

Many artists painted and drew Dickens in his lifetime. His two rivals for English literary fame, William Shakespeare and Jane Austen, are each in his or her own way shadowy. Not so Dickens. He was painted and engraved and photographed—we know what he looks like, except that we don't, really, because in his pictures, he never smiles. Forster attests to his playfulness and good humor, but a special moment in the present volume, not by Forster, comes in a sidebar by Malcolm Andrews, who employs eyewitness accounts to demonstrate why Dickens was such a sensation as a reader of his own work. After describing Dickens's acting skills, the way he not only voices every part, but also acts out facial expressions and characteristic actions and gestures, he writes, "But on some occasions, usually when he says something that makes the audience laugh heartily—he lets down the curtain from his face and smiles. And the smile turns to laughter as he laughs along with his audience. At those moments we come closest to him. The smile is quite wonderful; quick, curious, and beautiful. That smile is the secret of the man's whole nature." (p. 389) Surely this is true. What we love in Dickens is the playfulness (sometimes gay, sometimes somber) that overwhelms both us and himself. When we are reading his stories and novels, we are intently engaged with him in a profound form of play where anything can happen and amazing and affecting things very often do—one of my favorites is, again, in *Our Mutual Friend* (my favorite of his novels), when the failed gold-digger, Mr. Lammle (whose beard sparkles in the sunlight) administers a beating to the real villain, Fascination Fledgeby.

The novel is unique in the way that it gives us access to the inner life. It is the most subjective of art forms—even when the novelist appears to be describing places and people in a very objective, "I-am-a-camera" manner, he is revealing himself, word by word, sentence by sentence. The paradox of loving novels is that we believe both sides of the equation, both that we are seeing things through the novelist's sensibility and that what we are seeing is true. Perhaps generations of readers have loved Dickens because his style, which he himself called "inimitable," and his fascination with the world around him were both so extreme that he could not even aspire to an objective tone, but instead had to be swept away in his storytelling, and also swept away in his daily activities. On Dickens's 200th birthday, John Forster reminds us in this neatly done (and nicely supplemented) abridgement, that there has, indeed, been no one else like him, either on the page or walking down the street.

—Jane Smiley
CALIFORNIA, 2010

John Forster and Charles Dickens: A Literary Friendship

JOHN FORSTER, BORN IN APRIL 1812, was a couple of months younger than the man who became his great friend and the subject of his most famous work, Charles Dickens. Like Dickens, he came from relatively humble origins (Forster's father was a butcher in their hometown of Newcastle on Tyne), yet became prominent in London literary circles in the 1830s. Having distinguished himself at Newcastle's Royal Grammar School—a kindly uncle paid the fees—Forster enrolled at the University of Cambridge, but left after a month to pursue a law degree at the University of London. As Forster's biographer James Davis notes, Forster spent much of his time during his degree writing journalism, with his class setting up the *London University Magazine*. By the age of twenty he was drama critic for *The True Sun*, and became "Theatrical Examiner" for *The Examiner*, another key radical newspaper. Throughout his career he was to distinguish himself as a biographer; his publications included an acclaimed *Life and Adventures of Oliver Goldsmith*, 1848, the *Life of Landor*, 1868, and biographical essays on numerous figures including John Dryden and Daniel Defoe. He was also to draw upon his legal training to offer advice to his many author friends, as writing became increasingly professionalised, involving complex contracts with publishers and printers.[1] He is best remembered, though, as Dickens's first biographer.

The two men first met in May 1837, having each been eager to meet on the strength of one another's reputation as an author. Michael Slater, in his magisterial biography of Dickens, describes their almost immediate personal and professional intimacy in this way:

> Very quickly Forster became Dickens's trusted guide and adviser with regard to all aspects of his career. From the summer of this year onwards Forster records, "there was nothing written by him which I did not see before the world did, either in manuscript or proofs." Dickens relied on him implicitly as a proof corrector, for example, and was even happy for him to make minor textual alterations. Above all, Dickens was grateful for Forster's championship in his continued troubles with publishers. [2]

Writing his *Life of Dickens* over thirty years later, in the period immediately after Dickens's death in 1870, Forster offers the final proof of this absolute trust. He quotes Dickens's letters to him that commission him as his chosen biographer:

> 22nd April, 1848. "I desire no better for my fame, when my personal dustiness shall be past the control of my love of order, than such a biographer and such a critic." "You know me better," he wrote, resuming the same subject on the 6th of July, 1862, "than any other man does, or ever will" (v. 1, ch. 1).

Dickens's family shared this sentiment. As Dickens's sister-in-law Mary Hogarth put it, Forster was "the only person . . . who has the material—the knowledge and the power to write his Life."[3]

Indeed, Dickens had entrusted Forster with details of his childhood that came as a revelation to the author's adoring public when published in November 1871 in the first volume of the *Life*. David Copperfield's early experiences, as the inverted initials had hinted, were based on those of Charles Dickens; this eminently successful and wealthy author had been an impoverished factory child employed at a warehouse near the Thames to paste labels on bottles of boot blacking, and his father had been imprisoned for debt. Dickens presents his life as a "poor little drudge" as a secret shared only with Forster: "I have never, until I now impart it to this paper, in any burst of confidence with any one, my own wife not excepted, raised the curtain" on these scenes (v. 1, ch. 2). The public astonishment is summarized in this review: "Never perhaps has a fragment of biography wakened more interest and amazement than the first chapters of Mr Forster's biography."

LEFT: John Forster in his library by Edward Matthew Ward (detail), oil on canvas

(Robert Buchanan, February 1872, *St Paul's Magazine*).

Though this information scandalized some of Forster's readers—the depiction of Dickens's relationship to his parents and his use of his mother as a partial model for the hilarious Mrs. Nickleby and his father as a pattern for the memorable *Copperfield* character of Mr. Wilkins Micawber provoked particular criticism—Forster kept back other incendiary material about Dickens's relationships with his wife and mistress. A rags-to-riches narrative that presented Dickens as an entirely self-made man was in keeping with the Victorian ethos of "self-help," as Samuel Smiles famously called it in his 1859 book of short exemplary biographies. Though this revelation of childhood detail might seem indelicate, in demonstrating Dickens's remarkable energy and ability for self-fashioning it was not inconsistent with Forster's lifelong commitment to raising the dignity of the literary profession, a concern that he battled with throughout his career as a biographer. Dickens's separation from his wife Catherine, however, and his relationship with the young actress Ellen Ternan, were scandals that Forster endeavoured to, respectively, downplay and suppress.

In the *Life,* Forster largely avoids what he calls the "domesticities" of Dickens's deteriorating relationship with his wife, and his insistence in 1858 on a separation from her. Slater offers a sensitive account of Forster's difficult position here. He had a sincere friendship for Catherine, and as a bachelor until 1856, had been warmly welcomed as part of the Dickens family. Before his marriage to Eliza Colburn, another woman who remains unmentioned in the biography despite her acquaintance with Dickens, Forster wrote to Catherine, "I have never felt so strongly as within the last few months how much of the happiness of past years I owe to you." Yet "when he came to write the biography that his friend had virtually commissioned [. . .], felt himself constrained to present Dickens's narrative about ending his marriage without any 'balancing' comment from himself." [4] At his most critical, Forster does describe this phase of the biography as illustrative of "grave defects in Dickens's character" (v. 3, ch. 7). Though he treats this period as briefly as possible, this event does have a major impact upon the shape of the *Life,* as Forster's affectionate support for Catherine and his ineffective effort to prevent Dickens from rather cruelly publishing an angry announcement of his domestic reorganization were major factors in the cooling of their intimacy during the final decade of Dickens's career. In the final volume of the biography, then, Forster is much more reliant on Dickens's letters to his sister-in-law, daughters and other correspondents, rather than drawing on, as he had almost exclusively in the earlier volumes, Dickens's personal correspondence to him. Forster's reticence about Dickens's life with Catherine extends to their children, who are strangely shadowy presences in the biography. As J. W. T. Ley puts it in the only scholarly edition of the *Life,* published in 1928:

> Forster never once gives us an intimate domestic picture—never once shows us this man who wrote so glowingly of home felicity in his own home circle [. . .] We hear nothing of Mrs. Dickens beyond bare references, which are sometimes almost of a patronising character; and all that we are told about the children is facts—just facts.[5]

In his third volume, Forster avoids mention of perhaps the most important relationship of that part of Dickens's life, only naming Ellen Ternan in his reproduction of Dickens's will in the volume's appendices. Here, significantly, Ellen appears as the first named beneficiary. Dickens met the eighteen-year-old Ellen, or Nelly as he called her, in July 1857, having recruited her—together with her actress mother and sister—to perform with his amateur dramatic company. In Claire Tomalin's account of their romantic relationship of nearly thirteen years' duration she discusses the extraordinary concealment of this part of Dickens's life, pointing to the long legacy of Forster's exclusion and evasion: "Many Dickensians, from Forster on, have been determined to maintain the version of Dickens they regard as acceptable, even—as in Forster's case—when they know it to be untrue."[6] Forster similarly avoids detailing Dickens's early passion for his first, unrequited, love Maria Beadnell. She appears in the *Life* as one inspiration for Dora (v. 1, ch. 3), although later commentators have noted that Dickens's re-introduction to her in middle-age also provided a pattern for the voluble Flora Finching of *Little Dorrit.* He is diplomatically silent also about Dickens's intense relationship with Madame de la Rue, who Dickens hypnotised repeatedly while in Italy in an effort to cure her of a neurasthenic condition, causing Catherine understandable distress. Forster has long been accused of making overly light of Dickens's other male intimacies too. In his edition of the *Life*, Ley influentially stated that "Forster's love for the novelist was a jealous love."[7] This assessment, though I think unjust, has tended to stick, with various commentators criticizing Forster for diminishing the importance of Dickens's friendships with other—particularly younger—men, such as Wilkie Collins.

Selective in delineating Dickens's personal attachments, Forster focuses on his friend's literary life. As Dickens's informal literary agent, proof-reader, and critic (both in the feedback he gave Dickens and in the notices of his work he wrote for *The Examiner*) Forster was well placed to capture the, often intense, pressures of Dickens's professional life. He depicts in detail the challenges of publishing fiction in installments, working as editor and (in the case of *Master Humphrey's Clock*, sole) contributor, Dickens's interactions with his illustrators, and the demands of concurrent writing projects. Dickens, ever resourceful—as Forster notes he has only one professional failure across his entire career with *The Daily News*—soon finds ways to make the competing demands of his projects work to his advantage. He interleaves, for example, his tragic and comic writing to leave sufficient energy for each, as in the writing of the hilarities of Mr. Crummles and his theatrical family for *Nicholas Nickleby* alongside the grim world of Fagin's London and the vicious murder of Nancy for *Oliver Twist*. [8] Forster's attention to Dickens's writing in all these genres also offers a detailed picture of his efforts at social reform, apparent in his personal correspondence and journalism as well as his fiction. The *Life* shows Dickens campaigning on topics as varied as the abolition of public executions, the establishment of dedicated children's hospitals, and the state provision of quality education.

His punishing schedule reflects Dickens's persistent anxiety about money in his determination to establish himself beyond any risk of repeating his father's shameful financial ill-fortunes. What often feel like Dickens's super-human professional energies are also, and more urgently, fuelled by his need for a strong personal relationship with his public. In speeches, prefaces to his novels and periodicals, and in his journalism, Dickens constantly exhorts his audience to feel themselves to be personal friends. He aspired through a career of nearly forty years "to live," as he put it in the manifesto to *Household Words*, "in the Household affections, and to be numbered among the Household thoughts, of our readers. We hope to be the comrade and friend of many thousands of people, of both sexes, and of all ages and conditions, on whose faces we may never look" (March 30, 1850). In his other career as a hugely successful public reader of his own work, Dickens did look upon the faces of his fans, thriving on this close physical contact and the repeated confirmation of their affection for him. Forster gives an intimate insight into these mixed motivations, which finally led Dickens to work himself to death. He captures Dickens's relentless "work hard/ play hard" mentality, describing his friend's energetic approach to "leisure," involving, for example, elaborate family sports days and amateur theatrical performances. There are only moments of respite from responsibility, such as when he and Forster, having extended their holiday with friends for longer than planned, had to pawn their gold watches in Birmingham (v. 1, ch. 13).

As well as his privileged insight into Dickens as artist, the *Life* uniquely documents Forster's relationship with his "subject." Both noted for their capacity for friendship— a reputation which Forster maintained despite his sometimes off-putting brusque manner—I find this *Life* a moving testament to the emotional attachment and expressiveness possible for men in the nineteenth century. Forster's method of including Dickens's letters to "give also to the memoir what was attainable of the value of Autobiography" (v. 3, ch. 18), provides a reciprocal account of the friendship, expressed in their distinct voices. Far from the popular stereotype of the dry-eyed, unbending Victorian paterfamilias, Dickens and Forster are eloquent about the importance of their connection, and are emotionally expressive. They are surprisingly articulate at moments of loss, each providing a primary source of solace to the other in bereavement. This was the initial context for their friendship, which began when Forster visited Dickens at Hampstead, where he was struggling with the sudden death of his sister-in-law, Mary Hogarth: "More than ordinarily susceptible at the moment to all kindliest impressions, his heart opened itself to mine" (v. 1, ch. 6). We see the reverse process at a moment when Forster allows himself unusual prominence in the text. He introduces the year 1845 as follows: "It was of ill-omen to me, one of its earliest incidents being my only brother's death; but Dickens had a friend's true helpfulness in sorrow." Forster goes on to excerpt a remarkable letter in which Dickens consoles his friend with this assurance: "you have a Brother left. One bound to you by ties as strong as ever Nature forged" (v. 2, ch. 8). [9]

Forster proudly describes this as "a friendship which lasted without the interruption of a day for more than three and thirty years." Though he is looking back over this length of time Forster insists on his vivid recall of his first meeting with Dickens and of later, emotionally intense, moments of reunion: "I well remember noticing [. . .] a young man of my own age, whose keen animation of look would have arrested attention anywhere, and whose name, upon inquiry, I then for the first time heard" (v. 1, ch. 4). In a particularly moving section Forster recalls their shared eagerness to see one another again after Dickens has been away (for some months) in Italy. As he travels home Dickens writes (and Forster transcribes): "In the meantime I shall not write to you again . . . to enhance the pleasure (if anything *can* enhance the pleasure) of our meeting . . . I am opening my arms so wide!" Forster records a powerful flashback of Dickens's arrival:

I have but to write the words to bring back the eager face and figure, as they flashed upon me so suddenly this wintry Saturday night that almost before I could be conscious of his presence I felt the grasp of his hand. It is almost all I find it possible to remember of the brief, bright, meeting. Hardly did he seem to have come when he was gone (v. 2, ch. 8).

The emotional richness of this account contradicts a long-popular image of the Victorian biography as, in its emphasis on propriety, drained of life and passion. Virginia Woolf famously critiqued the genre of Victorian life writing for presenting great men "like the wax-figures now preserved in Westminster Abbey . . . effigies that have only a smooth superficial likeness to the body in the coffin." [10] However, while Forster is guilty of the charge of whitewashing, a major cause of modernist

distain, in his vibrant account of his relationship with Dickens, capturing Dickens's vital energy and physical presence, we can hardly accuse him of producing a wax-work.

In his book-length account of *John Forster and His Friendships*, Richard Renton describes Forster's almost "mesmeric" powers in forming attachments, calling his relationship with Dickens "the ideal friendship." [11] Their attachment was sometimes, however, less than ideal; it was strained, particularly, as noted above, by Dickens's treatment of Catherine, and by his insistence on pursuing a lucrative career in later life as public reader of his own works. Forster counseled against this, fearing for his friend's already delicate health and for the potential undermining of the dignity of literature through such showmanship, but was, again, ignored. Despite the severity of these differences in opinion between the two men in the period post 1858, the strength of the underlying relationship persisted. In his will Dickens gave testament to this in the description, "my dear and trusty friend John Forster", and in the appointment of Forster (the only non-family member other than Ellen Ternan, to appear in the will), together with Georgina Hogarth, as executor and guardian to Dickens's children. In this document, Dickens's legacy of their friendship overwrites the tensions within it, which were sometimes expressed in his less-than-complimentary references to Forster in his correspondence to others—his unsympathetic treatment of Forster's illnesses, for example—and in his incarnation of the most censuring aspects of his friend in the distinctly unappealing character of Podsnap in *Our Mutual Friend* (1865). [12] Podsnap, in his overbearing obsession with respectability and a decorum that will avoid bringing a "blush into the cheek of a young person" (*Our Mutual Friend*, chapter 11), can be seen to reflect the characteristics that Dickens was most frustrated by in his friend at this period. Dickens's will, however, anticipates Forster's *Life* in ironing out more ambivalent feeling in favor of an account of ideal friendship.

Forster's emphasis on their relationship led hostile early reviewers to suggest that the book "should not be called the Life of Dickens but the History of Dickens's Relations to Mr Forster" or "The autobiography of John Forster with recollections of Charles Dickens."[13] Dickens's friends and acquaintances tended to be more generous. Many wrote to Forster with additional information, much of which he included in revised editions. [14] Others, such as Dickens's friend and American publisher, James Fields, wrote to thank Forster for the comfort he offered: "the fun and pathos of the book brings his dear presence back to us again with intense vividness." [15] Richard Owen, another friend and colleague of Dickens and Forster, wrote thanking the latter for the similarly physical, almost tactile, sense of Dickens that the biography offered, envisaging the "pleasure for many evenings to come that Mrs. O & I shall have at our fireside, with you & our dear friend, whom you recall to life, completing the circle!" [16] Forster's particular capacity for friendship was marked at his death, six years after that of Dickens. *The Times* obituary remarked on Forster's "real tenderness and sympathy," whilst the inscription on his grave stone fittingly memorialized "the warmth of his affections" and "the lavish services in the midst of his crowded life / He rendered to his friends." [17]

This abridged edition endeavors to make this rich book, too long out of print, accessible to a new generation of Dickens enthusiasts, as we near the 2012 bi-centenary of the author's birth. Forster's text, reduced to a more manageable length but retaining all key moments of the biography and his own distinctive voice, is supplemented by extracts from Dickens's work and from recent criticism, biography and fiction. In presenting Dickens as editor, journalist, correspondent, and travel writer as well as novelist, this edition follows Forster's effort to present Dickens's extraordinary diversity and astonishing work rate which can only be fully recognized through an appreciation of the range of his writerly roles. This edition is generously illustrated with materials including original artwork from the serial parts of the novels, rare photographs and portraits of Dickens and his circle, and specially commissioned images from the Charles Dickens Museum of Dickens's personal possessions and favorite locations.

—Dr. Holly Furneaux
UNIVERSITY OF LEICESTER, 2010

[1] For a detailed account of Forster's career see James Davis, *John Forster: A Literary Life* (Leicester: Leicester University Press, 1983).

[2] Michael Slater, *Charles Dickens* (New Haven and London: Yale University Press, 2009), 102.

[3] *The Letters of Charles Dickens*, ed. by Madeline House and Graham Storey, Pilgrim edition, Volume 1 (Oxford: Clarendon, 1965), xv.

[4] Slater, *Dickens*, 435.

[5] John Forster, *The Life of Charles Dickens*, edited by J. W. T. Ley (London: Cecil Palmer, 1928), introduction, xix.

[6] Claire Tomalin, *The Invisible Woman, The Story of Nelly Ternan and Charles Dickens* (London: Penguin, 1991), 259.

[7] J. W. T. Ley, ed., *The Life*, introduction, pxviii. Philip Allingham, for example, uses the same language to refer to Forster's "jealousy of Dickens's younger friends." Philip Allingham, 'John Forster: Essayist, Historian, and Editor, 1812-1876,' The Victorian Web, http://www.victorianweb.org/authors/dickens/pva/pva35.html

[8] For a brilliant modern account of this see Slater, *Dickens*, 123.

[9] I give a more detailed account of the dynamics of this relationship in "Inscribing Friendship: John Forster's Life of Charles Dickens and the Writing of Male Intimacy in the Victorian Period," *Life Writing* (forthcoming, 2011.)

[10] Virginia Woolf, "The Art of Biography" in *The Death of the Moth* (London: Hogarth Press, 1981), 121.

[11] Richard Renton, *John Forster and His Friendships* (London: Chapman and Hall, 1912), 57, 91.

[12] For a fuller account of what Davies has described as Dickens's "attitude towards Forster of hostile attraction and defensive attack," see Davies, 176–180.

[13] *Saturday Review*, xxxiv (1872), 668; George Ford quoted by Davis, *Forster*, 257.

[14] See William J. Carlton, "Postscripts to Forster," *Dickensian* 58 (1962), 87–92.

[15] James T. Fields, *Biographical Notes and Personal Sketches* (Boston, 1881), 190.

[16] Richard Owen to John Forster, 14 November 1872, Frances Hirtzel Collection. Quoted by Gowan Dawson, "Richard Owen, Comparative Anatomy and the Reading of Dickens's Serial Fiction," paper given at the "Dickens and Science" Dickens Day conference, Institute of English Studies, London, 10 October 2009.

[17] Quoted in Davis, *Forster,* 260.

VOLUME I: 1812~1842

LEFT: Charles Dickens, oil on canvas by Daniel Maclise (detail), 1839

CHAPTER 1

CHILDHOOD

1812~1822

CHARLES DICKENS, THE MOST POPULAR NOVELIST of the century, and one of the greatest humorists that England has produced, was born at Landport in Portsea on Friday, the 7th of February, 1812.

His father, John Dickens, a clerk in the Navy-pay office, was at this time stationed in the Portsmouth dockyard. He had made acquaintance with the lady, Elizabeth Barrow, who became afterwards his wife, through her elder brother, Thomas Barrow, also engaged on the establishment at Somerset House; and she bore him in all a family of eight children, of whom two died in infancy. The eldest, Fanny (born 1810), was followed by Charles (entered in the baptismal register of Portsea as Charles John Huffham, though on the very rare occasions when he subscribed that name he wrote Huffam); by another son, named Alfred, who died in childhood; by Letitia (born 1816); by another daughter, Harriet, who died also in childhood; by Frederick (born 1820); by Alfred Lamert (born 1822); and by Augustus (born 1827); of all of whom only the second daughter now survives.

When his father was again brought up by his duties to London from Portsmouth, they went into lodgings in Norfolk Street, Middlesex Hospital; and it lived also in the child's memory that they had come away from Portsea in the snow. Their home, shortly

John Dickens

after, was again changed, on the elder Dickens being placed upon duty in Chatham dockyard; and the house where he lived in Chatham, which had a plain-looking whitewashed plaster front and a small garden before and behind, was in St. Mary's Place, otherwise called the Brook, and next door to a Baptist meeting-house called Providence Chapel, of which a Mr. Giles, to be presently mentioned, was minister.

Charles at this time was between four and five years old; and here he stayed till he was nine. Here the most durable of his early impressions were received; and the associations that were around him when he died were those which at the outset of his life had affected him most strongly.

The house called Gadshill Place stands on the strip of highest ground in the main road between Rochester and Gravesend. Often had we traveled past it together, years and years before it became his home, and never without some allusion to what he told me when first I saw it in his company, that amid the recollections connected with his childhood it held always a prominent place, for, upon first seeing it as he came from Chatham with his father, and looking up at it with much admiration, he had been promised that he might himself live in it, or in some such house, when he came to be a man, if he would only work hard enough. Which for a long time was his ambition. The story is a pleasant one, and receives authentic confirmation at the opening of one of his essays on traveling abroad, when as he passes along the road to Canterbury there crosses it a vision of his former self:

"So smooth was the old highroad, and so fresh were the horses, and so fast went I, that it was midway between Gravesend and Rochester, and the widening river was bearing the ships, white-sailed or black-smoked, out to sea, when I noticed by the wayside a very queer small boy.

"'Holloa!' said I to the very queer small boy, 'where do you live?'

"'At Chatham,' says he.

"'What do you do there?' says I.

"'I go to school,' says he.

"I took him up in a moment, and we went on. Presently, the very queer small boy says, 'This is Gadshill we are coming to, where Falstaff went out to rob those travelers, and ran away.'

"'You know something about Falstaff, eh?' said I.

"'All about him,' said the very queer small boy. 'I am old (I am nine), and I read all sorts of books. But do let us stop at the top of the hill, and look at the house there, if you please!'

"'You admire that house?' said I.

Ordnance Terrace: one of Dickens's childhood homes in Chatham

"'Bless you, sir,' said the very queer small boy, 'when I was not more than half as old as nine, it used to be a treat for me to be brought to look at it. And now I am nine, I come by myself to look at it. And ever since I can recollect, my father, seeing me so fond of it, has often said to me, If you were to be very persevering and were to work hard, you might some day come to live in it. Though that's impossible!' said the very queer small boy, drawing a low breath, and now staring at the house out of window with all his might.

"I was rather amazed to be told this by the very queer small boy; for that house happens to be my house, and I have reason to believe that what he said was true."

The queer small boy was indeed his very self. He was a very little and a very sickly boy. He was subject to attacks of violent spasm which disabled him for any active exertion. He has frequently been heard to say that his first desire for knowledge, and his earliest passion for reading, were awakened by his mother, who taught him the first rudiments not only of English, but also, a little later, of Latin.

Then followed the preparatory day-school, a school for girls and boys to which he went with his sister Fanny, and which was in a place called Rome (pronounced Room) Lane.

Of the "readings" and "imaginations" which he describes as brought away from Chatham, this authority can tell us. It is one of the many passages in Copperfield which are literally true, and its proper place is here. "My father had left a small collection of books in a little room up-stairs to which I had access (for it adjoined my own), and which nobody else in our house ever troubled. From that blessed little room, *Roderick Random*, *Peregrine Pickle*, *Humphrey Clinker*, *Tom Jones*, *the Vicar of Wakefield*, *Don Quixote*, *Gil Blas*, and *Robinson Crusoe* came out, a glorious host, to keep me company. They kept alive my fancy, and my hope of something beyond that place and time,—they, and the *Arabian Nights* and the *Tales of the Genii*,—and did me no harm; for whatever harm was in some of them was not there for me; I knew nothing of it. It is astonishing to me now how I found time, in the midst of my pourings and blunderings over heavier themes, to read those books as I did."

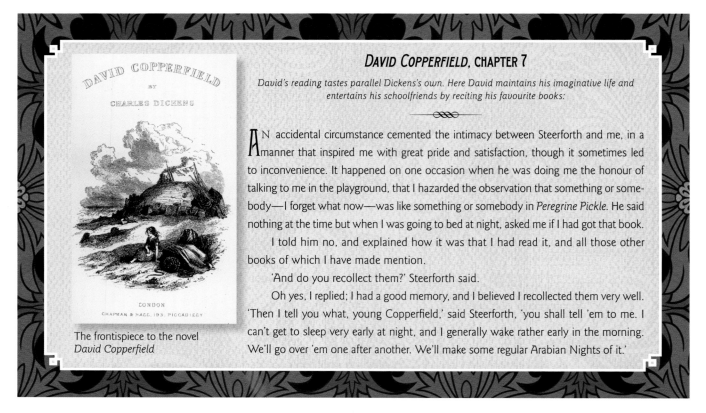

DAVID COPPERFIELD, CHAPTER 7

David's reading tastes parallel Dickens's own. Here David maintains his imaginative life and entertains his schoolfriends by reciting his favourite books:

⸺⸻⸺

AN accidental circumstance cemented the intimacy between Steerforth and me, in a manner that inspired me with great pride and satisfaction, though it sometimes led to inconvenience. It happened on one occasion when he was doing me the honour of talking to me in the playground, that I hazarded the observation that something or somebody—I forget what now—was like something or somebody in *Peregrine Pickle*. He said nothing at the time but when I was going to bed at night, asked me if I had got that book.

I told him no, and explained how it was that I had read it, and all those other books of which I have made mention.

'And do you recollect them?' Steerforth said.

Oh yes, I replied; I had a good memory, and I believed I recollected them very well. 'Then I tell you what, young Copperfield,' said Steerforth, 'you shall tell 'em to me. I can't get to sleep very early at night, and I generally wake rather early in the morning. We'll go over 'em one after another. We'll make some regular Arabian Nights of it.'

The frontispiece to the novel *David Copperfield*

Every word of this personal recollection had been written down as fact, some years before it found its way into *David Copperfield*; the only change in the fiction being his omission of the name of a cheap series of novelists then in course of publication, by which his father had become happily the owner of so large a lump of literary treasure in his small collection of books. The usual result followed. The child took to writing, himself, and became famous in his childish circle for having written a tragedy called *Misnar, the Sultan of India*, founded (and very literally founded, no doubt) on one of the *Tales of the Genii*. Nor was this his only distinction. He told a story offhand so well, and sang comic songs so especially well, that he used to be elevated on chairs and tables, both at home and abroad, for more effective display of these talents.

His chief ally and encourager in these displays was a youth of some ability, much older than himself, named James Lamert, stepson to his mother's sister, and therefore a sort of cousin, who was his great patron and friend in his childish days. Mary, the eldest daughter of Charles Barrow, himself a lieutenant in the navy, had for her first husband a commander in the navy called Allen; on whose death by drowning at Rio Janeiro she had joined her sister, the navy-pay clerk's wife, at Chatham; in which place she subsequently took for her second husband Dr. Lamert, an army-surgeon, whose son James, even after he had been sent to Sandhurst for his education, continued still to visit Chatham from time to time. He had a turn for private theatricals; and as his father's quarters were in the ordnance hospital there, a great rambling place otherwise at that time almost uninhabited, he had plenty of room in which to get up his entertainments. The staff-doctor himself played his part, and his portrait will be found in *Pickwick*.

During the last two years of Charles's residence at Chatham, he was sent to a school kept in Clover Lane by the young Baptist minister already named, Mr. William Giles. I have the picture of him here, very strongly in my mind, as a

RIGHT: Frontispiece to *David Copperfield* autograph edition, illustration by H.M. Brock, 1901

DAVID COPPERFIELD, CHAPTER II

*Many of Forster's first readers were shocked to discover
that the character of Wilkins Micawber was, in part, based on Dickens's father. Here, having been arrested for debt,
Micawber imparts his famous principle of economy to the young David Copperfield:*

AT last Mr Micawber's difficulties came to a crisis, and he was arrested early one morning, and carried over to the King's Bench Prison in the Borough [. . .]

On the first Sunday after he was taken there, I was to go and see him, and have dinner with him. [. . .]

Mr Micawber was waiting for me within the gate, and we went up to his room (top storey but one), and cried very much. He solemnly conjured me, I remember, to take warning by his fate; and to observe that if a man had twenty pounds a year for his income, and spent nineteen pounds nineteen shillings and sixpence, he would be happy, but that if he spent twenty pounds one he would be miserable. After which he borrowed a shilling of me for porter, gave me a written order on Mrs. Micawber for the amount, and put away his pocket-handkerchief, and cheered up.

sensitive, thoughtful, feeble-bodied little boy, with an unusual sort of knowledge and fancy for such a child, and with a dangerous kind of wandering intelligence that a teacher might turn to good or evil, happiness or misery, as he directed it. Nor does the influence of Mr. Giles, such as it was, seem to have been other than favorable. Charles had himself a not ungrateful sense in after-years that this first of his masters, in his little-cared-for childhood, had pronounced him to be a boy of capacity; and when, about half-way through the publication of *Pickwick*, his old teacher sent a silver snuff-box with admiring inscription to the "inimitable Boz," it reminded him of praise far more precious obtained by him at his first year's examination in the Clover Lane academy, when his recitation of a piece out of the *Humorist's Miscellany* about Doctor Bolus had received, unless his youthful vanity bewildered him, a double encore. A habit, the only bad one taught him by Mr. Giles, of taking for a time, in very moderate quantities, the snuff called Irish black-guard, was the result of this gift from his old master; but he abandoned it after some few years, and it was never resumed.

Not much over nine years old when his father was recalled from Chatham to Somerset House, and he had to leave this good master, and the old place endeared to him by recollections that clung to him afterwards all his life long. It was the birthplace of his fancy; and he hardly knew what store he had set by its busy varieties of change and scene, until he saw the falling cloud that was to hide its pictures from him forever.

The earliest impressions received and retained by him in London were of his father's money involvements; and now first he heard mentioned "the deed," representing that crisis of his father's affairs in fact which is ascribed in fiction to Mr. Micawber's.

He knew it in later days to have been a composition with creditors; though at this earlier date he was conscious of having confounded it with parchments of a much more demo-niacal description. One result from the awful document soon showed itself

A silver snuff box from 1852 inscribed with Dickens's initials and the date.

RIGHT: Photograph of Bayham Street residences

in enforced retrenchment. The family had to take up its abode in a house in Bayham Street, Camden-town.

Bayham Street was about the poorest part of the London suburbs then, and the house was a mean small tenement, with a wretched little back-garden abutting on a squalid court. Here was no place for new acquaintances to him: no boys were near with whom he might hope to become in any way familiar. A washerwoman lived next door, and a Bow-Street officer lived over the way. Many, many times has he spoken to me of this, and how he seemed at once to fall into a solitary condition apart from all other boys of his own age, and to sink into a neglected state at home which had been always quite unaccountable to him. "As I thought," he said on one occasion very bitterly, "in the little back-garret in Bayham Street, of all I had lost in losing Chatham, what would I have given, if I had had anything to give, to have been sent back to any other school, to have been taught something anywhere!" He was at another school already, not knowing it. The self-education forced upon him was teaching him, all unconsciously as yet, what, for the future that awaited him, it most behooved him to know.

How it came that, being what he was, he should now have fallen into the misery and neglect of the time about to be described, was a subject on which thoughts were frequently interchanged between us; and on one occasion he gave me a sketch of the character of his father, which, as I can here repeat it in the exact words employed by him,

will be the best preface I can make to what I feel that I have no alternative but to tell. "I know my father to be as kind-hearted and generous a man as ever lived in the world. Everything that I can remember of his conduct to his wife, or children, or friends, in sickness or affliction, is beyond all praise. By me, as a sick child, he has watched night and day, unweariedly and patiently, many nights and days. He never undertook any business, charge, or trust, that he did not zealously, conscientiously, punctually, honorably discharge. His industry has always been untiring. He was proud of me, in his way, and had a great admiration of the comic singing. But, in the ease of his temper, and the strait-ness of his means, he appeared to have utterly lost at this time the idea of educating me at all, and to have utterly put from him the notion that I had any claim upon him, in that regard, whatever. So I degenerated into cleaning his boots of a morning, and my own; and making myself useful in the work of the little house; and looking after my younger brothers and sisters (we were now six in all); and going on such poor errands as arose out of our poor way of living."

His sister Fanny was at about this time elected as a pupil to the Royal Academy of Music; and he has told me what a stab to his heart it was, thinking of his own disre-garded condition, to see her go away to begin her education, amid the tearful good wishes of everybody in the house.

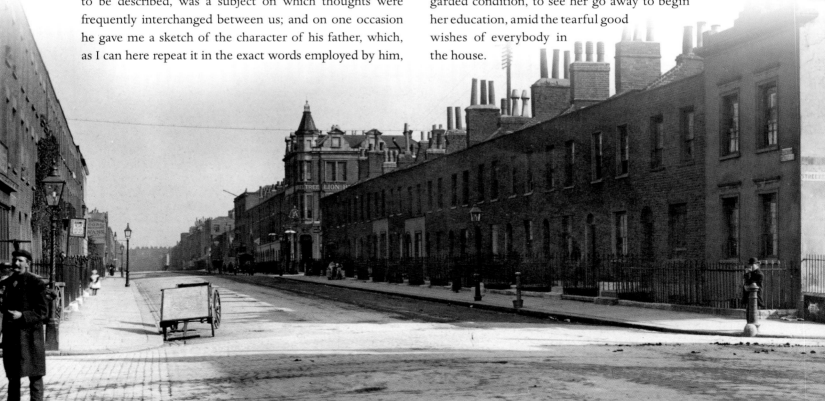

Dickens's boyhood residence on Bayham Street

Interior view of Bayham Street house

That part of his boyhood is now very near of which, when the days of fame and prosperity came to him, he felt the weight upon his memory as a painful burden until he could lighten it by sharing it with a friend; and an accident I will presently mention led him first to reveal it. There is, however, an interval of some months still to be described, of which, from conversations or letters that passed between us, after or because of this confidence, and that already have yielded fruit to these pages, I can supply some vague and desultory notices. The use thus made of them, it is due to myself to remark, was contemplated then; for though, long before his death, I had ceased to believe it likely that I should survive to write about him, he had never withdrawn the wish at this early time strongly expressed, or the confidences, not only then but to the very eve of his death reposed in me, that were to enable me to fulfill it.[1] The fulfillment indeed he had himself rendered more easy by partially uplifting the veil in *David Copperfield*.

The visits made from Bayham Street were chiefly to two connections of the family, his mother's elder brother and his godfather. The latter, who was a rigger, and mast-, oar-, and block-maker, lived at Limehouse in a substantial handsome sort of way, and was kind to his godchild. It was always a great treat to him to go to Mr. Huffham's; and the London night-sights as he returned were a perpetual joy and marvel. Here, too, the comic-singing accomplishment was brought into play so greatly to the admiration of one of the godfather's guests, an honest boat-builder, that he pronounced the little lad to be a "progidy." The visits to the uncle who was at this time fellow-clerk with his father, in Somerset House, were nearer home. Mr. Thomas Barrow, the eldest of his mother's family, had broken his leg in a fall; and, while laid up with this illness, his lodging was in Gerrard Street, Soho, in the upper part of the house of a worthy gentleman then recently deceased, a book-seller named Manson, father to the partner in the celebrated firm of Christie & Manson, whose widow at this time carried on the business. Attracted by the look of the lad as he went up-stairs, these good people lent him books to amuse him; among them Miss Porter's *Scottish Chiefs*, Holbein's *Dance of Death*, and George Colman's *Broad Grins*. The latter seized his fancy very much; and he was so impressed by its description of Covent Garden, in the piece called "The Elder Brother," that he stole down to the market by himself to compare it with the book. He remembered, as he said in telling me this, snuffing up the flavor of the faded cabbage-leaves as if it were the very breath of comic fiction. Nor was he far wrong, as comic fiction then and for some time after was. It was reserved for himself to give sweeter and fresher breath to it. Many years were to pass first, but he was beginning already to make the trial.

In Bayham Street, meanwhile, affairs were going on badly; the poor boy's visits to his uncle, while the latter was still kept a prisoner by his accident, were interrupted by another attack of fever; and on his recovery the mysterious "deed" had again come uppermost. His father's resources were so low, and all his expedients so thoroughly exhausted, that trial was to be made whether his mother might not come to the rescue. The time was arrived for her to exert herself, she said; and she "must do something." The godfather down at Limehouse was reported to have an Indian connection. People in the East Indies always sent their children home to be educated. She would set up a school. They would all grow rich by it. And then, thought the sick boy, "perhaps even I might go to school myself."

A house was soon found at number four, Gower Street north; a large brass plate on the door announced MRS. DICKENS'S ESTABLISHMENT; and the result I can give in the exact words of the then small actor in the comedy, whose hopes it had raised so high: "I left, at a great many other doors, a great many circulars calling attention to the merits of the establishment. Yet nobody ever came to school, nor do I recollect that anybody ever proposed to come, or that the least preparation was made to receive anybody. But I know that we got on very badly with the butcher and baker; that very often we had not too much for dinner; and that at last my father

was arrested." The interval between the sponging-house and the prison was passed by the sorrowful lad in running errands and carrying messages for the prisoner, delivered with swollen eyes and through shining tears; and the last words said to him by his father before he was finally carried to the Marshalsea were to the effect that the sun was set upon him forever. "I really believed at the time," said Dickens to me, "that they had broken my heart." He took afterwards ample revenge for this false alarm by making all the world laugh at them in *David Copperfield*.

Marshalsea yard

The same pawnbroker's shop, too, which was so well known to David, became not less familiar to Charles; and a good deal of notice was here taken of him by the pawnbroker, or by his principal clerk who officiated behind the counter, and who, while making out the duplicate, liked of all things to hear the lad conjugate a Latin verb and translate or decline his *musa* and *dominus*. Everything to this accompaniment went gradually; until, at last, even of the furniture of Gower Street number four there was nothing left except a few chairs, a kitchen table, and some beds. Then they encamped, as it were, in the two parlors of the emptied house, and lived there night and day.

All which is but the prelude to what remains to be described.

---

[1] The reader will forgive my quoting from a letter of the date of the 22d April, 1848. "I desire no better for my fame, when my personal dustiness shall be past the control of my love of order, than such a biographer and such a critic." "You know me better," he wrote, resuming the same subject on the 6th of July, 1862, "than any other man does, or ever will." In an entry of my diary during the interval between these years, I find a few words that not only mark the time when I first saw in its connected shape the autobiographical fragment which will form the substance of the second chapter of this biography, but also express his own feeling respecting it when written: "20 January, 1849. The description may make none of the impression on others that the reality made on him. . . . Highly probable that it may never see the light. No wish. Left to J. F. or others." The first number of *David Copperfield* appeared five months after this date; but though I knew, even before he adapted his fragment of autobiography to the eleventh number, that he had now abandoned the notion of completing it under his own name, the "no wish," or the discretion left me, was never in any way subsequently modified. What follows, from the same entry, refers to the manuscript of the fragment: "No blotting, as when writing fiction; but straight on, as when writing ordinary letter."

CHAPTER 2

HARD EXPERIENCES IN BOYHOOD

1822~1824

THE INCIDENTS TO BE TOLD NOW would probably never have been known to me, or indeed any of the occurrences of his childhood and youth, but for the accident of a question which I put to him one day in the March or April of 1847.

I asked if he remembered ever having seen in his boyhood our friend the elder Mr. Dilke, his father's acquaintance and contemporary, who had been a clerk in the same office in Somerset House to which Mr. John Dickens belonged. Yes, he said, he recollected seeing him at a house in Gerrard Street, where his uncle Barrow lodged during an illness, and Mr. Dilke had visited him. Never at any other time. Upon which I told him that some one else had been intended in the mention made to me, for that the reference implied not merely his being met accidentally, but his having had some juvenile employment in a warehouse near the Strand; at which place Mr. Dilke, being with the elder Dickens one day, had noticed him, and received, in return for the gift of a half-crown, a very low bow. He was silent for several minutes; I felt that I had unintentionally touched a painful place in his memory; and to Mr. Dilke I never spoke of the subject again. It was not, however, then, but some weeks later, that Dickens made further allusion to my thus having struck unconsciously upon a time of which he never could lose the remembrance while he remembered anything, and the recollection of which, at intervals, haunted him and made him miserable, even to that hour.

The person indirectly responsible for the scenes to be described was the young relative James Lamert, the cousin by his aunt's marriage of whom I have made frequent mention, who got up the plays at Chatham, and after passing at Sandhurst had been living with the family in Bayham Street in the hope of obtaining a commission in the army. This did

not come until long afterwards, when, in consideration of his father's services, he received it, and relinquished it then in favor of a younger brother; but he had meanwhile, before the family removed from Camden-town, ceased to live with them. The husband of a sister of his (of the same name as himself, being indeed his cousin, George Lamert), a man of some property, had recently embarked in an odd sort of commercial speculation, and had taken him into his office and his house, to assist in it. I give now the fragment of the autobiography of Dickens:

"This speculation was a rivalry of 'Warren's Blacking, 30, Strand,'—at that time very famous. One Jonathan Warren (the famous one was Robert), living at 30, Hungerford Stairs, or Market, Strand (for I forget which it was called then), claimed to have been the original inventor or proprietor of the blacking-recipe, and to have been deposed and ill used by his renowned relation. At last he put himself in the way of selling his recipe, and his name, and his 30, Hungerford Stairs, Strand (30, Strand, very large, and the intermediate direction very small), for an annuity; and he set forth by his agents that a little capital would make a great business of it. The man of some property was found in George Lamert, the cousin and brother-in-law of James. He bought this right and title, and went into the blacking-business and the blacking-premises.

"—In an evil hour for me, as I often bitterly thought. Its chief manager, James Lamert, the relative who had lived with us in Bayham Street, seeing how I was employed from day to day, and knowing what our domestic circumstances then were, proposed that I should go into the blacking-warehouse, to be as useful as I could, at a salary, I think, of six shillings a week. I am not clear whether it was six or seven. I am inclined to believe, from my uncertainty on this head, that it was six at first, and seven afterwards. At any rate, the offer was accepted very willingly by my father and mother, and on a Monday morning I went down to the blacking-warehouse to begin my business life.

"It is wonderful to me how I could have been so easily cast away at such an age. It is wonderful to me that, even

RIGHT: Old Hungerford Market from the river, London, watercolor by George "Sydney" Shepherd (detail), ca. 1810

Dickens transposes his childhood experiences of Warren's Blacking into David Copperfield's
"secret agony" under the employment of Murdstone and Grinby:

I KNOW enough of the world now, to have almost lost the capacity of being much surprised by anything; but it is a matter of some surprise to me, even now, that I can have been so easily thrown away at such an age. A child of excellent abilities, and with strong powers of observation, quick, eager, delicate, and soon hurt bodily or mentally, it seems wonderful to me that nobody should have made any sign in my behalf. But none was made; and I became, at ten years old, a little labouring hind in the service of Murdstone and Grinby.

Murdstone and Grinby's warehouse was at the waterside. It was down in Blackfriars. Modern improvements have altered the place; but it was the last house at the bottom of a narrow street, curving down hill to the river, with some stairs at the end, where people took boat. It was a crazy old house with a wharf of its own, abutting on the water when the tide was in, and on the mud when the tide was out, and literally overrun with rats. Its panelled rooms, discoloured with the dirt and smoke of a hundred years, I dare say; its decaying floors and staircase; the squeaking and scuffling of the old grey rats down in the cellars; and the dirt and rottenness of the place; are things, not of many years ago, in my mind, but of the present instant. They are all before me, just as they were in the evil hour when I went among them for the first time, with my trembling hand in Mr. Quinion's.

Murdstone and Grinby's trade was among a good many kinds of people, but an important branch of it was the supply of wines and spirits to certain packet ships. I forget now where they chiefly went, but I think there were some among them that made voyages both to the East and West Indies. I know that a great many empty bottles were one of the consequences of this traffic, and that certain men and boys were employed to examine them against the light, and reject those that were flawed, and to rinse and wash them. When the empty bottles ran short, there were labels to be pasted on full ones, or corks to be fitted to them, or seals to be put upon the corks, or finished bottles to be packed in casks. All this work was my work, and of the boys employed upon it I was one.

There were three or four of us, counting me. My working place was established in a corner of the warehouse, where Mr. Quinion could see me, when he chose to stand up on the bottom rail of his stool in the counting-house, and look at me through a window above the desk. Hither, on the first morning of my so auspiciously beginning life on my own account, the oldest of the regular boys was summoned to show me my business. His name was Mick Walker, and he wore a ragged apron and a paper cap. He informed me that his father was a bargeman, and walked, in a black velvet head-dress, in the Lord Mayor's Show. He also informed me that our principal associate would be another boy whom he introduced by the—to me—extraordinary name of Mealy Potatoes. I discovered, however, that this youth had not been christened by that name, but that it had been bestowed upon him in the warehouse, on account of his complexion, which was pale or mealy. Mealy's father was a waterman, who had the additional distinction of being a fireman, and was engaged as such at one of the large theatres; where some young relation of Mealy's—I think his little sister—did Imps in the Pantomimes.

No words can express the secret agony of my soul as I sunk into this companionship; compared these henceforth everyday associates with those of my happier childhood—not to say with Steerforth, Traddles, and the rest of those boys; and felt my hopes of growing up to be a learned and distinguished man, crushed in my bosom. The deep remembrance of the sense I had, of being utterly without hope now; of the shame I felt in my position; of the misery it was to my young heart to believe that day by day what I had learned, and thought, and delighted in, and raised my fancy and my emulation up by, would pass away from me, little by little, never to be brought back any more; cannot be written. As often as Mick Walker went away in the course of that forenoon, I mingled my tears with the water in which I was washing the bottles; and sobbed as if there were a flaw in my own breast, and it were in danger of bursting.

after my descent into the poor little drudge I had been since we came to London, no one had compassion enough on me—a child of singular abilities, quick, eager, delicate, and soon hurt, bodily or mentally—to suggest that something might have been spared, as certainly it might have been, to place me at any common school. Our friends, I take it, were tired out. No one made any sign. My father and mother were quite satisfied. They could hardly have been more so if I had been twenty years of age, distinguished at a grammar-school, and going to Cambridge.

"The blacking-warehouse was the last house on the left-hand side of the way, at old Hungerford Stairs. It was a crazy, tumble-down old house, abutting of course on the river, and literally overrun with rats. Its wainscoted rooms, and its rotten floors and staircase, and the old gray rats swarming down in the cellars, and the sound of their squeaking and scuffling coming up the stairs at all times, and the dirt and decay of the place, rise up visibly before me, as if I were there again. The counting-house was on the first floor, looking over the coal-barges and the river. There was a recess in it, in which I was to sit and work. My work was to cover the pots of paste-blacking; first with a piece of oil-paper, and then with a piece of blue paper; to tie them round with a string; and then to clip the paper close and neat, all round, until it looked as smart as a pot of ointment from an apothecary's shop. When a certain number of grosses of pots had attained this pitch of perfection, I was to paste on each a printed label, and then go on again with more pots. Two or three other boys were kept at similar duty down-stairs on similar wages. One of them came up, in a ragged apron and a paper cap, on the first Monday morning, to show me the trick of using the string and tying the knot. His name was Bob Fagin; and I took the liberty of using his name, long afterwards, in *Oliver Twist*.

"Our relative had kindly arranged to teach me something in the dinner-hour; from twelve to one, I think it was; every day. But an arrangement so incompatible with counting-house business soon died away, from no fault of his or mine; and, for the same reason, my small work-table, and my grosses of pots, my papers, string, scissors, paste-pot, and labels, by little and little, vanished out of the recess in the counting-house, and kept company with the other small work-tables, grosses of pots, papers, string, scissors, and paste-pots, down-stairs. It was not long before Bob Fagin and I, and another boy whose name was Paul Green, but who was currently believed to have been christened Poll (a belief which I transferred, long afterwards again, to Mr. Sweedlepipe, in *Martin Chuzzlewit*), worked generally, side by side. Bob Fagin was an orphan, and lived with his brother-in-law, a waterman. Poll Green's father had the additional distinction of being a fireman, and was employed at Drury Lane theatre; where another relation of Poll's, I think his little sister, did imps in the pantomimes.

"No words can express the secret agony of my soul as I sunk into this companionship; compared these every-day associates with those of my happier childhood; and felt my early hopes of growing up to be a learned and distinguished man, crushed in my breast. The deep remembrance of the sense I had of being utterly neglected and hopeless; of the shame I felt in my position; of the misery it was to my young heart to believe that, day by day, what I had learned, and thought, and delighted in, and raised my fancy and my emulation up by, was passing away from me, never to be brought back any more; cannot be written. My whole nature was so penetrated with the grief and humiliation of such considerations, that even now, famous and caressed and happy, I often forget in my dreams that I have a dear wife

Dickens depicted on the frontispiece to the Household Edition of Forster's *Life*, by Fred Barnard, 1892

Prison register with entry for John Dickens

and children; even that I am a man; and wander desolately back to that time of my life.

"My mother and my brothers and sisters (excepting Fanny in the Royal Academy of Music) were still encamped, with a young servant-girl from Chatham workhouse, in the two parlors in the emptied house in Gower Street north. It was a long way to go and return within the dinner-hour, and usually I either carried my dinner with me, or went and bought it at some neighboring shop. In the latter case, it was commonly a saveloy and a penny loaf; sometimes, a four-penny plate of beef from a cook's shop; sometimes, a plate of bread and cheese, and a glass of beer, from a miserable old public-house over the way: the Swan, if I remember right, or the Swan and something else that I have forgotten. Once, I remember tucking my own bread (which I had brought from home in the morning) under my arm, wrapped up in a piece of paper like a book, and going into the best dining-room in Johnson's alamode beef-house in Clare Court, Drury Lane, and magnificently ordering a small plate of alamode beef to eat with it. What the waiter thought of such a strange little apparition, coming in all alone, I don't know; but I can see him now, staring at me as I ate my dinner, and bringing up the other waiter to look. I gave him a halfpenny, and I wish, now, that he hadn't taken it."

I lose here for a little while the fragment of direct narrative, but I perfectly recollect that he used to describe

Saturday night as his great treat. It was a grand thing to walk home with six shillings in his pocket, and to look in at the shop-windows and think what it would buy. Hunt's roasted corn, as a British and patriotic substitute for coffee, was in great vogue just then; and the little fellow used to buy it, and roast it on the Sunday. There was a cheap periodical of selected pieces called the *Portfolio*, which he had also a great fancy for taking home with him. The new proposed "deed," meanwhile, had failed to propitiate his father's creditors; all hope of arrangement passed away; and the end was that his mother and her encampment in Gower Street north broke up and went to live in the Marshalsea. I am able at this point to resume his own account:

"The key of the house was sent back to the landlord, who was very glad to get it; and I (small Cain that I was, except that I had never done harm to any one) was handed over as a lodger to a reduced old lady, long known to our family, in Little College Street, Camden-town, who took children in to board, and had once done so at Brighton; and who, with a few alterations and embellishments, unconsciously began to sit for Mrs. Pipchin in *Dombey* when she took in me.

"Sundays, Fanny and I passed in the prison. I was at the academy in Tenterden Street, Hanover Square, at nine o'clock in the morning, to fetch her; and we walked back there together, at night.

"I know I do not exaggerate, unconsciously and unintentionally, the scantiness of my resources and the difficulties of my life. I know that if a shilling or so were given me by any one, I spent it in a dinner or a tea. I know that I worked, from morning to night, with common men and boys, a shabby child. I know that I tried, but ineffectually, not to anticipate my money, and to make it last the week through; by putting it away in a drawer I had in the counting-house, wrapped into six little parcels, each parcel containing the same amount and labeled with a different day. I know that I have lounged about the streets, insufficiently and unsatisfactorily fed. I know that, but for the mercy of God, I might easily have been, for any care that was taken of me, a little robber or a little vagabond.

"But I held some station at the blacking-warehouse too. Besides that my relative at the counting-house did what a man so occupied, and dealing with a thing so anomalous, could, to treat me as one upon a different footing from the rest, I never

DOMBEY AND SON, CHAPTER 8

In another authobiographical fragment within his fiction, Dickens recreates the landlady of his childhood in the severe Mrs. Pipchin:

THIS celebrated Mrs. Pipchin was a marvellous ill-favoured, ill-conditioned old lady, of a stooping figure, with a mottled face, like bad marble, a hook nose, and a hard grey eye, that looked as if it might have been hammered at on an anvil without sustaining any injury. Forty years at least had elapsed since the Peruvian mines had been the death of Mr. Pipchin; but his relict still wore black bombazeen, of such a lustreless, deep, dead, sombre shade, that gas itself couldn't light her up after dark, and her presence was a quencher to any number of candles. She was generally spoken of as 'a great manager' of children; and the secret of her management was, to give them everything that they didn't like, and nothing that they did—which was found to sweeten their dispositions very much. She was such a bitter old lady, that one was tempted to believe there had been some mistake in the application of the Peruvian machinery, and that all her waters of gladness and milk of human kindness, had been pumped out dry, instead of the mines.

said, to man or boy, how it was that I came to be there, or gave the least indication of being sorry that I was there. That I suffered in secret, and that I suffered exquisitely, no one ever knew but I. How much I suffered, it is, as I have said already, utterly beyond my power to tell. No man's imagination can overstep the reality. But I kept my own counsel, and I did my work. I knew from the first that, if I could not do my work as well as any of the rest, I could not hold myself above slight and contempt. I soon became at least as expeditious and as skillful with my hands as either of the other boys. Though perfectly familiar with them, my conduct and manners were different enough from theirs to place a space between

workhouse, from whose sharp little worldly and also kindly ways he took his first impression of the Marchioness in the *Old Curiosity Shop*. She also had a lodging in the neighborhood, that she might be early on the scene of her duties; and when Charles met her, as he would do occasionally, in his lounging-place by London Bridge, he would occupy the time before the gates opened by telling her quite astonishing fictions about the wharves and the tower. "But I hope I believed them myself," he would say. Besides breakfast, he had supper also in the prison, and got to his lodging generally at nine o'clock. The gates closed always at ten.

I must not omit what he told me of the landlord of this little lodging. He was a fat, good-natured, kind old gentleman. He was lame, and had a quiet old wife; and he had a very innocent grown-up son, who was lame too. They were all very kind to the boy. He was taken with one of his old attacks of spasm one night, and the whole three of them were about his bed until morning. They were all dead when he told me this; but in another form they still live very pleasantly as the Garland family in the *Old Curiosity Shop*.

His father's attempts to avoid going through the court having failed, all needful ceremonies had to be undertaken to obtain the benefit of the insolvent debtors' act; and in one of these little Charles had his part to play. One condition of the statute was that the wearing-apparel and personal matters retained were not to exceed twenty pounds sterling in value.

Still, the want felt most by him was the companionship of boys of his own age. He had no such acquaintance. Sometimes he remembered to have played on the coal-barges at dinner-time, with Poll Green and Bob Fagin; but those were rare occasions.

He generally strolled alone, about the back streets of the Adelphi, or explored the Adelphi arches. One of his favorite localities was a little public-house by the water-side, called the Fox-under-the-hill, approached by an underground passage which we once missed in looking for it together; and he had a vision which he has mentioned in *Copperfield* of sitting eating something on a bench outside, one fine evening, and looking at some coal-heavers dancing before the house. "I wonder what they thought of me," says David. He had himself already said the same in his fragment of autobiography.

A later, and not less characteristic, incident of the true story of this time found also a place, three or four years after it was written, in his now famous fiction. It preceded but by a short time the discharge, from the Marshalsea, of the elder Dickens; to whom a rather considerable legacy from a relative had accrued not long before ("some hundreds," I understood), and had been paid into court during his imprisonment. The scene to be described arose on the occasion of a petition drawn up by him before he left, praying, not for the abolition of imprisonment for debt, as David Copperfield relates, but for the less dignified but more accessible boon of a bounty to the prisoners to drink his majesty's health on his majesty's forthcoming birthday.

When the family left the Marshalsea they all went to lodge with the lady in Little College Street, a Mrs. Roylance, who has obtained unexpected immortality as Mrs. Pipchin; and they afterwards

Elizabeth Dickens painted by John Gilbert. As Peter Ackroyd describes it, Dickens's relationship to his mother was central to his life, but it was necessarily a complex one established on guilt and rejection but combined with a kind of hopeless love. "Dickens never forgave her for her willingness to send him back to the blacking warehouse." *Dickens* (London; Sinclair Stevenson, 1990), p. 95

DICKENS'S FOREMOST RECENT BIOGRAPHER, MICHAEL SLATER, REVEALS THE LEVEL OF ASTONISHMENT THAT FORSTER'S REVELATIONS PROVOKED. HE EXPLAINS THAT THE FIRST "REVIEWERS FOUND MUCH IN DICKENS'S POWERFULLY-WRITTEN ACCOUNT OF WHAT FORSTER CALLS HIS 'HARD EXPERIENCES IN BOYHOOD' THAT EXPLAINED WHY HE DEVELOPED INTO THE KIND OF NOVELIST HE DID":

Some fourteen months later, in November 1871, Forster published the first volume of his *Life of Charles Dickens* and the world was startled by another, and far more dramatic, explanation of himself by Dickens, this time the fragment of autobiography written by him over twenty years before and now presented by Forster in his second chapter. Here the public learned that young David Copperfield's grim experience of life in Murdstone and Grinby's warehouse echoed what had happened to Dickens himself, that the Micawbers were were modeled on his own parents, and their sojourn in the King's Bench Prison closely reflected what had happened in real life when John Dickens had been imprisoned for debt in the Marshalsea. To register just how sensational all this was to the vast majority of Dickens's readers, so many of whom felt themselves to be on terms of personal friendship with him, we need to remember that they knew virtually nothing of his life before he became a journalist in his late teens. This gap in his biographical record was usually filled with details about John Dickens's career in the Navy Pay Office and afterwards. 'The story of his life is soon told', said *The Times* in its obituary notice of Dickens on 10 June:

The son of Mr John Dickens, who held at one time a position in the Navy Pay Department, Charles Dickens was born at Portsmouth in the month of February, 1812. The duties of his father's office obliged him frequently to change his residence, and much of the future novelist's infancy was spent at Plymouth, Sheerness, Chatham, and other seaport towns. The European war, however, came to an end before he had completed his fourth year, and his father, finding his 'occupation gone', retired on a pension and came to London as a Parliamentary reporter for one of the daily papers. It was at first intended that young Charles should be sent to an attorney's office; but he had literary tastes, and eventually was permitted by his father to exchange the law for a post as a reporter on the staff of the *True Sun*.

All that his readers knew or surmised about Dickens's childhood, apart from the glimpse they had been given in the Cheap Edition preface to *Nickleby*, written contemporaneously with the autobiographical fragment, was what might be gleaned from some of his journalistic writings such as 'A Christmas Tree' (HW, 21 Dec. 1850) and 'Our School' (*HW*, 11 Oct. 1851), and especially some of the 'Uncommercial Traveller' pieces in *All the Year Round*. From these they would have derived a generalised impression of a secure middle-class background of nursemaids, children's parties, hampers and other treats, storybooks, academies (as schools for middle-class children were generally called), and so on. Forster's first volume therefore came as a revelation indeed. 'Never, perhaps,' wrote the Scottish poet and critic Robert Buchanan in the February 1872 issue of St Paul's Magazine, 'has a fragment of biography wakened more interest and amazement than the first chapters of Mr Forster's biography'. The Times review, serialised in two issues (7 and 26 Dec.) extended to over five columns, Forster's friend Whitwell Elwin devoted twenty two pages to it in the *Quarterly Review* (vol. 132, Jan.–April 1872), and the volume had already been nine times reprinted before the end of 1871.

From Michael Slater, *Charles Dickens* (New Haven and London: Yale University Press, 2009), pp. 619-621

occupied a small house in Somerstown. But, before this time, Charles was present with some of them in Tenterden Street to see his sister. Fanny received one of the prizes given to the pupils of the Royal Academy of Music. "I could not bear to think of myself—beyond the reach of all such honorable emulation and success. The tears ran down my face. I felt as if my heart were rent. I prayed, when I went to bed that night, to be lifted out of the humiliation and neglect in which I was. I never had suffered so much before. There was no envy in this." There was little need that he should say so. Extreme enjoyment in witnessing the exercise of her talents, the utmost pride in every success obtained by them, he manifested always to a degree otherwise quite unusual with him; and on the day of her funeral, which we passed together, I had most affecting proof of his tender and grateful memory of her in these childish days. A few more sentences, certainly not less touching than any that have gone before, will bring the story of them to its close. They stand here exactly as written by him:

"I am not sure that it was before this time, or after it, that the blacking-warehouse was removed to Chandos Street, Covent Garden. It is no matter. Next to the shop at the corner of Bedford Street in Chandos Street are two rather old-fashioned houses and shops adjoining one another. They were one then, or thrown into one, for the blacking-business; and had been a butter-shop. Opposite to them was, and is, a public-house, where I got my ale, under these new circumstances. The stones in the street may be smoothed by my small feet going across to it at dinner-time, and back again. The establishment was larger now, and we had one or two new boys. Bob Fagin and I had attained to great dexterity in tying up the pots. I forget how many we could do in five minutes. We worked, for the light's sake, near the second window as you come from Bedford Street; and we were so brisk at it that the people used to stop and look in. Sometimes there would be quite a little crowd there. I saw my father coming in at the door one day when we were very busy, and I wondered how he could bear it.

"Now, I generally had my dinner in the warehouse. Sometimes I brought it from home, so I was better off. I see myself coming across Russell Square from Somerstown, one morning, with some cold hotch-potch in a small basin tied up in a handkerchief. I had the same wanderings about the streets as I used to have, and was just as solitary and self-dependent as before; but I had not the same difficulty in merely living. I never, however, heard a word of being taken away, or of being otherwise than quite provided for.

"At last, one day, my father, and the relative so often mentioned, quarreled; quarreled by letter, for I took the letter from my father to him which caused the explosion, but quarreled very fiercely. It was about me. It may have had some backward reference, in part, for anything I know, to my employment at the window. All I am certain of is, that, soon after I had given him the letter, my cousin (he was a sort of cousin, by marriage) told me he was very much insulted about me, and that it was impossible to keep me after that. I cried very much, partly because it was so sudden, and partly because in his anger he was violent about my father, though gentle to me. Thomas, the old soldier, comforted me, and said he was sure it was for the best. With a relief so strange that it was like oppression, I went home.

"My mother set herself to accommodate the quarrel, and did so next day. She brought home a request for me to return next morning, and a high character of me, which I am very sure I deserved. My father said I should go back no more, and should go to school. I do not write resentfully or angrily; for I know how all these things have worked together to make me what I am; but I never afterwards forgot, I never shall forget, I never can forget, that my mother was warm for my being sent back.

"From that hour until this at which I write, no word of that part of my childhood which I have now gladly brought to a close has passed my lips to any human being. I have no idea how long it lasted; whether for a year, or much more, or less. From that hour until this my father and my mother have been stricken dumb upon it. I have never heard the least allusion to it, however far off and remote, from either of them. I have never, until I now impart it to this paper, in any burst of confidence with any one, my own wife not excepted, raised the curtain I then dropped, thank God."

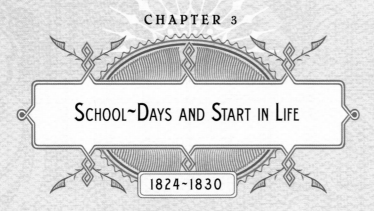

CHAPTER 3

SCHOOL~DAYS AND START IN LIFE

1824~1830

IN WHAT WAY THESE STRANGE EXPERIENCES of his boyhood affected him afterwards, this narrative of his life must show; but there were influences that made themselves felt even on his way to manhood.

His next move in life can be given in his own language: "There was a school in the Hampstead Road kept by Mr. Jones, a Welshman, to which my father dispatched me to ask for a card of terms. The boys were at dinner, and Mr. Jones was carving for them with a pair of holland sleeves on, when I acquitted myself of this commission. He came out, and gave me what I wanted; and hoped I should become a pupil. I did. At seven o'clock one morning, very soon afterwards, I went as day-scholar to Mr. Jones's establishment, which was in Mornington Place, and had its school-room sliced away by the Birmingham Railway, when that change came about. The school-room, however, was not threatened by directors or civil engineers then, and there was a board over the door, graced with the words WELLINGTON HOUSE ACADEMY."

At Wellington House Academy he remained nearly two years, being a little over fourteen years of age when he quitted it. In his minor writings as well as in *Copperfield* will be found general allusions to it, and there is a paper among his pieces reprinted from *Household Words* which purports specifically to describe it. To the account therein given of himself when he went to the school, as advanced enough, so safely had his memory retained its poor fragments of early schooling, to be put into *Virgil*, as getting sundry prizes, and as attaining to the eminent position of its first boy, one of his two schoolfellows with whom I have had communication makes objection; but both admit that the

general features of the place are reproduced with wonderful accuracy, and more especially in those points for which the school appears to have been much more notable than for anything connected with the scholarship of its pupils.

One who knew him in those early days, Mr. Owen P. Thomas, thus writes to me (February, 1871): "I had the honor of being Mr. Dickens's schoolfellow for about two years (1824-1826), both being day-scholars, at Mr. Jones's 'Classical and Commercial Academy,' as then inscribed in front of the house, and which was situated at the corner of Granby Street and the Hampstead Road.

"My recollection of Dickens whilst at school is that of a healthy-looking boy, small but well built, with a more than usual flow of spirits, inducing to harmless fun, seldom or never I think to mischief, to which so many lads at that age are prone. I cannot recall anything that then indicated he would hereafter become a literary celebrity; but perhaps he was too young then. He usually held his head more erect than lads ordinarily do, and there was a general smartness about him. His weekday dress of jacket and trowsers, I can clearly remember, was what is called pepper-and-salt; and, instead of the frill that most boys of his age wore then, he had a turn-down collar, so that he looked less youthful in consequence. He invented what we termed a 'lingo,' produced by the addition of a few letters of the same sound to every word; and it was our ambition, walking and talking thus along the street, to be considered foreigners. As an alternate amusement the present writer well remembers extemporizing tales of some sort, and reciting them offhand, with Dickens and Danson or Tobin walking on either side of him.

"After a lapse of years," Mr. Thomas continues, "I recognized the celebrated writer as the individual I had known so well as a boy and upon Mr. Dickens visiting Reading in December, 1854, to give one of his earliest readings for the benefit of the literary institute, of which he had become president on Mr. Justice Talfourd's death, we conversed about mutual schoolfellows, and among others Daniel Tobin was referred to, whom I remembered to have been Dickens's most intimate companion in the school-days (1824 to 1826). His reply was that Tobin either was then, or had previously been, assisting him in the capacity of amanuensis; but there is a subsequent mystery about Tobin, in connection with his friend and patron, which I have never been able to comprehend; for I understood shortly afterwards that there was entire separation between them, and it must have been an offense of some gravity to have sundered an acquaintance formed in early youth, and which had endured, greatly to Tobin's advantage, so long. He resided in our school-days in one of the now old and grimy-looking stone-fronted houses in George Street, Euston Road, a few doors from the Orange-tree tavern. It is the opinion of the other schoolfellow with whom we were intimate, Doctor Danson, that upon leaving school Mr. Dickens and Tobin entered the same solicitor's office, and this he thinks was either in or near Lincoln's Inn Fields."

Wellington Academy. Dickens's school

"OUR SCHOOL," *HOUSEHOLD WORDS*, 11 OCTOBER 1851

Early experiences are captured in Dickens's journalism as well as we have seen in his fiction:

THE master was supposed among us to know nothing, and one of the ushers was supposed to know everything. We are still inclined to think the first-named supposition perfectly correct. We have a general idea that its subject had been in the leather trade, and had bought us—meaning Our School—of another proprietor who was immensely learned. Whether this belief had any real foundation, we are not likely ever to know now. The only branches of education with which he showed the least acquaintance, were, ruling and corporally punishing. He was always ruling ciphering-books with a bloated mahogany ruler, or smiting the palms of offenders with the same diabolical instrument, or viciously drawing a pair of pantaloons tight with one of his large hands, and caning the wearer with the other. We have no doubt whatever that this occupation was the principal solace of his existence. [. . .] Our School was remarkable for white mice. Red-polls, linnets, and even canaries, were kept in desks, drawers, hat-boxes, and other strange refuges for birds; but white mice were the favourite stock. The boys trained the mice, much better than the masters trained the boys. We recall one white mouse, who lived in the cover of a Latin dictionary, who ran up ladders, drew Roman chariots, shouldered muskets, turned wheels, and even made a very creditable appearance on the stage as the Dog of Montargis. He might have achieved greater things, but for having the misfortune to mistake his way in a triumphal procession to the Capitol, when he fell into a deep inkstand, and was dyed black and drowned. The mice were the occasion of some most ingenious engineering, in the construction of their houses and instruments of performance. The famous one belonged to a company of proprietors, some of whom have since made Railroads, Engines, and Telegraphs; the chairman has erected mills and bridges in New Zealand.

The offense of Tobin went no deeper than the having at last worn out even Dickens's patience and kindness. His applications for relief were so incessantly repeated, that to cut him and them adrift altogether was the only way of escape from what had become an intolerable nuisance.

From Dickens himself I never heard much allusion to the school thus described; but I knew that, besides being the subject dealt with in *Household Words*, it had supplied some of the lighter traits of Salem House for *Copperfield*; and that to the fact of one of its tutors being afterwards engaged to teach a boy of Macready's, our common friend, Dickens used to point for one of the illustrations of his favorite theory as to the smallness of the world, and how things and persons apparently the most unlikely to meet were continually knocking up against each other. Dickens certainly had not quitted school many months before his father had made sufficient interest with an attorney of Gray's Inn, Mr. Edward Blackmore, to obtain him regular employment in his office. In this capacity of clerk, our only trustworthy glimpse of him we owe to the last-named gentleman, who has described briefly, and I do not doubt authentically, the services so rendered by him to the law. It cannot be said that they were noteworthy, though it might be difficult to find a more distinguished person who has borne the title, unless we make exception for the very father of literature himself, whom Chaucer, with amusing illustration of the way in which words change their meanings, calls "that conceited clerke Homere."

But, even thus, the process of education went on, defying what seemed to interrupt it; and in the amount of his present equipment for his needs of life, what he brought from the Wellington House Academy can have borne but the smallest proportion to his acquirement at Mr. Blackmore's. Yet to seek to identify, without help from himself, any passages in his books with those boyish law-experiences, would be idle and hopeless enough. In the earliest of his writings, and down to the very latest, he worked exhaustively the field which is opened by an attorney's office to a student of life and manners; but we have not now to deal with his numerous varieties of the genus clerk drawn thus for the amusement of others, but with the acquisitions which at present he was storing up for himself from the opportunities such offices opened to him. Nor would it be possible to have better illustrative comment on all these years than is furnished by his father's reply to a friend it was now hoped to interest on his behalf, which more than once I have heard him whimsically, but good-humoredly, imitate. "Pray, Mr. Dickens, where was your son educated?" "Why, indeed, sir—ha! ha!—he may be said to have educated himself!" Of the two kinds of education which Gibbon says that all men who rise above the common level receive,—the first, that of his teachers, and the second, more personal and more important, his own,—he had the advantage only of the last. It nevertheless sufficed for him.

Very nearly another eighteen months were now to be spent mainly in practical preparation for what he was, at this time, led finally to choose as an employment from which a fair income was certain with such talents as he possessed; his father already having taken to it, in these latter years, in aid of the family resources. In his father's house, which was at Hampstead through the first portion of the Mornington Street school time, then in the house out of Seymour Street mentioned by Dr. Danson, and afterwards, upon the elder Dickens going into the gallery, in Bentinck Street, Manchester Square, Charles had continued to live; and, influenced doubtless by the example before him, he took sudden determination to qualify himself thoroughly for what his father was lately become, a newspaper parliamentary reporter. He set resolutely, therefore, to the study of short-hand; and, for the additional help of such general information about books as a fairly-educated youth might be expected to have, as well as to satisfy some higher personal cravings, he became an assiduous attendant in the British Museum reading-room. He would frequently refer to these days as decidedly the usefulest to himself he had ever passed; and, judging from the results, they must have been so. No man who knew him in later years, and

talked to him familiarly of books and things, would have suspected his education in boyhood, almost entirely self-acquired as it was, to have been so rambling or haphazard as I have here described it. The secret consisted in this, that, whatever for the time he had to do, he lifted himself, there and then, to the level of, and at no time disregarded the rules that guided the hero of his novel. "Whatever I have tried to do in life, I have tried with all my heart to do well. What I have devoted myself to, I have devoted myself to completely. Never to put one hand to anything on which I could throw my whole self, and never to affect depreciation of my work, whatever it was, I find now to have been my golden rules."

What it was that made it not quite heart-breaking to the hero of the fiction, its readers know; and something of the same kind was now to enter into the actual experience of its writer. First let me say, however, that after subduing to his wants in marvelously quick time this unruly and unaccommodating servant of stenography, what he most desired was still not open to him. "There never was such a short-hand writer," has been often said to me by Mr. Beard, the friend he first made in that line when he entered the gallery, and with whom to the close of his life he maintained the friendliest intercourse. But there was no opening for him in the gallery yet. He had to pass nearly two years as a reporter for one of the offices in Doctors' Commons, practicing in this and the other law courts, before he became a sharer in parliamentary toils and triumphs; and what sustained his young hero through something of the same sort of trial was also his own support. He too had his Dora, at apparently the same hopeless elevation; striven for as the one only thing to be attained, and even more unattainable, for neither did he succeed nor happily did she die; but the one idol, like the other, supplying a motive to exertion for the time, and otherwise opening out to the idolater, both in fact and fiction, a highly unsubstantial, happy, foolish time. I used to laugh and tell him I had no belief in any but the book Dora, until the incident of a sudden reappearance of the real one in his life, nearly six years after *Copperfield* was written, convinced me there had been a more actual foundation for those chapters of his book than I was ready to suppose.

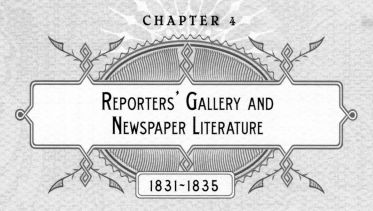

CHAPTER 4

REPORTERS' GALLERY AND NEWSPAPER LITERATURE

1831~1835

Dickens was nineteen years old when at last he entered the gallery. His father, with whom he still lived in Bentinck Street, had already, as we have seen, joined the gallery as a reporter for one of the morning papers, and was now in the more comfortable circumstances derived from the addition to his official pension which this praise-worthy labor insured; but his own engagement on the *Chronicle* dates somewhat later. His first parliamentary service was given to the *True Sun,* a journal which had then on its editorial staff some dear friends of mine, through whom I became myself a contributor to it, and afterwards, in common with all concerned, whether in its writing, reporting, printing, or publishing, a sharer in its difficulties. The most formidable of these arrived one day in a general strike of the reporters; and I well remember noticing at this dread time, on the staircase of the magnificent mansion we were lodged in, a young man of my own age, whose keen animation of look would have arrested attention anywhere, and whose name, upon inquiry, I then for the first time heard. It was coupled with the fact, which gave it interest even then, that "young Dickens" had been spokesman for the recalcitrant reporters, and conducted their case triumphantly. He was afterwards during two sessions engaged for the *Mirror of Parliament,* which one of his uncles by the mother's side originated and conducted; and finally, in his twenty-third year, he became a reporter for the *Morning Chronicle.*

A step far more momentous to him (though then he did not know it) he had taken shortly before. In the December number for 1833 of what then was called the *Old Monthly Magazine,* his first published piece of writing had seen the light. He has described himself dropping this paper ("Mr. Minns and his Cousin," as he afterwards entitled it, but which appeared in the magazine as "A Dinner at Poplar Walk") stealthily one evening at twilight, with fear and trembling, into a dark letter-box in a dark office up a dark court in Fleet Street; and he has told his agitation when it appeared in all the glory of print: "On which occasion I walked down to Westminster Hall, and turned into it for half an hour, because my eyes were so dimmed with joy and pride that they could not bear the street, and were not fit to be seen there."

He had purchased the magazine at a shop in the Strand; and exactly two years afterwards, in the younger member of a publishing firm who had called, at the chambers in Furnival's Inn to which he had moved soon after entering the gallery, with the proposal that originated Pickwick, he recognized the person he had bought that magazine from, and whom before or since he had never seen.

Mr. James Grant, a writer who was himself in the gallery with Dickens, and who states that among its eighty or ninety reporters he occupied the very highest rank, not merely for accuracy in reporting but for marvelous quickness in transcribing, has lately also told us that while there he was exceedingly reserved in his manners, and that, though showing the usual courtesies to all he was concerned with in his duties, the only personal intimacy he formed was with Mr. Thomas Beard, then too reporting for the *Morning Chronicle.* I have already mentioned the friendly and familiar relations maintained with this gentleman to the close of his life; and in confirmation of Mr. Grant's statement I can further say that the only other associate of these early reporting days to whom I ever heard him refer with special regard was the late Mr. Vincent Dowling, many years editor of *Bell's Life,* with whom he did not continue much personal intercourse, but of whose character as well as talents he had formed a very high opinion.

An anecdote of these reporting days, with its sequel, may be added from his own alleged relation, in which, however, mistakes occur that it seems strange he should have made. The story, as told, is that the late Lord Derby, when Mr. Stanley, had on some important occasion made

Overleaf: Westminster Hall, watercolor on paper by John Coney (detail), 1807

"Dinner at Poplar Walk," Old Monthly Magazine, December 1833

This is Dickens's first published piece. It is collected in Sketches by Boz, 1836, under the title "Mr. Minns and His Cousin":

MR. Augustus Minns was a bachelor, of about forty as he said—of about eight-and-forty as his friends said. He was always exceedingly clean, precise, and tidy; perhaps somewhat priggish, and the most retiring man in the world. He usually wore a brown frock-coat without a wrinkle, light inexplicables without a spot, a neat neckerchief with a remarkably neat tie, and boots without a fault; moreover, he always carried a brown silk umbrella with an ivory handle. He was a clerk in Somerset-house, or, as he said himself, he held 'a responsible situation under Government.' He had a good and increasing salary, in addition to some "10,000 pounds" of his own (invested in the funds), and he occupied a first floor in Tavistock-street, Covent-garden, where he had resided for twenty years, having been in the habit of quarrelling with his landlord the whole time: regularly giving notice of his intention to quit on the first day of every quarter, and as regularly countermanding it on the second. There were two classes of created objects which he held in the deepest and most unmingled horror; these were dogs, and children. He was not unamiable, but he could, at any time, have viewed the execution of a dog, or the assassination of an infant, with the liveliest satisfaction. Their habits were at variance with his love of order; and his love of order was as powerful as his love of life. Mr. Augustus Minns had no relations, in or near London, with the exception of his cousin, Mr. Octavius Budden, to whose son, whom he had never seen (for he disliked the father), he had consented to become godfather by proxy. Mr. Budden having realised a moderate fortune by exercising the trade or calling of a corn-chandler, and having a great predilection for the country, had purchased a cottage in the vicinity of Stamford-hill, whither he retired with the wife of his bosom, and his only son, Master Alexander Augustus Budden. One evening, as Mr. and Mrs. B. were admiring their son, discussing his various merits, talking over his education, and disputing whether the classics should be made an essential part thereof, the lady pressed so strongly upon her husband the propriety of cultivating the friendship of Mr. Minns in behalf of their son, that Mr. Budden at last made up his mind, that it should not be his fault if he and his cousin were not in future more intimate.

a speech which all the reporters found it necessary greatly to abridge; that its essential points had nevertheless been so well given in the Chronicle that Mr. Stanley, having need of it for himself in greater detail, had sent a request to the reporter to meet him in Carlton House Terrace and take down the entire speech; that Dickens attended and did the work accordingly, much to Mr. Stanley's satisfaction; and that, on his dining with Mr. Gladstone in recent years, and finding the aspect of the dining-room strangely familiar, he discovered afterwards on inquiry that it was there he had taken the speech. The story, as it actually occurred, is connected with the brief life of the *Mirror of Parliament*. It was not at any special desire of Mr. Stanley's, but for that new record of the debates, which had been started by one of the uncles of Dickens and professed to excel *Hansard* in giving verbatim reports, that the famous speech against O'Connell was taken as described. The young reporter went to the room in Carlton Terrace because the work of his uncle Barrow's publication required to be done there; and if, in later years, the great author was in the same room as the guest of the prime minister, it must have been but a month or two before he died, when for the first time he visited and breakfasted with Mr. Gladstone.

The other occupation had meanwhile not been lost sight of, and for this we are to go back a little. Since the first sketch appeared in the *Monthly Magazine*, nine others have enlivened the pages of later numbers of the same magazine, the last in February, 1835, and that which appeared in the preceding August having first had the signature of Boz.

This was the nickname of a pet child, his youngest brother Augustus, whom in honor of the Vicar of Wakefield he had dubbed Moses, which being facetiously pronounced through the nose became Boses, and being shortened became Boz. "Boz was a very familiar household word to me, long before I was an author, and so I came to adopt it." Thus had he fully invented his *Sketches by Boz* before they were even so called, or any one was ready

to give much attention to them; and the next invention needful to himself was some kind of payment in return for them. The magazine was owned as well as conducted at this time by a Mr. Holland, who had come back from Bolivar's South American campaigns with the rank of captain, and had hoped to make it a popular mouthpiece for his ardent liberalism. But this hope, as well as his own health, quite failed; and he had sorrowfully to decline receiving any more of the sketches when they had to cease as voluntary offerings. I do not think that either he or the

Dickens's signed pseudonym

George Cruikshank

CHARLES DICKENS TAKING DOWN AN ELECTION SPEECH OF LORD JOHN RUSSELL IN THE RAIN, WHILE TWO COLLEAGUES HELD A HANDKERCHIEF OVER HIS NOTEBOOK.

Charles Dickens reporting John Russell's speech at Exeter in Castle Yard

magazine lived many weeks after an evening I passed with him in Doughty Street in 1837, when he spoke in a very touching way of the failure of this and other enterprises of his life, and of the help that Dickens had been to him.

Nothing thus being forthcoming from the *Monthly*, it was of course but natural the sketches too should cease to be forthcoming; and, even before the above-named February number appeared, a new opening had been found for them. An evening offshoot to the *Morning Chronicle* had been lately in hand; and to a countryman of Black's engaged in the preparations for it, Mr. George Hogarth, Dickens was communicating from his rooms in Furnival's Inn, on the evening of Tuesday, the 20th of January, 1835, certain hopes and fancies he had formed. This was the beginning of his knowledge of an accomplished and kindly man, with whose family his relations were soon to become so intimate as to have an influence on all his future career. Mr. Hogarth had asked him, as a favor to himself, to write an original sketch for the first number of the enterprise, and in writing back to say with what readiness he should comply, and how anxiously he should desire to do his best for the person who had made the request, he mentioned what had arisen in his mind. It had occurred to him that he might not be unreasonably or improperly trespassing farther on Mr. Hogarth if, trusting to his kindness to refer the application to the proper quarter, he begged to ask whether it was probable, if he commenced a regular series of articles under some attractive title for the *Evening Chronicle*, its conductors would think he had any claim to *some* additional remuneration (of course, of no great amount) for doing so. In short, he wished to put it to the proprietors—first, whether a continuation of some chapters of light papers in the style of his street-sketches would be considered of use to the new journal; and secondly, if so, whether they would not think it fair and reasonable that, taking his share of the ordinary reporting business of the *Chronicle* besides, he should receive something for the papers beyond his ordinary salary as a reporter. The request was thought fair, he began the sketches, and his salary was raised from five to seven guineas a week.

Furnival's Inn, watercolor, pen and ink over graphite, by Samuel Ireland (detail), (d. 1800)

CHAPTER 5

FIRST BOOK, AND ORIGIN OF PICKWICK

1836

THE OPENING OF 1836 FOUND HIM collecting into two volumes the first series of *Sketches by Boz*, of which he had sold the copyright for a conditional payment of (I think) a hundred and fifty pounds to a young publisher named Macrone, whose acquaintance he had made through Mr. Ainsworth a few weeks before.[2] At this time also, we are told in a letter before quoted, the editorship of the *Monthly Magazine* having come into Mr. James Grant's hands, this gentleman, applying to him through its previous editor to know if he would again contribute to it, learned two things: the first, that he was going to be married; and the second, that, having entered into an arrangement to write a monthly serial, his duties in future would leave him small spare time. Both pieces of news were soon confirmed. The *Times* of the 26th of March, 1836, gave notice that on the 31st would be published the first shilling number of the *Posthumous Papers of the Pickwick Club*, edited by Boz; and the same journal of a few days later announced that on the 2nd of April Mr. Charles Dickens had married Catherine, the eldest daughter of Mr. George Hogarth, whom already we have met as his fellow-worker on the *Chronicle*. The honeymoon was passed in the neighborhood to which at all times of interest in his life he turned with a strange recurring fondness; and while the young couple are at the quiet little village of Chalk, on the road between Gravesend and Rochester, I will relate exactly the origin of the ever-memorable Mr. Pickwick.

A young publishing-house had started recently, among other enterprises ingenious rather than important, a Library of Fiction; among the authors they wished to enlist in it was the writer of the sketches in the *Monthly*; and, to the extent

of one paper during the past year, they had effected this through their editor, Mr. Charles Whitehead, a very ingenious and very unfortunate man."

And now comes another person on the scene.

"In November, 1835," continues Mr. Chapman, "we published a little book called the *Squib Annual*, with plates by Seymour; and it was during my visit to him to see after them that he said he should like to do a series of cockney-sporting plates of a superior sort to those he had already published. I said I thought they might do, if accompanied by letter-press and published in monthly parts; and, this being agreed to, we wrote to the author of *Three Courses and a Dessert*, and proposed it; but, receiving no answer, the scheme dropped for some months, till Seymour said he wished us to decide, as another job had offered which would fully occupy his time; and it was on this we decided to ask you to do it. Having opened already a connection with you for our Library of Fiction, we naturally applied to you to do the *Pickwick*; but I do not think we even mentioned our intention to Mr. Seymour, and I am quite sure that from the beginning to the end nobody but yourself had anything whatever to do with it. Our prospectus was out at the end of February, and it had all been arranged before that date."

The member of the firm who carried the application to him in Furnival's Inn was not the writer of this letter, but Mr. Hall, who had sold him two years before, not knowing that he was the purchaser, the magazine in which his first effusion was printed; and he has himself described what passed at the interview: "The idea propounded to me was that the monthly something should be a vehicle for certain plates to be executed by Mr. Seymour; and there was a notion, either on the part of that admirable humorous artist, or of my visitor, that a NIMROD CLUB, the members of which were to go out shooting, fishing, and so forth, and getting themselves into difficulties through their want of dexterity, would be the best means of introducing these. I objected, on consideration that, although born and partly bred in the country, I was no great sportsman, except in regard to all kinds of locomotion; that the idea was not novel, and had already been much used; that it would be infinitely better for the plates to arise naturally out of the text; and that I would like to take my own way, with a freer range of English

Charles John Huffam Dickens of Parish
Furnivals Inn, in this County. Bachelor
and *Catherine Thomson Hogarth* of *this* Parish
Spinster, a Minor
were married in this *Church* by *Licence* with Consent of
George Hogarth, the natural and
lawful Father of the said Minor { this *Second* Day of
April in the Year One thousand eight hundred and *Thirty-six*
By me *R.W. Morrell Curate*
This Marriage was solemnized between us { *Charles Dickens.*
Catherine Thomson Hogarth
In the Presence of { *Geo Hogarth Elizabth M Dickens*
Georgina Hogarth Thomas Beard
No. 201. *John Dickens*

Catherine Dickens (left, 1838) and Charles Dickens (right, 1837), chalk and crayon drawings by Samuel Laurence;
Marriage certificate (top) of Charles Dickens and Catherine Hogarth, April 2, 1836

Seymour's "The Dying Clown" for *Pickwick*
TOP LEFT: Robert Seymour

scenes and people, and was afraid I should ultimately do so in any case, whatever course I might prescribe to myself at starting. My views being deferred to, I thought of Mr. Pickwick, and wrote the first number; from the proof-sheets of which Mr. Seymour made his drawing of the club and his happy portrait of its founder. I connected Mr. Pickwick with a club, because of the original suggestion; and I put in Mr. Winkle expressly for the use of Mr. Seymour."

Mr. Hall was dead when this statement was first made, in the preface to the cheap edition in 1847; but Mr. Chapman clearly recollected his partner's account of the interview, and confirmed every part of it, in his letter of 1849,[3] with one exception. In giving Mr. Seymour credit for the figure by which all the habitable globe knows Mr. Pickwick, and which certainly at the outset helped to make him a reality, it had given the artist too much. The reader will hardly be so startled as I was on coming to the closing line of Mr. Chapman's confirmatory letter: "As this letter is to be historical, I may as well claim what little belongs to me in the matter, and that is the figure of Pickwick. Seymour's first sketch was of a

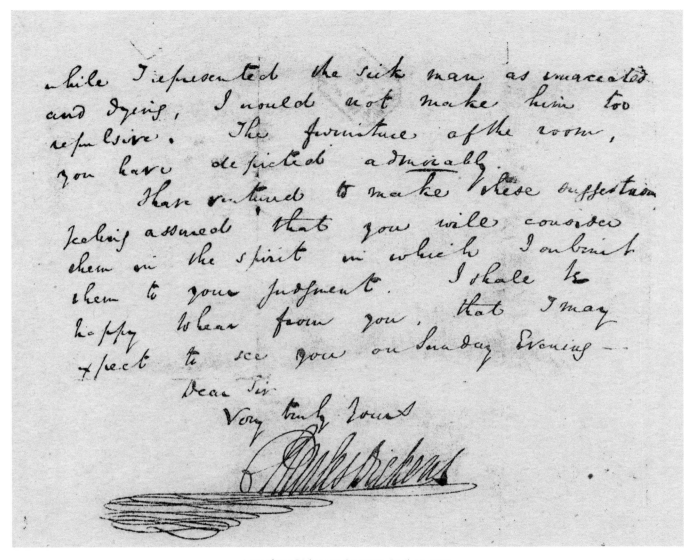

Letter from Dickens to Seymour, April 14, 1836

long, thin man. The present immortal one he made from my description of a friend of mine at Richmond, a fat old beau, who would wear, in spite of the ladies' protests, drab tights and black gaiters. His name was John Forster."

On the coincidences, resemblances, and surprises of life, Dickens liked especially to dwell, and few things moved his fancy so pleasantly. The world, he would say, was so much smaller than we thought it; we were all so connected by fate without knowing it; people supposed to be far apart were so constantly elbowing each other; and tomorrow bore so close a resemblance to nothing half so much as to yesterday. Here were the only two leading incidents of his own life before I knew him, his marriage and the first appearance of his Pickwick; and it turned out after all that I had some shadowy association with both. He was married on the anniversary of my birthday, and the original of the figure of Mr. Pickwick bore my name.[4]

The first number had not yet appeared when his *Sketches by Boz, Illustrative of Every-Day Life and Every-Day People*, came forth in two duodecimos with some capital

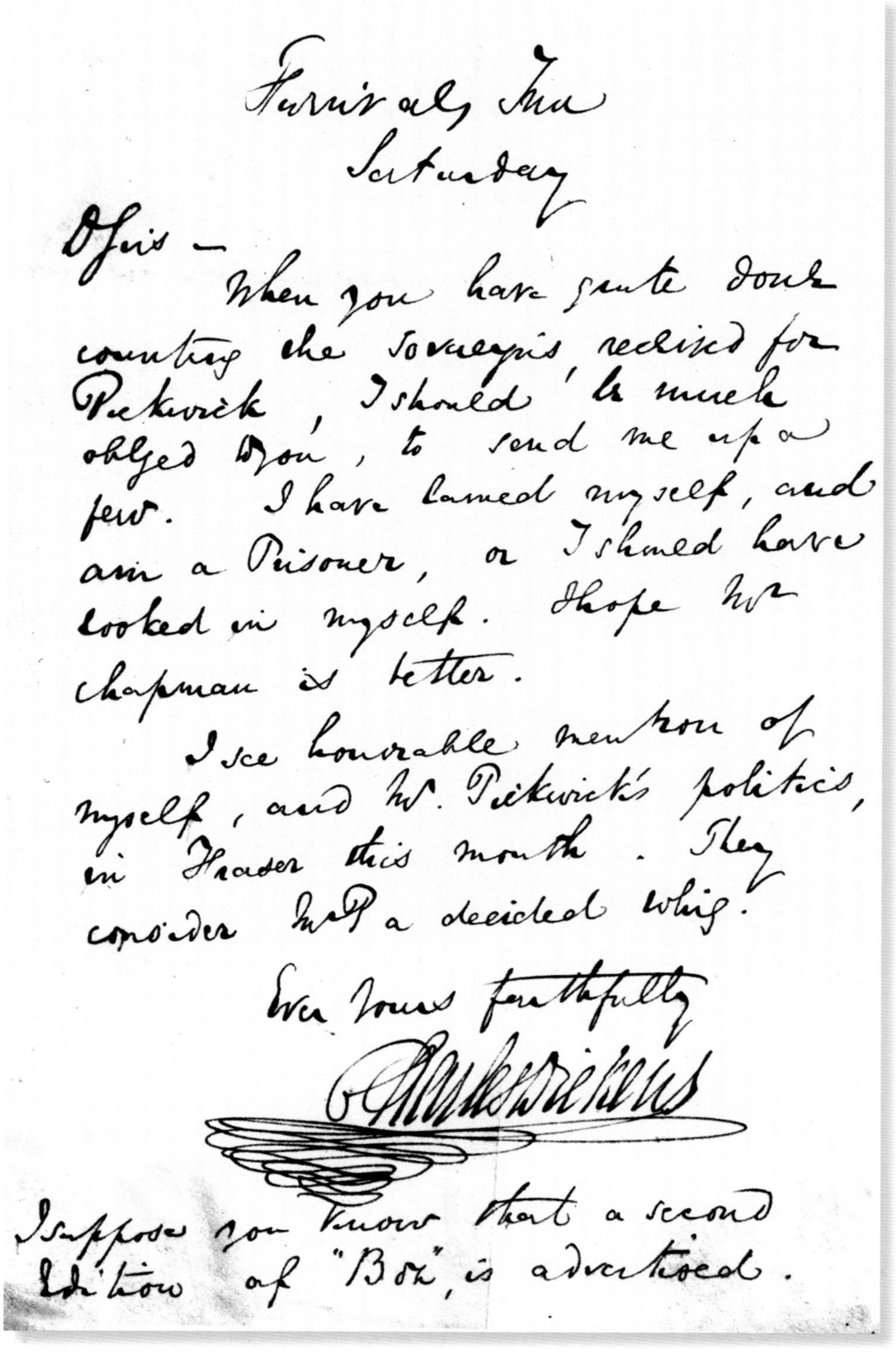

Furnivals Inn
Saturday

Dfsir —
When you have quite done counting the sovereigns received for Pickwick, I should be much obliged to you, to send me up a few. I have lamed myself, and am a Prisoner, or I should have looked in myself. I hope Mr Chapman is better.

I see honourable mention of myself, and Mr. Pickwick's politics, in Fraser this month. They consider me a decided whig.

Ever Yours faithfully

[signature: Charles Dickens]

I suppose you know that a second Edition of "Boz", is advertised.

Letter from Dickens to his publishers, Chapman and Hall, August 6, 1836

Unused design for *Sketches by Boz*, by George Cruikshank

FROM DICKENS'S PREFACE TO THE FIRST EDITION OF THE FIRST SERIES OF *SKETCHES BY BOZ*, FEBRUARY 1836

At this early point of his career, Dickens, much less sure of his audience, is glad to secure Cruikshank as a recognized name:

In humble imitation of a prudent course, universally adopted by aeronauts, the Author of these volumes throws them up as his pilot balloon, trusting it may catch favourable current, and devoutly and earnestly hoping it may *go off well*—a sentiment in which his Publisher cordially concurs.

Unlike the generality of pilot balloons which carry no car, in this one it is very possible for a man to embark, not only himself, but all his hopes of future fame, and all his chances of future success. Entertaining no considerable feeling of trepidation at the idea of making so perilous a voyage in so frail a machine, alone and unaccompanied, the Author was naturally desirous to secure the assistance and friendship of some well-known individual, who had frequently contributed to the success, though his well-earned reputation rendered it impossible for him ever to have shared the hazard, of similar undertakings. To whom, as possessing the requisite in an eminent degree, could he apply but to GEORGE CRUIKSHANK? The application was readily heard, and at once acceded to: this is their first voyage in company, but it may not be the last.

cuts by Cruikshank, and with a preface in which he spoke of the nervousness he should have had in venturing alone before the public, and of his delight in getting the help of Cruikshank, who had frequently contributed to the success, though his well-earned reputation rendered it impossible for him ever to have shared the hazard, of similar undertakings.

It very soon became apparent that there was no hazard here. The *Sketches* were much more talked about than the first two or three numbers of *Pickwick*, and I

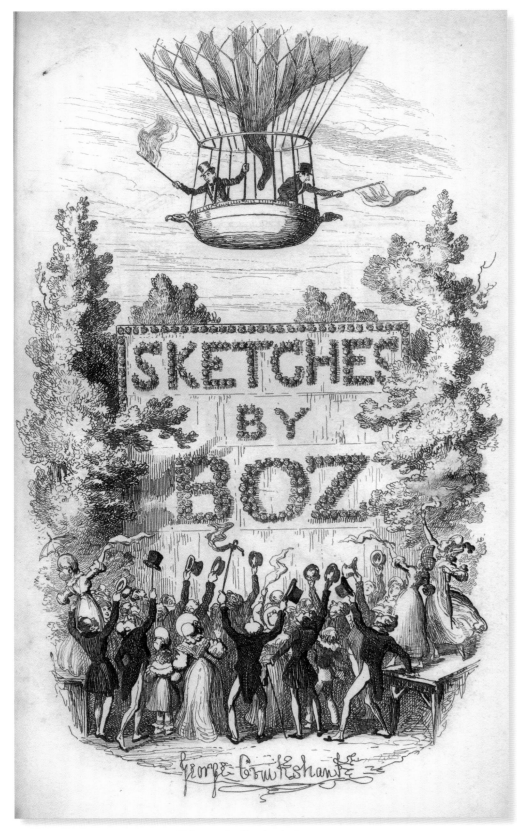

Title page for *Sketches by Boz*, 1836

St. James's Theatre.

Mr. HARLEY,

STAGE-MANAGER,

Has the honor to announce that

HIS BENEFIT

Is appointed for

This Evening, MONDAY, March 13th, 1837,

On which occasion will be performed

an original Comic Burletta, in One Act, Written by BOZ, called

IS SHE HIS WIFE ?

Or, SOMETHING SINGULAR !

Alfred Lovetown, Esq, Mr FORESTER,   Mr Peter Limbury, Mr GARDNER,

Felix Tapkins, Esq. (formerly of the India House Leadenhall Street, and now of Rustic Lodge near Reading,) Mr HARLEY.

Mrs Lovetown, Miss ALLISON,   Mrs Peter Limbury, Madame SALA.

Mr HARLEY

Will in the Character of

MR. PICKWICK

Make his First Visit

TO THE ST. JAMES'S THEATRE,

And relate, to a Scotch Air, his

EXPERIENCES

OF

"A White Bait Dinner at Blackwall,"

EDITED EXPRESSLY FOR HIM BY HIS BIOGRAPHER

"BOZ!"

The whole to conclude with, (by Particular Desire) for the **58th & Last Night this Season**

THE STRANGE
Gentleman.

Mr. Owen Overton (Mayor of a Small Town on the Road to Gretna, & useful at the St. James's Arms) Mr HOLLINGSWORTH

John Johnson (Detained at the St. James's Arms) Mr. SIDNEY,

The Strange Gentleman (Just Arrived at the St. James's Arms) Mr. HARLEY.

Charles Tomkins (Incognito at the St. James's Arms) Mr. FORESTER,

Tom Sparks (a One Eyed "Boots," at the St. James's Arms) Mr. GARDNER,

John.... Mr. WILLIAMSON,

Tom.... Waiters at the St. James's Arms Mr. MAY,

Will.... Mr. COULSON,

Julia Dobbs (Looking for a Husband at the St. James's Arms) Madame SALA.

Fanny Wilson (With an Appointment at the St. James's Arms) Miss SMITH,

Mary Wilson (her Sister awkwardly situated at the St. James's Arms) Miss JULIA SMITH

Mrs. Noakes (the Landlady at the St. James's Arms) Mrs PENSON,

Chambermaid, (at the St. James's Arms) Miss STUART.

Duet—"I know a Bank," .... Miss SMITH and Miss JULIA SMITH.

TICKETS, BOXES, and PRIVATE BOXES, may be obtained of Mr HARLEY, 14, Upper Gower Street, Bedford Square; and of Mr W. WARNE, at the Box-Office, at the Theatre, from Eleven until Six o'Clock daily.

Boxes 5s.--Second Price 3s.   Pit 3s.--Second Price 2s. Gallery 1s, 6d.--Second Price 1s.

VIVANT REX ET REGINA

Playbill for *The Strange Gentleman*

remember still with what hearty praise the book was first named to me by my dear friend Albany Fonblanque, as keen and clear a judge as ever lived either of books or men. Richly did it merit all the praise it had, and more, I will add, than he was ever disposed to give to it himself. He decidedly underrated it.

Between the first and the second numbers of *Pickwick*, the artist, Mr. Seymour, died by his own hand; and the number came out with three instead of four illustrations. There was at first a little difficulty in replacing him, and for a single number Mr. Buss was interposed. But before the fourth number a choice had been made, which as time went on was so thoroughly justified, that through the greater part of the wonderful career which was then beginning the connection was kept up, and Mr. Hablot Browne's name is not unworthily associated with the masterpieces of Dickens's genius. Dickens has himself described another change now made in the publication: "We started with a number of twenty-four pages and four illustrations. Mr. Seymour's sudden and lamented death before the second number was published, brought about a quick decision upon a point already in agitation: the number became one of thirty-two pages with only two illustrations, and remained so to the end."

The Session of 1836 terminated his connection with the gallery, and some fruits of his increased leisure showed themselves before the close of the year. His eldest sister's musical attainments and connections had introduced him to many cultivators and professors of that art; he was led to take much interest in Mr. Braham's enterprise at the St. James's theatre; and in aid of it he wrote a farce for Mr. Harley, founded upon one of his sketches, and the story and songs for an opera composed by his friend Mr. Hullah. Both the *Strange Gentleman*, acted in September, and the *Village Coquettes*, produced in December, 1836, had a good success; and the last is memorable to me for having brought me first into personal communication with Dickens.

---

[2] To this date belongs a visit paid him at Furnival's Inn in Mr. Macrone's company by the notorious Mr. N. P. Willis, who calls him "a young paragraphist for the *Morning Chronicle*," and thus sketches his residence and himself: "In the most crowded part of Holborn, within a door or two of the Bull-and-Mouth Inn, we pulled up at the entrance of a large building used for lawyers' chambers. I followed by a long flight of stairs to an upper story, and was ushered into an uncarpeted and bleak-looking room, with a deal table, two or three chairs and a few books, a small boy and Mr. Dickens, for the contents. I was only struck at first with one thing (and I made a memorandum of it that evening as the strongest instance I had seen of English obsequiousness to employers), the degree to which the poor author was overpowered with the honor of his publisher's visit! I remember saying to myself, as I sat down on a rickety chair, 'My good fellow, if you were in America with that fine face and your ready quill, you would have no need to be condescended to by a publisher.' Dickens was dressed very much as he has since described Dick Swiveller, *minus* the swell look. His hair was cropped close to his head, his clothes scant, though jauntily cut, and, after changing a ragged office-coat for a shabby blue, he stood by the door, collarless and buttoned up, the very personification, I thought, of a close sailer to the wind." I remember, while my friend lived, our laughing heartily at this description, hardly a word of which is true; and I give it now as no unfair specimen of the kind of garbage that since his death also has been served up only too plentifully by some of his own as well as by others of Mr. Willis's countrymen.

[3] The appeal was then made to him because of recent foolish statements by members of Mr. Seymour's family, which Dickens thus contradicted: "It is with great unwillingness that I notice some intangible and incoherent assertions which have been made, professedly on behalf of Mr. Seymour, to the effect that he had some share in the invention of this book, or of anything in it, not faithfully described in the foregoing paragraph. With the moderation that is due equally to my respect for the memory of a brother-artist, and to my self-respect, I confine myself to placing on record here the facts—That Mr. Seymour never originated or suggested an incident, a phrase, or a word, to be found in this book. That Mr. Seymour died when only twenty-four pages of this book were published, and when assuredly not forty-eight were written. That I believe I never saw Mr. Seymour's handwriting in my life. That I never saw Mr. Seymour but once in my life, and that was on the night before his death, when he certainly offered no suggestion whatsoever. That I saw him then in the presence of two persons, both living, perfectly acquainted with all these facts, and whose written testimony to them I possess. Lastly, that Mr. Edward Chapman (the survivor of the original firm of Chapman & Hall) has set down in writing, for similar preservation, his personal knowledge of the origin and progress of this book, of the monstrosity of the baseless assertions in question, and (tested by details) even of the self-evident impossibility of there being any truth in them." The "written testimony" alluded to is also in my possession, having been inclosed to me by Dickens, in 1867, with Mr. Chapman's letter here referred to.

[4] Whether Mr. Chapman spelt the name correctly, or has unconsciously deprived his fat beau of the letter "r," I cannot say; but experience tells me that the latter is probable. I have been trying all my life to get my own name spelt correctly, and have only very imperfectly succeeded.

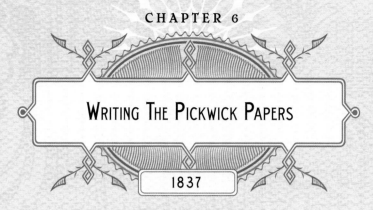

CHAPTER 6

WRITING THE PICKWICK PAPERS

1837

THE FIRST LETTER I HAD FROM HIM was at the close of 1836, from Furnival's Inn, when he sent me the book of his opera of the *Village Coquettes*, which had been published by Mr. Bentley; and this was followed, two months later, by his collected *Sketches*, both first and second series; which he desired me to receive "as a very small testimony of the donor's regard and obligations, as well as of his desire to cultivate and avail himself of a friendship which has been so pleasantly thrown in his way."

Very different was his face in those days from that which photography has made familiar to the present generation.

A look of youthfulness first attracted you, and then a candor and openness of expression which made you sure of the qualities within. The features were very good. He had a capital forehead, a firm nose with full wide nostril, eyes wonderfully beaming with intellect and running over with humor and cheerfulness, and a rather prominent mouth strongly marked with sensibility. The head was altogether well formed and symmetrical, and the air and carriage of it were extremely spirited. The hair so scant and grizzled in later days was then of a rich brown and most luxuriant abundance,

John Forster, oil painting by Daniel Maclise (detail), 1830

and the bearded face of his last two decades had hardly a vestige of hair or whisker; but there was that in the face as I first recollect it which no time could change, and which remained implanted on it unalterably to the last. This was the quickness, keenness, and practical power, the eager, restless, energetic outlook on each several feature, that seemed to tell so little of a student or writer of books, and so much of a man of action and business in the world. Light and motion flashed from every part of it.

Several unsuccessful efforts were made by each to get the other to his house before the door of either was opened at last. A son had been born to him on Twelfth-day (the 6th January, 1837), and before the close of the following month he and his wife were in the lodgings at Chalk they had occupied after their marriage. Early in March there is a letter from him accounting for the failure of a promise to call on me because of "a crew of house-agents and attorneys" through whom he had nearly missed his conveyance to Chalk, and been made "more than half wild besides." This was his last letter from Furnival's Inn. In that same month he went to 48, Doughty Street; and in his first letter to me from that address, dated at the close of the month, there is this passage: "We only called upon you a second time in the hope of getting you to dine with us, and were much disappointed not to find you. I have delayed writing a reply to your note, meaning to call upon you. I have been so much engaged, however, in the pleasant occupation of 'moving' that I have not had time; and I am obliged at last to write and say that I have been long engaged to the *Pickwick* publishers to a dinner in honor of that hero which comes off to-morrow. I am consequently unable to accept your kind invite, which I frankly own I should have liked much better."

That Saturday's celebration of his twelfth number, the anniversary of the birth of *Pickwick*, preceded by but a few weeks a personal sorrow which profoundly moved him. His wife's next younger sister, Mary, who lived with them, and by sweetness of nature even more than by graces of person had made herself the ideal of his life, died with a terrible suddenness that for the time completely bore him down. His grief and suffering were intense, and affected him, as will be seen, through many after-years. The publication of *Pickwick* was interrupted for two months, the effort of writing it not being possible to him. He moved for change of scene to Hampstead, and here, at the close of May, I visited him, and became first his guest. More than ordinarily susceptible at the moment to all kindliest impressions, his heart opened itself to mine. I left him as much his friend, and as entirely in his confidence, as if I had known him for years.

It was not until the fourth or fifth number of *Pickwick* (in the latter Sam Weller made his first appearance) that its importance began to be understood by "the trade," and on the eve of the issue of its sixth number, the 22nd August, 1836, he had signed an agreement with Mr. Bentley to undertake the editorship of a monthly magazine to be started the following January, to which he was to supply a serial story; and soon afterwards he had agreed with the same publisher to write two other tales, the first at a specified early date; the expressed remuneration in each case being certainly quite inadequate to the claims of a writer of any marked popularity. Under these Bentley agreements he was now writing, month by month, the first half of *Oliver Twist*, and, under his Chapman & Hall agreement, the last half of *Pickwick*.

His new story was now beginning largely to share attention with his *Pickwick Papers*, and it was delightful to see how real all its people became to him. What I had most, indeed, to notice in him, at the very outset of his career, was his indifference to any praise of his performances on the merely literary side, compared with the higher recognition of them as bits of actual life, with the meaning and purpose on their part, and the responsibility on his, of

Chalk House, Kent, where Charles and Catherine Dickens spent their honeymoon. Published in *Dickens-Land*, illustration by E. W. Haslehust, 1911

Sketch of Doughty Street residence

Mary Hogarth's grave, at Kensal Green Cemetery

realities rather than creatures of fancy. The exception that might be drawn from *Pickwick* is rather in seeming than substance. A first book has its immunities, and the distinction of this from the rest of the writings appears in what has been said of its origin. The plan of it was simply to amuse. It was to string together whimsical sketches of the pencil by entertaining sketches of the pen; and, at its beginning, where or how it was to end was as little known to himself as to any of its readers. But genius is a master as well as a servant, and when the laughter and fun were at their highest something graver made its appearance. He had to defend himself for this; and he said that, though the mere oddity of a new acquaintance was apt to impress one at first, the more serious qualities were discovered when we became

friends with the man. In other words he might have said that the change was become necessary for his own satisfaction. The book itself, in teaching him what his power was, had made him more conscious of what would be expected from its use; and this never afterwards quitted him. In what he was to do hereafter, as in all he was doing now, with *Pickwick* still to finish and *Oliver* only beginning, it constantly attended him. Nor could it well be otherwise, with all those fanciful creations so real, to a nature in itself so practical and earnest; and in this spirit I had well understood the letter accompanying what had been published of *Oliver* since its commencement the preceding February, which reached me the day after I visited him. Something to the effect of what has just been said, I had remarked publicly of the portion of

The Two Wellers at the Blue Boar, from *The Pickwick Papers*. Illustration by Cecil Charles Windsor Aldin, 1910

the story sent to me; and his instant warm-hearted acknowledgment, of which I permit myself to quote a line or two, showed me in what perfect agreement we were: "How can I thank you? Can I do better than by saying that the sense of poor Oliver's reality, which I know you have had from the first, has been the highest of all praise to me? None that has been lavished upon me have I felt half so much as that appreciation of my intent and meaning. You know I have ever done so, for it was your feeling for me and mine for you that first brought us together, and I hope will keep us so till

death do us part. Your notices make me grateful, but very proud: so have a care of them."

There was nothing written by him after this date which I did not see before the world did, either in manuscript or proofs; and in connection with the latter I shortly began to give him the help which he publicly mentioned twenty years later in dedicating his collected writings to me.

The number following this was the famous one in which the hero finds himself in the Fleet. He had as yet done nothing so remarkable, in blending humor with tragedy, as

Mary Hogarth died on May 7, 1837. The following day, Dickens wrote to her maternal grandfather, George Thompson:

On May 17, 1837, Dickens described his loss in a letter to his old friend Thomas Beard:

M Y Dear Sir,

It is my painful and melancholy duty to inform you, that poor Mary died here at three o Clock yesterday afternoon. She had been with us to the Theatre the evening before; was taken suddenly ill in the night; and breathed her last in my arms at the time I have mentioned. She lies here, and Mrs Hogarth who was present at her death has ever since remained insensible in this house.

We lost no time in procuring medical assistance, or in applying every remedy that skill and anxiety could suggest. The dear girl however sank beneath the attack. The medical men are of opinion that her heart had been diseased for a great length of time. Her general state of health, and above all the awful suddenness of her death induce me to think they are right.

You cannot conceive the misery in which this dreadful event has plunged us. Since our marriage she has been the grace and life of our home – the admired of all, for her beauty and excellence – I could have better spared a much nearer relation or an older friend, for she has been to us what we can never replace, and has left a blank which no one who ever know [stet] her can have the faintest hope of seeing supplied.

Believe me My Dear Sir
Affectionately and Truly Yours
Charles Dickens

Letter from Dickens to his friend Thomas Beard on mourning paper from Collins's farm, Hampstead, in which he describes the death of Mary

T HANK God she died in my arms, and the very last words she whispered were of me.

Of our sufferings at the time, and all through the dreary week that ensued, I will say nothing – no one can imagine what they were. You have seen a good deal of her, and can feel for us, and imagine what a blank she has left behind. The first burst of my grief has passed, and I can think and speak of her, calmly and dispassionately. I solemnly believe that so perfect a creature never breathed. I knew her inmost heart, and her real worth and value. She had not a fault. [. . .]

GAYNOR ARNOLD

THE INTENSITY OF DICKENS'S ATTACHMENT TO HIS SISTER-IN-LAW CONTINUES TO FASCINATE. FOR MODERN INTERPRETATIONS OF THIS RELATIONSHIP SEE PETER CAREY'S NOVEL *JACK MAGGS*, 1996, AND GAYNOR ARNOLD'S *GIRL IN A BLUE DRESS*, 2008. ARNOLD'S NOVEL IS NARRATED BY DOROTHEA GIBSON (CATHERINE DICKENS), WHO GIVES THIS ACCOUNT OF HER HUSBAND'S (ALFRED'S) REACTION TO THE SUDDEN DEATH OF HER YOUNGER SISTER (ALICE):

I mounted the stairs to Alice's bedroom. Each step of the two flights felt like the side of a mountain. My heart was nearly bursting as I paused for breath at the top. The door of her room was open. He was sitting on the bedstead with his arms locked around her. Her head was drooping on his breast, her eyes were closed, her face was colourless. I stood by the door, panting. He made no acknowledgement of my presence, but held her as if she were a baby, repeating her name, over and over. Then a great shaking sob came from him, so violent that it went through his entire body, and by necessity through hers: Oh, my darling girl! Please don't leave me. I can't do without you!' [. . .] Taking Alice's curling strands of chestnut hair, he put his lips to them before placing them carefully in his watch case, His hand shook, and he could hardly do it. But as he struggled, I couldn't help noticing he was wearing her ring on his little finger.

'You have taken her ring, Alfred?' 'Yes, I shall wear it as long as I live.'

'That is so beautifully devoted of you,' I said, my voice trembling with the effort not to censure him. 'But don't you think Mama may want the ring herself? Or perhaps I should like it.'

'Your mother? No. I am sure she will not begrudge it me. And I know you would not Dodo dear.'

I could see then that he was the tragic hero and Alice was the dead heroine, and I was simply standing in the wings. I knew at that moment that it was useless to speak of my own grief. I knew it was in vain to hope that he would wipe my tears and cherish me and tell me I was not to blame; that my jealousy was not the cause; that Alice's death was not my punishment for having evil thoughts. I knew he did not see my

Watercolor copy by F. G. Kitton of portrait (from memory) of Mary Hogarth by Hablot Knight Browne (Phiz)

anguish in the outpouring of his own. I could feel his massive grief filling the house, spilling out into the night. And I knew it would spill for ever into his books.

**Gaynor Arnold, *Girl in a Blue Dress*
(Birmingham: Tindal Street Press, 2008), p. 105**

his picture of what the poor side of a debtors' prison was in the days of which we have seen that he had himself had bitter experience; and we have but to recall, as it rises sharply to the memory, what is contained in this portion of a work that was not only among his earliest but his least considered as to plan, to understand what it was that not alone had given him his fame so early, but that in itself held the germ of the future that awaited him.

Every point was a telling one, and the truthfulness of the whole unerring. The dreadful restlessness of the place, undefined yet unceasing, unsatisfying and terrible, was pictured throughout with De Foe's minute reality; while points of character were handled in that greater style which connects with the richest oddities of humor an insight into principles of character universal as nature itself. When he resolved that Sam Weller should be occupant of the prison with Mr. Pickwick, he was perhaps thinking of his favorite Smollett, and how, when Peregrine Pickle was inmate of the Fleet, Hatchway and Pipes refused to leave him; but Fielding himself might have envied his way of setting about it. Nor is any portion of his picture less admirable than this. The comedy gradually deepening into tragedy; the shabby vagabonds who are the growth of debtors' prisons, contrasting with the poor simple creatures who are their sacrifices and victims; Mr. Mivins and Mr. Smangle side by side with the cobbler ruined by his legacy, who sleeps under the table to remind himself of his old four-poster; Mr. Pickwick's first night in the marshal's room, Sam Weller entertaining Stiggins in the snuggery, Jingle in decline, and the chancery prisoner dying; in all these scenes there was writing of the first order, a deep feeling of character, that delicate form of humor which has a quaintly pathetic turn in it as well, comedy of the richest and broadest kind, and the easy handling throughout of a master in his art. We place the picture by the side of those of the great writers of this style, of fiction in our language, and it does not fall by the comparison.

Of what the reception of the book had been up to this time, and of the popularity Dickens had won as its author, this also will be the proper place to speak. For its kind, its extent, and the absence of everything unreal or factitious in the causes that contributed to it, it is unexampled in literature. Here was a series of sketches, without the pretense to

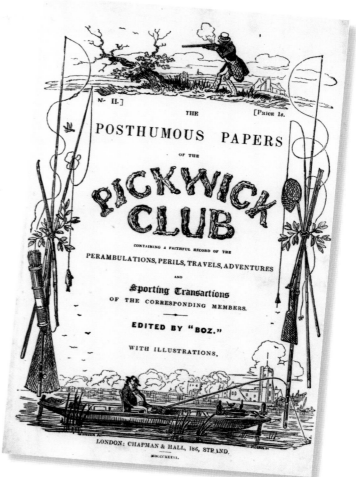

Cover to the monthly parts of *The Pickwick Papers*

such interest as attends a well-constructed story; put forth in a form apparently ephemeral as its purpose; having none that seemed higher than to exhibit some studies of cockney manners with help from a comic artist; and after four or five parts had appeared, without newspaper notice or puffing, and itself not subserving in the public anything false or unworthy, it sprang into a popularity that each part carried higher and higher, until people at this time talked of nothing else, tradesmen recommended their goods by using its name, and its sale, outstripping at a bound that of all the most famous books of the century, had reached to an almost fabulous number. Of part one, the binder prepared four hundred; and of part fifteen, his order was for more than forty thousand. Every class, the high equally with the low, was attracted to it. The charm of its gayety and good humor, its inexhaustible fun, its riotous overflow of animal spirits, its brightness and keenness of observation, and, above all, the incomparable ease of its many varieties of enjoyment, fascinated everybody.

I do not, for reasons to be hereafter stated, think the *Pickwick Papers* comparable to the later books; but, apart from the new vein of humor it opened, its wonderful freshness and its unflagging animal spirits, it has two characters that will probably continue to attract to it an unfading popularity. Its pre-eminent achievement is of course Sam Weller,—one of those people that take their place among the supreme successes of fiction, as one that nobody ever saw but everybody recognizes, at once perfectly natural and

intensely original. Sam Weller and Mr. Pickwick are the Sancho and the Quixote of Londoners, and as little likely to pass away as the old city itself.

I have to add what will complete the relation already given, in connection with his *Sketches*, of the uneasy sense accompanying his labor that it was yielding insufficient for himself while it enriched others, which is a needful part of his story at this time. At midsummer, 1837, replying to some inquiries, and sending his agreement with Mr. Bentley for the *Miscellany* under which he was writing *Oliver*, he went on: "It is a very extraordinary fact (I forgot it on Sunday) that I have NEVER HAD from him a copy of the agreement respecting the novel, which I never saw before or since I signed it at his house one morning long ago. Shall I ask

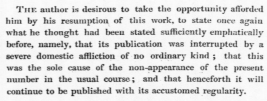

186, Strand, *June* 30, 1837.

ADDRESS

THE author is desirous to take the opportunity afforded him by his resumption of this work, to state once again what he thought had been stated sufficiently emphatically before, namely, that its publication was interrupted by a severe domestic affliction of no ordinary kind; that this was the sole cause of the non-appearance of the present number in the usual course; and that henceforth it will continue to be published with its accustomed regularity.

However superfluous this second notice may appear to many, it is rendered necessary by various idle speculations and absurdities which have been industriously propagated during the past month; which have reached the author's ears from many quarters, and have pained him exceedingly. By one set of intimate acquaintances, especially well informed, he has been killed outright; by another, driven mad; by a third, imprisoned for debt; by a fourth, sent per steamer to the United States; by a fifth, rendered incapable of any mental exertion for evermore—by all, in short, represented as doing anything but seeking in a few weeks' retirement the restoration of that cheerfulness and peace of which a sad bereavement had temporarily deprived him.

NOTICE TO CORRESPONDENTS.

WE receive every month an immense number of communications, purporting to be "suggestions" for the Pickwick Papers. We have no doubt that they are forwarded with the kindest intentions; but as it is wholly out of our power to make use of any such hints, and as we really have no time to peruse anonymous letters, we hope the writers will henceforth spare themselves a great deal of unnecessary and useless trouble.

Address to the reader in Part 15 of *The Pickwick Papers*, explaining the interruption in publication due to Dickens's grief at the death of Mary Hogarth

Mr. Pickwick Addresses the Club, by C.H. Green, 1890

him for a copy or no? I have looked at some memoranda I made at the time, and I *fear* he has my second novel on the same terms, under the same agreement. This is a bad lookout, but we must try and mend it. You will tell me you are very much surprised at my doing business in this way. So am I, for in most matters of labor and application I am punctuality itself. The truth is (though you do not need I should explain the matter to you, my dear fellow), that if I had allowed myself to be worried by these things, I could never have done as much as I have. But I much fear, in my desire to avoid present vexations, I have laid up a bitter store for the future." The second novel, which he had promised

in a complete form for a very early date, and had already selected subject and title for, was published four years later as *Barnaby Rudge*; but of the third he at present knew nothing but that he was expected to begin it, if not in the magazine, somewhere or other independently within a specified time.

The first appeal made, in taking action upon his letter, had reference to the immediate pressure of the *Barnaby* novel; but it also opened up the question of the great change of circumstances since these various agreements had been precipitately signed by him, the very different situation brought about by the extraordinary increase in the popularity of his writings, and the advantage it would be to both Mr. Bentley and himself to make

PICKWICK PAPERS, CHAPTER 41

When Mr Pickwick, wrongfully charged with "breach of promise,"
refuses to pay damages, he is taken to the Fleet debtor's prison.

IT was getting dark; that is to say, a few gas jets were kindled in this place which was never light, by way of compliment to the evening, which had set in outside. As it was rather warm, some of the tenants of the numerous little rooms which opened into the gallery on either hand, had set their doors ajar. Mr. Pickwick peeped into them as he passed along, with great curiosity and interest. Here, four or five great hulking fellows, just visible through a cloud of tobacco smoke, were engaged in noisy and riotous conversation over half-emptied pots of beer, or playing at all-fours with a very greasy pack of cards. In the adjoining room, some solitary tenant might be seen poring, by the light of a feeble tallow candle, over a bundle of soiled and tattered papers, yellow with dust and dropping to pieces from age, writing, for the hundredth time, some lengthened statement of his grievances, for the perusal of some great man whose eyes it would never reach, or whose heart it would never touch. In a third, a man, with his wife and a whole crowd of children, might be seen making up a scanty bed on the ground, or upon a few chairs, for the younger ones to pass the night in. And in a fourth, and a fifth, and a sixth, and a seventh, the noise, and the beer, and the tobacco smoke, and the cards, all came over again in greater force than before.

In the galleries themselves, and more especially on the stair-cases, there lingered a great number of people, who came there, some because their rooms were empty and lonesome, others because their rooms were full and hot; the greater part because they were restless and uncomfortable, and not possessed of the secret of exactly knowing what to do with themselves. There

were many classes of people here, from the labouring man in his fustian jacket, to the broken-down spendthrift in his shawl dressing-gown, most appropriately out at elbows; but there was the same air about them all—a kind of listless, jail-bird, careless swagger, a vagabondish who's-afraid sort of bearing, which is wholly indescribable in words, but which any man can understand in one moment if he wish, by setting foot in the nearest debtors' prison, and looking at the very first group of people he sees there, with the same interest as Mr. Pickwick did.

'It strikes me, Sam,' said Mr. Pickwick, leaning over the iron rail at the stair-head-'it strikes me, Sam, that imprisonment for debt is scarcely any punishment at all.'

'Think not, sir?' inquired Mr. Weller.

'You see how these fellows drink, and smoke, and roar,' replied Mr. Pickwick. 'It's quite impossible that they can mind it much.'

'Ah, that's just the wery thing, Sir,' rejoined Sam, 'they don't mind it; it's a reg'lar holiday to them—all porter and skittles. It's the t'other vuns as gets done over vith this sort o' thing; them down-hearted fellers as can't svig avay at the beer, nor play at skittles neither; them as vould pay if they could, and gets low by being boxed up. I'll tell you wot it is, sir; them as is always a-idlin' in public-houses it don't damage at all, and them as is alvays a-workin' wen they can, it damages too much. "It's unekal," as my father used to say wen his grog worn't made half-and-half: "it's unekal, and that's the fault on it."'

'I think you're right, Sam,' said Mr. Pickwick, after a few moments' reflection, 'quite right.'

more equitable adjustment of their relations. Some misunderstandings followed, but were closed by a compromise in September, 1837; by which the third novel was abandoned [5] on certain conditions, and *Barnaby* was undertaken to be finished by November, 1838. This involved a completion of the new story during the progress of *Oliver*, whatever might be required to follow on the close of *Pickwick*; and I doubted its wisdom. But it was accepted for the time.

He had meanwhile taken his wife abroad for a ten days' summer holiday, accompanied by the shrewd observant young artist, Mr. Hablot Browne, whose admirable illustrations to *Pickwick* had more than supplied Mr. Seymour's loss.

His later sea-side holiday was passed at Broadstairs, as were those of many subsequent years, and the little watering-place has been made memorable by his pleasant sketch of it.

Fleet Prison Courtyard, aquatint by Rowlandson and Pugin, 1808

After finishing *Pickwick* and resuming *Oliver*, the latter having been suspended by him during the recent disputes, he made his first visit to Brighton. The opening of his letter of Friday the 3rd of November is full of regrets that I had been unable to join them there: "It is a beautiful day, and we have been taking advantage of it, but the wind until to-day has been so high and the weather so stormy that Kate has been scarcely able to peep out of doors . . . Charles Kean was advertised for *Othello* 'for the benefit of Mrs. Sefton, having most kindly postponed for this one day his departure for London.' I have not heard whether he got to the theatre, but I am sure nobody else did. They do *The Honeymoon* to-night, on which occasion I mean to patronize the drama. We have a beautiful bay-windowed sitting-room here, fronting the sea, but I have seen nothing of B.'s brother who was to have shown me the lions, and my notions of the place are consequently somewhat confined: being limited to the pavilion, the chain-pier, and the sea. The last is quite enough for me, and, unless I am joined

RIGHT: Sam at the White Hart, from the *Posthumous Papers of the Pickwick Club*, by Charles Dickens, illustrated by Cecil Aldin, 1910 edition

Mr. Pickwick, from *Charles Dickens: A Gossip About His Life*, by Fred Barnard

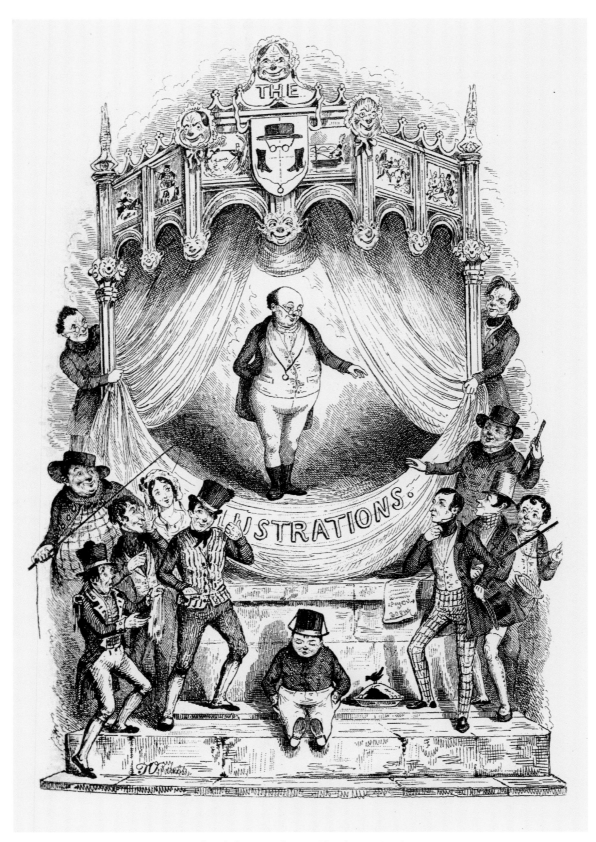

Pickwick characters illustrated by Thomas Onwhyn

Signature of Charles Dickens, 1853

by some male companion (do you think I shall be?), is most probably all I shall make acquaintance with. I am glad you like *Oliver* this month: especially glad that you particularize the first chapter. I hope to do great things with Nancy. If I can only work out the idea I have formed of her, and of the female who is to contrast with her, I think I may defy Mr.——and all his works. [6] I have had great difficulty in keeping my hands off Fagin and the rest of them in the evenings; but, as I came down for rest, I have resisted the temptation, and steadily applied myself to the labor of being idle . . . . We shall be at home at six o'clock, and I shall hope at least to see you that evening. I am afraid you will find this letter extremely dear at eightpence, but if the warmest assurances of friendship and attachment, and anxious lookings-forward to the pleasure of your society, be worth anything, throw them into the balance, together with a hundred good wishes and one hearty assurance that I am," etc. etc. "CHARLES DICKENS. No room for the flourish—I'll finish it the next time I write to you."

---

[5] I have a memorandum in Dickens's writing that five hundred pounds was to have been given for it, and an additional two hundred and fifty pounds on its sale reaching three thousand copies; but I feel certain it was surrendered on more favorable terms.

[6] The allusion was to the supposed author of a paper in the Quarterly Review (Oct. 1837), in the course of which there was much high praise, but where the writer said at the close, "Indications are not wanting that the particular vein of humor which has hitherto yielded so much attractive metal is worked out. . . . The fact is, Mr. Dickens writes too often and too fast. . . . If he persists much longer in this course, it requires no gift of prophecy to foretell his fate:—he has risen like a rocket, and he will come down like the stick."

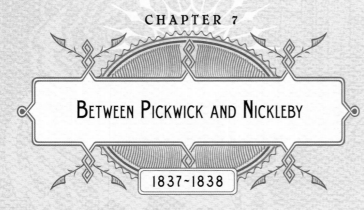

CHAPTER 7

BETWEEN PICKWICK AND NICKLEBY

1837~1838

Nᴏᴛ ʀᴇᴍᴏᴛᴇʟʏ ʙᴇᴀʀɪɴɢ on the stage, nevertheless, was the employment on which I found him busy at his return from Brighton; one result of his more satisfactory relations with Mr. Bentley having led to a promise to edit for him a life of the celebrated clown Grimaldi.

The manuscript had been prepared from autobiographical notes by a Mr. Egerton Wilks, and contained one or two stories told so badly, and so well worth better telling, that the hope of enlivening their dullness at the cost of very little labor constituted a sort of attraction for him. Except the preface, he did not write a line of this biography, such modifications or additions as he made having been dictated by him to his father; whom I found often in the supreme enjoyment of the office of amanuensis. He had also a most indifferent opinion of the mass of material which in general composed it, describing it to me as "twaddle," and his own modest estimate of the book, on its completion, may be guessed from the number of notes of admiration (no less than thirty) which accompanied his written mention to me of the sale with which it started in the first

week of its publication: "Seventeen hundred *Grimaldis* have been already sold, and the demand increases daily!!!!!!!!!!!!!!!!!!!!!!!!!!!!!!!!!!!"

Enormous meanwhile, and without objection audible on any side, had been the success of the completed *Pickwick*, which we celebrated by a dinner, with himself in the chair and Talfourd in the vice-chair, everybody in hearty good humor with every other body; and a copy of which I received from him on the 11th of December in the most luxurious of Hayday's bindings, with a note worth preserving for its closing allusion. The passage referred to in it was a comment, in delicately chosen words, that Leigh Hunt had made on the inscription at the grave in Kensal Green: "Chapman & Hall have just sent me, with a copy of our deed, three 'extra-super' bound copies of *Pickwick*, as per specimen inclosed.

The "deed" mentioned was one executed in the previous month to restore to him a third ownership in the book which had thus far enriched all concerned but himself. The original understanding respecting it Mr. Edward Chapman thus describes for me: "There was no agreement about *Pickwick* except a verbal one. Each number was to consist of a sheet and a half, for which we were to pay fifteen guineas; and we paid him for the first two numbers at once, as he required the money to go and get married with. We were also to pay more according to the sale, and I think *Pickwick* altogether cost us three thousand pounds." I had, however, always pressed so strongly the importance to him of some share in the copyright, that this at last was conceded in the deed above mentioned, though five years were to elapse before the right

Joseph Grimaldi by John Cawse
(black and white detail), 1807

Dickens placing his first literary contribution in the editor's box, by J. Stephenson, engraved by R. Herbert

the copyright, the entire ownership in which was then to revert to Dickens. The name of this new book, as all the world knows, was *The Life and Adventures of Nicholas Nickleby*; and between April, 1838, and October, 1839, it was begun and finished accordingly.

All through the interval of these arrangements *Oliver Twist* had been steadily continued. Month by month, for many months, it had run its opening course with the close of *Pickwick*, as we shall see it close with the opening of *Nickleby*; and the expectations of those who had built most confidently on the young novelist were more than confirmed. Here was the interest of a story simply but well constructed; and characters with the same impress of reality upon them, but more carefully and skillfully drawn. Nothing could be meaner than the subject, the progress of a parish or workhouse boy, nothing less so than its treatment. Thousands were attracted to him because he placed them in the midst of scenes and characters with which they were already themselves acquainted; and thousands were reading him with no less avidity because he introduced them to passages of nature and life of which they before knew nothing, but of the truth of which their own habits and senses sufficed to assure them. Only to genius are so revealed the affinities and sympathies of high and low, in regard to the customs and usages of life; and only a writer of the first rank can bear the application of such a test.

With such work as this in hand, it will hardly seem surprising that as the time for beginning *Nickleby* came on, and as he thought of his promise for November, he should have the sense of "something hanging over him like a hideous nightmare." He felt that he could not complete the *Barnaby Rudge* novel by the November of that year, as promised, and that the engagement he would have to break was unfitting him for engagements he might otherwise fulfill. He had undertaken what, in truth, was impossible. The labor of at once editing the *Miscellany* and supplying it with monthly portions of *Oliver* more than occupied all the time left him by other labors absolutely necessary.

Of the progress of his *Oliver*, and his habits of writing at the time, it may perhaps be worth giving some additional glimpses from his letters of 1838. "I was thinking about

should accrue; and it was only yielded as part consideration for a further agreement entered into at the same date (the 19th of November, 1837), whereby Dickens engaged to "write a new work, the title whereof shall be determined by him, of a similar character and of the same extent as the *Posthumous Papers of the Pickwick Club*," the first number of which was to be delivered on the 15th of the following March, and each of the numbers on the same day of each of the successive nineteen months; which was also to be the date of the payment to him, by Messrs. Chapman & Hall, of twenty several sums of one hundred and fifty pounds each for five years' use of

WALT WHITMAN

AMERICAN AUTHOR WALT WHITMAN, AN ENTHUSIASTIC READER OF DICKENS, REGULARLY DEFENDED HIM. HERE, HE ARGUES AGAINST A CRITIC FOR *THE GLOBE*, WHO HAD ASSERTED THAT DICKENS DELINEATES "THE HUMAN CHARACTER IN ITS LOWEST STAGE OF IGNORANCE, VICE AND DEGRADATION AND GIVES IT THE MOST UNBOUNDED SCOPE IN WICKEDNESS AND CRIME":

The mere fact of a man's delineating human character in its lowest stages of degradation, and giving it unbounded scope in every species of wickedness, proves neither his "democracy" nor its opposite. If it be done in such a way, as that a kind of charm is thrown all the time around the guilty personage described – in such a way that excuses and palliations for his vice are covertly conveyed, every now and then – such writings, most assuredly, would have no fair claim to rank among "the literature of democracy." But when these specimens of naked, ragged deformity, as ignorant as wicked, are drawn out before us, and surrounded with their fit accompaniments, filth and darkness, and the deepest discomfort – when crime is pourtrayed [sic], never so that by any possibility the reader can find the slightest temptation to go and do likewise – when our minds are led to the irresistible conclusion that iniquity is loathsome, and by the magic of the pen painter, have his pictures so stamped upon them that we ever after associated depraved actions with lowness and the very vulgarity of pollution – in such case, I say, the delineations of life in its lowest aspect, and even characterised by grossest ignorance and brutality, do not militate against their author's claim for admiration from all true democrats.

I consider Mr. Dickens to be a democratic writer.

The familiarity with low life wherein Mr. Dickens places his readers, is a wholesome familiarity. For those moving in a kindred sphere it is wholesome, because it holds out to them continually the spectacle of beings of their own grade, engaged either in worthy actions which are held up to emulation, and shown to be rewarded both in themselves and in their results – or engaged in avocations of guilt which in themselves and their results are fearful, and only to be thought of with shuddering. For the richer classes this familiarity is wholesome because they are taught to feel, in fancy, what poverty is, and what thousands of fellow-creatures, as good as they, toil on year after year, amid discouragements and evils, whose bare relation is ought to make the heart –sick. The rich cannot taste the distresses of want from their own experience, it is something if they are made to do so through the power of the pen.

He cannot comprehend, this critic tells us, how a writer can be called the champion of that class of mankind when he pictures it in colors so revolting. A good parent or teacher sometimes has to lay before those whom he would reform, the strong, naked, hideous, truth. But Dickens never maligns the poor. He puts the searing iron to wickedness, whether among poor or rich; and yet when he describes the guilty, poor and oppressed man, we are always in some way reminded how much need there is that certain systems of law and habit which led to this poverty and consequent crime should be remedied.

[. . .] As I think my humble lance, wielded in defence of Mr. Dickens, may meet the sight of the gentleman himself, I cannot lose the opportunity of saying how much I love and esteem him for what he has taught me through his writings – and for the genial influence that these writings spread around them wherever they go. Never having seen Boz in the body, we have yet had many a *tête-à-tête*. And I cannot tamely hear one whom I have long considered a personal friend, and a friend to his species, thus falsely and uncharitably and groundlessly attacked.

From Walt Whitman, "Boz and Democracy," *Brother Jonathan,* **26 February 1842, repr. in** *The Collected Writings of Walt Whitman: The Journalism,* **ed. by Herbert Bergman, Vol. I (New York: Peter Lang, 1998), pp. 35-38**

Oliver till dinner-time yesterday," he wrote on the 9th of March, [7] "and, just as I had fallen upon him tooth and nail, was called away to sit with Kate. I did eight slips, however, and hope to make them fifteen this morning." Three days before, a little daughter had been born to him, who became a little god-daughter to me.

On that day week, Monday, the 13th, after describing himself "sitting patiently at home waiting for *Oliver Twist* who has not yet arrived," which was his pleasant form of saying that his fancy had fallen into sluggishness that morning, he made addition not less pleasant as to some piece of painful news I had sent him, now forgotten: "I have not yet seen the paper, and you throw me into a fever. The comfort is, that all the strange and terrible things come uppermost, and that the good and pleasant things are mixed up with every moment of our existence so plentifully that we scarcely heed them." At the close of the month Mrs. Dickens was well enough to accompany him to Richmond, for now the time was come to start *Nickleby*; and, having been away from town when *Pickwick's* first number came out, he made it a superstition to be absent at all future similar times. The magazine-day of that April month, I remember, fell upon a Saturday, and the previous evening had brought me a peremptory summons: "Meet me at the Shakspeare on Saturday night at eight; order your horse at midnight, and ride back with me." Which was done accordingly. The smallest hour was sounding from St. Paul's into the night before we started, and the night was none of the pleasantest; but we carried news that lightened every part of the road, for the sale of *Nickleby* had reached that day the astonishing number of nearly fifty thousand! I left him working with unusual cheerfulness at *Oliver Twist* when I left the Star and Garter on the next day but one, after celebrating with both friends on the previous evening an anniversary which concerned us

all (their second and my twenty-sixth), and which we kept always in future at the same place, except when they were living out of England, for twenty successive years. It was a part of his love of regularity and order, as well as of his kindliness of nature, to place such friendly meetings as these under rules of habit and continuance.

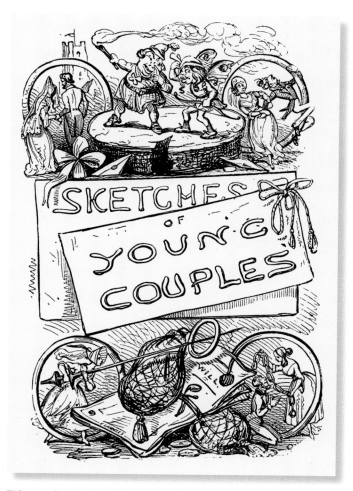

Title page for *Sketches of Young Couples,* 1840

---

[7] There is an earlier allusion I may quote, from a letter in January, for its mention of a small piece written by him at this time, but not included in his acknowledged writings: "I am as badly off as you. I have not done the *Young Gentlemen*, nor written the preface to Grimaldi, nor thought of *Oliver Twist*, or even supplied a subject for the plate." *The Young Gentlemen* was a small book of sketches which he wrote anonymously as the companion to a similar half-crown volume of *Young Ladies* (not written by him), for Messrs. Chapman & Hall. He added subsequently a like volume of *Young Couples*, also without his name.

CHAPTER 8

OLIVER TWIST

1838

THE WHOLE OF HIS TIME not occupied by *Nickleby* was now given to *Oliver*, and as the story shaped itself to its close it took extraordinary hold of him. I never knew him work so frequently after dinner, or to such late hours (a practice he afterwards abhorred), as during the final months of this task; which it was now his hope to complete before October, though its close in the magazine would not be due until the following March.

The publication had been announced for October, but the third-volume illustrations intercepted it a little. This part of the story, as we have seen, had been written in anticipation of the magazine, and the designs for it, having to be executed "in a lump," were necessarily done somewhat hastily. The matter supplied in advance of the monthly portions in the magazine formed the bulk of the last volume as published in the book; and for this the plates had to be prepared by Cruikshank also in advance of the magazine, to furnish them in time for the separate publication: Sikes and his dog, Fagin in the cell, and Rose Maylie and Oliver, being the three last.

The completed *Oliver Twist* found a circle of admirers, not so wide in its range as those of others of his books, but of a character and mark that made their honest liking for it, and steady advocacy of it,

important to his fame; and the book has held its ground in the first class of his writings. It deserves that place. The admitted exaggerations in *Pickwick* are incident to its club's extravaganza of adventure, of which they are part, and are easily separable from the reality of its wit and humor, and its incomparable freshness; but no such allowances were needed here. Make what deduction the too scrupulous reader of *Oliver* might please for "lowness" in the subject, the precision and the unexaggerated force of the delineation were not to be disputed. At the time of which I am speaking, the debtors' prisons described in *Pickwick*, the parochial management denounced in *Oliver*, and the Yorkshire schools exposed in *Nickleby*, were all actual existences,—which now have no vivider existence than in the forms he thus gave to them. With wiser purposes, he superseded the old petrifying process of the magician in the Arabian tale, and struck the prisons and parish abuses of his country, and its schools of neglect and crime, into palpable life forever.

Of the figures the book has made familiar to every one it is not my purpose to speak. To name one or two will be enough. Bumble and his wife; Charley Bates and the Artful Dodger; the cowardly charity-boy, Noah

Jacob's Island in the Thames, the site of Sike's death in *Oliver Twist*

Cut-out characters from *Oliver Twist*, engraved for a toy theatre edition, published by J. Redington

Claypole, whose *Such agony, please, sir,* puts the whole of a school-life into one phrase; the so-called merry old Jew, supple and black-hearted Fagin; and Bill Sikes, the bolder-faced bulky-legged ruffian, with his white hat and white shaggy dog,—who does not know them all, even to the least points of dress, look, and walk, and all the small peculiarities that express great points of character? I have omitted poor wretched Nancy; yet it is to be said of her, with such honest truthfulness her strength and weakness are shown, in the virtue that lies neighbored in her nature so closely by vice, that the people meant to be entirely virtuous show poorly beside her. But, though Rose and her lover are trivial enough beside Bill and his mistress, being indeed the weak part of the story, it is the book's pre-eminent merit that vice is nowhere made attractive in it.

And now, while *Oliver* was running a great career of popularity and success, the shadow of the tale of *Barnaby Rudge*, which he was to write on similar terms, and to begin in the *Miscellany* when the other should have ended, began to darken everything around him. We had much discussion respecting it, and I had no small difficulty in restraining him from throwing up the agreement altogether; but the real hardship of his position, and the

Poster of *Oliver Twist* characters for His Majesty's Theatre performance, 1905

considerate construction to be placed on every effort made by him to escape from obligations incurred in ignorance of the sacrifices implied by them, will be best understood from his own frank and honest statement. On the 21st of January, 1839, inclosing me the copy of a letter which he proposed to send to Mr. Bentley the following morning, he thus wrote: "From what I have already said to you, you will have been led to expect that I entertained some such intention. I know you will not endeavor to dissuade me from sending it. Go it MUST. It is no fiction to say that at present I *cannot* write this tale. The immense profits which *Oliver* has realized to its publisher and is still realizing; the paltry, wretched, miserable sum it brought to me (not equal to what is every day paid for a novel that sells fifteen hundred copies at most); the recollection of this, and the consciousness that I have still the slavery and drudgery of another work on the same journeyman-terms; the consciousness that my books are enriching everybody connected with them but myself, and that I, with such a

popularity as I have acquired, am struggling in old toils, and wasting my energies in the very height and freshness of my fame, and the best part of my life, to fill the pockets of others, while for those who are nearest and dearest to me I can realize little more than a genteel subsistence: all this puts me out of heart and spirits... I merely declare that I must have a postponement very common in all literary agreements; and for the time I have mentioned—six months from the conclusion of *Oliver* in the *Miscellany*—I wash my hands of any fresh accumulation of labor, and resolve to proceed as cheerfully as I can with that which already presses upon me."[8]

To describe what followed upon this is not necessary. It will suffice to state the results. Upon the appearance in the *Miscellany*, in the early months of 1839, of the last portion of *Oliver Twist*, its author, having been relieved altogether from his engagement to the magazine, handed over, in a familiar epistle from a parent to his child, the editorship to Mr. Ainsworth; and the still subsisting

Theater poster for *Oliver Twist*, woodcut. Published by Hartford, Conn.: Calhoun Print Co., ca. 1880s

Theater poster for *Oliver Twist*, color lithograph, England, early 20th c.

OLIVER TWIST, CHAPTER 2

Dickens's description of the workhouse in chapter 2 of Oliver Twist *was reprinted by* The Times *as part of its anti-poor law campaign:*

⬩⟶⟨⟩⟵⬩

THE members of this board were very sage, deep, philosophical men; and when they came to turn their attention to the workhouse, they found out at once, what ordinary folks would never have discovered—the poor people liked it! It was a regular place of public entertainment for the poorer classes; a tavern where there was nothing to pay; a public breakfast, dinner, tea, and supper all the year round; a brick and mortar elysium, where it was all play and no work. 'Oho!' said the board, looking very knowing; 'we are the fellows to set this to rights; we'll stop it all, in no time.' So, they established the rule, that all poor people should have the alternative (for they would compel nobody, not they), of being starved by a gradual process in the house, or by a quick one out of it. With this view, they contracted with the water-works to lay on an unlimited supply of water; and with a corn-factor to supply periodically small quantities of oatmeal; and issued three meals of thin gruel a day, with an onion twice a week, and half a roll of Sundays. They made a great many other wise and humane regulations, having reference to the ladies, which it is not necessary to repeat; kindly undertook to divorce poor married people, in consequence of the great expense of a suit in Doctors' Commons; and, instead of compelling a man to support his family, as they had theretofore done, took his family away from him, and made him a bachelor! There is no saying how many applicants for relief, under these last two heads, might have started up in all classes of society, if it had not been coupled with the workhouse; but the board were long-headed men, and had provided for this difficulty. The relief was inseparable from the workhouse and the gruel; and that frightened people.

For the first six months after Oliver Twist was removed, the system was in full operation. It was rather expensive at first, in consequence of the increase in the undertaker's bill, and the necessity of taking in the clothes of all the paupers, which fluttered loosely on their wasted, shrunken forms, after a week or two's gruel. But the number of workhouse inmates got thin as well as the paupers; and the board were in ecstasies.

The room in which the boys were fed, was a large stone hall, with a copper at one end: out of which the master, dressed in an apron for the purpose, and assisted by one or two women, ladled the gruel at mealtimes. Of this festive composition each boy had one porringer, and no more—except on occasions of great public rejoicing, when he had two ounces and a quarter of bread besides.

The bowls never wanted washing. The boys polished them with their spoons till they shone again; and when they had performed this operation (which never took very long, the spoons being nearly as large as the bowls), they would sit staring at the copper, with such eager eyes, as if they could have devoured the very bricks of which it was composed; employing themselves, meanwhile, in sucking their fingers most assiduously, with the view of catching up any stray splashes of gruel that might have been cast thereon. Boys have generally excellent appetites. Oliver Twist and his companions suffered the tortures of slow starvation for three months: at last they got so voracious and wild with hunger, that one boy, who was tall for his age, and hadn't been used to that sort of thing (for his father had kept a small cook-shop), hinted darkly to his companions, that unless he had another basin of gruel per diem, he was afraid he might some night happen to eat the boy who slept next him, who happened to be a weakly youth of tender age. He had a wild, hungry eye; and they implicitly believed him. A council was held; lots were cast who should walk up to the master after supper that evening, and ask for more; and it fell to Oliver Twist.

The evening arrived; the boys took their places. The master, in his cook's uniform, stationed himself at the copper; his pauper assistants ranged themselves behind him;

the gruel was served out; and a long grace was said over the short commons. The gruel disappeared; the boys whispered each other, and winked at Oliver; while his next neighbors nudged him. Child as he was, he was desperate with hunger, and reckless with misery. He rose from the table; and advancing to the master, basin and spoon in hand, said: somewhat alarmed at his own temerity:

'Please, sir, I want some more.'

The master was a fat, healthy man; but he turned very pale. He gazed in stupefied astonishment on the small rebel for some seconds, and then clung for support to the copper. The assistants were paralysed with wonder; the boys with fear.

'What!' said the master at length, in a faint voice.

'Please, sir,' replied Oliver, 'I want some more.'

The master aimed a blow at Oliver's head with the ladle; pinioned him in his arm; and shrieked aloud for the beadle.

The board were sitting in solemn conclave, when Mr. Bumble rushed into the room in great excitement, and addressing the gentleman in the high chair, said,

'Mr. Limbkins, I beg your pardon, sir! Oliver Twist has asked for more!'

There was a general start. Horror was depicted on every countenance.

'For *more!*' said Mr. Limbkins. 'Compose yourself, Bumble, and answer me distinctly. Do I understand that he asked for more, after he had eaten the supper allotted by the dietary?'

'He did, sir,' replied Bumble.

'That boy will be hung,' said the gentleman in the white waistcoat. 'I know that boy will be hung.'

Oliver asks for More, by Harold Copping, ca. 1924

LEFT: Monthly covers of the 1846 serial re-publication of *Oliver Twist*

RIGHT: "Oliver amazed by the Dodger's mode of going to work." Color lithograph of illustration for 1901 edition of *Oliver Twist* by George Cruikshank

Henry James remembered Oliver Twist as more Cruikshank's than Dickens's; it was such a thing of terribly vivid "images" (Henry James, *A Small Boy and Others*, 1913).

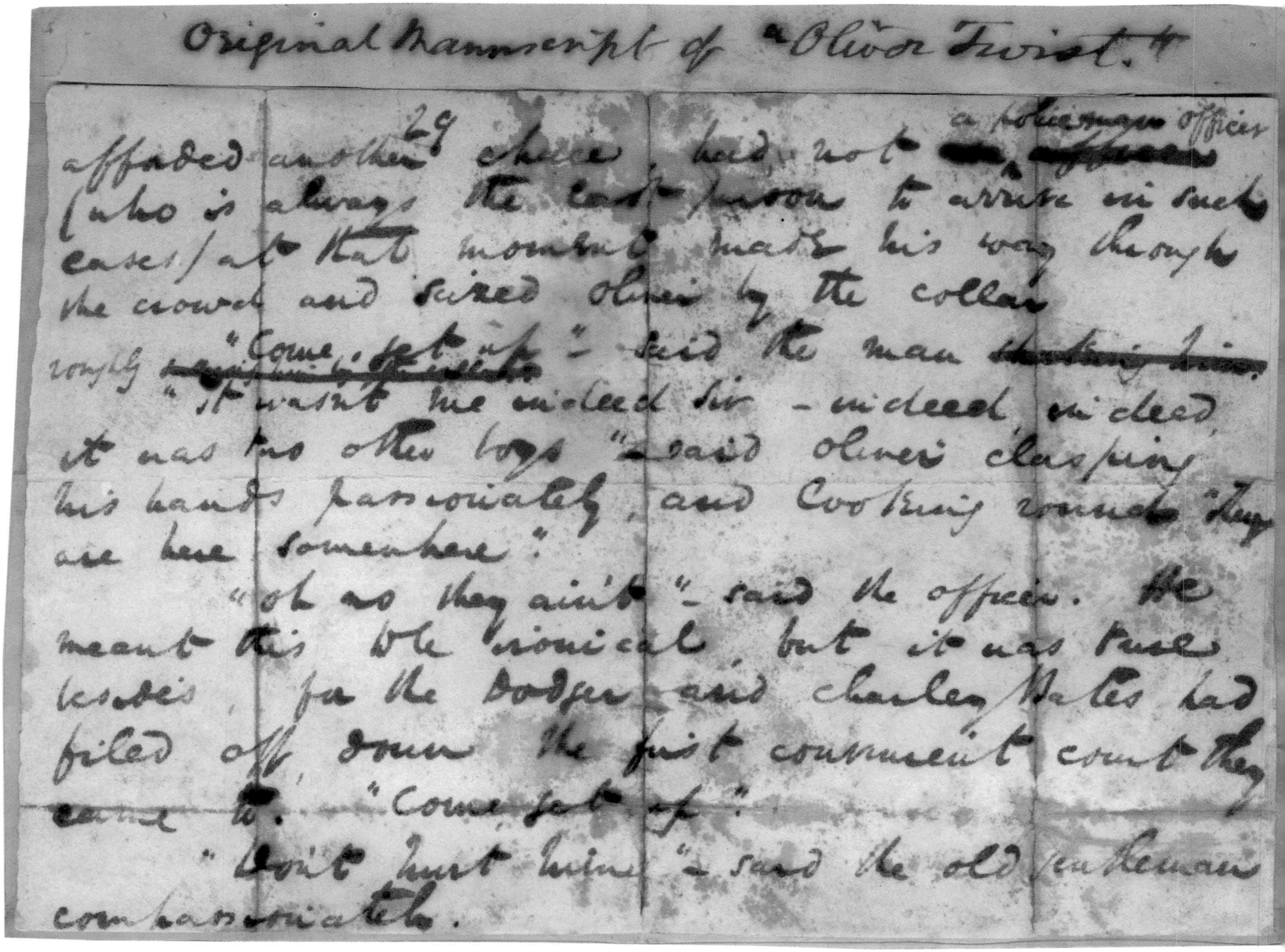

Original Manuscript of "Oliver Twist."

29

afforded another chase, had not ~~an officer~~ a policeman officer (who is always the last person to arrive in such cases) at that moment made his way through the crowd and seized Oliver by the collar.

roughly "Come, get up" – said the man ~~shaking him~~.

"It wasn't me indeed Sir – indeed indeed it was two other boys" – said Oliver clasping his hands passionately, and looking round "they are here somewhere".

"Oh no they ain't" – said the officer. He meant this to be ironical, but it was true besides, for the Dodger and Charley Bates had filed off, down the first convenient court they came to. "Come get up."

"Don't hurt him" – said the old gentleman compassionately.

Manuscript page from *Oliver Twist*

OLIVER TWIST, PREFACE

Dickens used the preface to the third, 1841, edition to respond to his critics. He professes to
"dim the false glitter surrounding something which really did exist, by showing it in its unattractive and repulsive truth."
Far from recommending a life of crime, Dickens suggests that his realism will have the opposite effect:

WHAT manner of life is that which is described in these pages, as the every-day existence of a Thief? What charms has it for the young and ill-disposed, what allurements for the most jolter-headed of juveniles? Here are no canterings upon moonlit heaths, no merry-makings in the snuggest of all possible caverns, none of the attractions of dress, no lace, no jack-boots, no crimson coats and ruffles, none of the dash and freedom with which 'the road' has been, time out of mind, invested. The cold, wet, shelterless midnight streets of London; the fowl and frowsy dens, where vice is closely packed and lacks the room to turn; the haunts of hunger and disease, the shabby rags that scarcely hold together; where are the attractions of these things? Have they no lesson, and do they not whisper something beyond the little-regarded warning of a moral precept?"

agreement to write *Barnaby Rudge* was, upon the overture of Mr. Bentley himself in June of the following year, 1840, also put an end to, on payment by Dickens, for the copyright of *Oliver Twist* and such printed stock as remained of the edition then on hand, of two thousand two hundred and fifty pounds. What was further incident to this transaction will be told hereafter; and a few words may meanwhile be taken, not without significance in regard to it, from the parent's familiar epistle. It describes the child as aged two years and two months

(so long had he watched over it); gives sundry pieces of advice concerning its circulation, and the importance thereto of light and pleasant articles of food; and concludes, after some general moralizing on the shiftings and changes of this world having taken so wonderful a turn that mail-coach guards were become no longer judges of horse-flesh, "I reap no gain or profit by parting from you, nor will any conveyance of your property be required, for in this respect you have always been literally Bentley's Miscellany and never mine."

[8] Upon receiving this letter I gently reminded him that I had made objection at the time to the arrangement on the failure of which he empowered me to bring about the settlement it was now proposed to supersede. I cannot give his reply, as it would be unbecoming to repeat the warmth of its expression to myself, but I preserve its first few lines to guard against any possible future misstatement: "If you suppose that anything in my letter could by the utmost latitude of construction imply the smallest dissatisfaction on my part, for God's sake dismiss such a thought from your mind. I have never had a momentary approach to doubt or discontent where you have been mediating for me. . . . I could say more, but you would think me foolish and rhapsodical; and such feeling as I have for you is better kept within one's own breast than vented in imperfect and inexpressive words."

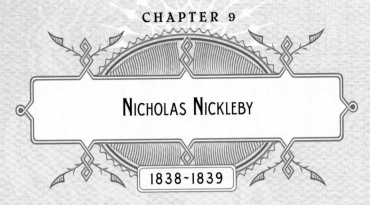

CHAPTER 9

NICHOLAS NICKLEBY

1838~1839

I WELL RECOLLECT THE DOUBT there was, mixed with the eager expectation which the announcement of his second serial story had awakened, whether the event would justify all that interest, and if indeed it were possible that the young writer could continue to walk steadily under the burden of the popularity laid upon him. The first number dispersed this cloud of a question in a burst of sunshine; and as much of the gayety of nations as had been eclipsed by old Mr. Pickwick's voluntary exile to Dulwich was restored by the cheerful confidence with which young Mr. Nicholas Nickleby stepped into his shoes. Everything that had given charm to the first book was here, with more attention to the important requisite of a story, and more wealth as well as truth of character.

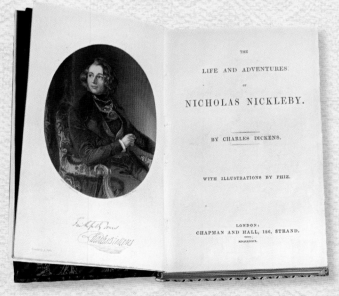

First edition of *Nicholas Nickleby*, with Daniel Maclise's portrait of Dickens, 1839

Nothing certainly could express better what the new book was at this time making manifest to its thousands of readers; not simply an astonishing variety in the creations of character, but what it was that made these creations so real; not merely the writer's wealth of genius, but the secret and form of his art. There never was any one who had less need to talk about his characters, because never were characters so surely revealed by themselves; and it was thus their reality made itself felt at once. They talked so well that everybody took to repeating what they said.

Who that recollects the numbers of *Nickleby* as they appeared can have forgotten how each number added to the general enjoyment? All that had given *Pickwick* its vast popularity, the overflowing mirth, hearty exuberance of humor, and genial kindliness of satire, had here the advantage of a better-laid design, more connected incidents, and greater precision of character. Everybody seemed immediately to know the Nickleby family as well as his own. Dotheboys, with all that rendered it, like a piece by Hogarth, both ludicrous and terrible, became a household word. Successive groups of Mantalinis, Kenwigses, Crummleses, introduced each its little world of reality, lighted up everywhere with truth and life, with capital observation, the quaintest drollery, and quite boundless mirth and fun. The brothers Cheeryble brought with them all the charities. With Smike came the first of those pathetic pictures that filled the world with pity for what cruelty, ignorance, or neglect may inflict upon the young. And Newman Noggs ushered in that class of the creatures of his fancy in which he took himself perhaps the most delight, and which the oftener he dealt with the more he seemed to know how to vary and render attractive: gentlemen by nature, however shocking bad their hats or ungenteel their dialects; philosophers of modest endurance, and needy but most respectable coats; a sort of humble angels of sympathy and self-denial, though without a particle of splendor or even good looks about them, except what an eye as fine as their own feelings might discern.

Thus rapidly may be indicated some elements that contributed to the sudden and astonishingly wide popularity of these books. I purposely reserve from my present notices of them, which are biographical rather than critical, any statement of the reasons for which I think them inferior in imagination and fancy to some of the later works; but there was continued and steady growth in them on the side of humor, observation, and character, while freshness and raciness of style continued to be an important help. There are faults of occasional exaggeration in the writing, but none that do not spring from animal spirits and good humor, or a pardonable excess, here and there, on the side of earnestness; and it has the rare virtue, whether gay or grave, of being always thoroughly intelligible and for the most part thoroughly natural, of suiting itself without effort to every change of mood, as quick, warm, and comprehensive as the sympathies it is taxed to express. The tone also is excellent. We are never repelled by egotism or conceit, and misplaced ridicule never disgusts us. When good is going on, we are sure to see all the beauty of it; and when there is evil, we are in no danger of mistaking it for good. No one can paint more picturesquely by an apposite epithet, or illustrate more happily by a choice allusion. Whatever he knows or feels, too, is always at his fingers' ends, and is present through whatever he is doing.

Of such notices as his letters give of his progress with *Nickleby*, which occupied him from February, 1838, to October, 1839, something may now be said. Soon after the agreement for it was signed, before the Christmas of 1837 was over, he went down into Yorkshire with Mr. Hablot Browne to look up the Cheap Schools in that county to which public attention had been painfully drawn by a law-case in the previous year; which had before been notorious for cruelties committed in them, whereof he had heard as early as in his childish days;[9] and which he was bent upon destroying if he could.

I soon heard the result of his journey; and the substance of that letter, returned to him for the purpose, is in his preface

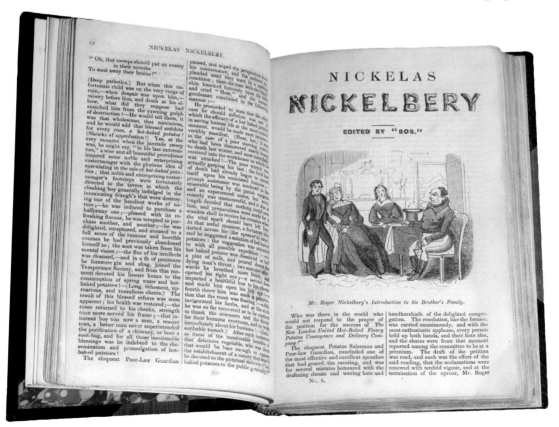

Nickelas Nickelbery, edited by "Bos" (T.P. Prest) was one of a number of serial plagiarists of Dickens's works.

Dotheboys Hall
Breaks up for Ever—
Nicholas Nickelby

> ### From Dickens's Preface to the 1848 edition of *Nicholas Nickleby*:
>
> *Here Dickens celebrates the power of fiction as a form of social reform, noting the effect of his novel in causing such institutions to close:*
>
> THIS story was begun within a few months after the publication of the completed *Pickwick Papers*. There were then, a good many cheap Yorkshire schools in existence. There are very few now [. . .]
>
> I went down into Yorkshire before I began this book, in very sever winter time which is pretty faithfully described herein. As I wanted to see a schoolmaster or two, and was forewarned that those gentlemen might, in their modesty, be shy of receiving a visit from the author of *Pickwick Papers*, I consulted with a professional friend here, who had a Yorkshire connection, and with whom I concerted a pious fraud. He gave me some letters of introduction, in the name, I think, of my travelling companions; they bore reference to a suppositious little boy who had been left with a widowed mother who didn't know what to do with him [. . .]
>
> In reference to these gentry, I may here quote a few words from the original preface to this book.
>
> 'It has afforded the Author great amusement and satisfaction, during the progress of this work, to learn, from country friends and from a variety of ludicrous statements concerning himself in provincial newspapers, that more than one Yorkshire schoolmaster lays claim to being the original of Mr. Squeers. One worthy, he has reason to believe, has actually consulted authorities learned in the law, as to his having good grounds on which to rest an action for libel; another, has meditated a journey to London, for the express purpose of committing an assault and battery on his traducer; a third, perfectly remembers being waited on, last January twelve-month, by two gentlemen, one of whom held him in conversation while the other took his likeness; and, although Mr. Squeers has but one eye, and he has two, and the published sketch does not resemble him (whoever he may be) in any other respect, still he and all his friends and neighbours know at once for whom it is meant, because—the character is so like him.

to the story written for the collected edition. He came back confirmed in his design, and in February set to work upon his first chapter. On his birthday he wrote to me, "I have begun! I wrote four slips last night, so you see the beginning is made. And what is more, I can go on: so I hope the book is in training at last." "The first chapter of *Nicholas* is done," he wrote two days later. "It took time, but I think answers the purpose as well as it could." Then, after a dozen days more, "I wrote twenty slips of *Nicholas* yesterday, left only four to do this morning (up at 8 o'clock too!), and have ordered my horse at one." I joined him as he expected, and we read together at dinner that day the first number of *Nicholas Nickleby*.

In the following number there was a difficulty which it was marvelous should not oftener have occurred to him in this form of publication. "I could not write a line till three o'clock," he says, describing the close of that number, "and have yet five slips to finish, and don't know what to put in them, for I have reached the point I meant to leave off with." He found easy remedy for such a miscalculation at his outset, and it was nearly his last as well as first misadventure of the kind: his difficulty in *Pickwick*, as he once told me, having always been, not the running short, but the running over: not the whip, but the drag, that was wanted.

The story was well in hand at the next letter to be quoted, for I limit myself to those only with allusions that are characteristic or illustrative. "I must be alone in my glory to-day," he wrote, "and see what I can do. I perpetrated a great amount of work yesterday, and have every day indeed since Monday, but I must buckle-to again and endeavor to get the steam up. If this were to go on long, I should 'bust' the boiler. I think Mrs. Nickleby's love-scene will come out rather unique."

72

to Miss Squeers. So that both the means
employed and the end produced were alike the most
natural in the world; for young ladies will
look forward to being married, and will
such other in the
to the altar, and will
attractions to the best advantage
down to the very end of time as they have done
from its beginning.

"Why, and here's Fanny in tears now!"
exclaimed Miss Snee as if in fresh amazement "What can be the matter!"

"Oh! you don't know Miss, of course
you don't know. Pray don't trouble yourself
to enquire" said Miss Squeers, producing that
change of countenance which children
call making a face.

"Well I'm sure" exclaimed Miss Snee.

"And who cares whether you are sure
or not ma'am." retorted Miss Squeers making
another face. "you are monstrous polite ma'am" said Miss Snee
"I shall not come to you to take
lessons in the art ma'am" retorted Miss Squeers.

Nicholas Nickleby, Chapter 8

*Dickens makes a powerful attack on the notorious Yorkshire schools in his depiction
of the cruelties of the Squeers' regime at Dotheboys Hall:*

'THERE,' said the schoolmaster as they stepped in together; 'this is our shop, Nickleby!'

It was such a crowded scene, and there were so many objects to attract attention, that, at first, Nicholas stared about him, really without seeing anything at all. By degrees, however, the place resolved itself into a bare and dirty room, with a couple of windows, whereof a tenth part might be of glass, the remainder being stopped up with old copy-books and paper. There were a couple of long old rickety desks, cut and notched, and inked, and damaged, in every possible way; two or three forms; a detached desk for Squeers; and another for his assistant. The ceiling was supported, like that of a barn, by cross-beams and rafters; and the walls were so stained and discoloured, that it was impossible to tell whether they had ever been touched with paint or whitewash.

But the pupils—the young noblemen! How the last faint traces of hope, the remotest glimmering of any good to be derived from his efforts in this den, faded from the mind of Nicholas as he looked in dismay around! Pale and haggard faces, lank and bony figures, children with the countenances of old men, deformities with irons upon their limbs, boys of stunted growth, and others whose long meagre legs would hardly bear their stooping bodies, all crowded on the view together; there were the bleared eye, the hare-lip, the crooked foot, and every ugliness or distortion that told of unnatural aversion conceived by parents for their offspring, or of young lives which, from the earliest dawn of infancy, had been one horrible endurance of cruelty and neglect. There were little faces which should have been handsome, darkened with the scowl of sullen, dogged suffering; there was childhood with the light of its eye quenched, its beauty gone, and its helplessness alone remaining; there were vicious-faced boys, brooding, with leaden eyes, like malefactors in a jail; and there were young creatures on whom the sins of their frail parents had descended, weeping even for the mercenary nurses they had known, and lonesome even in their loneliness. With every kindly sympathy and affection blasted in its birth, with every young and healthy feeling flogged and starved down, with every revengeful passion that can fester in swollen hearts, eating its evil way to their core in silence, what an incipient Hell was breeding here!

And yet this scene, painful as it was, had its grotesque features, which, in a less interested observer than Nicholas, might have provoked a smile. Mrs. Squeers stood at one of the desks, presiding over an immense basin of brimstone and treacle, of which delicious compound she administered a large instalment to each boy in succession: using for the purpose a common wooden spoon, which might have been originally manufactured for some gigantic top, and which widened every young gentleman's mouth considerably: they being all obliged, under heavy corporal penalties, to take in the whole of the bowl at a gasp. In another corner, huddled together for companionship, were the little boys who had arrived on the preceding night, three of them in very large leather breeches, and two in old trousers, a something tighter fit than drawers are usually worn; at no great distance from these was seated the juvenile son and heir of Mr. Squeers—a striking likeness of his father—kicking, with great vigour, under the hands of Smike, who was fitting upon him a pair of new boots that bore a most suspicious resemblance to those which the least of the little boys had worn on the journey down—as the little boy himself seemed to think, for he was regarding the appropriation with a look of most rueful amazement. Besides these, there was a long row of boys waiting, with countenances of no pleasant anticipation, to be treacled; and another file, who had just escaped from the infliction, making a variety of wry mouths indicative of anything but satisfaction. The whole were attired in such motley, ill-assorted, extraordinary garments, as would have been irresistibly ridiculous, but for the foul appearance of dirt, disorder, and disease, with which they were associated.

'Now,' said Squeers, giving the desk a great rap with his cane, which made half the little boys nearly jump out of their boots, 'is that physicking over?'

'Just over,' said Mrs. Squeers, choking the last boy in her hurry, and tapping the crown of his head with the wooden spoon to restore him. 'Here, you Smike; take away now. Look sharp!'

Smike shuffled out with the basin, and Mrs. Squeers having called up a little boy with a curly head, and wiped her hands upon it, hurried out after him into a species of washhouse, where there was a small fire and a large kettle, together with a number of little wooden bowls which were arranged upon a board.

Into these bowls, Mrs. Squeers, assisted by the hungry servant, poured a brown composition, which looked like diluted pincushions without the covers, and was called porridge. A minute wedge of brown bread was inserted in each bowl, and when they had eaten their porridge by means of the bread, the boys ate the bread itself, and had finished their breakfast; whereupon Mr. Squeers said, in a solemn voice, 'For what we have received, may the Lord make us truly thankful!'—and went away to his own.

"Nicholas Astonishes Mr. Squeers and Family," illustration by Hablot Knight Browne (Phiz), 1838

Nicholas distended his stomach with a bowl of porridge, for much the same reason which induces some savages to swallow earth—lest they should be inconveniently hungry when there is nothing to eat. Having further disposed of a slice of bread and butter, allotted to him in virtue of his office, he sat himself down, to wait for school-time.

He could not but observe how silent and sad the boys all seemed to be. There was none of the noise and clamour of a schoolroom; none of its boisterous play, or hearty mirth. The children sat crouching and shivering together, and seemed to lack the spirit to move about. The only pupil who evinced the slightest tendency towards locomotion or playfulness was Master Squeers, and as his chief amusement was to tread

upon the other boys' toes in his new boots, his flow of spirits was rather disagreeable than otherwise.

After some half-hour's delay, Mr. Squeers reappeared, and the boys took their places and their books, of which latter commodity the average might be about one to eight learners. A few minutes having elapsed, during which Mr. Squeers looked very profound, as if he had a perfect apprehension of what was inside all the books, and could say every word of their contents by heart if he only chose to take the trouble, that gentleman called up the first class.

Obedient to this summons there ranged themselves in front of the schoolmaster's desk, half-a-dozen scarecrows, out at knees and elbows, one of whom placed a torn and filthy book beneath his learned eye.

'This is the first class in English spelling and philosophy, Nickleby,' said Squeers, beckoning Nicholas to stand beside him. 'We'll get up a Latin one, and hand that over to you. Now, then, where's the first boy?'

'Please, sir, he's cleaning the backparlour window,' said the temporary head of the philosophical class.

'So he is, to be sure,' rejoined Squeers. 'We go upon the practical mode of teaching, Nickleby; the regular education system. C-l-e-a-n, clean, verb active, to make bright, to scour. W-i-n, win, d-e-r, der, winder, a casement. When the boy knows this out of book, he goes and does it. It's just the same principle as the use of the globes. Where's the second boy?'

'Please, sir, he's weeding the garden,' replied a small voice.

'To be sure,' said Squeers, by no means disconcerted. 'So he is. B-o-t, bot, t-i-n, tin, bottin, n-e-y, ney, bottinney, noun substantive, a knowledge of plants. When he has learned that bottinney means a knowledge of plants, he goes and knows 'em. That's our system, Nickleby: what do you think of it?'

NICHOLAS NICKLEBY, CHAPTER 37

*In this marvelous comic episode, Mrs. Nickleby tells her son about the attentions of the gentleman next door.
It is little wonder that Forster's readers were shocked to discover that Mrs. Nickleby was,
in part, modeled on Dickens's mother.*

'THERE can be no doubt,' said Mrs. Nickleby, 'that he IS a gentleman, and has the manners of a gentleman, and the appearance of a gentleman, although he does wear smalls and grey worsted stockings. That may be eccentricity, or he may be proud of his legs. I don't see why he shouldn't be. The Prince Regent was proud of his legs, and so was Daniel Lambert, who was also a fat man; HE was proud of his legs. So was Miss Biffin: she was—no,' added Mrs. Nickleby, correcting, herself, 'I think she had only toes, but the principle is the same.'

Nicholas looked on, quite amazed at the introduction of this new theme. Which seemed just what Mrs. Nickleby had expected him to be.

'You may well be surprised, Nicholas, my dear,' she said, 'I am sure I was. It came upon me like a flash of fire, and almost froze my blood. The bottom of his garden joins the bottom of ours, and of course I had several times seen him sitting among the scarlet-beans in his little arbour, or working at his little hot-beds. I used to think he stared rather, but I didn't take any particular notice of that, as we were newcomers, and he might be curious to see what we were like. But when he began to throw his cucumbers over our wall—'

'To throw his cucumbers over our wall!' repeated Nicholas, in great astonishment.

'Yes, Nicholas, my dear,' replied Mrs. Nickleby in a very serious tone; 'his cucumbers over our wall. And vegetable marrows likewise.'

'Confound his impudence!' said Nicholas, firing immediately. 'What does he mean by that?'

'I don't think he means it impertinently at all,' replied Mrs. Nickleby.

'What!' said Nicholas, 'cucumbers and vegetable marrows flying at the heads of the family as they walk in their own garden, and not meant impertinently! Why, mother—'

Nicholas stopped short; for there was an indescribable expression of placid triumph, mingled with a modest confusion, lingering between the borders of Mrs. Nickleby's nightcap, which arrested his attention suddenly.

'He must be a very weak, and foolish, and inconsiderate man,' said Mrs. Nickleby; 'blamable indeed—at least I suppose other people would consider him so; of course I can't be expected to express any opinion on that point, especially after always defending your poor dear papa when other people blamed him for making proposals to me; and to be sure there can be no doubt that he has taken a very singular way of showing it. Still at the same time, his attentions are—that is, as far as it goes, and to a certain extent of course—a flattering sort of thing; and although I should never dream of marrying again with a dear girl like Kate still unsettled in life—'

The steam doubtless rose dangerously high when such happy inspiration came. It was but a few numbers earlier than this, while that eccentric lady was imparting her confidences to Miss Knag, that Sydney Smith confessed himself vanquished by a humor against which his own had long striven to hold out. "*Nickleby* is *very good*," he wrote to Sir George Phillips after the sixth number. "I stood out against Mr. Dickens as long as I could, but he has conquered me."[10]

The close of the story was written at Broadstairs, from which (he had taken a house "two doors from the Albion

THE EXPERIENCE OF A PERSONAL INTIMACY WITH DICKENS'S CHARACTERS WAS WIDESPREAD FROM THE START OF HIS CAREER. AS THE *NATIONAL MAGAZINE* PUT IT IN 1837, "THE CHARACTERS AND SCENES OF THIS WRITER HAVE BECOME, TO AN EXTENT UNDREAMED OF IN ALL PREVIOUS CASES, PART OF OUR ACTUAL LIFE. THEIR INDIVIDUALITIES WHETHER MENTAL OR EXTERNAL, ARE AS FAMILIAR TO US AS THOSE OF OUR MOST INTIMATE ASSOCIATES, OR OUR MOST FREQUENT RESORTS." AMY CRUSE'S RESEARCH ON VICTORIAN READERS OFFERS FURTHER DETAIL:

Most of Dickens' readers had their particular friends among his creations, Henry Kingsley loved best Mr Pickwick, the Cheeryble brothers, Tom Pinch, and Captain Cuttle. William Morris specially favoured Joe Gargery and Mr Boffin 'Wot larks!' he would say, imitating the childlike enjoyment of Dickens's large hearted blacksmith, and 'Morning, morning!' with the genial nod of the Golden dustman. He delighted, too, in that remarkable old lady, Mr F's aunt. 'Bring him forward and I'll chuck him out o' winder', was his manner of expressing anger against any offender. Thackeray had a weakness for Mrs Steerforth [. . .] Trollope's sympathies went out to Bill Sikes. 'Poor Bill, I have a sort of love for him as he walks about with that dog of his, though I know it is necessary to hang him'. Even Agnes Wickfield, who might seem too immaculate to inspire any warm feeling, had, it is said, at least one adorer. A certain middle-aged gentleman fell deeply in love with her, and set out resolutely to find her counterpart that he might win her for his wife. Far and wide he sought, and many ladies he hopefully approached, but all in vain. Even advertisements failed to produce an acceptable candidate. At length, giving up the search, he settled down to celibacy, and solaced himself by writing long letters – which were found after his death – addressed to Miss Agnes Wickfield. Some of the younger Victorians grew up in such close familiarity with the Dickens people that these became their intimate life companions, meeting them at every turn of the road. Thus Francis Burnard says that his nursery governess was a Cornelia Blimber, and that at his first school one of his masters was 'a professor of Turveydropian deportment.' When he was eight years old he fell ill, and then he 'acted Paul Dombey to the life,' with a touch of Smike. At his next school there was a Toots, a Traddles, and a Mr Mell, and when he went to Eton he felt, as a new boy, 'like one of Squeers' queer collection at Dotheboys Hall'; and so the story goes on. Edmund Yates, Canon Ainger, Dean Hole, and Sir Edward Parry enjoyed a similar lifelong intimacy. Dickens tells how once, in York, a lady stopped him in the street and said, 'Mr Dickens, will you let me touch the hand that has filled my house with many friends', and there were readers all over the country ready to offer a similar tribute.

From Amy Cruse, *The Victorians and Their Books* (London: George Allen and Unwin, 1935), pp. 171-172

The Brothers Cheeryble, color lithograph based on illustration by Harold Copping for *Sketches from Dickens*, compiled by B.W. Matz, 1924

Portrait of W. C. Macready

so I reserve them till you come. It has been blowing great guns for the last three days, and last night (I wish you could have seen it!) there was such a sea! I staggered down to the pier, and, creeping under the lee of a large boat which was high and dry, watched it breaking for nearly an hour. Of course I came back wet through." On the afternoon of Wednesday, the 18th, he wrote again: "I shall not finish entirely before Friday, sending Hicks the last twenty pages of manuscript by the night-coach. I have had pretty stiff work, as you may suppose, and I have taken great pains. The discovery is made, Ralph is dead, the loves have come all right, Tim Linkinwater has proposed, and I have now only to break up Dotheboys and the book together. I am very anxious that you should see this conclusion before it leaves my hands, and I plainly see therefore that I must come to town myself on Saturday if I would not endanger the appearance of the number. So I have written to Hicks to send proofs to your chambers as soon as he can that evening; and, if you don't object, I will dine with you any time after five, and we will devote the night to a careful reading. I have not written to Macready, for they have not yet sent me the title-page of dedication, which is merely 'To W. C. Macready, Esq., the following pages are inscribed, as a slight token of admiration and regard, by his friend the Author.' Meanwhile will you let him know that I have fixed the Nickleby dinner for Saturday, the 5th of October? Place, the Albion in Aldersgate Street. Time, six for half-past exactly. . . . . I shall be more glad than I can tell you to see you again, and I look forward to Saturday, and the evenings that are to follow it, with most joyful anticipation. I have had a good notion for *Barnaby*, of which more anon."

Hotel, where we had that merry night two years ago") he wrote to me on the 9th September, 1839, "I am hard at it, but these windings-up wind slowly, and I shall think I have done great things if I have entirely finished by the 20th. Chapman & Hall came down yesterday with Browne's sketches, and dined here. They imparted their intentions as to a Nicklebeian fete which will make you laugh heartily—

[9] "I cannot call to mind now how I came to hear about Yorkshire schools when I was a not very robust child, sitting in by-places near Rochester castle, with a head full of Partridge, Strap, Tom Pipes, and Sancho Panza; but I know that my first impressions of them were picked up at that time."

[10] Moore, in his Diary (April, 1837), describes Sydney crying down Dickens at a dinner in the Row, "and evidently without having given him a fair trial."

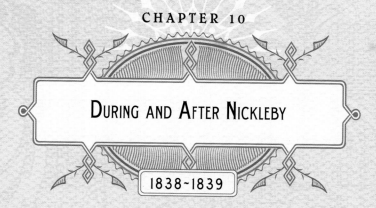

CHAPTER 10

DURING AND AFTER NICKLEBY

1838~1839

THE NAME OF HIS OLD gallery-companion may carry me back from the days to which the close of *Nickleby* had led me to those when it was only beginning. "This snow will take away the cold weather," he had written, in 1838, "and then for Twickenham." Here a cottage was taken, nearly all the summer was passed, and a familiar face there was Mr. Beard's. There, with Talfourd and with Thackeray and Jerrold, we had many friendly days, too; and the social charm of Maclise was seldom wanting. Nor was there anything that exercised a greater fascination over Dickens than the grand enjoyment of idleness, the ready self-abandonment to the luxury of laziness, which we both so laughed at in Maclise, under whose easy swing of indifference, always the most amusing at the most aggravating events and times, we knew that there was artist-work as eager, energy as unwearying, and observation almost as penetrating as Dickens's own. Edwin Landseer, all the world's favorite, and the excellent Stanfield, came a few months later, in the Devonshire-Terrace days; but another painter-friend was George Cattermole, who had then enough and to spare of fun as well as fancy to supply ordinary artists and humorists by the dozen, and wanted only a little more ballast and steadiness to have had all that could give attraction to good-fellowship.

A friend now especially welcome, too, was the novelist Mr. Ainsworth, who shared with us incessantly for the three following years in the companionship which began at his house; with whom we visited, during two of those years, friends of art and letters in his native Manchester, from among whom Dickens brought away his Brothers Cheeryble, and to whose sympathy in tastes and pursuits, accomplishments in literature, open-hearted

generous ways, and cordial hospitality, many of the pleasures of later years were due. Frederick Dickens, to whom soon after this a treasury clerkship was handsomely given, on Dickens's application, by Mr. Stanley of Alderley, known in and before those Manchester days, was for the present again living with his father, but passed much time in his brother's home; and another familiar face was that of Mr. Thomas Mitton, who had known him when himself a law-clerk in Lincoln's Inn, through whom there was introduction of the relatives of a friend and partner, Mr. Smithson, the gentleman connected with Yorkshire mentioned in his preface to *Nickleby*, who became very intimate in his house. These, his father and mother and

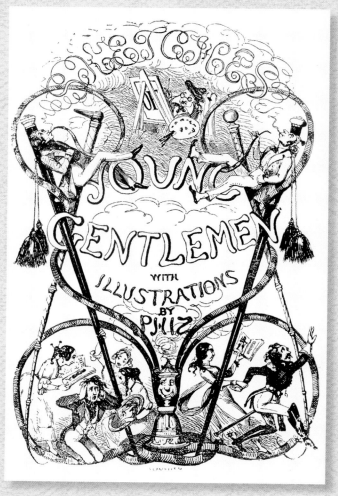

Cover design for "Sketches of Young Gentlemen," 1838

Daniel Maclise, Clarkson Stanfield, Charles Dickens and John Forster in carriage

their two younger sons, with members of his wife's family, and his married sisters and their husbands, Mr. and Mrs. Burnett and Mr. and Mrs. Austin, are figures that all associate themselves prominently with the days of Doughty Street and the cottages of Twickenham and Petersham as remembered by me in the summers of 1838 and 1839.

What else his letters of these years enable me to recall, that could possess any interest now, may be told in a dozen sentences. He wrote a farce by way of helping the Covent Garden manager which the actors could not agree about, and which he turned afterwards into a story called *The Lamplighter*. He entered his name among the students at the inn of the Middle Temple, though he did not eat dinners there until many years later. Between the completion of *Oliver* and its publication, Dickens went to see something of North Wales; and, joining him at Liverpool, I returned with him.[11] Soon after his arrival he had pleasant communication with

LEFT: Dickens's home at 1 Devonshire Terrace by H. M. Livens, published in *More Wanderings in London*, 1916

Lockhart, dining with him at Cruikshank's a little later; and this was the prelude to a *Quarterly* notice of *Oliver* by Mr. Ford, written at the instance of Lockhart, but without the raciness he would have put into it, in which amende was made for previous less favorable remarks in that review.

In the course of the year he was taken into Devonshire to select a home for his father, on the removal of the latter (who had long given up his reporting duties) from his London residence; and this he found in a cottage at Alphington, near Exeter, where he placed the elder Dickens with his wife and their youngest son.

The closing months of this year of 1839 had special interest for him. At the end of October another daughter was born to him, who bears the name of that dear friend of his and mine, Macready, whom he asked to be her godfather; and before the close of the year he had moved out of Doughty Street into Devonshire Terrace, a handsome house with a garden of considerable size, shut out from the New Road by a high brick wall facing the York Gate into Regent's Park. These various matters, and his attempts at

Devonshire Terrace entrance hall

the *Barnaby* novel on the conclusion of *Nickleby*, are the subject of his letters between October and December.

I will only add a couple of extracts from his letters while in Exeter arranging his father's and mother's new home. "I took a little house for them this morning" (5th March, 1839: from the New London Inn), "and if they are not pleased with it I shall be grievously disappointed. Exactly a mile beyond the city on the Plymouth road there are two white cottages: one is theirs and the other belongs to their landlady. I almost forget the number of rooms, but there is an excellent parlor with two other rooms on the ground floor, there is really a beautiful little room over the parlor which I am furnishing as a drawing-room, and there is a splendid garden. The paint and paper throughout is new and fresh and cheerful-looking, the place is clean beyond all description, and the neighborhood I suppose the most beautiful in

this most beautiful of English counties. Of the landlady, a Devonshire widow with whom I had the honor of taking lunch to-day, I must make most especial mention. She is a fat, infirm, splendidly-fresh-faced country dame, rising sixty and recovering from an attack 'on the nerves'—I thought they never went off the stones, but I find they try country air with the best of us. In the event of my mother's being ill at any time, I really think the vicinity of this good dame, the very picture of respectability and good humor, will be the greatest possible comfort. Her furniture and domestic arrangements are a capital picture, but that I reserve till I see you, when I anticipate a hearty laugh. She bears the highest character with the bankers and the clergyman (who formerly lived in my cottage himself), and is a kind-hearted worthy capital specimen of the sort of life, or I have no eye for the real and no idea of finding it out."

[11] I quote from a letter dated Llangollen, Friday morning, 3rd Nov. 1838: "I wrote to you last night, but by mistake the letter has gone on Heaven knows where in my portmanteau. I have only time to say, go straight to Liverpool by the first Birmingham train on Monday morning, and at the Adelphi Hotel in that town you will find me. I trust to you to see my dear Kate and bring the latest intelligence of her and the darlings. My best love to them."

CHAPTER 11

NEW LITERARY PROJECT

1839

THE TIME WAS NOW COME for him seriously to busy himself with a successor to *Pickwick* and *Nickleby*, which he had not, however, waited thus long before turning over thoroughly in his mind. *Nickleby's* success had so far outgone even the expectation raised by *Pickwick's*, that, without some handsome practical admission of this fact at the close, its publishers could hardly hope to retain him.

While he was at Petersham (July, 1839) he thus wrote to me: "I have been thinking that subject over. Indeed, I have been doing so to the great stoppage of *Nickleby* and the great worrying and fidgeting of myself. I have been thinking that if Chapman & Hall were to admit you into their confidence with respect to what they mean to do at the conclusion of *Nickleby*, without admitting me, it would help us very much. You know that I am well disposed towards them, and that if they do something handsome, even handsomer perhaps than they dreamt of doing, they will find it their interest, and will find me tractable. You know also that I have had straightforward offers from responsible men to publish anything for me at a percentage on the profits and take all the risk; but that I am unwilling to leave them, and have declared to you that if they behave with liberality to me I will not on any consideration, although to a certain extent I certainly and surely must gain by it. Knowing all this, I feel sure that if you were to put before them the glories of our new project, and, reminding them that when *Barnaby* is published I am clear of all engagements, were to tell them that if they wish to secure me and perpetuate our connection now is the time for them to step gallantly forward and make such proposals as will produce that result,—I feel quite sure that if this should be done by you, as you only can do

it, the result will be of the most vital importance to me and mine, and that a very great deal may be effected, thus, to recompense your friend for very small profits and very large work as yet. I shall see you, please God, on Tuesday night; and if they wait upon you on Wednesday, I shall remain in town until that evening."

"I should be willing to commence on the thirty-first of March, 1840, a new publication, consisting entirely of original matter, of which one number, price three-pence, should be published every week, and of which a certain amount of numbers should form a volume, to be published at regular intervals. The best general idea of the plan of the work might be given, perhaps, by reference to the *Spectator*, the *Tatler*, and Goldsmith's *Bee*; but it would be far more popular both in the subjects of which it treats and its mode of treating them.

"In addition to this general description of the contents, I may add that under particular heads I should strive to establish certain features in the work, which should be so many veins of interest and amusement running through the whole. Thus the Chapters on Chambers, which I have long thought and spoken of, might be very well incorporated with it; and a series of papers has occurred to me containing stories and descriptions of London as it was many years ago, as it is now, and as it will be many years hence, to which I would give some such title as The Relaxations of Gog and Magog, dividing them into portions like the *Arabian Nights*, and supposing Gog and Magog to entertain each other with such narrations in Guildhall all night long, and to break off every morning at daylight. An almost inexhaustible field of fun, raillery, and interest would be laid open by pursuing this idea.

"In order to give fresh novelty and interest to this undertaking, I should be ready to contract to go at any specified time (say in the midsummer or autumn of the year, when a sufficient quantity of matter in advance should have been prepared, or earlier if it were thought fit) either to Ireland or to America, and to write from thence a series of papers descriptive of the places and people I see, introducing local tales, traditions, and legends, something after the plan of Washington Irving's *Alhambra*. I should wish the republication of these papers in a separate form, with others to render the subject complete (if we should deem it advisable), to form part of the arrangement for the work; and I should wish the same provision to be made for the republication of the Gog and Magog series, or indeed any that I undertook.

"This is a very rough and slight outline of the project I have in view. I am ready to talk the matter over, to give any further explanations, to consider any suggestions, or to go into the details of the subject immediately. I say nothing of the novelty of such a publication nowadays, or its chances of success. Of course I think them very great, very great indeed,—almost beyond calculation,—or I should not seek to bind myself to anything so extensive.

"The heads of the terms upon which I should be prepared to go into this undertaking would be—That I be made a proprietor in the work and a sharer in the profits. That when I bind myself to write a certain portion of every number, I am insured, for that writing in every number, a certain sum of money. That those who assist me, and contribute the remainder of every number, shall be paid by the publishers immediately after its appearance, according to a scale to be calculated and agreed upon, on presenting my order for the amount to which they may be respectively entitled. Or, if the publishers prefer it, that they agree to pay me a certain sum for the *whole* of every number, and leave me to make such arrangements for that part which I may

Westminster Abbey and Hospital, from *London As It Is*. Color lithograph engraved and published by Thomas Shotter Boys, 1842

not write, as I think best. Of course I should require that for these payments, or any other outlay connected with the work, I am not held accountable in any way; and that no portion of them is to be considered as received by me on account of the profits. I need not add that some arrangement would have to be made, if I undertake my Travels, relative to the expenses of traveling.

"Now, I want our publishing friends to take these things into consideration, and to give me the views and proposals they would be disposed to entertain when they have maturely considered the matter."

The result of their consideration was, on the whole, satisfactory. An additional fifteen hundred pounds was to be paid at the close of *Nickleby*, the new adventure was to be undertaken, and Cattermole was to be joined with Browne as its illustrator. Nor was its plan much modified before starting, though it was felt by us all that, for the opening numbers at least, Dickens would have to be sole contributor, and that, whatever otherwise might be its attraction, or the success of the detached papers proposed by him, some reinforcement of them from time to time, by means of a story with his name continued at reasonable if not regular intervals, would be found absolutely necessary. Without any such planned story, however, the work did actually begin, its course afterwards being determined by circumstances stronger than any project he had formed. The agreement, drawn up in contemplation of a mere miscellany of detached papers or essays, and in which no mention of any story appeared, was signed at the end of March; and its terms were such as to place him in his only proper and legitimate position in regard to all such contracts, of being necessarily a gainer in any case, and, in the event of success, the greatest gainer of all concerned in the undertaking. All the risk of every kind was to be undergone by the publishers; and, as part of the expenses to be defrayed by them of each weekly number, he was to receive fifty pounds. Whatever the success or failure, this was always to be paid. The numbers were then to be accounted for separately, and half the realized profits paid to him, the other half going to the publishers; each number being held strictly responsible for itself, and the loss upon it, supposing any, not carried to the general account. The work was to be continued for twelve

months certain, with leave to the publishers then to close it; but if they elected to go on, he was himself bound to the enterprise for five years, and the ultimate copyright as well as profit was to be equally divided.

"Master Humphrey's clock"

Master Humphrey's Clock, Issue 1

Dickens carried out these plans for a new periodical in the initially successful Master Humphrey's Clock.
*The premise of stories told by Master Humphrey, introduced here, and his friends, didn't capture readers. Quickly declining sales
persuaded Dickens to give his audience what they really wanted, another serialized novel. Within two months of its
first publication, the miscellany was almost entirely taken up by* The Old Curiosity Shop.

THE reader must not expect to know where I live. At present, it is true, my abode may be a question of little or no import
to anybody; but if I should carry my readers with me, as I hope to do, and there should spring up between them and me
feelings of homely affection and regard attaching something of interest to matters ever so slightly connected with my fortunes
or my speculations, even my place of residence might one day have a kind of charm for them. Bearing this possible contingency
in mind, I wish them to understand, in the outset, that they must never expect to know it.

I am not a churlish old man. Friendless I can never be, for all mankind are my kindred, and I am on ill terms with no one
member of my great family. But for many years I have led a lonely, solitary life;—what wound I sought to heal, what sorrow to
forget, originally, matters not now; it is sufficient that retirement has become a habit with me, and that I am unwilling to break
the spell which for so long a time has shed its quiet influence upon my home and heart.

I live in a venerable suburb of London, in an old house which in bygone days was a famous resort for merry roysterers
and peerless ladies, long since departed. It is a silent, shady place, with a paved courtyard so full of echoes, that sometimes I
am tempted to believe that faint responses to the noises of old times linger there yet, and that these ghosts of sound haunt my
footsteps as I pace it up and down. I am the more confirmed in this belief, because, of late years, the echoes that attend my
walks have been less loud and marked than they were wont to be; and it is pleasanter to imagine in them the rustling of silk
brocade, and the light step of some lovely girl, than to recognise in their altered note the failing tread of an old man.

Six weeks before signature of this agreement, while a title was still undetermined, I had this letter from him: "I will dine with you. I intended to spend the evening in strict meditation (as I did last night); but perhaps I had better go out, lest all work and no play should make me a dull boy. *I* have a list of titles too, but the final title I have determined on—or something very near it. I have a notion of this old file in the queer house, opening the book by an account of himself, and, among other peculiarities, of his affection for an old quaint queer-cased clock; showing how that when they have sat alone together in the long evenings, he has got accustomed to its voice, and come to consider it as the voice of a friend; how its striking, in the night, has seemed like an assurance to him that it was still, a cheerful watcher at his chamber-door; and now its very face has seemed to have something of welcome in its dusty features, and to relax from its grimness when he has looked at it from his chimney-corner. Then I mean to tell how that he has kept odd manuscripts in the old, deep, dark, silent closet where the weights are; and taken them from thence to read (mixing up his enjoyments with some notion of his clock); and how, when the club came to be formed, they, by reason of their punctuality and his regard for this dumb servant, took their name from it. And thus I shall call the book either *Old Humphrey's Clock*, or *Master Humphrey's Clock*; beginning with a woodcut of old Humphrey and his clock, and explaining the why and wherefore. All Humphrey's own papers will be dated from 'my clock-side,' and I have divers thoughts about the best means of introducing the others. I thought about this all day yesterday and all last night till I went to bed. I am sure I can make a good thing of this opening, which I have thoroughly warmed up to in consequence."

CHAPTER 12

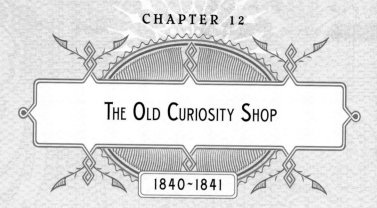

THE OLD CURIOSITY SHOP

1840~1841

DICKENS AND HIS WIFE, with Maclise and myself, visited Landor in Bath, and it was during three happy days we passed together there that the fancy which was shortly to take the form of Little Nell first occurred to its author,[12]—but as yet with the intention only of making out of it a tale of a few chapters. On the 1st of March we returned from Bath; and on the 4th I had this letter: "If you can manage to give me a call in the course of the day or evening, I wish you would. I am laboriously turning over in my mind how I can best effect the improvement we spoke of last night, which I will certainly make by hook or by crook, and which I would like you to see *before* it goes finally to the printer's. I have determined not to put that witch-story into number 3, for I am by no means satisfied of the effect of its contrast with Humphrey. I think of lengthening Humphrey, finishing the description of the society, and closing with the little child-story, which is SURE to be effective, especially after the old man's quiet way." Then there came hard upon this: "What do you think of the following double title for the beginning

The Old Curiosity Shop, Portsmouth Street, London

of that little tale? 'PERSONAL ADVENTURES OF MASTER HUMPHREY: *The Old Curiosity Shop.*' I have thought of *Master Humphrey's Tale, Master Humphrey's Narrative, A Passage in Master Humphrey's Life*—but I don't think any does as well as this. I have also thought of *The Old Curiosity Dealer and the Child* instead of *The Old Curiosity Shop.* Perpend. Topping waits."——And thus was taking gradual form, with less direct consciousness of design on his own part than I can remember in any other instance of all his career, a story which was to add largely to his popularity, more than any other of his works to make the bond between himself and his readers one of personal attachment, and very widely to increase the sense entertained of his powers as a pathetic as well as humorous writer.

He had very early himself become greatly taken with it. "I am very glad indeed," he wrote to me after the first half-dozen chapters, "that you think so well of the *Curiosity Shop*, and especially that what may be got out of Dick

109

remark of another of his letters. "I cannot yet discover that his aunt has any belief in him, or is in the least degree likely to send him a remittance, so that he will probably continue to be the sport of destiny."

To help his work he went twice to Broadstairs, in June and in September. From this he wrote to me (17th June), "It's now four o'clock, and I have been at work since half-past eight. I have really dried myself up into a condition which would almost justify me in pitching off the cliff, head first—but I must get richer before I indulge in a crowning luxury. Number 15, which I began to-day, I anticipate great things from. There is a description of getting gradually out of town, and passing through neighborhoods of distinct and various characters, with which, if I had read it as anybody else's writing, I think I should have been very much struck. The child and the old man are on their journey of course, and the subject is a very pretty one."

At this point it became necessary to close the first volume of the *Clock*, which was issued accordingly with a dedication to Rogers, and a preface to which allusion will be made hereafter. "I have opened the second volume," he wrote to me on the 9th of September, "with Kit; and I saw this morning looking out at the sea, as if a veil had been lifted up, an affecting thing that I can do with him by-and-by. Nous verrons." "I am glad you like that Kit number."

In the middle of October he returned to town, and by the end of the month he had so far advanced that the close of the story began to be not far distant. "Tell me what you think," he had written just before his return, "of 36 and 37? The way is clear for Kit now, and for a great effect at the last with the Marchioness."

At the opening of November, there seems to have been a wish on Maclise's part to try his hand at an illustration for the story; but I do not remember that it bore other fruit than a very pleasant day at Jack Straw's Castle, where Dickens read one of the later numbers to us. "Maclise and myself (alone in the carriage)," he wrote, "will be with you at two exactly. We propose driving out to Hampstead and

Little Nell and her Grandfather from *The Old Curiosity Shop*, illustration by Fred Barnard

strikes you. I *mean* to make much of him. I feel the story extremely myself, which I take to be a good sign; and am already warmly interested in it. I shall run it on now for four whole numbers together, to give it a fair chance." Every step lightened the road as it became more and more real with each character that appeared in it, and I still recall the glee with which he told me what he intended to do not only with Dick Swiveller, but with Septimus Brass, changed afterwards to Sampson. Undoubtedly, however, Dick was his favorite. "Dick's behavior in the matter of Miss Wackles will, I hope, give you satisfaction," is the

RIGHT: Grandpa's Favourite, from *The Old Curiosity Shop*, illustration by Harold Copping

way of doing it: what the actual doing it will be, God knows.
I can't preach to myself the schoolmaster's consolation,

The Old Curiosity Shop, by George Cattermole, 1841

The Little Marchioness, illustration for
The Old Curiosity Shop, by Kyd

Dick Swiveller book illustration, for
The Old Curiosity Shop, by Kyd

THE OLD CURIOSITY SHOP, CHAPTER 59

In a famous scene, the affable Dick Swiveller teaches the Marchioness,
"small servant" to the fearsome Sally Brass, to play cribbage:

'WELL—come in'—he said, after a little consideration. 'Here—sit down, and I'll teach you how to play.'

'Oh! I durstn't do it,' rejoined the small servant; 'Miss Sally 'ud kill me, if she know'd I come up here.'

'Have you got a fire down-stairs?' said Dick.

'A very little one,' replied the small servant.

'Miss Sally couldn't kill me if she know'd I went down there, so I'll come,' said Richard, putting the cards into his pocket. Why, how thin you are! What do you mean by it?'

'It ain't my fault.'

'Could you eat any bread and meat?' said Dick, taking down his hat. 'Yes? Ah! I thought so. Did you ever taste beer?' 'I had a sip of it once,' said the small servant.

'Here's a state of things!' cried Mr. Swiveller, raising his eyes to the ceiling. 'She never tasted it—it can't be tasted in a sip! Why, how old are you?'

'I don't know.'

Mr. Swiveller opened his eyes very wide, and appeared thoughtful for a moment; then, bidding the child mind the door until he came back, vanished straightway.

Presently, he returned, followed by the boy from the public-house, who bore in one hand a plate of bread and beef, and in the other a great pot, filled with some very fragrant compound, which sent forth a grateful steam, and was indeed choice purl, made after a particular recipe which Mr. Swiveller had imparted to the landlord, at a period when he was deep in his books and desirous to conciliate his friendship. Relieving the boy of his burden at the door, and charging his little companion to fasten it to prevent surprise, Mr. Swiveller followed her into the kitchen.

'There!' said Richard, putting the plate before her. 'First of all clear that off, and then you'll see what's next.'

The small servant needed no second bidding, and the plate was soon empty.

'Next,' said Dick, handing the purl, 'take a pull at that; but moderate your transports, you know, for you're not used to it. Well, is it good?'

'Oh! isn't it?' said the small servant.

Mr. Swiveller appeared gratified beyond all expression by this reply, and took a long draught himself, steadfastly regarding his companion while he did so. These preliminaries disposed of, he applied himself to teaching her the game, which she soon learnt tolerably well, being both sharp-witted and cunning.

'Now,' said Mr. Swiveller, putting two sixpences into a saucer, and trimming the wretched candle, when the cards had been cut and dealt, 'those are the stakes. If you win, you get 'em all. If I win, I get 'em. To make it seem more real and pleasant, I shall call you the Marchioness, do you hear?'

The small servant nodded.

'Then, Marchioness,' said Mr. Swiveller, 'fire away!'

The Marchioness, holding her cards very tight in both hands, considered which to play, and Mr. Swiveller, assuming the gay and fashionable air which such society required, took another pull at the tankard, and waited for her lead.

Dickens's cribbage board

The Death of Little Nell, engraving by George Cattermole

though I try. Dear Mary died yesterday, when I think of this sad story. I don't know what to say about dining to-morrow—perhaps you'll send up to-morrow morning for news? That'll be the best way. I have refused several invitations for this week and next, determining to go nowhere till I had done. I am afraid of disturbing the state I have been trying to get into, and having to fetch it all back again."

When I first began, *on your valued suggestion*, to keep my thoughts upon this ending of the tale, I resolved to try and do something which might be read by people about whom Death had been, with a softened feeling, and with consolation. . . . After you left last night, I took my desk up-stairs, and, writing until four o'clock this morning, finished the old story. It makes me very melancholy to think that all these people are lost to me forever, and I feel as if I never could become attached to any new set of characters." The words printed in italics, as underlined by himself, give me my share in the story which had gone so closely to his heart. I was responsible for its tragic ending. He had not thought of killing her, when, about half-way through, I asked him to consider whether it did not necessarily belong even to his own conception, after taking so mere a child through such a tragedy of sorrow, to lift her also out of the commonplace of ordinary happy endings so that the gentle

PILGRIM, VOL. 3

Dickens corresponded with other friends about his intense emotional response to writing the death of this character:

To Macready, ?6 Jan 1841

[. . .] I am slowly murdering the poor child, and grow wretched over it. It wrings my heart. Yet it must be.

From *Pilgrim*, vol. 3, p. 180

To Richard Monckton Milnes, 10 March 1841

[. . .] That Nellicide was the Act of Heaven, as you may see any of these fine mornings when you look about you. If you knew the pain it gave me—[. . .]

From *Pilgrim*, vol. 3, p. xii

As Madeline House and Graham Story argue, though:

THE letters show that Dickens's state of mind during the writing of the bulk of the book was itself buoyant and cheerful. Moreover, they provide no evidence that his thoughts, during the first 70 chapters, ever turned to his dead sister-in-law Mary Hogarth. Nell's creation had been haphazard; her death had been no part of a plan until Forster suggested it [. . .] she was no more than "the poor child" a dew days before he began to "murder" her."

The death of little Nell inspired extreme emotional reactions, both in Dickens and in his readers. It gave rise to Oscar Wilde's famous pronouncement: "One must have a heart of stone to read the death of little Nell without laughing" (quoted in Hesketh Pearson, *Life of Oscar Wilde* (London: Methuen, 1954), p. 235).

pure little figure and form should never change to the fancy. All that I meant he seized at once, and never turned aside from it again.

The published book was an extraordinary success, and, in America more especially, very greatly increased the writer's fame. The pathetic vein it had opened was perhaps mainly the cause of this, but opinion at home continued still to turn on the old characteristics,—the freshness of humor of which the pathos was but another form and product, the grasp of reality with which character had again been seized, the discernment of good under its least attractive forms and of evil in its most captivating disguises, the cordial wisdom and sound heart, the enjoyment and fun, luxuriant yet under proper control. No falling-off was found in these; and I doubt if any of his people have been more widely liked than Dick Swiveller and the Marchioness. The characters generally, indeed, work out their share in the purpose of the tale; the extravagances of some of them help to intensify its meaning; and the sayings and doings of the worst and the best alike have their point and applicability. Many an oversuspicious person will find advantage in remembering what a too liberal application of Foxey's principle of suspecting everybody brought Mr. Sampson Brass to; and many an overhasty judgment of poor human nature will unconsciously be checked, when it is remembered that Mr. Christopher Nubbles *did* come back to work out that shilling.

But the main idea and chief figure of the piece constitute its interest for most people, and give it rank upon the whole with the most attractive productions of English fiction. I am not acquainted with any story in the language more adapted to strengthen in the heart what most needs help and encouragement, to sustain kindly and innocent impulses, and to awaken everywhere the sleeping germs of good. It includes necessarily much pain, much uninterrupted sadness; and yet the brightness and sunshine quite overtop the gloom. The humor is so benevolent; the view of errors that have no depravity of heart in them is so indulgent; the quiet courage under calamity, the purity that nothing impure can soil, are so full of tender teaching. Its effect as a mere piece of art, too, considering the circumstances in which I have shown it to be written, I think very noteworthy.

JENNIFER HAYWARD

THE EXPERIENCE OF READING A DICKENS NOVEL IN INSTALLMENTS, THE FORM IN WHICH MANY OF HIS WORKS WERE FIRST PUBLISHED, PRODUCED PARTICULAR EFFECTS. AS JENNIFER HAYWARD HAS ARGUED, THE EPISODIC FORM OF PUBLICATION ALLOWED DICKENS TO EXPERIMENT WITH VARIOUS TECHNIQUES, SUCH AS THE CLIFFHANGER AND THE "CHARACTER INSTALLMENT," NOW MOST READILY ATTRIBUTED TO SOAP-OPERA. IN *OLIVER TWIST*, FOR EXAMPLE, DICKENS FINISHED THE JANUARY 1838 INSTALLMENT IN WHICH OLIVER IS FORCED BY BILL SIKES TO BREAK INTO A HOUSE AND IS DETECTED AND SHOT, WITH OLIVER BLEEDING FROM THE GUNSHOT WOUND FAINTING AND BEING DRAGGED ALONG BY SIKES. THE NUMBER FINISHES WITH THE WORDS "A COLD DEADLY FEELING CREPT OVER THE BOY'S HEART AND HE SAW OR HEARD NO MORE." BENTLEY'S READERS HAD TO WAIT A FULL THREE MONTHS TO LEARN WHAT HAPPENED TO HIM. ANTICIPATION ABOUT WHETHER A CHILD IN A DICKENS SERIAL HAD LIVED OR DIED GIVES RISE TO ONE OF THE MOST FAMOUS STORIES ABOUT DICKENS'S READERS. ACCORDING TO THE POPULAR TALE, NEW YORKERS CROWDED THE DOCKS IN BOSTON, AWAITING SHIPMENTS OF THE FINAL PART OF *THE OLD CURIOSITY SHOP* AND (ALLEGEDLY) SHOUTING UP TO THE SAILORS ON INCOMING SHIPS, "IS LITTLE NELL DEAD?" THIS CONCERN WITH THE FATE OF FICTIONAL CHARACTERS CERTAINLY HAS A PARALLEL IN RESPONSES TO MODERN SOAP OPERA NARRATIVES, WHERE CHARACTERS BEGIN TO FEEL PART OF OUR OWN WORLDS.

Please, Sir, can I have some more?
— Dickens, *Oliver Twist*

The appearance of a new tale by Mr. Dickens is an event of too great importance in the literary world – that part of it at least, which indulges in fiction – to be passed over without comment . . . This part is, however, doubtless, by this time in the hands of thousands of delighted readers, and thousands more of eager applicants and candidates are pressing to secure its next perusal. We will not unfairly interfere with their pleasure by giving the slightest insight into the nature of the mysteries wherewith the wizard is at present dealing. We will not even recommend its perusal, as everybody who reads a novel at all is sure to read this without recommendation, and as soon as he can lay his hands upon it. [*London Sunday Times*, May 8, 1864]

As is obvious from this review of *Our Mutual Friend*, popular serial novels became phenomena on the level of the O.J. Simpson trial or the first heady season of *Twin Peaks*. The sheer volume of discourse surrounding such fiction, which mobilized suspense and desire in highly profitable ways, enabled it to change the shape of the novel while creating a new genre that persists across time and technology to the present [. . .]

[Dickens developed] techniques and tropes now definitive of the serial form. Due to their sheer length and duration, serial narratives encourage plot and character developments such as returns from the dead, radical character transformations, and long-concealed secrets. Although all these tropes of course have a long and distinguished history in literature, they become thematically central to serial fiction and will be recognised as typical of the kind of "cheap ploys" for which soap operas are denigrated.

From Jennifer Hayward, *Consuming Pleasures: Active Audiences and Serial Fictions from Dickens to Soap Opera* (University Press of Kentucky, 1997) pp. 21, 45–46

Dickens and Little Nell statue, Clark Park, West Philadelphia

[12] I have mentioned the fact in my *Life of Landor*; and to the passage I here add the comment made by Dickens when he read it: "It was at a celebration of his birthday in the first of his Bath lodgings, 35, St. James's Square, that the fancy which took the form of Little Nell in the Curiosity Shop first dawned on the genius of its creator. No character in prose fiction was a greater favorite with Landor. He thought that, upon her, Juliet might for a moment have turned her eyes from Romeo, and that Desdemona might have taken her hair-breadth escapes to heart, so interesting and pathetic did she seem to him; and when, some years later, the circumstance I have named was recalled to him, he broke into one of those whimsical bursts of comical extravagance out of which arose the fancy of Boythorn. With tremendous emphasis he confirmed the fact, and added that he had never in his life regretted anything so much as his having failed to carry out an intention he had formed respecting it; for he meant to have purchased that house, 35, St. James's Square, and then and there to have burnt it to the ground, to the end that no meaner association should ever desecrate the birthplace of Nell. Then he would pause a little, become conscious of our sense of his absurdity, and break into a thundering peal of laughter." Dickens had himself proposed to tell this story as a contribution to my biography of our common friend, but his departure for America prevented him. "I see," he wrote to me, as soon as the published book reached him, "you have told, with what our friend would have called wonderful accuracy, the little St. James's Square story, which a certain faithless wretch was to have related."

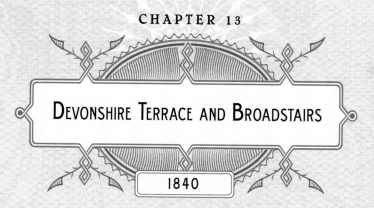

CHAPTER 13

DEVONSHIRE TERRACE AND BROADSTAIRS

1840

SOME AILMENTS WHICH DATED from an earlier period in his life made themselves felt in the spring of the year, as I remember, and increased horse-exercise was strongly recommended to him. "I find it will be positively necessary to go, for five days in the week, at least," he wrote to me in March, "on a perfect regimen of diet and exercise, and am anxious therefore not to delay treating for a horse." We were now in consequence, when he was not at the sea-side, much on horseback in suburban lanes and roads; and the spacious garden of his new house was also turned to healthful use at even his busiest times of work. I mark this, too, as the time when the first of his ravens took up residence there; and as the beginning of disputes with two of his neighbors about the smoking of the stable-chimney, which his groom Topping, a highly absurd little man with flaming red hair, so complicated by secret devices of his own, meant to conciliate each complainant alternately and having the effect of aggravating both, that law-proceedings were only barely avoided.

A graver incident, which occurred to him also among his earliest experiences as tenant of Devonshire Terrace, illustrates too well the always practical turn of his kindness and humanity not to deserve relation here. he was summoned, and obliged to sit, as juryman at an inquest on the body of a little child alleged to have been murdered by its mother; of which the result was, that, by his persevering exertion, seconded by the humane help of the coroner, Mr. Wakley, the verdict of himself and his fellow-jurymen charged her only with concealment of the birth. "The poor desolate creature dropped upon her knees before us with protestations that we were

right (protestations among the most affecting that I have ever heard in my life), and was carried away insensible. I caused some extra care to be taken of her in the prison, and counsel to be retained for her defense when she was tried at the Old Bailey; and her sentence was lenient, and her history and conduct proved that it was right." How much he felt the little incident, at the actual time of its occurrence, may be judged from the few lines written to me next morning: "Whether it was the poor baby, or its poor mother, or the coffin, or my fellow-jurymen, or what not, I can't say, but last night I had a most violent attack of sickness and indigestion, which not only prevented me from sleeping, but even from lying down. Accordingly Kate and I sat up through the dreary watches."

The day of the first publication of *Master Humphrey* (Saturday, 4th April) had by this time come, and, according to the rule observed in his two other great ventures, he left town with Mrs. Dickens on Friday, the 3rd. With Maclise we had been together at Richmond the previous night; and I joined him at Birmingham the day following with news of the sale of the whole sixty thousand copies to which the first working had been limited, and of orders already in hand for ten thousand more! The excitement of the success somewhat lengthened our holiday; and, after visiting Shakspeare's house at Stratford and Johnson's at Lichfield, we found our resources so straitened in returning, that, employing as our messenger of need his younger brother Alfred, who had joined us from Tamworth, where he was a student-engineer, we had to pawn our gold watches at Birmingham.

At the end of the following month he went to Broadstairs, and not many days before (on the 20th of May) a note from Mr. Jordan on behalf of Mr. Bentley opened the negotiations which transferred to Messrs. Chapman & Hall the agreement for *Barnaby Rudge*.

From the letters of his present Broadstairs visit, there is little further to add to their account of his progress with his story; but a couple more lines may be given for their characteristic expression of his invariable habit upon entering any new abode, whether to stay in it for days or for years. On a Monday night he arrived, and on the Tuesday (2nd of June) wrote to me, "Before I tasted bit or

The Harbor at Broadstairs, Kent, engraving

drop yesterday, I set out my writing-table with extreme taste and neatness, and improved the disposition of the furniture generally." He stayed till the end of June; when Maclise and myself joined him for the pleasure of posting back home with him and Mrs. Dickens, by way of his favorite Chatham and Rochester and Cobham, where we passed two agreeable days in revisiting well-remembered scenes. I had meanwhile brought to a close the treaty for repurchase of *Oliver* and surrender of *Barnaby*, upon terms which are succinctly stated in a letter written by him to Messrs. Chapman & Hall on the 2nd of July, the day after our return:

"The terms upon which you advance the money to-day for the purchase of the copyright and stock[13] of *Oliver* on my behalf are understood between us to be these. That this 2250£. is to be deducted from the purchase-money of a work by me entitled *Barnaby Rudge*, of which two chapters are now in your hands, and of which the whole is to be written within some convenient time to be agreed upon between us. But if it should not be written (which God forbid!) within five years, you are to have a lien to this amount on the property belonging to me that is now in your hands, namely, my shares in the stock and copyright of *Sketches by Boz*, *The Pickwick Papers*, *Nicholas Nickleby*, *Oliver Twist*, and *Master Humphrey's Clock*; in which we do not include any share of the current profits of the last-named work, which I shall remain at liberty to draw at the times stated in our agreement. Your purchase of *Barnaby Rudge* is made upon the following terms. It is to consist of matter sufficient for ten monthly numbers of the size of *Pickwick* and *Nickleby*, which you are, however, at liberty to divide and publish in fifteen smaller numbers if you think fit. The terms for the purchase of this edition in numbers, and for the copyright of the whole book for six months after the publication of the last number, are 3000£. At the expiration of the six months

"THE BEGGING~LETTER WRITER," *HOUSEHOLD WORDS*, 18 MAY 1850

Dickens turned his frustration at the myriad applications made to him for (usually!) pecuniary
assistance to humorous account in this journalistic sketch:

THE amount of money he annually diverts from wholesome and useful purposes in the United Kingdom, would be a set-off against the Window Tax. He is one of the most shameless frauds and impositions of this time. In his idleness, his mendacity, and the immeasurable harm he does to the deserving, dirtying the stream of true benevolence, and muddling the brains of foolish justices, with inability to distinguish between the base coin of distress, and the true currency we have always among us, he is more worthy of Norfolk Island than three-fourths of the worst characters who are sent there. Under any rational system, he would have been sent there long ago. I, the writer of this paper, have been, for some time, a chosen receiver of Begging Letters. For fourteen years, my house has been made as regular a Receiving House for such communications as any one of the great branch Post-Offices is for general correspondence. I ought to know something of the Begging-Letter Writer. He has besieged my door at all hours of the day and night; he has fought my servant; he has lain in ambush for me, going out and coming in; he has followed me out of town into the country; he has appeared at provincial hotels, where I have been staying for only a few hours; he has written to me from immense distances, when I have been out of England. He has fallen sick; he has died and been buried; he has come to life again, and again departed from this transitory scene: he has been his own son, his own mother, his own baby, his idiot brother, his uncle, his aunt, his aged grandfather. He has wanted a great-coat, to go to India in; a pound to set him up in life for ever; a pair of boots to take him to the coast of China; a hat to get him into a permanent situation under Government. He has frequently been exactly seven-and-sixpence short of independence. He has had such openings at Liverpool posts of great trust and confidence in merchants` houses, which nothing but seven-andsixpence was wanting to him to secure that I wonder he is not Mayor of that flourishing town at the present moment. [. . .] Once he wrote me rather a special letter, proposing relief in kind. He had got into a little trouble by leaving parcels of mud done up in brown paper, at people`s houses, on pretence of being a Railway Porter, in which character he received carriage money. This sportive fancy he expiated in the House of Correction. Not long after his release, and on a Sunday morning, he called with a letter (having first dusted himself all over), in which he gave me to understand that, being resolved to earn an honest livelihood, he had been travelling about the country with a cart of crockery. That he had been doing pretty well until the day before, when his horse had dropped down dead near Chatham, in Kent. That this had reduced him to the unpleasant necessity of getting into the shafts himself, and drawing the cart of crockery to London a somewhat exhausting pull of thirty miles. That he did not venture to ask again for money; but that if I would have the goodness TO LEAVE HIM OUT A DONKEY, he would call for the animal before breakfast!

the whole copyright reverts to me." The sequel was, as all the world knows, that Barnaby became successor to Little Nell, the money being repaid by the profits of the *Clock*; but I ought to mention also the more generous sequel that my own small service had, on my receiving from him, after not many days, an antique silver-mounted jug of great beauty of form and workmanship, but with a wealth far beyond jeweler's chasing or artist's design in the written words that accompanied it.[14] I accepted them to commemorate, not the help they would have far overpaid, but the gladness of his own escape from the last of the agreements that had hampered the opening of his career, and the better future that was now before him.

At the opening of August he was with Mrs. Dickens for some days in Devonshire, on a visit to his father, but he had to take his work with him; and, as he wrote to me, they had only one real holiday, when Dawlish, Teignmouth, Babbicombe, and Torquay were explored, returning to Exeter at night. In the beginning of September he was again at Broadstairs.

A few days later (the 15th) he wrote, "I have been rather surprised of late to have applications from Roman Catholic clergymen, demanding (rather pastorally, and with a kind of grave authority) assistance, literary employment, and so forth. At length it struck me that, through some channel or other, I must have been represented as belonging to that religion. Would you believe that in a letter from Lamert, at Cork, to my mother, which I saw last night, he says, 'What do the papers mean by saying that Charles is demented, and, further, *that he has turned Roman Catholic?*'—!" Of the begging-letter-writers, hinted at here, I ought earlier to have said something. In one of his detached essays he has described, without a particle of exaggeration, the extent to which he was made a victim by this class of swindler, and the extravagance of the devices practiced on him; but he

has not confessed, as he might, that for much of what he suffered he was himself responsible, by giving so largely, as at first he did, to almost every one who applied to him.

What at last brought him to his senses in this respect, I think, was the request made by the adventurer who had exhausted every other expedient, and who desired finally, after describing himself reduced to the condition of a traveling Cheap Jack in the smallest way of crockery, that a donkey might be left out for him next day, which he would duly call for. This I perfectly remember, and I much fear that the applicant was the Daniel Tobin before mentioned.

Of what occupied him in the way of literary labor in the autumn and winter months of the year, some description has been given; and, apart from what has already thus been said of his work at the closing chapters of *The Old Curiosity Shop*, nothing now calls for more special allusion, except that in his town-walks in November, impelled thereto by specimens recently discovered in his country-walks between Broadstairs and Ramsgate, he thoroughly explored the ballad literature of Seven-Dials, and took to singing himself, with an effect that justified his reputation for comic singing in his childhood, not a few of these wonderful productions.

---

[13] By way of a novelty to help off the stock, he had suggested (17th June), "Would it not be best to print new title-pages to the copies sheets and publish them as a new edition, with an interesting Preface? I am talking about all this as though the treaty were concluded, but I hope and trust that in effect it is, for negotiation and delay are worse to me than drawn daggers."

[14] "Accept from me" (July 8, 1840), "as a slight memorial of your attached companion, the poor keepsake which accompanies this. My heart is not an eloquent one on matters which touch it most, but suppose this claret-jug the urn in which it lies, and believe that its warmest and truest blood is yours. This was the object of my fruitless search, and your curiosity, on Friday. At first I scarcely knew what trifle (you will deem it valuable, I know, for the giver's sake) to send you; but I thought it would be pleasant to connect it with our jovial moments, and to let it add, to the wine we shall drink from it together, a flavor which the choicest vintage could never impart. Take it from my hand,—filled to the brim and running over with truth and earnestness. I have just taken one parting look at it, and it seems the most elegant thing in the world to me, for I lose sight of the vase in the crowd of welcome associations that are clustering and wreathing themselves about it."

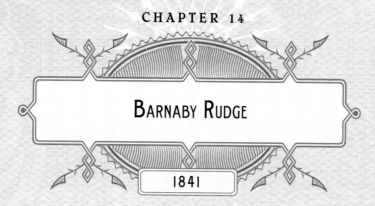

CHAPTER 14

BARNABY RUDGE

1841

THE LETTERS OF 1841 yield similar fruit as to his doings and sayings, and may in like manner first be consulted for the literary work he had in hand.

He had the advantage of beginning *Barnaby Rudge* with a fair amount of story in advance, which he had only to make suitable, by occasional readjustment of chapters, to publication in weekly portions; and on this he was engaged before the end of January. "I am at present" (22nd January, 1841) "in what Leigh Hunt would call a kind of impossible state,—thinking what on earth Master Humphrey can think of through four mortal pages. I added, here and there, to the last chapter of the *Curiosity Shop* yesterday, and it leaves me only four pages to write." Then on Friday the 29th . . . "By-the-by, don't engage yourself otherwise than to me for Sunday week, because it's my birthday. I have no doubt we shall have got over our troubles here by that time, and I purpose having a snug dinner in the study." We had the dinner, though the troubles were not over; but the next day another son was born to him. "Thank God," he wrote on the 9th, "quite well. I am thinking hard, and have just written to Browne inquiring when he will come and confer about the raven." He had by this time resolved to make that bird, whose accomplishments had been daily ripening and enlarging for the last twelve months to the increasing mirth and delight of all of us, a prominent figure in *Barnaby*.

The next letter mentioning *Barnaby* was from Brighton (25th February), whither he had flown for a week's quiet labor: "I have (it's four o'clock) done a very fair morning's work, at which I have sat very close, and been blessed besides with a clear view of the end of the volume. As the contents of one number usually require a day's thought at the very least, and often more, this puts me in great spirits. I think—that is, I hope—the story takes a great stride at this point, and takes it WELL. Nous verrons. Grip will be strong, and I build greatly on the Varden household."

Upon his return he had to lament a domestic calamity, which, for its connection with that famous personage in *Barnaby*, must be mentioned here. "You will be greatly shocked" (the letter is dated Friday evening, March 12, 1841) "and grieved to hear that the Raven is no more. He expired to-day at a few minutes after twelve o'clock at noon. He had been ailing for a few days, but we anticipated no serious result, conjecturing that a portion of the white paint he swallowed last summer might be lingering about his vitals without having any serious effect upon his

Frontispiece illustration to *Barnaby Rudge* by Gordon Frederick Browne, 1904. Autograph Edition

constitution. Yesterday afternoon he was taken so much worse that I sent an express for the medical gentleman (Mr. Herring), who promptly attended, and administered a powerful dose of castor oil. Under the influence of this medicine, he recovered so far as to be able at eight o'clock P.M. to bite Topping. His night was peaceful. This morning at daybreak he appeared better; received (agreeably to the doctor's directions) another dose of castor oil; and partook plentifully of some warm gruel, the flavor of which he appeared to relish. Towards eleven o'clock he was so much worse that it was found necessary to muffle the stable-knocker. At half-past, or thereabouts, he was heard talking to himself about the horse and Topping's family, and to add some incoherent expressions which are supposed to have been either a foreboding of his approaching disso-lution, or some wishes relative to the disposal of his little property: consisting chiefly of half-pence which he had buried in different parts of the garden. On the clock striking twelve he appeared slightly agitated, but he soon recovered, walked twice or thrice along the coach-house, stopped to bark, staggered, exclaimed *Halloa old girl!* (his favorite expression), and died.

In what way the loss was replaced, so that *Barnaby* should have the fruit of continued study of the habits of the family of birds which Grip had so nobly represented, Dickens has told in the preface to the story; and another, older, and larger Grip, obtained through Mr. Smithson, was installed in the stable, almost before the stuffed remains of his honored predecessor had been sent home in a glass case, by way of ornament to his master's study.

Days later he writes, "I finished the number yesterday, and, although I dined with Jeffrey, and was obliged to go to Lord Denman's afterwards (which made me late), have done eight slips of the *Lamplighter* for Mrs. Macrone, this morning. When I have got that off my mind, I shall try to go on steadily, fetching up the *Clock* lee-way." The *Lamp-lighter* was his old farce, which he now turned into a comic tale; and this, with other contributions given him by friends and edited by him as *Pic Nic Papers*, enabled him to help the

Fallen by the Wayside, from *Barnaby Rudge,* oil painting by Edgar Bundy, 1886

BARNABY RUDGE, CHAPTER 64

This disturbing novel depicts the anti-Papist riots of the late-eighteenth century.
In these vivid scenes, the rioters storm Newgate prison, an episode that clearly anticipates Dickens's depiction—
much later in his career—of French revolutionaries attacking the Bastille:

THE cry ran through the mob. Hammers began to rattle on the walls; and every man strove to reach the prison, and be among the foremost rank. Fighting their way through the press and struggle, as desperately as if they were in the midst of enemies rather than their own friends, the two men retreated with the locksmith between them, and dragged him through the very heart of the concourse.

And now the strokes began to fall like hail upon the gate, and on the strong building; for those who could not reach the door, spent their fierce rage on anything—even on the great blocks of stone, which shivered their weapons into fragments, and made their hands and arms to tingle as if the walls were active in their stout resistance, and dealt them back their blows. The clash of iron ringing upon iron, mingled with the deafening tumult and sounded high above it, as the great sledge-hammers rattled on the nailed and plated door: the sparks flew off in showers; men worked in gangs, and at short intervals relieved each other, that all their strength might be devoted to the work; but there stood the portal still, as grim and dark and strong as ever, and, saving for the dints upon its battered surface, quite unchanged.

While some brought all their energies to bear upon this toilsome task; and some, rearing ladders against the prison, tried to clamber to the summit of the walls they were too short to scale; and some again engaged a body of police a hundred strong, and beat them back and trod them under foot by force of numbers; others besieged the house on which the jailer had appeared, and driving in the door, brought out his furniture, and piled it up against the prison-gate, to make a bonfire which should burn it down. As soon as this device was understood, all those who had laboured hitherto, cast down their tools and helped to swell the heap; which reached half-way across the street, and was so high, that those who threw

more fuel on the top, got up by ladders. When all the keeper's goods were flung upon this costly pile, to the last fragment, they smeared it with the pitch, and tar, and rosin they had brought, and sprinkled it with turpentine. To all the woodwork round the prison-doors they did the like, leaving not a joist or beam untouched. This infernal christening performed, they fired the pile with lighted matches and with blazing tow, and then stood by, awaiting the result.

The furniture being very dry, and rendered more combustible by wax and oil, besides the arts they had used, took fire at once. The flames roared high and fiercely, blackening the prison-wall, and twining up its loftly front like burning serpents. At first they crowded round the blaze, and vented their exultation only in their looks: but when it grew hotter and fiercer—when it crackled, leaped, and roared, like a great furnace—when it shone upon the opposite houses, and lighted up not only the pale and wondering faces at the windows, but the inmost corners of each habitation—when through the deep red heat and glow, the fire was seen sporting and toying with the door, now clinging to its obdurate surface, now gliding off with fierce inconstancy and soaring high into the sky, anon returning to fold it in its burning grasp and lure it to its ruin—when it shone and gleamed so brightly that the church clock of St Sepulchre's so often pointing to the hour of death, was legible as in broad day, and the vane upon its steeple-top glittered in the unwonted light like something richly jewelled—when blackened stone and sombre brick grew ruddy in the deep reflection, and windows shone like burnished gold, dotting the longest distance in the fiery vista with their specks of brightness—when wall and tower, and roof and chimney-stack, seemed drunk, and in the flickering glare appeared to reel and stagger—when scores of objects, never seen before, burst out upon the view, and things the most familiar put on some new aspect—then the mob began to join the whirl, and with loud yells, and shouts, and clamour, such as happily is seldom heard, bestirred themselves to feed the fire, and keep it at its height.

Although the heat was so intense that the paint on the houses over against the prison, parched and crackled up, and swelling into boils, as it were from excess of torture, broke and crumbled away; although the glass fell from the window-sashes, and the lead and iron on the roofs blistered the incautious hand that touched them, and the sparrows in the eaves took wing, and rendered giddy by the smoke, fell fluttering down upon the blazing pile; still the fire was tended unceasingly by busy hands, and round it, men were going always. They never slackened in their zeal, or kept aloof, but pressed upon the flames so hard, that those in front had much ado to save themselves from being thrust in; if one man swooned or dropped, a dozen struggled for his place, and that although they knew the pain, and thirst, and pressure to be unendurable. Those who fell down in fainting-fits, and were not crushed or burnt, were carried to an inn-yard close at hand, and dashed with water from a pump; of which buckets full were passed from man to man among the crowd; but such was the strong desire of all to drink, and such the fighting to be first, that, for the most part, the whole contents were spilled upon the ground, without the lips of one man being moistened.

Meanwhile, and in the midst of all the roar and outcry, those who were nearest to the pile, heaped up again the burning fragments that came toppling down, and raked the fire about the door, which, although a sheet of flame, was still a door fast locked and barred, and kept them out. Great pieces of blazing wood were passed, besides, above the people's heads to such as stood about the ladders, and some of these, climbing up to the topmost stave, and holding on with one hand by the prison wall, exerted all their skill and force to cast these fire-brands on the roof, or down into the yards within. In many instances their efforts were successful; which occasioned a new and appalling addition to the horrors of the scene: for the prisoners within, seeing from between their bars that the fire caught in many places and thrived fiercely, and being all locked up in strong cells for the night, began to know that they were in danger of being burnt alive. This terrible fear, spreading from cell to cell and from yard to yard, vented itself in such dismal cries and wailings, and in such dreadful shrieks for help, that the whole jail resounded with the noise; which was loudly heard even above the shouting of the mob and roaring of the flames, and was so full of agony and despair, that it made the boldest tremble.

It was remarkable that these cries began in that quarter of the jail which fronted Newgate Street, where, it was well known, the men who were to suffer death on Thursday were confined. And not only were these four who had so short a time to live, the first to whom the dread of being burnt occurred, but they were, throughout, the most importunate of all: for they could be plainly heard, notwithstanding the great thickness of the walls, crying that the wind set that way, and that the flames would shortly reach them; and calling to the officers of the jail to come and quench the fire from a cistern which was in their yard, and full of water. Judging from what the crowd outside the walls could hear from time to time, these four doomed wretches never ceased to call for help; and that with as much distraction, and in as great a frenzy of attachment to existence, as though each had an honoured, happy life before him, instead of eight-and-forty hours of miserable imprisonment, and then a violent and shameful death.

widow of his old publisher in her straitened means by a gift of £300. He had finished his work of charity before he next wrote of *Barnaby Rudge*, but he was fetching up his lee-way lazily. "I am getting on" (29th of April) "very slowly. I want to stick to the story; and the fear of committing myself, because of the impossibility of trying back or altering a syllable, makes it much harder than it looks. It was too bad of me to give you the trouble of cutting the number, but I knew so well you would do it in the right places."

He left for Scotland after the middle of June, but he took work with him. "You may suppose," he wrote from Edinburgh on the 30th, "I have not done much work; but by Friday night's post from here I hope to send the first long chapter of a number and both the illustrations; from Loch Earn on Tuesday night, the closing chapter of that number; from the same place on Thursday night, the first long chapter of another, with both the illustrations; and, from some place which no man ever spelt but which sounds like Ballyhoolish, on Saturday, the closing chapter of that number, which will leave us all safe till I return to town."

This tale was Dickens's first attempt out of the sphere of the life of the day and its actual manners. Begun during the progress of *Oliver Twist*, it had been for some time laid aside; the form it ultimately took had been comprised only partially within its first design; and the story in its finished shape presented strongly a special purpose, the characteristic of all but his very earliest writings. Its scene is laid at the time when the incessant execution of men and women, comparatively innocent, disgraced every part of the country; demoralizing thousands, whom it also prepared for the scaffold. In Barnaby himself it was desired to show what sources of comfort there might be, for the patient and cheerful heart, in even the worst of all human afflictions; and in the hunted life of his outcast father, whose crime had entailed not that affliction only but other more fearful wretchedness, we have as powerful a picture as any in his writings of the inevitable and unfathomable consequences of sin. But, as the story went on, it was incident to these designs that what had been accomplished in its predecessor could hardly be attained here, in singleness of purpose, unity of idea, or harmony of treatment; and other defects supervened in the management of the plot. The interest with which the tale begins has ceased to be its interest before the close; and what has chiefly taken the reader's fancy at the outset almost wholly disappears in the power and passion with which, in the later chapters, the great riots are described.

So admirable is this description, however, that it would be hard to have to surrender it even for a more perfect structure of fable.

The story, which has unusually careful writing in it, and much manly upright thinking, has not so many people eagerly adopted as of kin by everybody, as its predecessors are famous for; but it has yet a fair proportion of such as take solid form within the mind and keep hold of the memory.

CHAPTER 15

PUBLIC DINNER IN EDINBURGH

1841

AMONG THE OCCURRENCES OF THE YEAR, apart from the tale he was writing, the birth of his fourth child and second son has been briefly mentioned. "I mean to call the boy Edgar," he wrote, the day after he was born (9th February), "a good honest Saxon name, I think." He changed his mind in a few days, however, on resolving to ask Landor to be godfather. This intention, as soon as formed, he announced to our excellent old friend, telling him it would give the child something to boast of, to be called Walter Landor, and that to call him so would do his own heart good. For, as to himself, whatever realities had gone out of the ceremony of christening, the meaning still remained in it of enabling him to form a relationship with friends he most loved; and as to the boy, he held that to give him a name to be proud of was to give him also another reason for doing nothing unworthy or untrue when he came to be a man. Walter, alas! only lived to manhood. He obtained a military cadetship through the kindness of Miss Coutts, and died at Calcutta on the last day of 1863, in his twenty-third year.

He hinted to me an intention soon to be carried out in a rather memorable manner: "I have done nothing to-day" (18th March: we had bought books together, the day before, at Tom Hill's sale) "but cut the *Swift*, looking into it with a delicious laziness in all manner of delightful places, and put poor Tom's books away. I had a letter from Edinburgh this morning, announcing that Jeffrey's visit to London will be the week after next; telling me that he drives about Edinburgh declaring there has been 'nothing so good as Nell since Cordelia,' which he writes also to all manner of people; and informing me of a desire in that romantic

town to give me greeting and welcome. For this and other reasons I am disposed to make Scotland my destination in June rather than Ireland. Think, *do* think, meantime (here are ten good weeks), whether you couldn't, by some effort worthy of the owner of the gigantic helmet, go with us. Think of such a fortnight,—York, Carlisle, Berwick, your own Borders, Edinburgh, Rob Roy's country, railroads,

Charles Dickens, by Pierre Morand, 1842

cathedrals, country inns, Arthur's Seat, lochs, glens, and home by sea. DO think of this, seriously, at leisure." It was very tempting, but not to be.

Early in April Jeffrey came, many feasts and entertainments welcoming him, of which he very sparingly partook; and before he left, the visit to Scotland in June was all duly arranged, to be initiated by the splendid welcome of a public dinner in Edinburgh, with Lord Jeffrey himself in the chair. Allan the painter had come up meanwhile, with increasing note of preparation; and it was while we were all regretting Wilkie's absence abroad, and Dickens with warrantable pride was saying how surely the great painter would have gone to this dinner, that the shock of his sudden death[15] came, and there was left but the sorrowful satisfaction of honoring his memory. There was one other change before the day. "I heard from Edinburgh this morning," he wrote on the 15th of June. "Jeffrey is not well enough to take the chair, so Wilson does. I think under all circumstances of politics, acquaintance, and *Edinburgh Review*, that it's much better as it is—Don't you?"

His first letter from Edinburgh, where he and Mrs. Dickens had taken up quarters at the Royal Hotel on their arrival the previous night, is dated the 23rd of June: "I have been this morning to the Parliament House, and am now introduced (I hope) to everybody in Edinburgh. The hotel is perfectly besieged, and I have been forced to take refuge in a sequestered apartment at the end of a long passage, wherein I write this letter. They talk of 300 at the dinner. We are very well off in point of rooms, having a handsome

Catherine Dickens, ca. 1846, from a painting by Daniel Maclise

sitting-room, another next to it for *Clock* purposes, a spacious bedroom, and large dressing-room adjoining. The castle is in front of the windows, and the view noble. There was a supper ready last night which would have been a dinner anywhere." This was his first practical experience of the honors his fame had won for him, and it found him as eager to receive as all were eager to give. Very interesting still, too, are those who took leading part in the celebration; and in his pleasant sketches of them there are some once famous and familiar figures not so well known to the present generation. Here, among the first, are Wilson and Robertson.

Nor have the most ordinary incidents of the visit any lack of interest for us now, in so far as they help to complete the picture of himself: "Allan has been squiring me about, all the morning. He and Fletcher have gone to a meeting of the dinner-stewards, and I take the opportunity of writing to you. They dine with us to-day, and we are going to-night to the theatre. M'Ian is playing there. I mean to leave a card for him before evening. We are engaged for every day of our stay, already; but the people I have seen are so very hearty and warm in their manner that much of the horrors of lionization gives way before it. I am glad to find that they propose giving me for a toast on Friday the Memory of Wilkie. I should have liked it better than anything, if I could have made my choice. Communicate all particulars to Mac. I would to God you were both here. Do dine together at the Gray's Inn on Friday, and think of me. If I don't drink my first glass of wine to you, may my pistols miss fire, and my mare slip her shoulder. All sorts of regard from Kate. She has gone with Miss Allan to see the house she was born in, etc. Write me soon, and long, etc."

His next letter was written the morning after the dinner, on Saturday, the 26th June: "The great event is over; and, being gone, I am a man again. It was the most brilliant affair you can conceive; the completest success possible, from first to last. The room was crammed, and more than seventy applicants for tickets were of necessity refused yesterday. Wilson was ill, but plucked up like a lion, and spoke famously." [16]

The parchment scroll of the city-freedom, recording the grounds on which it was voted, hung framed in his study to the last, and was one of his valued possessions.

The narrative of the trip to the Highlands must have a chapter to itself and its incidents of adventure and comedy. The latter chiefly were due to the guide who accompanied him, a quasi-Highlander himself, named a few pages back as Mr. Kindheart, whose real name was Mr. Angus Fletcher, and to whom it hardly needs that I should give other mention than will be supplied by such future notices of him as my friend's letters may contain. He had a wayward kind of talent, which he could never concentrate on a settled pursuit; and though at the time we knew him first he had taken up the profession of a sculptor, he abandoned it soon afterwards. The close of the poor fellow's life, alas!

Charles Dickens by Thomas Unwins, R.A.

was in only too sad agreement with all the previous course of it; but this will have mention hereafter. He is waiting now to introduce Dickens to the Highlands.

[15] Dickens refused to believe it at first. "My heart assures me Wilkie liveth," he wrote. "He is the sort of man who will be VERY old when he dies"—and certainly one would have said so.

[16] I now quote from Professor Wilson's speech: "Our friend has mingled in the common walks of life; he has made himself familiar with the lower orders of society. He has not been deterred by the aspect of vice and wickedness, and misery and guilt, from seeking a spirit of good in things evil, but has endeavored by the might of genius to transmute what was base into what is precious as the beaten gold. . . . But I shall be betrayed, if I go on much longer,—which it would be improper for me to do,—into something like a critical delineation of the genius of our illustrious guest. I shall not attempt that; but I cannot but express, in a few ineffectual words, the delight which every human bosom feels in the benign spirit which pervades all his creations. How kind and good a man he is, I need not say; nor what strength of genius he has acquired by that profound sympathy with his fellow-creatures, whether in prosperity or happiness, or overwhelmed with unfortunate circumstances, but who yet do not sink under their miseries, but trust to their own strength of endurance, to that principle of truth and honor and integrity which is no stranger to the uncultivated bosom, and which is found in the lowest abodes in as great strength as in the halls of nobles and the palaces of kings. Mr. Dickens is also a satirist. He satirizes human life, but he does not satirize it to degrade it. He does not wish to pull down what is high into the neighborhood of what is low. He does not seek to represent all virtue as a hollow thing, in which no confidence can be placed. He satirizes only the selfish, and the hard-hearted, and the cruel. Our distinguished guest may not have given us, as yet, a full and complete delineation of the female character. But this he has done: he has not endeavored to represent women as charming merely by the aid of accomplishments, however elegant and graceful. He has not depicted those accomplishments as their essentials, but has spoken of them rather as always inspired by a love of domesticity, by fidelity, by purity, by innocence, by charity, and by hope, which makes them discharge, under the most difficult circumstances, their duties, and which brings over their path in this world some glimpses of the light of heaven. Mr. Dickens may be assured that there is felt for him all over Scotland a sentiment of kindness, affection, admiration, and love; and I know for certain that the knowledge of these sentiments must make him happy."

CHAPTER 16

ADVENTURES IN THE HIGHLANDS

1841

FROM LOCH EARN HEAD DICKENS wrote on Monday, the 5th of July, having reached it, "wet through," at four that afternoon: "Having had a great deal to do in a crowded house on Saturday night at the theatre, we left Edinburgh yesterday morning at half-past seven, and traveled, with Fletcher for our guide, to a place called Stewart's Hotel, nine miles further than Callender. We had neglected to order rooms, and were obliged to make a sitting-room of our own bed-chamber [. . .] Being very tired (for we had not had more than three hours' sleep on the previous night) we lay till ten this morning, and at half-past eleven went through the Trossachs to Loch Katrine, where I walked from the hotel after tea last night. It is impossible to say what a glorious scene it was. It rained as it never does rain anywhere but here. We conveyed Kate up a rocky pass to go and see the island of the Lady of the Lake, but she gave in after the first five minutes, and we left her, very picturesque and uncomfortable, with Tom". . ."holding an umbrella over her head, while we climbed on. When we came back, she had gone into the carriage. We were wet through to the skin, and came on in that state four-and-twenty miles. . . ."

His next letter bore the date of "Ballechelish, Friday evening, ninth July, 1841, half-past nine, P.M.," and described what we had often longed to see together, the Pass of Glencoe. . . . "I can't go to bed without writing to you from here, though the post will not leave this place until we have left it and arrived at another. On looking over the route which Lord Murray made out for me, I found he had put down Thursday next for Abbotsford and Dryburgh Abbey, and a journey of seventy miles besides!

Therefore, and as I was happily able to steal a march upon myself at Loch Earn Head, and to finish in two days what I thought would take me three, we shall leave here to-morrow morning; and, by being a day earlier than we intended at all the places between this and Melrose (which we propose to reach by Wednesday night), we shall have a whole day for Scott's house and tomb, and still be at York on Saturday evening, and home, God willing, on Sunday . . . . We left Loch Earn Head last night, and went to a place called Killin, eight miles from it, where we slept. I walked some six miles with Fletcher after we got there, to see a waterfall; and truly it was a magnificent sight, foaming and crashing down three great steeps of riven rock; leaping over the first as far off as you could carry your eye, and rumbling and foaming down into a dizzy pool below you, with a deafening roar.. . . . Well, I will not bore you with my impressions of these tremendous wilds, but they really are fearful in their grandeur and amazing solitude. Wales is a mere toy compared with them.

"To-morrow at Oban. Sunday at Inverary. Monday at Tarbet. Tuesday at Glasgow (and that night at Hamilton). Wednesday at Melrose. Thursday at ditto. Friday I don't know where. Saturday at York. Sunday—how glad I shall be to shake hands with you!"

One more letter, brief, but overflowing at every word with his generous nature, must close the delightful series written from Scotland. It was dated from Inverary the day following his exciting adventure; promised me another from Melrose (which has unfortunately not been kept with the rest); and inclosed the invitation to a public dinner at Glasgow. "I have returned for answer that I am on my way home, on pressing business connected with my weekly publication, and can't stop. But I have offered to come down any day in September or October, and accept the honor then. Now, I shall come and return per mail; and, if this suits them, enter into a solemn league and covenant to come with me. *Do.* You must. I am sure you will. . . . Till my next, and always afterwards, God bless you. I got your welcome letter this morning, and have read it a hundred times. What a pleasure it is! Kate's best regards. I am dying for Sunday, and wouldn't stop now for twenty dinners of twenty thousand each."

CHAPTER 17

AGAIN AT BROADSTAIRS

1841

OON AFTER HIS RETURN, at the opening of August, he went to Broadstairs; and the direction in which that last question shows his thoughts to have been busy was that to which he turned his first holiday leisure. He sent me some rhymed squibs as his anonymous contribution to the fight the Liberals were then making against what was believed to be intended by the return to office of the Tories; ignorant as we were how much wiser than his party the statesman then at the head of it was, or how greatly what we all most desired would be advanced by the very success that had been most disheartening. I doubt indeed if he ever enjoyed anything more than the power of thus taking part occasionally, unknown to outsiders, in the sharp conflict the press was waging at the time. "By Jove, how radical I am getting!" he wrote to me (13th August). "I wax stronger and stronger in the true principles every day. I don't know whether it's the sea, or no, but so it is." He would at times even talk, in moments of sudden indignation at the political outlook, of carrying off himself and his household gods, like Coriolanus, to a world elsewhere! "Thank God there is a Van Diemen's Land. That's my comfort. Now, I wonder if I should make a good settler! I wonder, if I went to a new colony with my head, hands, legs, and health, I should force myself to the top of the social milk-pot and live upon the cream! What do you think? Upon my word, I believe I should."

Of matters in which he had been specially interested before he quitted London, one or two may properly be named. He had always sympathized, almost as strongly as Archbishop Whately did, with Dr. Elliotson's mesmeric investigations; and, reinforced as these were in the present year by the displays of a Belgian youth whom another friend, Mr. Chauncy Hare Townshend, brought over to England, the subject, which to the last had an attraction for him, was for the time rather ardently followed up. The improvement during the last few years in the London prisons was another matter of eager and pleased inquiry with him; and he took frequent means of stating what in this respect had been done, since even the date when his *Sketches* were written, by two most efficient public officers at Clerkenwell and Tothill Fields, Mr. Chesterton and Lieutenant Tracey, whom the course of these inquiries turned into private friends.

In the middle of August (Monday, 16th) I had announcement that he was coming up for special purposes: "... I shall be in town on Saturday morning and go straight to you. A letter has come from little Hall begging that when I do come to town I will dine there, as they wish to talk about the new story. I have written to say that I will do so on Saturday, and we will go together; but I shall be by no means good company. . . . I have more than half a mind to start a bookseller of my own. I could; with good capital too, as you know; and ready to spend it."

Small causes of displeasure had been growing out of the *Clock*, and were almost unavoidably incident to the position in which he found himself respecting it. Its discontinuance had become necessary, the strain upon himself being too great without the help from others which experience had shown to be impracticable; but I thought he had not met the difficulty wisely by undertaking, which already he had done, to begin a new story so early as the following March. On his arrival, therefore, we decided on another plan, with which we went armed that Saturday afternoon to his publishers, and of which the result will be best told by himself. He had returned to Broadstairs the following morning, and next day (Monday, the 23rd of August) he wrote to me in very enthusiastic terms of the share I had taken in what he calls "the development on Saturday afternoon; when I thought Chapman very manly and sensible, Hall morally and physically feeble though perfectly well intentioned, and both the statement and reception of the project quite triumphant. Didn't you think so too?" A fortnight later, Tuesday, the 7th of September, the

Painting of the Dickens children: Charley, Wally, Mamie, and Katey, plus Grip the Raven, produced by Daniel Maclise at Catherine Dickens's request (1841). Catherine took it with her on the expedition to America.

accepted to the full extent, gave yet the assurance needed to quiet natural apprehensions. All this, including an arrangement for publication of such notes as might occur to him on the journey, took but a few days.

"Now" (19th September) "to astonish you. After balancing, considering, and weighing the matter in every point of view, I HAVE MADE UP MY MIND (WITH GOD'S LEAVE) TO GO TO AMERICA—AND TO START AS SOON AFTER CHRISTMAS AS IT WILL BE SAFE TO GO."

Three days later than that which announced his resolve, the subject was resumed: "I wrote to Chapman & Hall asking them what they thought of it, and saying I meant to keep a note-book, and publish it for half a guinea or thereabouts, on my return. They instantly sent the warmest possible reply, and said they had taken it for granted I would go, and had been speaking of it only the day before.

His next letter was the unexpected arrival which came by hand from Devonshire Terrace, when I thought him still by the sea: "This is to give you notice that I am coming to breakfast with you this morning on my way to Broadstairs. I repeat it, sir,—on my way to Broadstairs. For, directly I got Macready's note yesterday I went to Canterbury, and came on by day-coach for the express purpose of talking with him; which I did between 11 and 12 last night in Clarence Terrace. The American preliminaries are necessarily startling, and, to a gentleman of my temperament, destroy rest, sleep, appetite, and work, unless definitely arranged. Macready has quite decided me in respect of time and so forth. The instant I have wrung a reluctant consent from Kate, I shall take our joint passage in the mail-packet for next January." His next letter, two days later from Broadstairs, informed me of the result of the Macready conference: "Only a word. Kate is quite reconciled. 'Anne' (her maid) goes, and is amazingly cheerful and light of heart upon it."

His wife's younger brother had died with the same unexpected suddenness that attended her younger sister's death; and the event had followed close upon the decease of Mrs. Hogarth's mother while on a visit to her daughter and Mr. Hogarth. "As no steps had been taken towards the funeral," he wrote (25th October) in reply to my offer of such service as I could render, "I thought it best at once to bestir myself; and not even you could have saved my going to the cemetery. It is a great trial to me to give up Mary's grave; greater than I can possibly express. I thought of moving her to the catacombs and saying nothing about it; but then I remembered that the poor old lady is buried next her at her own desire, and could not find it in my heart, directly she is laid in the earth, to take her grandchild away. The desire to be buried next her is as strong upon me now as it was five years ago; and I *know* (for I don't think there ever was love like that I bear her) that it will never diminish and by whose side, if it please God to leave me in possession of sense to signify my wishes, my bones, whenever or wherever I die, will one day be laid."

We had some days of much enjoyment at the end of the year, when Landor came up from Bath for the christening of his godson; and the "Britannia," which was to take the travelers from us in January, brought over to them in December all sorts of cordialities, anticipations, and stretchings-forth of palms, in token of the welcome awaiting them. On New Year's Eve they dined with me, and I with them on New Year's Day; when (his house having been taken for the period of his absence by General Sir John Wilson) we sealed up his wine-cellar, after opening therein some sparkling Moselle in honor of the ceremony, and drinking it then and there to his happy return. Next morning (it was a Sunday) I accompanied them to Liverpool, Maclise having been suddenly stayed by his mother's death; the intervening day and its occupations have been humorously sketched in his American book; and on the 4th they sailed. I never saw the Britannia after I stepped from her deck back to the small steamer that had taken us to her. "How little I thought" (were the last lines of his first American letter), "the first time you mounted the shapeless coat, that I should have such a sad association with its back as when I saw it by the paddle-box of that small steamer!"

CHAPTER 19

FIRST IMPRESSIONS OF AMERICA

1842

THE FIRST LINES OF THAT LETTER were written as soon as he got sight of earth again, from the banks of Newfoundland, on Monday, the 17th of January, the fourteenth day from their departure: even then so far from Halifax that they could not expect to make it before Wednesday night, or to reach Boston until Saturday or Sunday. They had not been fortunate in the passage. During the whole voyage the weather had been unprecedentedly bad, the wind for the most part dead against them, the wet intolerable, the sea horribly disturbed, the days dark, and the nights fearful. On the previous Monday night it had blown a hurricane, beginning at five in the afternoon and raging all night. His description of the storm is published, and the peculiarities of a steamer's behavior in such circumstances are hit off as if he had been all his life a sailor.

He stood out against sickness only for the day following that on which they sailed.

For the three following days he kept his bed, miserable enough, and had not, until the eighth day of the voyage, six days before the date of his letter, been able to get to work at the dinner-table. What he then observed of his fellow-travelers, and had to tell of their life on board, has been set forth in his *Notes* with delightful humor; but in

its first freshness I received it in this letter, and some whimsical passages, then suppressed, there will be no harm in printing now:

"We have 86 passengers; and such a strange collection of beasts never was got together upon the sea, since the days of the Ark. I have never been in the saloon since the first day; the noise, the smell, and the closeness being quite intolerable. I have only been on deck once!—and then I was surprised and disappointed at the smallness of the panorama. The sea, running as it does and has done, is very stupendous, and viewed from the air or some great height would be grand no doubt. But seen from the wet and rolling decks, in this weather and these circumstances, it only impresses one giddily and painfully. I was very glad to turn away, and come below again."

Their "way of passing the time" will be found in the *Notes* much as it was written to me; except that there was one point connected with the card-playing which he feared might overtax the credulity of his readers, but which he protested had occurred more than once: "Apropos of rolling, I have forgotten to mention that in playing whist we are obliged to put the tricks in our pockets, to keep them from disappearing altogether; and that five or six times in the course of every rubber we are all flung from our seats, roll out at different doors, and keep on rolling until we are picked up by stewards. This has become such a matter of course, that we go through it with perfect gravity, and, when we are bolstered up on our sofas again, resume our conversation or our game at the point where it was interrupted."

The next day's landing at Halifax, and delivery of the mails, are sketched in the *Notes*; but not his personal part in what followed: "Then, sir, comes a breathless man who has been already into the ship and out again, shouting

Charles Dickens in 1841, pencil on paper by Count D'Orsay, sketched shortly before the author's first trip to the United States in December 1841, and signed by Dickens

AMERICAN NOTES, CHAPTER 2

Dickens experiences sea-sickness on his voyage to America with characteristic hyperbole:

I SAY nothing of what may be called the domestic noises of the ship: such as the breaking of glass and crockery, the tumbling down of stewards, the gambols, overhead, of loose casks and truant dozens of bottled porter, and the very remarkable and far from exhilarating sounds raised in their various state-rooms by the seventy passengers who were too ill to get up to breakfast. I say nothing of them: for although I lay listening to this concert for three or four days, I don't think I heard it for more than a quarter of a minute, at the expiration of which term, I lay down again, excessively sea-sick.

Not sea-sick, be it understood, in the ordinary acceptation of the term: I wish I had been: but in a form which I have never seen or heard described, though I have no doubt it is very common. I lay there, all the day long, quite coolly and contentedly; with no sense of weariness, with no desire to get up, or get better, or take the air; with no curiosity, or care, or regret, of any sort or degree, saving that I think I can remember, in this universal indifference, having a kind of lazy joy—of fiendish delight, if anything so lethargic can be dignified with the title—in the fact of my wife being too ill to talk to me. [. . .]

Once—once—I found myself on deck. I don't know how I got there, or what possessed me to go there, but there I was; and completely dressed too, with a huge pea-coat on, and a pair of boots such as no weak man in his senses could ever have got into. I found myself standing, when a gleam of consciousness came upon me, holding on to something. I don't know what. I think it was the boatswain: or it may have been the pump: or possibly the cow. I can't say how long I had been there; whether a day or a minute. I recollect trying to think about something (about anything in the whole wide world, I was not particular) without the smallest effect. I could not even make out which was the sea, and which the sky, for the horizon seemed drunk, and was flying wildly about in all directions.

my name as he tears along. I stop, arm in arm with the little doctor whom I have taken ashore for oysters. The breathless man introduces himself as The Speaker of the House of Assembly; will drag me away to his house; and will have a carriage and his wife sent down for Kate, who is laid up with a hideously swoln face. Then he drags me up to the Governor's house (Lord Falkland is the governor), and then Heaven knows where; concluding with both houses of parliament, which happen to meet for the session that very day, and are opened by a mock speech from the throne delivered by the governor, with one of Lord Grey's sons for his aide-de-camp, and a great host of officers about him. I wish you could have seen the crowds cheering the inimitable[18] in the streets. I wish you could have seen judges, law-officers, bishops, and law-makers welcoming the inimitable."

He resumed his letter at Tremont House on Saturday, the 28th of January, having reached Boston that day week at five in the afternoon; and, as his first American experience is very lightly glanced at in the *Notes*, a fuller picture will perhaps be welcome. "As the Cunard boats have a wharf of their own at the custom-house, and that a narrow one, we were a long time (an hour at least) working in. I was standing in full fig on the paddle-box beside the captain, staring about me, when suddenly, long before we were moored to the wharf, a dozen men came leaping on board at the peril of their lives, with great bundles of newspapers under their arms; worsted comforters (very much the worse for wear) round their necks; and so forth. 'Aha!' says I, 'this is like our London Bridge;' believing of course that these visitors were news-boys. But what do you think of their being EDITORS? And what do you think of their tearing violently up to me and beginning to shake hands like madmen? Oh! if you could have seen how I wrung their wrists!

by the high price (three pounds sterling each) of the tickets. There is to be a ball next Monday week at New York, and 150 names appear on the list of the committee. There is to be a dinner in the same place, in the same week, to which I have had an invitation with every known name in America appended to it. But what can I tell you about any of these things which will give you the slightest notion of the enthusiastic greeting they give me, or the cry that runs through the whole country? I have had deputations from the Far West, who have come from more than two thousand miles' distance: from the lakes, the rivers, the back-woods, the log houses, the cities, factories, villages, and towns. Authorities from nearly all the States have written to me. I have heard from the universities, Congress, Senate, and bodies, public and private, of every sort and kind."

There were but two days more before the post left for England, and the close of this part of his letter sketched the engagements that awaited him on leaving Boston: "We leave here next Saturday. We go to a place called Worcester, about 75 miles off, to the house of the governor of this place; and stay with him all Sunday. On Monday we go on by railroad about 50 miles further to a town called Springfield, where I am met by a 'reception committee' from Hartford 20 miles further, and carried on by the multitude: I am sure I don't know how, but I shouldn't wonder if they appear with a triumphal car. On Wednesday I have a public dinner there. On Friday I shall be obliged to present myself in public again, at a place called New Haven, about 30 miles further. On Saturday evening I hope to be at New York; and there I shall stay ten days or a fortnight. You will suppose that I have enough to do. I am sitting for a portrait and for a bust. I have the correspondence of a secretary of state, and the engagements of a fashionable physician. I have a secretary whom I take on with me. He is a young man of the name of Q.; was strongly recommended to me; is most modest, obliging, silent, and willing; and does his work well. He boards and lodges at my expense when we travel; and his salary is ten dollars per month—about two pounds five of our English money. There will be dinners and balls at Washington, Philadelphia, Baltimore, and I believe everywhere. In Canada, I have promised to play at the theatre with the officers, for the benefit of a charity.

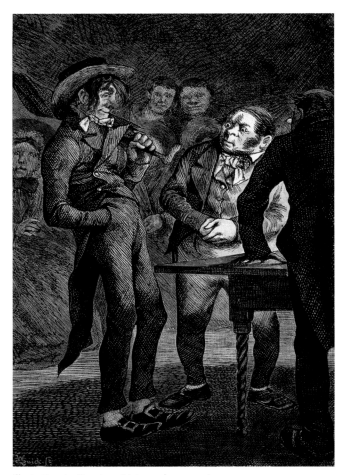

Illustration to *American Notes*, color engraving.

"A Mr. Alexander, to whom I had written from England promising to sit for a portrait, was on board directly we touched the land, and brought us here in his carriage. Then, after sending a present of most beautiful flowers, he left us to ourselves, and we thanked him for it."

What further he had to say of that week's experience finds its first public utterance here. "How can I tell you," he continues, "what has happened since that first day? How can I give you the faintest notion of my reception here; of the crowds that pour in and out the whole day; of the people that line the streets when I go out; of the cheering when I went to the theatre; of the copies of verses, letters of congratulation, welcomes of all kinds, balls, dinners, assemblies without end? There is to be a public dinner to me here in Boston, next Tuesday, and great dissatisfaction has been given to the many

MARTIN CHUZZLEWIT, CHAPTER 16

Dickens presents a more explicit critique of the American newspaper industry on Martin Chuzzlewit's arrival in New York:

'HERE'S this morning's New York Sewer!' cried one. 'Here's this morning's New York Stabber! Here's the New York Family Spy! Here's the New York Private Listener! Here's the New York Peeper! Here's the New York Plunderer! Here's the New York Keyhole Reporter! Here's the New York Rowdy Journal! Here's all the New York papers! Here's full particulars of the patriotic locofoco movement yesterday, in which the whigs was so chawed up; and the last Alabama gouging case; and the interesting Arkansas dooel with Bowie knives; and all the Political, Commercial, and Fashionable News. Here they are! Here they are! Here's the papers, here's the papers!'

'Here's the Sewer!' cried another. 'Here's the New York Sewer! Here's some of the twelfth thousand of to-day's Sewer, with the best accounts of the markets, and all the shipping news, and four whole columns of country correspondence, and a full account of the Ball at Mrs. White's last night, where all the beauty and fashion of New York was assembled; with the Sewer's own particulars of the private lives of all the ladies that was there! Here's the Sewer! Here's some of the twelfth thousand of the New York Sewer! Here's the Sewer's exposure of the Wall Street Gang, and the Sewer's exposure of the Washington Gang, and the Sewer's exclusive account of a flagrant act of dishonesty committed by the Secretary of State when he was eight years old; now communicated, at a great expense, by his own nurse. Here's the Sewer! Here's the New York Sewer, in its twelfth thousand, with a whole column of New Yorkers to be shown up, and all their names printed! Here's the Sewer's article upon the Judge that tried him, day afore yesterday, for libel, and the Sewer's tribute to the independent Jury that didn't convict him, and the Sewer's account of what they might have expected if they had! Here's the Sewer, here's the Sewer! Here's the wide-awake Sewer; always on the lookout; the leading Journal of the United States, now in its twelfth thousand, and still a-printing off:—Here's the New York Sewer!'

"On looking back through these sheets, I am astonished to find how little I have told you, and how much I have, even now, in store which shall be yours by word of mouth. The American poor, the American factories, the institutions of all kinds—I have a book, already. There is no man in this town, or in this State of New England, who has not a blazing fire and a meat dinner every day of his life. A flaming sword in the air would not attract so much attention as a beggar in the streets. There are no charity uniforms, no wearisome repetition of the same dull ugly dress, in that blind school.

"All are attired after their own tastes, and every boy and girl has his or her individuality as distinct and unimpaired as you would find it in their own homes. At the theatres, all the ladies sit in the fronts of the boxes. The gallery are as quiet as the dress circle at dear Drury Lane.

A man with seven heads would be no sight at all, compared with one who couldn't read and write."

Unmistakably to be seen, in this earliest of his letters, is the quite fresh and unalloyed impression first received by him at this memorable visit; and it is due, as well to himself as to the great country which welcomed him, that this should be considered independently of any modification it afterwards underwent. Of the fervency and universality of the welcome there could indeed be no doubt, and as little that it sprang from feelings honorable both to giver and receiver. The sources of Dickens's popularity in England

OVERLEAF: View of the City of Boston from Dochester Heights, by Robert Havell, ca. 1841

were in truth multiplied many-fold in America. The hearty, cordial, and humane side of his genius had fascinated them quite as much; but there was also something beyond this. The cheerful temper that had given new beauty to the commonest forms of life, the abounding humor which had added largely to all innocent enjoyment, the honorable and in those days rare distinction of America which left no home in the Union inaccessible to such advantages, had made Dickens the object everywhere of grateful admiration, for the most part of personal affection. But even this was not all. I do not say it either to lessen or to increase the value of the tribute, but to express simply what it was; and there cannot be a question that the young English author, whom by his language they claimed equally for their own, was almost universally regarded by the Americans as a kind of embodied protest against what they believed to be worst in the institutions of England, depressing and overshadowing in a social sense, and adverse to purely intellectual influences. In all the papers of every grade in the Union, of which many were sent to me at the time, the feeling of triumph over the mother-country in this particular is everywhere predominant. You worship titles, they said, and military heroes, and millionaires, and we of the New World want to show you, by extending the kind of homage that the Old World reserves for kings and conquerors, to a young man with nothing to distinguish him but his heart and his genius, what it is we think in these parts worthier of honor, than birth, or wealth, a title, or a sword.

"A triumph has been prepared for him," wrote Mr. Ticknor to our dear friend Kenyon, "in which the whole country will join. He will have a progress through the States unequaled since Lafayette's." Daniel Webster told the Americans that Dickens had done more already to ameliorate the condition of the English poor than all the statesmen Great Britain had sent into Parliament.

[18] This word, applied to him by his old master; Mr. Giles was for a long time the epithet we called him by.

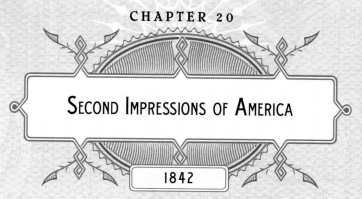

CHAPTER 20

SECOND IMPRESSIONS OF AMERICA

1842

His SECOND LETTER, radiant with the same kindly warmth that gave always pre-eminent charm to his genius, was dated from the Carlton Hotel, New York, on the 14th February, but its only allusion of any public interest was to the beginning of his agitation of the question of international copyright. He went to America with no express intention of starting this question in any way, and certainly with no belief that such remark upon it as a person in his position could alone be expected to make would be resented strongly by any sections of the American people. But he was not long left in doubt on this head. He had spoken upon it twice publicly, "to the great indignation of some of the editors here, who are attacking me for so doing, right and left."

"Carlton House, New York: Thursday, February Seventeenth, 1842. . . . As there is a sailing-packet from here to England to-morrow which is warranted (by the owners) to be a marvelous fast sailer, and as it appears most probable that she will reach home (I write the word with a pang) before the Cunard steamer of next month, I indite this letter. And lest this letter should reach you before another letter which I dispatched from here last Monday, let me say in the first place that I *did* dispatch a brief epistle to you on that day, together with a newspaper, and a pamphlet touching the Boz ball; and that I put in the post-office at Boston another newspaper for you containing an account of the dinner, which was just about to come off, you remember, when I wrote to you from that city.

"We left Boston on the fifth, and went away with the governor of the city to stay till Monday at his house at Worcester. He married a sister of Bancroft's, and another sister of Bancroft's went down with us. The village of Worcester is one of the prettiest in New England. . . . On Monday morning at nine o'clock we started again by railroad and went on to Springfield, where a deputation of two were waiting, and everything was in readiness that the utmost attention could suggest. Owing to the mildness of the weather, the Connecticut river was 'open,' videlicet not frozen, and they had a steamboat ready to carry us on to Hartford; thus saving a land-journey of only twenty-five miles, but on such roads at this time of year that it takes nearly twelve hours to accomplish! The boat was very small, the river full of floating blocks of ice, and the depth where we went (to avoid the ice and the current) not more than a few inches. After two hours and a half of this queer traveling, we got to Hartford. There, there was quite an English inn; except in respect of the bedrooms, which are always uncomfortable; and the best committee of management that has yet presented itself. They kept us more quiet, and were more considerate and thoughtful, even to their own exclusion, than any I have yet had to deal with. Kate's face being horribly bad, I determined to give her a rest here; and accordingly wrote to get rid of my engagement at New Haven, on that plea. We remained in this town until the eleventh: holding a formal levee every day for two hours, and receiving on each from two hundred to three hundred people. At five o'clock on the afternoon of the eleventh, we set off (still by railroad) for New Haven, which we reached about eight o'clock. The moment we had had tea, we were forced to open another levee for the students and professors of the college (the largest in the States), and the townspeople. I suppose we shook hands, before going to bed, with considerably more than five hundred people; and I stood, as a matter of course, the whole time. . . .

After a hasty breakfast we started off; and after another levee on the deck (actually on the deck), and 'three times three for Dickens,' moved towards New York.

"About half-past 2 we arrived here. In half an hour more, we reached this hotel, where a very splendid suite of rooms was prepared for us; and where everything is very comfortable, and no doubt (as at Boston) *enormously* dear. Just as we sat down to dinner, David Colden made his appearance; and when he had gone, and we were taking our wine, Washington Irving came in alone, with open arms. And here he stopped, until ten o'clock at night."

DICKENS OBJECTED TO THE ABSENCE OF AN INTERNATIONAL COPYRIGHT LAW, AS ROBERT PATTEN EXPLAINS:

The principal law affecting Dickens's copyright during his lifetime was 5 & 6 Vict. C. 45, the 1842 Copyright Amendment Act that secured to the author, heirs, and assigns copyright for 42 years or seven years after the author's death, whichever was longer. This statute, justified on the grounds that it encourages 'the Production of Literary Works of lasting Benefit to the World', gave authors and their estates a much longer-term interest in their writings

[. . .] A] deficiency in the earlier copyright acts was the absence of regulation about copies of British authors printed abroad, for sale in the colonies or other countries, and copies of titles by foreign nationals imported into Britain. When Dickens travelled to America in the winter and spring of 1842, he spoke out, frequently, in favour of an 'international'—by which he meant, at a minimum, a 'bi-national'—copyright agreement with America granting reciprocal privileges to subjects or citizens of other countries [. . .]

American authors, too, could be printed and sold in Britain without any copyright agreement. Some of them, like William Cullen Bryant and Washington Irving, wanted revenue from their British sales and some protection for American writings against the flood of cheaper British imports, and therefore supported Dickens's position. But the American press, goaded by sensationalist publishers, protectionist printers, and politicians disingenuously rallying around the notion that cheap knowledge was a public benefit, hurled execrations upon Dickens's head. He returned home somewhat damaged in reputation and feelings, and in *Martin Chuzzlewit* he satirised cut-throat, 'piratical', and hypocritical, American journalism. For the next ten years Dickens refused to 'enter into any negotiation' for the transmission of early proofs to America, a resolution he ended when Harper's offered £360 to

"Boz (Charles Dickens)," engraving by Winkle, ca. 1843, after Maclise's 1839 painting

serialise *Bleak House* in their magazine simultaneously with its British issue.

From Robert Patten, "Copyright,"
***The Oxford Reader's Companion to Dickens**, ed. by Paul Schlicke*
(Oxford: OUP, 2000), pp. 123–124

"Having got so far, I shall divide my discourse into four points. First, the ball. Secondly, some slight specimens of a certain phase of character in the Americans. Thirdly, international copyright. Fourthly, my life here, and projects to be carried out while I remain.

"Firstly, the ball. It came off last Monday (vide pamphlet.) 'At a quarter-past 9, exactly' (I quote the printed order of proceeding), we were waited upon by 'David Colden, Esquire, and General George Morris;' habited, the former in full ball costume, the latter in the full dress uniform of Heaven knows what regiment of militia. The scene on our entrance was very striking. There were three thousand people present in full dress; from the roof to the floor, the theatre was decorated magnificently; and the light, glitter, glare, show, noise, and cheering, baffle my descriptive powers... We began to dance—Heaven knows how we did it, for there was no room. And we continued dancing until, being no longer able even to stand, we slipped away quietly, and came back to the hotel.

The newspapers were if possible unusually loquacious; and in their accounts of me, and my seeings, sayings, and doings on the Saturday night and Sunday before, they describe my manner, mode of speaking, dressing, and so forth. In doing this, they report that I am a very charming fellow (of course), and have a very free and easy way with me; 'which,' say they, 'at first amused a few fashionables;' but soon pleased them exceedingly. Another paper, coming after the ball, dwells upon its splendor and brilliancy; hugs itself and its readers upon all that Dickens saw, and winds up by gravely expressing its conviction that Dickens was never in such society in England as he has seen in New York, and that its high and striking tone cannot fail to make an indelible impression on his mind! For the same reason I am always represented, whenever I appear in public, as being 'very pale;' 'apparently thunderstruck;' and utterly confounded by all I see. . . . You recognize the queer vanity which is at the root of all this?

"Twenty-fourth February.

"I proceed to my third head: the international copyright question.

"I believe there is no country on the face of the earth where there is less freedom of opinion on any subject in reference to which there is a broad difference of opinion, than

in this.—There!—I write the words with reluctance, disappointment, and sorrow; but I believe it from the bottom of my soul. I spoke, as you know, of international copyright, at Boston; and I spoke of it again at Hartford. My friends were paralyzed with wonder at such audacious daring. The notion that I, a man alone by himself, in America, should venture to suggest to the Americans that there was one point on which they were neither just to their own countrymen nor to us, actually struck the boldest dumb! Washington Irving, Prescott, Hoffman, Bryant, Halleck, Dana, Washington Allston—every man who writes in this country is devoted to the question, and not one of them *dares* to raise his voice and complain of the atrocious state of the law. It is nothing that of all men living I am the greatest loser by it. It is nothing that I have a claim to speak and be heard.

"The *New York Herald*, which you will receive with this, is the *Satirist* of America; but having a great circulation (on account of its commercial intelligence and early news) it can afford to secure the best reporters. . . . My speech is done, upon the whole, with remarkable accuracy. There are a great many typographical errors in it; and by the omission of one or two words, or the substitution of one word for another, it is often materially weakened. Thus, I did not say that I 'claimed' my right, but that I 'asserted' it; and I did not say that I had 'some claim,' but that I had 'a most righteous claim,' to speak. But altogether it is very correct."

Washington Irving was chairman of this dinner, and, having from the first a dread that he should break down in his speech, the catastrophe came accordingly. Near him sat the Cambridge professor who had come with Dickens by boat from New Haven, with whom already a warm friendship had been formed that lasted for life, and who has pleasantly sketched what happened. Mr. Felton saw Irving constantly in the interval of preparation, and could not but despond at his daily iterated foreboding of *I shall certainly break down*; though besides the real dread there was a sly humor which heightened its whimsical horror with an irresistible drollery. But the professor plucked up hope a little when the night came and he

OVERLEAF: View of New York Harbor from Brooklyn Heights, by F. Palmer, published by Nathaniel Currier, 1849

Ticket to Boz Ball at Park Theatre, New York, 1842

saw that Irving had laid under his plate the manuscript of his speech. During dinner, nevertheless, his old foreboding cry was still heard, and "at last the moment arrived; Mr. Irving rose; and the deafening and long-continued applause by no means lessened his apprehension. He began in his pleasant voice; got through two or three sentences pretty easily, but in the next hesitated; and, after one or two attempts to go on, gave it up, with a graceful allusion to the tournament and the troop of knights all armed and eager for the fray; and ended with the toast CHARLES DICKENS, THE GUEST OF THE NATION. *There!* said he, as he resumed his seat amid applause as great as had greeted his rising. He had so great a love for Irving that it was painful to speak of him as at any disadvantage, and of the New York dinner he wrote only in its connection with his own copyright speeches.

"The effect of all this copyright agitation at least has been to awaken a great sensation on both sides of the subject; the respectable newspapers and reviews taking up the cudgels as strongly in my favor, as the others have done against me. Some of the vagabonds take great credit to themselves (grant us patience!) for having made me popular by publishing my books in newspapers: as if there were no England, no Scotland, no Germany, no place but America in the whole world.

"I will tell you what I should like, my dear friend, always supposing that your judgment concurs with mine, and that you would take the trouble to get such a document. I should like to have a short letter addressed to me by the principal English authors who signed the international copyright petition, expressive of their sense that I have done my duty to the cause. I am sure I deserve it, but I don't wish it on that ground. It is because its publication in the best journals here would unquestionably do great good. As the gauntlet is down, let us go on. Clay has already sent a gentleman to me express from Washington (where I shall be on the 6th or 7th of next month) to declare his strong interest in the matter, his cordial approval of the 'manly' course I have held in reference to it, and his desire to stir in it if possible. I have lighted up such a blaze that a meeting of the foremost people on the other side (very respectfully and properly conducted in reference to me, personally, I am bound to say) was held in this town t'other night. And it would be a thousand pities if we did not strike as hard as we can, now that the iron is so hot.

"On Monday morning, the 28th, we leave for Philadelphia. There I shall only stay three days. Thence we go to Baltimore, and there I shall only stay three days. Thence to Washington, where we may stay perhaps ten days; perhaps not so long. Thence to Virginia, where we may halt for one day; and thence to Charleston, where we may pass a week perhaps, and where we shall very likely remain until your March letters reach us, through David Colden.

"We mean to return home in a packet-ship,—not a steamer. Her name is the George Washington, and she will sail from here, for Liverpool, on the seventh of June. At that season of the year they are seldom more than three weeks making the voyage; and I never will trust myself upon the wide ocean, if it please Heaven, in a steamer again.

"When we reach Baltimore, we are in the regions of slavery. It exists there, in its least shocking and most mitigated form; but there it is. They whisper, here (they dare only whisper, you know, and that below their breaths), that on that place, and all through the South, there is a dull gloomy cloud on which the very word seems written. I shall be able to say, one of these days, that I accepted no public mark of respect in any place where slavery was;—and that's something.

"The ladies of America are decidedly and unquestionably beautiful. Their complexions are not so good as those of Englishwomen; their beauty does not last so long; and their figures are very inferior. But they are most beautiful. I still reserve my opinion of the national character,—just whispering that I tremble for a radical coming here, unless he is a radical on principle, by reason and reflection, and from the sense of right. I fear that if he were anything else, he would return home a Tory. . . . Twenty-seventh February. Sunday.

"There begins to be great consternation here, in reference to the Cunard packet which (we suppose) left Liverpool on the fourth. She has not yet arrived. We scarcely know what to do with ourselves in our extreme anxiety to get letters from home. I have really had serious thoughts of going back to Boston, alone, to be nearer news. We have determined to remain here until Tuesday afternoon, if she should not arrive before, and to send Mr. Q. and the luggage on to Philadelphia to-morrow morning.

"I have in my portmanteau a petition for an international copyright law, signed by all the best American writers, with Washington Irving at their head. They have requested me to hand it to Clay for presentation, and to back it with any remarks I may think proper to offer. So 'Hoo-roar for the principle, as the money-lender said ven he wouldn't renoo the bill.'

"Carlton House, New York, February twenty-eighth, 1842. . . . The Caledonia, I grieve and regret to say, has not arrived. If she left England to her time, she has been four-and-twenty days at sea. There is no news of her; and on the nights of the fourteenth and eighteenth it blew a terrible gale, which almost justifies the worst suspicions. For myself, I have hardly any hope of her; having seen enough, in our passage out, to convince me that steaming across the ocean in heavy weather is as yet an experiment of the utmost hazard.

"It would be difficult to tell you, my dear fellow, what an impression this has made upon our minds, or with what intense anxiety and suspense we have been waiting for your letters from home. We were to have gone South to-day, but linger here until to-morrow afternoon (having sent the secretary and luggage forward) for one more chance of news.

"P.S. Washington Irving is a *great* fellow. We have laughed most heartily together. He is just the man he ought to be. So is Doctor Channing, with whom I have had an interesting correspondence since I saw him last at Boston. Halleck is a merry little man. Bryant a sad one, and very reserved. Washington Allston the painter (who wrote *Monaldi*) is a fine specimen of a glorious old genius. Longfellow, whose volume of poems I have got for you, is a frank accomplished man as well as a fine writer, and will be in town 'next fall.' Tell Macready that I suspect prices here must have rather altered since his time. I paid our fortnight's bill here, last night. We have dined out every day (except when I was laid up with a sore throat), and only had in all four bottles of wine. The bill was 70£. English!!!"

On the very day when the Caledonia was due in Boston (the 18th of February) it was learned in London that she had undergone misadventure; that, her decks having been swept and her rudder torn away, though happily no lives were lost, she had returned disabled to Cork; and that the Acadia, having received her passengers and mails, was to sail with them from Liverpool next day.

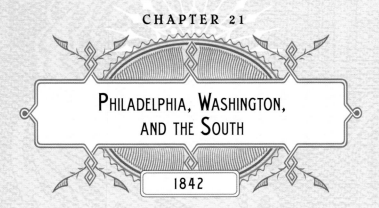

CHAPTER 21

PHILADELPHIA, WASHINGTON, AND THE SOUTH

1842

DICKENS'S NEXT LETTER was begun in the "United States Hotel, Philadelphia," and bore date "Sunday, sixth March, 1842." It treated of much dealt with afterwards at greater length in the *Notes*, but the freshness and vivacity of the first impressions in it have surprised me. I do not, however, print any passage here which has not its own interest independently of anything contained in that book. The rule will be continued, as in the portions of letters already given, of not transcribing anything before printed, or anything having even but a near resemblance to descriptions that appear in the *Notes*.

"I have often asked Americans in London which were the better railroads,—ours or theirs? They have taken time for reflection, and generally replied on mature consideration that they rather thought we excelled; in respect of the punctuality with which we arrived at our stations, and the smoothness of our traveling. I wish you could see what an American railroad is, in some parts where I now have seen them. I won't say I wish you could feel what it is, because that would be an unchristian and savage aspiration. It is never inclosed, or warded off. You walk down the main street of a large town; and, slap-dash, headlong, pell-mell, down the middle of the street, with pigs burrowing, and boys flying kites and playing marbles, and men smoking, and women talking, and children crawling, close to the very rails, there comes tearing along a mad locomotive with its train of cars, scattering a red-hot shower of sparks (from its wood fire) in all directions; screeching, hissing, yelling, and panting; and nobody one atom more concerned than if it were a hundred miles away.

"The cars are like very shabby omnibuses,—only larger; holding sixty or seventy people. The seats, instead of being placed long ways, are put cross-wise, back to front. Each holds two. There is a long row of these on each side of the caravan, and a narrow passage up the centre. The windows are usually all closed, and there is very often, in addition, a hot, close, most intolerable charcoal stove in a red-hot glow. The heat and closeness are quite insupportable. But this is the characteristic of all American houses, of all the public institutions, chapels, theatres, and prisons. From the constant use of the hard anthracite coal in these beastly furnaces, a perfectly new class of diseases is springing up in the country.

"In the ladies' car, there is no smoking of tobacco allowed. All gentlemen who have ladies with them sit in this car; and it is usually very full. Before it, is the gentlemen's car; which is something narrower. As I had a window close to me yesterday which commanded this gentlemen's car, I looked at it pretty often, perforce. The flashes of saliva flew so perpetually and incessantly out of the windows all the way, that it looked as though they were ripping open feather-beds inside, and letting the wind dispose of the feathers. But this spitting is universal.

In the courts of law, the judge has his spittoon on the bench, the counsel have theirs, the witness has his, the prisoner his, and the crier his. The jury are accommodated at the rate of three men to a spittoon (or spit-box as they call it here); and the spectators in the gallery are provided for, as so many men who in the course of nature expectorate without cessation. There are spit-boxes in every steamboat, bar-room, public dining-room, house of office, and place of general resort, no matter what it be. In the hospitals, the students are requested, by placard, to use the boxes provided for them, and not to spit upon the stairs. I have twice seen gentlemen, at evening parties in New York, turn aside when they were not engaged in conversation, and spit upon the drawing-room carpet. And in every bar-room and hotel passage the stone floor looks as if it were paved with open oysters—from the quantity of this kind of deposit which tessellates it all over. . . .

"The institutions at Boston, and at Hartford, are most admirable. It would be very difficult indeed to improve upon them. But this is not so at New York; where there is an ill-managed lunatic asylum, a bad jail, a dismal workhouse,

AMERICAN NOTES, CHAPTER 8

Dickens's growing disgust at the chewing and expectoration of tobacco reached a peak when he visited the Senate in Washington:

THE Senate is a dignified and decorous body, and its proceedings are conducted with much gravity and order. Both houses are handsomely carpeted; but the state to which these carpets are reduced by the universal disregard of the spittoon with which every honourable member is accommodated, and the extraordinary improvements on the pattern which are squirted and dabbled upon it in every direction, do not admit of being described. I will merely observe, that I strongly recommend all strangers not to look at the floor; and if they happen to drop anything, though it be their purse, not to pick it up with an ungloved hand on any account.

It is somewhat remarkable too, at first, to say the least, to see so many honourable members with swelled faces; and it is scarcely less remarkable to discover that this appearance is caused by the quantity of tobacco they contrive to stow within the hollow of the cheek. It is strange enough too, to see an honourable gentleman leaning back in his tilted chair with his legs on the desk before him, shaping a convenient 'plug' with his penknife, and when it is quite ready for use, shooting the old one from his mouth, as from a pop-gun, and clapping the new one in its place.

passages where no one stays; has no drop of water, or ray of light, or visitor, or help of any kind; and there he remains until the magistrate's arrival. If he die (as one man did not long ago), he is half eaten by the rats in an hour's time (as this man was). I expressed, on seeing these places the other night, the disgust I felt, and which it would be impossible to repress.

"When a man is hanged in New York, he is walked out of one of these cells, without any condemned sermon or other religious formalities, straight into the narrow jail-yard, which may be about the width of Cranbourn Alley. There, a gibbet is erected, which is of curious construction; for the culprit stands on the earth with the rope about his neck, which passes through a pulley in the top of the 'Tree' (see *Newgate Calendar* passim), and is attached to a weight something heavier than the man. This weight, being suddenly let go, drags the rope down with it, and sends the criminal flying up fourteen feet into the air; while the judge, and jury, and five-and-twenty citizens (whose presence is required by the law), stand by, that they may afterwards certify to the fact. This yard is a very dismal place; and when I looked at it, I thought the practice infinitely superior to ours: much more solemn, and far less degrading and indecent.

"There is another prison near New York which is a house of correction. The convicts labor in stone-quarries near at hand, but the jail has no covered yards or shops, so that when the weather is wet (as it was when I was there) each man is shut up in his own little cell, all the live-long day. Imagine them in number 400, and in every one a man locked up; this one with his hands through the bars of his grate, this one in bed (in the middle of the day, remember), and this one flung down in a heap upon the ground with his head against the bars like a wild beast. Make the rain pour down in torrents outside. Put the everlasting stove in the midst; hot, suffocating, and vaporous, as a witch's cauldron. Add a smell like that of a thousand old mildewed umbrellas wet through, and a thousand dirty-clothes-bags musty, moist, and fusty, and you will have some idea—a very feeble one, my dear friend, on my word—of this place yesterday week.

"Washington, Sunday, March the Thirteenth, 1842. I must tell you a slight experience I had in Philadelphia. My

and a perfectly intolerable place of police-imprisonment. A man is found drunk in the streets, and is thrown into a cell below the surface of the earth; profoundly dark; so full of noisome vapors that when you enter it with a candle you see a ring about the light, like that which surrounds the moon in wet and cloudy weather; and so offensive and disgusting in its filthy odors that you *cannot bear* its stench. He is shut up within an iron door, in a series of vaulted

rooms had been ordered for a week, but, in consequence of Kate's illness, only Mr. Q. and the luggage had gone on. Mr. Q. always lives at the table-d'hote, so that while we were in New York our rooms were empty. The landlord not only charged me half the full rent for the time during which the rooms were reserved for us (which was quite right), but charged me also *for board for myself and Kate and Anne, at the rate of nine dollars per day* for the same period, when we were actually living, at the same expense, in New York!!! I *did* remonstrate upon this head, but was coolly told it was the custom (which I have since been assured is a lie), and had nothing for it but to pay the amount. What else could I do? I was going away by the steamboat at five o'clock in the morning; and the landlord knew perfectly well that my disputing an item of his bill would draw down upon me the sacred wrath of the newspapers, which would one and all demand in capitals if THIS was the gratitude of the man whom America had received as she had never received any other man but La Fayette?

"I had to dress in a hurry, and follow Kate to Carey's the bookseller's, where there was a party. He married a sister of Leslie's. There are three Miss Leslies here, very accomplished; and one of them has copied all her brother's principal pictures. These copies hang about the room. We got away from this as soon as we could; and next morning had to turn out at five. In the morning I had received and shaken hands with five hundred people, so you may suppose that I was pretty well tired. Indeed, I am obliged to be very careful of myself; to avoid smoking and drinking; to get to bed soon; and to be particular in respect of what I eat. . . . You cannot think how bilious and trying the climate is. One day it is hot summer, without a breath of air; the next, twenty degrees below freezing, with a wind blowing that cuts your skin like steel. These changes have occurred here several times since last Wednesday night.

"I have altered my route, and don't mean to go to Charleston. The country, all the way from here, is nothing but a dismal swamp; there is a bad night of sea-coasting in the journey; the equinoctial gales are blowing hard; and Clay (a most *charming* fellow, by-the-by), whom I have consulted, strongly dissuades me. The weather is intensely hot there; the spring fever is coming on; and there is very little to see, after all.

"We therefore go next Wednesday night to Richmond, which we shall reach on Thursday. There we shall stop three days; my object being to see some tobacco-plantations. Then we shall go by James River back to Baltimore, which we have already passed through, and where we shall stay two days. Then we shall go West at once, straight through the most gigantic part of this continent: across the Alleghany Mountains, and over a prairie.

"STILL AT WASHINGTON, Fifteenth March, 1842. . . . It is impossible, my dear friend, to tell you what we felt when Mr. Q. (who is a fearfully sentimental genius, but heartily interested in all that concerns us) came to where we were dining last Sunday, and sent in a note to the effect that the Caledonia[19] had arrived! Being really assured of her safety, we felt as if the distance between us and home were diminished by at least one-half. There was great joy everywhere here, for she had been quite despaired of, but our joy was beyond all telling. This news came on by express. Last night your letters reached us. I was dining with a club (for I can't avoid a dinner of that sort, now and then), and Kate sent me a note about nine o'clock to say they were here. But she didn't open them—which I consider heroic—until I came home. That was about half-past ten; and we read them until nearly two in the morning.

"I have the privilege of appearing on the floor of both Houses here, and go to them every day. They are very handsome and commodious. There is a great deal of bad speaking, but there are a great many very remarkable men, in the legislature: such as John Quincy Adams, Clay, Preston, Calhoun, and others: with whom I need scarcely add I have been placed in the friendliest relations. Adams is a fine old fellow—

United States Capitol, Washington, D.C., ink, watercolor and wash on paper, by Alexander Jackson Davis, 1834

MARTIN CHUZZLEWIT, CHAPTER 23

In Martin Chuzzlewit, *Dickens has his hero and his faithful friend and servant Mark Tapley*
attempt to settle in the feverish Mississippi swampland of 'Eden':

AS they proceeded further on their track, and came more and more towards their journey's end, the monotonous desolation of the scene increased to that degree, that for any redeeming feature it presented to their eyes, they might have entered, in the body, on the grim domains of Giant Despair. A flat morass, bestrewn with fallen timber; a marsh on which the good growth of the earth seemed to have been wrecked and cast away, that from its decomposing ashes vile and ugly things might rise; where the very trees took the aspect of huge weeds, begotten of the slime from which they sprung, by the hot sun that burnt them up; where fatal maladies, seeking whom they might infect, came forth at night in misty shapes, and creeping out upon the water, hunted them like spectres until day; where even the blessed sun, shining down on festering elements of corruption and disease, became a horror; this was the realm of Hope through which they moved.

At last they stopped. At Eden too. The waters of the Deluge might have left it but a week before; so choked with slime and matted growth was the hideous swamp which bore that name.

There being no depth of water close in shore, they landed from the vessel's boat, with all their goods beside them. There were a few log-houses visible among the dark trees; the best, a cow-shed or a rude stable; but for the wharves, the market-place, the public buildings—

'Here comes an Edener,' said Mark. 'He'll get us help to carry these things up. Keep a good heart, sir. Hallo there!'

The man advanced toward them through the thickening gloom, very slowly; leaning on a stick. As he drew nearer, they observed that he was pale and worn, and that his anxious eyes were deeply sunken in his head. His dress of homespun blue hung about him in rags; his feet and head were bare. He sat down on a stump half-way, and beckoned them to come to him. When they complied, he put his hand upon his side as if in pain, and while he fetched his breath stared at them, wondering.

'Strangers!' he exclaimed, as soon as he could speak.

'The very same,' said Mark. 'How are you, sir?'

'I've had the fever very bad,' he answered faintly. 'I haven't stood upright these many weeks. Those are your notions I see,' pointing to their property.

'Yes, sir,' said Mark, 'they are. You couldn't recommend us some one as would lend a hand to help carry 'em up to the—to the town, could you, sir?'

'My eldest son would do it if he could,' replied the man; 'but today he has his chill upon him, and is lying wrapped up in the blankets. My youngest died last week.'

'I'm sorry for it, governor, with all my heart,' said Mark, shaking him by the hand. 'Don't mind us. Come along with me, and I'll give you an arm back. The goods is safe enough, sir'—to Martin—'there ain't many people about, to make away with 'em. What a comfort that is!'

'No,' cried the man. 'You must look for such folk here,' knocking his stick upon the ground, 'or yonder in the bush, towards the north. We've buried most of 'em. The rest have gone away. Them that we have here, don't come out at night.'

'The night air ain't quite wholesome, I suppose?' said Mark.

'It's deadly poison,' was the settler's answer.

seventy-six years old, but with most surprising vigor, memory, readiness, and pluck. Clay is perfectly enchanting; an irresistible man. There are some very notable specimens, too, out of the West. Splendid men to look at, hard to deceive, prompt to act, lions in energy, Crichtons in varied accomplishments, Indians in quickness of eye and gesture, Americans in affectionate and generous impulse. It would be difficult to exaggerate the nobility of some of these glorious fellows.

"I said I wouldn't write anything more concerning the American people, for two months. Second thoughts are best. I shall not change, and may as well speak out—to *you*. They are friendly, earnest, hospitable, kind, frank, very often accomplished, far less prejudiced than you would suppose, warm-hearted, fervent, and enthusiastic. They are chivalrous in their universal politeness to women, courteous, obliging, disinterested; and, when they conceive a perfect affection for a man (as I may venture to say of myself), entirely devoted to him. I have received thousands of people of all ranks and grades, and have never once been asked an offensive or unpolite question,—except by Englishmen, who, when they have been 'located' here for some years, are worse than the devil in his blackest painting. The State is a parent to its people; has a parental care and watch over all poor children, women laboring of child, sick persons, and captives. The common men render you assistance in the streets, and would revolt from the offer of a piece of money. The desire to oblige is universal; and I have never once traveled in a public conveyance without making some generous acquaintance whom I have been sorry to part from, and who has in many cases come on miles, to see us again. But I don't like the country. I would not live here, on any consideration. It goes against the grain with me. It would with you. I think it impossible, utterly impossible, for any Englishman to live here and be happy. I have a confidence that I must be right, because I have everything, God knows, to lead me to the opposite conclusion; and yet I cannot resist coming to this one. As to the causes, they are too many to enter upon here. . . .

"Richmond, in Virginia. Thursday Night, March 17. "Irving was with me at Washington yesterday, and *wept heartily* at parting. He is a fine fellow, when you know him well; and you would relish him, my dear friend, of all things. We have laughed together at some absurdities we have encountered in company, quite in my vociferous Devonshire-Terrace style. The 'Merrikin' government has treated him, he says, most liberally and handsomely in every respect. He thinks of sailing for Liverpool on the 7th of April, passing a short time in London, and then going to Paris. Perhaps you may meet him. If you do, he will know that you are my dearest friend, and will open his whole heart to you at once. His secretary of legation, Mr. Coggleswell, is a man of very remarkable information, a great traveler, a good talker, and a scholar.

"We had intended to go to Baltimore from Richmond, by a place called Norfolk; but, one of the boats being under repair, I found we should probably be detained at this Norfolk two days. Therefore we came back here yesterday, by the road we had traveled before; lay here last night; and go on to Baltimore this afternoon, at four o'clock. It is a journey of only two hours and a half. Richmond is a prettily situated town, but, like other towns in slave districts (as the planters themselves admit), has an aspect of decay and gloom which to an unaccustomed eye is *most* distressing. In the black car (for they don't let them sit with the whites), on the railroad as we went there, were a mother and family, whom the steamer was conveying away, to sell; retaining the man (the husband and father, I mean) on his plantation. The children cried the whole way.

"Yesterday, on board the boat, a slave-owner and two constables were our fellow-passengers. They were coming here in search of two negroes who had run away on the previous day. On the bridge at Richmond there is a notice against fast driving over it, as it is rotten and crazy: penalty—for whites, five dollars; for slaves, fifteen stripes. My heart is lightened as if a great load had been taken from it, when I think that we are turning our backs on this accursed and detested system. I really don't think I could have borne it any longer. It is all very well to say 'be silent on the subject.' They won't let you be silent. They will ask you what you think of it; and will expatiate on slavery as if it were one of the greatest blessings of mankind. 'It's not,' said a hard, bad-looking fellow to me the other day, 'it's not the interest of a man to use his slaves ill. It's damned nonsense that you hear in England.'—I told him quietly that it was not a man's interest to get drunk, or to steal, or to game, or to indulge in any other vice, but he *did* indulge in it for all that; that cruelty, and the abuse of irresponsible power, were two of the bad passions of human nature, with the gratification of which, considerations of interest or of ruin, had nothing whatever to do; and that, while every candid man must admit that even a slave might

American Notes, Chapter 9

In American Notes, *Dickens presents a powerful critique of slavery:*

THIS singular kind of coaching terminates at Fredericksburgh, whence there is a railway to Richmond. The tract of country through which it takes its course was once productive; but the soil has been exhausted by the system of employing a great amount of slave labour in forcing crops, without strengthening the land: and it is now little better than a sandy desert overgrown with trees. Dreary and uninteresting as its aspect is, I was glad to the heart to find anything on which one of the curses of this horrible institution has fallen; and had greater pleasure in contemplating the withered ground, than the richest and most thriving cultivation in the same place could possibly have afforded me.

In this district, as in all others where slavery sits brooding, (I have frequently heard this admitted, even by those who are its warmest advocates:) there is an air of ruin and decay abroad, which is inseparable from the system. The barns and outhouses are mouldering away; the sheds are patched and half roofless; the log cabins (built in Virginia with external chimneys made of clay or wood) are squalid in the last degree. There is no look of decent comfort anywhere. The miserable stations by the railway side, the great wild wood-yards, whence the engine is supplied with fuel; the negro children rolling on the ground before the cabin doors, with dogs and pigs; the biped beasts of burden slinking past: gloom and dejection are upon them all.

In the negro car belonging to the train in which we made this journey, were a mother and her children who had just been purchased; the husband and father being left behind with their old owner. The children cried the whole way, and the mother was misery's picture. The champion of Life, Liberty, and the Pursuit of Happiness, who had bought them, rode in the same train; and, every time we stopped, got down to see that they were safe. The black in Sinbad's Travels with one eye in the middle of his forehead which shone like a burning coal, was nature's aristocrat compared with this white gentleman.

be happy enough with a good master, all human beings knew that bad masters, cruel masters, and masters who disgraced the form they bore, were matters of experience and history, whose existence was as undisputed as that of slaves themselves. He was a little taken aback by this, and asked me if I believed in the Bible. Yes, I said, but if any man could prove to me that it sanctioned slavery, I would place no further credence in it.

. . . "We were desperately tired at Richmond, as we went to a great many places and received a very great number of visitors. We appoint usually two hours in every day for this latter purpose, and have our room so full at that period that it is difficult to move or breathe. Before we left Richmond, a gentleman told me, when I really was so exhausted that I could hardly stand, that 'three people of great fashion' were much offended by having been told, when they called last evening, that I was tired and not visible, then, but would be 'at home' from twelve to two next day! Another gentleman (no doubt of great fashion also) sent a letter to me two hours after I had gone to bed, preparatory to rising at four next morning, with instructions to the slave who brought it to knock me up and wait for an answer!"

---

[19] This was the Acadia with the Caledonia mail.

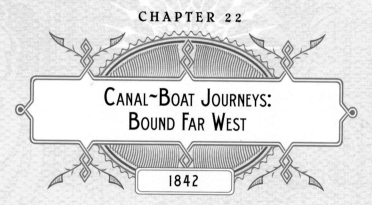

CHAPTER 22

CANAL-BOAT JOURNEYS: BOUND FAR WEST

1842

HIS NEXT LETTER WAS BEGUN from "on board the canal-boat. Going to Pittsburgh. Monday, March twenty-eighth, 1842. Several of the descriptive masterpieces of the book are in it, with such touches of original freshness as might fairly have justified a reproduction of them in their first form. Among these are the Harrisburg coach on its way through the Susquehanna valley; the railroad across the mountain; the brown-forester of the Mississippi, the interrogative man in pepper-and-salt, and the affecting scene of the emigrants put ashore as the steamer passes up the Ohio. But all that I may here give, bearing any resemblance to what is given in the *Notes*, are the opening sketch of the small creature on the top of the queer stage-coach, to which the printed version fails to do adequate justice, and an experience to which the interest belongs of having suggested the settlement of Eden in *Martin Chuzzlewit*. . . . "We left Baltimore last Thursday, the twenty-fourth, at half-past eight in the morning, by railroad; and got to a place called York, about twelve. There we dined, and took a stage-coach for Harrisburg; twenty-five miles further. This stage-coach was like nothing so much as the body of one of the swings you see at a fair set upon four wheels and roofed and covered at the sides with painted canvas. There were twelve *inside*! I, thank my stars, was on the box. The luggage was on the roof; among it, a good-sized dining-table, and a big rocking-chair. We also took up an intoxicated gentleman, who sat for ten miles between me and the coachman; and another intoxicated gentleman who got up behind, but in the course of a mile or two fell off without hurting himself, and was seen in the distant perspective reeling back to the grog-shop where we had

found him. There were four horses to this land-ark, of course; but we did not perform the journey until after half-past six o'clock that night. . . . The first half of the journey was tame enough, but the second lay through the valley of the Susquehanah (I think I spell it right, but I haven't that *American Geography* at hand), which is very beautiful. . . .

"We had all next morning in Harrisburg, as the canal-boat was not to start until three o'clock in the afternoon. The officials called upon me before I had finished breakfast; and, as the town is the seat of the Pennsylvanian legislature, I went up to the Capitol. I was very much interested in looking over a number of treaties made with the poor Indians, their signatures being rough drawings of the creatures or weapons they are called after; and the extraordinary drawing of these emblems, showing the queer, unused, shaky manner in which each man has held the pen, struck me very much.

"The innkeeper was the most attentive, civil, and obliging person I ever saw in my life. On being asked for his bill, he said there was no bill: the honor and pleasure, etc. being more than sufficient. I did not permit this, of course, and begged Mr. Q. to explain to him that, traveling four strong, I could not hear of it on any account.

"And now I come to the Canal-Boat. Bless your heart and soul, my dear fellow,—if you could only see us on board the canal-boat! Let me think, for a moment, at what time of the day or night I should best like you to see us. In the morning? Between five and six in the morning, shall I say? Well! you *would* like to see me, standing on the deck, fishing the dirty water out of the canal with a tin ladle chained to the boat by a long chain; pouring the same into a tin basin (also chained up in like manner); and scrubbing my face with the jack towel. At night, shall I say? I don't know that you *would* like to look into the cabin at night, only to see me lying on a temporary shelf exactly the width of this sheet of paper when it's open (*I measured it this morning*),[20] with one man above me, and another below; and, in all, eight-and-twenty in a low cabin, which you can't stand upright in with your hat on. I don't think you would like to look in at breakfast-time either, for then these shelves have only just been taken down and put away, and the atmosphere of the place is, as you may suppose, by no means fresh; though there *are* upon the table tea and coffee, and bread and butter, and salmon, and shad, and liver, and steak, and potatoes, and pickles, and ham, and pudding, and sausages; and three-and-thirty people sitting round it, eating and drinking; and savory bottles of gin, and whiskey, and brandy, and rum, in the bar hard by; and seven-and-twenty out of the eight-and-twenty men, in foul linen, with yellow streams from half-chewed tobacco trickling down their chins. Perhaps the best time for you to take a peep would be the present: eleven o'clock in the forenoon: when the barber is at his shaving, and the gentlemen are lounging about the stove waiting for their turns, and not more than seventeen are spitting in concert, and two or three are walking overhead (lying down on the luggage every time the man at the helm calls 'Bridge!'), and I am writing this in the ladies' cabin, which is a part of the gentlemen's, and only screened off by a red curtain. Indeed, it exactly resembles the dwarf's private apartment in a caravan at a fair; and the gentlemen, generally, represent the spectators at a penny a head. The place is just as clean and just as large as that caravan you and I were in at Greenwich Fair last past. Outside, it is exactly like any canal-boat you have seen near the Regent's Park, or elsewhere.

"We expect to reach Pittsburgh to-night, between eight and nine o'clock; and there we ardently hope to find your March letters awaiting us. We have had, with the exception of Friday afternoon, exquisite weather, but cold. Clear star-light and moonlight nights. The canal has run, for the most part, by the side of the Susquehanah and Iwanata rivers; and has been carried through tremendous obstacles. Yesterday we crossed the mountain. This is done *by railroad.* . . . You dine at an inn upon the mountain; and, including the half-hour allowed for the meal, are rather more than five hours performing this strange part of the journey. The people north and 'down east' have terrible legends of its danger; but they appear to be exceedingly careful, and don't go to work at all wildly. There are some queer precipices close to the rails, certainly; but every precaution is taken, I am inclined to think, that such difficulties, and such a vast work, will admit of."

He resumed his letter, "on board the steamboat from Pittsburgh to Cincinnati, April the 1st, 1842. A very tremulous steamboat, which makes my hand shake. This morning, my dear friend, this very morning, which, passing by without bringing news from England, would have seen us on our way to St. Louis (via Cincinnati and Louisville) with sad hearts and dejected countenances, and the prospect of remaining for at least three weeks longer without any intelligence of those so inexpressibly dear to us—this very morning, bright and lucky morning that it was, a great packet was brought to our bedroom door, from HOME.

"Let me see. I should tell you, first, that we got to Pittsburgh between eight and nine o'clock of the evening of the day on which I left off at the top of this sheet.

"Pittsburgh is like Birmingham—at least its townsfolks say so; and I didn't contradict them. It is, in one respect. There is a great deal of smoke in it. I quite offended a man at our yesterday's levee, who supposed I was 'now quite at home,' by telling him that the notion of London being so dark a place was a popular mistake. We had very queer customers at our receptions, I do assure you.

"Still in the Same Boat. April the Second, 1842. Many, many happy returns of the day. It's only eight o'clock in the morning now, but we mean to drink your health after dinner, in a bumper; and scores of Richmond dinners to us! We have some wine (a present sent on board by our Pittsburgh landlord) in our own cabin; and we shall tap it to good purpose, I assure you; wishing you all manner and kinds of happiness, and a long life to ourselves that we may be partakers of it. We have wondered a hundred times already, whether you and Mac will dine anywhere together, in honor of the day. I say yes, but Kate says no. She predicts that you'll ask Mac, and he won't go. I have not yet heard from him.

"We have a better cabin here than we had on board the Britannia; the berths being much wider, and the den having two doors: one opening on the ladies' cabin, and one upon a little gallery in the stern of the boat. We expect to be at Cincinnati some time on Monday morning, and we carry about fifty passengers. The cabin for meals goes right through the boat, from the prow to the stern, and is very long; only a small portion of it being divided off, by a partition of wood and ground glass, for the ladies. We breakfast at half-after seven, dine at one, and sup at six. Nobody will sit down to any one of these meals, though the dishes are smoking on the board, until the ladies have appeared and taken their chairs. It was the same in the canal-boat.

"My friend the New Englander is perhaps the most intolerable bore on this vast continent. He drones, and snuffles, and writes poems, and talks small philosophy and metaphysics, and never *will* be quiet, under any circumstances. He is going to a great temperance convention at Cincinnati; along with a doctor of whom I saw something at Pittsburgh. The doctor, in addition to being everything that the New Englander is, is a phrenologist besides. I dodge them about the boat. Whenever I appear on deck, I see them bearing down upon me—and fly. The New Englander was very anxious last night that he and I should 'form a magnetic chain,' and magnetize the doctor, for the benefit of all incredulous passengers; but I declined on the plea of tremendous occupation in the way of letter-writing.

"And, speaking of magnetism, let me tell you that the other night at Pittsburgh, there being present only Mr. Q. and the portrait-painter, Kate sat down, laughing, for me to try my hand upon her. I had been holding forth upon the subject rather luminously, and asserting that I thought I could exercise the influence, but had never tried. In six minutes, I magnetized her into hysterics, and then into the magnetic sleep. I tried again next night, and she fell into the slumber in little more than two minutes. . . . I can wake her with perfect ease; but I confess (not being prepared for anything so sudden and complete) I was on the first occasion rather alarmed."

He resumed his letter, on "Sunday, April the third," with allusion to a general who had called upon him in Washington with two literary ladies, and had written to him next day for an immediate interview, as "the two LL's" were ambitious of the honor of a personal introduction. "Besides the doctor and the dread New Englander, we have on board that valiant general who wrote to me about the 'two LL's.' He is perhaps the most horrible bore in this country. And I am quite serious when I say that I do not believe there are, on the whole earth besides, so many intensified bores as in these United States. No man can form an adequate idea of the real meaning of the word, without coming here. There are no particular characters on board, with these three exceptions. Indeed, I seldom see the passengers but at meal-times, as I read and write

in our own little state-room. . . . I have smuggled two chairs into our crib, and write this on a book upon my knee. Everything is in the neatest order, of course; and my shaving-tackle, dressing-case, brushes, books, and papers, are arranged with as much precision as if we were going to remain here a month. Thank God we are not.

"The average width of the river rather exceeds that of the Thames at Greenwich. In parts it is much broader; and then there is usually a green island, covered with trees, dividing it into two streams. Occasionally we stop for a few minutes at a small town, or village (I ought to say city, everything is a city here); but the banks are for the most part deep solitudes, overgrown with trees, which, in these western latitudes, are already in leaf, and very green. . . .

"Cincinnati. Fourth April, 1842. We arrived here this morning: about three o'clock, I believe, but I was fast asleep in my berth. I turned out soon after six, dressed, and breakfasted on board. About half-after eight, we came ashore and drove to the hotel, to which we had written on from Pittsburgh ordering rooms; and which is within a stone's throw of the boat-wharf. Before I had issued an official notification that we were 'not at home,' two Judges called, on the part of the inhabitants, to know when we would receive the townspeople. We appointed to-morrow morning, from half-past eleven to one; arranged to go out, with these two gentlemen, to see the town, *at* one; and were fixed for an evening party to-morrow night at the house of one of them. On Wednesday morning we go on by the mail-boat to Louisville, a trip of fourteen hours; and from that place proceed in the next good boat to St. Louis, which is a voyage of four days. Finding from my judicial friends (well-informed and most agreeable gentlemen) this morning that the prairie travel to Chicago is a very fatiguing one, and that the lakes are stormy, sea-sicky, and not over safe at this season, I wrote by our captain to St. Louis (for the boat that brought us here goes on there) to the effect, that I should not take the lake route, but should come back here; and should visit the prairies, which are within thirty miles of St. Louis, immediately on my arrival there. . . ."

---

[20] Sixteen inches exactly.

CHAPTER 23

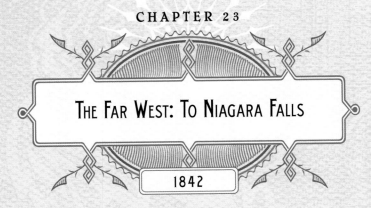

THE FAR WEST: TO NIAGARA FALLS

1842

THE NEXT LETTER DESCRIBED his experiences in the Far West, his stay in St. Louis, his visit to a prairie, the return to Cincinnati, and, after a stage-coach ride from that city to Columbus, the travel thence to Sandusky, and so, by Lake Erie, to the Falls of Niagara. All these subjects appear in the *Notes*, but nothing printed there is repeated in the extracts now to be given. Of the closing passages of his journey, when he turned from Columbus in the direction of home, the story, here for the first time told, is in his most characteristic vein; the account that will be found of the prairie will probably be preferred to what is given in the *Notes*; the Cincinnati sketches are very pleasant; and even such a description as that of the Niagara Falls, of which so much is made in the book, has here an independent novelty and freshness. The first vividness is in his letter.

The captain of the boat that had dropped them at Cincinnati and gone to St. Louis had stayed in the latter place until they were able to join and return with him; this letter bears date accordingly, "On board the Messenger again. Going from St. Louis back to Cincinnati. Friday, fifteenth April, 1842;" and its first paragraph is an outline of the movements which it afterwards describes in detail. "We remained in Cincinnati one whole day after the date of my last, and left on Wednesday morning, the 6th. We reached Louisville soon after midnight on the same night; and slept there. Next day at one o'clock we put ourselves on board another steamer, and traveled on until Sunday evening, the tenth; when we reached St. Louis at about nine o'clock. The next day we devoted to seeing the city. Next day, Tuesday, the twelfth, I started off with a party of men (we were fourteen in all) to see a prairie; returned to St. Louis about noon on the thirteenth; attended

a soiree and ball—not a dinner—given in my honor that night; and yesterday afternoon at four o'clock we turned our faces homewards. Thank Heaven!

"Cincinnati is only fifty years old, but is a very beautiful city; I think the prettiest place I have seen here, except Boston. It has risen out of the forest like an Arabian-Night city; is well laid out; ornamented in the suburbs with pretty villas; and above all, for this is a very rare feature in America, has smooth turf-plots and well-kept gardens. There happened to be a great temperance festival; and the procession mustered under, and passed, our windows early in the morning. I suppose they were twenty thousand strong, at least.

"In the evening we went to a party at Judge Walker's, and were introduced to at least one hundred and fifty first-rate bores, separately and singly. I was required to sit down by the greater part of them, and talk![21] In the night we were serenaded (as we usually are in every place we come to), and very well serenaded, I assure you.

"The last 200 miles of the voyage from Cincinnati to St. Louis are upon the Mississippi, for you come down the Ohio to its mouth. It is well for society that this Mississippi, the renowned father of waters, had no children who take after him. It is the beastliest river in the world.". . . (His description is in the *Notes*.)

"Conceive the pleasure of rushing down this stream by night (as we did last night) at the rate of fifteen miles an hour; striking against floating blocks of timber every instant; and dreading some infernal blow at every bump. The helmsman in these boats is in a little glass house upon the roof. In the Mississippi, another man stands in the very head of the vessel, listening and watching intently; listening, because they can tell in dark nights by the noise when any great obstruction is at hand. This man holds the rope of a large bell which hangs close to the wheel-house, and whenever he pulls it the engine is to stop directly, and not to stir until he rings again. Last night, this bell rang at least once in every five minutes; and at each alarm there was a concussion which nearly flung one out of bed. . . .

"We had a very crowded levee in St. Louis. Of course the paper had an account of it. If I were to drop a letter in the street, it would be in the newspaper next day, and nobody would think its publication an outrage. The editor objected to my hair, as not curling sufficiently. He admitted an eye; but objected again to dress, as being somewhat foppish, 'and indeed perhaps rather flash.' 'But such,' he benevolently adds, 'are the differences between American and English taste—rendered more apparent, perhaps, by all the other gentlemen present being dressed in black.' Oh that you could have seen the other gentlemen! . . .

"They won't let me alone about slavery. A certain judge in St. Louis went so far yesterday that I fell upon him (to the indescribable horror of the man who brought him) and told him a piece of my mind. I said that I was very averse to speaking on the subject here, and always forbore, if possible; but when he pitied our national ignorance of the truths of slavery, I must remind him that we went upon indisputable records, obtained after many years of careful investigation, and at all sorts of self-sacrifice, and that I believed we were much more competent to judge of its atrocity and horror than he who had been brought up in the midst of it. I told him that I could sympathize with men who admitted it to be a dreadful evil, but frankly confessed their inability to devise a means of getting rid of it; but that men who spoke of it as a blessing, as a matter of course, as a state of things to be desired, were out of the pale of reason; and that for them to speak of ignorance or prejudice was an absurdity too ridiculous to be combated. ". . .

"Same Boat, Saturday, Sixteenth April, 1842." Nothing is repeated that will be found in his printed description of the jaunt to the looking-glass prairie:

"But about the prairie—it is not, I must confess, so good in its way as this; but I'll tell you all about that too, and leave you to judge for yourself. Tuesday the 12th was the day fixed; and we were to start at five in the morning—sharp. I turned out at four; shaved and dressed; got some bread and milk; and, throwing up the window, looked down into the street. Deuce a coach was there, nor did anybody seem to be stirring in the house. I waited until half-past five; but no preparations being visible even then, I left Mr. Q. to look out, and lay down upon the bed again. There I slept until nearly seven, when I was called. . . . Exclusive of Mr. Q. and myself, there were twelve of my committee in the party: all lawyers except one. He was an intelligent, mild,

well-informed gentleman of my own age,—the Unitarian minister of the place. With him, and two other companions, I got into the first coach. . . .

"We halted at so good an inn at Lebanon that we resolved to return there at night, if possible. One would scarcely find a better village alehouse of a homely kind in England. During our halt I walked into the village, and met a *dwelling-house* coming down-hill at a good round trot, drawn by some twenty oxen! We resumed our journey as soon as possible, and got upon the looking-glass prairie at sunset. We halted near a solitary log house for the sake of its water; unpacked the baskets; formed an encampment with the carriages; and dined.

"Now, a prairie is undoubtedly worth seeing—but more, that one may say one has seen it, than for any sublimity it possesses in itself. Like most things, great or small, in this country, you hear of it with considerable exaggerations. Basil Hall was really quite right in depreciating the general character of the scenery. The widely-famed Far West is not to be compared with even the tamest portions of Scotland or Wales. You stand upon the prairie, and see the unbroken horizon all round you. You are on a great plain, which is like a sea without water. I am exceedingly fond of wild and lonely scenery, and believe that I have the faculty of being as much impressed by it as any man living. But the prairie fell, by far, short of my preconceived idea. I felt no such emotions as I do in crossing Salisbury Plain. The excessive flatness of the scene makes it dreary, but tame. I would say to every man who can't see a prairie—go to Salisbury Plain, Marlborough Downs, or any of the broad, high, open lands near the sea. Many of them are fully as impressive, and Salisbury Plain is *decidedly* more so.

"We got back to St. Louis soon after twelve at noon; and I rested during the remainder of the day. The soiree came off at night, in a very good ball-room at our inn,—the Planter's House. The whole of the guests were introduced to us, singly. We were glad enough, you may believe, to come away at midnight; and were very tired. Yesterday, I wore a blouse. To-day, a fur coat. Trying changes!

"In the Same Boat, Sunday, Sixteenth April, 1842. The inns in these outlandish corners of the world would astonish you by their goodness. The Planter's House is as large as the Middlesex Hospital, and built very much on our hospital plan, with long wards abundantly ventilated, and plain whitewashed walls. They had a famous notion of sending up at breakfast-time large glasses of new milk with blocks of ice in them as clear as crystal. Our table was abundantly supplied indeed at every meal. One day when Kate and I were dining alone together, in our own room, we counted sixteen dishes on the table at the same time.

"The society is pretty rough, and intolerably conceited. All the inhabitants are young. *I didn't see one gray head in St. Louis.* There is an island close by, called Bloody Island. It is the dueling-ground of St. Louis; and is so called from the last fatal duel which was fought there.

"Sandusky, Sunday, Twenty-fourth April, 1842. We went ashore at Louisville this night week, and slept at the hotel, in which we had put up before. The Messenger being abominably slow, we got our luggage out next morning, and started on again at eleven o'clock in the Benjamin Franklin mail-boat: a splendid vessel, with a cabin more than two hundred feet long, and little state-rooms affording proportionate conveniences. She got in at Cincinnati by one o'clock next morning, when we landed in the dark and went back to our old hotel.

"We remained at Cincinnati all Tuesday the nineteenth, and all that night. At eight o'clock on Wednesday morning the twentieth, we left in the mail-stage for Columbus: Anne, Kate, and Mr. Q. inside; I on the box. The distance is a hundred and twenty miles; the road macadamized; and, for an American road, very good. We were three-and-twenty hours performing the journey. We traveled all night; reached Columbus at seven in the morning; breakfasted; and went to bed until dinner-time. At night we held a levee for half an hour, and the people poured in as they always do: each gentleman with a lady on each arm, exactly like the Chorus to God Save the Queen. I wish you could see them, that you might know what a splendid comparison this is. They wear their clothes precisely as the chorus people do; and stand—supposing Kate and me to be in the centre of the stage, with our backs to the footlights—just as the company would, on the first night of the season. They shake hands exactly after the manner of the guests at a ball at the Adelphi or the Haymarket; receive any facetiousness on my part as

if there were a stage direction 'all laugh;' and have rather more difficulty in 'getting off' than the last gentlemen, in white pantaloons, polished boots, and berlins, usually display, under the most trying circumstances.

"Next morning, that is to say, on Friday, the 22nd, at seven o'clock exactly, we resumed our journey. The stage from Columbus to this place only running thrice a week, and not on that day, I bargained for an 'exclusive extra' with four horses; for which I paid forty dollars, or eight pounds English: the horses changing, as they would if it were the regular stage. To insure our getting on properly, the proprietors sent an agent on the box; and, with no other company but him and a hamper full of eatables and drinkables, we went upon our way. It is impossible to convey an adequate idea to you of the kind of road over which we traveled. I can only say that it was, at the best, but a track through the wild forest, and among the swamps, bogs, and morasses of the withered bush. A great portion of it was what is called a 'corduroy road:' which is made by throwing round logs or whole trees into a swamp, and leaving them to settle there. Good Heaven! if you only felt one of the least of the jolts with which the coach falls from log to log! It is like nothing but going up a steep flight of stairs in an omnibus. Now the coach flung us in a heap on its floor, and now crushed our heads against its roof. Now one side of it was deep in the mire, and we were holding on to the other. Now it was lying on the horses' tails, and now again upon its back. But it never, never was in any position, attitude, or kind of motion, to which we are accustomed in coaches; or made the smallest approach to our experience of the proceedings of any sort of vehicle that goes on wheels.

"Still, the day was beautiful, the air delicious, and we were *alone*; with no tobacco-spittle, or eternal prosy conversation about dollars and politics (the only two subjects they ever converse about, or can converse upon), to bore us. We really enjoyed it; made a joke of the being knocked about; and were quite merry. At two o'clock we stopped in the wood to open our hamper and dine; and we drank to our darlings and all friends at home. Then we started again and went on until ten o'clock at night: when we reached a place called Lower Sandusky, sixty-two miles from our starting-point. The last three hours of the journey were not very pleasant; for it lightened—awfully: every flash very vivid, very blue, and very long; and, the wood being so dense that the branches on either side of the track rattled and broke against the coach, it was rather a dangerous neighborhood for a thunder-storm.

"The inn at which we halted was a rough log house. The people were all abed, and we had to knock them up. We had the queerest sleeping-room, with two doors, one opposite the other; both opening directly on the wild black country, and neither having any lock or bolt. The effect of these opposite doors was, that one was always blowing the other open: an ingenuity in the art of building, which I don't remember to have met with before. You should have seen me, in my shirt, blockading them with portmanteaus, and desperately endeavoring to make the room tidy! But the blockading was really needful, for in my dressing-case I have about 250l. in gold; and for the amount of the middle figure in that scarce metal there are not a few men in the West who would murder their fathers. Apropos of this golden store, consider at your leisure the strange state of things in this country. It has *no money*; really no money. The bank-paper won't pass; the newspapers are full of advertisements from tradesmen who sell by barter; and American gold is not to be had, or purchased. I bought sovereigns, English sovereigns, at first; but as I could get none of them at Cincinnati, to this day, I have had to purchase French gold; 20-franc pieces; with which I am traveling as if I were in Paris!

"There was an old gentleman in the log inn at Lower Sandusky who treats with the Indians on the part of the American government, and has just concluded a treaty with the Wyandot Indians at that place to remove next year to some land provided for them west of the Mississippi, a little way beyond St. Louis. He described his negotiation to me, and their reluctance to go, exceedingly well. They are a fine people, but degraded and broken down. If you could see any of their men and women on a race-course in England, you would not know them from gipsies.

"We are in a small house here, but a very comfortable one, and the people are exceedingly obliging. Their demeanor in these country parts is invariably morose, sullen, clownish, and repulsive. I should think there is not, on the face of the earth, a people so entirely destitute of humor, vivacity, or the capacity of enjoyment. It is most remarkable. I am quite serious when I say that I have not heard a hearty laugh these six weeks, except my own; nor have I seen a merry face on any shoulders but a black man's. Lounging listlessly about; idling in bar-rooms; smoking; spitting; and lolling on the pavement in rocking-chairs, outside the shop-doors; are the only recreations.

"We are wishing very much for a boat; for we hope to find our letters at Buffalo. It is half-past one; and, as there is no boat in sight, we are fain (sorely against our wills) to order an early dinner.

"Tuesday, April Twenty-sixth, 1842. Niagara Falls!!! (Upon the English[22] Side.) I don't know at what length I might have written you from Sandusky, my beloved friend, if a steamer had not come in sight just as I finished the last unintelligible sheet! (oh! the ink in these parts!): whereupon I was obliged to pack up bag and baggage, to swallow a hasty apology for a dinner, and to hurry my train on board with all the speed I might. She was a fine steamship, four hundred tons burden, name the Constitution, had very few passengers on board, and had bountiful and handsome accommodation. It's all very fine talking about Lake Erie, but it won't do for persons who are liable to sea-sickness. We were all sick. It's almost as bad in that respect as the Atlantic. The waves are very short, and horribly constant. We reached Buffalo at six this morning; went ashore to breakfast; sent to the post-office forthwith; and received— oh! who or what can say with how much pleasure and what unspeakable delight!—our English letters!

"We lay all Sunday night at a town (and a beautiful town too) called Cleveland; on Lake Erie. The people poured on board, in crowds, by six on Monday morning, to see me; and a party of 'gentlemen' actually planted themselves before our little cabin, and stared in at the door and windows *while I was washing, and Kate lay in bed.*

"I never in my life was in such a state of excitement as coming from Buffalo here, this morning. You come by rail-road, and are nigh two hours upon the way. I looked out for the spray, and listened for the roar, as far beyond the bounds of possibility as though, landing in Liverpool, I were to listen for the music of your pleasant voice in Lincoln's Inn Fields.

OVERLEAF: Niagara Falls, painted and engraved by W. J. Bennett, 1829

AMERICAN NOTES, CHAPTER 12

*Dickens gives a rather nostalgic account of his meeting
with a Choctaw chief in* American Notes:

———⊶⊷———

THERE chanced to be on board this boat, in addition to the usual dreary crowd of passengers, one Pitchlynn, a chief of the Choctaw tribe of Indians, who SENT IN HIS CARD to me, and with whom I had the pleasure of a long conversation.

He spoke English perfectly well, though he had not begun to learn the language, he told me, until he was a young man grown. He had read many books; and Scott's poetry appeared to have left a strong impression on his mind: especially the opening of The Lady of the Lake, and the great battle scene in Marmion, in which, no doubt from the congeniality of the subjects to his own pursuits and tastes, he had great interest and delight. He appeared to understand correctly all he had read; and whatever fiction had enlisted his sympathy in its belief, had done so keenly and earnestly. I might almost say fiercely. He was dressed in our ordinary everyday costume, which hung about his fine figure loosely, and with indifferent grace. On my telling him that I regretted not to see him in his own attire, he threw up his right arm, for a moment, as though he were brandishing some heavy weapon, and answered, as he let it fall again, that his race were losing many things besides their dress, and would soon be seen upon the earth no more: but he wore it at home, he added proudly.

He told me that he had been away from his home, west of the Mississippi, seventeen months: and was now returning. He had been chiefly at Washington on some negotiations pending between his Tribe and the Government: which were not settled yet (he said in a melancholy way), and he feared never would be: for what could a few poor Indians do, against such well-skilled men of business as the whites? He had no love for Washington; tired of towns and cities very soon; and longed for the Forest and the Prairie.

I asked him what he thought of Congress? He answered, with a smile, that it wanted dignity, in an Indian's eyes.

He would very much like, he said, to see England before he died; and spoke with much interest about the great things to be seen there. When I told him of that chamber in the British Museum wherein are preserved household memorials of a race that ceased to be, thousands of years ago, he was very attentive, and it was not hard to see that he had a reference in his mind to the gradual fading away of his own people.

This led us to speak of Mr. Catlin's gallery, which he praised highly: observing that his own portrait was among the collection, and that all the likenesses were 'elegant.' Mr. Cooper, he said, had painted the Red Man well; and so would I, he knew, if I would go home with him and hunt buffaloes, which he was quite anxious I should do. When I told him that supposing I went, I should not be very likely to damage the buffaloes much, he took it as a great joke and laughed heartily.

He was a remarkably handsome man; some years past forty, I should judge; with long black hair, an aquiline nose, broad cheek-bones, a sunburnt complexion, and a very bright, keen, dark, and piercing eye. There were but twenty thousand of the Choctaws left, he said, and their number was decreasing every day. A few of his brother chiefs had been obliged to become civilised, and to make themselves acquainted with what the whites knew, for it was their only chance of existence. But they were not many; and the rest were as they always had been. He dwelt on this: and said several times that unless they tried to assimilate themselves to their conquerors, they must be swept away before the strides of civilised society.

At last, when the train stopped, I saw two great white clouds rising up from the depths of the earth,—nothing more. They rose up slowly, gently, majestically, into the air. I dragged Kate down a deep and slippery path leading to the ferry-boat; bullied Anne for not coming fast enough; perspired at every pore; and felt, it is impossible to say how, as the sound grew louder and louder in my ears, and yet nothing could be seen for the mist.

"I was not disappointed—but I could make out nothing. In an instant I was blinded by the spray, and wet to the skin. I saw the water tearing madly down from some immense height, but could get no idea of shape, or situation, or anything but vague immensity. But when we were seated in the boat, and crossing at the very foot of the cataract—then I began to feel what it was. Directly I had changed my clothes at the inn I went out again, taking Kate with me, and hurried to the Horse-shoe Fall. I went down alone, into the very basin. It would be hard

Peter Perkins Pitchlynn, a Choctaw Indian Chief, by Charles Fenderich, 1842

for a man to stand nearer God than he does there. There was a bright rainbow at my feet; and from that I looked up to—great Heaven! to *what* a fall of bright green water! The broad, deep, mighty stream seems to die in the act of falling; and from its unfathomable grave arises that tremendous ghost of spray and mist which is never laid, and has been haunting this place with the same dread solemnity—perhaps from the creation of the world.

"We purpose remaining here a week. In my next I will try to give you some idea of my impressions, and to tell you how they change with every day. At present it is impossible. I can only say that the first effect of this tremendous spectacle on me was peace of mind—tranquillity—great thoughts of eternal rest and happiness—nothing of terror. I can shudder at the recollection of Glencoe (dear friend, with Heaven's leave we must see Glencoe together), but whenever I think of Niagara I shall think of its beauty."

[21] A young lady's account of this party, written next morning, and quoted in one of the American memoirs of Dickens, enables us to contemplate his suffering from the point of view of those who inflicted it: "I went last evening to a party at Judge Walker's, given to the hero of the day.... When we reached the house, Mr. Dickens had left the crowded rooms, and was in the hall with his wife, about taking his departure when we entered the door. We were introduced to him in our wrapping; and in the flurry and embarrassment of the meeting, one of the party dropped a parcel, containing shoes, gloves, etc. Mr. Dickens, stooping, gathered them up and restored them with a laughing remark, and we bounded up-stairs to get our things off. Hastening down again, we found him with Mrs. Dickens seated upon a sofa, surrounded by a group of ladies; Judge Walker having requested him to delay his departure for a few moments, for the gratification of some tardy friends who had just arrived, ourselves among the number. Declining to re-enter the rooms where he had already taken leave of the guests, he had seated himself in the hall. He is young and handsome, has a mellow, beautiful eye, fine brow, and abundant hair. His mouth is large, and his smile so bright it seemed to shed light and happiness all about him. His manner is easy, negligent, but not elegant. His dress was foppish; in fact, he was overdressed, yet his garments were worn so easily they appeared to be a necessary part of him. (!) He had a dark coat, with lighter pantaloons; a black waistcoat, embroidered with colored flowers; and about his neck, covering his white shirt-front, was a black neckcloth, also embroidered in colors, in which were placed two large diamond pins connected by a chain. A gold watch-chain, and a large red rose in his button-hole, completed his toilet. He appeared a little weary, but answered the remarks made to him—for he originated none—in an agreeable manner. Mr. Beard's portrait of Fagin was so placed in the room that we could see it from where we stood surrounding him. One of the ladies asked him if it was his idea of the Jew. He replied, 'Very nearly.' Another, laughingly, requested that he would give her the rose he wore, as a memento. He shook his head and said, 'That will not do; he could not give it to one; the others would be jealous.' A half-dozen then insisted on having it, whereupon he proposed to divide the leaves among them. In taking the rose from his coat, either by design or accident, the leaves loosened and fell upon the floor, and amid considerable laughter the ladies stooped and gathered them. He remained some twenty minutes, perhaps, in the hall, and then took his leave. I must confess to considerable disappointment in the personal of my idol. I felt that his throne was shaken, although it never could be destroyed." This appalling picture supplements and very sufficiently explains the mournful passage in the text.

[22] Ten dashes underneath the word.

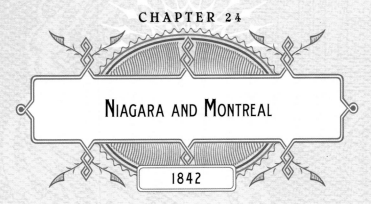

CHAPTER 24

NIAGARA AND MONTREAL

1842

MY FRIEND WAS BETTER than his word, and two more letters reached me before his return. The opening of the first was written from Niagara on the 3rd, and its close from Montreal on the 12th, of May; from which latter city also, on the 26th of that month, the last of all was written.

Much of the first of these letters had reference to the international copyright agitation, and gave strong expression to the indignation awakened in him (nor less in some of the best men of America) by the adoption, at a public meeting in Boston itself, of a memorial against any change of the law, in the course of which it was stated that, if English authors were invested with any control over the republication of their own books, it would be no longer possible for American editors to alter and adapt them to the American taste. This deliberate declaration, however, unsparing as Dickens's anger at it was, in effect vanquished him. He saw the hopelessness of pursuing further any present effort to bring about the change desired; and he took the determination not only to drop any allusion to it in his proposed book, but to try what effect might be produced, when he should again be in England, by a league of English authors to suspend further intercourse with American publishers while the law should remain as it is. On his return he made accordingly a public appeal to this effect, stating his own intention for the future to forego all profit derivable from the authorized transmission of early proofs across the Atlantic; but his hopes in this particular also were doomed to disappointment.

"Niagara Falls, Tuesday, Third May, 1842." "The conclusion of this letter was dated from "Montreal, Thursday, twelfth May," This will be a very short and stupid letter, my dear friend; for the post leaves here much earlier than I expected, and all my grand designs for being unusually brilliant fall to the ground. I will write you *one line* by the next Cunard boat,—reserving all else until our happy and long long looked-for meeting.

"We have been to Toronto and Kingston; experiencing attentions at each which I should have difficulty in describing. The wild and rabid toryism of Toronto is, I speak seriously, *appalling*. English kindness is very different from American. People send their horses and carriages for your use, but they don't exact as payment the right of being always under your nose. We had no less than *five* carriages at Kingston waiting our pleasure at one time; not to mention the commodore's barge and crew, and a beautiful government steamer. We dined with Sir Charles Bagot last Sunday. Lord Mulgrave was to have met us yesterday at Lachine; but, as he was windbound in his yacht and couldn't get in, Sir Richard Jackson sent his drag four-in-hand, with two other young fellows who are also his aides, and in we came in grand style.

"The Theatricals (I think I told you I had been invited to play with the officers of the Coldstream Guards here) are *A Roland for an Oliver; Two o'Clock in the Morning*; and either the *Young Widow*, or *Deaf as a Post*. Ladies (unprofessional) are going to play, for the first time. I wrote to Mitchell at New York for a wig for Mr. Snobbington, which has arrived, and is brilliant. If they had done *Love, Law, and Physick*, as at first proposed, I was already 'up' in Flexible, having played it of old, before my authorship days; but if it should be Splash in the *Young Widow*, you will have to do me the favor to imagine me in a smart livery-coat, shiny black hat and cockade, white knee-cords, white top-boots, blue stock, small whip, red cheeks, and dark eyebrows. Conceive Topping's state of mind if I bring this dress home and put it on unexpectedly! . . . God bless you, dear friend. I can say nothing about the seventh, the day on which we sail. It is impossible. Words cannot express what we feel, now that the time is so near. . . ."

His last letter, dated from "Peasco's Hotel, Montreal, Canada, twenty-sixth of May," described the private theatricals, and inclosed me a bill of the play.

"This, like my last, will be a stupid letter, because both Kate and I are thrown into such a state of excitement by the near approach of the seventh of June that we can do nothing, and think of nothing.

Dickens in the character
of Sir Charles Coldstream
in Don Boucicault's play
Used Up. Painting by
Augustus Egg. 1849

"The play came off last night. The audience, between five and six hundred strong, were invited as to a party; a regular table with refreshments being spread in the lobby and saloon. We had the band of the twenty-third (one of the finest in the service) in the orchestra, the theatre was lighted with gas, the scenery was excellent, and the properties were all brought from private houses. Sir Charles Bagot, Sir Richard Jackson, and their staffs were present; and as the military portion of the audience were all in full uniform, it was really a splendid scene.

"But only think of Kate playing! and playing devilish well, I assure you! All the ladies were capital, and we had no wait or hitch for an instant. You may suppose this, when I tell you that we began at eight, and had the curtain down at eleven. It is their custom here, to prevent heart-burnings in a very heart-burning town, whenever they have played in private, to repeat the performances in public. So, on Saturday (substituting, of course, real actresses for the ladies), we repeat the two first pieces to a paying audience, for the manager's benefit. . . .

"As the time draws nearer, we get FEVERED with anxiety for home. . . . Kiss our darlings for us. We shall soon meet, please God, and be happier and merrier than ever we were, in all our lives. . . . Oh, home—home—home—home—home—home—HOME!!!!!!!!!!!"

173

John Forster

so high that we have no choice but to return by land. No steamer can come out of Ramsgate, and the Margate boat lay out all night on Wednesday with all her passengers on board. You may be sure of us therefore on Saturday at 5, for I have determined to leave here to-morrow, as we could not otherwise manage it in time; and have engaged an omnibus to bring the whole caravan by the overland route. . . . We cannot open a window, or a door; legs are of no use on the terrace; and the Margate boats can only take people aboard at Herne Bay!" He brought with him all that remained to be done of his second volume except the last two chapters, including that to which he has referred as "introductory;" and on the following Wednesday (5th of October) he told me that the first of these was done. "I want you very much to come and dine to-day that we may repair to Drury-lane together; and let us say half-past four, or there is no time to be comfortable. I am going out to Tottenham this morning, on a cheerless mission I would willingly have avoided. Hone, of the *Every Day Book*, is dying; and sent Cruikshank yesterday to beg me to go and see him, as, having read no books but mine of late, he wanted to see and shake hands with me before (as George said) 'he went.' There is no help for it, of course; so to Tottenham I repair, this morning. I worked all day, and till midnight; and finished the slavery chapter yesterday."

On the 10th of October I heard from him that the chapter intended to be introductory to the *Notes* was written, and waiting our conference whether or not it should be printed. We decided against it. The book appeared on the 18th of October and before the close of the year four large editions had been sold. In my opinion it thoroughly deserved the estimate formed of it by one connected with America by the strongest social affections, and otherwise in all respects an honourable, high-minded, upright judge. "You have been very tender," wrote Lord Jeffrey, "to our sensitive friends beyond sea, and my whole heart goes along with every word you have written. I think that you have perfectly accomplished all that you profess or undertake to do, and that the world has never yet seen a more faithful, graphic, amusing, kind-hearted narrative."

The printers were now hard at work, and in the last week of September he wrote: "I send you proofs as far as Niagara . . . I am rather holiday-making this week . . . taking principal part in a regatta here yesterday, very pretty and gay indeed. We think of coming up in time for Macready's opening, when perhaps you will give us a chop; and of course you and Mac will dine with us the next day? I shall leave nothing of the book to do after coming home, please God, but the two chapters on slavery and the people which I could manage easily in a week."

On the last day of the month I had the last of his letters during this Broadstairs visit. "Strange as it may appear to you" (25th of September), "the sea is running

CHAPTER 2

FIRST YEAR OF MARTIN CHUZZLEWIT

1843

THE CORNISH TRIP HAD COME OFF, meanwhile, with such unexpected and continued attraction for us that we were well into the third week of absence before we turned our faces homeward. Railways helped us then not much; but where the roads were inaccessible to post-horses, we walked. Tintagel was visited, and no part of mountain or sea consecrated by the legends of Arthur was left unexplored. We ascended to the cradle of the highest tower of Mount St. Michael, and descended into several mines. Land and sea yielded each its marvels to us; but of all the impressions brought away, of which some afterwards took forms as lasting as they could receive from the most delightful art, I doubt if any were the source of such deep emotion to us all as a sunset we saw at Land's-end. Stanfield knew the wonders of the Continent, the glories of Ireland were native to Maclise, I was familiar from boyhood with border and Scottish scenery, and Dickens was fresh from Niagara; but there was something in the sinking of the sun behind the Atlantic that autumn afternoon, as we viewed it together from the top of the rock projecting farthest into the sea, which each in his turn declared to have no parallel in memory.

"Blessed star of morning!" wrote Dickens to Felton while yet the glow of its enjoyment was upon him. "Such a trip as we had into Cornwall just after Longfellow went away! . . . Sometimes we travelled all night, sometimes all day, sometimes both. . . . Heavens!. . . I never laughed in my life as I did on this journey. It would have done you good to hear me. I was choking and gasping and bursting the buckle off the back of my stock, all the way. And Stanfield got into such apoplectic entanglements that we were often obliged to beat him on the back with portmanteaus before we could recover him.

Seriously, I do believe there never was such a trip. And they made such sketches, those two men, in the most romantic of our halting-places, that you would have sworn we had the Spirit of Beauty with us, as well as the Spirit of Fun."[34]

The waterfall I led him to was among the records of the famous holiday, celebrated also by Thackeray in one of his pen-and-ink pleasantries, which were sent by both painters to the next year's Academy; and so eager was Dickens to possess this landscape by Maclise which included the likeness of a member of his family, yet so anxious that our friend should be spared the sacrifice which he knew would follow an avowal of his wish, that he bought it under a feigned name before the Academy opened, and steadily refused to take back the money which on discovery of the artifice Maclise pressed upon him.[35] Our friend, who already had munificently given him a charming drawing of his four eldest children to accompany him and his wife to America, had his generous way nevertheless; and as a voluntary offering four years later, painted Mrs. Dickens on a canvas of the same size as the picture of her husband in 1839.

"Behold finally the title of the new book," was the first note I had from Dickens (12th of November) after our return; "don't lose it, for I have no copy." Title and even story had been undetermined while we travelled, from the lingering wish he still had to begin it among those Cornish scenes; but this intention had now been finally abandoned, and the reader lost nothing by his substitution for the lighthouse or mine in Cornwall, of the Wiltshire-village forge on the windy autumn evening which opens the tale of *Martin Chuzzlewit*. Into that name he finally settled, but only after much deliberation, as a mention of his changes will show. Martin was the prefix to all, but the surname varied from its first form of Sweezleden, Sweezleback, and Sweezlewag, to those of Chuzzletoe, Chuzzleboy, Chubblewig, and Chuzzlewig; nor was Chuzzlewit chosen at last until after more hesitation and discussion. What he had sent me in his letter as finally adopted, ran thus: "The Life and Adventures of Martin Chuzzlewig, his family, friends, and enemies. Comprising all his wills and his ways. With an historical record of what he did and what he didn't. The whole forming a complete key to the house of Chuzzlewig." All which latter portion of the title was of course dropped as the work became modified, in its progress, by changes at first not contemplated; but as early as the third number he sent me the plan of "old Martin's plot to degrade and punish Pecksniff," and the difficulties he encountered in departing from other portions of his scheme were such as to render him, in his subsequent stories, more bent upon constructive care at the outset, and adherence as far as might be to any design he had formed.

The first number, which appeared in January 1843, had not been quite finished when he wrote to me on the 8th of December: "The Chuzzlewit copy makes so much more than I supposed, that the number is nearly done. Thank God!"

Another piece of his writing that claims mention at the close of 1842 was a prologue contributed to the *Patrician's Daughter*, Mr. Westland Marston's first dramatic effort, which had attracted him by the beauty of its composition less than by the courage with which its subject had been chosen from the actual life of the time.

"Not light its import, and not poor its mien; Yourselves the actors, and your homes the scene."

This was the date, too, of Mr. Browning's tragedy of the *Blot on the 'Scutcheon*, which I took upon myself, after reading it in the manuscript, privately to impart to Dickens; and I was not mistaken in the belief that it would profoundly touch him. "Browning's play," he wrote (25th of November), "has thrown me into a perfect passion of sorrow. To say that there is anything in its subject save what is lovely, true, deeply affecting, full of the best emotion, the most earnest feeling, and the most true and tender source of interest, is to say that there is no light in the sun, and no heat in blood. It is full of genius, natural and great thoughts, profound and yet simple and beautiful in its vigour."

Catherine Dickens, engraving after Daniel Maclise, 1848

Eighteen hundred and forty-three[25] opened with the most vigorous prosecution of his *Chuzzlewit* labour. "I hope the number will be very good," he wrote to me of number two (8th of January). "I have been hammering away, and at home all day. Ditto yesterday; except for two hours in the afternoon, when I ploughed through snow half a foot deep, round about the wilds of Willesden." For the present, however, I shall glance only briefly from time to time at his progress with the earlier portions of the story on which he was thus engaged until the midsummer of 1844. Disappointments arose in connection with it, unexpected and strange, which had important influence upon him: but, I reserve the mention of these for awhile, that I may speak of the leading incidents of 1843.

"I am in a difficulty," he wrote (12th of February), "and am coming down to you some time to-day or to-night. I couldn't write a line yesterday; not a word, though I really tried hard. In a kind of despair I started off at half-past two with my pair of petticoats to Richmond; and dined there!! Oh what a lovely day it was in those parts." His pair of petticoats were Mrs. Dickens and her sister Georgina: the latter, since his return from America, having become part of his household, of which she remained a member until his death; and he had just reason to be proud of the steadiness, depth, and devotion of her friendship. Not many days after that holiday at Richmond, a slight unstudied outline in pencil was made by Maclise of the three who formed the party there, as we all sat together; and never did a touch so light carry with it more truth of observation. The likenesses of all are excellent; and I here preserve the drawing because nothing ever done of Dickens himself has conveyed more vividly his look and bearing at this yet youthful time.

There was a statement of the reviewer of the *American Notes* in the *Edinburgh* to the effect, that, if he had been rightly informed, Dickens had gone to America as a kind of missionary in the cause of international copyright; to which a prompt contradiction had been given in the *Times*. "I deny it," wrote Dickens, "wholly. He is wrongly informed; and reports, without enquiry, a piece of information which I could only characterize by using one of the shortest and strongest words in the language."

The disputes that had arisen out of the American book, I may add, stretched over great part of the year. It will quite suffice, however, to say here that the ground taken by him in his letters written on the spot, and printed in my former volume, which in all the more material statements his book invited public judgment upon and which he was moved to reopen in *Chuzzlewit*, was so kept by him against all comers, that none of the counter-statements or arguments dislodged him from a square inch of it. But the controversy is dead now; and he took occasion, on his later visit to America, to write its epitaph.

I soon after joined him at a cottage he rented in Finchley; and here, walking and talking in the green lanes as the midsummer months were coming on, his introduction of Mrs. Gamp, and the uses to which he should apply that remarkable personage, first occurred to him. In his preface to the book he speaks of her as a fair representation, at the time it was published, of the hired attendant on the poor in sickness: but he might have added that the rich were no better off, for Mrs. Gamp's original was in reality a person hired by a most distinguished friend of his own, a lady, to take charge of an invalid very dear to her; and the common habit of this nurse in the sick room, among other Gampish peculiarities, was to rub her nose along the top of the tall fender.

There followed a celebration, in which one of these entertainers was the guest and which owed hardly less to Dickens's exertions, when, at the Star-and-garter at Richmond in the autumn, we wished Macready good-speed on his way to America. Dickens took the chair at that dinner; and with Stanfield, Maclise, and myself, was in the following week to have accompanied the great actor to Liverpool to say good-bye to him on board the Cunard ship, and bring his wife back to London after their leave-taking; when a

Georgina Hogarth, Catherine Dickens, and Charles Dickens, by Daniel Maclise, 1843

word from our excellent friend Captain Marryat, startling to all of us except Dickens himself, struck him out of our party. Marryat thought that Macready might suffer in the States by any public mention of his having been attended on his way by the author of the *American Notes* and *Martin Chuzzlewit*, and our friend at once agreed with him. "Your main and foremost reason," he wrote to me, "for doubting Marryat's judgment, I can at once destroy. It has occurred to me many times; I have mentioned the thing to Kate more than once; and I had intended *not* to go on board, charging Radley to let nothing be said of my being in his house. I have been prevented from giving any expression to my fears by a misgiving that I should seem to attach, if I did so, too much importance to my own doings. But now that I have Marryat at my back, I have not the least hesitation in saying that I am certain he is right. I have very great

Mr. Pecksniff and Old Martin Chuzzlewit, by Harold Copping, ca. 1924

week was at Manchester, presiding at the opening of its great Athenaeum, when Mr. Cobden and Mr. Disraeli also "assisted." Here he spoke mainly on a matter always nearest his heart, the education of the very poor. He protested against the danger of calling a little learning dangerous; declared his preference for the very least of the little over none at all; proposed to substitute for the old a new doggerel,

Though house and lands be never got,

Learning can give what they can *not*; told his listeners of the real and paramount danger we had lately taken Longfellow to see in the nightly refuges of London, "thousands of immortal creatures condemned without alternative or choice to tread, not what our great poet calls the primrose path to the everlasting bonfire, but one of jagged flints and stones laid down by brutal ignorance."

The same spirit impelled him to give eager welcome to the remarkable institution of Ragged schools, which, begun by a shoemaker of Southampton and a chimney-sweep of Windsor and carried on by a peer of the realm, has had results of incalculable importance to society.

The year of which I am writing was its first, as this in which I write is its last; and in the interval, out of three hundred thousand children to whom it has given some sort of education, it is computed also to have given to a third of that number the means of honest employment.[26]

Active as he had been in the now ending year, and great as were its varieties of employment; his genius in its highest mood, his energy unwearied in good work, and his capacity for enjoyment without limit; he was able to signalize its closing months by an achievement supremely fortunate, which but for disappointments the year had also brought might never have been thought of. He had not begun until a week after his return from Manchester, where the fancy first occurred to him, and before the end of November he had finished, his memorable *Christmas Carol*.

It was the work of such odd moments of leisure as were left him out of the time taken up by two numbers of his *Chuzzlewit*; and though begun with but the special design of adding something to the *Chuzzlewit* balance, I can testify to the accuracy of his own account of what befell him in its composition, with what a strange mastery it seized him

apprehensions that the *Nickleby* dedication will damage Macready. Marryat is wrong in supposing it is not printed in the American editions, for I have myself seen it in the shop windows of several cities. If I were to go on board with him, I have not the least doubt that the fact would be placarded all over New York, before he had shaved himself in Boston. And that there are thousands of men in America who would pick a quarrel with him on the mere statement of his being my friend, I have no more doubt than I have of my existence. You have only doubted Marryat because it is impossible for any man to know what they are in their own country, who has not seen them there."

He returned to town "for good" on Monday the 2nd of October, and from the Wednesday to the Friday of that

Martin Chuzzlewit, Chapter 19

Martin Chuzzlewit presents an extraordinary cast of memorable characters, including the audacious hypocrite, Pecksniff, Mrs. Gamp and her "friend" (or alter-ego) Mrs. Harris:

HE was a fat old woman, this Mrs. Gamp, with a husky voice and a moist eye, which she had a remarkable power of turning up, and only showing the white of it. Having very little neck, it cost her some trouble to look over herself, if one may say so, at those to whom she talked. She wore a very rusty black gown, rather the worse for snuff, and a shawl and bonnet to correspond. In these dilapidated articles of dress she had, on principle, arrayed herself, time out of mind, on such occasions as the present; for this at once expressed a decent amount of veneration for the deceased, and invited the next of kin to present her with a fresher suit of weeds; an appeal so frequently successful, that the very fetch and ghost of Mrs. Gamp, bonnet and all, might be seen hanging up, any hour in the day, in at least a dozen of the second-hand clothes shops about Holborn. The face of Mrs. Gamp—the nose in particular—was somewhat red and swollen, and it was difficult to enjoy her society without becoming conscious of a smell of spirits. Like most persons who have attained to great eminence in their profession, she took to hers very kindly; insomuch that, setting aside her natural predilections as a woman, she went to a lying-in or a laying-out with equal zest and relish.

'Ah!' repeated Mrs. Gamp; for it was always a safe sentiment in cases of mourning. 'Ah dear! When Gamp was summoned to his long home, and I see him a-lying in Guy's Hospital with a penny-piece on each eye, and his wooden leg under his left arm, I thought I should have fainted away. But I bore up.'

If certain whispers current in the Kingsgate Street circles had any truth in them, she had indeed borne up surprisingly; and had exerted such uncommon fortitude as to dispose of Mr. Gamp's remains for the benefit of science. But it should be added, in fairnes, that this had happened twenty years before; and that Mr. and Mrs. Gamp had long been separated on the ground of incompatibility of temper in their drink.

'You have become indifferent since then, I suppose?' said Mr. Pecksniff. 'Use is second nature, Mrs. Gamp.'

'You may well say second nater, sir,' returned that lady. 'One's first ways is to find sich things a trial to the feelings, and so is one's lasting custom. If it wasn't for the nerve a little sip of liquor gives me (I never was able to do more than taste it), I never could go through with what I sometimes has to do. "Mrs. Harris," I says, at the very last case as ever I acted in, which it was but a young person, "Mrs. Harris," I says, "leave the bottle on the chimley-piece, and don't ask me to take none, but let me put my lips to it when I am so dispoged, and then I will do what I'm engaged to do, according to the best of my ability." "Mrs. Gamp," she says, in answer, "if ever there was a sober creetur to be got at eighteen pence a day for working people, and three and six for gentlefolks—night watching,"' said Mrs. Gamp with emphasis, '"being a extra charge—you are that inwallable person." "Mrs. Harris," I says to her, "don't name the charge, for if I could afford to lay all my feller creetus out for nothink, I would gladly do it, sich is the love I bears 'em. But what I always says to them as has the management of matters, Mrs. Harris"'—here she kept her eye on Mr. Pecksniff—'"be they gents or be they ladies, is, don't ask me whether I won't take none, or whether I will, but leave the bottle on the chimley-piece, and let me put my lips to it when I am so dispoged."'

I OFFER no apology for entreating the attention of the readers of *The Daily News* to an effort which has been making for some three years and a half, and which is making now, to introduce among the most miserable and neglected outcasts in London, some knowledge of the commonest principles of morality and religion; to commence their recognition as immortal human creatures, before the Gaol Chaplain becomes their only schoolmaster; to suggest to Society that its duty to this wretched throng, foredoomed to crime and punishment, rightfully begins at some distance from the police office; and that the careless maintenance from year to year, in this, the capital city of the world, of a vast hopeless nursery of ignorance, misery and vice; a breeding place for the hulks and jails: is horrible to contemplate. This attempt is being made in certain of the most obscure and squalid parts of the Metropolis, where rooms are opened, at night, for the gratuitous instruction of all comers, children or adults, under the title of RAGGED SCHOOLS. The name implies the purpose. They who are too ragged, wretched, filthy, and forlorn, to enter any other place: who could gain admission into no charity school, and who would be driven from any church door; are invited to come in here, and find some people not depraved, willing to teach them something, and show them some sympathy, and stretch a hand out, which is not the iron hand of Law, for their correction. [. . .] For the instruction, and as a first step in the reformation, of such unhappy beings, the Ragged Schools were founded. I was first attracted to the subject, and indeed was first made conscious of their existence, about two years ago, or more, by seeing an advertisement in the papers dated from West Street, Saffron Hill, stating "That a room had been opened and supported in that wretched neighbourhood for upwards of twelve months, where religious instruction had been imparted to the poor", and explaining in a few words what was meant by Ragged Schools as a generic term, including, then, four or five similar places of instruction. I wrote to the masters of this particular school to make some further inquiries, and went myself soon afterwards.

It was a hot summer night; and the air of Field Lane and Saffron Hill was not improved by such weather, nor were the people in those streets very sober or honest company. Being unacquainted with the exact locality of the school, I was fain to make some inquiries about it. These were very jocosely received in general; but everybody knew where it was, and gave the right direction to it. The prevailing idea among the loungers (the greater part of them the very sweepings of the streets and station houses) seemed to be, that the teachers were quixotic, and the school upon the whole "a lark". But there was certainly a kind of rough respect for the intention, and (as I have said) nobody denied the school or its whereabouts, or refused assistance in directing to it. It consisted at that time of either two or three—I forget which-miserable rooms, upstairs in a miserable house. In the best of these, the pupils in the female school were being taught to read and write; and though there were among the number, many wretched creatures steeped in degradation to the lips, they were tolerably quiet, and listened with apparent earnestness and patience to their instructors. The appearance of this room was sad and melancholy, of course—how could it be otherwise!—but, on the whole, encouraging. The close, low chamber at the back, in which the boys were crowded, was so foul and stifling as to be, at first, almost insupportable. But its moral aspect was so far worse than its physical, that this was soon forgotten. Huddled together on a bench about the room, and shown out by some flaring candles stuck against the walls, were a crowd of boys, varying from mere infants to young men; sellers of fruit, herbs, lucifer-matches, flints;

sleepers under the dry arches of bridges; young thieves and beggars—with nothing natural to youth about them: with nothing frank, ingenuous, or pleasant in their faces; low-browed, vicious, cunning, wicked; abandoned of all help but this; speeding downward to destruction; and UNUTTERABLY IGNORANT. This, Reader, was one room as full as it could hold; but these were only grains in sample of a Multitude that are perpetually sifting through these schools; in sample of a Multitude who had within them once, and perhaps have now, the elements of men as good as you or I, and maybe infinitely better; in sample of a Multitude among whose doomed and sinful ranks (oh, think of this, and think of them!) the child of any man upon this earth, however lofty his degree, must, as by Destiny and Fate, be found, if, at its birth, it were consigned to such an infancy and nurture, as these fallen creatures had! This was the Class I saw at the Ragged School. They could not be trusted with books; they could only be instructed orally; they were difficult of reduction to anything like attention, obedience, or decent behaviour; their benighted ignorance in reference to the Deity, or to any social duty (how could they guess at any social duty, being so discarded by all social teachers but the gaoler and the hangman!) was terrible to see. Yet, even here, and among these, something had been done already. The Ragged School was of recent date and very poor; but he had inculcated some association with the name of the Almighty, which was not an oath, and had taught them to look forward in a hymn (they sang it) to another life, which would correct the miseries and woes of this.

View of old houses with the open part of the Fleet Ditch, near Field Lane, London, 1851

Mr. Pecksniff, from *Charles Dickens: A Gossip About His Life*, by Fred Barnard

for itself, how he wept over it, and laughed, and wept again, and excited himself to an extraordinary degree, and how he walked thinking of it fifteen and twenty miles about the black streets of London, many and many a night after all sober folks had gone to bed. And when it was done, as he told our friend Mr. Felton in America, he let himself loose like a madman.

Eighteen hundred and forty-four was but fifteen days old when a third son (his fifth child, which received the name of its godfather Francis Jeffrey) was born.

A CHRISTMAS CAROL, STAVE 3

In A Christmas Carol, Dickens, continuing his concern for the education of the poor,
has the Ghost of Christmas Present introduce Scrooge to Ignorance and Want:

FROM the foldings of its robe, it brought two children; wretched, abject, frightful, hideous, miserable. They knelt down at its feet, and clung upon the outside of its garment.

"Oh, Man! look here. Look, look, down here!" exclaimed the Ghost.

They were a boy and girl. Yellow, meagre, ragged, scowling, wolfish; but prostrate, too, in their humility. Where graceful youth should have filled their features out, and touched them with its freshest tints, a stale and shrivelled hand, like that of age, had pinched, and twisted them, and pulled them into shreds. Where angels might have sat enthroned, devils lurked, and glared out menacing. No change, no degradation, no perversion of humanity, in any grade, through all the mysteries of wonderful creation, has monsters half so horrible and dread.

Scrooge started back, appalled. Having them shown to him in this way, he tried to say they were fine children, but the words choked themselves, rather than be parties to a lie of such enormous magnitude.

"Spirit! are they yours?" Scrooge could say no more.

"They are Man's," said the Spirit, looking down upon them. "And they cling to me, appealing from their fathers. This boy is Ignorance. This girl is Want. Beware them both, and all of their degree, but most of all beware this boy, for on his brow I see that written which is Doom, unless the writing be erased. Deny it!" cried the Spirit, stretching out its hand towards the city. "Slander those who tell it ye! Admit it for your factious purposes, and make it worse. And bide the end!"

---

[23] Printed in the *Atlantic Monthly* shortly after his death, and since collected, by Mr. James T. Fields of Boston, with several of later date addressed to himself, and much correspondence having reference to other writers, into a pleasing volume entitled *Yesterdays with Authors*.

[24] This is mentioned in Mr. O. Driscoll's agreeable little Memoir, but supposed to refer to Maclise's portrait of Dickens.

[25] In one of the letters to his American friend Mr. Felton there is a glimpse of Christmas sports which had escaped my memory, and for which a corner may be found here, inasmuch as these gambols were characteristic of him at the pleasant old season, and were frequently renewed in future years. "The best of it is" (31 Dec. 1842) "that Forster and I have purchased between us the entire stock-in-trade of a conjuror, the practice and display whereof is entrusted to me. . . . In those tricks which require a confederate I am assisted (by reason of his imperturbable good humour) by Stanfield, who always does his part exactly the wrong way, to the unspeakable delight of all beholders. We come out on a small scale to-night, at Forster's, where we see the old year out and the new one in." *Atlantic Monthly*, July 1871.

[26] "After a period of 27 years, from a single school of five small infants, the work has grown into a cluster of some 300 schools, an aggregate of nearly 30,000 children, and a body of 3000 voluntary teachers, most of them the sons and daughters of toil. . . . Of more than 300,000 children which, on the most moderate calculation, we have a right to conclude have passed through these schools since their commencement, I venture to affirm that more than 100,000 of both sexes have been placed out in various ways, in emigration, in the marine, in trades, and in domestic service. For many consecutive years I have contributed prizes to thousands of the scholars; and let no one omit to call to mind what these children were, whence they came, and whither they were going without this merciful intervention. They would have been added to the perilous swarm of the wild, the lawless, the wretched, and the ignorant, instead of being, as by God's blessing they are, decent and comfortable, earning an honest livelihood, and adorning the community to which they belong." Letter of Lord Shaftesbury in *The Times* of the 13th of November, 1871.

CHAPTER 3

CHUZZLEWIT DISAPPOINTMENTS AND CHRISTMAS CAROL

1843~1844

CHUZZLEWIT HAD FALLEN SHORT of all the expectations formed of it in regard to sale. By much the most masterly of his writings hitherto, the public had rallied to it in far less numbers than to any of its predecessors. The primary cause of this, there is little doubt, had been the change to weekly issues in the form of publication of his last two stories; for into everything in this world mere habit enters more largely than we are apt to suppose. Nor had the temporary withdrawal to America been favourable to an immediate resumption by his readers of their old and intimate relations. This also is to be added, that the excitement by which a popular reputation is kept up to the highest selling mark, will always be subject to lulls too capricious for explanation. But whatever the causes, here was the undeniable fact of a grave depreciation of sale in his writings, unaccompanied by any falling off either in themselves or in the writer's reputation. It was very temporary; but it was present, and to be dealt with accordingly. The forty and fifty thousand purchasers of *Pickwick* and *Nickleby*, the sixty and seventy thousand of the early numbers of the enterprize in which the *Old Curiosity Shop* and *Barnaby Rudge* appeared, had fallen to little over twenty thousand. They rose somewhat on Martin's ominous announcement, at the end of the fourth number, that he'd *go to America*; but though it was believed that this resolve, which Dickens adopted as suddenly as his hero, might increase the number of his readers, that reason influenced him less than the challenge to make good his *Notes* which every mail had been bringing him from unsparing assailants beyond the Atlantic. The substantial effect of the American episode upon the sale was yet by no means great. A couple of thousand additional purchasers were added, but the highest number at any time reached before the story closed was twenty-three thousand. Its sale, since, has ranked next after *Pickwick* and *Copperfield*.

We were now, however, to have a truth brought home to us which few that have had real or varied experience in such matters can have failed to be impressed by—that publishers are bitter bad judges of an author, and are seldom safe persons to consult in regard to the fate or fortunes that may probably await him. Describing the agreement for this book in September 1841, I spoke of a provision against the improbable event of its profits proving inadequate to certain necessary repayments. In this unlikely case, which was to be ascertained by the proceeds of the first five numbers, the publishers were to have power to appropriate fifty pounds a month out of the two hundred pounds payable for authorship in the expenses of each number; but though this had been introduced with my knowledge, I knew also too much of the antecedent relations of the parties to regard it as other than a mere form to satisfy the attorneys in the case. The fifth number, which landed Martin and Mark in America, and the sixth, which described their first experiences, were published; and on the eve of the seventh, in which Mrs. Gamp was to make her first appearance, I heard with infinite pain that from Mr. Hall, the younger partner of the firm which had enriched itself by *Pickwick* and *Nickleby*, and a very kind well-disposed man, there had dropped an inconsiderate hint to the writer of those books that it might be desirable to put the clause in force. It had escaped him without his thinking of all that it involved; certainly the senior partner, whatever amount of as thoughtless sanction he had at the moment given to it, always much regretted it, and made endeavours to exhibit his regret; but the mischief was done, and for the time was irreparable.

The communication he had desired me to make to his printers had taken them too much by surprise to enable them to form a clear judgment respecting it; and they replied by suggestions which were in effect a confession of that want of confidence in themselves. They enlarged upon the great results that would follow a reissue of his writings in a cheap form; they strongly urged such an undertaking; and they offered to invest to any desired amount in the establishment of a magazine or other periodical to be edited by him. The possible dangers, in short, incident to their assuming the position of publishers as well as printers of new works from his pen, seemed at first to be so much greater than on closer examination they were found to be, that at the outset they shrank from encountering them. And hence the remarkable letter I shall now quote (1st of November, 1843).

"Don't be startled by the novelty and extent of my project. Both startled me at first; but I am well assured of its wisdom and necessity... I should unquestionably fade away from the public eye for a year, and enlarge my stock of description and observation by seeing countries new to me; which it is most necessary to me that I should see, and which with an increasing family I can scarcely hope to see at all, unless I see them now. Already for some time I have had this hope and intention before me; and though not having made money yet, I find or fancy that I can put myself in the position to accomplish it. And this is the course I have before me. At the close of *Chuzzlewit* (by which time the debt will have been materially reduced) I purpose drawing from Chapman and Hall my share of the subscription—bills, or money, will do equally well. I design to tell them that it is not likely I shall do anything for a year; that, in the meantime, I make no arrangement whatever with any one; and our business matters rest *in statu quo*. The same to Bradbury and Evans. I shall let the house if I can; if not, leave it to be let. I shall take all the family, and two servants—three at most—to some place which I know beforehand to be CHEAP and in a delightful climate, in Normandy or Brittany, to which I shall go over, first, and where I shall rent some house for six or eight months. During that time, I shall walk through Switzerland, cross the Alps, travel through France and Italy; take Kate perhaps to Rome and Venice, but not elsewhere; and in short see everything that is to be seen. I shall write my descriptions to you from time to time, exactly as I did in America; and you will be able to judge whether or not a new and attractive book may not be made on such ground. At the same time I shall be able to turn over the story I have in my mind, and which I have a strong notion might be published with great advantage, *first in Paris*—but that's another matter to be talked over. And of course I have not yet settled, either, whether any book about the travel, or this, should be the first."

I had certainly not much after reading this letter, written amid all the distractions of his work, with both the *Carol* and *Chuzzlewit* in hand; but such insufficient breath as was left to me I spent against the project, and in favour of far more consideration than he had given to it, before anything should be settled. "I expected you," he wrote next day (the 2nd of November), "to be startled. If I was startled myself, when I first got this project of foreign travel into my head, MONTHS AGO, how much more must you be, on whom it comes fresh: numbering only hours! Still, I am very resolute upon it—very. I am convinced that my expenses abroad would not be more than half of my expenses here; the influence of change and nature upon me, enormous. You know, as well as I, that I think *Chuzzlewit* in a hundred points immeasurably the best of my stories. That I feel my power now, more than I ever did. That I have a greater confidence in myself than I ever had. I said MYSELF IN MY NOTE TO YOU—ANTICIPATING WHAT YOU PUT TO ME—THAT IT WAS A QUESTION *what* I SHOULD COME OUT WITH, FIRST. The travel-book, if to be done at all, would cost me very little trouble; and surely would go very far to pay charges, whenever published. We have spoken of the baby, and of leaving it here with Catherine's mother. Moving the children into France could not, in any ordinary course of things, do them anything but good.

There were difficulties, still to be strongly urged, against taking any present step to a final resolve; and he gave way a little. But the pressure was soon renewed. "I have been," he wrote (10th of November), "all day in *Chuzzlewit* agonies—conceiving only. I hope to bring forth to-morrow. Will you come here at six? I want to say a word or two about the cover of the *Carol* and the advertising, and to consult you on a nice point in the tale.

It will come wonderfully I think. Mac will call here soon after, and we can then all three go to Bulwer's together. And do, my dear fellow, do for God's sake turn over about Chapman and Hall, and look upon my project as a *settled thing*. If you object to see them, I must write to them." My reluctance as to the question affecting his old publishers was connected with the little story, which, amid all his perturbations and troubles and "*Chuzzlewit* agonies," he was steadily carrying to its close; and which remains a splendid proof of how thoroughly he was borne out in the assertion just before

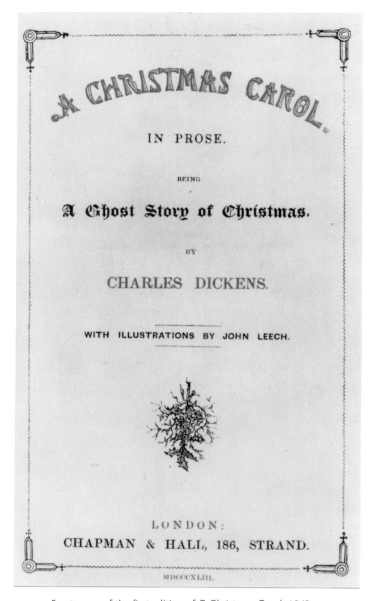

A CHRISTMAS CAROL.

IN PROSE.

BEING

A Ghost Story of Christmas.

BY

CHARLES DICKENS.

WITH ILLUSTRATIONS BY JOHN LEECH.

LONDON:
CHAPMAN & HALL, 186, STRAND.

MDCCCXLIII.

Front cover of the first edition of *A Christmas Carol*, 1843

made, of the sense of his power felt by him, and his confidence that it had never been greater than when his readers were thus falling off from him. He had entrusted the Carol for publication on his own account, under the usual terms of commission, to the firm he had been so long associated with; and at such a moment to tell them, short of absolute necessity, his intention to quit them altogether, I thought a needless putting in peril of the little book's chances. He

yielded to this argument; but the issue, as will be found, was less fortunate than I hoped.

He replied on the following day (19th of November) to the comment I had made upon it. "I was most horribly put out for a little while; for I had got up early to go at it, and was full of interest in what I had to do. But having eased my

RIGHT: *Scrooge and the children,* by Harold Copping

mind by that note to you, and taken a turn or two up and down the room, I went at it again, and soon got so interested that I blazed away till 9 last night; only stopping ten minutes for dinner! I suppose I wrote eight printed pages of *Chuzzlewit* yesterday. The consequence is that I could finish to-day, but am taking it easy, and making myself laugh very much." The very next day, unhappily, there came to himself a repetition of precisely similar trouble in exaggerated form, and to me a fresh reminder of what was gradually settling into a fixed resolve. "I am quite serious and sober when I say, that I have very grave thoughts of keeping my whole menagerie in Italy, three years."

Of the book which awoke such varied feelings and was the occasion of such vicissitudes of fortune, some notice is now due; and this, following still as yet my former rule, will be not so much critical as biographical. He had left for Italy before the completed tale was published, and its reception for a time was exactly what his just-quoted letter prefigures. It had forced itself up in public opinion without forcing itself up in sale.

In construction and conduct of story *Martin Chuzzlewit* is defective, character and description constituting the chief part of its strength. But what it lost as a story by the American episode it gained in the other direction; young Martin, by happy use of a bitter experience, casting off his slough of selfishness in the poisonous swamp of Eden.

Sending me the second chapter of his eighth number on the 15th of August, he gave me the latest tidings from America. "I gather from a letter I have had this morning that Martin has made them all stark staring raving mad across the water. I wish you would consider this. Don't you think the time has come when I ought to state that such public entertainments as I received in the States were either accepted before I went out, or in the first week after my arrival there; and that as soon as I began to have any acquaintance with the country, I set my face against any public recognition whatever but that which was forced upon me to the destruction of my peace and comfort—and made no secret of my real sentiments." We did not agree as to this, and the notion was abandoned; though his correspondent had not

overstated the violence of the outbreak in the States when those chapters exploded upon them. But though an angry they are a good humoured and a very placable people; and, as time moved on a little, the laughter on that side of the Atlantic became quite as great as our amusement on this side, at the astonishing fun and comicality of these scenes. With a little reflection the Americans had doubtless begun to find out that the advantage was not all with us, nor the laughter wholly against them.

Certainly Dickens thus far had done nothing of which, as in this novel, the details were filled in with such minute and incomparable skill; where the wealth of comic circumstance was lavished in such overflowing abundance on single types of character; or where generally, as throughout the story, the intensity of his observation of individual humours and vices had taken so many varieties of imaginative form. Everything in *Chuzzlewit* indeed had grown under treatment, as will be commonly the case in the handling of a man of genius, who never knows where any given conception may lead him, out of the wealth of resource in development and incident which it has itself created.

But this is a chapter of disappointments, and I have now to state, that as *Martin Chuzzlewit's* success was to seem to him at first only distant and problematical, so even the prodigious immediate success of the *Christmas Carol* itself was not to be an unmitigated pleasure. Never had a little book an outset so full of brilliancy of promise. Published but a few days before Christmas, it was hailed on every side with enthusiastic greeting. The first edition of six thousand copies was sold the first day, and on the third of January 1844 he wrote to me that "two thousand of the three printed for second and third editions are already taken by the trade." But a very few weeks were to pass before the darker side of the picture came. "Such a night as I have passed!" he wrote to me on Saturday morning the 10th of February. "I really believed I should never get up again, until I had passed through all the horrors of a fever. I found the *Carol* accounts awaiting me, and they were the cause of it. The first six thousand copies show a profit of £230! And the last four will yield as much more.

IN OUR FASCINATION WITH DICKENS'S MOST POPULAR CHRISTMAS WRITING AND THE PERSISTENT RETELLING OF THIS TALE ACROSS A RANGE OF MEDIA, "WE ARE," AS PAUL DAVIES ARGUES, "STILL CREATING THE CULTURE-TEXT OF THE CAROL":

The text of *A Christmas Carol* is fixed in Dickens's words, but the culture-text, the Carol as it has been re-created in the century and a half since it first appeared, changes as the reasons for the its retelling change [. . .]

The *Carol* is the sum of all its versions, of all its revisions, parodies and piracies. It is a much the Hollywood animation or the Henry Winkler re-creation as it is the fine facsimile complete with copies of the original illustrations by John Leech. Disguised as Lionel Barrymore or Mister Magoo, Scrooge had become common cultural property and is as deeply embedded in our consciousness as George Washington or Dick Whittington, Merlin or Moses. His reorginations since 1843 have produced a culture-text of remarkable diversity. Reappearing in new guises from page to page and from age to age, Scrooge is a protean figure always in process of reformation.

From Paul Davis, *The Lives and Times of Ebenezer Scrooge* (New Haven: Yale UP, 1990), pp. 4-5

Scrooge is visited by the Ghost of Jacob Marley, his former business partner. LEFT: illustration by Arthur Rackham, published in 1915, RIGHT: illustration by John Leech, first published in 1843

I had set my heart and soul upon a Thousand, clear. What a wonderful thing it is, that such a great success should occasion me such intolerable anxiety and disappointment! My year's bills, unpaid, are so terrific, that all the energy and determination I can possibly exert will be required to clear me before I go abroad; which, if next June come and find me alive, I shall do. Good Heaven, if I had only taken heart a year ago! Do come soon, as I am very anxious to talk with you. We can send round to Mac after you arrive, and tell him to join us at Hampstead or elsewhere. I was so utterly knocked down last night, that I came up to the contemplation of all these things quite bold this morning. If I can let the house for this season, I will be off to some seaside place as soon as a tenant offers. I am not afraid, if I reduce my expenses; but if I do not, I shall be ruined past all mortal hope of redemption."

The ultimate result was that his publishers were changed, and the immediate result that his departure for Italy became a settled thing; but a word may be said on these Carol accounts before mention is made of his new publishing arrangements.[27] Want of judgment had been shown in not adjusting the expenses of production with a more equable regard to the selling price, but even as it was, before the close of the year, he had received £726 from a sale of fifteen thousand copies; and the difference between this and the amount realised by the same proportion of the sale of the successor to the Carol, undoubtedly justified him in the discontent now expressed. Of that second tale, as well as of the third and fourth, more than double the numbers of the Carol were at once sold, and of course there was no complaint of any want of success: but the truth really was, as to all the Christmas stories issued in this form, that the price charged, while too large for the public addressed by them, was too little to remunerate their outlay; and when in later years he put forth similar fancies for Christmas, charging for them fewer pence than the shillings required for these, he counted his purchasers, with fairly corresponding gains to himself, not by tens but by hundreds of thousands.[28]

It was necessary now that negotiations should be resumed with his printers, but before any step was taken Messrs. Chapman and Hall were informed of his intention not to open fresh publishing relations with them after

Chuzzlewit should have closed. Then followed deliberations and discussions, many and grave, which settled themselves at last into the form of an agreement with Messrs. Bradbury and Evans executed on the first of June 1844; by which, upon advance made to him of £2800, he assigned to them a fourth share in whatever he might write during the next ensuing eight years, to which the agreement was to be strictly limited. There were the usual protecting clauses, but no interest was to be paid, and no obligations were imposed as to what works should be written, if any, or the form of them; the only farther stipulation having reference to the event of a periodical being undertaken whereof Dickens might be only partially editor or author, in which case his proprietorship of copyright and profits was to be two thirds instead of three fourths. There was an understanding, at the time this agreement was signed, that a successor to the Carol would be ready for the Christmas of 1844; but no other promise was asked or made in regard to any other book, nor had he himself decided what form to give to his experiences of Italy, if he should even finally determine to publish them at all.

Between this agreement and his journey six weeks elapsed, and there were one or two characteristic incidents before his departure: but mention must first be interposed of the success quite without alloy that also attended the little book, and carried off in excitement and delight every trace of doubt or misgiving.

"Blessings on your kind heart!" wrote Jeffrey to the author of the Carol. "You should be happy yourself, for you may be sure you have done more good by this little publication, fostered more kindly feelings, and prompted more positive acts of beneficence, than can be traced to all the pulpits and confessionals in Christendom since Christmas 1842." "Who can listen," exclaimed Thackeray, "to objections regarding such a book as this? It seems to me a national benefit, and to every man or woman who reads it a personal kindness." Such praise expressed what men of genius felt and said; but the small volume had other tributes, less usual and not less genuine. There poured upon its author daily, all through that Christmas time, letters from complete strangers to him which I remember reading with a wonder of pleasure; not literary at all, but of the simplest domestic

A CHRISTMAS CAROL, STAVE 3

Notwithstanding half a century of criticism exploring a darker Dickens, his association with the spirit and customs of Christmas remains strong. For many, as the wealth of screen adaptations attest, Christmas celebrations are not complete without a helping of A Christmas Carol, *and an imaginative involvement in Mrs. Cratchit's Christmas dinner.*

SUCH a bustle ensued that you might have thought a goose the rarest of all birds; a feathered phenomenon, to which a black swan was a matter of course—and in truth it was something very like it in that house. Mrs. Cratchit made the gravy (ready beforehand in a little saucepan) hissing hot; Master Peter mashed the potatoes with incredible vigour; Miss Belinda sweetened up the apple-sauce; Martha dusted the hot plates; Bob took Tiny Tim beside him in a tiny corner at the table; the two young Cratchits set chairs for everybody, not forgetting themselves, and mounting guard upon their posts, crammed spoons into their mouths, lest they should shriek for goose before their turn came to be helped. At last the dishes were set on, and grace was said. It was succeeded by a breathless pause, as Mrs. Cratchit, looking slowly all along the carving-knife, prepared to plunge it in the breast; but when she did, and when the long expected gush of stuffing issued forth, one murmur of delight arose all round the board, and even Tiny Tim, excited by the two young Cratchits, beat on the table with the handle of his knife, and feebly cried Hurrah!

There never was such a goose. Bob said he didn't believe there ever was such a goose cooked. Its tenderness and flavour, size and cheapness, were the themes of universal admiration. Eked out by apple-sauce and mashed potatoes, it was a sufficient dinner for the whole family; indeed, as Mrs. Cratchit said with great delight (surveying one small atom of a bone upon the dish), they hadn't ate it all at last! Yet every one had had enough, and the youngest Cratchits in particular, were steeped in sage

and onion to the eyebrows! But now, the plates being changed by Miss Belinda, Mrs. Cratchit left the room alone—too nervous to bear witnesses—to take the pudding up and bring it in.

Suppose it should not be done enough! Suppose it should break in turning out! Suppose somebody should have got over the wall of the back-yard, and stolen it, while they were merry with the goose—a supposition at which the two young Cratchits became livid! All sorts of horrors were supposed.

Hallo! A great deal of steam! The pudding was out of the copper. A smell like a washing-day! That was the cloth. A smell like an eating-house and a pastrycook's next door to each other, with a laundress's next door to that! That was the pudding! In half a minute Mrs. Cratchit entered—flushed, but smiling proudly—with the pudding, like a speckled cannon-ball, so hard and firm, blazing in half of half-a-quartern of ignited brandy, and bedight with Christmas holly stuck into the top.

Oh, a wonderful pudding! Bob Cratchit said, and calmly too, that he regarded it as the greatest success achieved by Mrs. Cratchit since their marriage. Mrs. Cratchit said that now the weight was off her mind, she would confess she had had her doubts about the quantity of flour. Everybody had something to say about it, but nobody said or thought it was at all a small pudding for a large family. It would have been flat heresy to do so. Any Cratchit would have blushed to hint at such a thing.

Bob Cratchit and Tiny Tim, illustration for *Character Sketches from Dickens* compiled by B.W. Matz. Color lithograph after Harold Copping, 1924

Mr. Fezziwig's Ball, by
John Leech, 1843

kind; of which the general burden was to tell him, amid many confidences about their homes, how the *Carol* had come to be read aloud there, and was to be kept upon a little shelf by itself, and was to do them all no end of good. Anything more to be said of it will not add much to this.

There was indeed nobody that had not some interest in the message of the *Christmas Carol*. It told the selfish man to rid himself of selfishness; the just man to make himself generous; and the good-natured man to enlarge the sphere of his good nature. Its cheery voice of faith and hope, ringing from one end of the island to the other, carried pleasant warning alike to all, that if the duties of Christmas were wanting no good could come of its outward observances; that it must shine upon the cold hearth and warm it, and into the sorrowful heart and comfort it; that it must be kindness, benevolence, charity, mercy, and forbearance,

or its plum pudding would turn to bile, and its roast beef be indigestible.[29] Nor could any man have said it with the same appropriateness as Dickens. What was marked in him to the last was manifest now. He had identified himself with Christmas fancies.

Its life and spirits, its humour in riotous abundance, of right belonged to him. Its imaginations as well as kindly thoughts were his; and its privilege to light up with some sort of comfort the squalidest places, he had made his own. Christmas Day was not more social or welcome: New Year's Day not more new: Twelfth Night not more full of characters. The duty of diffusing enjoyment had never been taught by a more abundant, mirthful, thoughtful, ever-seasonable writer.

RIGHT: *Bob Cratchit's Christmas Dinner*, by Harold Copping

[27] It may interest the reader, and be something of a curiosity of literature, if I give the expenses of the first edition of 6000, and of the 7000 more which constituted the five following editions, with the profit of the remaining 2000 which completed the sale of 15,000:

Christmas Carol.
1st Edition, 6000 No.

1843.	£	s.	d.
Dec. Printing	74	2	9
Paper	89	2	0
Drawings and Engravings	49	18	0
Two Steel Plates	1	4	0
Printing Plates	15	17	6
Paper for do	7	12	0
Colouring Plates	120	0	0
Binding	180	0	0
Incidents and Advertising	168	7	8
Commission	99	4	6
	£805	8	5

2nd to the 7th Edition, making 7000 Copies

1844.	£	s.	d.
Jan. Printing	58	18	0
Paper	103	19	0
Printing Plates	17	10	0
Paper	8	17	4
Colouring Plates	140	0	0
Binding	199	18	2
Incidents and Advertising	83	5	8
Commission	107	18	10
	£720	7	0

2000 more, represented by the last item in the subjoined balance, were sold before the close of the year, leaving a remainder of 70 copies.

1843.	£	s.	d.
Dec. Balance of a/c to			
Mr. Dickens's credit	186	16	7
1844.			
Jan. to April. Do. Do.	349	12	0
May to Dec. Do. Do.	189	11	5
Amount of Profit on the Work	£726	0	0

[28] In November 1865 he wrote to me that the sale of his Christmas fancy for that year (*Dr. Marigold's Prescriptions*) had gone up, in the first week, to 250,000.

[29] A characteristic letter of this date, which will explain itself, has been kindly sent to me by the gentleman it was written to, Mr. James Verry Staples, of Bristol:—"Third of April, 1844. I have been very much gratified by the receipt of your interesting letter, and I assure you that it would have given me heartfelt satisfaction to have been in your place when you read my little *Carol* to the Poor in your neighbourhood. I have great faith in the poor; to the best of my ability I always endeavour to present them in a favourable light to the rich; and I shall never cease, I hope, until I die, to advocate their being made as happy and as wise as the circumstances of their condition, in its utmost improvement, will admit of their becoming. I mention this to assure you of two things. Firstly, that I try to deserve their attention; and secondly, that any such marks of their approval and confidence as you relate to me are most acceptable to my feelings, and go at once to my heart."

CHAPTER 4

YEAR OF DEPARTURE FOR ITALY

1844

I

N THE PREVIOUS FEBRUARY, on the 26TH and 28TH respectively, he had taken the chair at two great meetings, in Liverpool of the Mechanics' Institution, and in Birmingham of the Polytechnic Institution, to which reference is made by him in a letter of the 21st. I quote the allusion because it shows thus early the sensitive regard to his position as a man of letters, and his scrupulous consideration for the feelings as well as interest of the class, which he manifested in many various and often greatly self-sacrificing ways all through his life. "Advise me on the following point. And as I must write to-night, having already lost a post, advise me by bearer. This Liverpool Institution, which is wealthy and has a high grammar-school the masters of which receive in salaries upwards of £2000 a year (indeed its extent horrifies me; I am struggling through its papers this morning), writes me yesterday by its secretary a business letter about the order of the proceedings on Monday; and it begins thus. 'I beg to send you prefixed, with the best respects of our committee, a bank order for twenty pounds in payment of the expenses contingent on your visit to Liverpool.'—And there, sure enough, it is. Now my impulse was, *and is*, decidedly to return it. Twenty pounds is not of moment to me; and any sacrifice of independence is worth it twenty times' twenty times told. But haggling in my mind is a doubt whether that would be proper, and not boastful (in an inexplicable way); and whether as an author, I have a right to put myself on a basis which the professors of literature in other forms *connected with the Institution* cannot afford to occupy. Don't you see? But of course you do. The case stands thus. The Manchester Institution, being in debt, appeals to me as it were *in forma pauperis*, and makes no such provision as I have named.

The Birmingham Institution, just struggling into life with great difficulty, applies to me on the same grounds. But the Leeds people (thriving) write to me, making the expenses a distinct matter of business; and the Liverpool, as a point of delicacy, say nothing about it to the last minute, and then send the money. Now, what in the name of goodness ought I to do?—I am as much puzzled with the cheque as Colonel Jack was with his gold. If it would have settled the matter to put it in the fire yesterday, I should certainly have done it. Your opinion is requested. I think I shall have grounds for a very good speech at Brummagem; but I am not sure about Liverpool: having misgivings of over-gentility." My opinion was clearly for sending the money back, which accordingly was done.

Both speeches, duly delivered to enthusiastic listeners at the places named, were good, and both, with suitable variations, had the same theme: telling his popular audience in Birmingham that the principle of their institute, education comprehensive and unsectarian, was the only safe one, for that without danger no society could go on punishing men for preferring vice to virtue without giving them the means of knowing what virtue was; and reminding his genteeler audience in Liverpool, that if happily they had been themselves well taught, so much the more should they seek to extend the benefit to all, since, whatever the precedence due to rank, wealth, or intellect, there was yet a nobility beyond them, expressed unaffectedly by the poet's verse and in the power of education to confer.

He underwent some suffering, which he might have spared himself, at his return. "I saw the *Carol* last night," he wrote to me of a dramatic performance of the little story at the Adelphi. "Better than usual, and Wright seems to enjoy Bob Cratchit, but *heart-breaking* to me. Oh Heaven! if any forecast of *this* was ever in my mind! Yet O. Smith was drearily better than I expected. It is a great comfort to have that kind of meat under done; and his face is quite perfect." Of what he suffered from these adaptations of his books, multiplied remorselessly at every theatre, I have forborne to speak, but it was the subject of complaint with him incessantly; and more or less satisfied as he was with individual performances, such as Mr. Yates's Quilp or Mantalini and Mrs. Keeley's Smike or Dot, there was only one, that of Barnaby Rudge by the Miss Fortescue who became afterwards Lady Gardner, on which I ever heard him dwell with a thorough liking. It is true that to the dramatizations of his next and other following Christmas stories he gave help himself; but, even then, all such efforts to assist special representations were mere attempts to render more tolerable what he had no power to prevent, and, with a few rare exceptions, they were never very successful.

Another and graver wrong was the piracy of his writings, every one of which had been reproduced with merely such colourable changes of title, incidents, and names of characters, as were believed to be sufficient to evade the law and adapt them to "penny" purchasers. So shamelessly had this been going on ever since the days of *Pickwick*, in so many outrageous ways[30] and with all but impunity, that a course repeatedly urged by Talfourd and myself was at last taken in the present year with the *Christmas Carol* and the *Chuzzlewit* pirates. Upon a case of such peculiar flagrancy, however, that the vice-chancellor would not even hear Dickens's counsel; and what it cost our dear friend Talfourd to suppress his speech exceeded

by very much the labour and pains with which he had prepared it. "The pirates," wrote Dickens to me, after leaving the court on the 18th of January, "are beaten flat. They are bruised, bloody, battered, smashed, squelched, and utterly undone." The undertaking to which he had at last to submit was, that upon ample public apology, and payment of all costs, the offenders should be let go; but the real result was that, after infinite vexation and trouble, he had himself to pay all the costs incurred on his own behalf; and, a couple of years later, upon repetition of the wrong he had suffered in so gross a form that proceedings were again advised by Talfourd and others, he wrote to me from Switzerland the condition of mind to which his experience had brought him. "My feeling about the——is the feeling common, I suppose, to three fourths of the reflecting part of the community in our happiest of all possible countries; and that is, that it is better to suffer a great wrong than to have recourse to the much greater wrong of the law. I shall not easily forget the expense, and anxiety, and horrible injustice of the *Carol* case, wherein, in asserting the plainest right on earth, I was really treated as if I were the robber instead of the robbed. Upon the whole, I certainly

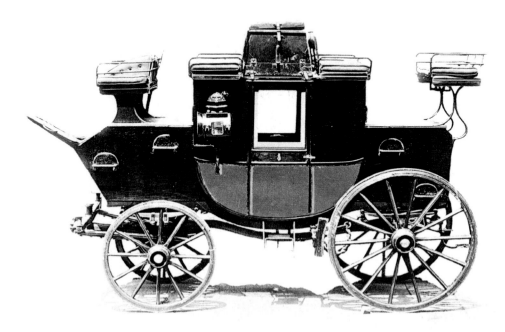

A carriage design by Barker and Co., Chandos Street, London, 19th century. Dickens was one of their customers.

would much rather NOT proceed. What do you think of sending in a grave protest against what has been done in this case, on account of the immense amount of piracy to which I am daily exposed, and because I have been already met in the court of chancery with the legal doctrine that silence under such wrongs barred my remedy: to which Talfourd's written opinion might be appended as proof that we stopped under no discouragement.

The preparation for departure was now actively going forward, and especially his enquiries for two important adjuncts thereto, a courier and a carriage. As to the latter it occurred to him that he might perhaps get for little money "some good old shabby devil of a coach—one of those vast phantoms that hide themselves in a corner of the Pantechnicon;" and exactly such a one he found there; sitting himself inside it, a perfect Sentimental Traveller, while the managing man told him its history. "As for comfort—let me see—it is about the size of your library; with night-lamps and day-lamps and pockets and imperials and leathern cellars, and the most extraordinary contrivances. Joking apart, it is a wonderful machine. And when you see it (if you *do* see it) you will roar at it first, and will then proclaim it to be 'perfectly brilliant, my dear

fellow.'" It was marked sixty pounds; he got it for five-and-forty; and my own emotions respecting it he had described by anticipation quite correctly. In finding a courier he was even more fortunate; and these successes were followed by a third apparently very promising, but in the result less satisfactory. His house was let to not very careful people.

The last incident before Dickens's departure was a farewell dinner to him at Greenwich, which took also the form of a celebration for the completion of *Chuzzlewit*, or, as the Ballantynes used to call it in Scott's case, a christening dinner; when Lord Normanby took the chair, and I remember sitting next the great painter Turner, who had come with Stanfield, and had enveloped his throat, that sultry summer day, in a huge red belcher-handkerchief which nothing would induce him to remove. He was not otherwise demonstrative, but enjoyed himself in a quiet silent way, less perhaps at the speeches than at the changing lights on the river. Carlyle did not come; telling me in his reply to the invitation that he truly loved Dickens, having discerned in the inner man of him a real music of the genuine kind, but that he'd rather testify to this in some other form than that of dining out in the dogdays.

---

[30] In a letter on the subject of copyright published by Thomas Hood after Dickens's return from America, he described what had passed between himself and one of these pirates who had issued a *Master Humphrey's Clock* edited by Bos. "Sir," said the man to Hood, "if you had observed the name, it was Bos, not Boz; s, sir, not z; and, besides, it would have been no piracy, sir, even with the z, because *Master Humphrey's Clock*, you see, sir, was not published as by Boz, but by Charles Dickens!"

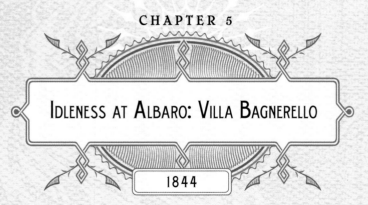

CHAPTER 5

IDLENESS AT ALBARO: VILLA BAGNERELLO

1844

THE TRAVELLING PARTY ARRIVED at Marseilles on the evening of Sunday the 14th of July. Not being able to get vetturino horses in Paris, they had come on, post; paying for nine horses but bringing only four, and thereby saving a shilling a mile out of what the four would have cost in England. So great thus far, however, had been the cost of travel, that "what with distance, caravan, sight-seeing, and everything," two hundred pounds would be nearly swallowed up before they were at their destination. The success otherwise had been complete. The children had not cried in their worst troubles, the carriage had gone lightly over abominable roads, and the courier had proved himself a perfect gem. "Surrounded by strange and perfectly novel circumstances," Dickens wrote to me from Marseilles, "I feel as if I had a new head on side by side with my old one."

His first experience in a foreign tongue he made immediately on landing, when he had gone to the bank for money, and after delivering with most laborious distinctness a rather long address in French to the clerk behind the counter, was disconcerted by that functionary's cool enquiry in the native-born Lombard-street manner, "How would you like to take it, sir?" He took it, as everybody must, in five-franc pieces, and a most inconvenient coinage he found it; for he required so much that he had to carry it in a couple of small sacks, and was always "turning hot about suddenly" taking it into his head that he had lost them.

The evening of Tuesday the 16th of July saw him in a villa at Albaro, the suburb of Genoa in which, upon the advice of our Gore-house friends, he had resolved to pass the summer months before taking up his quarters in the city. His wish was to have had Lord Byron's house there, but

it had fallen into neglect and become the refuge of a third-rate wine-shop. The matter had then been left to Angus Fletcher who just now lived near Genoa, and he had taken at a rent absurdly above its value[31] an unpicturesque and uninteresting dwelling, which at once impressed its new tenant with its likeness to a pink jail. "It is," he said to me, "the most perfectly lonely, rusty, stagnant old staggerer of a domain that you can possibly imagine."

The heat tried him less than he expected, excepting always the sirocco, which, near the sea as they were, and right in the course of the wind as it blew against the house, made everything hotter than if there had been no wind. "One feels it most, on first getting up. Then, it is really so oppressive that a strong determination is necessary to enable one to go on dressing; one's tendency being to tumble down anywhere and lie there." It seemed to hit him, he said, behind the knee, and made his legs so shake that he could not walk or stand. He had unfortunately a whole week of this without intermission, soon after his arrival; but then came a storm, with wind from the mountains; and he could bear the ordinary heat very well. What at first had been a home-discomfort, the bare walls, lofty ceilings, icy floors, and lattice blinds, soon became agreeable; there were regular afternoon breezes from the sea; in his courtyard was a well of very pure and very cold water; there were new milk and eggs by the bucketful, and, to protect from the summer insects these and other dainties, there were fresh vine-leaves by the thousand; and he satisfied himself, by the experience of a day or two in the city, that he had done well to come first to its suburb by the sea. What startled and disappointed him most were the frequent cloudy days.[32] He opened his third letter (3rd of August) by telling me there was a thick November fog, that rain was pouring incessantly, and that he did not remember to have seen in his life, at that time of year, such cloudy weather as he had seen beneath Italian skies.

In his second letter from Albaro there was more of this subject; and an outbreak of whimsical enthusiasm in it, meant especially for Maclise, is followed by some

RIGHT: Dickens's daughter Katey painted by her second husband, Carlo Perugini, ca. 1874

"Won't it do to-morrow?" "I want it now," you would reply; and he would say, "No, no, there can be no hurry!" He remonstrated against the cruelty. But everywhere there was deference, courtesy, more than civility. "In a cafe a little tumbler of ice costs something less than threepence, and if you give the waiter in addition what you would not offer to an English beggar, say, the third of a halfpenny, he is profoundly grateful." The attentions received from English residents were unremitting.

The light, eager, active figure soon made itself familiar in the streets of Genoa, and he never went into them without bringing some oddity away. I soon heard of the strada Nuova and strada Balbi; of the broadest of the two as narrower than Albany-street, and of the other as less wide than Drury-lane or Wych-street; but both filled with palaces of noble architecture and of such vast dimensions that as many windows as there are days in the year might be counted in one of them, and this not covering by any means the largest plot of ground.

With the theatres of course he soon became acquainted, and of that of the puppets he wrote to me again and again with humorous rapture.

The living performers he did not think so good, a disbe-lief in Italian actors having been always a heresy with him, and the deplorable length of dialogue to the small amount of action in their plays making them sadly tiresome. The first that he saw at the principal theatre was a version of Balzac's *Pere Goriot.* "The domestic Lear I thought at first was going to be very clever. But he was too pitiful—perhaps the Italian reality would be. He was immensely applauded, though." He afterwards saw a version of Dumas' prepos-terous play of *Kean*, in which most of the representatives of English actors wore red hats with steeple crowns, and very loose blouses with broad belts and buckles round their waists. "There was a mysterious person called the Prince of Var-lees" (Wales), "the youngest and slimmest man in the company, whose badinage in Kean's dressing-room was irre-sistible; and the dresser wore top-boots, a Greek skull-cap, a black velvet jacket, and leather breeches. One or two of the actors looked very hard at me to see how I was touched by these English peculiarities—especially when Kean kissed his male friends on both cheeks." The arrangements of the

house, which he described as larger than Drury-lane, he thought excellent. Instead of a ticket for the private box he had taken on the first tier, he received the usual key for admis-sion which let him in as if he lived there; and for the whole set-out, "quite as comfortable and private as a box at our opera," paid only eight and fourpence English. The opera itself had not its regular performers until after Christmas, but in the summer there was a good comic company, and he saw the *Scaramuccia* and the *Barber of Seville* brightly and pleasantly done. There was also a day theatre, beginning at half past four in the afternoon; but beyond the novelty of looking on at the covered stage as he sat in the fresh pleasant air, he did not find much amusement in the Goldoni comedy put before him. There came later a Russian circus, which the unusual rains of that summer prematurely extinguished.

He had hired rooms in the Peschiere from the first of the following October; and so ended the house-hunting for his winter residence, that had taken him so often to the city. The Peschiere was the largest palace in Genoa let on hire, and had the advantage of standing on a height aloof from the town, surrounded by its own gardens.

In the middle of August he dined with the French consul-general, and there will now be no impropriety in printing his agreeable sketch of the dinner. "There was present, among other Genoese, the Marquis di Negri: a very fat and much older Jerdan, with the same thickness of speech and size of tongue. He was Byron's friend, keeps open house here, writes poetry, improvises, and is a very good old Blunderbore; just the sort of instrument to make an artesian well with, anywhere."

This, too, was the year of other uncomfortable glories of France in the last three years of her Orleans dynasty; among them the Tahiti business, as politicians may remember; and so hot became rumours of war with England at the opening of September that Dickens had serious thoughts of at once striking his tent. One of his letters was filled with the conflicting doubts in which they lived for nigh a fortnight, every day's arrival contradicting the arrival of the day before: so that, as he told me, you met a man in the street to-day, who told you there would certainly be war in a week; and you met the same man in the street to-morrow, and he swore he always knew there

PICTURES FROM ITALY, CHAPTER 3

In his letters from Italy, Dickens delights in the comedy of the ridiculous at the puppet theatre.
Here he transposes that experience into his travelogue:

THE Theatre of Puppets, or Marionetti—a famous company from Milan—is, without any exception, the drollest exhibition I ever beheld in my life. I never saw anything so exquisitely ridiculous. They LOOK between four and five feet high, but are really much smaller; for when a musician in the orchestra happens to put his hat on the stage, it becomes alarmingly gigantic, and almost blots out an actor. They usually play a comedy, and a ballet. The comic man in the comedy I saw one summer night, is a waiter in an hotel. There never was such a locomotive actor, since the world began. Great pains are taken with him. He has extra joints in his legs: and a practical eye, with which he winks at the pit, in a manner that is absolutely insupportable to a stranger, but which the initiated audience, mainly composed of the common people, receive (so they do everything else) quite as a matter of course, and as if he were a man. His spirits are prodigious. He continually shakes his legs, and winks his eye. And there is a heavy father with grey hair, who sits down on the regular conventional stage-bank, and blesses his daughter in the regular conventional way, who is tremendous. No one would suppose it possible that anything short of a real man could be so tedious. It is the triumph of art.

In the ballet, an Enchanter runs away with the Bride, in the very hour of her nuptials. He brings her to his cave, and tries to soothe her. They sit down on a sofa (the regular sofa! in the regular place, O. P. Second Entrance!) and a procession of musicians enters; one creature playing a drum, and knocking himself off his legs at every blow. These failing to delight her, dancers appear. Four first; then two; THE two; the flesh-coloured two. The way in which they dance; the height to which they spring; the impossible and inhuman extent to which they pirouette; the revelation of their preposterous legs; the coming down with a pause, on the very tips of their toes, when the music requires it; the gentleman's retiring up, when it is the lady's turn; and the lady's retiring up, when it is the gentleman's turn; the final passion of a pas-de-deux; and the going off with a bound!—I shall never see a real ballet, with a composed countenance again.

would be nothing but peace; and you met him again the day after, and he said it all depended *now* on something perfectly new and unheard of before, which somebody else said had just come to the knowledge of some consul in some dispatch which said something about some telegraph which had been at work somewhere, signalizing some prodigious intelligence. However, it all passed harmlessly away, leaving him undisturbed opportunity to avail himself of a pleasure that arose out of the consul-general's dinner party, and to be present at a great reception given shortly after on the occasion of his daughter's birthday.

Of course all news from England, and especially visits paid him by English friends who might be travelling in Italy, were a great delight. This was the year when O'Connell was released from prison by the judgment of the Lords on appeal. "I have no faith in O'Connell taking the great position he might upon this: being beleaguered by vanity always. Denman delights me. I am glad to think I have always liked him so well. I am sure that whenever he makes a mistake, it *is* a mistake; and that no man lives who has a grander and nobler scorn of every mean and dastard action. I would to Heaven it were decorous to pay him some public tribute of respect . . . O'Connell's speeches are the old thing: fretty, boastful, frothy, waspish at the voices in the crowd, and all that: but with no true greatness. . . . What a relief to turn to that noble letter of Carlyle's" (in which a timely testimony had been borne to the truthfulness and honour of Mazzini), "which I think above all praise. My love to him." Among his English visitors were Mr. Tagart's family, on their way from a scientific congress at Milan; and Peter (now become Lord) Robertson from Rome, of whose talk he wrote very pleasantly. The same letter told me, too, something of his reading. Jerrold's *Story of a Feather* he had derived much enjoyment from. "Gauntwolf's sickness and the career of that snuff box, masterly.[34] I have been deep in Voyages and Travels, and in De Foe. Tennyson I have also been reading, again and again. What a great creature he is! . . . What about the *Goldsmith*? Apropos, I am all eagerness to write a story about the length of that most delightful of all stories, the *Vicar of Wakefield*."

In the second week of September he went to meet his brother Frederick at Marseilles, and bring him back over the Cornice road to pass a fortnight's holiday at Genoa.

In four days they were at Albaro, and the morning after their arrival Dickens underwent the terrible shock of seeing his brother very nearly drowned in the bay. He swam out into too strong a current,[35] and was only narrowly saved by the accident of a fishing-boat preparing to leave the harbour at the time. "It was a world of horror and anguish," Dickens wrote to me, "crowded into four or five minutes of dreadful agitation; and, to complete the terror of it, Georgy, Charlotte" (the nurse), "and the children were on a rock in full view of it all, crying, as you may suppose, like mad creatures." His own bathing was from the rock, and, as he had already told me, of the most primitive kind. He went in whenever he pleased, broke his head against sharp stones if he went in with that end foremost, floundered about till he was all over bruises, and then climbed and staggered out again.

I will add another personal touch, also Masaniello-like, which marks the beginning of a change which, though confined for the present to his foreign residence and removed when he came to England, was resumed somewhat later, and in a few more years wholly altered the aspect of his face. "The moustaches are glorious, glorious. I have cut them shorter, and trimmed them a little at the ends to improve the shape. They are charming, charming. Without them, life would be a blank."

---

[31] He regretted one chance missed by his eccentric friend, which he described to me just before he left Italy. "I saw last night an old palazzo of the Doria, six miles from here, upon the sea, which De la Rue urged Fletcher to take for us, when he was bent on that detestable villa Bagnerello; which villa the Genoese have hired, time out of mind, for one-fourth of what I paid, as they told him again and again before he made the agreement. This is one of the strangest old palaces in Italy, surrounded by beautiful woods of great trees (an immense rarity here) some miles in extent: and has upon the terrace a high tower, formerly a prison for offenders against the family, and a defence against the pirates. The present Doria lets it as it stands for £40 English—for the year. . . . And the grounds are no expense; being proudly maintained by the Doria, who spends this rent, when he gets it, in repairing the roof and windows. It is a wonderful house; full of the most unaccountable pictures and most incredible furniture: every room in it like the most quaint and fanciful of Cattermole's pictures; and how many rooms I am afraid to say." 2nd of June, 1845.

[32] "We have had a London sky until to-day," he wrote on the 20th of July, "gray and cloudy as you please: but I am most disappointed, I think, in the evenings, which are as commonplace as need be; for there is no twilight, and as to the stars giving more light here than elsewhere, that is humbug." The summer of 1844 seems to have been, however, an unusually stormy and wet season. He wrote to me on the 21st of October that they had had, so far, only four really clear days since they came to Italy.

[33] I send my heart up to thee, all my heart
In this my singing!
For the stars help me, and the sea bears part;
The very night is clinging
Closer to Venice' streets to leave one space
Above me, whence thy face
May light my joyous heart to thee its dwelling-place.

Written to express Maclise's subject in the Academy catalogue.

[34] A characteristic message for Jerrold came in a later letter (12th of May, 1845): "I wish you would suggest to Jerrold for me as a Caudle subject (if he pursue that idea). 'Mr. Caudle has incidentally remarked that the house-maid is good-looking.'"

[35] Of the dangers of the bay he had before written to me (10th of August). "A monk was drowned here on Saturday evening. He was bathing with two other monks, who bolted when he cried out that he was sinking—in consequence, I suppose, of his certainty of going to Heaven."

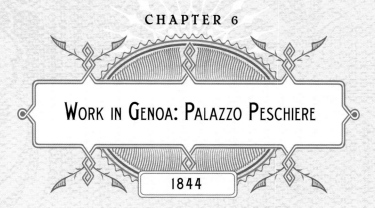

CHAPTER 6

Work in Genoa: Palazzo Peschiere

1844

In the last week of September they moved from Albaro into Genoa, amid a violent storm of wind and wet, "great guns blowing," the lightning incessant, and the rain driving down in a dense thick cloud. But the worst of the storm was over when they reached the Peschiere. As they passed into it along the stately old terraces, flanked on either side with antique sculptured figures, all the seven fountains were playing in its gardens, and the sun was shining brightly on its groves of camellias and orange-trees.

It was a wonderful place, and I soon became familiar with the several rooms that were to form their home for the rest of their stay in Italy. In the centre was the grand sala, fifty feet high, of an area larger than "the dining-room of the Academy," and painted, walls and ceiling, with frescoes three hundred years old, "as fresh as if the colours had been laid on yesterday." On the same floor as this great hall were a drawing-room, and a dining-room,[36] both covered also with frescoes still bright enough to make them thoroughly cheerful, and both so nicely proportioned as to give to their bigness all the effect of snugness.[37] Out of these opened three other chambers that were turned into sleeping-rooms and nurseries. Adjoining the sala, right and left, were the two best bedrooms; "in size and shape like those at Windsor-castle but greatly higher;" both having altars, a range of three windows with stone balconies, floors tesselated in patterns of black and white stone, and walls painted every inch: on the left, nymphs pursued by satyrs "as large as life and as wicked;" on the right, "Phaeton larger than life, with horses bigger than Meux and Co.'s, tumbling

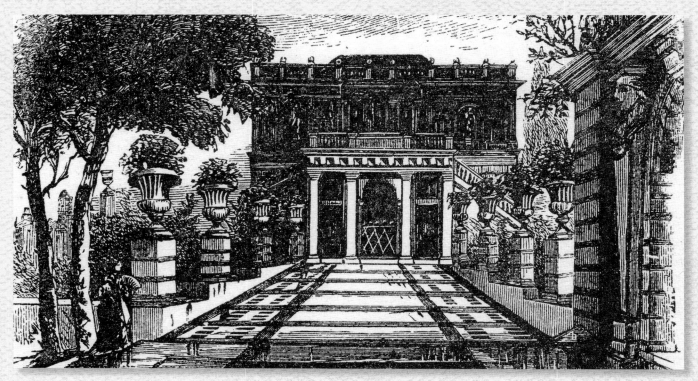

Palazzo Peschiere, Genoa

headlong down into the best bed." The right-hand one he occupied with his wife, and of the left took possession as a study; writing behind a big screen he had lugged into it, and placed by one of the windows, from which he could see over the city, as he wrote, as far as the lighthouse in its harbour. Distant little over a mile as the crow flew, flashing five times in four minutes, and on dark nights, as if by magic, illuminating brightly the whole palace-front every time it shone, this lighthouse was one of the wonders of Genoa.

When it had all become more familiar to him, he was fond of dilating on its beauties; and even the dreary sound of the chaunting from neighbouring mass-performances, as it floated in at all the open windows, which at first was a sad trouble, came to have its charm for him. I remember a vivid account he gave me of a great festa on the hill behind the house, when the people alternately danced under tents in the open air and rushed to say a prayer or two in an adjoining church bright with red and gold and blue and silver; so many minutes of dancing, and of praying, in regular turns of each. But the view over into Genoa, on clear bright days, was a never failing enjoyment. The whole city then, without an atom of smoke, and with every possible variety of tower and steeple pointing up into the sky, lay stretched out below his windows. To the right and left were lofty hills, with every indentation in their rugged sides sharply discernible; and on one side of the harbour stretched away into the dim bright distance the whole of the Cornice, its first highest range of mountains hoary with snow. Sitting down one Spring day to write to me, he thus spoke of the sea and of the garden. "Beyond the town is the wide expanse of the Mediterranean, as blue, at this moment, as the most pure and vivid prussian blue on Mac's palette when it is newly set; and on the horizon there is a red flush, seen nowhere as it is here. Immediately below the windows are the gardens of the house, with gold fish swimming and diving in the fountains; and below them, at the foot of a steep slope, the public garden and drive, where the walks are marked out by hedges of pink roses, which blush and shine through the green trees and vines, close up to the balconies of these windows."

The subject for his new Christmas story he had chosen, but he had not found a title for it, or the machinery to work it with; when, at the moment of what seemed to be

The Tower of the Chimes, illustration for *The Chimes*, by Daniel Maclise, 1844

his greatest trouble, both reliefs came. Sitting down one morning resolute for work, though against the grain, his hand being out and everything inviting to idleness, such a peal of chimes arose from the city as he found to be "maddening." Only two days later, however, came a letter in which not a syllable was written but "We have heard THE CHIMES at midnight, Master Shallow!" and I knew he had discovered what he wanted.

"It's a great thing to have my title, and see my way how to work the bells. Let them clash upon me now from all the churches and convents in Genoa, I see nothing but the old London belfry I have set them in. In my mind's eye, Horatio. I like more and more my notion of making, in this little book, a great blow for the poor. Something powerful, I think

I can do, but I want to be tender too, and cheerful; as like the *Carol* in that respect as may be, and as unlike it as such a thing can be. The duration of the action will resemble it a little, but I trust to the novelty of the machinery to carry that off; and if my design be anything at all, it has a grip upon the very throat of the time." (8th of October.)

The picture I am now to give of him at work should be prefaced by a word or two that may throw light on the design he was working at. It was a large theme for so small an instrument; and the disproportion was not more characteristic of the man, than the throes of suffering and passion to be presently undergone by him for results that many men would smile at. He was bent, as he says, on striking a blow for the poor. They had always been his clients, they had never been forgotten in any of his books, but here nothing else was to be remembered. He had become, in short, terribly earnest in the matter. Several months before he left England, I had noticed in him the habit of more gravely regarding many things before passed lightly enough; the hopelessness of any true solution of either political or social problems by the ordinary Downing-street methods had been startlingly impressed on him in Carlyle's writings; and in the parliamentary talk of that day he had come to have as little faith for the putting down of any serious evil, as in a then notorious city Alderman's gabble for the putting down of suicide. The latter had stirred his indignation to its depths just before he came to Italy, and his increased opportunities of solitary reflection since had strengthened and extended it. When he came therefore to think of his new story for Christmas time, he resolved to make it a plea for the poor. He did not want it to resemble his *Carol*, but the same kind of moral was in his mind. He was to try and convert Society, as he had converted Scrooge, by showing that its happiness rested on the same foundations as those of the individual, which are mercy and charity not less than justice. Whether right or wrong in these assumptions, need not be questioned here, where facts are merely stated to render intelligible what will follow; he had not made politics at any time a study, and they were always an instinct with him rather than a science; but the instinct was wholesome and sound, and to set class against class never ceased to be as odious to him as he thought it righteous at all times

to help each to a kindlier knowledge of the other. And so, here in Italy, amid the grand surroundings of this Palazzo Peschiere, the hero of his imagination was to be a sorry old drudge of a London ticket-porter, who in his anxiety not to distrust or think hardly of the rich, has fallen into the opposite extreme of distrusting the poor.

From such distrust it is the object of the story to reclaim him; and, to the writer of it, the tale became itself of less moment than what he thus intended it to enforce. Far beyond mere vanity in authorship went the passionate zeal with which he began, and the exultation with which he finished, this task. When we met at its close, he was fresh from Venice, which had impressed him as "the wonder" and "the new sensation" of the world: but well do I remember how high above it all arose the hope that filled his mind. "Ah!" he said to me, "when I saw those places, how I thought that to leave one's hand upon the time, lastingly upon the

Trotty Veck, by Kyd [Joseph Clayton Clarke]

THE CHIMES, CHAPTER 3, THIRD QUARTER

In The Chimes, *the spirits of the bells (like those of Christmases past, present, and future in* A Christmas Carol) *redeem the poor man, Trotty Veck, who has lost his faith in the humanity of the poor:*

TROTTY'S first excess of fear was gone. But he had felt tenderly and gratefully towards the Bells, as you have seen; and when he heard himself arraigned as one who had offended them so weightily, his heart was touched with penitence and grief.

'If you knew,' said Trotty, clasping his hands earnestly—'or perhaps you do know—if you know how often you have kept me company; how often you have cheered me up when I've been low; how you were quite the plaything of my little daughter Meg (almost the only one she ever had) when first her mother died, and she and me were left alone; you won't bear malice for a hasty word!'

'Who hears in us, the Chimes, one note bespeaking disregard, or stern regard, of any hope, or joy, or pain, or sorrow, of the many-sorrowed throng; who hears us make response to any creed that gauges human passions and affections, as it gauges the amount of miserable food on which humanity may pine and wither; does us wrong. That wrong you have done us!' said the Bell.

'I have!' said Trotty. 'Oh forgive me!'

'Who hears us echo the dull vermin of the earth: the Putters Down of crushed and broken natures, formed to be raised up higher than such maggots of the time can crawl or can conceive,' pursued the Goblin of the Bell; 'who does so, does us wrong. And you have done us wrong!'

'Not meaning it,' said Trotty. 'In my ignorance. Not meaning it!'

'Lastly, and most of all,' pursued the Bell. 'Who turns his back upon the fallen and disfigured of his kind; abandons them as vile; and does not trace and track with pitying eyes the unfenced precipice by which they fell from good—grasping in their fall some tufts and shreds of that lost soil, and clinging to them still when bruised and dying in the gulf below; does wrong to Heaven and man, to time and to eternity. And you have done that wrong!'

'Spare me!' cried Trotty, falling on his knees; 'for Mercy's sake!'

time, with one tender touch for the mass of toiling people that nothing could obliterate, would be to lift oneself above the dust of all the Doges in their graves, and stand upon a giant's staircase that Sampson couldn't overthrow!" In varying forms this ambition was in all his life.

Another incident of these days will exhibit aspirations of a more solemn import that were not less part of his nature. It was depth of sentiment rather than clearness of faith which kept safe the belief on which they rested against all doubt or question of its sacredness, but every year seemed to strengthen it in him. "Let me tell you," he wrote (30th of September), "of a curious dream I had, last Monday night; and of the fragments of reality I can collect; which helped to make it up. I have had a return of

rheumatism in my back, and knotted round my waist like a girdle of pain; and had laid awake nearly all that night under the infliction, when I fell asleep and dreamed this dream. Observe that throughout I was as real, animated, and full of passion as Macready (God bless him!) in the last scene of *Macbeth*. In an indistinct place, which was quite sublime in its indistinctness, I was visited by a Spirit. I could not make out the face, nor do I recollect that I desired to do so. It wore a blue drapery, as the Madonna might in a picture by Raphael; and bore no resemblance to any one I have known except in stature. I think (but I am not sure) that I recognized the voice. Anyway, I knew it was poor Mary's spirit. I was not at all afraid, but in a great delight, so that I wept very much, and stretching out my arms to it called it 'Dear.' At this, I thought it recoiled; and I felt immediately, that not being of my gross nature, I ought not to have addressed it so familiarly. 'Forgive me!' I said. 'We poor living creatures are only able to express ourselves by looks and words. I have used the word most natural to our affections; and you know my heart.' It was so full of compassion and sorrow for me—which I knew spiritually, for, as I have said, I didn't perceive its emotions by its face—that it cut me to the heart; and I said, sobbing, 'Oh! give me some token that you have really visited me!' 'Form a wish,' it said. I thought, reasoning with myself: 'If I form a selfish wish, it will vanish.' So I hastily discarded such hopes and anxieties of my own as came into my mind, and said, 'Mrs. Hogarth is surrounded with great distresses'—observe, I never thought of saying 'your mother' as to a mortal creature—'will you extricate her?' 'Yes.' 'And her extrication is to be a certainty to me, that this has really happened?' 'Yes.' 'But answer me one other question!' I said, in an agony of entreaty lest it should leave me. 'What is the True religion?' As it paused a moment without replying, I said—Good God in such an agony of haste, lest it should go away!—'You think, as I do, that the Form of religion does not so greatly matter, if we try to do good? or,' I said, observing that it still hesitated, and was moved with the greatest compassion for me, 'perhaps the Roman Catholic is the best? perhaps it makes one think of God oftener, and believe in him more steadily?' 'For *you*,' said the Spirit, full of such heavenly tenderness for me, that I felt as if my heart would break; 'for *you*, it is the best!' Then I awoke, with the tears running down my face, and myself in exactly the condition of the dream. It was just dawn. I called up Kate, and repeated it three or four times over, that I might not unconsciously make it plainer or stronger afterwards. It was exactly this. Free from all hurry, nonsense, or confusion, whatever. Now, the strings I can gather up, leading to this, were three. The first you know, from the main subject of my last letter. The second was, that there is a great altar in our bed-room, at which some family who once inhabited this palace had mass performed in old time: and I had observed within myself, before going to bed, that there was a mark in the wall, above the sanctuary, where a religious picture used to be; and I had wondered within myself what the subject might have been, and what the face

was like. Thirdly, I had been listening to the convent bells (which ring at intervals in the night), and so had thought, no doubt, of Roman Catholic services. And yet, for all this, put the case of that wish being fulfilled by any agency in which I had no hand; and I wonder whether I should regard it as a dream, or an actual Vision!" It was perhaps natural that he should omit, from his own considerations awakened by the dream, the very first that would have risen in any mind to which his was intimately known—that it strengthens other evidences, of which there are many in his life, of his not having escaped those trying regions of reflection which most men of thought and all men of genius have at some time to pass through. In such disturbing fancies during the next year or two, I may add that the book which helped him most was the *Life of Arnold*. "I respect and reverence his memory," he wrote to me in the middle of October, in reply to my mention of what had most attracted myself in it, "beyond all expression. I must have that book. Every sentence that you quote from it is the text-book of my faith."

He kept his promise that I should hear from him while writing, and I had frequent letters when he was fairly in his work. "With my steam very much up, I find it a great trial to be so far off from you, and consequently to have no one (always excepting Kate and Georgy) to whom to expatiate on my day's work. And I want a crowded street to plunge into at night. And I want to be 'on the spot' as it were. But apart from such things, the life I lead is favourable to work." In his next letter: "I am in regular, ferocious excitement with the *Chimes*; get up at seven; have a cold bath before breakfast; and blaze away, wrathful and red-hot, until three o'clock or so; when I usually knock off (unless it rains) for the day . . . I am fierce to finish in a spirit bearing some affinity to those of truth and mercy, and to shame the cruel and the canting. I have not forgotten my catechism. 'Yes verily, and with God's help, so I will!'"

Within a week he had completed his first part, or quarter. "I send you to-day" (18th of October), "by mail, the first and longest of the four divisions. This is great for the first week, which is usually up-hill. I have kept a copy in shorthand in case of accidents. I hope to send you a parcel every Monday until the whole is done. I do not wish to influence you, but it has a great hold upon me, and has affected me, in the doing, in divers strong ways, deeply, forcibly.

ROBERT NEWSOM

DECIDED ANTI-ROMAN CATHOLIC PREJUDICE PERMEATES DICKENS'S ACCOUNTS OF ITALY AND, LATER, SWITZERLAND. THIS MYS-
TERIOUS DREAM, HOWEVER, IS A MOMENT WHERE, AS ROBERT NEWSOM HAS ARGUED, THE AMBIVALENCE OF DICKENS'S PROFESSED
REPULSION BECOMES CLEAR:

As much as Dickens disliked the enthusiasm of Evangeli-
cals and Dissenters his strongest religious antipathies were
aroused by Roman Catholicism, and unfortunately he was by no
means unusual among English Protestants in the strength of his
prejudice. For whereas the age saw a gradual but steady decline
in intolerant attitudes directed at Dissenters and Jews there were
notable Victorian outbreaks of anti-Roman Catholic feeling, especially occasioned by the Oxford Movement and the high drama of
John Henry Newman's conversion in 1845, and the so-called 'Papal
Aggression' scare of 1851, which was sparked by the decision of
Rome to reinstate a Roman Catholic hierarchy in Great Britain. In
these outbreaks Dickens was a spirited participant [. . .]

Although on good personal terms with many Catholics and
sympathetic to individuals persecuted for their Catholicism (as, for
example, in his treatment of the Gordon Riots of 1780 in *Barnaby
Rudge*) Dickens was perfectly convinced that Roman Catholicim
embodied the worst evils of the past, that it was the epitome of
ignorance and superstition, slavish obedience to priestly authority, and unwholesome asceticism—as well, of course, as the
whole gamut of cruelties represented by the Inquisition. Only
a few months before his death, in a letter to John Forster, he
referred to Roman Catholicism as 'that curse upon the world' (29
April 1870). The interpolated tale of 'The Five Sisters of York' in
Nicholas Nickleby is an early and elaborate warning against the
Catholic Church's gloomy, otherworldly call to take the veil (*NN*
6). The vanity, degredation, and cruelty of Catholicism are insistent
themes in *Pictures From Italy* (1846), where Dickens's taste for the
macabre is well satisfied by multitudes of relics and skeletons of
saints dressed up in rich vestments and jewels. The Pope's celebration of High Mass strikes him as 'droll and tawdry' (*PI* 'Rome').
There are jibes at the Oxford Movement in *Bleak House*, and
the evils of Chancery in that novel are often imagistically linked
with Roman Catholicism. More outspoken is the account of the
Reformation ('which set the people free from their slavery to the
priests') in *A Child's History of England* (1851–3). Without defending Henry VIII or the destruction of the monasteries as such (for
'the King's officers and men punished the good monks with the

bad' and 'demolished many beautiful things and many valuable
libraries' and otherwise 'did great injustice'), Dickens nonethe-
less believes 'that many of these religious establishments were
religious in nothing but name, and were crammed with lazy, indo-
lent, and sensual monks. There is no doubt that they imposed
upon the people in every possible way; that they had images
moved by wires, which they pretended were miraculously moved
by Heaven; that they had among them a whole tun measure of
teeth, all purporting to have come out of the head of one saint,
who must indeed have been a very extraordinary person with that
enormous allowance of grinders...and that all these bits of rubbish
were called Relics, and adored by the ignorant people' (*CHE* 27).
This is strong language, and while one can find similarly strong
views in the novels of Charles Kingsley and Charlotte Brontë, for
example—it exceeds Dickens's bigotry under other religious heads.

Passionate denunciations are often a sign of ambivalence, and
Dickens's repulsions are frequently compounded with attractions.
A strange dream experienced during his Italian journey in 1844
suggests this may have been the case here. In it, the spirit of his
beloved Mary Hogarth visits him, wearing 'a blue drapery as the
Madonna might in a picture by Raphael.' After begging for a sign
that the visit is real, Dickens goes on to ask, 'What is the True religion? ... You think, as I do, that the Form of religion does not so
greatly matter, if we try to do good?—or ... perhaps the Roman
Catholic is the best?' To which Mary replies, 'for you, it is the best!'
In recounting the dream to Forster, Dickens analyses the 'fragments
of reality' that 'helped to make it up', but he later receives the sign
he has asked for that the visitation was real (the extrication of his
mother-in-law from distressing circumstances) and exclaims, 'I
wonder whether I should regard it as a dream, or an actual Vision!'
(Forster 4.5) Dickens certainly never after this wandered Rome-
ward, nor wavered in his detestation of Roman Catholicism, but
the dream surely hints at a much more complicated religious character than the explicit expressions of distaste denote.

From Robert Newsom, "Roman Catholic Church,"
***The Oxford Reader's Companion to Dickens*, ed. by Paul Schlicke**
(Oxford: OUP, 2000), pp. 510–511

With the second part or quarter, after a week's interval, came announcement of the enlargement of his plan, by which he hoped better to carry out the scheme of the story, and to get, for its following part, an effect for his heroine that would increase the tragic interest. "I am still in stout heart with the tale. I think it well-timed and a good thought; and as you know I wouldn't say so to anybody else, I don't mind saying freely thus much. It has great possession of me every moment in the day; and drags me where it will. . . . If you only could have read it all at once!—But you never would have done that, anyway, for I never should have been able to keep it to myself; so that's nonsense. I hope you'll like it. I would give a hundred pounds (and think it cheap) to see you read it. . . . Never mind."

That was the first hint of an intention of which I was soon to hear more; but meanwhile, after eight more days, the third part came, with the scene from which he expected so much, and with a mention of what the writing of it had cost him. "This book (whether in the Hajji Baba sense or not I can't say, but certainly in the literal one) has made my face white in a foreign land. My cheeks, which were beginning to fill out, have sunk again; my eyes have grown immensely large; my hair is very lank; and the head inside the hair is hot and giddy. Read the scene at the end of the third part, twice. I wouldn't write it twice, for something. . . . You will see that I have substituted the name of Lilian for Jessie. It is prettier in sound, and suits my music better. I mention this, lest you should wonder who and what I mean by that name. To-morrow I shall begin afresh (starting the next part with a broad grin, and ending it with the very soul of jollity and happiness); and I hope to finish by next Monday at latest. Perhaps on Saturday. I hope you will like the little book. Since I conceived, at the beginning of the second part, what must happen in the third, I have undergone as much sorrow and agitation as if the thing were real; and have wakened up with it at night. I was obliged to lock myself in when I finished it yesterday, for my face was swollen for the time to twice its proper size, and was hugely ridiculous.". . . His letter ended abruptly. "I am going for a long walk, to clear my head. I feel that I am very shakey from work, and throw down my pen for the day. There! (That's where it fell.)" A huge blot represented it, and, as Hamlet says, the rest was silence.

Two days later, answering a letter from me that had reached in the interval, he gave sprightlier account of himself, and described a happy change in the weather. Up to this time, he protested, they had not had more than four or five clear days. All the time he had been writing they had been wild and stormy. "Wind, hail, rain, thunder and lightning. To-day," just before he sent me his last manuscript, "has been November slack-baked, the sirocco having come back; and to-night it blows great guns with a raging storm." "Weather worse," he wrote after three Mondays, "than any November English weather I have ever beheld, or any weather I have had experience of anywhere. So horrible to-day that all power has been rained and gloomed out of me. Yesterday, in pure determination to get the better of it, I walked twelve miles in mountain rain. You never saw it rain. Scotland and America are nothing to it." But now all this was over. "The weather changed on Saturday night, and has been glorious ever since. I am afraid to say more in its favour, lest it should change again." It did not. I think there were no more complainings. I heard now of autumn days with the mountain wind lovely, enjoyable, exquisite past expression. I heard of mountain walks behind the Peschiere, most beautiful and fresh, among which, and along the beds of dry rivers and torrents, he could "pelt away," in any dress, without encountering a soul but the contadini. I heard of his starting off one day after finishing work, "fifteen miles to dinner—oh my stars! at such an inn!!!" On another day, of a party to dinner at their pleasant little banker's at Quinto six miles off, to which, while the ladies drove, he was able "to walk in the sun of the middle of the day and to walk home again at night."

A visit from him to London was to be expected almost immediately! That all remonstrance would be idle, under the restless excitement his work had awakened, I well knew. It was not merely the wish he had, natural enough, to see the last proofs and the woodcuts before the day of publication, which he could not otherwise do; but it was the stronger and more eager wish, before that final launch, to have a vivider sense than letters could give him of the effect of what he had been doing. "If I come, I shall put up at Cuttris's" (then the Piazza-hotel in Covent-garden) "that I may be close to you. Don't say to anybody, except our immediate friends, that I am coming. Then I shall not be bothered. If I should preserve my present fierce writing humour, in any pass I may run to Venice, Bologna, and Florence, before I turn my face towards Lincoln's-inn-fields; and come to England by Milan and Turin."

But the close of his letter revealed more than its opening of the reason, not at once so frankly confessed, for the long winter-journey he was about to make; and if it be thought that, in printing the passage, I take a liberty with my friend, it will be found that equal liberty is taken with myself, whom it goodnaturedly caricatures; so that the reader can enjoy his laugh at either or both. "Shall I confess to you, I particularly want Carlyle above all to see it before the rest of the world, when it is done; and I should like to inflict the little story on him and on dear old gallant Macready with my own lips, and to have Stanny and the other Mac sitting by. Now, if you was a real gent, you'd get up a little circle for me, one wet evening, when I come to town: and would say, 'My boy (SIR, will you have the goodness to leave those books alone and to go downstairs—WHAT the Devil are you doing! And mind, sir, I can see nobody—do you hear? Nobody. I am particularly engaged with a gentleman from Asia)—My boy, would you give us that little Christmas book (a little Christmas book of Dickens's, Macready, which I'm anxious you should hear); and don't slur it, now, or be too fast, Dickens, please!'—I say, if you was a real gent, something to this effect might happen. I shall be under sailing orders the moment I have finished. And I shall produce myself (please God) in London on the very day you name. For one week: to the hour."

The wish was complied with, of course; and that night in Lincoln's-inn-fields led to rather memorable issues. His next letter told me the little tale was done. "Third of November, 1844. Half-past two, afternoon. Thank God! I have finished the *Chimes*. This moment. I take up my pen again to-day; to say only that much; and to add that I have had what women call 'a real good cry!'" Very genuine all this, it is hardly necessary to say. The little book thus completed was not one of his greater successes, and it raised him up some objectors; but there was that in it which more than repaid the suffering its writing cost him, and the enmity its opinions provoked; and in his own heart it had a cherished corner to the last.

He resumed his letter on the fourth of November. "Here is the brave courier measuring bits of maps with a carving-fork, and going up mountains on a teaspoon. He and I start on Wednesday for Parma, Modena, Bologna, Venice, Verona, Brescia, and Milan. Milan being within a reasonable journey from here, Kate and Georgy will come to meet me when I arrive there on my way towards England; and will bring me all letters from you. I shall be there on the 18th. . . . Now, you know my punctiwality. Frost, ice, flooded rivers, steamers, horses, passports, and custom-houses may damage it. But my design is, to walk into Cuttris's coffee-room on Sunday the 1st of December, in good time for dinner. I shall look for you at the farther table by the fire—where we generally go. . . . But the party for the night following? I know you have consented to the party. Let me see. Don't have any one, this particular night, to dinner, but let it be a summons for the special purpose at half-past 6. Carlyle, indispensable, and I should like his wife of all things: *her* judgment would be invaluable. You will ask Mac, and why not his sister? Stanny and Jerrold I should particularly wish; Edwin Landseer; Blanchard; perhaps Harness; and what say you to Fonblanque and Fox? I leave it to you. You know the effect I want to try . . . Think the *Chimes* a letter, my dear fellow, and forgive this. I will not fail to write to you on my travels. Most probably from Venice. And when I meet you (in sound health I hope) oh Heaven! what a week we will have."

---

[36] "Into which we might put your large room—I wish we could!—away in one corner, and dine without knowing it."

[37] "Very vast you will say, and very dreary; but it is not so really. The paintings are so fresh, and the proportions so agreeable to the eye, that the effect is not only cheerful but snug. . . . We are a little incommoded by applications from strangers to go over the interior. The paintings were designed by Michael Angelo, and have a great reputation. . . . Certain of these frescoes were reported officially to the Fine Art Commissioners by Wilson as the best in Italy . . . I allowed a party of priests to be shown the great hall yesterday . . . It is in perfect repair, and the doors almost shut—which is quite a miraculous circumstance. I wish you could see it, my dear F. Gracious Heavens! if you could only come back with me, wouldn't I soon flash on your astonished sight." (6th of October.)

CHAPTER 7

ITALIAN TRAVEL

1844

So it all fell out accordingly. He parted from his disconsolate wife, as he told me in his first letter from Ferrara, on Wednesday the 6th of November: left her shut up in her palace like a baron's lady in the time of the crusades; and had his first real experience of the wonders of Italy. He saw Parma, Modena, Bologna, Ferrara, Venice, Verona, and Mantua. As to all which the impressions conveyed to me in his letters have been more or less given in his published Pictures. They are charmingly expressed.

"I must not," he said, "anticipate myself. But, my dear fellow, nothing in the world that ever you have heard of Venice, is equal to the magnificent and stupendous reality.

The wildest visions of the Arabian Nights are nothing to the piazza of Saint Mark, and the first impression of the inside of the church. The gorgeous and wonderful reality of Venice is beyond the fancy of the wildest dreamer. Opium couldn't build such a place, and enchantment couldn't shadow it forth in a vision. All that I have heard of it, read of it in truth or fiction, fancied of it, is left thousands of miles behind. You know that I am liable to disappointment in such things from over-expectation, but Venice is above, beyond, out of all reach of coming near, the imagination of a man. It has never been rated high enough. It is a thing you would shed tears to see. I feel cruel not to have brought Kate and Georgy; positively cruel and base. Canaletti and Stanny, miraculous in their truth. Turner, very noble.

But the reality itself, beyond all pen or pencil. I never saw the thing before that I should be afraid to describe. But to tell what Venice is, I feel to be an impossibility. And here I sit alone, writing it: with nothing to urge me on, or goad me to that estimate, which, speaking of it to anyone I loved,

and being spoken to in return, would lead me to form. In the sober solitude of a famous inn; with the great bell of Saint Mark ringing twelve at my elbow; with three arched windows in my room (two stories high) looking down upon the grand canal and away, beyond, to where the sun went down to-night in a blaze; and thinking over again those silent speaking faces of Titian and Tintoretto; I swear (uncooled by any humbug I have seen) that Venice is *the* wonder and the new sensation of the world!"

Five days later, Sunday the 17th, he was at Lodi, from which he wrote to me that he had been, like Leigh Hunt's pig, up "all manner of streets" since he left his palazzo; that with one exception he had not on any night given up more than five hours to rest; that all the days except two had been bad ("the last two foggy as Blackfriars-bridge on Lord Mayor's day"); and that the cold had been dismal. But what cheerful, keen, observant eyes he carried everywhere; and, in the midst of new and unaccustomed scenes, and of objects and remains of art for which no previous study had prepared him.

In the same letter he described the Inns. "It is a great thing—quite a matter of course—with English travellers, to decry the Italian inns. Of course you have no comforts that you are used to in England; and travelling alone, you dine in your bedroom always. Which is opposed to our habits. But they are immeasurably better than you would suppose. The attendants are very quick; very punctual; and so obliging, if you speak to them politely, that you would be a beast not to look cheerful, and take everything pleasantly.

He closed his Lodi letter next day at Milan, whither his wife and her sister had made an eighty miles journey from Genoa, to pass a couple of days with him in Prospero's old Dukedom before he left for London. "We shall go our several ways on Thursday morning, and I am still bent on appearing at Cuttris's on Sunday the first, as if I had walked thither from Devonshire-terrace. In the meantime I shall not write to you again . . . to enhance the pleasure (if anything *can* enhance the pleasure) of our meeting . . . I am opening my arms so wide!" One more letter I had nevertheless; written at Strasburg on Monday night the 25th; to tell me I might look for him one day earlier, so rapid had been his progress. He had been in bed only once, at Friburg for

PICTURES FROM ITALY, CHAPTER 7

Dickens captures his experience of the sublimity of Venice in this reverie:

IN the luxurious wonder of so rare a dream, I took but little heed of time, and had but little understanding of its flight. But there were days and nights in it; and when the sun was high, and when the rays of lamps were crooked in the running water, I was still afloat, I thought: plashing the slippery walls and houses with the cleavings of the tide, as my black boat, borne upon it, skimmed along the streets.

Sometimes, alighting at the doors of churches and vast palaces, I wandered on, from room to room, from aisle to aisle, through labyrinths of rich altars, ancient monuments; decayed apartments where the furniture, half awful, half grotesque, was mouldering away. Pictures were there, replete with such enduring beauty and expression: with such passion, truth and power: that they seemed so many young and fresh realities among a host of spectres. I thought these, often intermingled with the old days of the city: with its beauties, tyrants, captains, patriots, merchants, counters, priests: nay, with its very stones, and bricks, and public places; all of which lived again, about me, on the walls. Then, coming down some marble staircase where the water lapped and oozed against the lower steps, I passed into my boat again, and went on in my dream.

Floating down narrow lanes, where carpenters, at work with plane and chisel in their shops, tossed the light shaving straight upon the water, where it lay like weed, or ebbed away before me in a tangled heap. Past open doors, decayed and rotten from long steeping in the wet, through which some scanty patch of vine shone green and bright, making unusual shadows on the pavement with its trembling leaves. Past quays and terraces, where women, gracefully veiled, were passing and repassing, and where idlers were reclining in the sunshine, on flag-stones and on flights of steps. Past bridges, where there were idlers too; loitering and looking over. Below stone balconies, erected at a giddy height, before the loftiest windows of the loftiest houses. Past plots of garden, theatres, shrines, prodigious

piles of architecture—Gothic—Saracenic—fanciful with all the fancies of all times and countries. Past buildings that were high, and low, and black, and white, and straight, and crooked; mean and grand, crazy and strong. Twining among a tangled lot of boats and barges, and shooting out at last into a Grand Canal! There, in the errant fancy of my dream, I saw old Shylock passing to and fro upon a bridge, all built upon with shops and humming with the tongues of men; a form I seemed to know for Desdemona's, leaned down through a latticed blind to pluck a flower. And, in the dream, I thought that Shakespeare's spirit was abroad upon the water somewhere: stealing through the city.

At night, when two votive lamps burnt before an image of the Virgin, in a gallery outside the great cathedral, near the roof, I fancied that the great piazza of the Winged Lion was a blaze of cheerful light, and that its whole arcade was thronged with people; while crowds were diverting themselves in splendid coffee-houses opening from it—which were never shut, I thought, but open all night long. When the bronze giants struck the hour of midnight on the bell, I thought the life and animation of the city were all centred here; and as I rowed away, abreast the silent quays, I only saw them dotted, here and there, with sleeping boatmen wrapped up in their cloaks, and lying at full length upon the stones.

But close about the quays and churches, palaces and prisons sucking at their walls, and welling up into the secret places of the town: crept the water always. Noiseless and watchful: coiled round and round it, in its many folds, like an old serpent: waiting for the time, I thought, when people should look down into its depths for any stone of the old city that had claimed to be its mistress.

Thus it floated me away, until I awoke in the old market-place at Verona. I have, many and many a time, thought since, of this strange Dream upon the water: half-wondering if it lie there yet, and if its name be Venice.

two or three hours, since he left Milan; and he had sledged through the snow on the top of the Simplon in the midst of prodigious cold. "I am sitting here *in* a wood-fire, and drinking brandy and water scalding hot, with a faint idea of coming warm in time. My face is at present tingling with the frost and wind, as I suppose the cymbals may, when that turbaned turk attached to the life guards' band has been newly clashing at them in St. James's-park. I am in hopes it may be the preliminary agony of returning animation."

There was certainly no want of animation when we met. I have but to write the words to bring back the eager face and figure, as they flashed upon me so suddenly this wintry Saturday night that almost before I could be conscious of his presence I felt the grasp of his hand. It is almost all I find it possible to remember of the brief, bright, meeting. Hardly did he seem to have come when he was gone. But all that the visit proposed he accomplished. He saw his little book in its final form for publication; and, to a select few brought together on Monday the 2nd of December at my house, had the opportunity of reading it aloud.

An occasion rather memorable, in which was the germ of those readings to larger audiences by which, as much as by his books, the world knew him in his later life; but of which no detail beyond the fact remains in my memory, and all are now dead who were present at it excepting only Mr. Carlyle and myself. When I expressed to Dickens, after he left us, my grief that he had had so tempestuous a journey for such brief enjoyment, he replied that the visit had been one happiness and delight to him. "I would not recall an inch of the way to or from you, if it had been twenty times as long and twenty thousand times as wintry. It was worth any travel—anything! With the soil of the road in the very grain of my cheeks, I swear I wouldn't have missed that week, that first night of our meeting, that one evening of the reading at your rooms, aye, and the second reading too, for any easily stated or conceived consideration."

He wrote from Paris, at which he had stopped on his way back to see Macready, whom an engagement to act there with Mr. Mitchell's English company had prevented from joining us in Lincoln's-inn-fields. There had been no

Dickens reading *The Chimes* to his friends at Forster's home, 58 Lincoln Inn Fields, Monday, December 2nd, 1844. Sketch by Daniel Maclise.

such frost and snow since 1829, and he gave dismal report of the city. And then came allusion to a project we had started on the night of the reading, that a private play should be got up by us on his return from Italy. He left Paris on the night of the 13th with the malle poste, which did not reach Marseilles till fifteen hours behind its time, after three days and three nights travelling over horrible roads. Then, in a confusion between the two rival packets for Genoa, he unwillingly detained one of them more than an hour from sailing; and only managed at last to get to her just as she was moving out of harbour. As he went up the side, he saw a strange sensation among the angry travellers whom he had detained so long; heard a voice exclaim "I am blarmed if it ain't DICKENS!" and stood in the centre of a group of *Five Americans*! But the pleasantest part of the story is that they were, one and all, glad to see him; that their chief man, or leader, who had met him in New York, at once introduced them all round with the remark, "Personally our countrymen, and you, can fix it friendly sir, I do expectuate;" and that, through the stormy passage to Genoa which followed, they were excellent friends. For the greater part of the time, it is true, Dickens had to keep to his cabin; but he contrived to get enjoyment out of them nevertheless.

Basilica di San Giovanni e Paolo, print after Giovanni Battista Borghesi

CHAPTER 8

LAST MONTHS IN ITALY

1845

ON THE 22ND OF DECEMBER he had resumed his ordinary Genoa life; and of a letter from Jeffrey, to whom he had dedicated his little book, he wrote as "most energetic and enthusiastic."

Of his purpose to start for the south of Italy in the middle of January, taking his wife with him, his letter the following week told me; dwelling on all he had missed, in that first Italian Christmas, of our old enjoyments of the season in England; and closing its pleasant talk with a postscript at midnight. "First of January, 1845. Many many many happy returns of the day! A life of happy years! The Baby is dressed in thunder, lightning, rain, and wind. His birth is most portentous here."

It was of ill-omen to me, one of its earliest incidents being my only brother's death; but Dickens had a friend's true helpfulness in sorrow, and a portion of what he then wrote to me I permit myself to preserve in a note [38] for what it relates of his own sad experiences and solemn beliefs and hopes. The journey southward began on the 20th January, and five days later I had a letter written from La Scala, at a little inn, "supported on low brick arches like a British haystack," the bed in their room "like a mangle," the ceiling without lath or plaster, nothing to speak of available for comfort or decency, and nothing particular to eat or drink. "But for all this I have become attached to the country and I don't care who knows it." They had left Pisa that morning and Carrara the day before: at the latter place an ovation awaiting him, the result of the zeal of our eccentric friend Fletcher, who happened to be staying there with an English marble-merchant.[39] "There is a beautiful little theatre there, built of marble; and they had it illuminated that night, in my honour. There was

really a very fair opera: but it is curious that the chorus has been always, time out of mind, made up of labourers in the quarries, who don't know a note of music, and sing entirely by ear. It was crammed to excess, and I had a great reception; a deputation waiting upon us in the box, and the orchestra turning out in a body afterwards and serenading us at Mr. Walton's." Between this and Rome they had a somewhat wild journey;[40] and before Radicofani was reached, there were disturbing rumours of bandits and even uncomfortable whispers as to their night's lodging-place. "I really began to think we might have an adventure; and as I had brought (like an ass) a bag of Napoleons with me from Genoa, I called up all the theatrical ways of letting off pistols that I could call to mind, and was the more disposed to fire them from not having any." It ended in no worse adventure, however, than a somewhat exciting dialogue with an old professional beggar at Radicofani itself, in which he was obliged to confess that he came off second-best.

The first impression of Rome was disappointing. It was the evening of the 30th of January, and the cloudy sky, dull cold rain, and muddy footways, he was prepared for; but he was not prepared for the long streets of commonplace shops and houses like Paris or any other capital, the busy people, the equipages, the ordinary walkers up and down. "It was no more my Rome, degraded and fallen and lying asleep in the sun among a heap of ruins, than Lincoln's-inn-fields is. So I really went to bed in a very indifferent humour." That all this yielded to later and worthier impressions I need hardly say; and he had never in his life, he told me afterwards, been so moved or overcome by any sight as by that of the Coliseum, "except perhaps by the first contemplation of the Falls of Niagara." He went to Naples for the interval before the holy week; and his first letter from it was to say that he had found the wonderful aspects of Rome before he left, and that for loneliness and grandeur of ruin nothing could transcend the southern side of the Campagna. But farther and farther south the weather had become worse; and for a week before his letter (the 11th of February), the only bright sky he had seen was just as the sun was coming up across the sea at Terracina. "Of which place, a beautiful one, you can get a very good idea by imagining something as totally unlike the scenery in *Fra Diavolo* as possible." He thought the bay less striking at Naples than at Genoa, the shape of the latter being more perfect in its beauty, and the smaller size enabling you to see it all at once, and feel it more like an exquisite picture. The city he conceived the greatest dislike to.[41] "The condition of the common people here is abject and shocking. I am afraid the conventional idea of the picturesque is associated with such misery and degradation that a new picturesque will have to be established as the world goes onward. Except Fondi, there is nothing on earth that I have seen so dirty as Naples. He was again at Rome on Sunday the second of March.

After the ceremonies of the holy week, of which the descriptions sent to me were reproduced in his book, he went to Florence,[42] which lived always afterwards in his memory with Venice, and with Genoa. He thought these the three great Italian cities. "There are some places here,[43]—oh Heaven how fine! I wish you could see the tower of the palazzo Vecchio as it lies before me at this moment, on the opposite bank of the Arno! But I will tell you more about it, and about all Florence, from my shady arm-chair up among the Peschiere oranges. I shall not be sorry to sit down in it again."

Before he left Florence (on the 4th of April) I heard of a "very pleasant and very merry day" at Lord Holland's; and I ought to have mentioned how much he was gratified, at Naples, by the attentions of the English Minister there, Mr. Temple, Lord Palmerston's brother, whom he described as a man supremely agreeable, with everything about him in perfect taste, and with that truest gentleman-manner which has its root in kindness and generosity of nature. He was back at home in the Peschiere on Wednesday the ninth of April. Here he continued to write to me every week, for as long as he remained, of whatever he had seen: with no definite purpose as yet, but the pleasure of interchanging with myself the impressions and emotions undergone by him.

Two more months were to finish his Italian holiday, and I do not think he enjoyed any part of it so much as its close. He had formed a real friendship for Genoa, was greatly attached to the social circle he had drawn round him there, and liked rest after his travel all the more for the little excitement of living its activities over again, week by week, in these letters to me. And so, from his "shady arm-chair

up among the Peschiere oranges," I had at regular intervals what he called his rambling talk; went over with him again all the roads he had taken; and of the more important scenes and cities, such as Venice, Rome, and Naples, received such rich filling-in to the first outlines sent, as fairly justified the title of *Pictures* finally chosen for them.

The weather all the time too had been without a flaw. "Since our return," he wrote on the 27th April, "we have had charming spring days. The garden is one grove of roses; we have left off fires; and we breakfast and dine again in the great hall, with the windows open. To-day we have rain, but rain was rather wanted I believe, so it gives offence to nobody. As far as I have had an opportunity of judging yet, the spring is the most delightful time in this country. But for all that I am looking with eagerness to the tenth of June, impatient to renew our happy old walks and old talks in dear old home."

His last letter from Genoa was written on the 7th of June, not from the Peschiere, but from a neighbouring palace, "Brignole Rosso," into which he had fled from the miseries of moving. "They are all at sixes and sevens up at the Peschiere, as you may suppose; and Roche is in a condition of tremendous excitement, engaged in settling the inventory with the house-agent, who has just told me he is the devil himself. I had been appealed to, and had contented myself with this expression of opinion. 'Signor Noli, you are an old impostor!' 'Illustrissimo,' said Signor Noli in reply, 'your servant is the devil himself: sent on earth to torture me.' I look occasionally towards the Peschiere (it is visible from this room), expecting to see one of them flying out of a window.

He came home by the Great St. Gothard, and was quite carried away by what he saw of Switzerland. The country was so divine that he should have wondered indeed if its sons and daughters had ever been other than a patriotic people. Yet, infinitely above the country he had left as he ranked it in its natural splendours, there was something more enchanting than these that he lost in leaving Italy; and he expressed this delightfully in the letter from Lucerne (14TH of June) which closes the narrative of his Italian life.

"We came over the St. Gothard, which has been open only eight days. The road is cut through the snow, and the carriage winds along a narrow path between two massive

PICTURES FROM ITALY, CHAPTER 11

*Possibly the most dramatic exploit that Dickens recounts of his Italian travels
is his expedition to the mouth of Vesuvius:*

THE rising of the moon soon afterwards, revives the flagging spirits of the bearers. Stimulating each other with their usual watchword, 'Courage, friend! It is to eat macaroni!' they press on, gallantly, for the summit.

From tingeing the top of the snow above us, with a band of light, and pouring it in a stream through the valley below, while we have been ascending in the dark, the moon soon lights the whole white mountain-side, and the broad sea down below, and tiny Naples in the distance, and every village in the country round. The whole prospect is in this lovely state, when we come upon the platform on the mountain-top—the region of Fire—an exhausted crater formed of great masses of gigantic cinders, like blocks of stone from some tremendous waterfall, burnt up; from every chink and crevice of which, hot, sulphurous smoke is pouring out: while, from another conical-shaped hill, the present crater, rising abruptly from this platform at the end, great sheets of fire are streaming forth: reddening the night with flame, blackening it with smoke, and spotting it with red-hot stones and cinders, that fly up into the air like feathers, and fall down like lead. What words can paint the gloom and grandeur of this scene!

The broken ground; the smoke; the sense of suffocation from the sulphur: the fear of falling down through the crevices in the yawning ground; the stopping, every now and then, for somebody who is missing in the dark (for the dense smoke now obscures the moon); the intolerable noise of the thirty; and the hoarse roaring of the mountain; make it a scene of such confusion, at the same time, that we reel again. But, dragging the ladies through it, and across another exhausted crater to the foot of the present Volcano, we approach close to it on the windy side, and then sit down among the hot ashes at its foot, and look up in silence; faintly estimating the action that is going on within, from its being full a hundred feet higher, at this minute, than it was six weeks ago.

There is something in the fire and roar, that generates an irresistible desire to get nearer to it. We cannot rest long, without starting off, two of us, on our hands and knees, accompanied by the head-guide, to climb to the brim of the flaming crater, and try to look in. Meanwhile, the thirty yell, as with one voice, that it is a dangerous proceeding, and call to us to come back; frightening the rest of the party out of their wits.

What with their noise, and what with the trembling of the thin crust of ground, that seems about to open underneath our feet and plunge us in the burning gulf below (which is the real danger, if there be any); and what with the flashing of the fire in our faces, and the shower of red-hot ashes that is raining down, and the choking smoke and sulphur; we may well feel giddy and irrational, like drunken men. But, we contrive to climb up to the brim, and look down, for a moment, into the Hell of boiling fire below. Then, we all three come rolling down; blackened, and singed, and scorched, and hot, and giddy: and each with his dress alight in half-a-dozen places.

snow walls, twenty feet high or more. Vast plains of snow range up the mountain-sides above the road, itself seven thousand feet above the sea; and tremendous waterfalls, hewing out arches for themselves in the vast drifts, go thundering down from precipices into deep chasms, here and there and everywhere: the blue water tearing through the white snow with an awful beauty that is most sublime. The pass itself, the mere pass over the top, is not so fine, I think, as the Simplon; and there is no plain upon the summit, for the moment it is reached the descent begins. So that the loneliness and wildness of the Simplon are not equalled *there*. But being much higher, the ascent and the descent range over a much greater space of country; and on both sides there are places of terrible grandeur, unsurpassable, I should imagine, in the world. The Devil's Bridge, terrific! The whole descent between Andermatt (where we slept on Friday night) and Altdorf, William Tell's town, which we passed through yesterday afternoon, is the highest sublimation of all you can imagine in the way of Swiss scenery. Oh God! what a beautiful country it is! How poor and shrunken, beside it, is Italy in its brightest aspect!

"If the Swiss villages look beautiful to me in winter, their summer aspect is most charming: most fascinating: most delicious. Shut in by high mountains capped with perpetual snow; and dotting a rich carpet of the softest turf, overshadowed by great trees; they seem so many little havens of refuge from the troubles and miseries of great towns. The cleanliness of the little baby-houses of inns is wonderful to those who come from Italy. But the beautiful Italian manners, the sweet language, the quick recognition of a pleasant look or cheerful word; the captivating expression of a desire to oblige in everything; are left behind the Alps. Remembering them, I sigh for the dirt again: the brick floors, bare walls, unplaistered ceilings, and broken windows."

We met at Brussels; Maclise, Jerrold, myself, and the travellers; passed a delightful week in Flanders together; and were in England at the close of June.

View of Naples, Italy, by Carl Wilhelm Gotzloff, 19th century

[38] "I feel the distance between us now, indeed. I would to Heaven, my dearest friend, that I could remind you in a manner more lively and affectionate than this dull sheet of paper can put on, that you have a Brother left. One bound to you by ties as strong as ever Nature forged. By ties never to be broken, weakened, changed in any way—but to be knotted tighter up, if that be possible, until the same end comes to them as has come to these. That end but the bright beginning of a happier union, I believe; and have never more strongly and religiously believed (and oh! Forster, with what a sore heart I have thanked God for it) than when that shadow has fallen on my own hearth, and made it cold and dark as suddenly as in the home of that poor girl you tell me of. . . . When you write to me again, the pain of this will have passed. No consolation can be so certain and so lasting to you as that softened and manly sorrow which springs up from the memory of the Dead. I read your heart as easily as if I held it in my hand, this moment. And I know—I know, my dear friend—that before the ground is green above him, you will be content that what was capable of death in him, should lie there. . . . I am glad to think it was so easy, and full of peace. What can we hope for more, when our own time comes!—The day when he visited us in our old house is as fresh to me as if it had been yesterday. I remember him as well as I remember you. . . . I have many things to say, but cannot say them now. Your attached and loving friend for life, and far, I hope, beyond it. C. D." (8th of January, 1845.)

[39] "A Yorkshireman, who talks Yorkshire Italian with the drollest and pleasantest effect; a jolly, hospitable excellent fellow; as odd yet kindly a mixture of shrewdness and simplicity as I have ever seen. He is the only Englishman in these parts who has been able to erect an English household out of Italian servants, but he has done it to admiration. It would be a capital country-house at home; and for staying in 'first-rate.' (I find myself inadvertently quoting Tom Thumb.) Mr. Walton is a man of an extraordinarily kind heart, and has a compassionate regard for Fletcher to whom his house is open as a home, which is half affecting and half ludicrous. He paid the other day a hundred pounds for him, which he knows he will never see a penny of again." C. D. to J. F. (25th of January, 1845.)

[40] "Do you think," he wrote from Ronciglione on the 29th January, "in your state room, when the fog makes your white blinds yellow, and the wind howls in the brick and mortar gulf behind that square perspective, with a middle distance of two ladder-tops and a background of Drury-lane sky—when the wind howls, I say, as if its eldest brother, born in Lincoln's-inn-fields, had gone to sea and was making a fortune on the Atlantic—at such times do you ever think of houseless Dick?"

[41] He makes no mention in his book of the pauper burial-place at Naples, to which the reference made in his letters is striking enough for preservation. "In Naples, the burying place of the poor people is a great paved yard with three hundred and sixty-five pits in it: every one covered by a square stone which is fastened down. One of these pits is opened every night in the year; the bodies of the pauper dead are collected in the city; brought out in a cart (like that I told you of at Rome); and flung in, uncoffined. Some lime is then cast down into the pit; and it is sealed up until a year is past, and its turn again comes round. Every night there is a pit opened; and every night that same pit is sealed up again, for a twelvemonth. The cart has a red lamp attached, and at about ten o'clock at night you see it glaring through the streets of Naples: stopping at the doors of hospitals and prisons, and such places, to increase its freight: and then rattling off again. Attached to the new cemetery (a very pretty one, and well kept: immeasurably better in all respects than Pere-la-Chaise) there is another similar yard, but not so large.". . . In connection with the same subject he adds: "About Naples, the dead are borne along the street, uncovered, on an open bier; which is sometimes hoisted on a sort of palanquin, covered with a cloth of scarlet and gold. This exposure of the deceased is not peculiar to that part of Italy; for about midway between Rome and Genoa we encountered a funeral procession attendant on the body of a woman, which was presented in its usual dress, to my eyes (looking from my elevated seat on the box of a travelling carriage) as if she were alive, and resting on her bed. An attendant priest was chanting lustily—and as badly as the priests invariably do. Their noise is horrible. . . ."

[42] The reader will perhaps think with me that what he noticed, on the roads in Tuscany more than in any others, of wayside crosses and religious memorials, may be worth preserving. . . . "You know that in the streets and corners of roads, there are all sorts of crosses and similar memorials to be seen in Italy. The most curious are, I think, in Tuscany. There is very seldom a figure on the cross, though there is sometimes a face; but they are remarkable for being garnished with little models in wood of every possible object that can be connected with the Saviour's death. The cock that crowed when Peter had denied his master thrice, is generally perched on the tip-top; and an ornithological phenomenon he always is. Under him is the inscription. Then, hung on to the cross-beam, are the spear, the reed with the sponge of vinegar and water at the end, the coat without seam for which the soldiers cast lots, the dice-box with which they threw for it, the hammer that drove in the nails, the pincers that pulled them out, the ladder which was set against the cross, the crown of thorns, the instrument of flagellation, the lantern with which Mary went to the tomb—I suppose; I can think of no other—and the sword with which Peter smote the high priest's servant. A perfect toyshop of little objects; repeated at every four or five miles all along the highway."

[43] Of his visit to Fiesole I have spoken in my LIFE OF LANDOR. "Ten years after Landor had lost this home, an Englishman travelling in Italy, his friend and mine, visited the neighbourhood for his sake, drove out from Florence to Fiesole, and asked his coachman which was the villa in which the Landor family lived. 'He was a dull dog, and pointed to Boccaccio's. I didn't believe him. He was so deuced ready that I knew he lied. I went up to the convent, which is on a height, and was leaning over a dwarf wall basking in the noble view over a vast range of hill and valley, when a little peasant girl came up and began to point out the localities. Ecco la villa Landora! was one of the first half-dozen sentences she spoke. My heart swelled as Landor's would have done when I looked down upon it, nestling among its olive-trees and vines, and with its upper windows (there are five above the door) open to the setting sun. Over the centre of these there is another story, set upon the housetop like a tower; and all Italy, except its sea, is melted down into the glowing landscape it commands. I plucked a leaf of ivy from the convent-garden as I looked; and here it is. 'For Landor. With my love.' So wrote Mr. Dickens to me from Florence on the and of April 1845; and when I turned over Landor's papers in the same month after an interval of exactly twenty years, the ivy-leaf was found carefully enclosed, with the letter in which I had sent it." Dickens had asked him before leaving what he would most wish to have in remembrance of Italy. "An ivy-leaf from Fiesole," said Landor.

CHAPTER 9

AGAIN IN ENGLAND

1845~1846

HIS FIRST LETTER AFTER again taking possession of Devonshire-terrace revived a subject on which opinions had been from time to time interchanged during his absence, and to which there was allusion in the agreement executed before his departure. The desire was still as strong with him as when he started *Master Humphrey's Clock* to establish a periodical, that, while relieving his own pen by enabling him to receive frequent help from other writers, might yet retain always the popularity of his name. "I really think I have an idea, and not a bad one, for the periodical. I have turned it over, the last two days, very much in my mind: and think it positively good. I incline still to weekly; price three halfpence, if possible; partly original, partly select; notices of books, notices of theatres, notices of all good things, notices of all bad ones; *Carol* philosophy, cheerful views, sharp anatomization of humbug, jolly good temper; papers always in season, pat to the time of year; and a vein of glowing, hearty, generous, mirthful, beaming reference in everything to Home, and Fireside. And I would call it, sir,—

THE CRICKET.
A cheerful creature that chirrups on the Hearth.
Natural History.

"Now, don't decide hastily till you've heard what I would do. I would come out, sir, with a prospectus on the subject of the Cricket that should put everybody in a good temper, and make such a dash at people's fenders and arm-chairs as hasn't been made for many a long day. I could approach them in a different mode under this

name, and in a more winning and immediate way, than under any other.

My objection, incident more or less to every such scheme, was the risk of losing its general advantage by making it too specially dependent on individual characteristics; but there was much in favour of the present notion, and its plan had been modified so far, in the discussions that followed, as to involve less absolute personal identification with Dickens,—when discussion, project, everything was swept away by a larger scheme, in its extent and its danger more suitable to the wild and hazardous enterprises of that prodigious year (1845) of excitement and disaster. In this more tremendous adventure, already hinted at on a previous page, we all became involved; and the chirp of the Cricket, delayed in consequence until Christmas, was heard then in circumstances quite other than those that were first intended. The change he thus announced to me about half way through the summer. "What do you think of a notion that has occurred to me in connection with our abandoned little weekly? It would be a delicate and beautiful fancy for a Christmas book, making the Cricket a little household god—silent in the wrong and sorrow of the tale, and loud again when all went well and happy." The reader will not need to be told that thus originated the story of the *Cricket on the Hearth*, a Fairy Tale of Home, which had a great popularity in the Christmas days of 1845. Its sale at the outset doubled that of both its predecessors.

"ARE we to have that play??? Have I spoken of it, ever since I came home from London, as a settled thing! I do not know if I have ever told you seriously, but I have often thought, that I should certainly have been as successful on the boards as I have been between them. I assure you, when I was on the stage at Montreal (not having played for years) I was as much astonished at the reality and ease, to myself, of what I did as if I had been another man. See how oddly things come about! When I was about twenty, and knew three or four successive years of Mathews's At Homes from sitting in the pit to hear them, I wrote to Bartley who was stage manager at Covent-garden, and told him how young I was, and exactly what I thought I could do; and that I believed I had a strong perception of character and oddity, and a natural power of reproducing in my own person what

THE CRICKET ON THE HEARTH, CHAPTER 1, CHIRP THE FIRST

The cheery fireside scenes of The Cricket on the Hearth *are darkened by John Peerybingle's suspicion (proved misplaced) of his wife's infidelity. Such a plot shows the complexity of Dickens's famous domestic "fairytales":*

THAT this song of the kettle's was a song of invitation and welcome to somebody out of doors: to somebody at that moment coming on, towards the snug small home and the crisp fire: there is no doubt whatever. Mrs. Peerybingle knew it, perfectly, as she sat musing before the hearth. It's a dark night, sang the kettle, and the rotten leaves are lying by the way; and, above, all is mist and darkness, and, below, all is mire and clay; and there's only one relief in all the sad and murky air; and I don't know that it is one, for it's nothing but a glare; of deep and angry crimson, where the sun and wind together; set a brand upon the clouds for being guilty of such weather; and the widest open country is a long dull streak of black; and there's hoar-frost on the finger-post, and thaw upon the track; and the ice it isn't water, and the water isn't free; and you couldn't say that anything is what it ought to be; but he's coming, coming, coming!—

And here, if you like, the Cricket DID chime in! with a Chirrup, Chirrup, Chirrup of such magnitude, by way of chorus; with a voice so astoundingly disproportionate to its size, as compared with the kettle; (size! you couldn't see it!) that if it had then and there burst itself like an overcharged gun, if it had fallen a victim on the spot, and chirruped its little body into fifty pieces, it would have seemed a natural and inevitable consequence, for which it had expressly laboured.

I observed in others. There must have been something in the letter that struck the authorities, for Bartley wrote to me, almost immediately, to say that they were busy getting up the *Hunchback* (so they were!) but that they would communicate with me again, in a fortnight. Punctual to the time, another letter came: with an appointment to do anything of Mathews's I pleased, before him and Charles Kemble, on a certain day at the theatre. My sister Fanny was in the secret, and was to go with me to play the songs. I was laid up, when the day came, with a terrible bad cold and an inflammation of the face; the beginning, by the bye, of that annoyance in one ear to which I am subject at this day. I wrote to say so, and added that I would resume my application next season. I made a great splash in the gallery soon afterwards; the *Chronicle* opened to me; I had a distinction in the little world of the newspaper, which made me like it; began to write; didn't want money; had never thought of the stage, but as a means of getting it; gradually left off turning my thoughts that way; and never resumed the idea. I never told you this, did I? See how near I may have been, to another sort of life.

"This was at the time when I was at Doctors' Commons as a shorthand writer for the proctors. And I recollect I wrote the letter from a little office I had there, where the answer came also. It wasn't a very good living (though not a *very* bad one), and was wearily uncertain; which made me think of the Theatre in quite a business-like way. I went to some theatre every night, with a very few exceptions, for at least three years: really studying the bills first, and going to where there was the best acting: and always to see Mathews whenever he played. I practised immensely (even such things as walking in and out, and sitting down in a chair): often four, five, six hours a day: shut up in my own room, or walking about in the fields. I prescribed to myself, too, a sort of Hamiltonian system for learning parts; and learnt a great number. I haven't even lost the habit now, for I knew my Canadian parts immediately, though they were new to me. I must have done a good deal: for, just as Macready found me out, they used to challenge me at Braham's: and Yates, who was knowing enough in those things, wasn't to be parried at all. It was just the same, that day at Keeley's, when they were getting up the *Chuzzlewit* last June."

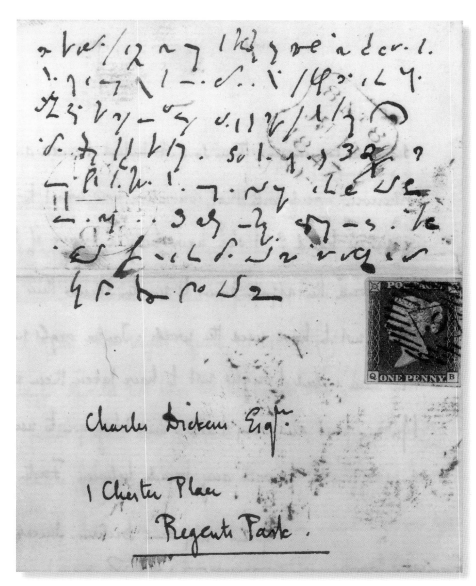

Dickens's shorthand

In less than three weeks after his return we had selected our play, cast our parts, and all but engaged our theatre; as I find by a note from my friend of the 22nd of July, in which the good natured laugh can give now no offence, since all who might have objected to it have long gone from us. Fanny Kelly, the friend of Charles Lamb, and a genuine successor to the old school of actresses in which the Mrs. Orgers and Miss Popes were bred, was not more delightful on the stage than impracticable when off, and the little theatre in Dean-street which the Duke of Devonshire's munificence had enabled her to build, and which with any ordinary good sense might handsomely have realized both its uses, as a private school for young actresses and a place of public amusement, was made useless for both by her mere whims and fancies. "Heavens! Such a scene as I have had with Miss Kelly here, this morning! She wanted us put off until the theatre should be cleaned and brushed up a bit, and she would and she would not, for she is eager to have us and alarmed when she thinks of us. By the foot of Pharaoh, it was a great scene! Especially when she choked, and had the glass of water brought. She exaggerates the importance of our occupation, dreads the least prejudice against the establishment in the minds of any of our company, says the place already has quite ruined her, and with tears in her eyes protests that any jokes at her additional expense in print would drive her mad. By the body of Caesar, the scene was incredible! It's like a preposterous dream." Something of our play is disclosed by the oaths a la Bobadil, and of our actors by "the jokes" poor Miss Kelly was afraid of. We had chosen EVERY MAN IN HIS HUMOUR, with special regard to the singleness and individuality of the "humours" portrayed in it; and our company included the leaders of a journal then in its earliest years, but already not more renowned as the most successful joker of jokes yet known in England, than famous for that exclusive use of its laughter and satire for objects the highest or most harmless which makes it still so enjoyable a companion to mirth-loving right-minded men. Maclise took earnest part with us, and was to have acted, but fell away on the eve of the rehearsals; and Stanfield, who went so far as to rehearse Downright twice, then took fright and also ran away: but Jerrold, who played Master Stephen, brought with him Lemon, who took Brainworm; Leech, to whom Master Matthew was given; A'Beckett, who had condescended to the small part of William; and Mr. Leigh, who had Oliver Cob. I played Kitely, and Bobadil fell to Dickens, who took upon him the redoubtable Captain long before he stood in his dress at the footlights; humouring the completeness of his assumption by talking and writing Bobadil, till the dullest of our party were touched and stirred to something of his own heartiness of enjoyment. One or two hints of these have been given, and I will only add to them his refusal of my wish that he should go and see some special performance of the Gamester. "Man of the House. *Gamester!* By the foot of Pharaoh, I will *not* see the *Gamester*. Man shall not force, nor horses drag, this poor gentleman-like carcass into the presence of the *Gamester*. I have said it. . . . The player Mac hath bidden me to eat and likewise drink with him, thyself, and short-necked Fox to-night—An' I go not, I am a hog, and not a soldier. But an' thou goest not—Beware citizen! Look to it. . . . Thine as thou meritest. BOBADIL (Captain). Unto Master Kitely. These."

The play was played on the 21st of September with a success that out-ran the wildest expectation; and turned our little enterprise into one of the small sensations of the day. The applause of the theatre found so loud an echo in the press, that for the time nothing else was talked about in private circles; and after a week or two we had to yield (we did not find it difficult) to a pressure of demand for more public performance in a larger theatre, by which a useful charity received important help, and its committee showed their gratitude by an entertainment to us at the Clarendon, a month or two later, when Lord Lansdowne took the chair. There was also another performance by us at the same theatre, before the close of the year, of a play by Beaumont and Fletcher. I may not farther indicate the enjoyments that attended the success, and gave always to the first of our series of performances a pre-eminently pleasant place in memory.

Graver things now claim a notice which need not be proportioned to their gravity, because, though they had an immediate effect on Dickens's fortunes, they do not otherwise form part of his story. But first let me say, he was at Broadstairs for three weeks in the autumn; we had the private play on his return; and a month later, on the 28th of October, a sixth child and fourth son, named Alfred Tennyson after his godfathers d'Orsay and Tennyson, was born in Devonshire-terrace. In the preparation for the proposed new Daily Paper to which reference has been made, he was now actively assisting, and had all but consented to the publication of his name.

I entertained at this time, for more than one powerful reason, the greatest misgiving of his intended share in the adventure. It was not fully revealed until later on what difficult terms, physical as well as mental, Dickens held the tenure of his imaginative life; but already I knew enough to doubt the wisdom of what he was at present undertaking. In all intellectual labour, his will prevailed so strongly when he fixed it on any object of desire, that what else its attainment might exact was never duly measured; and this led to frequent strain and unconscious waste of what no man could less afford to spare.

The morning after his last note I heard again. "I have been so very unwell this morning, with giddiness, and headache,

Dickens as Captain Bobadil, in Ben Johnson's play *Every Man in His Humour*, engraving after an 1846 painting by C.R. Leslie

and botheration of one sort or other, that I didn't get up till noon: and, shunning Fleet-street" (the office of the proposed new paper), "am now going for a country walk, in the course of which you will find me, if you feel disposed to come away in the carriage that goes to you with this. It is to call for a pull of the first part of the *Cricket*, and will bring you, if you like, by way of Hampstead to me, and subsequently to dinner. There is much I should like to discuss, if you can manage it. It's the loss of my walks, I suppose; but I am as giddy as if I were drunk, and can hardly see." I gave far from sufficient importance

at the time to the frequency of complaints of this kind, or to the recurrence, at almost regular periods after the year following the present, of those spasms in the side of which he has recorded an instance in the recollections of his childhood, and of which he had an attack in Genoa; but though not conscious of it to its full extent, this consideration was among those that influenced me in a determination to endeavour to turn him from what could not but be regarded as full of peril. His health, however, had no real prominence in my letter; and it is strange now to observe that it appears

Scene from Ben Jonson's *Every Man in His Humour*, oil on canvas by Daniel Maclise, painted
1847–1848

as an argument in his reply. I had simply put before him, in the strongest form, all the considerations drawn from his genius and fame that should deter him from the labour and responsibility of a daily paper, not less than from the party and political involvements incident to it; and here was the material part of the answer made. "Many thanks for your affectionate letter, which is full of generous truth. These considerations weigh with me, *heavily*: but I think I descry in these times, greater stimulants to such an effort; greater chance of some fair recognition of it; greater means of persevering in it, or retiring from it unscratched by any weapon one should care for; than at any other period. And most of all I have, sometimes, that possibility of failing health or fading popularity before me, which beckons me to such a venture when it comes within my reach."

But it does not fall within my plan to describe more than the issue, which was to be accounted so far at least fortunate that it established a journal which has advocated steadily improvements in the condition of all classes, rich as well as poor, and has been able, during late momentous occurrences, to give wider scope to its influence by its enterprise and liberality. To that result, the great writer whose name gave its earliest attraction to the *Daily News* was not enabled to contribute much; but from him it

Forster's copy of the *Every Man in His Humour* playbill. It is embellished by Daniel Maclise's sketches of Dickens and Forster in the roles of Captain Bobadil and Kitely.

certainly received the first impress of the opinions it has since consistently maintained. Its prospectus is before me in his handwriting, but it bears upon itself sufficiently the character of his hand and mind. The paper would be kept free, it said, from personal influence or party bias; and would be devoted to the advocacy of all rational and honest means by which wrong might be redressed, just rights maintained, and the happiness and welfare of society promoted.

The day for the appearance of its first number was that which was to follow Peel's speech for the repeal of the corn laws; but, brief as my allusions to the subject are, the remark should be made that even before this day came there were interruptions to the work of preparation, at one time very grave, which threw such "changes of vexation" on Dickens's personal relations to the venture as went far to destroy both his faith and his pleasure in it. No opinion need be offered as to where most of the blame lay, and it would be useless now to apportion the share that might possibly have belonged to himself; but, owing to this cause, his editorial work began with such diminished ardour that its brief continuance could not but be looked for. A little note written "before going home" at six o'clock in the morning of Wednesday the 21st of January 1846, to tell me they had "been at press three quarters of an hour, and were out before the *Times*," marks the beginning; and a note written in the night of Monday the 9th of February, "tired to death and quite worn out," to say that he had just resigned his editorial functions, describes the end. I had not been unprepared.

Front page of the first issue of *The Daily News*, January 21, 1846

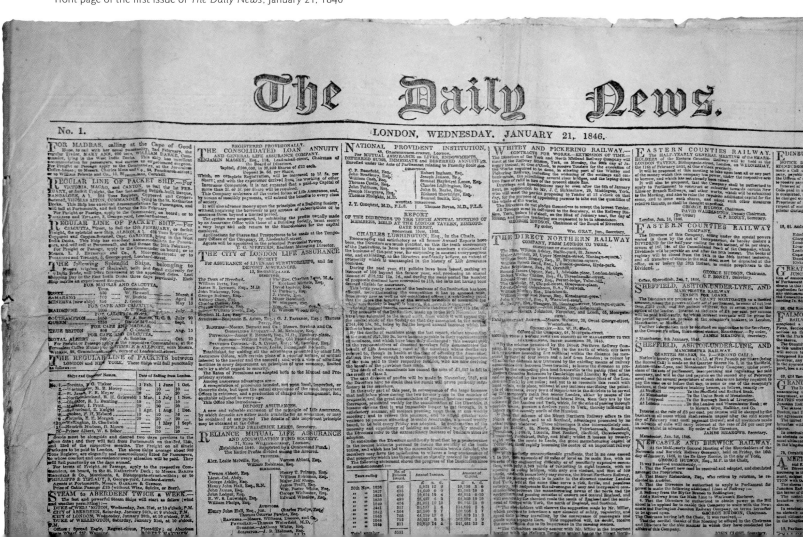

PILGRIM, VOL. 4

The Pilgrim *editors reprint the following advertisement for* The Daily News, *which "appeared in* The Morning Herald *and* Morning Chronicle *of 1 Dec, and elsewhere (but not in* The Times *said to have refused it)":*

NEW morning paper, to be commenced early in the New Year. —THE DAILY NEWS. A Morning Newspaper of Liberal Politics and thorough Independence. The leading features of the Paper may be briefly stated under the following heads:—Its City News and Commercial Intelligence, collected from the highest sources, will be scrupulously impartial, and always early. In Scientific and Business Information on every topic connected with Railways, whether in actual operation, in progress, or projected, will be found to be complete. An extensive system of Foreign Correspondence in all parts of the world has been for some time, and is now, in course of organisation. Its Parliamentary Reports, its Law Reports, and every other item of such matter, will be furnished by gentlemen of the highest qualifications. Among the writers of its Leading Articles, its Criticism on Books, the Drama, Music and the Fine Arts, are some of the most distinguished names of this time. The Literary Department of the Daily News will be under the direction of Mr Charles Dickens. The Counting-house, and Office for Advertisements intended for insertion in the Daily News, will be at No. 90 Fleet-street, London; to which place any communications for the Editor should be addressed, until the publishing offices in Whitefriars shall be completed.

To the supreme control which he had quitted, I succeeded, retaining it very reluctantly for the greater part of that weary, anxious, laborious year; but in little more than four months from the day the paper started, the whole of Dickens's connection with the *Daily News*, even that of contributing letters with his signature, had ceased. As he said in the preface to the republished *Pictures*, it was a mistake to have disturbed the old relations between himself and his readers, in so departing from his old pursuits. It had however been "a brief mistake;" the departure had been only "for a moment;" and now those pursuits were "joyfully" to be resumed in Switzerland. Upon the latter point we had much discussion; but he was bent on again removing himself from London, and his glimpse of the Swiss mountains on his coming from Italy had given him a passion to visit them again. "I don't think," he wrote to me, "I *could* shut out the paper sufficiently, here, to write well. No . . . I will write my book in Lausanne and in Genoa, and forget everything else if I can; and by living in Switzerland for the summer, and in Italy or France for the winter, I shall be saving money while I write." So therefore it was finally determined.

I may add, he took much interest in the establishment of the General Theatrical Fund, of which he remained a trustee until his death. It had originated in the fact that the Funds of the two large theatres, themselves then disused for theatrical performances, were no longer available for the ordinary members of the profession; and on the occasion of his presiding at its first dinner in April he said, very happily, that now the statue of Shakespeare outside the door of Drury-lane, as emphatically as his bust inside the church of Stratford-on-Avon, *pointed out his grave.* I am tempted also to mention as felicitous a word which I heard fall from him at one of the many private dinners that were got up in those days of parting to give him friendliest farewell. "Nothing is ever so good as it is thought," said Lord Melbourne. "And nothing so bad," interposed Dickens.

The last incidents were that he again obtained Roche for his travelling servant, and that he let his Devonshire-terrace house to Sir James Duke for twelve months, the entire proposed term of his absence. On the 30th of May they all dined with me, and on the following day left England.

TITANIA DICKENS TO BOTTOM, THE DAILY NEWS.

Come rest in this bosom, my own stricken donkey,
Nor heed *Times*, nor *Chronicle*, *Grandm'a*, nor *Flunkey*;
Though the leaders are scorned of my own *Daily News*,
I who wrote them, to read them will never refuse.

What's an editor made for, if he isn't the brick,
Circulation or none, to his paper to stick?

I know not, I ask not, if they buy you or not,
I but know that I edit thee—therefore they ought.

Thou hast called me thy "Dickens" in moments of bliss,
Still *the* Dickens I'll play with thee even in this;
While there's shot in the locker thy fortune is mine,
While a copper is left I am *thy* Valentine!

From 'Mephistopheles,' Feb. 14, 1846.

Dickens and Titania Cartoon from "Mephistopheles," "Titania Dickens to Bottom, *The Daily News*," Febuary 14, 1846

CHAPTER 10

A HOME IN SWITZERLAND

1846

HALTING ONLY AT OSTEND, Verviers, Coblentz, and Mannheim, they reached Strasburg on the seventh of June: the beauty of the weather[59] showing them the Rhine at its best. At Mayence there had come aboard their boat a German, who soon after accosted Mrs. Dickens on deck in excellent English: "Your countryman Mr. Dickens is travelling this way just now, our papers say. Do you know him, or have you passed him anywhere?" Explanations ensuing, it turned out, by one of the odd chances my friend thought himself always singled out for, that he had with him a letter of introduction to the brother of this gentleman; who then spoke to him of the popularity of his books in Germany, and of the many persons he had seen reading them in the steamboats as he came along. Dickens remarking at this how great his own vexation was not to be able himself to speak a word of German, "Oh dear! that needn't trouble you," rejoined the other; "for even in so small a town as ours, where we are mostly primitive people and have few travellers, I could make a party of at least forty people who understand and speak English as well as I do, and of at least as many more who could manage to read you in the original." His town was Worms, which Dickens afterwards saw, ". . . a fine old place, though greatly shrunken and decayed in respect of its population; with a picturesque old cathedral standing on the brink of the Rhine, and some brave old churches shut up, and so hemmed in and overgrown with vineyards that they look as if they were turning into leaves and grapes."

From Strasburg they went by rail on the 8th to Bale, from which they started for Lausanne next day, in three coaches, two horses to each, taking three days for the journey. The travellers reached the hotel Gibbon at Lausanne on the evening of Thursday the 11th of June; having been tempted as they came along to rest somewhat short of it, by a delightful glimpse of Neuchatel. "On consideration however I thought it best to come on here, in case I should find, when I begin to write, that I want streets sometimes. In which case, Geneva (which I hope would answer the purpose) is only four and twenty miles away."

He at once began house-hunting, and had two days' hard work of it. He found the greater part of those let to the English like small villas in the Regent's-park, with verandahs, glass-doors opening on lawns, and alcoves overlooking the lake and mountains. One he was tempted by, higher up the hill, "poised above the town like a ship on a high wave;" but the possible fury of its winter winds deterred him. And so he again fell back upon the very first place he had seen, Rosemont, quite a doll's house; with two pretty little salons, a dining-room, hall, and kitchen, on the ground floor; and with just enough bedrooms upstairs to leave the family one to spare. "It is beautifully situated on the hill that rises from the lake, within ten minutes' walk of this hotel, and furnished, though scantily as all here are, better than others, on account of its having being built and fitted up (the little salons in the Parisian way) by the landlady and her husband for themselves. They lived now in a smaller house like a porter's lodge, just within the gate. A portion of the grounds is farmed by a farmer, and *he* lives close by; so that, while it is secluded, it is not at all lonely." The rent was to be ten pounds a month for half a year, with reduction to eight for the second half, if he should stay so long; and the rooms and furniture were to be described to me, so that according to custom I should be quite at home there, as soon as, also according to a custom well-known, his own ingenious re-arrangements and improvements in the chairs and tables should be completed. "I shall merely observe at present therefore, that my little study is upstairs, and looks out, from two French windows opening into a balcony, on the lake and mountains; and that there are roses enough to smother the whole establishment of the *Daily News* in. Likewise,

there is a pavilion in the garden, which has but two rooms in it; in one of which, I think you shall do your work when you come. As to bowers for reading and smoking, there are as many scattered about the grounds, as there are in Chalk-farm tea-gardens. But the Rosemont bowers are really beautiful. Will you come to the bowers. . . ?"

Very pleasant were the earliest impressions of Switzerland with which this first letter closed. "The country is delightful in the extreme—as leafy, green, and shady, as England; full of deep glens, and branchy places (rather a Leigh Huntish expression), and bright with all sorts of flowers in profusion.[44] It abounds in singing birds besides—very pleasant after Italy; and the moonlight on the lake is noble. Prodigious mountains rise up from its opposite shore (it is eight or nine miles across, at this point), and the Simplon, the St. Gothard, Mont Blanc, and all the Alpine wonders are piled there, in tremendous grandeur. The cultivation is uncommonly rich and profuse. There are all manner of walks, vineyards, green lanes, cornfields, and pastures full of hay. The general neatness is as remarkable as in England. There are no priests or monks in the streets, and the people appear to be industrious and thriving. French (and very intelligible and pleasant French) seems to be the universal language. I never saw so many booksellers' shops crammed within the same space, as in the steep up-and-down streets of Lausanne."

In the heart of these things he was now to live and work for at least six months; and, as the love of nature was as much a passion with him in his intervals of leisure, as the craving for crowds and streets when he was busy with the creatures of his fancy, no man was better qualified to enjoy what was thus open to him from his little farm.

Regular evening walks of nine or ten miles were named in the same letter (22nd of June) as having been begun;[45] and thoughts of his books were already stirring in him. "An odd shadowy undefined idea is at work within me, that I could connect a great battle-field somehow with my little Christmas story. Shapeless visions of the repose and peace pervading it in after-time; with the corn

Lausanne, Switzerland, ca. 1890–1900

and grass growing over the slain, and people singing at the plough; are so perpetually floating before me, that I cannot but think there may turn out to be something good in them when I see them more plainly. . . . I want to get Four Numbers of the monthly book done here, and the Christmas book.

If all goes well, and nothing changes, and I can accomplish this by the end of November, I shall run over to you in England for a few days with a light heart, and leave Roche to move the caravan to Paris in the meanwhile. His letter ended with a promise to tell me, when next he wrote, of the small colony of English who seemed ready to give him even more than the usual welcome. Two visits had thus early been paid him by Mr. Haldimand, formerly a member of the English parliament, an accomplished man, who, with his sister Mrs. Marcet (the well-known authoress), had long made Lausanne his home. He had a very fine seat just below Rosemont, and his character and station had made him quite the little sovereign of the place. "He has founded and endowed all sorts of hospitals and institutions here, and he gives a dinner to-morrow to introduce our neighbours, whoever they are."

He found them to be happily the kind of people who rendered entirely pleasant those frank and cordial hospitalities which the charm of his personal intercourse made every one so eager to offer him. The dinner at Mr. Haldimand's was followed by dinners from the guests he met there; from an English lady married to a Swiss, Mr. and Mrs. Cerjat, clever and agreeable both, far beyond the common; from her sister wedded to an Englishman, Mr. and Mrs. Goff; and from Mr. and Mrs. Watson of Rockingham-castle in Northamptonshire, who had taken the Elysee on Dickens giving it up, and with whom, as with Mr. Haldimand, his relations continued to be very intimate long after he left Lausanne.

Only a couple of weeks, themselves not idle ones, had passed over him at Rosemont when he made a dash at the beginning of his real work; from which indeed he had only been detained so long by the non-arrival of a box dispatched from London before his own departure, containing not his proper writing materials only, but certain quaint little bronze figures that thus early stood upon his desk, and were as much needed for the easy flow of his writing as blue ink or quill pens. "I have not been idle" (28th of June) "since I have been here, though at first I was 'kept out' of the big box as you know. I had a good deal to write for Lord John about the Ragged schools. I set to work and did that. A good deal for Miss Coutts, in reference to her charitable projects. I set to work and did *that*. Half of the children's New Testament[46] to write, or pretty nearly.

I set to work and did *that*. Next I cleared off the greater part of such correspondence as I had rashly pledged myself to; and then. . . .

BEGAN DOMBEY!

I performed this feat yesterday—only wrote the first slip—but there it is, and it is a plunge straight over head and ears into the story. . . . Besides all this, I have really gone with great vigour at the French, where I find myself greatly assisted by the Italian; and am subject to two descriptions of mental fits in reference to the Christmas book: one, of the suddenest and wildest enthusiasm; one, of solitary and anxious consideration. . . . By the way, as I was unpacking the big box I took hold of a book, and said to 'Them,'— 'Now, whatever passage my thumb rests on, I shall take as having reference to my work.' It was TRISTRAM SHANDY, and opened at these words, 'What a work it is likely to turn out! Let us begin it!'"

The same letter told me that he still inclined strongly to "the field of battle notion" for his Christmas volume, but was not as yet advanced in it; being curious first to see whether its capacity seemed to strike me at all. My only objection was to his adventure of opening two stories at once, of which he did not yet see the full danger; but for the moment the Christmas fancy was laid aside, and not resumed, except in passing allusions, until after the close of August, when the first two numbers of *Dombey* were done. The interval supplied fresh illustration of his life in his new home, not without much interest; and as I have shown what a pleasant social circle, "wonderfully friendly and hospitable"to the last, already had grouped itself round him in Lausanne, and how full of "matter to be heard and learn'd" he found such institutions as its prison and blind school.

Dickens developed his battlefield idea into this powerful opening for his Christmas book of 1846:

❧

ONCE upon a time, it matters little when, and in stalwart England, it matters little where, a fierce battle was fought. It was fought upon a long summer day when the waving grass was green. Many a wild flower formed by the Almighty Hand to be a perfumed goblet for the dew, felt its enamelled cup filled high with blood that day, and shrinking dropped. Many an insect deriving its delicate colour from harmless leaves and herbs, was stained anew that day by dying men, and marked its frightened way with an unnatural track. The painted butterfly took blood into the air upon the edges of its wings. The stream ran red. The trodden ground became a quagmire, whence, from sullen pools collected in the prints of human feet and horses' hoofs, the one prevailing hue still lowered and glimmered at the sun.

Heaven keep us from a knowledge of the sights the moon beheld upon that field, when, coming up above the black line of distant rising-ground, softened and blurred at the edge by trees, she rose into the sky and looked upon the plain, strewn with upturned faces that had once at mothers' breasts sought mothers' eyes, or slumbered happily. Heaven keep us from a knowledge of the secrets whispered afterwards upon the tainted wind that blew across the scene of that day's work and that night's death and suffering! Many a lonely moon was bright upon the battle-ground, and many a star kept mournful watch upon it, and many a wind from every quarter of the earth blew over it, before the traces of the fight were worn away.

They lurked and lingered for a long time, but survived in little things; for, Nature, far above the evil passions of men, soon recovered Her serenity, and smiled upon the guilty battle-ground as she had done before, when it was innocent. The larks sang high above it; the swallows skimmed and dipped and flitted to and fro; the shadows of the flying clouds pursued each other swiftly, over grass and corn and turnip-field and wood, and over roof and church-spire in the nestling town among the trees, away into the bright distance on the borders of the sky and earth, where the red sunsets faded. Crops were sown, and grew up, and were gathered in; the stream that had been crimsoned, turned a watermill; men whistled at the plough; gleaners and haymakers were seen in quiet groups at work; sheep and oxen pastured; boys whooped and called, in fields, to scare away the birds; smoke rose from cottage chimneys; sabbath bells rang peacefully; old people lived and died; the timid creatures of the field, the simple flowers of the bush and garden, grew and withered in their destined terms: and all upon the fierce and bloody battle-ground, where thousands upon thousands had been killed in the great fight. But, there were deep green patches in the growing corn at first, that people looked at awfully. Year after year they re-appeared; and it was known that underneath those fertile spots, heaps of men and horses lay buried, indiscriminately, enriching the ground. The husbandmen who ploughed those places, shrunk from the great worms abounding there; and the sheaves they yielded, were, for many a long year, called the Battle Sheaves, and set apart; and no one ever knew a Battle Sheaf to be among the last load at a Harvest Home. For a long time, every furrow that was turned, revealed some fragments of the fight. For a long time, there were wounded trees upon the battle-ground; and scraps of hacked and broken fence and wall, where deadly struggles had been made; and trampled parts where not a leaf or blade would grow. For a long time, no village girl would dress her hair or bosom with the sweetest flower from that field of death: and after many a year had come and gone, the berries growing there, were still believed to leave too deep a stain upon the hand that plucked them.

THE LIFE OF OUR LORD, FROM CHAPTERS 1 AND 2

Dickens's retelling of the New Testament solely for his children (it was first published in 1934)
gives an insight into his Protestant humanism and, in its personal touches,
his relationships with his young family:

MY dear children, I am very anxious that you should know something about the History of Jesus Christ. For everybody ought to know about Him. No one ever lived, who was so good, so kind, so gentle, and so sorry for all people who did wrong, or were in anyway ill or miserable, as he was. And as he is now in Heaven, where we hope to go, and all to meet each other after we are dead, and there be happy always together, you never can think what a good place Heaven, is without knowing who he was and what he did. He was born, a long long time ago—nearly Two Thousand years ago—at a place called Bethlehem. His father and mother lived in a city called Nazareth, but they were forced, by business to travel to Bethlehem. His father's name was Joseph, and his mother's name was Mary. [. . .]

At the time there was a very good man indeed, named John, who was the son of a woman named Elizabeth—the cousin of Mary. And people being wicked, and violent, and killing each other, and not minding their duty towards God, John (to teach them better) went about the country, preaching to them, and entreating them to be better men and women. And because he loved them more than himself, and didn't mind himself when he was doing them good, he was poorly dressed in the skin of a camel, and ate little but some insects called locusts, which he found as he travelled: and wild honey, which the bees left in the Hollow Trees. You never saw a locust, because they belong to that country near Jerusalem, which is a great way off. So do camels, but I think you have seen a camel? At all events they are brought over here, sometimes; and if you would like to see one, I will shew you one.

---

[44] "The green woods and green shades about here," he says in another letter, "are more like Cobham in Kent, than anything we dream of at the foot of the Alpine passes."

[45] To these the heat interposed occasional difficulties. "Setting off last night" (5th of July) "at six o'clock, in accordance with my usual custom, for a long walk, I was really quite floored when I got to the top of a long steep hill leading out of the town—the same by which we entered it. I believe the great heats, however, seldom last more than a week at a time; there are always very long twilights, and very delicious evenings; and now that there is moonlight, the nights are wonderful. The peacefulness and grandeur of the Mountains and the Lake are indescribable. There comes a rush of sweet smells with the morning air too, which is quite peculiar to the country."

[46] This was an abstract, in plain language for the use of his children, of the narrative in the Four Gospels. Allusion was made, shortly after his death, to the existence of such a manuscript, with expression of a wish that it might be published; but nothing would have shocked himself so much as any suggestion of that kind. The little piece was of a peculiarly private character, written for his children, and exclusively and strictly for their use only.

CHAPTER 11

SWISS PEOPLE AND SCENERY

1846

WHAT AT ONCE HAD STRUCK HIM as the wonderful feature in the mountain scenery was its everchanging and yet unchanging aspect. It was never twice like the same thing to him. Shifting and altering, advancing and retreating, fifty times a day, it was unalterable only in its grandeur. The lake itself too had every kind of varying beauty for him. By moonlight it was indescribably solemn; and before the coming on of a storm had a strange property in it of being disturbed, while yet the sky remained clear and the evening bright, which he found to be mysterious and impressive in an especial degree. Such a storm had come among his earliest and most grateful experiences; a degree of heat worse even than in Italy[47] having disabled him at the outset for all exertion until the lightning, thunder, and rain arrived. The letter telling me this (5th July) described the fruit as so abundant in the little farm, that the trees of the orchard in front of his house were bending beneath it; spoke of a field of wheat sloping down to the side window of his dining-room as already cut and carried; and said that the roses, which the hurricane of rain had swept away, were come back lovelier and in greater numbers than ever.

The first great gathering of the Swiss peasantry which he saw was in the third week after his arrival, when a country fete was held at a place called The Signal; a deep green wood, on the sides and summit of a very high hill overlooking the town and all the country round; and he gave me very pleasant account of it. "There were various booths for eating and drinking, and the selling of trinkets and sweetmeats; and in one place there was a great circle cleared, in which the common people waltzed and polka'd, without cessation, to the music of a band. There was a great roundabout for children (oh my stars what a family were proprietors of it! A sunburnt father and mother, a humpbacked boy, a great poodle-dog possessed of all sorts of accomplishments, and a young murderer of seventeen who turned the machinery); and there were some games of chance and skill established under trees. It was very pretty. In some of the drinking booths there were parties of German peasants, twenty together perhaps, singing national drinking-songs, and making a most exhilarating and musical chorus by rattling their cups and glasses on the table and drinking them against each other, to a regular tune. You know it as a stage dodge, but the real thing is splendid. Farther down the hill, other peasants were rifle-shooting for prizes, at targets set on the other side of a deep ravine, from two to three hundred yards off. It was quite fearful to see the astonishing accuracy of their aim, and how, every time a rifle awakened the ten thousand echoes of the green glen, some men crouching behind a little wall immediately in front of the targets, sprung up with large numbers in their hands denoting where the ball had struck the bull's eye—and then in a moment disappeared again."

Meanwhile, day by day, he was steadily moving on with his first number; feeling sometimes the want of streets in an "extraordinary nervousness it would be hardly possible to describe," that would come upon him after he had been writing all day; but at all other times finding the repose of the place very favourable to industry. "I am writing slowly at first, of course" (5th of July), "but I hope I shall have finished the first number in the course of a fortnight at farthest. I have done the first chapter, and begun another. I say nothing of the merits thus far, or of the idea beyond what is known to you; because I prefer that you should come as fresh as may be upon them. I shall certainly have a great surprise for people at the end of the fourth number;[48] and I think there is a new and peculiar sort of interest, involving the necessity of a little bit of delicate treatment whereof I will expound my idea to you by and by. When I have done this number, I may take a run to Chamounix perhaps. . . . My thoughts have necessarily been called away from the Christmas book. The first *Dombey* done, I think I should fly off to that, whenever the idea presented itself vividly before me. I still cherish the Battle fancy, though it is nothing but a fancy as yet." A week later he told me that he hoped to

DOMBEY AND SON, CHAPTER 16

The surprise Dickens had in mind was the death of the eponymous son, Paul:

PAUL had never risen from his little bed. He lay there, listening to the noises in the street, quite tranquilly; not caring much how the time went, but watching it and watching everything about him with observing eyes.

When the sunbeams struck into his room through the rustling blinds, and quivered on the opposite wall like golden water, he knew that evening was coming on, and that the sky was red and beautiful. As the reflection died away, and a gloom went creeping up the wall, he watched it deepen, deepen, deepen, into night. Then he thought how the long streets were dotted with lamps, and how the peaceful stars were shining overhead. His fancy had a strange tendency to wander to the river, which he knew was flowing through the great city; and now he thought how black it was, and how deep it would look, reflecting the hosts of stars—and more than all, how steadily it rolled away to meet the sea.

As it grew later in the night, and footsteps in the street became so rare that he could hear them coming, count them as they passed, and lose them in the hollow distance, he would lie and watch the many-coloured ring about the candle, and wait patiently for day. His only trouble was, the swift and rapid river. He felt forced, sometimes, to try to stop it—to stem it with his childish hands—or choke its way with sand—and when he saw it coming on, resistless, he cried out! But a word from Florence, who was always at his side, restored him to himself; and leaning his poor head upon her breast, he told Floy of his dream, and smiled.

Sister and brother wound their arms around each other, and the golden light came streaming in, and fell upon them, locked together.

'How fast the river runs, between its green banks and the rushes, 'Floy! But it's very near the sea. I hear the waves! They always said so!'

Presently he told her the motion of the boat upon the stream was lulling him to rest. How green the banks were now, how bright the flowers growing on them, and how tall the rushes! Now the boat was out at sea, but gliding smoothly on. And now there was a shore before him. Who stood on the bank—!

He put his hands together, as he had been used to do at his prayers. He did not remove his arms to do it; but they saw him fold them so, behind her neck.

'Mama is like you, Floy. I know her by the face! But tell them that the print upon the stairs at school is not divine enough. The light about the head is shining on me as I go!'

The golden ripple on the wall came back again, and nothing else stirred in the room. The old, old fashion! The fashion that came in with our first garments, and will last unchanged until our race has run its course, and the wide firmament is rolled up like a scroll. The old, old fashion—Death!

Oh thank GOD, all who see it, for that older fashion yet, of Immortality! And look upon us, angels of young children, with regards not quite estranged, when the swift river bears us to the ocean!

'Dear me, dear me! To think,' said Miss Tox, bursting out afresh that night, as if her heart were broken, 'that Dombey and Son should be a Daughter after all!'

---

finish the first number by that day week or thereabouts, when he should then run and look for his Christmas book in the glaciers at Chamounix. His progress to this point had been pleasing him. "I think *Dombey* very strong—with great capacity in its leading idea; plenty of character that is likely to tell; and some rollicking facetiousness, to say nothing of pathos. I hope you will soon judge of it for yourself, however; and I know you will say what you think. I have been very constantly at work." Six days later I heard that he had still eight slips to write, and for a week had put off Chamounix.

But though the fourth chapter yet was incomplete, he could repress no longer the desire to write to me of what he was doing (18th of July). "I think the general idea of *Dombey* is interesting and new, and has great material in it. But I don't like to discuss it with you till you have read number one, for fear I should spoil its effect. When done—about Wednesday or Thursday, please God—I will send it in two days' posts, seven letters each day.. . . . One word more. What do you think, as a name for the Christmas book, of THE BATTLE OF LIFE? It is not a name I have conned at all, but has just occurred to me in connection with that foggy idea. If I can see my way, I think I will take it next, and clear it off. If you knew how it hangs about me, I am sure you would say

so too. It would be an immense relief to have it done, and nothing standing in the way of *Dombey*."

His next letter (written on the second of August) described his own first real experience of mountain-travel. "I begin my letter to-night, but only begin, for we returned from Chamounix in time for dinner just now, and are pretty considerably done up. We went by a mountain pass not often crossed by ladies, called the Col de Balme, where your imagination may picture Kate and Georgy on mules *for ten hours at a stretch*, riding up and down the most frightful precipices. We returned by the pass of the Tete Noire, which Talfourd knows, and which is of a different character, but astonishingly fine too. Mont Blanc, and the Valley of

Mer de Glace, Mont Blanc, Chamonix Valley, France, late 19th century

Chamounix, and the Mer de Glace, and all the wonders of that most wonderful place, are above and beyond one's wildest expectations. I cannot imagine anything in nature more stupendous or sublime. If I were to write about it now, I should quite rave—such prodigious impressions are rampant within me. . . . You may suppose that the mule-travelling is pretty primitive. Each person takes a carpet-bag strapped on the mule behind himself or herself: and that is all the baggage that can be carried. A guide, a thorough-bred mountaineer, walks all the way, leading the lady's mule; I say the lady's par excellence, in compliment to Kate; and all the rest struggle on as they please. The cavalcade stops at a lone hut for an hour and a half in the middle of the day, and lunches brilliantly on whatever it can get. Going by that Col de Balme pass, you climb up and up and up for five hours and more, and look—from a mere unguarded ledge of path on the side of the precipice—into such awful valleys, that at last you are firm in the belief that you have got above everything in the world, and that there can be nothing earthly overhead. Just as you arrive at this conclusion, a different (and oh Heaven! what a free and wonderful) air comes blowing on your face; you cross a ridge of snow; and lying before you (wholly unseen till then), towering up into the distant sky, is the vast range of Mont Blanc, with attendant mountains diminished by its majestic side into mere dwarfs tapering up into innumerable rude Gothic pinnacles; deserts of ice and snow; forests of firs on mountain sides, of no account at all in the enormous scene; villages down in the hollow, that you can shut out with a finger; waterfalls, avalanches, pyramids and towers of ice, torrents, bridges; mountain upon mountain until the very sky is blocked away, and you must look up, overhead, to see it. Good God, what a country Switzerland is, and what a concentration of it is to be beheld from that one spot!

A few days' rest after his return were interposed, before he began his second number; and until the latter has been completed, and the Christmas story taken in hand, I do not admit the reader to his full confidences about his writing. But there were other subjects that amused and engaged him up to that date, as well when he was idle as when again

Castle of Chillon, by Weber, ca. 1910

he was at work, to which expression so full of character is given in his letters that they properly find mention here.

Between the second and the ninth of August he went down one evening to the lake, five minutes after sunset, when the sky was covered with sullen black clouds reflected in the deep water, and saw the Castle of Chillon. He thought it the best deserving and least exaggerated in repute, of all the places he had seen. "The insupportable solitude and dreariness of the white walls and towers, the sluggish moat and drawbridge, and the lonely ramparts, I never saw the like of. But there is a court-yard inside; surrounded by prisons, oubliettes, and old chambers of torture; so terrifically sad, that death itself is not more sorrowful. And oh! a wicked old Grand Duke's bedchamber upstairs in the tower, with a secret staircase down into the chapel, where the bats were wheeling about; and Bonnivard's dungeon; and a horrible trap whence prisoners were cast out into the lake; and a stake all burnt and crackled up, that still stands in the torture-ante-chamber to the saloon of justice (!)—what tremendous places! Good God, the greatest mystery in all the earth, to me, is how or why the world was tolerated by its Creator through the good old times, and wasn't dashed to fragments."

On the ninth of August he wrote to me that there was to be a prodigious fete that day in Lausanne, in honour of the first anniversary of the proclamation of the New Constitution:[49] "beginning at sunrise with the firing of great guns, and twice two thousand rounds of rifles by two thousand men; proceeding at eleven o'clock with a great service, and some speechifying, in the church; and ending to-night with a great ball in the public promenade, and a general illumination of the town." The authorities had invited him to a place of honour in the ceremony; and though he did not go ("having been up till three o'clock in the morning, and being fast asleep at the appointed time"), the reply that sent his thanks expressed also his sympathy. The issue was told in two postscripts to his letter, and showed him to be so far right. "P.S. 6 o'clock afternoon. The fete going on, in great force. Not one of 'the old party' to be seen. I went down with one to the ground before dinner, and nothing would induce him to go within the barrier with me. Yet what they call a revolution was nothing but a change of government. Thirty-six thousand people, in this small canton, petitioned against the Jesuits—God knows with good reason. The Government chose to call them 'a mob.' So, to prove that they were not, they turned the Government out. I honour them for it. They are a genuine people, these Swiss. There is better metal in them than in all the stars and stripes of all the fustian banners of the so-called, and falsely called, U-nited States. They are a thorn in the sides of European despots, and a good wholesome people to live near Jesuit-ridden Kings on the brighter side of the mountains." "P.P.S. August 10th. . . . The fete went off as quietly as I supposed it would; and they danced all night."

---

[47] "When it is very hot, it is hotter than in Italy. The over-hanging roofs of the houses, and the quantity of wood employed in their construction (where they use tile and brick in Italy), render them perfect forcing-houses. The walls and floors, hot to the hand all the night through, interfere with sleep; and thunder is almost always booming and rumbling among the mountains." Besides this, though there were no mosquitoes as in Genoa, there was at first a plague of flies, more distressing even than at Albaro. "They cover everything eatable, fall into everything drinkable, stagger into the wet ink of newly-written words and make tracks on the writing paper, clog their legs in the lather on your chin while you are shaving in the morning, and drive you frantic at any time when there is daylight if you fall asleep."

[48] The life of Paul was nevertheless prolonged to the fifth number.

[49] Out of the excitements consequent on the public festivities arose some domestic inconveniences. I will give one of them. "Fanchette the cook, distracted by the forthcoming fete, madly refused to buy a duck yesterday as ordered by the Brave, and a battle of life ensued between those two powers. The Brave is of opinion that 'datter woman have went mad.' But she seems calm to-day; and I suppose won't poison the family. . . ."

CHAPTER 12

SKETCHES CHIEFLY PERSONAL

1846

Sᴏᴍᴇ sᴋᴇᴛᴄʜᴇs ꜰʀᴏᴍ ᴛʜᴇ ʟɪꜰᴇ in his pleasantest vein now claim to be taken from the same series of letters; and I will prefix one or two less important notices, for the most part personal also, that have characteristic mention of his opinions in them.

Home-politics he criticized in what he wrote on the 24th of August, much in the spirit of his last excellent remark on the Protestant and Catholic cantons; having no sympathy with the course taken by the whigs in regard to Ireland after they had defeated Peel on his coercion bill, and resumed the government. "I am perfectly appalled by the hesitation and cowardice of the whigs. To bring in that arms bill, bear the brunt of the attack upon it, take out the obnoxious clauses, still retain the bill, and finally withdraw it, seems to me the meanest and most halting way of going to work that ever was taken. I cannot believe in them. Lord John must be helpless among them. They seem somehow or other never to know what cards they hold in their hands, and to play them out blindfold. The contrast with Peel (as he was last) is, I agree with you, certainly not favourable." Referring in the same letter to the reluctance of public men of all parties to give the needful help to schemes of emigration, he ascribed it to a secret belief "in the gentle politico-economical principle that a surplus population must and ought to starve;" in which for himself he never could see anything but disaster for all who trusted to it.

It was now the opening of the second week in August; and before he finally addressed himself to the second number of *Dombey*, he had again turned a lingering look in the direction of his Christmas book. "It would be such a great relief to me to get that small story out of the way." Wisely, however, again he refrained, and went on with

Dombey; at which he had been working for a little time when he described to me (24th of August) a visit from two English travellers, of one of whom with the slightest possible touch he gives a speaking likeness.[50]

"Not having your letter as usual, I sat down to write to you on speculation yesterday, but lapsed in my uncertainty into *Dombey*, and worked at it all day. It was, as it has been since last Tuesday morning, incessantly raining regular mountain rain. After dinner, at a little after seven o'clock, I was walking up and down under the little colonnade in the garden, racking my brain about *Dombeys* and *Battles of Lives*, when two travel-stained-looking men approached, of whom one, in a very limp and melancholy straw hat, ducked, perpetually to me as he came up the walk. I couldn't make them out at all; and it wasn't till I got close up to them that I recognised A. and (in the straw hat) N. They had come from Geneva by the steamer, and taken a scrambling dinner on board. I gave them some fine Rhine wine, and cigars innumerable."

His next letter described a day's party of the Cerjats, Watsons, and Haldimands, among the neighbouring hills, which, contrary to his custom while at work, he had been unable to resist the temptation of joining. They went to a mountain-lake twelve miles off, had dinner at the public-house on the lake, and returned home by Vevay at which they rested for tea.

But the most agreeable addition to their own special circle was referred to in his first September letter, just when he was coming to the close of his second number of *Dombey*. "There are two nice girls here, the Ladies Taylor, daughters of Lord Headfort. Their mother was daughter (I think) of Sir John Stevenson, and Moore dedicated one part of the Irish Melodies to her. They inherit the musical taste, and sing very well. A proposal is on foot for our all bundling off on Tuesday (16 strong) to the top of the Great St. Bernard. But the weather seems to have broken, and the autumn rains to have set in; which I devoutly hope will break up the party. It would be a most serious hindrance to me, just now; but I have rashly promised. Do you know young Romilly? He is coming over from Geneva when 'the reading' comes off, and is a fine fellow I am told. There is not a bad little theatre here; and by way of an artificial crowd, I should certainly have got it open with an amateur company, if we were not so few that the only thing we want is the audience.". . . The "reading" named by

Little Dorrit, Book 2, chapter 1

Several years later, Dickens was to draw on his memories of this ascent in writing Little Dorrit:

———— ⚬⚬⚬ ————

IN the autumn of the year, Darkness and Night were creeping up to the highest ridges of the Alps.

It was vintage time in the valleys on the Swiss side of the Pass of the Great Saint Bernard, and along the banks of the Lake of Geneva.

The air there was charged with the scent of gathered grapes. Baskets, troughs, and tubs of grapes stood in the dim village doorways, stopped the steep and narrow village streets, and had been carrying all day along the roads and lanes. Grapes, split and crushed under foot, lay about everywhere. The child carried in a sling by the laden peasant woman toiling home, was quieted with picked-up grapes; the idiot sunning his big goitre under the leaves of the wooden chalet by the way to the Waterfall, sat Munching grapes; the breath of the cows and goats was redolent of leaves and stalks of grapes; the company in every little cabaret were eating, drinking, talking grapes. A pity that no ripe touch of this generous abundance could be given to the thin, hard, stony wine, which after all was made from the grapes!

The air had been warm and transparent through the whole of the bright day. Shining metal spires and church-roofs, distant and rarely seen, had sparkled in the view; and the snowy mountain-tops had been so clear that unaccustomed eyes, cancelling the intervening country, and slighting their rugged heights for something fabulous, would have measured them as within a few hours easy reach. Mountain-peaks of great celebrity in the valleys, whence no trace of their existence was visible sometimes for months together, had been since morning plain and near in the blue sky. And now, when it was dark below, though they seemed solemnly to recede, like spectres who were going to vanish, as the red dye of the sunset faded out of them and left them coldly white, they were yet distinctly defined in their loneliness above the mists and shadows. Seen from these solitudes, and from the Pass of the Great Saint Bernard, which was one of them, the ascending Night came up the mountain like a rising water. When it at last rose to the walls of the convent of the Great Saint Bernard, it was as if that weather-beaten structure were another Ark, and floated on the shadowy waves.

Darkness, outstripping some visitors on mules, had risen thus to the rough convent walls, when those travellers were yet climbing the mountain. As the heat of the glowing day when they had stopped to drink at the streams of melted ice and snow, was changed to the searching cold of the frosty rarefied night air at a great height, so the fresh beauty of the lower journey had yielded to barrenness and desolation. A craggy track, up which the mules in single file scrambled and turned from block to block, as though they were ascending the broken staircase of a gigantic ruin, was their way now. No trees were to be seen, nor any vegetable growth save a poor brown scrubby moss, freezing in the chinks of rock. Blackened skeleton arms of wood by the wayside pointed upward to the convent as if the ghosts of former travellers overwhelmed by the snow haunted the scene of their distress. Icicle-hung caves and cellars built for refuges from sudden storms, were like so many whispers of the perils of the place; never-resting wreaths and mazes of mist wandered about, hunted by a moaning wind; and snow, the besetting danger of the mountain, against which all its defences were taken, drifted sharply down.

The file of mules, jaded by their day's work, turned and wound slowly up the deep ascent; the foremost led by a guide on foot, in his broad-brimmed hat and round jacket, carrying a mountain staff or two upon his shoulder, with whom another guide conversed. There was no speaking among the string of riders. The sharp cold, the fatigue of the journey, and a new sensation of a catching in the breath, partly as if they had just emerged from very clear crisp water, and partly as if they had been sobbing, kept them silent.

At length, a light on the summit of the rocky staircase gleamed through the snow and mist. The guides called to the mules, the mules pricked up their drooping heads, the travellers' tongues were loosened, and in a sudden burst of slipping, climbing, jingling, clinking, and talking, they arrived at the convent door.

him was that of his first number, which was to "come off" as soon as I could get the proofs out to him; but which the changes needful to be made, and to be mentioned hereafter, still delayed. The St. Bernard holiday, which within sight of his Christmas-book labour he would fain have thrown over, came off as proposed very fortunately for the reader, who might otherwise have lost one of his pleasantest descriptions.

The last letter sent me before he fell upon his self-appointed task for Christmas, contained a delightful account of the trip to the Great St. Bernard. It was dated on the sixth of September.

"The weather obstinately clearing, we started off last Tuesday for the Great St. Bernard, returning here on Friday afternoon.

"The party consisted of eleven people and two servants—Haldimand, Mr. and Mrs. Cerjat and one daughter, Mr. and Mrs. Watson, two Ladies Taylor, Kate, Georgy, and I. We were wonderfully unanimous and cheerful; went away from here by the steamer; found at its destination a whole omnibus provided by the Brave (who went on in advance everywhere); rode therein to Bex; found two large carriages ready to take us to Martigny; slept there; and proceeded up the mountain on mules next day. Although the St. Bernard convent is, as I dare say you know, the highest inhabited spot but one in the world, the ascent is extremely gradual and uncommonly easy: really presenting no difficulties at all, until within the last league, when the ascent, lying through a place called the valley of desolation, is very awful and tremendous, and the road is rendered toilsome by scattered rocks and melting snow. The convent is a most extraordinary place, full of great vaulted passages, divided from each other with iron gratings; and presenting a series of the most astonishing little dormitories, where the windows are so small (on account of the cold and snow), that it is as much as one can do to get one's head out of them. Here we slept: supping, thirty strong, in a rambling room with a great wood-fire in it set apart for that purpose; with a grim monk, in a high black sugar-loaf hat with a great knob at the top of it, carving the dishes. At five o'clock in the morning the chapel bell rang in the dismallest way for matins: and I, lying in bed close to the chapel, and being awakened by the solemn organ and the chaunting, thought for a moment I had died in the night and passed into the unknown world.

"It is the most distinct and individual place I have seen, even in this transcendent country. But, for the Saint Bernard holy fathers and convent in themselves, I am sorry to say that they are a piece of as sheer humbug as we ever learnt to believe in, in our young days. Trashy French sentiment and the dogs (of which, by the bye, there are only three remaining) have done it all. They are a lazy set of fellows; not over fond of going out themselves; employing servants to clear the road (which has not been important or much used as a pass these hundred years); rich; and driving a good trade in Innkeeping: the convent being a common tavern in everything but the sign. No charge is made for their hospitality, to be sure; but you are shown to a box in the chapel, where everybody puts in more than could, with any show of face, be charged for the entertainment; and from this the establishment derives a right good income. As to the self-sacrifice of living up there, they are obliged to go there young, it is true, to be inured to the climate: but it is an infinitely more exciting and various life than any other convent can offer; with constant change and company through the whole summer; with a hospital for invalids down in the valley, which affords another change; and with an annual begging-journey to Geneva and this place and all the places round for one brother or other, which affords farther change. The brother who carved at our supper could speak some English, and had just had *Pickwick* given him!—what a humbug he will think me when he tries to understand it! If I had had any other book of mine with me, I would have given it him, that I might have had some chance of being intelligible. . . ."

---

[50] Ten days before there had been a visit from Mr. Ainsworth and his daughters on their way to Geneva. "I breakfasted with him at the hotel Gibbon next morning and they dined here afterwards, and we walked about all day, talking of our old days at Kensal-lodge." The same letter told me: "We had a regatta at Ouchy the other day, mainly supported by the contributions of the English handfull. It concluded with a rowing-match by women, which was very funny. I wish you could have seen Roche appear on the Lake, rowing, in an immense boat, Cook, Anne, two nurses, Katey, Mamey, Walley, Chickenstalker, and Baby; no boatmen or other degrading assistance; and all sorts of Swiss tubs splashing about them . . . Senior is coming here to-morrow, I believe, with his wife; and they talk of Brunel and his wife as on their way. We dine at Haldimand's to meet Senior—which solitary and most interesting piece of intelligence is all the news I know of . . . Take care you don't back out of your Paris engagement; but that we really do have (please God) some happy hours there. Kate, Georgy, Mamey, Katey, Charley, Walley, Chickenstalker, and Baby, send loves. . . . I am all anxiety and fever to know what we start Dombey with!"

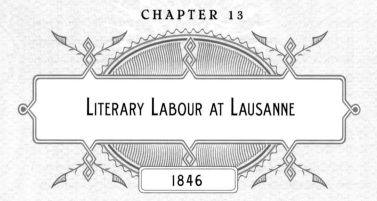

CHAPTER 13

LITERARY LABOUR AT LAUSANNE

1846

$\mathcal{S}$OMETHING OF THE OTHER SIDE of the medal has now to be presented. His letters enable us to see him amid his troubles and difficulties of writing, as faithfully as in his leisure and enjoyments; and when, to the picture thus given of Dickens's home life in Switzerland, some account has been added of the vicissitudes of literary labour undergone in the interval, as complete a representation of the man will be afforded as could be taken from any period of his career. Of the larger life whereof it is part, the Lausanne life is indeed a perfect microcosm, wanting only the London streets. At his heart there was a genuine love of nature at all times; and strange as it may seem to connect this with such forms of humorous delineation as are most identified with his genius, it is yet the literal truth that the impressions of this noble Swiss scenery were with him during the work of many subsequent years: a present and actual, though it might be seldom a directly conscious, influence. When he said afterwards, that, while writing the book on which he is now engaged, he had not seen less clearly each step of the wooden midshipman's staircase, each pew of the church in which Florence was married, or each bed in the dormitory of Doctor Blimber's establishment, because he was himself at the time by the lake of Geneva, he might as truly have said that he saw them all the more clearly even because of that circumstance. He worked his humour to its greatest results by the freedom and force of his imagination; and while the smallest or commonest objects around him were food for the one, the other might have pined or perished without additional higher aliment. Dickens had little love for Wordsworth, but he was himself an example of the truth the great poet never tired of enforcing, that Nature has subtle

helps for all who are admitted to become free of her wonders and mysteries.

Dickens proposed to himself, it will be remembered, to write at Lausanne not only the first four numbers of his larger book, but the Christmas book suggested to him by his fancy of a battle field; and reserving what is to be said of *Dombey* to a later chapter, this and its successor will deal only with what he finished as well as began in Switzerland, and will show at what cost even so much was achieved amid his other and larger engagements.

He had restless fancies and misgivings before he settled to his first notion. "I have been thinking this last day or two," he wrote on the 25th of July, "that good Christmas characters might be grown out of the idea of a man imprisoned for ten or fifteen years; his imprisonment being the gap between the people and circumstances of the first part and the altered people and circumstances of the second, and his own changed mind. Though I shall probably proceed with the Battle idea, I should like to know what you think of this one?" It was afterwards used in a modified shape for the *Tale of Two Cities*. "I shall begin the little story straightway," he wrote a few weeks later; "but I have been dimly conceiving a very ghostly and wild idea, which I suppose I must now reserve for the next Christmas book. Nous verrons. It will mature in the streets of Paris by night, as well as in London." This took ultimately the form of the *Haunted Man*, which was not written until the winter of 1848. At last I knew that his first slip was done, and that even his eager busy fancy would not turn him back again.

But other unsatisfied wants and cravings had meanwhile broken out in him, of which I heard near the close of the second number of *Dombey*. The first he had finished at the end of July; and the second, which he began on the 8th of August, he was still at work upon in the first week of September, when this remarkable announcement came to me. It was his first detailed confession of what he felt so continuously, and if that were possible even more strongly, as the years went on, that there is no single passage in any of his letters which throws such a flood of illuminative light into the portions of his life which always awaken the greatest interest. Very much that is to follow must be read by it. "You can hardly imagine," he wrote on the 30th of

"In the breathless interval" (Rosemont: 3rd of October) "between our return from Geneva and the arrival of the Talfourds (expected in an hour or two), I cannot do better than write to you. For I think you will be well pleased if I anticipate my promise, and Monday, at the same time. I have been greatly better at Geneva, though I still am made uneasy by occasional giddiness and headache: attributable, I have not the least doubt, to the absence of streets. There is an idea here, too, that people are occasionally made despondent and sluggish in their spirits by this great mass of still water, lake Leman. At any rate I have been very uncomfortable: at any rate I am, I hope, greatly better: and (lastly) at any rate I hope and trust, *now*, the Christmas book will come in due course!! I have had three very good days' work at Geneva, and trust I may finish the second part (the third is the shortest) by this day week. Whenever I finish it, I will send you the first two together. I do not think they can begin to illustrate it, until the third arrives; for it is a single minded story, as it were, and an artist should know the end: which I don't think very likely, unless he reads it." Then, after relating a superhuman effort he was making to lodge his visitors in his doll's house ("I didn't like the idea of turning them out at night. It is so dark in these lanes, and groves, when the moon's not bright"), he sketched for me what he possibly might, and really did, accomplish. He would by great effort finish the small book on the 20th; would fly to Geneva for a week to work a little at *Dombey*, if he felt "pretty sound;" in any case would finish his number three by the 10th of November; and on that day would start for Paris: "so that, instead of resting unprofitably here, I shall be using my interval of idleness to make the journey and get into a new house, and shall hope so to put a pinch of salt on the tail of the sliding number in advance. . . . I am horrified at the idea of getting the blues (and bloodshots) again." Though I did not then know how gravely ill he had been, I was fain to remind him that it was bad economy to make business out of rest itself; but I received prompt confirmation that all was falling out as he wished. The Talfourds stayed two days: "and I think they were very happy. He was in his best aspect; the manner so well known to us, not the less loveable for being laughable; and if you could have seen him going round and round the coach that brought them, as a preliminary to paying the voiturier to whom he couldn't speak, in a currency he didn't understand, you never would have forgotten it." His friends left Lausanne on the 5th; and five days later he sent me two-thirds of the manuscript of his Christmas book.

---

[51] The storm of rain formerly mentioned by him had not been repeated, but the weather had become unsettled, and he thus referred to the rainfall which made that summer so disastrous in England. "What a storm that must have been in London! I wish we could get something like it, here. . . . It is thundering while I write, but I fear it don't look black enough for a clearance. The echoes in the mountains are of such a stupendous sort, that a peal of thunder five or ten minutes long, is here the commonest of circumstances. . . ." That was early in August, and at the close of the month he wrote: "I forgot to tell you that yesterday week, at half-past 7 in the morning, we had a smart shock of an earthquake, lasting, perhaps, a quarter of a minute. It awoke me in bed. The sensation was so curious and unlike any other, that I called out at the top of my voice I was sure it was an earthquake."

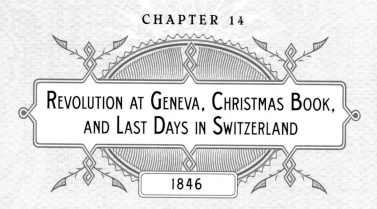

CHAPTER 14

REVOLUTION AT GENEVA, CHRISTMAS BOOK, AND LAST DAYS IN SWITZERLAND

1846

I SEND YOU IN TWELVE LETTERS, counting this as one, the first two parts (thirty-five slips) of the Christmas book. I have two present anxieties respecting it. One to know that you have received it safely; and the second to know how it strikes you. Be sure you read the first and second parts together. . . . There seems to me to be interest in it, and a pretty idea; and it is unlike the others. . . . There will be some minor points for consideration: as, the necessity for some slight alterations in one or two of the Doctor's speeches in the first part; and whether it should be called 'The Battle of Life. A Love Story'—to express both a love story in the common acceptation of the phrase, and also a story of love; with one or two other things of that sort. We can moot these by and by. I made a tremendous day's work of it yesterday and was horribly excited—so I am going to rush out, as fast as I can: being a little used up, and sick. . . . But never say die! I have been to the glass to look at my eye. Pretty bright!"

I made it brighter next day by telling him that the first number of *Dombey* had outstripped in sale the first of *Chuzzlewit* by more than twelve thousand copies; and his next letter, sending the close of his little tale, showed his need of the comfort my pleasant news had given him. "I really do not know what this story is worth. I am so floored: wanting sleep, and never having had my head free from it for this month past. I think there are some places in this last part which I may bring better together in the proof, and where a touch or two may be of service; particularly in the scene between Craggs and Michael Warden, where, as it stands, the interest seems anticipated. But I shall have the benefit of your suggestions, and my own then cooler head, I hope; and I will be very careful with the proofs, and keep them

by me as long as I can. . . I am flying to Geneva to-morrow morning." (That was on the 18th of October; and on the 20th he wrote from Geneva.) "We came here yesterday, and we shall probably remain until Katey's birthday, which is next Thursday week. I shall fall to work on number three of *Dombey* as soon as I can."

Of the "revolution" he had written to me a week before, from Lausanne; where the news had just reached them, that, upon the Federal Diet decreeing the expulsion of the Jesuits, the Roman Catholic cantons had risen against the decree, the result being that the Protestants had deposed the grand council and established a provisional government, dissolving the Catholic league. His interest in this, and prompt seizure of what really was brought into issue by the conflict, is every way characteristic of Dickens. "You will know," he wrote from Lausanne on the 11th of October, "long before you get this, all about the revolution at Geneva. There were stories of plots against the Government when I was there, but I didn't believe them; for all sorts of lies are always afloat against the radicals, and wherever there is a consul from a Catholic Power the most monstrous fictions are in perpetual circulation against them: as in this very place, where the Sardinian consul was gravely whispering the other day that a society called the Homicides had been formed, whereof the president of the council of state, the O'Connell of Switzerland and a clever fellow, was a member; who were sworn on skulls and cross-bones to exterminate men of property, and so forth. There was a great stir here, on the day of the fight in Geneva. We heard the guns (they shook this house) all day; and seven hundred men marched out of this town of Lausanne to go and help the radical party—arriving at Geneva just after it was all over.

"It is a horribly ungentlemanly thing to say here, though I *do* say it without the least reserve—but my sympathy is all with the radicals. I don't know any subject on which this indomitable people have so good a right to a strong feeling as Catholicity—if not as a religion, clearly as a means of social degradation. They know what it is. They live close to it. They have Italy beyond their mountains. They can compare the effect of the two systems at any time in their own valleys; and their dread of it, and their horror of the introduction of Catholic priests and emissaries into their towns, seems to me the most rational feeling in the world. Apart from this, you have no conception of the preposterous, insolent little aristocracy of Geneva: the most ridiculous caricature the fancy can suggest of what we know in England. I was talking to two famous gentlemen (very intelligent men) of that place, not long ago, who came over to invite me to a sort of reception there—which I declined. Really their talk about 'the people' and 'the masses,' and the necessity they would shortly be under of shooting a few of them as an example for the rest, was a kind of monstrosity one might have heard at Genoa."

Such traces of the "revolution" as he found upon his present visit to Geneva he described in writing to me from the hotel de l'Ecu on the 20th of October. "You never would suppose from the look of this town that there had been anything revolutionary going on. Over the window of my old bedroom there is a great hole made by a cannon-ball in the house-front; and two of the bridges are under repair. But these are small tokens which anything else might have brought about as well. The people are all at work. The little streets are rife with every sight and sound of industry; the place is as quiet by ten o'clock as Lincoln's-inn-fields; and the only outward and visible sign of public interest in political events is a little group at every street corner, reading a public announcement from the new Government of the forthcoming election of state-officers, in which the people are reminded of their importance as a republican institution, and desired to bear in mind their dignity in all their proceedings."

But revolutions may be small as well as their heroes, and while he thus was sending me his Gamin de Geneve I was sending him news of a sudden change in Whitefriars which had quite as vivid interest for him. Not much could be told him at first, but his curiosity instantly arose to fever pitch. "In reference to that *Daily News* revolution," he wrote from Geneva on the 26th, "I have been walking and wondering all day through a perfect Miss Burney's Vauxhall of conjectural dark walks. Heaven send you enlighten me fully on Wednesday, or number three will suffer!" Two days later he resumed, as he was beginning his journey back to Lausanne. "I am in a great state of excitement on account of your intelligence, and desperately anxious to know all about

it. I shall be put out to an unspeakable extent if I don't find your letter awaiting me. God knows there has been small comfort for either of us in the *D. N.*'s nine months." There was not much to tell then, and there is less now; but at last the discomfort was over for us both, as I had been unable to reconcile myself to a longer continuance of the service I had given in Whitefriars since he quitted it.

The time was now shortening for him at Lausanne; but before my sketches of his pleasant days there close, the little story of his Christmas book may be made complete by a few extracts from the letters that followed immediately upon the departure of the Talfourds.

Yet it was probably here the fact, as with the *Chimes*, that the serious parts were too much interwoven with the tale to render the subject altogether suitable to the old mirth-bringing season; but this had also some advantages. The story is all about two sisters, the younger of whom, Marion, sacrifices her own affection to give happiness to the elder, Grace. But Grace had already made the same sacrifice for this younger sister; life's first and hardest battle had been won by her before the incidents begin; and when she is first seen, she is busying herself to bring about her sister's marriage with Alfred Heathfield, whom she has herself loved, and whom she has kept wholly unconscious, by a quiet change in her bearing to him, of what his own still disengaged heart would certainly not have rejected. Marion, however, had earlier discovered this, though it is not until her victory over herself that Alfred knows it; and meanwhile he is become her betrothed. The sisters thus shown at the opening, one believing her love undiscovered and the other bent for the sake of that love on surrendering her own, each practising concealment and both unselfishly true, form a pretty and tender picture. The second part is intended to give to Marion's flight the character of an elopement; and so to manage this as to show her all the time unchanged to the man she is pledged to, yet flying from, was the author's difficulty. One Michael Warden is the *deus ex machina* by whom it is solved, hardly with the usual skill; but there is much art in rendering his pretensions to the hand of Marion, whose husband he becomes after an interval of years, the means of closing against him all hope of success, in the very hour when her own

THE BATTLE OF LIFE, CHAPTER 3

In this, Dickens's fourth Christmas book, there is a change of heart, characteristic of these writings,
that moves a cynical male to humanism. Rather than being brought about by supernatural elements,
this is worked through the self-sacrificing love of two sisters, Grace and Marion. They are reunited in this scene:

AH! what was that, emerging from its shadow; standing on its threshold! That figure, with its white garments rustling in the evening air; its head laid down upon her father's breast, and pressed against it to his loving heart! O God! was it a vision that came bursting from the old man's arms, and with a cry, and with a waving of its hands, and with a wild precipitation of itself upon her in its boundless love, sank down in her embrace!

'Oh, Marion, Marion! Oh, my sister! Oh, my heart's dear love! Oh, joy and happiness unutterable, so to meet again!'

It was no dream, no phantom conjured up by hope and fear, but Marion, sweet Marion! So beautiful, so happy, so unalloyed by care and trial, so elevated and exalted in her loveliness, that as the setting sun shone brightly on her upturned face, she might have been a spirit visiting the earth upon some healing mission.

Clinging to her sister, who had dropped upon a seat and bent down over her—and smiling through her tears—and kneeling, close before her, with both arms twining round her, and never turning for an instant from her face—and with the glory of the setting sun upon her brow, and with the soft tranquillity of evening gathering around them—Marion at length broke silence; her voice, so calm, low, clear, and pleasant, well-tuned to the time.

'When this was my dear home, Grace, as it will be now again—"Stay, my sweet love! A moment! O Marion, to hear you speak again.'

She could not bear the voice she loved so well, at first.

'When this was my dear home, Grace, as it will be now again, I loved him from my soul. I loved him most devotedly. I would have died for him, though I was so young. I never slighted his affection in my secret breast for one brief instant. It was far beyond all price to me. Although it is so long ago, and past, and gone, and everything is wholly changed, I could not bear to think that you, who love so well, should

think I did not truly love him once. I never loved him better, Grace, than when he left this very scene upon this very day. I never loved him better, dear one, than I did that night when I left here.'

Her sister, bending over her, could look into her face, and hold her fast.

'But he had gained, unconsciously,' said Marion, with a gentle smile, 'another heart, before I knew that I had one to give him. That heart—yours, my sister!—was so yielded up, in all its other tenderness, to me; was so devoted, and so noble; that it plucked its love away, and kept its secret from all eyes but mine—Ah! what other eyes were quickened by such tenderness and gratitude!—and was content to sacrifice itself to me. But, I knew something of its depths. I knew the struggle it had made. I knew its high, inestimable worth to him, and his appreciation of it, let him love me as he would. I knew the debt I owed it. I had its great example every day before me. What you had done for me, I knew that I could do, Grace, if I would, for you. I never laid my head down on my pillow, but I prayed with tears to do it. I never laid my head down on my pillow, but I thought of Alfred's own words on the day of his departure, and how truly he had said (for I knew that, knowing you) that there were victories gained every day, in struggling hearts, to which these fields of battle were nothing. Thinking more and more upon the great endurance cheerfully sustained, and never known or cared for, that there must be, every day and hour, in that great strife of which he spoke, my trial seemed to grow light and easy. And He who knows our hearts, my dearest, at this moment, and who knows there is no drop of bitterness or grief—of anything but unmixed happiness—in mine, enabled me to make the resolution that I never would be Alfred's wife. That he should be my brother, and your husband, if the course I took could bring that happy end to pass; but that I never would (Grace, I then loved him dearly, dearly!) be his wife!'

act might seem to be opening it to him. During the same interval Grace, believing Marion to be gone with Warden, becomes Alfred's wife; and not until reunion after six years' absence is the truth entirely known to her. The struggle, to all of them, has been filled and chastened with sorrow; but joy revisits them at its close. Hearts are not broken by the duties laid upon them; nor is life shown to be such a perishable holiday, that amidst noble sorrow and generous self-denial it must lose its capacity for happiness. The tale thus justifies its place in the Christmas series.

"I wonder whether you foresaw the end of the Christmas book! There are two or three places in which I can make it prettier, I think, by slight alterations. . . . I trust to Heaven you may like it. What an affecting story I could have made of it in one octavo volume. Oh to think of the printers transforming my kindly cynical old father into Doctor Taddler!" (28th of October.)

I had managed, as a glad surprise for him, to enlist both Stanfield and Maclise in the illustration of the story, in addition to the distinguished artists whom the publishers had engaged for it, Leech and Richard Doyle; and among the subjects contributed by Stanfield are three morsels of English landscape which had a singular charm for Dickens at the time, and seem to me still of their kind quite faultless. I may add a curious fact, never mentioned until now. In the illustration which closes the second part of the story, where the festivities to welcome the bridegroom at the top of the page contrast with the flight of the bride represented below, Leech made the mistake of supposing that Michael Warden had taken part in the elopement, and has introduced his figure with that of Marion. We did not discover this until too late for remedy, the publication having then been delayed, for these drawings, to the utmost limit; and it is highly characteristic of Dickens, and of the true regard he had for this fine artist, that, knowing the pain he must give in such circumstances by objection or complaint, he preferred to pass it silently. Nobody made remark upon it, and there the illustration still stands; but any one who reads the tale carefully will at once perceive what havoc it makes of one of the most delicate turns in it.

John Leech's illustrations to *The Battle of Life*, 1846

BOTTOM: Leech, as Forster notes, makes the error of including Michael Warden in the scene of Marion's departure.

Of the few days that remained of his Lausanne life, before he journeyed to Paris, there is not much requiring to be said. His work had continued during the whole of the month before departure to occupy him so entirely as to leave room for little else, and even occasional letters to very dear friends at home were intermitted.

Then, as the inevitable time approached, he cast about him for such comfort as the coming change might bring, to set against the sorrow of it; and began to think of Paris, "'in a less romantic and more homely contemplation of the picture,' as not wholly undesirable. I have no doubt that constant change, too, is indispensable to me when I am at work: and at times something more than a doubt will force itself upon me whether there is not something in a Swiss valley that disagrees with me. Certainly, whenever I live in Switzerland again, it shall be on the hill-top. Something of the *goitre* and *cretin* influence seems to settle on my spirits sometimes, on the lower ground.[52] How sorry, ah yes! how sorry I shall be to leave the little society nevertheless. We have been thoroughly good-humoured and agreeable together, and I'll always give a hurrah for the Swiss and Switzerland."

He had begun his third number of *Dombey* on the 26th of October, on the 4th of the following month he was half through it, on the 7th he was in the "agonies" of its last chapter, and on the 9th, one day before that proposed for its completion, all was done. This was marvellously rapid work, after what else he had undergone; but within a week, Monday the 16th being the day for departure, they were to strike their tents, and troubled and sad were the few days thus left him for preparation and farewell.

He shall himself describe how they travelled post to Paris, occupying five days. "We got through the journey charmingly, though not quite so quickly as we hoped. The children as good as usual, and even Skittles jolly to the last. (That name has long superseded Sampson Brass, by the bye. I call him so, from something skittle-playing and public-housey in his countenance.) We have been up at five every morning, and on the road before seven. We were three carriages: a sort of wagon, with a cabriolet attached, for the luggage; a ramshackle villainous old swing upon wheels (hired at Geneva), for the children; and for ourselves, that travelling chariot which I was so kind as to bring here for sale. It was very cold indeed crossing the Jura—nothing but fog and frost; but when we were out of Switzerland and across the French frontier, it became warmer, and continued so. We stopped at between six and seven each evening; had two rather queer inns, wild French country inns; but the rest good. They were three hours and a half examining the luggage at the frontier custom-house—atop of a mountain, in a hard and biting frost; where Anne and Roche had sharp work I assure you, and the latter insisted on volunteering the most astonishing and unnecessary lies about my books, for the mere pleasure of deceiving the officials. When we were out of the mountain country, we came at a good pace, but were a day late in getting to our hotel here."

They were in Paris when that was written; at the hotel Brighton; which they had reached in the evening of Friday the 20th of November.

---

[52] "I may tell you," he wrote to me from Paris at the end of November, "now it is all over. I don't know whether it was the hot summer, or the anxiety of the two new books coupled with *D. N.* remembrances and reminders, but I was in that state in Switzerland, when my spirits sunk so, I felt myself in serious danger. Yet I had little pain in my side; excepting that time at Genoa I have hardly had any since poor Mary died, when it came on so badly; and I walked my fifteen miles a day constantly, at a great pace."

CHAPTER 15

THREE MONTHS IN PARIS

1846~1847

NO MAN ENJOYED BRIEF residence in a hotel more than Dickens, but "several tons of luggage, other tons of servants, and other tons of children" are not desirable accompaniments to this kind of life; and his first day in Paris did not close before he had offered for an "eligible mansion." That same Saturday night he took a "colossal" walk about the city, of which the brilliancy and brightness almost frightened him; and among other things that attracted his notice was "rather a good book announced in a bookseller's window as Les Mysteres de Londres par Sir Trollopp. Do you know him?"

Next day he took another long walk about the streets, and lost himself fifty times. This was Sunday, and he hardly knew what to say of it, as he saw it there and then. The bitter observance of that day he always sharply resisted, believing a little rational enjoyment to be not opposed to either rest or religion; but here was another matter. "The dirty churches, and the clattering carts and waggons, and the open shops (I don't think I passed fifty shut up, in all my strollings in and out), and the work-a-day dresses and drudgeries, are not comfortable. Open theatres and so forth I am well used to, of course, by this time; but so much toil and sweat on what one would like to see, apart from religious observances, a sensible holiday, is painful."

The date of his letter was the 22nd of November, and it had three postscripts.[53] The first, "Monday afternoon," told me a house was taken; that, unless the agreement should break off on any unforeseen fight between Roche and the agent ("a French Mrs. Gamp"), I was to address him at No. 48, Rue de Courcelles, Faubourg St. Honore; and that he would merely then advert to the premises as in

his belief the "most ridiculous, extraordinary, unparalleled, and preposterous" in the whole world; being something between a baby-house, a "shades," a haunted castle, and a mad kind of clock.

His following letter nevertheless sent more, even in the form of an additional protestation that never till I saw it should the place be described. "I will merely observe that it is fifty yards long, and eighteen feet high, and that the bedrooms are exactly like opera-boxes. It has its little court-yard and garden, and porter's house, and cordon to open the door, and so forth; and is a Paris mansion in little. There is a gleam of reason in the drawing-room. Being a gentleman's house, and not one furnished to let, it has some very curious things in it; some of the oddest things you ever beheld in your life; and an infinity of easy chairs and sofas. . . . Bad weather. It is snowing hard. There is not a door or window here—but that's nothing! There's not a door or window in all Paris—that shuts."

My visit was not yet due, however, and what occupied or interested him in the interval may first be told. He had not been two days in Paris when a letter from his father made him very anxious for the health of his eldest sister. "I was going to the play (a melodrama in eight acts, five hours long), but hadn't the heart to leave home after my father's letter," he is writing on the 30th of November, "and sent Georgy and Kate by themselves. There seems to be no doubt whatever that Fanny is in a consumption." She had broken down in an attempt to sing at a party in Manchester; and subsequent examination by Sir Charles Bell's son, who was present and took much interest in her, too sadly revealed the cause. "He advised that neither she nor Burnett should be told the truth, and my father has not disclosed it. In worldly circumstances they are very comfortable, and they are very much respected. They seem to be happy together, and Burnett has a great deal of teaching. You remember my fears about her when she was in London the time of Alfred's marriage, and that I said she looked to me as if she were in a decline?" Kate took her to Elliotson, who said that her lungs were certainly not affected then. And she cried for joy. Don't you think it would be better for her to be brought up, if possible, to see Elliotson again? I am deeply, deeply grieved about it." This course was taken, and for a time there seemed room for hope; but the result will be seen. In the same letter I heard of poor Charles Sheridan, well known to us both, dying of the same terrible disease; and his chief, Lord Normanby, whose many acts of sympathy and kindness had inspired strong regard in Dickens, he had already found "as informal and good-natured as ever, but not so gay as usual, and having an anxious, haggard way with him, as if his responsibilities were more than he had bargained for." Nor, to account for this, had Dickens far to seek, when a little leisure enabled him to see something of what was passing in Paris in that last year of Louis Philippe's reign.

What first impressed him most unfavourably was a glimpse in the Champs Elysees, of the King himself coming in from the country. "There were two carriages. His was surrounded by horseguards. It went at a great pace, and he sat very far back in a corner of it, I promise you. It was strange to an Englishman to see the Prefet of Police riding on horseback some hundreds of yards in advance of the cortege, turning his head incessantly from side to side, like a figure in a Dutch clock, and scrutinizing everybody and everything, as if he suspected all the twigs in all the trees in the long avenue."

But these and other political indications were only, as they generally prove to be, the outward signs of maladies more deeply-seated. He saw almost everywhere signs of canker eating into the heart of the people themselves. "It is a wicked and detestable place, though wonderfully attractive; and there can be no better summary of it, after all, than Hogarth's unmentionable phrase." He sent me no letter that did not contribute something of observation or character. He went at first rather frequently to the Morgue, until shocked by something so repulsive that he had not courage for a long time to go back; and on that same occasion he had

View of Pont Neuf, Paris, engraving by Martens after a dagurreotype by Lerebours, 1842

Not many days after I left, all Paris was crowding to the sale of a lady of the demi-monde, Marie du Plessis, who had led the most brilliant and abandoned of lives, and left behind her the most exquisite furniture and the most voluptuous and sumptuous bijouterie. Dickens wished at one time to have pointed the moral of this life and death of which there was great talk in Paris while we were together. The disease of satiety, which only less often than hunger passes for a broken heart, had killed her. "What do you want?" asked the most famous of the Paris physicians, at a loss for her exact complaint. At last she answered: "To see my mother." She was sent for; and there came a simple Breton peasant-woman clad in the quaint garb of her province, who prayed by her bed until she died. Wonderful was the admiration and sympathy; and it culminated when Eugene Sue bought her prayer-book at the sale. Our last talk before I quitted Paris, after dinner at the Embassy, was of the danger underlying all this, and of the signs also visible everywhere of the Napoleon-worship which the Orleanists themselves had most favoured. Accident brought Dickens to England a fortnight later, when again we met together, at Gore-house, the self-contained reticent man whose doubtful inheritance was thus rapidly preparing to fall to him.

The accident was the having underwritten his number of *Dombey* by two pages, which there was not time to supply otherwise than by coming to London to write them.[55] This was done accordingly; but another greater trouble followed. He had hardly returned to Paris when his eldest son, whom I had brought to England with me and placed in the house of Doctor Major, then head-master of King's-college-school, was attacked by scarlet fever; and this closed prematurely Dickens's residence in Paris. But though he and his wife at once came over, and were followed after some days by the children and their aunt, the isolation of the little invalid could not so soon be broken through. His father at last saw him, nearly a month before the rest, in a lodging in Albany-street, where his grandmother, Mrs. Hogarth, had devoted herself to the charge of him.

An elderly charwoman employed about the place had shown so much sympathy in the family trouble, that Mrs. Hogarth specially told her of the approaching visit, and who it was that was coming to the sick-room. "Lawk ma'am!" she said. "Is the young gentleman upstairs the son of the man that put together *Dombey*?" Reassured upon this point, she explained her question by declaring that she never thought there was a man that *could* have put together *Dombey*. Being pressed farther as to what her notion was of this mystery of a *Dombey* (for it was known she could not read), it turned out that she lodged at a snuff-shop kept by a person named Douglas, where there were several other lodgers; and that on the first Monday of every month there was a Tea, and the landlord read the month's number of *Dombey*, those only of the lodgers who subscribed to the tea partaking of that luxury, but all having the benefit of the reading; and the impression produced on the old charwoman revealed itself in the remark with which she closed her account of it. "Lawk ma'am! I thought that three or four men must have put together *Dombey*!"

---

[53] It had also the mention of another floating fancy for the weekly periodical which was still and always present to his mind, and which settled down at last, as the reader knows, into *Household Words*. "As to the Review, I strongly incline to the notion of a kind of *Spectator* (Addison's)—very cheap, and pretty frequent. We must have it thoroughly discussed. It would be a great thing to found something. If the mark between a sort of *Spectator*, and a different sort of *Athenaeum*, could be well hit, my belief is that a deal might be done. But it should be something with a marked and distinctive and obvious difference, in its design, from any other existing periodical."

[54] Some smaller items of family news were in the same letter. "Mamey and Katey have come out in Parisian dresses, and look very fine. They are not proud, and send their loves. Skittles is cutting teeth, and gets cross towards evening. Frankey is smaller than ever, and Walter very large. Charley in statu quo. Everything is enormously dear. Fuel, stupendously so. In airing the house, we burnt five pounds' worth of firewood in one week!! We mix it with coal now, as we used to do in Italy, and find the fires much warmer. To warm the house thoroughly, this singular habitation requires fires on the ground floor. We burn three. . . ."

[55] ". . . I am horrified to find that the first chapter makes at least two pages less than I had supposed, and I have a terrible apprehension that there will not be copy enough for the number! As it could not possibly come out short, and as there would be no greater possibility of sending to me, in this short month, to supply what may be wanted, I decide—after the first burst of nervousness is gone—to follow this letter by Diligence to-morrow morning. The malle poste is full for days and days. I shall hope to be with you some time on Friday." C. D. to J. F., Paris: Wednesday, 17th February, 1847.

CHAPTER 16

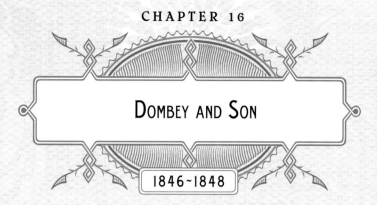

DOMBEY AND SON

1846~1848

THOUGH HIS PROPOSED NEW "book in shilling numbers" had been mentioned to me three months before he quitted England, he knew little himself at that time or when he left excepting the fact, then also named, that it was to do with Pride what its predecessor had done with Selfishness. But this limit he soon overpassed; and the succession of independent groups of character, surprising for the variety of their forms and handling, with which he enlarged and enriched his plan, went far beyond the range of the passion of Mr. Dombey and Mr. Dombey's second wife.

Obvious causes have led to grave under-estimates of this novel. Its first five numbers forced up interest and expectation so high that the rest of necessity fell short; but it is not therefore true of the general conception that thus the wine of it had been drawn, and only the lees left. In the treatment of acknowledged masterpieces in literature it not seldom occurs that the genius and the art of the master have not pulled together to the close; but if a work of imagination is to forfeit its higher meed of praise because its pace at starting has not been uniformly kept, hard measure would have to be dealt to books of undeniable greatness. Among other critical severities it was said here, that Paul died at the beginning not for any need of the story, but only to interest its readers somewhat more; and that Mr. Dombey relented at the end for just the same reason. What is now to be told will show how little ground existed for either imputation. The so-called "violent change" in the hero has more lately been revived in the notices of Mr. Taine, who says of it that *"it spoils a fine novel;"* but it will be seen that in the apparent change no unnaturalness of change was involved, and certainly the adoption of it was not a sacrifice

to "public morality." While every other portion of the tale had to submit to such varieties in development as the characters themselves entailed, the design affecting Paul and his father had been planned from the opening, and was carried without alteration to the close. And of the perfect honesty with which Dickens himself repelled such charges as those to which I have adverted, when he wrote the preface to his collected edition, remarkable proof appears in the letter to myself which accompanied the manuscript of his proposed first number. No other line of the tale had at this time been placed on paper.

Several letters now expressed his anxiety and care about the illustrations. A nervous dread of caricature in the face of his merchant-hero, had led him to indicate by a living person the type of city-gentleman he would have

Mr. Dombey and James Carker, 1848

rarely anything but disappointment; and that of all notions to connect with him the most preposterous would be that which directly reversed these relations, and depicted him as receiving from any artist the inspiration he was always vainly striving to give. An assertion of this kind was contradicted in my first volume; but it has since been repeated so explicitly, that to prevent any possible misconstruction from a silence I would fain have persisted in, the distasteful subject is again reluctantly introduced.

It originated with a literary friend of the excellent artist by whom *Oliver Twist* was illustrated from month to month, during the earlier part of its monthly issue. This gentleman stated, in a paper written and published in America, that Mr. Cruikshank, by executing the plates before opportunity was afforded him of seeing the letter press, had suggested to the writer the finest effects in his story; and to this, opposing my clear recollection of all the time the tale was in progress, it became my duty to say that within my own personal knowledge the alleged fact was not true. "Dickens," the artist is reported as saying to his admirer, "ferreted out that bundle of drawings, and when he came to the one which represents Fagin in the cell, he silently studied it for half an hour, and told me he was tempted to change the whole plot of his story. . . . I consented to let him write up to my designs; and that was the way in which Fagin, Sikes, and Nancy were created." Happily I was able to add the complete refutation of this folly by producing a letter of Dickens written at the time, which proved incontestably that the closing illustrations, including the two specially named in support of the preposterous charge, Sikes and his Dog, and Fagin in his Cell, had not even been seen by Dickens until his finished book was on the eve of appearance.

Resuming the *Dombey* letters I find him on the 30th of August in better heart about his illustrator. "I shall gladly acquiesce in whatever more changes or omissions you propose. "Browne is certainly interesting himself, and taking pains. I think the cover very good: perhaps with a little too much in it, but that is an ungrateful objection."

The second week of September brought me the finished MS. of number two; and his letter of the 3rd of October, noticing objections taken to it, gives additional touches to this picture of him while at work. The matter that engages

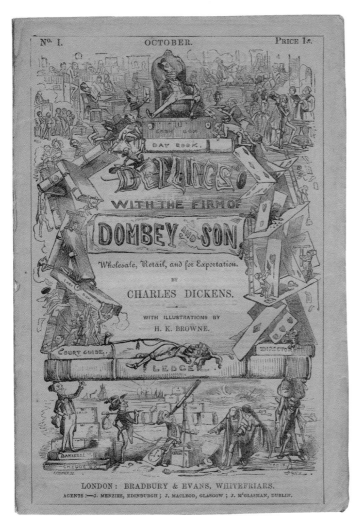

A monthly part of *Dombey and Son*, with illustrations by Hablot Knight Browne (Phiz)

had the artist select; and this is all he meant by his reiterated urgent request, "I do wish he could get a glimpse of A, for he is the very Dombey."

In itself amusing, it has now the important use of showing, once for all, in regard to Dickens's intercourse with his artists, that they certainly had not an easy time with him; that, even beyond what is ordinary between author and illustrator, his requirements were exacting; that he was apt, as he has said himself, to build up temples in his mind not always makeable with hands; that in the results he had

PREFACE TO THE CHEAP EDITION OF *DOMBEY AND SON* (1858):

Though he believed that Prefaces should be brief, advising other authors to avoid justification of their works in this form, Dickens, as Forster notes, often used the prefaces to later editions of his novels to respond to his critics. Here he defends himself from accusations of crowd-pleasing in his plotting of Dombey's reformation:

I MAKE so bold as to believe that the faculty (or the habit) of closely and carefully observing the characters of men is a rare one. I have not even found, within my experience, that the faculty (or the habit) of closely and carefully observing so much as the faces of men, is a general one by any means. The two commonest mistakes in judgement that I suppose to arise from the former default, are, the confounding of shyness with arrogance, and the not understanding that an obstinate nature exists in a permanent struggle with itself. Mr. Dombey undergoes no violent internal change, either in the book, or in life. A sense of his injustice is within him all along. The more he represses it, the more unjust he necessarily is. Internal shame and external circumstances may bring the contest to the surface in a week, or a day; but it has been a contest for years, and is only fought out then, after a long balance of victory. It is ten years since I dismissed Mr. Dombey. I have not been impatient to offer this critical remark upon him, and I offer it with some confidence. I began this book by the lake of Geneva, and went on with it for some months in France. The association between the writing and the place of writing is so curiously strong in my mind, that, at this day, although I know every stair in the little Midshipman's house, and could swear to every pew in the church in which Florence was married, or to every young gentleman's bedstead in Doctor Blimber's establishment, I yet confusedly imagine Captain Cuttle as secluding himself from Mrs. Mac Stinger among the mountains of Switzerland. Similarly, when I am reminded by any chance of what it was the waves were always saying, I wander in my fancy for a whole winter night about the streets of Paris—as I really did, with a heavy heart, on the night when my little friend and I parted company.

him is one of his masterpieces. There is nothing in all his writings more perfect, for what it shows of his best qualities, than the life and death of Paul Dombey. The comedy is admirable; nothing strained, everything hearty and wholesome in the laughter and fun; all who contribute to the mirth, Doctor Blimber and his pupils, Mr. Toots, the Chicks and the Toodles, Miss Tox and the Major, Paul and Mrs. Pipchin, up to his highest mark; and the serious scenes never falling short of it, from the death of Paul's mother in the first number, to that of Paul himself in the fifth, which, as a writer of genius with hardly exaggeration said, threw a whole nation into mourning. But see how eagerly this fine writer takes every suggestion, how little of self-esteem and self-sufficiency there is, with what a consciousness of the tendency of his humour to exuberance he surrenders what is needful to restrain it, and of what small account to him is any special piece of work in his care and his considerateness for the general design.

Meanwhile his first number had been launched with a sale that transcended his hopes and brought back *Nickleby* days. The *Dombey* success "is BRILLIANT!" he wrote to me on the 11th. "I had put before me thirty thousand as the limit of the most extreme success, saying that if we should reach that, I should be more than satisfied and more than happy; you will judge how happy I am! I read the second number here last night to the most prodigious and uproarious delight of the circle. I never saw or heard people laugh so. You will allow me to observe that my reading of the Major has merit." What a valley of the shadow he had just been passing, in his journey through his Christmas book, has before been told; but always, and with only too much eagerness, he sprang up under pressure. "A week of perfect idleness," he wrote to me on the 26th, "has brought me round again—idleness so rusting and devouring, so complete and unbroken, that I am quite glad to write the

heading of the first chapter of number three to-day. I shall be slow at first, I fear, in consequence of that change of the plan. But I allow myself nearly three weeks for the number; designing, at present, to start for Paris on the 16th of November. Full particulars in future bills. Just going to bed. I think I can make a good effect, on the after story, of the feeling created by the additional number before Paul's death." . . . Five more days confirmed him in this hope. "I am at work at *Dombey* with good speed, thank God. All well here. Country stupendously beautiful. Mountains covered with snow. Rich, crisp weather." There was one drawback. The second number had gone out to him, and the illustrations he found to be so "dreadfully bad" that they made him "curl his legs up." They made him also more than usually anxious in regard to a special illustration on which he set much store, for the part he had in hand.

". . . I hope to finish the number by next Tuesday or Wednesday. It is hard writing under these bird-of-passage circumstances, but I have no reason to complain, God knows, having come to no knot yet. . . . I hope you will like Mrs. Pipchin's establishment. It is from the life, and I was there—I don't suppose I was eight years old; but I remember it all as well, and certainly understood it as well, as I do now. We should be devilish sharp in what we do to children. I thought of that passage in my small life, at Geneva. *Shall I leave you my life in MS. when I die? There are some things in it that would touch you very much, and that might go on the same shelf with the first volume of Holcroft's.*"

On the Monday week after that was written he left Lausanne for Paris, and my first letter to him there was to say that he had overwritten his number by three pages. "I have taken out about two pages and a half," he wrote by return from the hotel Brighton, "and the rest I must ask you to take out with the assurance that you will satisfy me in whatever you do. The sale, prodigious indeed! I am very thankful."

And then came something of a damper to his spirits, as he thus toiled along. He saw public allusion made to a review that had appeared in the *Times* of his Christmas book, and it momentarily touched what he too truly called his morbid susceptibility to exasperation. "I see that the

Left: Frontispiece to *Dombey and Son,* by W. Rainey

'good old Times' are again at issue with the inimitable B. Another touch of a blunt razor on B.'s nervous system.— Friday morning. Inimitable very mouldy and dull. Hardly able to work. Dreamed of *Timeses* all night. Disposed to go to New Zealand and start a magazine."

But soon he sprang up, as usual, more erect for the moment's pressure; and after not many days I heard that the number was as good as done. His letter was very brief, and told me that he had worked so hard the day before (Tuesday, the 12th of January), and so incessantly, night as well as morning, that he had breakfasted and lain in bed till midday. "I hope I have been very successful." There was but one small chapter more to write, in which he and his little friend were to part company for ever; and the greater part of the night of the day on which it was written, Thursday the 14th, he was wandering desolate and sad about the streets of Paris. I arrived there the following morning on my visit; and as I alighted from the malle-poste, a little before eight o'clock, found him waiting for me at the gate of the post-office bureau.

I left him on the 2nd of February with his writing-table in readiness for number six; but on the 4th, enclosing me subjects for illustration, he told me he was "not under weigh yet. Can't begin." Then, on the 7th, his birthday, he wrote to warn me he should be late. "Could not begin before Thursday last, and find it very difficult indeed to fall into the new vein of the story. I see no hope of finishing before the 16th at the earliest, in which case the steam will have to be put on for this short month. But it can't be helped. Perhaps I shall get a rush of inspiration. . . . I will send the chapters as I write them, and you must not wait, of course, for me to read the end in type. To transfer to Florence, instantly, all the previous interest, is what I am aiming at. For that, all sorts of other points must be thrown aside in this number. . . . We are going to dine again at the Embassy to-day—with a very ill will on my part. All well. I hope when I write next I shall report myself in better cue. . . . I have had a tremendous outpouring from Jeffrey about the last part, which he thinks the best thing past, present, or to come."[56] Three more days and I had the MS. of the completed chapter, nearly half the number (in which as printed it stands second, the small middle chapter having

Five ~~five~~ chapters.

THE STORY

OF

LITTLE DOMBEY.

I.

his Wife's

Rich MR DOMBEY sat in the corner of ~~the~~ darkened ~~room bedchamber~~
~~rich~~ rick Mr Dombeys
in the great arm-chair by the bedside, and Son lay
tucked up warm in a little basket ~~bedstead~~, care-
placed
fully ~~disposed~~ on a low settee ~~immediately~~ in front
of the fire and close to it, as if his constitution
were analogous to that of a muffin, and it was
essential to toast him brown while he was very
new.

Rich MR Dombey was about eight-and-forty years of age.
Son about eight-and-forty minutes. *N* Dombey
was rather bald, rather red, and ~~though a hand~~ *rather*
~~some well made many too~~ stern and pompous in

B

Rich Mr Dombey's son

"The Story of Little Dombey." Dickens's edited reading copy. In 1858, a decade after publishing *Dombey and Son*, Dickens reworked the character of Paul Dombey as a tear-jerking piece for his public readings. It was the first reading to be taken from a novel.

been transposed to its place). "I have taken the most prodigious pains with it; the difficulty, immediately after Paul's death, being very great. May you like it! My head aches over it now (I write at one o'clock in the morning), and I am strange to it. . . . I think I shall manage Dombey's second wife (introduced by the Major), and the beginning of that business in his present state of mind, very naturally and well. . . . Paul's death has amazed Paris. All sorts of people are open-mouthed with admiration."

I shall not farther dwell upon it in any detail. It extended over the whole of the year; and the interest and passion of it, when to himself both became centred in Florence and in Edith Dombey, took stronger hold of him, and more powerfully affected him, than had been the case in any of his previous writings, I think, excepting only the close of the Old Curiosity Shop.

Edith's worst qualities are but the perversion of what should have been her best. A false education in her, and a tyrant passion in her husband, make them other than Nature meant; and both show how life may run its evil course against the higher dispensations.

As the catastrophe came in view, a nice point in the management of [Edith's] character and destiny arose. I quote from a letter of the 19th of November, when he was busy with his fourteenth part. "Of course she hates Carker in the most deadly degree. I have not elaborated that, now, because (as I was explaining to Browne the other day) I have relied on it very much for the effect of her death. But I have no question that what you suggest will be an improvement. The strongest place to put it in, would be the close of the chapter immediately before this last one. I want to make the two first chapters as light as I can, but I will try to do it, solemnly, in that place." Then came the effect of this fourteenth number on Jeffrey; raising the question of whether the end might not come by other means than her death, and bringing with it a more bitter humiliation for her destroyer. While engaged on the fifteenth (21st December) Dickens thus wrote to me: "I am thoroughly delighted that you like what I sent. I enclose designs. Shadow-plate, poor. But I think Mr. Dombey admirable. One of the prettiest things in the book ought to be at the end of the chapter I am writing now. But in Florence's marriage, and in her subsequent return to her father, I see a brilliant opportunity.

"The Wooden Midshipman on the Look Out," illustration for *Dombey and Son*, by Hablot Knight Browne (Phiz)

. . . Note from Jeffrey this morning, who won't believe (positively refuses) that Edith is Carker's mistress. What do you think of a kind of inverted Maid's Tragedy, and a tremendous scene of her undeceiving Carker, and giving him to know that she never meant that?" So it was done; and when he sent me the chapter in which Edith says adieu to Florence, I had nothing but praise and pleasure to express. "I need not say," he wrote in reply, "I can't, how delighted and overjoyed I am by what you say and feel of it. I propose to show Dombey twice more; and in the end, leave him exactly

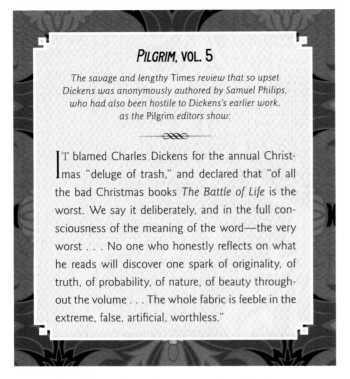

PILGRIM, VOL. 5

The savage and lengthy Times *review that so upset Dickens was anonymously authored by Samuel Philips, who had also been hostile to Dickens's earlier work, as the* Pilgrim *editors show:*

IT blamed Charles Dickens for the annual Christmas "deluge of trash," and declared that "of all the bad Christmas books *The Battle of Life* is the worst. We say it deliberately, and in the full consciousness of the meaning of the word—the very worst . . . No one who honestly reflects on what he reads will discover one spark of originality, of truth, of probability, of nature, of beauty throughout the volume . . . The whole fabric is feeble in the extreme, false, artificial, worthless."

The Little Wooden Midshipman trade sign of Messrs. Imray, Laurie, Norie, and Wilson Ltd. Chart Publishers, Leadenhall Street, London. Dickens saw it at their premises—which he reimagines as those of Sol Gills. (On display at the Charles Dickens Museum, London.)

as you describe." The end came; and, at the last moment when correction was possible, this note arrived. "I suddenly remember that I have forgotten Diogenes. Will you put him in the last little chapter? After the word 'favourite' in reference to Miss Tox, you can add, 'except with Diogenes, who is growing old and wilful.' Or, on the last page of all, after 'and with them two children: boy and girl' (I quote from memory), you might say 'and an old dog is generally in their company,' or to that effect. Just what you think best."

That was on Saturday the 25th of March, 1848. But as the confidences revealed in this chapter have dealt wholly with the leading currents of interest, there is yet room for a word on incidental persons in the story, of whom I have seen other so-called confidences alleged which it will be only right to state have really no authority. And first let me say what unquestionable evidence these characters give of the unimpaired freshness, richness, variety, and fitness of Dickens's invention at this time. So vivid and life-like were all these people, to the very youngest of the young gentlemen, that it became natural eagerly to seek out for them actual prototypes; but I think I can say with some confidence of them all, that, whatever single traits may have been taken from persons known to him (a practice with all writers, and very specially with Dickens), only two had living originals. His own experience of Mrs. Pipchin has been related; I had myself some knowledge of Miss Blimber; and the Little Wooden Midshipman did actually (perhaps does still) occupy his post of observation in Leadenhall-street.

DOMBEY AND SON, CHAPTER 27

*Though Dickens has long been critizised for his presentaion of insipid women, Edith Dombey's
searing analysis of the marriage market shows his acute awareness of sexual politics and his
ability to write powerful, self-aware women:*

MRS. Skewton reposed on her sofa, and Edith sat apart, by her harp, in silence. The mother, trifling with her fan, looked stealthily at the daughter more than once, but the daughter, brooding gloomily with downcast eyes, was not to be disturbed.

Thus they remained for a long hour, without a word, until Mrs. Skewton's maid appeared, according to custom, to prepare her gradually for night. At night, she should have been a skeleton, with dart and hour-glass, rather than a woman, this attendant; for her touch was as the touch of Death. The painted object shrivelled underneath her hand; the form collapsed, the hair dropped off, the arched dark eyebrows changed to scanty tufts of grey; the pale lips shrunk, the skin became cadaverous and loose; an old, worn, yellow, nodding woman, with red eyes, alone remained in Cleopatra's place, huddled up, like a slovenly bundle, in a greasy flannel gown.

The very voice was changed, as it addressed Edith, when they were alone again.

'Why don't you tell me,' it said sharply, 'that he is coming here to-morrow by appointment?'

'Because you know it,' returned Edith, 'Mother.'

The mocking emphasis she laid on that one word!

'You know he has bought me,' she resumed. 'Or that he will, to-morrow. He has considered of his bargain; he has shown it to his friend; he is even rather proud of it; he thinks that it will suit him, and may be had sufficiently cheap; and he will buy to-morrow. God, that I have lived for this, and that I feel it!'

Compress into one handsome face the conscious self-abasement, and the burning indignation of a hundred women, strong in passion and in pride; and there it hid itself with two white shuddering arms.

'What do you mean?' returned the angry mother. 'Haven't you from a child—'

'A child!' said Edith, looking at her, 'when was I a child? What childhood did you ever leave to me? I was a woman—artful, designing, mercenary, laying snares for men—before I knew myself, or you, or even understood the base and wretched aim of every new display I learnt. You gave birth to a woman. Look upon her. She is in her pride tonight.'

---

[56] "Edinburgh, 31st January, 1847. Oh, my dear, dear Dickens! what a No. 5 you have now given us! I have so cried and sobbed over it last night, and again this morning; and felt my heart purified by those tears, and blessed and loved you for making me shed them; and I never can bless and love you enough. Since the divine Nelly was found dead on her humble couch, beneath the snow and the ivy, there has been nothing like the actual dying of that sweet Paul, in the summer sunshine of that lofty room. And the long vista that leads us so gently and sadly, and yet so gracefully and winningly, to the plain consummation! Every trait so true, and so touching—and yet lightened by the fearless innocence which goes playfully to the brink of the grave, and that pure affection which bears the unstained spirit, on its soft and lambent flash, at once to its source in eternity.". . . In the same letter he told him of his having been reading the *Battle of Life* again, charmed with its sweet writing and generous sentiments.

CHAPTER 17

SPLENDID STROLLING

1847~1852

DEVONSHIRE TERRACE remaining still in possession of Sir James Duke, a house was taken in Chester-place, Regent's-park, where, on the 18th of April, his fifth son, to whom he gave the name of Sydney Smith Haldimand, was born.[57] Exactly a month before, we had attended together the funeral, at Highgate, of his publisher Mr. William Hall, his old regard for whom had survived the recent temporary cloud, and with whom he had the association as well of his first success, as of much kindly intercourse not forgotten at this sad time. Of the summer months that followed, the greater part was passed by him at Brighton or Broadstairs; and the chief employment of his leisure, in the intervals of Dombey, was the management of an enterprise originating in the success of our private play, of which the design was to benefit a great man of letters.

The purpose and the name had hardly been announced, when, with the statesmanlike attention to literature and its followers for which Lord John Russell has been eccentric among English politicians, a civil-list pension of two hundred a year was granted to Leigh Hunt; but though this modified our plan so far as to strike out of it performances meant to be given in London, so much was still thought necessary as might clear off past liabilities, and enable one of the most genuine of writers better to enjoy the easier future that had at last been opened to him. Reserving therefore anything realized beyond a certain sum for a dramatic author of merit, Mr. John Poole, to whom help had become also important, it was proposed to give, on Leigh Hunt's behalf, two representations of Ben Jonson's comedy, one at Manchester and the other at Liverpool, to be varied by different farces in each place; and with a prologue of

Talfourd's which Dickens was to deliver in Manchester, while a similar address by Sir Edward Bulwer Lytton was to be spoken by me in Liverpool. Among the artists and writers associated in the scheme were Mr. Frank Stone, Mr. Augustus Egg, Mr. John Leech, and Mr. George Cruikshank; Mr. Douglas Jerrold, Mr. Mark Lemon, Mr. Dudley Costello, and Mr. George Henry Lewes; the general management and supreme control being given to Dickens.

Leading men in both cities contributed largely to the design, and my friend Mr. Alexander Ireland of Manchester has lately sent me some letters not more characteristic of the energy of Dickens in regard to it than of the eagerness of every one addressed to give what help they could. Making personal mention of his fellow-sharers in the enterprise he describes the troop, in one of those letters, as "the most easily governable company of actors on earth;" and to this he had doubtless brought them, but not very easily. They deserved the term applied to them by Maclise, who had invented it first for Macready, on his being driven to "star" in the provinces when his managements in London closed. They were "splendid strollers."[58]

On Monday the 26th July we played at Manchester, and on Wednesday the 28th at Liverpool; the comedy being followed on the first night by *A Good Night's Rest* and *Turning the Tables*, and on the second by *Comfortable Lodgings, or Paris in 1750*; and the receipts being, on the first night £440 12s., and on the second, £463 8s. 6d. But though the married members of the company who took their wives defrayed that part of the cost, and every one who acted paid three pounds ten to the benefit-fund for his hotel charges, the expenses were necessarily so great that the profit was reduced to four hundred guineas, and, handsomely as this realised the design, expectations had been raised to five hundred. There was just that shade of disappointment, therefore, when, shortly after we came back and Dickens had returned to Broadstairs, I was startled by a letter from him. On the 3rd of August he had written: "All well. Children" (who had been going through whooping cough) "immensely improved. Business arising out of the late blaze of triumph, worse than ever." Then came what startled me, the very next day. As if his business were not enough, it had occurred to him that he might add the much longed-for

James Henry Leigh Hunt by Margaret Gillies, watercolor and gouache on ivory, 1838–1846

DEVONSHIRE HOUSE.

ON FRIDAY EVENING, MAY 16th, 1851,
THE AMATEUR COMPANY
OF THE
GUILD OF LITERATURE AND ART,
WILL HAVE THE HONOR OF PERFORMING, FOR THE FIRST TIME,
IN THE PRESENCE OF
HER MAJESTY THE QUEEN,
AND
HIS ROYAL HIGHNESS THE PRINCE ALBERT,
A NEW COMEDY, IN FIVE ACTS, BY SIR EDWARD BULWER LYTTON, BART.,
CALLED

NOT SO BAD AS WE SEEM:
OR,
MANY SIDES TO A CHARACTER.

Playbill of the Royal Performance of *Not So Bad as We Seem*, performed at Devonshire House, May 16th, 1851

hundred pounds to the benefit-fund by a little jeu d'esprit in form of a history of the trip, to be published with illustrations from the artists; and his notion was to write it in the character of Mrs. Gamp. It was to be, in the phraseology of that notorious woman, a new "Piljians Projiss;" and was to bear upon the title page its description as an Account of a late Expedition into the North, for an Amateur Theatrical Benefit, written by Mrs. Gamp (who was an eye-witness), Inscribed to Mrs. Harris, Edited by Charles Dickens, and published, with illustrations on wood by so and so, in aid of the Benefit-fund. Alas! it perished prematurely, as I feared it would, from failure of the artists to furnish needful nourishment. Of course it could not live alone. Without suitable illustration it must have lost its point and pleasantry. "Mac will make a little garland of the ladies for the title-page. Egg and Stone will themselves originate something fanciful, and I will settle with Cruikshank and Leech. I have no doubt the little thing will be droll and attractive." So it certainly would have been, if the Thanes of art had not fallen from him; but on their desertion it had to be abandoned after the first few pages were written.

One letter made mention of other matters of interest. His accounts for the first half-year of *Dombey* were so much in excess of what had been expected from the new publishing arrangements, that from this date all embarrassments connected with money were brought to a close.

Memorandum.— Special.

It is proposed that the company shall dine together at the Bedford Hotel Covent Garden, on Wednesday next at half past 5, in order that the whole of the dresses may be tried on there, after dinner, while there is yet ample time before the Dress Rehearsal for making any needful alterations.

Those gentlemen who assent to this arrangement will have the kindness, this morning, to attach their names to this paper.

Charles Dickens

Devonshire House
28th April, 1857.

J Forster,   Mark Lemon
D. Jerrold,   Robert Bell
Mark Lemon
R. H. Horne
E Huntington
N Wilson
Dudley Costello
F. Stone
Charles Knight
Wilkie Collins
Augustus Egg

Rehearsal notice concerning the Amateur Players, signed by Forster, Douglas Jerrold, Wilkie Collins, and other members of the company, 1851

His future profits varied of course with his varying sales, but there was always enough, and savings were now to begin.

"The Government is about to issue a Sanitary commission, and Lord John, I am right well pleased to say, has appointed Henry Austin secretary." Mr. Austin, who afterwards held the same office under the Sanitary act, had married his youngest sister Letitia; and of his two youngest brothers I may add that Alfred, also a civil-engineer, became one of the sanitary inspectors, and that Augustus was now placed in a city employment by Mr. Thomas Chapman, which after a little time he surrendered, and then found his way to America.

Devonshire-terrace meanwhile had been left by his tenant; and coming up joyfully himself to take possession, he brought for completion in his old home an important chapter of *Dombey*. On the way he lost his portmanteau, but "Thank God! the MS. of the chapter wasn't in it. Whenever I travel, and have anything of that valuable article, I always carry it in my pocket." He had begun at this time to find difficulties in writing at Broadstairs, of which he told me on his return. "Vagrant music is getting to that height here, and is so impossible to be escaped from, that I fear Broadstairs and I must part company in time to come. Unless it pours of rain, I cannot write half-an-hour without the most excruciating organs, fiddles, bells, or glee-singers. There is a violin of the most torturing kind under the window now (time, ten in the morning) and an Italian box of music on the steps—both in full blast."

He was to be in London at the end of the month: but I had from him meanwhile his preface[59] for his first completed book in the popular edition (*Pickwick* being now issued in that form, with an illustration by Leslie); and sending me shortly after (12th of Sept.) the first few slips of the story of the *Haunted Man* proposed for his next Christmas book, he told me he must finish it in less than a month if it was to be done at all, *Dombey* having now become very importunate. This prepared me for his letter of a week's later date. "Have been at work all day, and am seedy in consequence. *Dombey* takes so much time, and requires to be so carefully done, that I really begin to have serious doubts whether it is wise to go on with the Christmas book. Your kind help is invoked. What do you think? Would there be any distinctly bad effect in holding this idea over for another twelve-month? saying nothing whatever till November; and then announcing in the *Dombey* that its occupation of my entire time prevents the continuance of the Christmas series until next year, when it is proposed to be renewed. There might not be anything in that but a possibility of an extra lift for the little book when it did come—eh? On the other hand, I am very loath to lose the money. And still more so to leave any gap at Christmas firesides which I ought to fill."

The year's closing incidents were his chairmanship at a meeting of the Leeds Mechanics' Society on the 1st of December, and his opening of the Glasgow Athenaeum on the 28TH; where, to immense assemblages in both, he contrasted the obstinacy and cruelty of the Power of ignorance with the docility and gentleness of the Power of knowledge; pointed the use of popular institutes in supplementing what is learnt first in life, by the later education for its employments and equipment for its domesticities and virtues, which the grown person needs from day to day as much as the child its reading and writing; and he closed at Glasgow with allusion to a bazaar set on foot by the ladies of the city, under patronage of the Queen, for adding books to its Athenaeum library.

On the last day but one of the old year he wrote to me from Edinburgh. "We came over this afternoon, leaving Glasgow at one o'clock. Alison lives in style in a handsome country house out of Glasgow, and is a capital fellow, with an agreeable wife, nice little daughter, cheerful niece, all things pleasant in his household. I went over the prison and lunatic asylum with him yesterday;[60] at the Lord Provost's had gorgeous state-lunch with the Town Council; and was entertained at a great dinner-party at night.

Dickens threw himself into the new scheme with all his old energy; and prefatory mention may be made of our difficulty in selection of a suitable play to alternate with our old Ben Jonson. The *Alchemist* had been such a favourite with some of us, that, before finally laying it aside, we went through two or three rehearsals, in which I recollect thinking Dickens's Sir Epicure Mammon as good as anything he had done; and now the same trouble, with the same result, arising from a vain desire to please everybody, was taken successively with Beaumont and Fletcher's *Beggar's Bush*, and Goldsmith's *Good Natured Man*, with

Jerrold's characteristic drama of the *Rent Day*, and Bulwer's masterly comedy of *Money*. Choice was at last made of Shakespeare's *Merry Wives*, in which Lemon played Falstaff, I took again the jealous husband as in Jonson's play, and Dickens was Justice Shallow; to which was added a farce, *Love, Law, and Physick*, in which Dickens took the part he had acted long ago, before his days of authorship; and, besides the professional actresses engaged, we had for our Dame Quickly the lady to whom the world owes incomparably the best *Concordance* to Shakespeare that has ever been published, Mrs. Cowden Clarke. The success was undoubtedly very great. At Manchester, Liverpool, and Edinburgh there were single representations; but Birmingham and Glasgow had each two nights, and two were given at the Haymarket, on one of which the Queen and Prince were present. The gross receipts from the nine performances, before the necessary large deductions for London and local charges, were two thousand five hundred and fifty-one pounds and eightpence.[61] The first representation was in London on the 15th of April,

The Amateur Player's production of *Not so Bad as we Seem*, as depicted by the *Illustrated London News*, May 24, 1851

the last in Glasgow on the 20th of July, and everywhere Dickens was the leading figure.

My allusion to the last of these splendid strollings in aid of what we believed to be the interests of men of letters, shall be as brief as I can make it. Two winters after the present, at the close of November 1850, in the great hall of Lord Lytton's old family mansion in Knebworth-park, there were three private performances by the original actors in Ben Jonson's *Every Man in His Humour*. All the circumstances and surroundings were very brilliant; some of the gentlemen of the county played both in the comedy and farces; our generous host was profuse of all noble encouragement; and amid the general pleasure and excitement hopes rose high. Without discussing now, however, what will have to be stated hereafter, it suffices to say that the enterprise was set on foot, and the "Guild of Literature and Art" originated at Knebworth. A five-act comedy was to be written by Sir Edward Lytton, and, when a certain sum of money had been obtained by public representations of it, the details of the scheme were to be drawn up, and appeal made to those whom it addressed more especially. In a very few months everything was ready, except a farce which Dickens was to have written to follow the comedy, and which unexpected cares of management and preparation were held to absolve him from. There was substituted a new farce of Lemon's, to which, however, Dickens soon contributed so many jokes and so much Gampish and other fun of his own, that it came to be in effect a joint piece of authorship; and Gabblewig, which the manager took to himself, was one of those personation parts requiring five or six changes of face, voice, and gait in the course of it, from which, as we have seen, he derived all the early theatrical ambition that the elder Mathews had awakened in him. "You have no idea," he continued, "of the immensity of the work as the time advances, for the Duke even throws the whole of the audience on us, or he would get (he says) into all manner of scrapes." The Duke of Devonshire had offered his house in Piccadilly for the first representations, and in his princely way discharged all the expenses attending them. A moveable theatre was built and set up in the great drawing-room, and the library was turned into a green-room.

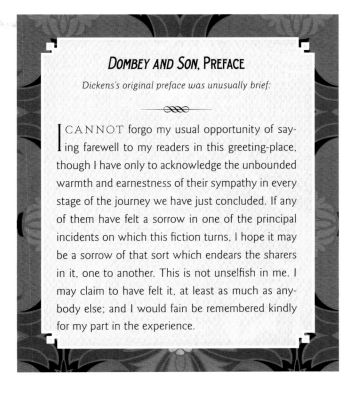

DOMBEY AND SON, PREFACE

Dickens's original preface was unusually brief:

I CANNOT forgo my usual opportunity of saying farewell to my readers in this greeting-place, though I have only to acknowledge the unbounded warmth and earnestness of their sympathy in every stage of the journey we have just concluded. If any of them have felt a sorrow in one of the principal incidents on which this fiction turns, I hope it may be a sorrow of that sort which endears the sharers in it, one to another. This is not unselfish in me. I may claim to have felt it, at least as much as anybody else; and I would fain be remembered kindly for my part in the experience.

Not so Bad as We Seem was played for the first time at Devonshire-house on the 27th of May, 1851, before the Queen and Prince and as large an audience as places could be found for; *Mr. Nightingale's Diary* being the name given to the farce. The success abundantly realised the expectations formed; and, after many representations at the Hanover-square Rooms in London, strolling began in the country, and was continued at intervals for considerable portions of this and the following year. "We have had prodigious houses, though smaller rooms (as to their actual size) than I had hoped for. The Duke was at Derby, and no end of minor radiances. Into the room at Newcastle (where Lord Carlisle was by the bye) they squeezed six hundred people, at twelve and sixpence, into a space reasonably capable of holding three hundred. Last night, in a hall built like a theatre, with pit, boxes, and gallery, we had about twelve hundred—I dare say more. We dine at two to-day (it is now one) and go to Sheffield at four, arriving there at about ten. I had been as fresh as a daisy; walked from Nottingham to Derby, and from Newcastle here; but seem to have had my nerves crumpled up last night, and have an excruciating headache."

Manchester and Liverpool closed the trip with enormous success at both places; and Sir Edward Lytton was present at a public dinner which was given in the former city, Dickens's brief word about it being written as he was setting foot in the train that was to bring him to London. "Bulwer spoke brilliantly at the Manchester dinner, and his earnestness and determination about the Guild was most impressive. It carried everything before it. They are now getting up annual subscriptions, and will give us a revenue to begin with. I swear I believe that people to be the greatest in the world. At Liverpool I had a Round Robin on the stage after the play was over, a place being left for your signature, and as I am going to have it framed, I'll tell Green to send it to Lincoln's-inn-fields. You have no idea how good Tenniel, Topham, and Collins have been in what they had to do."

These names, distinguished in art and letters, represent additions to the company who had joined the enterprise; and the last of them, Mr. Wilkie Collins, became, for all the rest of the life of Dickens, one of his dearest and most valued friends.

---

[57] He entered the Royal Navy, and survived his father only a year and eleven months. He was a Lieutenant, at the time of his death from a sharp attack of bronchitis; being then on board the P. and O. steamer "Malta," invalided from his ship the Topaze, and on his way home. He was buried at sea on the 2nd of May, 1872. Poor fellow! He was the smallest in size of all the children, in his manhood reaching only to a little over five feet; and throughout his childhood was never called by any other name than the "Ocean Spectre," from a strange little weird yet most attractive look in his large wondering eyes, very happily caught in a sketch in oils by the good Frank Stone, done at Bonchurch in September 1849 and remaining in his aunt's possession. "Stone has painted," Dickens then wrote to me, "the Ocean Spectre, and made a very pretty little picture of him." It was a strange chance that led his father to invent this playful name for one whom the ocean did indeed take to itself at last.

[58] I think it right to place on record here Leigh Hunt's own allusion to the incident (Autobiography, p. 432), though it will be thought to have too favourable a tone, and I could have wished that other names had also found mention in it. But I have already (p. 211) stated quite unaffectedly my own opinion of the very modest pretensions of the whole affair, and these kind words of Hunt may stand valeant quantum. "Simultaneous with the latest movement about the pension was one on the part of my admirable friend Dickens and other distinguished men, Forsters and Jerrolds, who, combining kindly purpose with an amateur inclination for the stage, had condescended to show to the public what excellent actors they could have been, had they so pleased,—what excellent actors, indeed, some of them were. . . . They proposed . . . a benefit for myself, . . . and the piece performed on the occasion was Ben Jonson's *Every Man in his Humour*. . . . If anything had been needed to show how men of letters include actors, on the common principle of the greater including the less, these gentlemen would have furnished it. Mr. Dickens's Bobadil had a spirit in it of intellectual apprehension beyond anything the existing stage has shown . . . and Mr. Forster delivered the verses of Ben Jonson with a musical flow and a sense of their grace and beauty unknown, I believe, to the recitation of actors at present.

[59] "Do you see anything to object to in it? I have never had so much difficulty, I think, in setting about any slight thing; for I really didn't know that I had a word to say, and nothing seems to live 'twixt what I have said and silence. The advantage of it is, that the latter part opens an idea for future prefaces all through the series, and may serve perhaps to make a feature of them." (7th of September, 1847.)

[60] "Tremendous distress at Glasgow, and a truly damnable jail, exhibiting the separate system in a most absurd and hideous form. Governor practical and intelligent; very anxious for the associated silent system; and much comforted by my fault-finding." (30th of December.)

[61] I give the sums taken at the several theatres. Haymarket, £319 14s.; Manchester, £266 12s. 6d.; Liverpool, £467 6s. 6d.; Birmingham, £327 10s., and £262 18s. 6d.; Edinburgh, £325 1s. 6d.; Glasgow, £471 7s. 8d., and (at half the prices of the first night) £210 10s.

CHAPTER 18

SEASIDE HOLIDAYS

1848~1851

THE PORTION OF DICKENS'S LIFE over which his adventures of strolling extended was in other respects not without interest; and this chapter will deal with some of his seaside holidays before I pass to the publication in 1848 of the story of The Haunted Man, and to the establishment in 1850 of the Periodical which had been in his thoughts for half a dozen years before, and has had foreshadowings nearly as frequent in my pages.

Among the incidents of 1848 before the holiday season came, were the dethronement of Louis Philippe, and birth of the second French republic.

Somewhat earlier than usual this summer, on the close of the Shakespeare-house performances, he tried Broadstairs once more, having no important writing in hand: but in the brief interval before leaving he saw a thing of celebrity in those days, the Chinese Junk; and I had all the details in so good a description that I could not resist the temptation of using some parts of it at the time. "Drive down to the Blackwall railway," he wrote to me, "and for a matter of eighteen-pence you are at the Chinese Empire in no time. Well, if there be any one thing in the world that this extraordinary craft is not at all like, that thing is a ship of any kind. So narrow, so long, so grotesque; so low in the middle, so high at each end, like a China pen-tray; with no rigging, with nowhere to go to aloft; with mats for sails, great warped cigars for masts, gaudy dragons and sea-monsters disporting themselves from stem to stern, and *on* the stern a gigantic cock of impossible aspect, defying the world (as well he may) to produce his equal,—it would look more at home at the top of a public building, or at the top of a mountain, or in an avenue of trees, or down in a mine,

than afloat on the water. As for the Chinese lounging on the deck, the most extravagant imagination would never dare to suppose them to be mariners. Imagine a ship's crew, without a profile among them, in gauze pinafores and plaited hair; wearing stiff clogs a quarter of a foot thick in the sole; and lying at night in little scented boxes, like backgammon men or chess-pieces, or mother-of-pearl counters!"

"Yes, there can be no question that this is Finality in perfection; and it is a great advantage to have the doctrine so beautifully worked out, and shut up in a corner of a dock near a fashionable white-bait house for the edification of man. Thousands of years have passed away since the first junk was built on this model, and the last junk ever launched was no better for that waste and desert of time. The mimic eye painted on their prows to assist them in finding their way, has opened as wide and seen as far as any actual organ of sight in all the interval through the whole immense extent of that strange country. It has been set in the flowery head to as little purpose for thousands of years. With all their patient and ingenious but never advancing art, and with all their rich and diligent agricultural cultivation, not a new twist or curve has been given to a ball of ivory, and not a blade of experience has been grown."

Other letters of the summer from Broadstairs will complete what he wrote from the same place last year on Mr. Cruikshank's efforts in the cause of temperance, and will enable me to say, what I know he wished to be remembered in his story, that there was no subject on which through his whole life he felt more strongly than this. No man advocated temperance, even as far as possible its legislative enforcement, with greater earnestness; but he made important reservations. Not thinking drunkenness to be a vice inborn, or incident to the poor more than to other people, he never would agree that the existence of a gin-shop was the alpha and omega of it. Believing it to be, *the* "national horror," he also believed that many operative causes had to do with having made it so; and his objection to the temperance agitation was that these were left out of account altogether. This was consistently Dickens's "platform" throughout the years he was known to me; and holding it to be within the reach as well as the scope of legislation, which even our political magnates have been discovering lately, he thought intemperance to be but the one result that, out of all those arising from the absence of legislation, was the most wretched. For him, drunkenness had a teeming and reproachful history anterior to the drunken stage; and he thought it the first duty of the moralist bent upon annihilating the gin-shop, to "strike deep and spare not" at those previous remediable evils. Certainly this was not the way of Mr. Cruikshank, any more than it is that of the many excellent people who take part in temperance agitations. His former tale of the *Bottle*, as told by his admirable pencil, was that of a decent working man, father of a boy and a girl, living in comfort and good esteem until near the middle age, when, happening unluckily to have a goose for dinner one day in the bosom of his thriving family, he jocularly sends out for a bottle of gin, persuades his wife, until then a picture of neatness and good housewifery, to take a little drop after the stuffing, and the whole family from that moment drink themselves to destruction. The sequel, of which Dickens now wrote to me, traced the lives of the boy and girl after the wretched deaths of their drunken parents, through gin-shop, beer-shop, and dancing-rooms, up to their trial for robbery, when the boy is convicted, dying aboard the hulks; and the girl, desolate and mad after her acquittal, flings herself from London-bridge into the night-darkened river.

This led to some remark on Hogarth's method in such matters, and I am glad to be able to preserve this fine criticism of that great Englishman, by a writer who closely resembled him in genius; as another generation will be probably more apt than our own to discover. "Hogarth avoided the Drunkard's Progress, I conceive, precisely because the causes of drunkenness among the poor were so numerous and widely spread, and lurked so sorrowfully deep and far down in all human misery, neglect, and despair, that even *his* pencil could not bring them fairly and justly into the light. It was never his plan to be content with only showing the effect. I cannot but bethink me that it was not until this year of grace 1848 that a Bishop of London first came out respecting something wrong in poor men's social accommodations, and I am confirmed in my suspicion that Hogarth had many meanings which have not grown obsolete in a century."

Of what otherwise occupied him at Broadstairs in 1848 there is not much to mention until the close of his holiday. He used to say that he never went for more than a couple of days from his own home without something befalling him that never happened to anyone else, and his Broadstairs adventure of the present summer verged closer on tragedy than comedy. Returning there one day in August after bringing up his boys to school, it had been arranged that his wife should meet him at Margate; but he had walked impatiently far beyond the place for meeting when at last he caught sight of her, not in the small chaise but in a large carriage and pair followed by an excited crowd, and with the youth that should have been driving the little pony bruised and bandaged on the box behind the two prancing horses. "You may faintly imagine my amazement at encountering this carriage, and the strange people, and Kate, and the crowd, and the bandaged one, and all the rest of it." And then in a line or two I had the story. "At the top of a steep hill on the road, with a ditch on each side, the pony bolted, upon which what does John do but jump out! He says he was thrown out, but it cannot be. The reins immediately became entangled in the wheels, and away went the pony down the hill madly, with Kate inside rending the Isle of Thanet with her screams. The accident might have been a fearful one, if the pony had not, thank Heaven, on getting to the bottom, pitched over the side; breaking the shaft and cutting her hind legs, but in the most extraordinary manner smashing her own way apart. She tumbled down, a bundle of legs with her head tucked underneath, and left the chaise standing on the bank! A Captain Devaynes and his wife were passing in their carriage at the moment, saw the accident with no power of preventing it, got Kate out, laid her on the grass, and behaved with infinite kindness. All's well that ends well, and I think she's really none the worse for the fright. John is in bed a good deal bruised, but without any broken bone, and likely soon to come right; though for the present plastered all over, and, like Squeers, a brown-paper parcel chock-full of nothing but groans. The women generally have no sympathy for him whatever; and the nurse says, with indignation, how could he go and leave an unprotected female in the shay!"

RIGHT: Gin Lane by William Hogarth, London, 1751

Holiday incidents there were many, but none that need detain us. This was really a summer idleness: for it was the interval between two of his important undertakings, there was no periodical yet to make demands on him, and only the task of finishing his *Haunted Man* for Christmas lay ahead.

Not till the close of September I heard of work intruding itself, in a letter twitting me for a broken promise in not joining him: "We are reasonably jolly, but rurally so; going to bed o' nights at ten, and bathing o' mornings at half-past seven. . . Dim visions of divers things are floating around me; and I must go to work, head foremost, when I get home. I am glad, after all, that I have not been at it here; for I am all the better for my idleness, no doubt. . . ."

His first seaside holiday in 1849 was at Brighton, where he passed some weeks in February; and not, I am bound to add, without the usual *un*usual adventure to signalize his visit. He had not been a week in his lodgings, where Leech and his wife joined him, when both his landlord and the daughter of his landlord went raving mad, and the lodgers were driven away to the Bedford hotel. "If you could have heard the cursing and crying of the two; could have seen the physician and nurse quoited out into the passage by the madman at the hazard of their lives; could have seen Leech and me flying to the doctor's rescue; could have seen our wives pulling us back; could have seen the M.D. faint with fear; could have seen three other M.D.'s come to his aid; with an atmosphere of Mrs. Gamps, strait-waistcoats, struggling friends and servants, surrounding the whole; you would have said it was quite worthy of me, and quite in keeping with my usual proceedings." The letter ended with a word on what then his thoughts were full of, but for which no name had yet been found. "A sea-fog to-day, but yesterday inexpressibly delicious. My mind running, like a high sea, on names—not satisfied yet, though." When he next wrote from the seaside, in the beginning of July, he had found the name; had started his book; and was "rushing to Broadstairs" to write the fourth number of *David Copperfield*.

In the middle of July the number was nearly done, and he was still doubtful where to pass his longer summer holiday. Leech wished to join him in it, and both desired a change from Broadstairs. At first he thought of Folke-stone, but disappointment there led to a sudden change. "I

propose" (15th of July) "returning to town to-morrow by the boat from Ramsgate, and going off to Weymouth or the Isle of Wight, or both, early the next morning." A few days after, his choice was made.

He had taken a house at Bonchurch, attracted there by the friend who had made it a place of interest for him during the last few years, the Reverend James White, with whose name and its associations my mind connects insepa-rably many of Dickens's happiest hours. To pay him fitting tribute would not be easy, if here it were called for. In the kindly shrewd Scotch face, a keen sensitiveness to plea-sure and pain was the first thing that struck any common observer. Cheerfulness and gloom coursed over it so rapidly that no one could question the tale they told. But the relish of his life had outlived its more than usual share of sorrows; and quaint sly humour, love of jest and merriment, capital knowledge of books, and sagacious quips at men, made his companionship delightful.

He began with an excess of liking. Of the Undercliff he was full of admiration. "From the top of the highest downs," he wrote in his second letter (28th of July) "there are views which are only to be equalled on the Genoese shore of the Mediterranean; the variety of walks is extraordinary; things are cheap, and everybody is civil. The waterfall acts wonder-fully, and the sea bathing is delicious. Best of all, the place is certainly cold rather than hot, in the summer time. The evenings have been even chilly. . . ."

He wrote again on the first of August. "I have just begun to get into work. We are expecting the Queen to come by very soon, in grand array, and are going to let off ever so many guns. I had a letter from Jeffrey yesterday morning, just as I was going to write to him. He has evidently been very ill, and I begin to have fears for his recovery. It is a very pathetic letter, as to his state of mind; but only in a tranquil contemplation of death, which I think very noble." His next letter, four days later, described himself as continuing still at work; but also taking part in dinners at Blackgang, and picnics of "tremendous success" on Shanklin Down.

After a few more days I heard of progress with his writing in spite of all festivities. "I have made it a rule that the inimitable is invisible, until two every day. I shall have half the number done, please God, to-morrow. I have not worked quickly here yet, but I don't know what I *may* do. Divers cogitations have occupied my mind at intervals, respecting the dim design." The design was the weekly periodical so often in his thoughts, of which more will appear in my next chapter. His letter closed with intimations of discomfort in his health; of an obstinate cough; and of a determination he had formed to mount daily to the top of the downs. "It makes a great difference in the climate to get a blow there and come down again." Then I heard of the doctor "stethoscoping" him, of his hope that all was right in that quarter, and of rubbings "a la St. John Long" being ordered for his chest. But the mirth still went on. "There has been a Doctor Lankester at Sandown, a very good merry fellow, who has made one at the picnics, and whom I went over and dined with, along with Danby (I remember your liking for Danby, and don't wonder at it), Leech, and White." A letter towards the close of August resumed yet more of his ordinary tone. "We had games and forfeits last night at White's. Davy Roberts's pretty little daughter is there for a week, with her husband, Bicknell's son."

My visit was due at the opening of September, but a few days earlier came the full revelation of which only a passing shadow had reached in two or three previous letters. "Before I think of beginning my next number, I perhaps cannot do better than give you an imperfect description of the results of the climate of Bonchurch after a few weeks' residence. The first salubrious effect of which the Patient becomes conscious is an almost continual feeling of sickness, accompanied with great prostration of strength, so that his legs tremble under him, and his arms quiver when he wants to take hold of any object. An extraordinary disposition to sleep (except at night, when his rest, in the event of his having any, is broken by incessant dreams) is always present at the same time; and, if he have anything to do requiring thought and attention, this overpowers him to such a degree that he can only do it in snatches: lying down on beds in the fitful intervals. Extreme depression of mind, and a disposition to shed tears from morning to night, developes itself at the same period. If the Patient happen to have been a good walker, he finds ten miles an insupportable distance; in the achievement of which his legs are so unsteady, that he goes from side to side of the road, like a drunken man. If he happen to have ever possessed any energy of any kind, he finds it quenched in a dull, stupid languor. I find, from all sorts of hints from Kate, Georgina, and the Leeches, that they are all affected more or less in the same way, and find it very difficult to make head against."

These were grave imputations against one of the prettiest places in England; but of the generally depressing influence of that Undercliff on particular temperaments,

I had already enough experience to abate something of the surprise with which I read the letter. What it too bluntly puts aside are the sufferings other than his own, projected and sheltered by what only aggravated his; but my visit gave me proof that he had really very little overstated the effect upon himself. Making allowance, which sometimes he failed to do, for special peculiarities, and for the excitability never absent when he had in hand an undertaking such as *Copperfield*, I

Dickens's house at Bonchurch (Winterbourne, on the Isle of Wight), where he continued work on *David Copperfield*

DAVID COPPERFIELD, CHAPTER 15

Mr Dick, having been cruelly treated by his family, is taken in by David's aunt Betsy Copperfield. The "touching delineation"
of this character sees him become an eccentric father figure to David, as well as a struggling author, dogged by writer's block.
Here he and a young David go kite-flying together:

———— ❦ ————

MR. Dick and I soon became the best of friends, and very often, when his day's work was done, went out together to fly the great kite. Every day of his life he had a long sitting at the Memorial, which never made the least progress, however hard he laboured, for King Charles the First always strayed into it, sooner or later, and then it was thrown aside, and another one begun. The patience and hope with which he bore these perpetual disappointments, the mild perception he had that there was something wrong about King Charles the First, the feeble efforts he made to keep him out, and the certainty with which he came in, and tumbled the Memorial out of all shape, made a deep impression on me. What Mr. Dick supposed would come of the Memorial, if it were completed; where he thought it was to go, or what he thought it was to do; he knew no more than anybody else, I believe. Nor was it at all necessary that he should trouble himself with such questions, for if anything were certain under the sun, it was certain that the Memorial never would be finished. It was quite an affecting sight, I used to think, to see him with the kite when it was up a great height in the air. What he had told me, in his room, about his belief in its disseminating the statements pasted on it, which were nothing but old leaves of abortive Memorials, might have been a fancy with him sometimes; but not when he was out, looking up at the kite in the sky, and feeling it pull and tug at his hand. He never looked so serene as he did then. I used to fancy, as I sat by him of an evening, on a green slope, and saw him watch the kite high in the quiet air, that it lifted his mind out of its confusion, and bore it (such was my boyish thought) into the skies. As he wound the string in and it came lower and lower down out of the beautiful light, until it fluttered to the ground, and lay there like a dead thing, he seemed to wake gradually out of a dream; and I remember to have seen him take it up, and look about him in a lost way, as if they had both come down together, so that I pitied him with all my heart.

Illustration for the Household Edition of *David Copperfield*, by Fred Barnard, ca. 1870

observed a nervous tendency to misgivings and apprehensions to the last degree unusual with him, which seemed to make the commonest things difficult; and though he stayed out his time, and brought away nothing that his happier associations with the place and its residents did not long survive, he never returned to Bonchurch.

In the month that remained he completed his fifth number, and with the proof there came the reply to some questions of which I hardly remember more than that they referred to doubts of mine; one being as to the propriety of the kind of delusion he had first given to poor Mr. Dick,[62] which I thought a little too farcical for that really touching delineation of character.

"Browne has sketched an uncommonly characteristic and capital Mr. Micawber for the next number. I hope the present number is a good one. I hear nothing but pleasant accounts of the general satisfaction."

The same letter told me of an intention to go to Broadstairs, put aside by doubtful reports of its sanitary condition; but it will be seen presently that there was another graver interruption. With his work well off his hands, however, he had been getting on better where he was; and they had all been very merry. "Yes," he said, writing after a couple of days (23rd of September), "we have been sufficiently rollicking since I finished the number; and have had great games at rounders every afternoon, with all Bonchurch looking on; but I begin to long for a little peace and solitude. And now for my less pleasing piece of news. The sea has been running very high, and Leech, while bathing, was knocked over by a bad blow from a great wave on the forehead. He is in bed, and had twenty of his namesakes on his temples this morning. When I heard of him just now, he was asleep—which he had not been all night." He closed his letter hopefully, but next day (24th September) I had less favourable report. "Leech has been very ill with congestion of the brain ever since I wrote, and being still in excessive pain has had ice to his head continuously, and been bled in the arm besides. Beard and I sat up there, all night." On the 26th he wrote, "My plans are all unsettled by Leech's illness; as of course I do not like to leave this place while I can be of any service to him and his good little wife. But all visitors are gone to-day, and Winterbourne once more left to the engaging family of the inimitable B. Ever since I wrote to you Leech has been seriously worse, and again very heavily bled. The night before last he was in

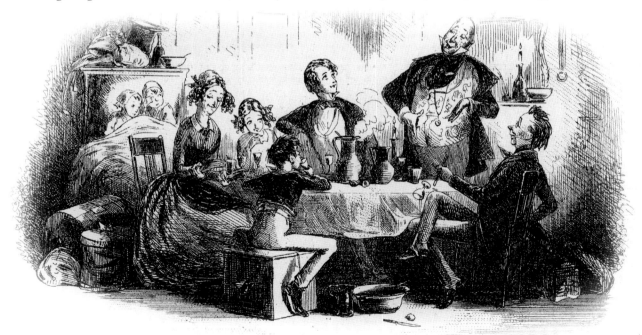

"Mr. Micawber Delivers Some Valedictory Remarks," illustration by Hablot Knight Browne (Phiz), 1850

IN the Autumn-time of the year, when the great metropolis is so much hotter, so much noisier, so much more dusty or so much more water-carted, so much more crowded, so much more disturbing and distracting in all respects, than it usually is, a quiet sea-beach becomes indeed a blessed spot. Half awake and half asleep, this idle morning in our sunny window on the edge of a chalk-cliff in the old-fashioned watering-place to which we are a faithful resorter, we feel a lazy inclination to sketch its picture.

The place seems to respond. Sky, sea, beach, and village, lie as still before us as if they were sitting for the picture. It is dead low-water. A ripple plays among the ripening corn upon the cliff, as if it were faintly trying from recollection to imitate the sea; and the world of butterflies hovering over the crop of radish-seed are as restless in their little way as the gulls are in their larger manner when the wind blows. But the ocean lies winking in the sunlight like a drowsy lion its glassy waters scarcely curve upon the shore the fishing-boats in the tiny harbour are all stranded in the mud our two colliers (our watering-place has a maritime trade employing that amount of shipping) have not an inch of water within a quarter of a mile of them, and turn, exhausted, on their sides, like faint fish of an antediluvian species. Rusty cables and chains, ropes and rings, undermost parts of posts and piles and confused timber-defences against the waves, lie strewn about, in a brown litter of tangled sea-weed and fallen cliff which looks as if a family of giants had been making tea here for ages, and had observed an untidy custom of throwing their tea-leaves on the shore.

In truth, our watering-place itself has been left somewhat high and dry by the tide of years. Concerned as we are for its honour, we must reluctantly admit that the time when this pretty little semicircular sweep of houses, tapering off at the end of the wooden pier into a point in the sea, was a gay place, and when the lighthouse overlooking it shone at daybreak on company dispersing from public balls, is but dimly traditional now. There is a bleak chamber in our watering-place which is yet called the Assembly `Rooms,` and understood to be available on hire for balls or concerts; and, some few seasons since, an ancient little gentleman came down and stayed at the hotel, who said that he had danced there, in bygone ages, with the Honourable Miss Peepy, well known to have been the Beauty of her day and the cruel occasion of innumerable duels. But he was so old and shrivelled, and so very rheumatic in the legs, that it demanded more imagination than our watering-place can usually muster, to believe him; therefore, except the Master of the `Rooms` (who to this hour wears kneebreeches, and who confirmed the statement with tears in his eyes), nobody did believe in the little lame old gentleman, or even in the Honourable Miss Peepy, long deceased.

[. . .]We have a pier—a queer old wooden pier, fortunately without the slightest pretensions to architecture, and very picturesque in consequence. Boats are hauled up upon it, ropes are coiled all over it; lobster-pots, nets, masts, oars, spars, sails, ballast, and rickety capstans, make a perfect labyrinth of it. For ever hovering about this pier, with their hands in their pockets, or leaning over the rough bulwark it opposes to the sea, gazing through telescopes which they carry about in the same profound receptacles, are the Boatmen of our watering-place. Looking at them, you would say that surely these must be the laziest boatmen in the world. They lounge about, in obstinate and inflexible pantaloons that are apparently made of wood, the whole season through. Whether talking together about the shipping in the Channel, or gruffly unbending over mugs of beer at the publichouse, you would consider them the slowest of men. The chances are a thousand to one that you might stay here for ten seasons, and never see a boatman in a hurry. A certain expression about his loose hands, when they are not in his pockets, as if he were carrying a considerable lump of iron in each, without any inconvenience, suggests strength, but he never seems to use it. He has the appearance of perpetually strolling, running is too inappropriate a word to be thought of to seed. The only subject on which he seems to feel any

"*Familiar in their Mouths as* HOUSEHOLD WORDS."—Shakespeare.

HOUSEHOLD WORDS.

A WEEKLY JOURNAL.

CONDUCTED BY CHARLES DICKENS.

Nº. 130.] SATURDAY, SEPTEMBER 18, 1852. [Price 2*d*.

Running head to *Household Words*

approach to enthusiasm, is pitch. He pitches everything he can lay hold of, the pier, the palings, his boat, his house, when there is nothing else left he turns to and even pitches his hat, or his rough-weather clothing. Do not judge him by deceitful appearances. These are among the bravest and most skilful mariners that exist. Let a gale arise and swell into a storm, let a sea run that might appal the stoutest heart that ever beat, let the Light-boat on these dangerous sands throw up a rocket in the night, or let them hear through the angry roar the sig- nalguns of a ship in distress, and these men spring up into activity so dauntless, so valiant, and heroic, that the world cannot surpass it. Cavillers may object that they chiefly live upon the salvage of valuable cargoes. So they do, and God knows it is no great living that they get out of the deadly risks they run. But put that hope of gain aside. Let these rough fel- lows be asked, in any storm, who volunteers for the life-boat to save some perishing souls, as poor and empty-handed as themselves, whose lives the perfection of human reason does not rate at the value of a farthing each; and that boat will be manned, as surely and as cheerfully, as if a thousand pounds were told down on the weather-beaten pier. For this, and for the recollection of their comrades whom we have known, whom the raging sea has engulfed before their children`s eyes in such brave efforts, whom the secret sand has buried, we hold the boatmen of our watering-place in our love and hon- our, and are tender of the fame they well deserve.

So many children are brought down to our watering- place that, when they are not out of doors, as they usually are in fine weather, it is wonderful where they are put: the whole village seeming much too small to hold them under cover. In the afternoons, you see no end of salt and sandy little boots drying on upper window-sills. At bathing-time in the morning, the little bay re-echoes with every shrill vari- ety of shriek and splash after which, if the weather be at all fresh, the sands teem with small blue mottled legs. The sands are the children`s great resort. They cluster there, like ants: so busy burying their particular friends, and making castles with infinite labour which the next tide overthrows, that it is curious to consider how their play, to the music of the sea, foreshadows the realities of their after lives.

It is curious, too, to observe a natural ease of approach that there seems to be between the children and the boat- men. They mutually make acquaintance, and take individual likings, without any help. You will come upon one of those slow heavy fellows sitting down patiently mending a little ship for a mite of a boy, whom he could crush to death by throwing his lightest pair of trousers on him. You will be sensible of the oddest contrast between the smooth little creature, and the rough man who seems to be carved out of hard-grained wood between the delicate hand expec- tantly held out, and the immense thumb and finger that can hardly feel the rigging of thread they mend between the small voice and the gruff growl and yet there is a natural propriety in the companionship: always to be noted in con- fidence between a child and a person who has any merit of reality and genuineness: which is admirably pleasant.

PATTEN EXPLAINS THE CONTEXT OF PRODUCTION AND CONSUMPTION IN THE VICTORIAN SERIAL PUBLISHING INDUSTRY:

Victorians did not read their literature piecemeal. Novels came out physically divided into volumes: many titles appeared in three volumes, but fiction might be packaged in two, four, five or even eight separate volumes, sometimes released in stages, monthly or bimonthly. And many readers didn't buy these volumes, which were expensive; instead, they checked them out from a for-profit circulating library, one volume at a time. A large number of novels first appeared in the pages of monthly or weekly magazines: Dickens's *Oliver Twist, The Old Curiosity Shop, Barnaby Rudge, Hard Times, A Tale of Two Cities*, and *Great Expectations*, Elizabeth Gaskell's *North and South*, George Eliot's *Romola*, Margaret Oliphant's *Miss Marjoribanks*, Anthony Trollope's *Frimley Parsonage*, and Joseph Conrad's *Lord Jim* are just a few of the hundreds of novels Victorian readers encountered in periodicals. Sales of novels in magazines far exceeded sales in volumes: an initial print order for a three-volume title ("three-deckers" in the terms of the trade) might be between 500 and 1000 copies (Sir Walter Scott's novels often sold ten times that amount), whereas magazine sales in the 1840s achieved 8000 or more per month (*The Old Curiosity Shop* reached nearly 100,000 by its conclusion), mid-century weeklies topped 100,000 and in 1896 the *Strand Magazine*, buoyed by Arthur Conan Doyle's *Sherlock Holmes* tales, sold 60,000 copies of the July number to the United States and another 392,000 to the home market. And from the 1830s to the 1870s fiction also appeared in individually self-contained parts issued weekly or monthly and running for a year or more. Some of these serialisations sold 50,000 or more copies of each instalment.

[. . .] Fiction became, not a luxury item, but a household one. Something of that change in the conceptualisation of fiction is reflected in the titles of Dickens's two weekly journals, incorporating fiction, that he owned and edited from 1850 to his death. The first was called *Household Words*, the title taken from Shakespeare's *Henry V*, "*Familiar in their Mouths as HOUSEHOLD WORDS*". The second, which he initiated to supplant the first and ruin the publisher with whom he had quarrelled, was entitled *All the Year Round*, suggesting that this weekly commodity was part of weekend shopping, along with the groceries, and that buying it and reading it were routine, repetitive parts of one's life, 24/7/365.

[. . .] Recent critics have speculated on the physiological rhythms periodical publications exploited and reinforced. Serial fictions were likened to trains and other moving vehicles, thrusting forward, terminating in suspense or temporary resolution time after time, and tracking the young protagonist's battle to win a place for himself, and to marry. These were concepts easily mapped onto male patterns of pleasure. But serials also attracted large audiences of females, who may have been drawn, in part, by structures that repeated monthly, that formed new consensual communities ratified by the presence of healthy young families in the final part, that appealed to sentiment and compassion, and that advocated nurturing even the neediest and most abject members of society. Thus serials answered males fantasies, rocketing forward, propelled by suspense, heroes and heroines in danger, and domestic arrangements under assault. They enacted female desires, as, at the end of individual parts and the novel as a whole, serials rebirthed nurturing worlds. Serials also deployed nostalgia, backward glances to earlier parts and better times. Dickens deplored sentimentalising earlier eras, but his novels are themselves full of evocations of simpler, pastoral times, insulated from the corruptions and speed of the city. At the same time, his fictions recognise stagnation: decaying houses and institutions and families testify to the imperative to adapt to change. In all these ways, then, serial publication's rhythms inherently addressed and accommodated to the industrial world, which reformed human bodies and psyches under the regimes of temporal control and repetitive labor.

From Robert L. Patten, "Publishing in Parts," *in Palgrave Advances in Charles Dickens Studies*, ed. John Bowen and Robert Patten (Basingstoke: Palgrave, 2006) pp. 11-12, 19, 32-33

such an alarming state of restlessness, which nothing could relieve, that I proposed to Mrs. Leech to try magnetism. Accordingly, in the middle of the night I fell to; and after a very fatiguing bout of it, put him to sleep for an hour and thirty-five minutes. A change came on in the sleep, and he is decidedly better. I talked to the astounded little Mrs. Leech across him, when he was asleep, as if he had been a truss of hay. . . . What do you think of my setting up in the magnetic line with a large brass plate? 'Terms, twenty-five guineas per nap.'" When he wrote again on the 30th, he had completed his sixth number; and he was next day to leave for Broadstairs with his wife, her sister, and the two little girls. "I will merely add that I entreat to be kindly remembered to Thackeray" (who had a dangerous illness at this time); "that I think I have, without a doubt, *got* the Periodical notion; and that I am writing under the depressing and discomforting influence of paying off the tribe of bills that pour in upon an unfortunate family-young-man on the eve of a residence like this. So no more at present from the disgusted, though still inimitable, and always affectionate B."

He stayed at Broadstairs till he had finished his number seven, and what else chiefly occupied him were thoughts about the Periodical of which account will presently be given.

His visit to the little watering-place in the following year was signalised by his completion of the most famous of his novels, and his letters otherwise were occupied by elaborate managerial preparation for the private performances at Kneb-worth. But again the plague of itinerant music flung him into such fevers of irritation, that he finally resolved against any renewed attempt to carry on important work here; and the summer of 1851, when he was only busy with miscellaneous writing, was the last of his regular residences in the place. He then let his London house for the brief remainder of its term; ran away at the end of May, when some grave family sorrows had befallen him, from the crowds and excitements of the Great Exhibition; and with intervals of absence, chiefly at the Guild representations, stayed in his favourite Fort-house by the sea until October, when he took possession of Tavistock-house.

Vague mention of a "next book" escaped in a letter at the end of July, on which I counselled longer abstinence. "Good advice," he replied, "but difficult: I wish you'd come to us and preach another kind of abstinence. Fancy the Preventive men finding a lot of brandy in barrels on the rocks here, the day before yesterday! Nobody knows anything about the barrels, of course. They were intended to have been landed with the next tide, and to have been just covered at low water. But the water being unusually low, the tops of the barrels became revealed to Preventive telescopes, and descent was made upon the brandy. They are always at it, hereabouts, I have no doubt. And of course B would not have had any of it. O dear no! certainly not."

His reading was considerable and very various at these intervals of labour, and in this particular summer took in all the minor tales as well as the plays of Voltaire, several of the novels (old favourites with him) of Paul de Kock, Ruskin's *Lamps of Architecture*, and a surprising number of books of African and other travel for which he had insatiable relish: but the notices of all this in his letters were few.

I joined him for the August regatta and stayed a pleasant fortnight. His paper on "Our Watering-place" appeared while I was there, and great was the local excitement.

His own restlessness with fancies for a new book had now risen beyond bounds, and for the time he was eager to open it in that prettiest quaintest bit of English landscape, Strood valley, which reminded him always of a Swiss scene. I had not left him many days when these lines followed me. "I very nearly packed up a portmanteau and went away, the day before yesterday, into the mountains of Switzerland, alone! Still the victim of an intolerable restlessness, I shouldn't be at all surprised if I wrote to you one of these mornings from under Mont Blanc. I sit down between whiles to think of a new story, and, as it begins to grow, such a torment of a desire to be anywhere but where I am; and to be going I don't know where, I don't know why; takes hold of me, that it is like being *driven away*. If I had had a passport, I sincerely believe I should have gone to Switzerland the night before last. I should have remembered our engagement—say, at Paris, and have come back for it; but should probably have left by the next express train."

At the end of November, when he had settled himself in his new London abode, the book was begun; and as generally happened with the more important incidents of his life, but always accidentally, begun on a Friday.

THE HAUNTED MAN AND THE GHOST'S BARGAIN, CHAPTER 1

*In this final Christmas book, Dickens presents a fascinating study of the operation of memory.
It is unsurprising that Freud was an attentive reader of Dickens, given their shared interest
in the the effects of past experience on character.*

"IF I could forget my sorrow and wrong, I would," the Ghost repeated. "If I could forget my sorrow and my wrong, I would!"

"Evil spirit of myself," returned the haunted man, in a low, trembling tone, "my life is darkened by that incessant whisper."

"It is an echo," said the Phantom.

"If it be an echo of my thoughts—as now, indeed, I know it is," rejoined the haunted man, "why should I, therefore, be tormented? It is not a selfish thought.I suffer it to range beyond myself. All men and women have their sorrows,—most of them their wrongs; ingratitude, and sordid jealousy, and interest, besetting all degrees of life. Who would not forget their sorrows and their wrongs?"

"Who would not, truly, and be happier and better for it?" said the Phantom.

"These revolutions of years, which we commemorate," proceeded Redlaw, "what do THEY recall!Are there any minds in which they do not re-awaken some sorrow, or some trouble?What is the remembrance of the old man who was here to-night? A tissue of sorrow and trouble."

"But common natures," said the Phantom, with its evil smile upon its glassy face, "unenlightened minds and ordinary spirits, do not feel or reason on these things like men of higher cultivation and profounder thought."

"Tempter," answered Redlaw, "whose hollow look and voice I dread more than words can express, and from whom some dim foreshadowing of greater fear is stealing over me while I speak, I hear again an echo of my own mind."

"Receive it as a proof that I am powerful," returned the Ghost. "Hear what I offer! Forget the sorrow, wrong, and trouble you have known!"

"Forget them!" he repeated.

"I have the power to cancel their remembrance—to leave but very faint, confused traces of them, that will die out soon," returned the Spectre. "Say! Is it done?"

"Stay!" cried the haunted man, arresting by a terrified gesture the uplifted hand. "I tremble with distrust and doubt of you; and the dim fear you cast upon me deepens into a nameless horror I can hardly bear.—I would not deprive myself of any kindly recollection, or any sympathy that is good for me, or others. What shall I lose, if I assent to this? What else will pass from my remembrance?"

"No knowledge; no result of study; nothing but the intertwisted chain of feelings and associations, each in its turn dependent on, and nourished by, the banished recollections.Those will go."

"Are they so many?" said the haunted man, reflecting in alarm.

"They have been wont to show themselves in the fire, in music, in the wind, in the dead stillness of the night, in the revolving years," returned the Phantom scornfully.

"In nothing else?"

The Phantom held its peace.

---

[62] It stood originally thus: "'Do you recollect the date,' said Mr. Dick, looking earnestly at me, and taking up his pen to note it down, 'when that bull got into the china warehouse and did so much mischief?' I was very much surprised by the inquiry; but remembering a song about such an occurrence that was once popular at Salem House, and thinking he might want to quote it, replied that I believed it was on St. Patrick's Day. 'Yes, I know,' said Mr. Dick—'in the morning; but what year?' I could give no information on this point." Original MS. of *Copperfield*.

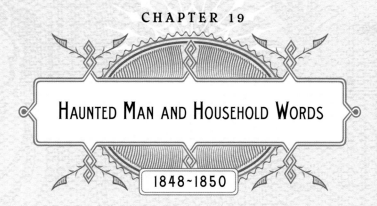

CHAPTER 19

HAUNTED MAN AND HOUSEHOLD WORDS

1848~1850

I$_T$ HAS BEEN SEEN THAT his fancy for his Christmas book of 1848 first arose to him at Lausanne in the summer of 1846, and that, after writing its opening pages in the autumn of the following year, he laid it aside under the pressure of his Dombey. These lines were in the letter that closed his 1848 Broadstairs holiday. "At last I am a mentally matooring of the Christmas book—or, as poor Macrone[63] used to write, 'booke,' 'boke,' 'buke,' &c." It was the first labour to which he applied himself at his return.

In London it soon came to maturity; was published duly as *The Haunted Man, or the Ghost's Bargain*; sold largely, beginning with a subscription of twenty thousand; and had a great success on the Adelphi stage, to which it was rather cleverly adapted by Lemon. Out of heaped-up images of gloomy and wintry fancies, the supernatural takes a shape which is not forced or violent; and the dialogue which is no dialogue, but a kind of dreary dreamy echo, is a piece of ghostly imagination better than Mrs. Radcliffe. The boon desired is granted and the bargain struck. He is not only to lose his own recollection of grief and wrong, but to destroy the like memory in all whom he approaches.

"You must suppose," he wrote to me (21st of November), "that the Ghost's saving clause gives him those glimpses without which it would be impossible to carry out the idea. Of course my point is that bad and good are inextricably linked in remembrance, and that you could not choose the enjoyment of recollecting only the good. To have all the best of it you must remember the worst also. My intention in the other point you mention is, that he should not know himself how he communicates the gift, whether by look or touch; and that it should diffuse itself in its own way in each

case. I can make this clearer by a very few lines in the second part. It is not only necessary to be so, for the variety of the story, but I think it makes the thing wilder and stranger." Critical niceties are indeed out of place, where wildness and strangeness in the means matter less than that there should be clearness in the drift and intention. Dickens leaves no doubt as to this. He thoroughly makes out his fancy, that no man should so far question the mysterious dispensations of evil in this world as to desire to lose the recollection of such injustice or misery as he may suppose it to have done to himself. There may have been sorrow, but there was the kindness that assuaged it; there may have been wrong, but there was the charity that forgave it; and with both are connected inseparably so many thoughts that soften and exalt whatever else is in the sense of memory, that what is good and pleasurable in life would cease to continue so if these were forgotten. The old proverb does not tell you to forget that you may forgive, but to forgive that you may forget. It is forgiveness of wrong, for forgetfulness of the evil that was in it; such as poor old Lear begged of Cordelia.

The design for his much-thought-of new Periodical was still "dim," as we have seen, when the first cogitation of it at Bonchurch occupied him; but the expediency of making it clearer came soon after with a visit from Mr. Evans, who brought his half-year's accounts of sales, and some small disappointment for him in those of *Copperfield*. "The accounts are rather shy, after *Dombey*, and what you said comes true after all. I am not sorry I cannot bring myself to care much for what opinions people may form; and I have a strong belief, that, if any of my books are read years hence, *Dombey* will be remembered as among the best of them: but passing influences are important for the time, and as *Chuzzlewit* with its small sale sent me up, *Dombey's* large sale has tumbled me down. Not very much, however, in real truth. These accounts only include the first three numbers, have of course been burdened with all the heavy expenses of number one, and ought not in reason to be complained of. But it is clear to me that the Periodical must be set agoing in the spring; and I have already been busy, at odd half-hours, in shadowing forth a name and an idea. Evans says they have but one opinion repeated to them of *Copperfield*, and they feel very confident about it. A steady twenty-five thousand, which it is now on the verge of, will do very well. The back numbers are always going off. Read the enclosed"

It was a letter from a Russian man of letters, dated from St. Petersburg and signed "Trinarch Ivansvitch Wredenskii," sending him a translation of *Dombey* into Russian; and informing him that his works, which before had only been translated in the journals, and with certain omissions, had now been translated in their entire form by his correspondent.

The week before he left Bonchurch I again had news of the old and often recurring fancy. "The old notion of the Periodical, which has been agitating itself in my mind for so long, I really think is at last gradually growing into form." That was on the 24th of September; and on the 7th of October, from Broadstairs, I had something of the form it had been taking. "I do great injustice to my floating ideas (pretty speedily and comfortably settling down into orderly arrangement) by saying anything about the Periodical now: but my notion is a weekly journal, price either three-halfpence or two-pence, matter in part original and in part selected, and always having, if possible, a little good poetry. . . . The original matter to be essays, reviews, letters, theatrical criticisms, &c, &c, as amusing as possible, but all distinctly and boldly going to what in one's own view ought to be the spirit of the people and the time. . . . Now to bind all this together, and to get a character established as it were which any of the writers may maintain without difficulty, I want to suppose a certain SHADOW, which may go into any place, by sunlight, moonlight, starlight, fire-light, candlelight, and be in all homes, and all nooks and corners, and be supposed to be cognisant of everything, and go everywhere, without the least difficulty. Which may be in the Theatre, the Palace, the House of Commons, the Prisons, the Unions, the Churches, on the Railroad, on the Sea, abroad and at home: a kind of semi-omniscient, omnipresent, intangible creature. I don't think it would do to call the paper THE SHADOW: but I want something tacked to that title, to express the notion of its being a cheerful, useful, and always welcome Shadow."

Excellent the idea doubtless, and so described in his letter that hardly anything more characteristic survives

him. But I could not make anything out of it that had a quite feasible look. The ordinary ground of miscellaneous reading, selection, and compilation out of which it was to spring, seemed to me no proper soil for the imaginative produce it was meant to bear. Not to trouble the reader now with objections given him in detail, my judgment was clear against his plan; less for any doubt of the effect if its parts could be brought to combine, than for my belief that it was not in that view practicable; and though he did not immediately accept my reasons, he acquiesced in them ultimately. "I do not lay much stress on your grave doubts about Periodical, but more anon." The more anon resolved itself into conversations out of which the shape given to the project was that which it finally took.

It was to be a weekly miscellany of general literature; and its stated objects were to be, to contribute to the entertainment and instruction of all classes of readers, and to help in the discussion of the more important social questions of the time. It was to comprise short stories by others as well as himself; matters of passing interest in the liveliest form that could be given to them; subjects suggested by books that might most be attracting attention; and poetry in every number if possible, but in any case something of romantic fancy. This was to be a cardinal point. This was all finally settled by the close of 1849, when a general announcement of the intended adventure was made. There remained only a title and an assistant editor; and I am happy now to remember that for the latter important duty Mr. Wills was chosen at my suggestion. He discharged his duties with admirable patience and ability for twenty years, and Dickens's later life had no more intimate friend.

The title took some time and occupied many letters. One of the first thought-of has now the curious interest of having foreshadowed, by the motto proposed to accompany it, the title of the series of *All the Year Round* which he was led to substitute for the older series in 1859. "THE ROBIN. With this motto from Goldsmith. '*The redbreast, celebrated for its affection to mankind, continues with us, the year round.*'" That however was rejected. Then came: "MANKIND. This I think very good." It followed the other nevertheless. After it came: "And here a strange idea, but with decided advantages. 'CHARLES DICKENS. A weekly journal designed for

Dickens explicitly lays out his aspiration to a sense of personal fellowship with his readers of all classes in this "Preliminary Word" to introduce his new periodical:

THE name that we have chosen for this publication expresses, generally, the desire we have at heart in originating it.

We aspire to live in the Household affections, and to be numbered among the Household thoughts, of our readers. We hope to be the comrade and friend of many thousands of people, of both sexes, and of all ages and conditions, on whose faces we may never look. We seek to bring into innumerable homes, from the stirring world around us, the knowledge of many social wonders, good and evil, that are not calculated to render any of us less ardently persevering in ourselves, less tolerant of one another, less faithful in the progress of mankind, less thankful for the privilege of living in this summer-dawn of time.

No mere utilitarian spirit, no iron binding of the mind to grim realities, will give a harsh tone to our Household Words. In the bosoms of the young and old, of the well-to-do and of the poor, we would tenderly cherish that light of Fancy which is inherent in the human breast; which, according to its nurture, burns with an inspiring flame, or sinks into a sullen glare, but which (or woe betide that day!) can never be extinguished. To show to all, that in all familiar things, even in those which are repellant on the surface, there is Romance enough, if we will find it out:—to teach the hardest workers at this whirling wheel of toil, that their lot is not necessarily a moody, brutal fact, excluded from the sympathies and graces of imagination; to bring the greater and the lesser in degree, together, upon that wide field, and mutually dispose them to a better acquaintance and a kinder understanding—is one main object of our *Household Words* .

The mightier inventions of this age are not, to our thinking, all material, but have a kind of souls in their stupendous bodies which may find expression in *Household Words*. The traveller whom we accompany on his railroad or his steamboat journey, may gain, we hope, some compensation for incidents which these later generations have outlived, in new associations with the Power that bears him onward; with the habitations and the ways of life of crowds of his fellow creatures among whom he passes like the wind; even with the towering chimneys he may see, spirting out fire and smoke upon the prospect. The swart giants, Slaves of the Lamp of Knowledge, have their thousand and one tales, no less than the Genii of the East; and these, in all their wild, grotesque, and fanciful aspects, in all their many phases of endurance, in all their many moving lessons of compassion and consideration, we design to tell.

Our *Household Words* will not be echoes of the present time alone, but of the past too. Neither will they treat of the hopes, the enterprises, triumphs, joys, and sorrows, of this country only, but, in some degree, of those every nation upon earth. For nothing can be a source of real interest in one of them, without concerning all the rest.

We have considered what an ambition it is to be admitted into many homes with affection and confidence; to be regarded as a friend by children and old people; to be thought of in affliction and in happiness; to people the sick room with airy shapes 'that give delight and hurt not,' and to be associated with the harmless laughter and the gentle tears of many hearths. We know the great responsibility of such a privilege; its vast reward; the pictures that it conjures up, in hours of solitary labour, of a multitude moved by one sympathy; the solemn hopes which it awakens in the labourer's breast, that he may be free from self-reproach in looking back at last upon his work, and that his name may be remembered in his race in time to come, and borne by the dear objects of his love with pride. The hand that writes these faltering lines, happily associated with some Household Words before to-day, has known enough of such experiences to enter an earnest spirit upon this new task, and with an awakened sense of all that it involves.

the instruction and entertainment of all classes of readers. CONDUCTED BY HIMSELF.'" Still, there was something wanting in that also. Next day arrived: "I really think if there *be* anything wanting in the other name, that this is very pretty, and just supplies it. THE HOUSEHOLD VOICE. I have thought of many others, as—THE HOUSEHOLD GUEST. THE HOUSEHOLD FACE. THE COMRADE. THE MICROSCOPE. THE HIGHWAY OF LIFE. THE LEVER. THE ROLLING YEARS. THE HOLLY TREE (with two lines from Southey for a motto). EVERYTHING, But I rather think the VOICE is it." It was near indeed; but the following day came, "HOUSEHOLD WORDS. This is a very pretty name:" and the choice was made.

The first number appeared on Saturday the 30th of March 1850, and contained among other things the beginning of a story by a very original writer, Mrs. Gaskell, for whose powers he had a high admiration, and with whom he had friendly intercourse during many years. Other opportunities will arise for mention of those with whom this new labour brought him into personal communication, but I may at once say that of all the writers, before unknown, whom his journal helped to make familiar to a wide world of readers, he had the strongest personal interest in Mr. Sala, and placed at once in the highest rank his capabilities of help in such an enterprise.[64]

---

[63] The mention of this name may remind me to state that I have received, in reference to the account in my first volume of Dickens's repurchase of his Sketches from Mr. Macrone, a letter from the solicitor and friend of that gentleman so expressed that I could have greatly wished to revise my narrative into nearer agreement with its writer's wish. But farther enquiry, and an examination of the books of Messrs. Chapman and Hall, have confirmed the statement given. Mr. Hansard is in error in supposing that "unsold impressions" of the books were included in the transaction (the necessary requirement being simply that the small remainders on hand should be transferred with a view to being "wasted"): I know myself that it could not have included any supposed right of Mr. Macrone to have a novel written for him, because upon that whole matter, and his continued unauthorised advertisements of the tale, I decided myself the reference against him: and Mr. Hansard may be assured that the £2000 was paid for the copyright alone. For the same copyright, a year before, Dickens had received £250, both the first and second series being included in the payment; and he had already had about the same sum as his half share of the profits of sales. I quote the close of Mr. Hansard's letter. "Macrone no doubt was an adventurer, but he was sanguine to the highest degree. He was a dreamer of dreams, putting no restraint on his exultant hopes by the reflection that he was not dealing justly towards others. But reproach has fallen upon him from wrong quarters. He died in poverty, and his creditors received nothing from his estate. But that was because he had paid away all he had, and all he had derived from trust and credit, to authors." This may have been so, but Dickens was not among the authors so benefited. The Sketches repurchased for the high price I have named never afterwards really justified such an outlay.

[64] Mr. Sala's first paper appeared in September 1851, and in the same month of the following year I had an allusion in a letter from Dickens which I shall hope to have Mr. Sala's forgiveness for printing. "That was very good indeed of Sala's" (some essay he had written). "He was twenty guineas in advance, by the bye, and I told Wills delicately to make him a present of it. I find him a very conscientious fellow. When he gets money ahead, he is not like the imbecile youth who so often do the like in Wellington-street" (the office of *Household Words*) "and walk off, but only works more industriously. I think he improves with everything he does. He looks sharply at the alterations in his articles, I observe; and takes the hint next time."

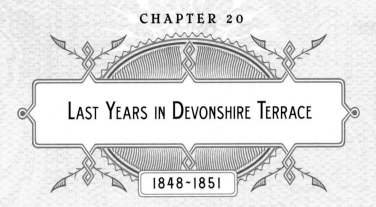

CHAPTER 20

LAST YEARS IN DEVONSHIRE TERRACE

1848~1851

EXCEPTING ALWAYS THE HAUNTS and associations of his childhood, Dickens had no particular sentiment of locality, and any special regard for houses he had lived in was not a thing noticeable in him. But he cared most for Devonshire-terrace, perhaps for the bit of ground attached to it; and it was with regret he suddenly discovered, at the close of 1847, that he should have to resign it "next lady-day three years. I had thought the lease two years more." To that brief remaining time belong some incidents of which I have still to give account; and I connect them with the house in which he lived during the progress of what is generally thought his greatest book, and of what I think were his happiest years.

We had never had such intimate confidences as in the interval since his return from Paris; but these have been used in my narrative of the childhood and boyish experiences, and what remain are incidental only. Of the fragment of autobiography there also given, the origin has been told; but the intention of leaving such a record had been in his mind, we now see, at an earlier date; and it was the very depth of our interest in the opening of his fragment that led to the larger design in which it became absorbed. "I hardly know why I write this," was his own comment on one of his personal revelations, "but the more than friendship which has grown between us seems to force it on me in my present mood. We shall speak of it all, you and I, Heaven grant, wisely and wonderingly many and many a time in after years. In the meanwhile I am more at rest for having opened all my heart and mind to you. . . . This day eleven years, poor dear Mary died."

That was written on the seventh of May 1848, but another sadness impending at the time was taking his thoughts still farther back; to when he trotted about with his little elder sister in the small garden to the house at Portsea. The faint hope for her which Elliotson had given him in Paris had since completely broken down; and I was to hear, in less than two months after the letter just quoted, how nearly the end was come. "A change took place in poor Fanny," he wrote on the 5th of July, "about the middle of the day yesterday, which took me out there last night. Her cough suddenly ceased almost, and, strange to say, she immediately became aware of her hopeless state; to which she resigned herself, after an hour's unrest and struggle, with extraordinary sweetness and constancy. She said she was quite calm and happy, relied upon the mediation of Christ, and had no terror at all. She had worked very hard, even when ill; but believed that was in her nature, and neither regretted nor complained of it." After not many weeks she died, and the little child who was her last anxiety did not long survive her.

In all the latter part of the year Dickens's thoughts were turning much to the form his next book should assume. A suggestion that he should write it in the first person, by way of change, had been thrown out by me, which he took at once very gravely; and this, with other things, though as yet not dreaming of any public use of his own personal and private recollections, conspired to bring about that resolve. The determination once taken, with what a singular truthfulness he contrived to blend the fact with the fiction may be shown by a small occurrence of this time. It has been inferred, from the vividness of the boy-impressions of Yarmouth in David's earliest experiences, that the place must have been familiar to his own boyhood: but the truth was that at the close of 1848 he first saw that celebrated sea-port. One of its earlier months had been signalised by an adventure in which Leech, Lemon, and myself took part with him, when, obtaining horses from Salisbury, we passed the whole of a March day in riding over every part of the Plain; visiting Stonehenge, and exploring Hazlitt's "hut" at Winterslow, birthplace of some of his finest essays; altogether with so brilliant a success that now (13th of November) he proposed to "repeat the Salisbury Plain idea in a new direction in mid-winter, to wit, Blackgang Chine in the Isle of Wight, with dark winter cliffs and roaring oceans." But mid-winter brought with it too much dreariness of its own. . . and on the last day of the year he bethought him "it would

Devonshire Terrace, London. Dickens's home from 1839–1851

be better to make an outburst to some old cathedral city we don't know, and what do you say to Norwich and Stanfield-hall?" Thither accordingly the three friends went, illness at the last disabling me; and of the result I heard (12th of January, 1849) that Stanfield-hall, the scene of a recent frightful tragedy, had nothing attractive unless the term might be applied to "a murderous look that seemed to invite such a crime. Norwich, a disappointment" (one pleasant face "transformeth a city," but he was unable yet to connect it with our delightful friend Elwin); "all save its place of execution, which we found fit for a gigantic scoundrel's exit. But the success of the trip, for me, was to come. Yarmouth, sir, where we went afterwards, is the

strangest place in the wide world: one hundred and forty-six miles of hill-less marsh between it and London. More when we meet. I shall certainly try my hand at it." He made it the home of his "little Em'ly."

Everything now was taking that direction with him; and soon, to give his own account of it, his mind was upon names "running like a high sea." Four days after the date of the last-quoted letter ("all over happily, thank God, by four o'clock this morning") there came the birth of his eighth child and sixth son; whom at first he meant to call by Oliver Goldsmith's name, but settled afterwards into that of Henry Fielding; and to whom that early friend Ainsworth who had first made us

DAVID COPPERFIELD, CHAPTER 3

David Copperfield visits Mr. Peggotty's Houseboat at Yarmouth:

I WAS quite tired, and very glad, when we saw Yarmouth. It looked rather spongy and soppy, I thought, as I carried my eye over the great dull waste that lay across the river; and I could not help wondering, if the world were really as round as my geography book said, how any part of it came to be so flat. But I reflected that Yarmouth might be situated at one of the poles; which would account for it.

As we drew a little nearer, and saw the whole adjacent prospect lying a straight low line under the sky, I hinted to Peggotty that a mound or so might have improved it; and also that if the land had been a little more separated from the sea, and the town and the tide had not been quite so much mixed up, like toast and water, it would have been nicer. But Peggotty said, with greater emphasis than usual, that we must take things as we found them, and that, for her part, she was proud to call herself a Yarmouth Bloater.

When we got into the street (which was strange enough to me) and smelt the fish, and pitch, and oakum, and tar, and saw the sailors walking about, and the carts jingling up and down over the stones, I felt that I had done so busy a place an injustice; and said as much to Peggotty, who heard my expressions of delight with great complacency, and told me it was well known (I suppose to those who had the good fortune to be born Bloaters) that Yarmouth was, upon the whole, the finest place in the universe.

'Here's my Am!' screamed Peggotty, 'growed out of knowledge!'

He was waiting for us, in fact, at the public-house; and asked me how I found myself, like an old acquaintance. I did not feel, at first, that I knew him as well as he knew me, because he had never come to our house since the night I was born, and naturally he had the advantage of me. But our intimacy was much advanced by his taking me on his back to carry me home. He was, now, a huge, strong fellow of six feet high, broad in proportion, and round-shouldered; but with a simpering boy's face and curly light hair that gave him quite a sheepish look. He was dressed in a canvas jacket, and a pair of such very stiff trousers that they would have stood quite as well alone, without any legs in them. And you couldn't so properly have said he wore a hat, as that he was covered in a-top, like an old building, with something pitchy.

Ham carrying me on his back and a small box of ours under his arm, and Peggotty carrying another small box of ours, we turned down lanes bestrewn with bits of chips and little hillocks of sand, and went past gas-works, rope-walks, boat-builders' yards, shipwrights' yards, ship-breakers' yards, caulkers' yards, riggers' lofts, smiths' forges, and a great litter of such places, until we came out upon the dull waste I had already seen at a distance; when Ham said,

'Yon's our house, Mas'r Davy!'

I looked in all directions, as far as I could stare over the wilderness, and away at the sea, and away at the river, but no house could I make out. There was a black barge, or some other kind of superannuated boat, not far off, high and dry on the ground, with an iron funnel sticking out of it for a chimney and smoking very cosily; but nothing else in the way of a habitation that was visible to me.

'That's not it?' said I. 'That ship-looking thing?'

'That's it, Mas'r Davy,' returned Ham.

If it had been Aladdin's palace, roc's egg and all, I suppose I could not have been more charmed with the romantic idea of living in it. There was a delightful door cut in the side, and it was roofed in, and there were little windows in it; but the wonderful charm of it was, that it was a real boat which had no doubt been upon the water hundreds of times, and which had never been intended to be lived in, on dry land. That was the captivation of it to me. If it had ever been meant to be lived in, I might have thought it small, or inconvenient, or lonely; but never having been designed for any such use, it became a perfect abode.

Mr. Peggotty's Houseboat, illustration from *David Copperfield* by Fred Barnard, engraved by the Dalziels for the Household Edition of *David Copperfield*, ca. 1870

known to each other, welcome and pleasant companion always, was asked to be godfather. "Deepest despondency, as usual, in commencing, besets me;" is the opening of the letter in which he speaks of what of course was always one of his first anxieties, the selection of a name. In this particular instance he had been undergoing doubts and misgivings to more than the usual degree. It was not until the 23rd of February he got to anything like the shape of a feasible title. It is singular that it should never have occurred to him, while the name was thus strangely as by accident bringing itself together, that the initials were but his own reversed; but he was much startled when I pointed this out, and protested it was just in keeping with the fates and chances which were always befalling him. "Why else," he said, "should I

so obstinately have kept to that name when once it turned up?"

"I wish," he wrote on the 26th of February, "you would look over carefully the titles now enclosed, and tell me to which you most incline. You will see that they give up *Mag* altogether, and refer exclusively to one name—that which I last sent you. I doubt whether I could, on the whole, get a better name.

"1. *The Copperfield Disclosures.* Being the personal history, experience, and observation, of Mr. David Copperfield the Younger, of Blunderstone House.

"2. *The Copperfield Records.* Being the personal history, experience, and observation, of Mr. David Copperfield the Younger, of Copperfield Cottage.

"3. *The Last Living Speech and Confession of David*

DICKENS'S LETTER TO THE EDITOR OF *THE TIMES*, 13 NOVEMBER 1849

Appalled by the behavior of the crowd at the public hanging of Mr. and Mrs. Manning (found guilty of murdering Mrs. Manning's lover for his money), Dickens wrote to The Times *attacking the spectacle of public execution:*

I WAS a witness of the execution at Horsemonger Lane this morning. I went there with the intention of observing the crowd gathered to behold it, and I had excellent opportunities of doing so, at intervals all through the night, and continuously from day-break until after the spectacle was over... I believe that a sight so inconceivably awful as the wickedness and levity of the immense crowd collected at that execution this morning could be imagined by no man, and could be presented in no heathen land under the sun. The horrors of the gibbet and of the crime which brought the wretched murderers to it faded in my mind before the atrocious bearing, looks, and language of the assembled spectators. When I came upon the scene at midnight, the shrillness of the cries and howls that were raised from time to time, denoting that they came from a concourse of boys and girls already assembled in the best places, made my blood run cold. As the night went on, screeching, and laughing, and yelling in strong chorus of parodies on negro melodies, with substitutions of 'Mrs. Manning' for 'Susannah', and the like, were added to these. When the day dawned, thieves, low prostitutes, ruffians, and vagabonds of every kind, flocked on to the ground, with every variety of offensive and foul behaviour. Fightings, faintings, whistlings, imitations of Punch, brutal jokes, tumultuous demonstrations of indecent delight when swooning women were dragged out of the crowd by the police, with their dresses disordered, gave a new zest to the general entertainment. When the sun rose brightly-as it did-it gilded thousands upon thousands of upturned faces, so inexpressibly odious in their brutal mirth or callousness, that a man had cause to feel ashamed of the shape he wore, and to shrink from himself, as fashioned in the image of the Devil. When the two miserable creatures who attracted all this ghastly sight about them were turned quivering into the air, there was no more emotion, no more pity, no more thought that two immortal souls had gone to judgement, no more restraint in any of the previous obscenities, than if the name of Christ had never been heard in this world, and there were no belief among men but that they perished like the beasts.

Copperfield Junior, of Blunderstone Lodge, who was never executed at the Old Bailey. Being his personal history found among his papers.

"4. *The Copperfield Survey of the World as it Rolled.* Being the personal history, experience, and observation, of David Copperfield the Younger, of Blunderstone Rookery.

"5. *The Last Will and Testament of Mr. David Copperfield.* Being his personal history left as a legacy.

"6. *Copperfield, Complete.* Being the whole personal history and experience of Mr. David Copperfield of Blunderstone House, which he never meant to be published on any account.

Or, the opening words of No. 6 might be *Copperfield's Entire*; and *The Copperfield Confessions* might open Nos. 1 and 2. Now, WHAT SAY YOU?"

What I said is to be inferred from what he wrote back on the 28th. "The *Survey* has been my favourite from the first. Kate picked it out from the rest, without my saying anything about it. Georgy too. You hit upon it, on the first glance. Therefore I have no doubt that it is indisputably the best title; and I will stick to it." There was a change nevertheless. His completion of the second chapter defined to himself, more clearly than before, the character of the book; and the propriety of rejecting everything not strictly personal from the name given to it. The words proposed, therefore, became ultimately these only: "The Personal History, Adventures, Experience, and Observation of David Copperfield the Younger, of Blunderstone Rookery, which he never meant to be published on any account." And the letter which told me that with this name it was finally to be launched on the first of May, told me also (19th April) the difficulties that still beset him at the opening.

The preceding month was that of the start of *David Copperfield*, and to one more dinner (on the 12th) I may especially refer for those who were present at it. Carlyle and Mrs. Carlyle came, Thackeray and Rogers, Mrs. Gaskell and Kenyon, Jerrold and Hablot Browne, with Mr. and Mrs. Tagart; and it was a delight to see the enjoyment of Dickens at Carlyle's laughing reply to questions about his health, that he was, in the language of Mr. Peggotty's housekeeper, a lorn lone creature and everything went contrairy with him.

This chapter would far outrun its limits if I spoke of other as pleasant gatherings under Dickens's roof during the years which I am now more particularly describing; when, besides the dinners, the musical enjoyments and dancings, as his children became able to take part in them, were incessant. "Remember that for my Biography!" he said to me gravely on twelfth-day in 1849, after telling me what he had done the night before; and as gravely I now redeem my laughing promise that I would. Little Mary and her sister Kate had taken much pains to teach their father the polka, that he might dance it with them at their brother's birthday festivity (held this year on the 7th, as the 6th was a Sunday); and in the middle of the previous night as he lay in bed, the fear had fallen on him suddenly that the step was forgotten, and then and there, in that wintry dark cold night, he got out of bed to practise it. Anything *more* characteristic could certainly not be told; unless I could have shown him dancing it afterwards, and far excelling the youngest performer in untiring vigour and vivacity.

Some incidents that belong specially to the three years that closed his residence in the home thus associated with not the least interesting part of his career, will farther show what now were his occupations and ways of life. In the summer of 1849 he came up from Broadstairs to attend a Mansion-house dinner, which the lord mayor of that day had been moved by a laudable ambition to give to "literature and art," which he supposed would be adequately represented by the Royal Academy, the contributors to *Punch*, Dickens, and one or two newspaper men. On the whole the result was not cheering; the worthy chief

magistrate, no doubt quite undesignedly, expressing too much surprise at the unaccustomed faces around him to be altogether complimentary. In general (this was the tone) we are in the habit of having princes, dukes, ministers, and what not for our guests, but what a delight, all the greater for being unusual, to see gentlemen like you! In other words, what could possibly be pleasanter than for people satiated with greatness to get for a while by way of change into the butler's pantry? This in substance was Dickens's account to me next day, and his reason for having been very careful in his acknowledgment of the toast of "the Novelists."

Of an incident towards the close of the year, though it had important practical results, brief mention will here suffice. We saw the Mannings executed on the walls of Horse-monger-lane gaol; and with the letter which Dickens wrote next day to the *Times* descriptive of what we had witnessed on that memorable morning, there began an active agitation against public executions which never ceased until the salutary change was effected which has worked so well.

A little earlier in that winter we had together taken his eldest son to Eton, and a little later he had a great sorrow. "Poor dear Jeffrey!" he wrote to me on the 29th January, 1850. "I bought a *Times* at the station yesterday morning, and was so stunned by the announcement, that I felt it in that wounded part of me, almost directly; and the bad symptoms (modified) returned within a few hours. I had a letter from him in extraordinary good spirits within this week or two—he was better, he said, than he had been for a long time—and I sent him proof-sheets of the number only last Wednesday. I say nothing of his wonderful abilities and great career, but he was a most affectionate and devoted friend to me; and though no man could wish to live and die more happily, so old in years and yet so young in faculties and sympathies, I am very very deeply grieved for his loss." He was justly entitled to feel pride in being able so to word his tribute of sorrowing affection. Jeffrey had completed with consummate success, if ever man did, the work appointed him in this world; and few, after a life of such activities, have left a memory so unstained and pure. But other and sharper sorrows awaited Dickens.

RIGHT: William Charles Macready (1793-1873), actor and theatre manager, oil on canvas by John Jackson, 1821

The chief occupation of the past and present year, *David Copperfield*, will have a chapter to itself, and in this may be touched but lightly. Once fairly in it, the story bore him irresistibly along; certainly with less trouble to himself in the composition, beyond that ardent sympathy with the creatures of the fancy which always made so absolutely real to him their sufferings or sorrows; and he was probably never less harassed by interruptions or breaks in his invention. His principal hesitation occurred in connection with the child-wife Dora, who had become a great favourite as he went on; and it was shortly after her fate had been decided, in the early autumn of 1850, but before she breathed her last, that a third daughter was born to him, to whom he gave his dying little heroine's name. On these and other points, without forestalling what waits to be said of the composition of this fine story, a few illustrative words from his letters will properly find a place here. "*Copperfield* half done," he wrote of the second number on the 6th of June. "I feel, thank God, quite confident in the story. I have a move in it ready for this month; another for next; and another for the next."

The year following did not open with favourable omen, both the child and its mother having severe illness. The former rallied however, and "little Dora is getting on bravely, thank God!" was his bulletin of the early part of February. Soon after, it was resolved to make trial of Great Malvern for Mrs. Dickens; and lodgings were taken there in March, Dickens and her sister accompanying her, and the children being left in London. "It is a most beautiful place," he wrote to me (15th of March). This was the month, as we have seen, when the performances for the Guild were in active preparation, and it was also the date of the farewell dinner to our friend Macready on his quitting the stage.

Dickens had to return to London after the middle of March for business connected with a charitable home established at Shepherd's-bush by Miss Coutts, in the benevolent hope of rescuing fallen women by testing their fitness for emigration, of which future mention will be made, and which largely and regularly occupied his time for several years.

On this occasion his stay was prolonged by the illness of his father. His health had been failing latterly, and graver symptoms were now spoken of. "I saw my poor father twice yesterday," he wrote to me on the 27th, "the second time between ten and eleven at night. In the morning I thought him not so well. At night, as well as any one in such a situation could be." Next day he was so much better that his son went back to Malvern, and even gave us grounds for hope that we might yet have his presence in Hertfordshire to advise on some questions connected with the comedy which Sir Edward Lytton had written for the Guild. But the end came suddenly. I returned from Knebworth to London, supposing that some accident had detained him at Malvern; and at my house this letter waited me. "Devonshire-terrace, Monday, thirty-first of March 1851. . . . My poor father died this morning at five and twenty minutes to six. They had sent for me to Malvern, but I passed John on the railway; for I came up with the intention of hurrying down to Bulwer Lytton's to-day before you should have left. I arrived at eleven last night, and was in Keppel-street at a quarter past eleven. But he did not know me, nor any one. He began to sink at about noon yesterday, and never rallied afterwards. I remained there until he died—O so quietly. . . . I hardly know what to do. I am going up to Highgate to get the ground. Perhaps you may like to go, and I should like it if you do. I will not leave here before two o'clock. I think I must go down to Malvern again, at night, to know what is to be done about the children's mourning; and as you are returning to Bulwer's I should like to have gone that way, if *Bradshaw* gave me any hope of doing it. I wish most particularly to see you, I needn't say. I must not let myself be distracted by anything—and God knows I have left a sad sight!—from the scheme on which so much depends. Most part of the alterations proposed I think good." Mr. John Dickens was laid in Highgate Cemetery on the 5th of April; and the stone placed over him by the son who has made his name a famous one in England, bore tribute to his "zealous, useful, cheerful spirit." What more is to be said of him will be most becomingly said in speaking of *David Copperfield*. While the book was in course of being written, all that had been best in him came more and more vividly back to its author's memory; as time wore on, nothing else was remembered; and five years before his own death, after using in one of his letters to me a phrase

FROM "HOME FOR HOMELESS WOMEN," *HOUSEHOLD WORDS*, 23 APRIL 1853 REPRINTED IN
THE DENT UNIFORM EDITION OF DICKENS'S JOURNALISM, VOL 3, ED. BY MICHAEL SLATER

*Dickens describes his establishment and running, with wealthy philanthropist Angela Burdett Coutts,
of Urania Cottage, a "Home for Homeless Women." This domestic language distinguishes the enterprise from existing,
more forbiddingly named, institutions such as The British Penitent Female Refuge:*

FIVE years and a half ago, certain ladies, grieved to think that numbers of their own sex were wandering about the streets in degradation, passing through and through the prisons all their lives, or hopelessly perishing in other ways, resolved to try the experiment on a limited on a limited scale of a Home for the reclamation and emigration of women. As it was clear to them that there could be little or no hope in this country for the greater part of those who might become the objects of their charity, they determined to receive into their Home, only those who distinctly accepted this condition: That they came there to be ultimately sent abroad (whither, was at the discretion of the ladies); and that they also came there, to remain for such length of time as considered necessary as a term of probation, and for instruction in the means of obtaining an honest livelihood. The object of the Home was twofold. First, to replace young women who had already lost their characters and lapsed into guilt, into a situation of hope. Secondly, to save other young women who were in danger of falling into the like condition, and give them an opportunity of flying from crime when they and it stood face to face.

The projectors of this establishment, in undertaking it, were sustained by nothing but the high object of making some unhappy women a blessing to themselves and others instead of a curse, and raising up among the solitudes of a new world some virtuous homes, much needed there, from the sorrow and ruin of the old. They had no romantic visions or extravagant expectations. They were prepared for many failures and disappointments, and to consider their enterprise rewarded, if they in time succeeded with one third or one half of the cases they received.

As the experience of this small Institution, even under the many disadvantages of a beginning, may be useful and interesting, this paper will contain an exact account of its progress and results.

It was (and is) established in a detached house with a garden. The house was never designed for any such purpose, and is only adapted to it, in being retired and not immediately overlooked. It is capable of containing thirteen inmates besides two Superintendents. Excluding from consideration ten young women now in the house, there have been received in all, since November eighteen hundred and forty seven, fifty-six inmates. They have belonged to no particular class, but have been starving needlewomen of good character, poor needlewomen who have robbed their furnished lodgings, violent girls committed to prison for disturbances in ill-conducted workhouses, poor girls from Ragged Schools, destitute girls who have applied at Police offices for relief, young women from the streets: young women of the same class taken from the prisons after undergoing punishment there as disorderly characters, or for shoplifting, or for thefts from the person: domestic servants who have been seduced, and two young women held to bail for attempting suicide. No class has been favored more than another; and misfortune and distress are a sufficient introduction. It is not usual to receive women of more than five or six-and-twenty; the average age in the fifty-six cases would probably be about twenty. In some instances there have been very great personal attractions; in others, the girls have been very homely and plain. The reception has been wholly irrespective of such sources of interest. Nearly all have been extremely ignorant.

Of these fifty-six cases, seven went away by their own desire during their probation; ten were sent away for misconduct in the Home; seven ran away; three emigrated and relapsed on the passage out; thirty (of whom seven are now married) on their arrival in Australia or elsewhere, entered into a good service, acquired a good character, and have done so well ever since as to establish a strong prepossession in favour of others sent out from the same quarter. [. . .]

rather out of the common with him, this was added: "I find this looks like my poor father, whom I regard as a better man the longer I live."

He was at this time under promise to take the chair at the General Theatrical Fund on the 14th of April. Great efforts were made to relieve him from the promise; but such special importance was attached to his being present, and the Fund so sorely then required help, that, no change of day being found possible for the actors who desired to attend, he yielded to the pressure put upon him; of which the result was to throw upon me a sad responsibility. The reader will understand why, even at this distance of time; my allusion to it is brief.

The train from Malvern brought him up only five minutes short of the hour appointed for the dinner, and we first met that day at the London Tavern. I never heard him to greater advantage than in the speech that followed. His liking for this Fund was the fact of its not confining its benefits to any special or exclusive body of actors, but opening them generously to all.

Half an hour before he rose to speak I had been called out of the room. It was the servant from Devonshire-terrace to tell me his child Dora was suddenly dead. She had not been strong from her birth; but there was just at this time no cause for special fear, when unexpected convulsions came, and the frail little life passed away. My decision had to be formed at once; and I satisfied myself that it would be best to permit his part of the proceedings to close before the truth was told to him. But as he went on, after the sentences I have quoted, to speak of actors having to come from scenes of sickness, of suffering, aye, even of death itself, to play their parts before us, my part was very difficult. "Yet how often is it with all of us," he proceeded to say, and I remember to this hour with what anguish I listened to words that had for myself alone, in all the crowded room, their full significance: "how often is it with all of us, that in our several spheres we have to do violence to our feelings, and to hide our hearts in carrying on this fight of life, if we would bravely discharge in it our duties and responsibilities." In the disclosure that followed when he left the chair, Mr. Lemon, who was present, assisted me; and I left this good friend with him next day, when I went myself to Malvern and brought back Mrs. Dickens and her sister. The little child lies in a grave at Highgate near that of Mr. and Mrs. John Dickens; and on the stone which covers her is now written also her father's name, and those of two of her brothers.

One more public discussion he took part in, before quitting London for the rest of the summer; and what he said (it was a meeting, with Lord Carlisle in the chair, in aid of Sanitary reform) very pregnantly illustrates what was remarked by me on a former page. He declared his belief that neither education nor religion could do anything really useful in social improvement until the way had been paved for their ministrations by cleanliness and decency.

Shortly after the Sanitary meeting came the first Guild performances; and then Dickens left Devonshire-terrace, never to return to it. "I have been" (15th of September) "tremendously at work these two days; eight hours at a stretch yesterday, and six hours and a half to-day, with the Ham and Steerforth chapter, which has completely knocked me over—utterly defeated me!" "I am" (21st of October) "within three pages of the shore; and am strangely divided, as usual in such cases, between sorrow and joy. Oh, my dear Forster, if I were to say half of what *Copperfield* makes me feel to-night, how strangely, even to you, I should be turned inside out! I seem to be sending some part of myself into the Shadowy World."

LEFT: Angela Georgina Burdett-Coutts, oil on panel by unknown artist (detail), ca. 1840

VOLUME III: 1852~1870

LEFT: *Charles Dickens by Ben Gurney, New York, 1867*

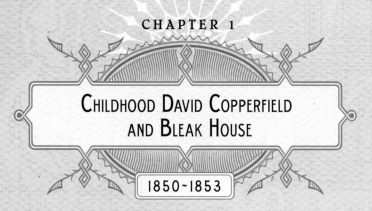

CHAPTER 1

CHILDHOOD DAVID COPPERFIELD AND BLEAK HOUSE

1850~1853

DICKENS NEVER STOOD so high in reputation as at the completion of *Copperfield*. The popularity it obtained at the outset increased to a degree not approached by any previous book excepting *Pickwick*. "You gratify me more than I can tell you," he wrote to Bulwer Lytton (July 1850), "by what you say about *Copperfield*, because I hope myself that some heretofore deficient qualities are there." If the power was not greater than in *Chuzzlewit*, the subject had more attractiveness; there was more variety of incident, with a freer play of character; and there was withal a suspicion, which though general and vague had sharpened interest not a little, that underneath the fiction lay something of the author's life. How much, was not known by the world until he had passed away.

"I have had the queerest adventure this morning," he wrote (28th of December 1849) on the eve of his tenth number, "the receipt of the enclosed from Miss Mowcher! It is serio-comic, but there is no doubt one is wrong in being tempted to such a use of power." Thinking a grotesque little oddity among his acquaintance to be safe from recognition, he had done what Smollett did sometimes, but never Fielding, and given way, in the first outburst of fun that had broken out around the fancy, to the temptation of copying too closely peculiarities of figure and face amounting in effect to deformity. He was shocked at discovering the pain he had given, and a copy is before me of the assurances by way of reply which he at once sent to the complainant. That he was grieved and surprised beyond measure. That he had not intended her altogether. That all his characters, being made up out of many people, were composite, and never individual. That the chair (for table) and other matters were

undoubtedly from her, but that other traits were not hers at all; and that in Miss Mowcher's "Ain't I volatile" his friends had quite correctly recognized the favourite utterance of a different person. That he felt nevertheless he had done wrong, and would now do anything to repair it. That he had intended to employ the character in an unpleasant way, but he would, whatever the risk or inconvenience, change it all, so that nothing but an agreeable impression should be left. The reader will remember how this was managed, and that the thirty-second chapter went far to undo what the twenty-second had done.

A much earlier instance is the only one known to me where a character in one of his books intended to be odious was copied wholly from a living original. The use of such material, never without danger, might have been justifiable here if anywhere, and he had himself a satisfaction in always admitting the identity of Mr. Fang in *Oliver Twist* with Mr. Laing of Hatton-garden. But the avowal of his purpose in that case, and his mode of setting about it, mark strongly a difference of procedure from that which, following great examples, he adopted in his later books.

He wrote accordingly (from Doughty-street on the 3rd of June 1837) to Mr. Haines, a gentleman who then had general supervision over the police reports for the daily papers. "In my next number of *Oliver Twist* I must have a magistrate; and, casting about for a magistrate whose harshness and insolence would render him a fit subject to be *shown up*, I have as a necessary consequence stumbled upon Mr. Laing of Hatton-garden celebrity. I know the man's character perfectly well; but as it would be necessary to describe his personal appearance also, I ought to have seen him, which (fortunately or unfortunately as the case may be) I have never done. In this dilemma it occurred to me that perhaps I might under your auspices be smuggled into the Hatton-garden office for a few moments some morning. If you can further my object I shall be really very greatly obliged to you." The opportunity was found; the magistrate was brought up before the novelist; and shortly after, on some fresh outbreak of intolerable temper, the home-secretary found it an easy and popular step to remove Mr. Laing from the bench.

This was a comfort to everybody, saving only the principal person; but the instance was highly exceptional,

David Copperfield, illustration by Kyd from *Character Sketches from Charles Dickens*, ca. 1890

Mr. Micawber, illustration by Kyd from *Character Sketches from Charles Dickens*, ca. 1890

and it rarely indeed happens that to the individual objection natural in every such case some consideration should not be paid. In the book that followed *Copperfield*, two characters appeared having resemblances in manner and speech to two distinguished writers too vivid to be mistaken by their personal friends. To Lawrence Boythorn, under whom Landor figured, no objection was made; but Harold Skimpole, recognizable for Leigh Hunt, led to much remark; the difference being, that ludicrous traits were employed in the first to enrich without impairing an attractive person in the tale, whereas to the last was assigned a part in the plot which no fascinating foibles or gaieties of speech could redeem from contempt.

Though a want of consideration was thus shown to the friend whom the character would be likely to recall to many readers, it is nevertheless very certain that the intention of Dickens was not at first, or at any time, an unkind one. He erred from thoughtlessness only. What led him to the subject

at all, he has himself stated. Hunt's philosophy of moneyed obligations, always, though loudly, half jocosely proclaimed, and his ostentatious wilfulness in the humouring of that or any other theme on which he cared for the time to expatiate, had so often seemed to Dickens to be whimsical and attractive that, wanting an "airy quality" for the man he invented, this of Hunt occurred to him; and "partly for that reason, and partly, he has since often grieved to think, for the pleasure it afforded to find a delightful manner reproducing itself under his hand, he yielded to the temptation of too often making the character speak like his old friend."

The pleasant sparkling airy talk, which could not be mistaken, identified with odious qualities a friend only known to the writer by attractive ones; and for this there was no excuse. Perhaps the only person acquainted with the original who failed to recognize the copy, was the original himself (a common case); but good-natured friends in time told Hunt everything, and painful explanations followed,

Aunt Betsey seeing off trespassing Donkey boys, scene from *David Copperfield*,
illustrated by Felix Octavius Carr, ca. 1873

where nothing was possible to Dickens but what amounted to a friendly evasion of the points really at issue. The time for redress had gone. I yet well remember with what eager earnestness, on one of these occasions, he strove to set Hunt up again in his own esteem. "Separate in your own mind," he said to him, "what you see of yourself from what other people tell you that they see. As it has given you so much pain, I take it at its worst, and say I am deeply sorry, and that I feel I did wrong in doing it. I should otherwise have taken it at its best, and ridden off upon what I strongly feel to be the truth, that there is nothing in it that *should* have given you pain. The character is not you, for there are traits in it common to fifty thousand people besides, and I did not fancy you would ever recognize it. Under similar disguises my own father and mother are in my books, and you might as well see your likeness in Micawber." The distinction is that the foibles

Advertisement for French adaptation of *David Copperfield*, 1884

of Mr. Micawber and of Mrs. Nickleby, however laughable, make neither of them in speech or character less loveable; and that this is not to be said of Skimpole's.

The Micawber offence otherwise was not grave. We have seen in what way Dickens was moved or inspired by the rough lessons of his boyhood, and the groundwork of the character was then undoubtedly laid; but the rhetorical exuberance impressed itself upon him later, and from this, as it expanded and developed in a thousand amusing ways, the full-length figure took its great charm. No one could know the elder Dickens without secretly liking him the better for these flourishes of speech, which adapted themselves so readily to his gloom as well as to his cheerfulness, that it was difficult not to fancy they had helped him considerably in both, and had rendered more tolerable to him, if also more possible, the shade and sunshine of his chequered life.

It is a tribute to the generally healthful and manly tone of the story of *Copperfield* that such should be the outcome of the eccentricities of this leading personage in it; and the superiority in this respect of Micawber over Skimpole is one of many indications of the inferiority of *Bleak House* to its predecessor. With leading resemblances that make it difficult to say which character best represents the principle or no principle of impecuniosity, there cannot be any doubt which has the advantage in moral and intellectual development. It is genuine humour against personal satire. Between the worldly circumstances of the two, there is nothing to choose; but as to everything else it is the difference between shabbiness and greatness. Skimpole's sunny talk might be expected to please as much as Micawber's gorgeous speech, the design of both being to take the edge off poverty. But in the one we have no relief from attendant meanness or

distress, and we drop down from the airiest fancies into sordidness and pain; whereas in the other nothing pitiful or merely selfish ever touches us. At its lowest depth of what is worst, we never doubt that something better must turn up; and of a man who sells his bedstead that he may entertain his friend, we altogether refuse to think nothing but badly. This is throughout the free and cheery style of *Copperfield*.

The masterpieces of Dickens's humour are not in it; but he has nowhere given such variety of play to his invention, and the book is unapproached among his writings for its completeness of effect and uniform pleasantness of tone.

What has to be said hereafter of those writings generally, will properly restrict what is said here, as in previous instances, mainly to personal illustration. The *Copperfield* disclosures formerly made will for ever connect the book with the author's individual story; but too much has been assumed, from those revelations, of a full identity of Dickens with his hero, and of a supposed intention that his own character as well as parts of his career should be expressed in the narrative. It is right to warn the reader as to this. He can judge for himself how far the childish experiences are likely to have given the turn to Dickens's genius; whether their bitterness had so burnt into his nature, as, in the hatred of oppression, the revolt against abuse of power, and the war with injustice under every form displayed in his earliest books, to have reproduced itself only; and to what extent mere compassion for his own childhood may account for the strange fascination always exerted over him by child-suffering and sorrow.

Consider Copperfield thus in his proper place in the story, and sequence as well as connection will be given to the varieties of its childish adventure. The first warm nest

Leigh Hunt

BLEAK HOUSE, CHAPTER 6

Leigh Hunt's offense at being portrayed as the responsibility-evading Harold Skimpole is easily understood:

WHEN we went downstairs, we were presented to Mr. Skimpole, who was standing before the fire telling Richard how fond he used to be, in his school-time, of football. He was a little bright creature with a rather large head, but a delicate face and a sweet voice, and there was a perfect charm in him. All he said was so free from effort and spontaneous and was said with such a captivating gaiety that it was fascinating to hear him talk. Being of a more slender figure than Mr. Jarndyce and having a richer complexion, with browner hair, he looked younger. Indeed, he had more the appearance in all respects of a damaged young man than a well-preserved elderly one. There was an easy negligence in his manner and even in his dress (his hair carelessly disposed, and his neckkerchief loose and flowing, as I have seen artists paint their own portraits) which I could not separate from the idea of a romantic youth who had undergone some unique process of depreciation. It struck me as being not at all like the manner or appearance of a man who had advanced in life by the usual road of years, cares, and experiences.

I gathered from the conversation that Mr. Skimpole had been educated for the medical profession and had once lived, in his professional capacity, in the household of a German prince. He told us, however, that as he had always been a mere child in point of weights and measures and had never known anything about them (except that they disgusted him), he had never been able to prescribe with the requisite accuracy of detail. In fact, he said, he had no head for detail. And he told us, with great humour, that when he was wanted to bleed the prince or physic any of his people, he was generally found lying on his back in bed, reading the newspapers or making fancy-sketches in pencil, and couldn't come. The prince, at last, objecting to this, "in which," said Mr. Skimpole, in the frankest manner, "he was perfectly right," the engagement terminated, and Mr. Skimpole having (as he added with delightful gaiety) "nothing to live upon but love, fell in love, and married, and surrounded himself with rosy cheeks." His good friend Jarndyce and some other of his good friends then helped him, in quicker or slower succession, to several openings in life, but to no purpose, for he must confess to two of the oldest infirmities in the world: one was that he had no idea of time, the other that he had no idea of money. In consequence of which he never kept an appointment, never could transact any business, and never knew the value of anything! Well! So he had got on in life, and here he was! He was very fond of reading the papers, very fond of making fancy-sketches with a pencil, very fond of nature, very fond of art. All he asked of society was to let him live. THAT wasn't much. His wants were few. Give him the papers, conversation, music, mutton, coffee, landscape, fruit in the season, a few sheets of Bristol-board, and a little claret, and he asked no more. He was a mere child in the world, but he didn't cry for the moon. He said to the world, "Go your several ways in peace! Wear red coats, blue coats, lawn sleeves; put pens behind your ears, wear aprons; go after glory, holiness, commerce, trade, any object you prefer; only—let Harold Skimpole live!"

of love in which his vain fond mother, and her quaint kind servant, cherish him; the quick-following contrast of hard dependence and servile treatment; the escape from that premature and dwarfed maturity by natural relapse into a more perfect childhood; the then leisurely growth of emotions and faculties into manhood; these are component parts of a character consistently drawn. The sum of its achievement is to be a successful cultivation of letters; and often as such imaginary discipline has been the theme of fiction, there are not many happier conceptions of it. The ideal and real parts of the boy's nature receive development in the proportions which contribute best to the end desired; the readiness for impulsive attachments that had put him into the leading of others, has underneath it a

base of truthfulness on which at last he rests in safety; the practical man is the outcome of the fanciful youth; and a more than equivalent for the graces of his visionary days, is found in the active sympathies that life has opened to him. Many experiences have come within its range, and his heart has had room for all. Our interest in him cannot but be increased by knowing how much he expresses of what the author had himself gone through; but David includes far less than this, and infinitely more.

Of its method, and its author's generally, in the delineation of character, something will have to be said on a later page. The author's own favourite people in it, I think, were the Peggotty group; and perhaps he was not far wrong. It has been their fate, as with all the leading figures of his invention, to pass their names into the language, and become types; and he has nowhere given happier embodiment to that purity of homely goodness, which, by the kindly and all-reconciling influences of humour, may exalt into comeliness and even grandeur the clumsiest forms of humanity. What has been indicated in the style of the book as its greatest charm is here felt most strongly. The ludicrous so helps the pathos, and the humour so uplifts and refines the sentiment, that mere rude affection and simple manliness in these Yarmouth boatmen, passed through the fires of unmerited suffering and heroic endurance, take forms half-chivalrous half-sublime. It is one of the cants of critical superiority to make supercilious mention of the serious passages in this great writer; but the storm and shipwreck at the close of *Copperfield*, when the body of the seducer is flung dead upon the shore amid the ruins of the home he has wasted and by the side of the man whose heart he has broken, the one as unconscious of what he had failed to reach as the other of what he has perished to save, is a description that may compare with the most impressive in the language.

There are other people drawn into this catastrophe who are among the failures of natural delineation in the book. But though Miss Dartle is curiously unpleasant, there are some natural traits in her (which Dickens's least life-like people are never without); and it was from one of his lady

Frontispiece to *David Copperfield*, by Hablot Knight Browne (Phiz), 1850

friends, very familiar to him indeed, he copied her peculiarity of never saying anything outright, but hinting it merely, and making more of it that way. Of Mrs. Steerforth it may also be worth remembering that Thackeray had something of a fondness for her. "I knew how it would be when I began," says a pleasant letter all about himself written immediately after she appeared in the story. "My letters to my mother are like this, but then she likes 'em—like Mrs. Steerforth: don't you like Mrs. Steerforth?"

Of the heroines who divide so equally between them the impulsive, easily swayed, not disloyal but sorely distracted affections of the hero, the spoilt foolishness and tenderness of the loving little child-wife, Dora, is more attractive than the too unfailing wisdom and self-sacrificing goodness of the angel-wife, Agnes. The scenes of the courtship and housekeeping are matchless; and the glimpses of Doctors' Commons, opening those views, by Mr. Spenlow, of man's vanity of expectation and inconsistency of conduct

LEFT: Mr. Peggotty, illustration for *David Copperfield*, by Fred Barnard

David Copperfield, Chapter 11

David Copperfield is introduced to the rhetorical
exuberance of Mr. Micawber:

'I AM,' said the stranger, 'thank Heaven, quite well. I have received a letter from Mr. Murdstone, in which he mentions that he would desire me to receive into an apartment in the rear of my house, which is at present unoccupied—and is, in short, to be let as a—in short,' said the stranger, with a smile and in a burst of confidence, 'as a bedroom—the young beginner whom I have now the pleasure to—' and the stranger waved his hand, and settled his chin in his shirt-collar.

'This is Mr. Micawber,' said Mr. Quinion to me.

'Ahem!' said the stranger, 'that is my name.'

'Mr. Micawber,' said Mr. Quinion, 'is known to Mr. Murdstone. He takes orders for us on commission, when he can get any. He has been written to by Mr. Murdstone, on the subject of your lodgings, and he will receive you as a lodger.'

'My address,' said Mr. Micawber, 'is Windsor Terrace, City Road. I—in short,' said Mr. Micawber, with the same genteel air, and in another burst of confidence—'I live there.'

I made him a bow.

'Under the impression,' said Mr. Micawber, 'that your peregrinations in this metropolis have not as yet been extensive, and that you might have some difficulty in penetrating the arcana of the Modern Babylon in the direction of the City Road,—in short,' said Mr. Micawber, in another burst of confidence, 'that you might lose yourself—I shall be happy to call this evening, and install you in the knowledge of the nearest way.'

in neglecting the sacred duty of making a will, on which he largely moralizes the day before he dies intestate, form a background highly appropriate to David's domesticities. This was among the reproductions of personal experience in the book; but it was a sadder knowledge that came with the conviction some years later, that David's contrasts in his earliest married life between his happiness enjoyed and his happiness once anticipated, the "vague unhappy loss or want of something" of which he so frequently complains, reflected also a personal experience which had not been supplied in fact so successfully as in fiction.

Bleak House followed *Copperfield*, which in some respects it copied in the autobiographical form by means of extracts from the personal relation of its heroine. But the distinction between the narrative of David and the diary of Esther, like that between Micawber and Skimpole, marks the superiority of the first to its successor. To represent a storyteller as giving the most surprising vividness to manners, motives, and

characters of which we are to believe her, all the time, as artlessly unconscious, as she is also entirely ignorant of the good qualities in herself she is naively revealing in the story, was a difficult enterprise, full of hazard in any case, not worth success, and certainly not successful. Ingenuity is more apparent than freshness, the invention is neither easy nor unstrained, and though the old marvellous power over the real is again abundantly manifest, there is some alloy of the artificial. Nor can this be said of Esther's relation without some general application to the book of which it forms so large a part. The novel is nevertheless, in the very important particular of construction, perhaps the best thing done by Dickens.

In his later writings he had been assiduously cultivating this essential of his art, and here he brought it very nearly to perfection. Of the tendency of composing a story piecemeal to induce greater concern for the part than for the whole, he

RIGHT: Micawber by E. Sherard Kennedy, 1873

Uriah Heep and David Copperfield, illustration for the Household Edition of *David Copperfield* by Fred Barnard, ca. 1870

had been always conscious; but I remember a remark also made by him to the effect that to read a story in parts had no less a tendency to prevent the reader's noticing how thoroughly a work so presented might be calculated for perusal as a whole. Look back from the last to the first page of the present novel, and not even in the highest examples of this kind of elaborate care will it be found, that event leads more closely to event, or that the separate incidents have been planned with a more studied consideration of the bearing they are severally to have on the general result. Nothing is introduced at random, everything tends to the catastrophe, the various lines of the plot converge and fit to its centre, and to the larger interest all the rest is irresistibly drawn. The heart of the story is a Chancery suit. On this the plot hinges, and on incidents connected with it, trivial or important, the passion and suffering turn exclusively. Chance words, or the deeds of chance people, to

appearance irrelevant, are found everywhere influencing the course taken by a train of incidents of which the issue is life or death, happiness or misery, to men and women perfectly unknown to them, and to whom they are unknown. Even the fits of the little law-stationer's servant help directly in the chain of small things that lead indirectly to Lady Dedlock's death. One strong chain of interest holds together Chesney Wold and its inmates, Bleak House and the Jarndyce group, Chancery with its sorry and sordid neighbourhood. The characters multiply as the tale advances, but in each the drift is the same. "There's no great odds betwixt my noble and learned brother and myself," says the grotesque proprietor of the rag and bottle shop under the wall of Lincoln's-inn, "they call me Lord Chancellor and my shop Chancery, and we both of us grub on in a muddle." *Edax rerum* the motto of both, but with a difference. Out of the lumber of the shop emerge slowly some fragments of evidence by which the

David Copperfield and the friendly waiter, illustration by Harold Copping for *Character Sketches from Dickens*, compiled by B.W. Matz, 1924

chief actors in the story are sensibly affected, and to which Chancery itself might have succumbed if its devouring capacities had been less complete. But by the time there is found among the lumber the will which puts all to rights in the Jarndyce suit, it is found to be too late to put anything to rights. The costs have swallowed up the estate, and there is an end of the matter.

What in one sense is a merit however may in others be a defect, and this book has suffered by the very completeness with which its Chancery moral is worked out. The didactic in Dickens's earlier novels derived its strength from being merely incidental to interest of a higher and more permanent kind, and not in a small degree from the playful sportiveness and fancy that lighted up its graver illustrations. Here it is of sterner stuff, too little relieved, and all-pervading.

What in one sense is a merit however may in others be a defect, and this book has suffered by the very completeness with which its Chancery moral is worked out. The didactic in Dickens's earlier novels derived its strength from being merely incidental to interest of a higher and more permanent kind, and not in a small degree from the playful sportiveness and fancy that lighted up its graver illustrations. Here it is of sterner stuff, too little relieved, and all-pervading. The fog so marvellously painted in the opening chapter has hardly cleared away when there arises, in *Jarndyce v. Jarndyce*, as bad an atmosphere to breathe in; and thenceforward to the end, clinging round the people of the story as they come or go, in dreary mist or in heavy cloud, it is rarely absent. Dickens has himself described his purpose to have been to dwell on the romantic side of familiar things.

"We arrive unexpectedly at Mr. Peggotty's Fireside," Hablot Knight Browne (Phiz), 1850

BLEAK HOUSE

BY

CHARLES DICKENS.

LONDON:

BRADBURY & EVANS BOUVERIE STREET

1853

The title page for *Bleak House*, by Hablot Knight Browne (Phiz)

his manner of telling them, the things he tells us are always true. I wish that he could think it right to limit his brilliant exaggeration to works written only for public amusement; and when he takes up a subject of high national importance, such as that which he handled in *Hard Times*, that he would use severer and more accurate analysis."

The home incidents of the summer and autumn of 1855 may be mentioned briefly. It was a year of much unsettled discontent with him, and upon return from a short trip to Paris with Mr. Wilkie Collins, he flung himself rather hotly into agitation with the administrative reformers, and spoke at one of the great meetings in Drury-lane Theatre. In the following month (April) he took occasion, even from the chair of the General Theatrical Fund, to give renewed expression to political dissatisfactions. In the summer he threw open to many friends his Tavistock House Theatre, having secured for its "lessee and manager Mr. Crummles;" for its poet Mr. Wilkie Collins, in an "entirely new and original domestic melodrama;" and for its scene-painter "Mr. Stanfield, R.A."[71] *The Lighthouse*, by Mr. Wilkie Collins, was then produced, its actors being Mr. Crummles the manager (Dickens in other words), the Author of the play, Mr. Lemon and Mr. Egg, and the manager's sister-in-law and eldest daughter. It was followed by the Guild farce of *Mr. Nightingale's Diary*, in which besides the performers named, and Dickens in his old personation part, the manager's youngest daughter and Mr. Frank Stone assisted. The success was wonderful; and in the three delighted audiences who crowded to what the bills described as "the smallest theatre in the world," were not a few of the notabilities of London.

Then came the beginning of *Nobody's Fault*, as *Little Dorrit* continued to be called by him up to the eve of its publication; a flight to Folkestone to help his sluggish fancy; and his return to London in October to preside at a dinner to Thackeray on his going to lecture in America. It was a muster of more than sixty admiring entertainers, and Dickens's speech gave happy expression to the spirit that animated all, telling Thackeray not alone how much his friendship was prized by those present, and how proud they were of his genius, but offering him in the name of the tens of thousands absent who had never touched his hand

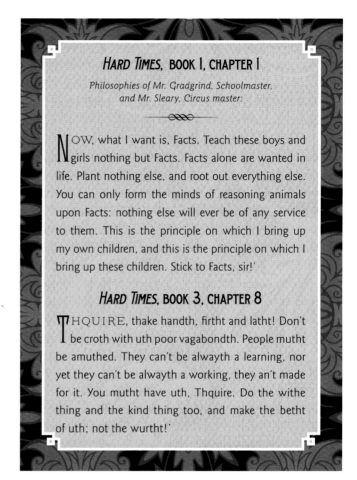

HARD TIMES, BOOK 1, CHAPTER 1

Philosophies of Mr. Gradgrind, Schoolmaster, and Mr. Sleary, Circus master:

NOW, what I want is, Facts. Teach these boys and girls nothing but Facts. Facts alone are wanted in life. Plant nothing else, and root out everything else. You can only form the minds of reasoning animals upon Facts: nothing else will ever be of any service to them. This is the principle on which I bring up my own children, and this is the principle on which I bring up these children. Stick to Facts, sir!'

HARD TIMES, BOOK 3, CHAPTER 8

THQUIRE, thake handth, firtht and latht! Don't be croth with uth poor vagabondth. People mutht be amuthed. They can't be alwayth a learning, nor yet they can't be alwayth a working, they an't made for it. You mutht have uth, Thquire. Do the withe thing and the kind thing too, and make the betht of uth; not the wurtht!'

or seen his face, life-long thanks for the treasures of mirth, wit, and wisdom within the yellow-covered numbers of *Pendennis* and *Vanity Fair*.

Dickens went to Paris early in October, and at its close was brought again to London by the sudden death of a friend, much deplored by himself, and still more so by a distinguished lady who had his loyal service at all times. An incident before his return to France is worth brief relation. He had sallied out for one of his night walks, full of thoughts of his story, one wintery rainy evening (the 8th of November), and "pulled himself up," outside the door of Whitechapel Workhouse, at a strange sight which arrested him there. Against the dreary enclosure of the house were leaning, in the midst of the downpouring rain and storm, what seemed to be seven heaps of rags: "dumb, wet, silent horrors" he described them, "sphinxes set up

THE SMALLEST THEATRE IN THE WORLD!

TAVISTOCK HOUSE.

LESSEE AND MANAGER - - - MR. CRUMMLES.

On Tuesday Evening, June 19th, 1855, will be presented, AT EXACTLY EIGHT O'CLOCK,

AN ENTIRELY NEW AND ORIGINAL

DOMESTIC MELO-DRAMA, IN TWO ACTS, BY MR. WILKIE COLLINS,

NOW FIRST PERFORMED, CALLED

THE LIGHTHOUSE.

THE SCENERY PAINTED BY MR. STANFIELD, R.A.

AARON GURNOCK, *the head Light-keeper*	. .	. MR. CRUMMLES.
MARTIN GURNOCK, *his son; the second Light-keeper*		. MR. WILKIE COLLINS.
JACOB DALE, *the third Light-keeper*	. .	. MR. MARK LEMON.
SAMUEL FURLEY, *a Pilot*	. .	. MR. AUGUSTUS EGG, A.R.A.

THE RELIEF OF LIGHT-KEEPERS, BY MR. CHARLES DICKENS, JUNIOR, MR. EDWARD HOGARTH, MR. ALFRED AINGER, and MR. WILLIAM WEBSTER.

THE SHIPWRECKED LADY	. .	. MISS HOGARTH.
PHŒBE .	. . . .	. MISS DICKENS.

Who will sing a new Ballad, the Music by MR. LINLEY, *the Words by* MR. CRUMMLES, *entitled*

THE SONG OF THE WRECK.

I.
THE wind blew high, the waters raved,
A Ship drove on the land,
A hundred human creatures saved,
Kneeled down upon the sand.
Three-score were drowned, three-score were thrown
Upon the black rocks wild;
And thus among them left alone,
They found one helpless child.

II.
A Seaman rough, to shipwreck bred,
Stood out from all the rest,
And gently laid the lonely head
Upon his honest breast.
And trav'ling o'er the Desert wide,
It was a solemn joy
To see them, ever side by side,
The sailor and the boy.

III.
In famine, sickness, hunger, thirst,
The two were still but one,
Until the strong man drooped the first,
And felt his labours done.
Then to a trusty friend he spake:
"Across this Desert wide
"O take the poor boy for my sake!"
And kissed the child, and died.

IV.
Toiling along in weary plight
Through heavy jungle-mire,
These two came later every night
To warm them at the fire,
Until the Captain said one day:
"O seaman good and kind,
"To save thyself now come away
"And leave the boy behind!"

V.
The child was slumb'ring near the blaze:
"O Captain let him rest
"Until it sinks, when GOD's own ways
"Shall teach us what is best!"
They watched the whiten'd ashey heap,
They touched the child in vain,
They did not leave him there asleep,
He never woke again.

HALF-AN-HOUR FOR REFRESHMENT.

TO CONCLUDE WITH

The Guild Amateur-Company's Farce, in One Act, by MR. CRUMMLES and MR. MARK LEMON;

MR. NIGHTINGALE'S DIARY.

MR. NIGHTINGALE	. . . .	MR. FRANK STONE, A.R.A.
MR. GABBLEWIG, *of the Middle Temple*	. .	
CHARLEY BIT, *a Boots*	. . .	
MR. POULTER, *a Pedestrian and Cold Water Drinker*	.	MR. CRUMMLES.
CAPTAIN BLOWER, *an Invalid*	. . .	
A RESPECTABLE FEMALE	. . .	
A DEAF SEXTON	. . . .	
TIP, *Mr. Gabblewig's Tiger*	. . .	MR. AUGUSTUS EGG, A.R.A.
CHRISTOPHER, *a Charity Boy*	. . .	
SLAP, *Professionally Mr. Flormiville, a Country Actor*	.	
MR. TICKLE, *Inventor of the celebrated Compounds*	.	MR. MARK LEMON.
A VIRTUOUS YOUNG PERSON IN THE CON- FIDENCE OF MARIA	. . . .	
LITHERS, *Landlord of the Water Lily*	. . .	MR. WILKIE COLLINS.
ROSINA, *Mr. Nightingale's Niece*	. . .	MISS KATE DICKENS.
SUSAN, *her Maid* .	. . .	MISS HOGARTH.

Composer and Director of the Music, MR. FRANCESCO BERGER, who will Preside at the Piano-forte.

Costume Makers, MESSRS. NATHAN, *of Titchbourne Street, Haymarket.* *Perruquier,* MR. WILSON, *of the Strand.*
Machinery and Properties by MR. IRELAND, *of the Theatre Royal, Adelphi.*

Playbill for *The Lighthouse*, paired (as *Not So Bad As We Seem* had been four years earlier) with the farce *Mr. Nightingale's Diary*, June 19, 1855

against that dead wall, and no one likely to be at the pains of solving them until the General Overthrow." He sent in his card to the Master. Against him there was no ground of complaint; he gave prompt personal attention; but the casual ward was full, and there was no help. The rag-heaps were all girls, and Dickens gave each a shilling. One girl, "twenty or so," had been without food a day and night. "Look at me," she said, as she clutched the shilling, and without thanks shuffled off. So with the rest. There was not a single "thank you." A crowd meanwhile, only less poor than these objects of misery, had gathered round the scene; but though they saw the seven shillings given away they asked for no relief to themselves, they recognized in their sad wild way the other greater wretchedness, and made room in silence for Dickens to walk on.

Not more tolerant of the way in which laws meant to be most humane are too often administered in England, he left in a day or two to resume his *Little Dorrit* in Paris. But before his life there is described, some sketches from his holiday trip to Italy with Mr. Wilkie Collins and Mr. Augustus Egg, and from his three summer visits to Boulogne, claim to themselves two intervening chapters.

---

[65] I subjoin the dozen titles successively proposed for *Bleak House*. 1. "Tom-all-Alone's. The Ruined House;" 2. "Tom-all-Alone's. The Solitary House that was always shut up;" 3. "Bleak House Academy;" 4. "The East Wind;" 5. "Tom-all-Alone's. The Ruined [House, Building, Factory, Mill] that got into Chancery and never got out;" 6. "Tom-all-Alone's. The Solitary House where the Grass grew;" 7. "Tom-all-Alone's. The Solitary House that was always shut up and never Lighted;" 8. "Tom-all-Alone's. The Ruined Mill, that got into Chancery and never got out;" 9. "Tom-all-Alone's. The Solitary House where the Wind howled;" 10. "Tom-all-Alone's. The Ruined House that got into Chancery and never got out;" 11. "Bleak House and the East Wind. How they both got into Chancery and never got out;" 12. "Bleak House."

[66] He was greatly interested in the movement for closing town and city graves (see the close of the 11th chapter of *Bleak House*), and providing places of burial under State supervision.

[67] Baron Tauchnitz, describing to me his long and uninterrupted friendly intercourse with Dickens, has this remark: "I give also a passage from one of his letters written at the time when he sent his son Charles, through my mediation, to Leipzig. He says in it what he desires for his son. 'I want him to have all interest in, and to acquire a knowledge of, the life around him, and to be treated like a gentleman though pampered in nothing. By punctuality in all things, great or small, I set great store.'"

[68] The reading occupied nearly three hours: double the time devoted to it in the later years.

[69] On the 28th of Dec., 1854 he wrote from Bradford: "The hall is enormous, and they expect to seat 3700 people to-night! Notwithstanding which, it seems to me a tolerably easy place—except that the width of the platform is so very great to the eye at first." From Folkestone, on his way to Paris, he wrote in the autumn of 1855: "16th of Sept. I am going to read for them here, on the 5th of next month, and have answered in the last fortnight thirty applications to do the like all over England, Ireland, and Scotland. Fancy my having to come from Paris in December, to do this, at Peterborough, Birmingham, and Sheffield—old promises." Again: 23rd of Sept. "I am going to read here, next Friday week. There are (as there are everywhere) a Literary Institution and a Working Men's Institution, which have not the slightest sympathy or connexion. The stalls are five shillings, but I have made them fix the working men's admission at threepence, and I hope it may bring them together. The event comes off in a carpenter's shop, as the biggest place that can be got." In 1857, at Paxton's request, he read his *Carol* at Coventry for the Institute.

[70] It is well to remember, too, what he wrote about the story to Charles Knight. It had no design, he said, to damage the really useful truths of Political Economy, but was wholly directed against "those who see figures and averages, and nothing else; who would take the average of cold in the Crimea during twelve months as a reason for clothing a soldier in nankeen on a night when he would be frozen to death in fur; and who would comfort the labourer in travelling twelve miles a day to and from his work, by telling him that the average distance of one inhabited place from another, on the whole area of England, is not more than four miles."

[71] For the scene of the Eddystone Lighthouse at this little play, afterwards placed in a frame in the hall at Gadshill, a thousand guineas was given at the Dickens sale. It occupied the great painter only one or two mornings, and Dickens will tell how it originated. Walking on Hampstead Heath to think over his Theatrical Fund speech, he met Mr. Lemon, and they went together to Stanfield. "He has been very ill, and he told us that large pictures are too much for him, and he must confine himself to small ones. But I would not have this, I declared he must paint bigger ones than ever, and what would he think of beginning upon an act-drop for a proposed vast theatre at Tavistock House? He laughed and caught at this, we cheered him up very much, and he said he was quite a man again." April, 1855.

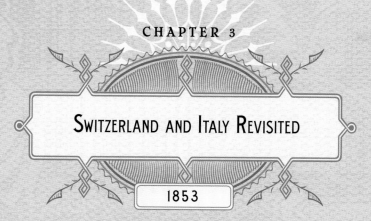

CHAPTER 3

SWITZERLAND AND ITALY REVISITED

1853

THE FIRST NEWS of the three travellers was from Chamounix, on the 20th of October; and in it there was little made of the fatigue, and much of the enjoyment, of their Swiss travel. Great attention and cleanliness at the inns, very small windows and very bleak passages, doors opening to wintery blasts, overhanging eaves and external galleries, plenty of milk, honey, cows, and goats, much singing towards sunset on mountain sides, mountains almost too solemn to look at—that was the picture of it, with the country everywhere in one of its finest aspects, as winter began to close in. They had started from Geneva the previous morning at four, and in their day's travel Dickens had again noticed what he spoke of formerly, the ill-favoured look of the people in the valleys owing to their hard and stern climate. On the day the letter was written they had been up to the Mer de Glace, finding it not so beautiful in colour as in summer, but grander in its desolation; the green ice, like the greater part of the ascent, being covered with snow. The only place new to Dickens was Berne: "a surprisingly picturesque old Swiss town, with a view of the Alps from the outside of it singularly beautiful in the morning light." Everything else was familiar to him: though at that winter season, when the inns were shutting up, and all who could afford it were off to Geneva, most things in the valley struck him with a new aspect. From such of his old friends as he found at Lausanne, where a day or two's rest was taken, he had the gladdest of greetings; "and the wonderful manner in which they turned out in the wettest morning ever beheld for a Godspeed down the Lake was really quite pathetic."

Before October closed, the travellers had reached Genoa, having been thirty-one consecutive hours on the road from Milan. They arrived in somewhat damaged condition, and took up their lodging in the top rooms of the Croce di Malta, "overlooking the port and sea pleasantly and airily enough, but it was no joke to get so high, and the apartment is rather vast and faded." The warmth of personal greeting that here awaited Dickens was given no less to the friends who accompanied him, and though the reader may not share in such private confidences as would show the sensation created by his reappearance, and the jovial hours that were passed among old associates, he will perhaps be interested to know how far the intervening years had changed the aspect of things and places made pleasantly familiar to us in his former letters. He wrote to his sister-in-law that the old walks were pretty much the same as ever except that there had been building behind the Peschiere up the San Bartolomeo hill, and the whole town towards San Pietro d'Arena had been quite changed. The Bisagno looked just the same, stony just then, having very little water in it; the vicoli were fragrant with the same old flavour of "very rotten cheese kept in very hot blankets;" and everywhere he saw the mezzaro as of yore. The Jesuits' College in the Strada Nuova was become, under the changed government, the Hotel de Ville, and a splendid caffe with a terrace-garden had arisen between it and Palavicini's old palace. "Pal himself has gone to the dogs." Another new and handsome caffe had been built in the Piazza Carlo Felice, between the old one of the Bei Arti and the Strada Carlo Felice; and the Teatro Diurno had now stone galleries and seats, like an ancient amphitheatre. He observed an extraordinary increase everywhere else, since he was last in the splendid city, of "life, growth, and enterprise;" and he declared his old conviction to be confirmed that for picturesque beauty and character there was nothing in Italy, Venice excepted, "near brilliant old Genoa."

The voyage thence to Naples, written from the latter place, is too capital a description to be lost. The steamer in which they embarked was "the new express English ship," but they found her to be already more than full of passengers from Marseilles (among them an old friend, Sir Emerson Tennent, with his family), and everything in confusion. There were no places at the captain's table, dinner

had to be taken on deck, no berth or sleeping accommodation was available, and heavy first-class fares had to be paid. Thus they made their way to Leghorn, where worse awaited them. The authorities proved to be not favourable to the "crack" English-officered vessel (she had just been started for the India mail); and her papers not being examined in time, it was too late to steam away again that day, and she had to lie all night long off the lighthouse. "The scene on board beggars description. Ladies on the tables; gentlemen under the tables; bed-room appliances not usually beheld in public airing themselves in positions where

soup-tureens had been lately developing themselves; and ladies and gentlemen lying indiscriminately on the open deck, arranged like spoons on a sideboard. No mattresses, no blankets, nothing. Towards midnight attempts were made, by means of awning and flags, to make this latter scene remotely approach an Australian encampment; and we three (Collins, Egg, and self) lay together on the bare planks covered with our coats. We were all gradually dozing off, when a perfectly tropical rain fell, and in a moment drowned the whole ship. The rest of the night we passed upon the stairs, with an immense jumble of men

Left: Illustration of Dickens and his characters, by J.R. Brown, 1889–90

Coliseum at Rome, ca. 1872

and women. There were excellent officers aboard, and, in the morning, the first mate lent me his cabin to wash in—which I afterwards lent to Egg and Collins. Then we, the Emerson Tennents, the captain, the doctor, and the second officer, went off on a jaunt together to Pisa, as the ship was to lie all day at Leghorn. Last night, I had the steward's own cabin, opening on deck, all to myself. It had been previously occupied by some desolate lady who went ashore at Civita Vecchia. There was little or no sea, thank Heaven, all the trip; but the rain was heavier than any I have ever seen, and the lightning very constant and vivid. We were, with the crew, some 200 people—provided with boats, at the utmost stretch, for one hundred perhaps. I could not help thinking what would happen if we met with any accident: the crew being chiefly Maltese, and evidently fellows who would cut off alone in the largest boat, on the least alarm; the speed very high; and the running, thro' all the narrow rocky channels. Thank God, however, here we are."

At Naples some days were passed very merrily; going up Vesuvius and into the buried cities, with Layard who had joined them, and with the Tennents.

From Naples they went to Rome, where they found Lockhart, "fearfully weak and broken, yet hopeful of himself too" (he died the following year); smoked and drank punch with David Roberts, then painting everyday with Louis Haghe in St. Peter's; and took the old walks. The Coliseum, Appian Way, and Streets of Tombs, seemed desolate and grand as ever; but generally, Dickens adds, "I discovered the Roman antiquities to be *smaller* than my imagination in nine years had made them. The Electric Telegraph now goes like a sunbeam through the cruel old heart of the Coliseum—a suggestive thing to think about, I fancied. The Pantheon I thought even nobler than of yore." The amusements were of course an attraction; and nothing at the Opera amused the party of three English more, than another party of four Americans who sat behind them in the pit. The opera was excellently done, and the price of the stalls one and threepence English. At Milan, on the other hand, the Scala was fallen from its old estate, dirty, gloomy, dull, and the performance execrable.

Another theatre of the smallest pretension Dickens sought out with avidity in Rome, and eagerly enjoyed.

He had heard it said in his old time in Genoa that the finest Marionetti were here; and now, after great difficulty, he discovered the company in a sort of stable attached to a decayed palace. "It was a wet night, and there was no audience but a party of French officers and ourselves. We all sat together. I never saw anything more amazing than the performance—altogether only an hour long, but managed by as many as ten people, for we saw them all go behind, at the ringing of a bell. The saving of a young lady by a good fairy from the machinations of an enchanter, coupled with the comic business of her servant Pulcinella (the Roman Punch) formed the plot of the first piece. There was a ballet afterwards, on the same scale, and we really came away quite enchanted with the delicate drollery of the thing. French officers more than ditto."

Of the great enemy to the health of the now capital of the kingdom of Italy, Dickens remarked in the same letter. "I have been led into some curious speculations by the existence and progress of the Malaria about Rome. Isn't it very extraordinary to think of its encroaching and encroaching on the Eternal City as if it were commissioned to swallow it up. This year it has been extremely bad, and has long outstayed its usual time. Rome has been very unhealthy, and is not free now. Few people care to be out at the bad times of sunset and sunrise, and the streets are like a desert at night. I walk out from the Coliseum through the Street of Tombs to the ruins of the old Appian Way—pass no human being, and see no human habitation but ruined houses from which the people have fled, and where it is Death to sleep: these houses being three miles outside a gate of Rome at its farthest extent. Imagine this phantom knocking at the gates of Rome; passing them; creeping along the streets; haunting the aisles and pillars of the churches; year by year more encroaching, and more impossible of avoidance."

From Rome they posted to Florence, reaching it in three days and a half, on the morning of the 20th of November; having then been out six weeks, with only three days' rain; and in another week they were at Venice. "The fine weather has accompanied us here," Dickens wrote on the 28th of November, "the place of all others where it is necessary, and the city has been a blaze of sunlight and blue sky (with an extremely clear cold air) ever since we have been in it. If you could see it at this moment you would never forget it. We live in the same house that I lived in nine years ago, and have the same sitting-room—close to the Bridge of Sighs and the Palace of the Doges. The room is at the corner of the house, and there is a narrow street of water running round the side: so that we have the Grand Canal before the two front windows, and this wild little street at the corner window: into which, too, our three bedrooms look. We established a gondola as soon as we arrived, and we slide out of the hall on to the water twenty times a day. Last night we go downstairs at half-past eight, step into the gondola, slide away on the black water, ripple and plash swiftly along for a mile or two, land at a broad flight of steps, and

View of the Grand Canal, Venice, Italy. Engraved by Martens after daguerreotype by Lerebours, 1842

instantly walk into the most brilliant and beautiful theatre conceivable—all silver and blue, and precious little fringes made of glittering prisms of glass. There we sit until half-past eleven, come out again (gondolier asleep outside the box-door), and in a moment are on the black silent water, floating away as if there were no dry building in the world. It stops, and in a moment we are out again, upon the broad solid Piazza of St. Mark, brilliantly lighted with gas, very like the Palais Royal at Paris, only far more handsome, and shining with no end of caffes. The two old pillars and the enormous bell-tower are as gruff and solid against the exquisite starlight as if they were a thousand miles from the sea or any undermining water: and the front of the cathedral, overlaid with golden mosaics and beautiful colours, is like a thousand rainbows even in the night."

His formerly expressed notions as to art and pictures in Italy received confirmation at this visit. "I am more than ever confirmed in my conviction that one of the great uses of travelling is to encourage a man to think for himself, to be bold enough always to declare without offence that he *does* think for himself, and to overcome the villainous meanness of professing what other people have professed when he knows (if he has capacity to originate an opinion) that his profession is untrue. The intolerable nonsense against which genteel taste and subserviency are afraid to rise, in connection with art, is astounding. Egg's honest amazement and consternation when he saw some of the most trumpeted things was what the Americans call 'a caution.' In the very same hour and minute there were scores of people falling into conventional raptures with that very poor Apollo, and passing over the most beautiful little figures and heads in the whole Vatican because they were not expressly set up to be worshipped. So in this place."

The last place visited was Turin, where the travellers arrived on the 5th of December, finding it, with a brightly shining sun, intensely cold and freezing hard. "There are double windows to all the rooms, but the Alpine air comes down and numbs my feet as I write (in a cap and shawl) within six feet of the fire." "This is a remarkably agreeable place. A beautiful town, prosperous, thriving, growing prodigiously, as Genoa is; crowded with busy inhabitants; full of noble streets and squares. The Alps, now covered deep with snow, are close upon it, and here and there seem almost ready to tumble into the houses. The contrast this part of Italy presents to the rest, is amazing. Beautifully made railroads, admirably managed; cheerful, active people; spirit, energy, life, progress.

There were incidents of the Austrian occupation as to which Dickens thought the ordinary style of comment unfair; and his closing remark on their police is well worth preserving. "I am strongly inclined to think that our countrymen are to blame in the matter of the Austrian vexations to travellers that have been complained of. Their manner is so very bad, they are so extraordinarily suspicious, so determined to be done by everybody, and give so much offence. Now, the Austrian police are very strict, but they really know how to do business, and they do it. And if you treat them like gentlemen, they will always respond. When we first crossed the Austrian frontier, and were ushered into the police office, I took off my hat. The officer immediately took off his, and was as polite—still doing his duty, without any compromise—as it was possible to be. When we came to Venice, the arrangements were very strict, but were so business-like that the smallest possible amount of inconvenience consistent with strictness ensued. At Turin and at Genoa there are no such stoppages at all; but in any other part of Italy, give me an Austrian in preference to a native functionary. At Naples it is done in a beggarly, shambling, bungling, tardy, vulgar way; but I am strengthened in my old impression that Naples is one of the most odious places on the face of the earth. The general degradation oppresses me like foul air."

CHAPTER 4

THREE SUMMERS AT BOULOGNE

1853, 1854, 1856

DICKENS WAS IN BOULOGNE, in 1853, from the middle of June to the end of September, and for the next three months, as we have seen, was in Switzerland and Italy. In the following year he went again to Boulogne in June, and stayed, after finishing *Hard Times*, until far into October. In February of 1855 he was for a fortnight in Paris with Mr. Wilkie Collins; not taking up his more prolonged residence there until the winter. From November 1855 to the end of April 1856 he made the French capital his home, working at *Little Dorrit* during all those months. Then, after a month's interval in Dover and London, he took up his third summer residence in Boulogne, whither his younger children had gone direct from Paris; and stayed until September, finishing *Little Dorrit* in London in the spring of 1857.

Of the first of these visits, a few lively notes of humour and character out of his letters will tell the story sufficiently. The second and third had points of more attractiveness. Those were the years of the French-English alliance, of the great exposition of English paintings, of the return of the troops from the Crimea, and of the visit of the Prince Consort to the Emperor; such interest as Dickens took in these several matters appearing in his letters with the usual vividness, and the story of his continental life coming out with amusing distinctness in the successive pictures they paint with so much warmth and colour. Another chapter will be given to Paris. This deals only with Boulogne.

For his first summer residence, in June 1853, he had taken a house on the high ground near the Calais road; an odd French place with the strangest little rooms and halls, but standing in the midst of a large garden, with wood and waterfall, a conservatory opening on a great bank of roses,

and paths and gates on one side to the ramparts, on the other to the sea. Above all there was a capital proprietor and landlord, by whom the cost of keeping up gardens and wood (which he called a forest) was defrayed, while he gave his tenant the whole range of both and all the flowers for nothing, sold him the garden produce as it was wanted, and kept a cow on the estate to supply the family milk. "If this were but 300 miles farther off," wrote Dickens, "how the English would rave about it! I do assure you that there are picturesque people, and town, and country, about this place, that quite fill up the eye and fancy. As to the fishing people (whose dress can have changed neither in colour nor in form for many many years), and their quarter of the town cobweb-hung with great brown nets across the narrow up-hill streets, they are as good as Naples, every bit." His description both of house and landlord, of which I tested the exactness when I visited him, was in the old pleasant vein; requiring no connection with himself to give it interest, but, by the charm and ease with which everything picturesque or characteristic was disclosed, placed in the domain of art.

Then came the charm of the letter, his description of his landlord, lightly sketched by him in print as M. Loyal-Devasseur, but here filled in with the most attractive touches his loving hand could give. "But the landlord—M. Beaucourt—is wonderful. Everybody here has two surnames (I cannot conceive why), and M. Beaucourt, as he is always called, is by rights M. Beaucourt-Mutuel. He is a portly jolly fellow with a fine open face; lives on the hill behind, just outside the top of the garden; and was a linen draper in the town, where he still has a shop, but is supposed to have mortgaged his business and to be in difficulties—all along of this place, which he has planted with his own hands; which he cultivates all day; and which he never on any consideration speaks of but as 'the Property.' He is extraordinarily popular in Boulogne (the people in the shops invariably brightening up at the mention of his name, and congratulating us on being his tenants), and really seems to deserve it."

On the 3rd of July there came a fresh trait of the good fellow of a landlord. "Fancy what Beaucourt told me last night. When he 'conceived the inspiration' of planting the property ten years ago, he went over to England to buy the trees, took a small cottage in the market-gardens at Putney,

"Our French Watering Place," _Household Words_, 4 November 1854

Dickens's amiable landlord appears in his sketch of Boulogne:

⸺⸺⸺

BUT we can never henceforth separate our French watering-place from our own landlord of two summers, M. Loyal Devasseur, citizen and town-councillor. Permit us to have the pleasure of presenting M. Loyal Devasseur.

His own family name is simply Loyal; but, as he is married, and as in that part of France a husband always adds to his own name the family name of his wife, he writes himself Loyal Devasseur. He owns a compact little estate of some twenty or thirty acres on a lofty hill-side, and on it he has built two country houses, which he lets furnished. They are by many degrees the best houses that are so let near our French watering-place; we have had the honour of living in both, and can testify. [. . .]

Aforetime, M. Loyal was a tradesman in the town. You can transact business with no present tradesman in the town, and give your card `chez M. Loyal,` but a brighter face shines upon you directly. We doubt if there is, ever was, or ever will be, a man so universally pleasant in the minds of people as M. Loyal is in the minds of the citizens of our French watering-place. They rub their hands and laugh when they speak of him. Ah, but he is such a good child, such a brave boy, such a generous spirit, that Monsieur Loyal! It is the honest truth. M. Loyal`s nature is the nature of a gentleman. He cultivates his ground with his own hands (assisted by one little labourer, who falls into a fit now and then); and he digs and delves from morn to eve in prodigious perspirations `works always,` as he says but, cover him with dust, mud, weeds, water, any stains you will, you never can cover the gentleman in M. Loyal. A portly, upright, broad-shouldered, brown-faced man, whose soldierly bearing gives him the appearance of being taller than he is, look into the bright eye of M. Loyal, standing before you in his working-blouse and cap, not particularly well shaved, and, it may be, very earthy, and you shall discern in M. Loyal a gentleman whose true politeness is ingrain, and confirmation of whose word by his bond you would blush to think of. Not without reason is M. Loyal when he tells that story, in his own vivacious way, of his travelling to Fulham, near London, to buy all these hundreds and hundreds of trees you now see upon the Property, then a bare, bleak hill; and of his sojourning in Fulham three months; and of his jovial evenings with the market-gardeners; and of the crowning banquet before his departure, when the market-gardeners rose as one man, clinked their glasses all together (as the custom at Fulham is), and cried, `Vive Loyal!`

M. Loyal has an agreeable wife, but no family; and he loves to drill the children of his tenants, or run races with them, or do anything with them, or for them, that is good-natured. He is of a highly convivial temperament, and his hospitality is unbounded. Billet a soldier on him, and he is delighted. Five-and-thirty soldiers had M. Loyal billeted on him this present summer, and they all got fat and red-faced in two days. It became a legend among the troops that whosoever got billeted on M. Loyal rolled in clover; and so it fell out that the fortunate man who drew the billet `M. Loyal Devasseur` always leaped into the air, though in heavy marching order. [. . .]

Long ago a family of children and a mother were left in one of his houses without money, a whole year. M. Loyal anything but as rich as we wish he had been had not the heart to say `you must go;` so they stayed on and stayed on, and paying-tenants who would have come in couldn`t come in, and at last they managed to get helped home across the water; and M. Loyal kissed the whole group, and said, `Adieu, my poor infants!` and sat down in their deserted salon and smoked his pipe of peace. `The rent, M. Loyal?` `Eh! well! The rent!` M. Loyal shakes his head. `Le bon Dieu,` says M. Loyal presently, `will recompense me,` and he laughs and smokes his pipe of peace. May he smoke it on the Property, and not be recompensed, these fifty years!

lived there three months, held a symposium every night attended by the principal gardeners of Fulham, Putney, Kew, and Hammersmith (which he calls Hamsterdam), and wound up with a supper at which the market-gardeners rose, clinked their glasses, and exclaimed with one accord (I quote him exactly) VIVE BEAUCOURT! He was a captain in the National Guard, and Cavaignac his general. Brave Capitaine Beaucourt! said Cavaignac, you must receive a decoration. My General, said Beaucourt, No! It is enough for me that I have done my duty. I go to lay the first stone of a house upon a Property I have—that house shall be my decoration. (Regard that house!)" Addition to the picture came in a letter of the 24th of July: with a droll glimpse of Shakespeare at the theatre, and of the Saturday's pig-market.

"We went to the theatre last night, to see the *Midsummer Night's Dream*—of the Opera Comique. It is a beautiful little theatre now, with a very good company; and the nonsense of the piece was done with a sense quite confounding in that connexion. Willy Am Shay Kes Peer; Sirzhon Foll Stayffe; Lor Lattimeer; and that celebrated Maid of Honour to Queen Elizabeth, Meees Oleeveeir—were the principal characters."

He had meanwhile gathered friendly faces round him. Frank Stone went over with his family to a house taken for him on the St. Omer road by Dickens, who was joined in the chateau by Mr. and Mrs. Leech and Mr. Wilkie Collins. "Leech says that when he stepped from the boat after their stormy passage, he was received by the congregated spectators with a distinct round of applause as by far the most intensely and unutterably miserable looking object that had yet appeared. The laughter was tumultuous, and he wishes his friends to know that altogether he made an immense hit." So passed the summer months: excursions with these friends to Amiens and Beauvais relieving the work upon his novel, and the trip to Italy, already described, following on its completion.

In June, 1854, M. Beaucourt had again received his famous tenant, but in another cottage or chateau (to him convertible terms) on the much cherished property, placed on the very summit of the hill with a private road leading out to the Column, a really pretty place, rooms larger than in the other house, a noble sea view, everywhere nice prospects, good garden, and plenty of sloping turf.[72] It was called the

Villa du Camp de Droite, and here Dickens stayed, as I have intimated, until the eve of his winter residence in Paris.

The formation of the Northern Camp at Boulogne began the week after he had finished *Hard Times*, and he watched its progress, as it increased and extended itself along the cliffs towards Calais, with the liveliest amusement. At first he was startled by the suddenness with which soldiers overran the roads, became billeted in every house, made the bridges red with their trowsers, and "sprang upon the pier like fantastic mustard and cress when boats were expected, many of them never having seen the sea before." But the good behaviour of the men had a reconciling effect, and their ingenuity delighted him. The quickness with which they raised whole streets of mud-huts, less picturesque than the tents,[73] but (like most unpicturesque things) more comfortable, was like an Arabian Nights' tale. "Each little street holds 144 men, and every corner-door has the number of the street upon it as soon as it is put up; and the postmen can fall to work as easily as in the Rue de Rivoli at Paris." His patience was again a little tried when he found baggage-wagons ploughing up his favourite walks, and trumpeters in twos and threes teaching newly-recruited trumpeters in all the sylvan places, and making the echoes hideous. But this had its amusement too. "I met to-day a weazen sun-burnt youth from the south with such an immense regimental shako on, that he looked like a sort of lucifer match-box, evidently blowing his life rapidly out, under the auspices of two magnificent creatures all hair and lungs, of such breadth across the shoulders that I couldn't see their breast-buttons when I stood in front of them."

The interest culminated as the visit of the Prince Consort approached with its attendant glories of illuminations and reviews. Beaucourt's excitement became intense. The Villa du Camp de Droite was to be a blaze of triumph on the night of the arrival; Dickens, who had carried over with him the meteor flag of England and set it streaming over a haystack in his field,[74] now hoisted the French colours over the British Jack in honour of the national alliance; the Emperor was to subside to the station of a general officer, so that all the rejoicings should be in honour of the Prince; and there was to be a review in the open country near Wimereux, when "at one stage of the maneuvres (I am too excited to spell the word but you know what I mean)" the whole hundred thousand men in the camp of the North were to be placed before the Prince's eyes, to show him what a division of the French army might be. "I believe everything I hear," said Dickens. It was the state of mind of Hood's country gentleman after the fire at the Houses of Parliament. "Beaucourt, as one of the town council, receives summonses to turn out and debate about something, or receive somebody, every five minutes. Whenever I look out of window, or go to the door, I see an immense black object at Beaucourt's porch like a boat set up on end in the air with a pair of white trowsers below it. This is the cocked hat of an official Huissier, newly arrived with a summons, whose head is thrown back as he is in the act of drinking Beaucourt's wine." The day came at last, and all Boulogne turned out for its holiday; "but I" Dickens wrote, "had by this cooled down a little, and, reserving myself for the illuminations, I abandoned the great men and set off upon my usual country walk. See my reward. Coming home by the Calais road, covered with dust, I suddenly find myself face to face with Albert and Napoleon, jogging along in the pleasantest way, a little in front, talking extremely loud about the view, and attended by a brilliant staff of some sixty or seventy horsemen, with a couple of our royal grooms with their red coats riding oddly enough in the midst of the magnates. I took off my wide-awake without stopping to stare, whereupon the Emperor pulled off his cocked hat; and Albert (seeing, I suppose, that it was an Englishman) pulled off his. Then we went our several ways. The Emperor is broader across the chest than in the old times when we used to see him so often at Gore-house, and stoops more in the shoulders. Indeed his carriage thereabouts is like Fonblanque's."[75] The town he described as "one great flag" for the rest of the visit; and to the success of the illuminations he contributed largely himself by leading off splendidly with a hundred and twenty wax candles blazing in his seventeen front windows, and visible from that great height over all the place. "On the first eruption Beaucourt *danced and screamed* on the grass before the door; and when he was more composed, set off with Madame Beaucourt to look at the house from every possible quarter, and, he said, collect the suffrages of his compatriots."

When leaving Paris for his third visit to Boulogne, at the beginning of June 1856, he had not written a word of the ninth number of his new book, and did not expect for another month to "see land from the running sea of *Little Dorrit.*" He had resumed the house he first occupied, the cottage or villa "des Moulineaux," and after dawdling about his garden for a few days with surprising industry in a French farmer garb of blue blouse, leathern belt, and military cap, which he had mounted as "the only one for complete comfort," he wrote to me that he was getting "Now to work again—to work! The story lies before me, I hope, strong and clear. Not to be easily told; but nothing of that sort IS to be easily done that *I* know of." At work it became his habit to sit late, and then, putting off his usual walk until night, to lie down among the roses reading until after tea ("middle-aged Love in a blouse and belt"), when he went down to the pier. "The said pier at evening is a phase of the place we never see, and which I hardly knew. But I never did behold such specimens of the youth of my country, male and female, as pervade that place. They are really, in their vulgarity and insolence, quite disheartening. One is so fearfully ashamed of them, and they contrast so very unfavourably with the natives." Mr. Wilkie Collins was again his companion in the summer weeks, and the presence of Jerrold for the greater part of the time added much to his enjoyment.

Besides the graver work which Mr. Wilkie Collins and himself were busy with, in these months, and by which *Household Words* mainly was to profit, some lighter matters occupied the leisure of both.

There were to be, at Christmas, theatricals again at Tavistock House; in which the children, with the help of their father and other friends, were to follow up the success of the *Lighthouse* by again acquitting themselves as grown-up actors; and Mr. Collins was busy preparing for them a new drama to be called *The Frozen Deep*, while Dickens was sketching a farce for Mr. Lemon to fill in. But this pleasant employment had sudden and sad interruption.

An epidemic broke out in the town, affecting the children of several families known to Dickens, among them that of his friend Mr. Gilbert A'Becket; who, upon arriving from Paris, and finding a favourite little son stricken dangerously, sank himself under an illness from

RIGHT: Wilkie Collins, oil on panel by Sir John Everett Millais (detail), 1850

A LIST OF DICKENS'S AND COLLINS'S LITERARY COLLABORATIONS

From 1854 onward Dickens and Wilkie Collins collaborated regularly. Their joint work, sometimes,
especially in the Christmas writings, involved other contributors, listed here:

1854: "The Seven Poor Travellers," in the Extra Christmas Number of *Household Words* (14 December) with Eliza Lynn, Adelaide Anne Procter, and George Augustus Sala.

1855: "The Holly Tree Inn," in the Extra Christmas Number of *Household Words* (15 December) with William Howitt, Harriet Parr, and Adelaide Anne Procter.

1856: "The Wreck of the Golden Mary," in in the Extra Christmas Number of *Household Words* (6 December) with Percy Fitzgerald, Adelaide Anne Procter, Harriet Parr, and James White.

1857: *The Frozen Deep*, initially performed in the converted schoolroom of Dickens's London residence, Tavistock House, on January 6th; "The Lazy Tour of Two Idle Apprentices" in *Household Words* (3-31 October); "The Perils of Certain English Prisoners" in the Extra Christmas Number of *Household Words* (7 December) without the assistance of other staff writers.

1858: "A House to Let" in the Extra Christmas Number of *Household Words* (7 December) with Elizabeth Gaskell and Adelaide Anne Procter.

1859: "The Haunted House" in the Extra Christmas Number of *All the Year Round* (13 December) with Elizabeth Gaskell, Adelaide Anne Procter, George Augustus Sala, and Hesba Stretton.

1860: "A Message from the Sea" in the Extra Christmas Number of *All the Year Round* (13 December) with Robert Buchanan or Henry F. Chorley, Charles Collins, Amelia B. Edwards, and Harriet Parr.

1861: "Tom Tiddler's Ground" in the Extra Christmas Number of *All the Year Round* (12 December) with John Harwood, Charles Collins, and Amelia B. Edwards.

1867: "No Thoroughfare" in the Extra Christmas Number of *All the Year Round* (12 December) without the assistance of other staff writers.

Lillian Nayder, *Unequal Partners: Charles Dickens, Wilkie Collins, and Victorian Authorship*.
London and Ithaca: Cornell University Press, 2002. xi-xii

which he had been suffering, and died two days after the boy. "He had for three days shown symptoms of rallying, and we had some hope of his recovery; but he sank and died, and never even knew that the child had gone before him. A sad, sad story." Dickens meanwhile had sent his own children home with his wife, and the rest soon followed. Poor M. Beaucourt was inconsolable. "The desolation of the place is wretched. When Mamey and Katey went, Beaucourt came in and wept. He really is almost broken-hearted about it. He had planted all manner of flowers for next month, and has thrown down the spade and left off weeding the garden, so that it looks something like a dreary bird-cage with all manner of grasses and chickweeds sticking through the bars and lying in the sand. 'Such a loss too,' he says, 'for Monsieur Dickens!' Then he looks in at the kitchen window (which seems to be his only relief), and sighs himself up the hill home."[76]

The interval of residence in Paris between these two last visits to Boulogne is now to be described.

Dickens's home from 1851-1860, located at Tavistock Square. He and Collins first staged *The Frozen Deep* there in 1857.

[72] Besides the old friends before named, Thackeray and his family were here in the early weeks, living "in a melancholy but very good chateau on the Paris road, where their landlord (a Baron) has supplied them, T. tells me, with one milk-jug as the entire crockery of the establishment." Our friend soon tired of this, going off to Spa, and on his return, after ascending the hill to smoke a farewell cigar with Dickens, left for London and Scotland in October.

[73] Another of his letters questioned even the picturesqueness a little, for he discovered that on a sunny day the white tents, seen from a distance, looked exactly like an immense washing establishment with all the linen put out to dry.

[74] "Whence it can be seen for miles and miles, to the glory of England and the joy of Beaucourt."

[75] The picture had changed drearily in less than a year and a half, when (17th of Feb. 1856) Dickens thus wrote from Paris. "I suppose mortal man out of bed never looked so ill and worn as the Emperor does just now. He passed close by me on horseback, as I was coming in at the door on Friday, and I never saw so haggard a face. Some English saluted him, and he lifted his hand to his hat as slowly, painfully, and laboriously, as if his arm were made of lead. I think he must be in pain."

[76] I cannot take leave of M. Beaucourt without saying that I am necessarily silent as to the most touching traits recorded of him by Dickens, because they refer to the generosity shown by him to an English family in occupation of another of his houses, in connection with whom his losses must have been considerable, but for whom he had nothing but help and sympathy. Replying to some questions about them, put by Dickens one day, he had only enlarged on their sacrifices and self-denials. "Ah that family, unfortunate! 'And you, Monsieur Beaucourt,' I said to him, 'you are unfortunate too, God knows!' Upon which he said in the pleasantest way in the world, Ah, Monsieur Dickens, thank you, don't speak of it!—And backed himself down the avenue with his cap in his hand, as if he were going to back himself straight into the evening star, without the ceremony of dying first. I never did see such a gentle, kind heart."

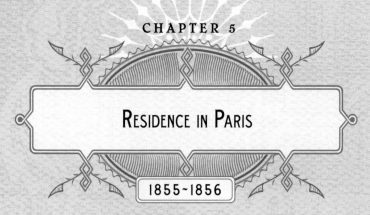

CHAPTER 5

RESIDENCE IN PARIS

1855~1856

In Paris Dickens's life was passed among artists, and in the exercise of his own art. His associates were writers, painters, actors, or musicians, and when he wanted relief from any strain of work he found it at the theatre. The years since his last residence in the great city had made him better known, and the increased attentions pleased him. He had to help in preparing for a translation of his books into French; and this, with continued labour at the story he had in hand, occupied him as long as he remained. It will be all best told by extracts from his letters; in which the people he met, the theatres he visited, and the incidents, public or private, that seemed to him worthy of mention, reappear with the old force and liveliness.

In October, Dickens's longer residence began. He betook himself with his family, after two unsuccessful attempts in the new region of the Rue Balzac and Rue Lord Byron, to an apartment in the Avenue des Champs Elysees. Over him was an English bachelor with an establishment consisting of an English groom and five English horses. "The concierge and his wife told us that his name was *Six*, which drove me nearly mad until we discovered it to be *Sykes*." The situation was a good one, very cheerful for himself and with amusement for his children. It was a quarter of a mile above Franconi's on the other side of the way, and within a door or two of the Jardin d'Hiver. The Exposition was just below; the Barriere de l'Etoile from a quarter to half a mile below; and all Paris, including Emperor and Empress coming from and returning to St. Cloud, thronged past the windows in open carriages or on horseback, all day long. Now it was he found himself more of a celebrity than when he had wintered in the city nine years before;[77] the feuilleton of the *Moniteur* was

filled daily with a translation of *Chuzzlewit*; and he had soon to consider the proposal I have named, to publish in French his collected novels and tales.[78] Before he had been a week in his new abode, Ary Scheffer, "a frank and noble fellow," had made his acquaintance; introduced him to several distinguished Frenchmen; and expressed the wish to paint him.

To Scheffer was also due an advantage obtained for my friend's two little daughters of which they may always keep the memory with pride. "Mamey and Katey are learning Italian, and their master is Manin of Venetian fame, the best and the noblest of those unhappy gentlemen. He came here with a wife and a beloved daughter, and they are both dead. Scheffer made him known to me, and has been, I understand, wonderfully generous and good to him." Nor may I omit to state the enjoyment afforded him, not only by the presence in Paris during the winter of Mr. Wilkie Collins and of Mr. and Mrs. White of Bonchurch, but by the many friends from England whom the Art Exposition brought over. Sir Alexander Cockburn was one of these; Edwin Landseer, Charles Robert Leslie, and William Boxall, were others. Macready left his retreat at Sherborne to make him a visit of several days. Thackeray went to and fro all the time between London and his mother's house, also in the Champs Elysees, where his daughters were. And Paris for the time was the home of Robert Lytton, who belonged to the Embassy, of the Sartorises, of the Brownings, and of others whom Dickens liked and cared for.

The success of a most agreeable little piece by our old friend Regnier took him next to the Francais, where Plessy's acting enchanted him. "Of course the interest of it turns upon a flawed piece of living china (*that* seems to be positively essential), but, as in most of these cases, if you will accept the position in which you find the people, you have nothing more to bother your morality about." The theatre in the Rue Richelieu, however, was not generally his favourite resort. He used to talk of it whimsically as a kind of tomb, where you went, as the Eastern people did in the stories, to think of your unsuccessful loves and dead relations.

At a theatre of a yet heavier school than the Francais he had a drearier experience. "On Wednesday we went to the

Odeon to see a new piece, in four acts and in verse, called *Michel Cervantes*. I suppose such an infernal dose of ditch water never was concocted. But there were certain passages, describing the suppression of public opinion in Madrid, which were received with a shout of savage application to France that made one stare again!

The last piece he went to see before leaving Paris was a French version of *As You Like It*; but he found two acts of it to be more than enough. "In *Comme il vous Plaira* nobody had anything to do but to sit down as often as possible on as many stones and trunks of trees as possible. When I had seen Jacques seat himself on 17 roots of trees, and 25 grey stones, which was at the end of the second act, I came away."

But great as was the pleasure thus derived from the theatre, he was, in the matter of social intercourse, even more indebted to distinguished men connected with it by authorship or acting. At Scribe's he was entertained frequently; and "very handsome and pleasant" was his account of the dinners, as of all the belongings, of the prolific dramatist—a charming place in Paris, a fine estate in the country, capital carriage, handsome pair of horses, "all made, as he says, by his pen." One of the guests the first evening was Auber, "a stolid little elderly man, rather petulant in manner," who told Dickens he had once lived "at Stock Noonton" (Stoke Newington) to study English, but had forgotten it all. "Louis Philippe had invited him to meet the Queen of England, and when L. P. presented him, the Queen said, 'We are such old acquaintances through M. Auber's works, that an introduction is quite unnecessary.'" They met again a few nights later, with the author of the *History of the Girondins*, at the hospitable table of M. Pichot, to whom Lamartine had expressed a strong desire again to meet Dickens as "un des grands amis de son imagination." "He continues to be precisely as we formerly knew him, both in appearance and manner; highly prepossessing, and with a sort of calm passion about him, very taking indeed. We talked of De Foe[79] and Richardson, and of that wonderful genius for the minutest details in a narrative, which has given them so much fame in France. I found him frank and unaffected, and full of curious knowledge of the French common people. He informed the company at dinner that he had rarely met a foreigner who spoke French so easily as your inimitable correspondent, whereat your

correspondent blushed modestly, and almost immediately afterwards so nearly choked himself with the bone of a fowl (which is still in his throat), that he sat in torture for ten minutes with a strong apprehension that he was going to make the good Pichot famous by dying like the little Hunchback at his table. Scribe and his wife were of the party, but had to go away at the ice-time because it was the first representation at the Opera Comique of a new opera by Auber and himself, of which very great expectations have been formed. It was very curious to see him—the author of 400 pieces—getting nervous as the time approached, and pulling out his watch every minute. At last he dashed out as if he were going into what a friend of mine calls a plunge-bath. Whereat she rose and followed. She is the most extraordinary woman I ever beheld; for her eldest son must be thirty, and she has the figure of five-and-twenty, and is strikingly handsome. So graceful too, that her manner of rising, curtseying, laughing, and going out after him, was pleasanter than the pleasantest thing I have ever seen done on the stage." The opera Dickens himself saw a week later, and wrote of it as "most charming. Delightful music, an excellent story, immense stage tact, capital scenic arrangements, and the most delightful little prima donna ever seen or heard, in the person of Marie Cabel. It is called *Manon Lescaut*—from the old romance—and is charming throughout. She sings a laughing song in it which is received with madness, and which is the only real laughing song that ever was written. Auber told me that when it was first rehearsed, it made a great effect upon the orchestra; and that he could not have had a better compliment upon its freshness than the musical director paid him, in coming and clapping him on the shoulder with 'Bravo, jeune homme! Cela promet bien!'"

At the house of another great artist, Madame Viardot, the sister of Malibran, Dickens dined to meet Georges Sands, that lady having appointed the day and hour for the interesting festival, which came off duly on the 10th of January. "I suppose it to be impossible to imagine anybody more unlike my preconceptions than the illustrious Sand. Just the kind of woman in appearance whom you might suppose to be the Queen's monthly nurse. Chubby, matronly, swarthy, black-eyed. Nothing of the blue-stocking about her, except a little final way of settling all your opinions with hers, which I take to have been acquired in the country where she lives,

lives, and in the domination of a small circle. A singularly ordinary woman in appearance and manner. The dinner was very good and remarkably unpretending.

"Emile Girardin," wrote Dickens on the 23rd of March, "was here yesterday, and he says that Peace is to be formally announced at Paris to-morrow amid general apathy." But the French are never wholly apathetic to their own exploits; and a display with a touch of excitement in it had been witnessed a couple of months before on the entry of the troops from the Crimea,[80] when the Zouaves, as they marched past, pleased Dickens most. "A remarkable body of men," he wrote, "wild, dangerous, and picturesque. Close-cropped head, red skull cap, Greek jacket, full red petticoat trowsers trimmed with yellow, and high white gaiters—the most sensible things for the purpose I know, and coming into use in the line. A man with such things on his legs is always free there, and ready for a muddy march; and might flounder through roads two feet deep in mud, and, simply by changing his gaiters (he has another pair in his haversack), be clean and comfortable and wholesome again, directly. Plenty of beard and moustache, and the musket carried reverse-wise with the stock over the shoulder, make up the sunburnt Zouave."

It was the festival time of the New Year, and Dickens was fairly lost in a mystery of amazement at where the money could come from that everybody was spending on the etrennes they were giving to everybody else. All the famous shops on the Boulevards had been blockaded for more than a week. "There is now a line of wooden stalls, three miles long, on each side of that immense thoroughfare; and wherever a retiring house or two admits of a double line, there it is. All sorts of objects from shoes and sabots, through porcelain and crystal, up to live fowls and

George Sand, engraving after portrait by Auguste Charpentier, ca. 1830s

rabbits which are played for at a sort of dwarf skittles (to their immense disturbance, as the ball rolls under them and shakes them off their shelves and perches whenever it is delivered by a vigorous hand), are on sale in this great Fair. And what you may get in the way of ornament for two-pence, is astounding." Unhappily there came dark and rainy weather, and one of the improvements of the Empire ended, as so many others did, in slush and misery.

Some sketches connected with the Art Exposition in the winter of 1855, and with the fulfilment of Ary Scheffer's design to paint the portrait of Dickens, may close these Paris pictures. He did not think that English art showed to advantage beside the French. It seemed to him small, shrunken, insignificant, "niggling."

To the sittings at Ary Scheffer's some troubles as well as many pleasures were incident, and both had mention in his letters. "You may faintly imagine what I have suffered from sitting to Scheffer every day since I came back. He is a most noble fellow, and I have the greatest pleasure in his society, and have made all sorts of acquaintances at his house; but I can scarcely express how uneasy and unsettled it makes me to have to sit, sit, sit, with *Little Dorrit* on my mind, and the Christmas business too—though that is now happily dismissed. On Monday afternoon, *and all day on Wednesday*, I am going to sit again. And the crowning feature is, that I do not discern the slightest resemblance, either in his portrait or his brother's! They both peg away at me at the same time."

That was at the close of November. January came, and the end of the sittings was supposed to be at hand. "The nightmare portrait is nearly done; and Scheffer promises that an interminable sitting next Saturday, beginning at 10

Mrs. Kate Perugini (neé Dickens)

o'clock in the morning, shall finish it. It is a fine spirited head, painted at his very best, and with a very easy and natural appearance in it. But it does not look to me at all like, nor does it strike me that if I saw it in a gallery I should suppose myself to be the original." Still this was not the last. March had come before the portrait was done. "Scheffer finished yesterday; and Collins, who has a good eye for pictures, says that there is no man living who could do the painting about the eyes. As a work of art I see in it spirit combined with perfect ease, and yet I don't see myself. So I come to the conclusion that I never *do* see myself. I shall be very curious to know the effect of it upon you."

Dickens left Paris at the end of April, and, after the summer in Boulogne which has been described, passed the winter in London, giving to his theatrical enterprise nearly all the time that *Little Dorrit* did not claim from him. His book was finished in the following spring; was inscribed to Clarkson Stanfield; and now claims to have something said about it.

---

[77] "It is surprising what a change nine years have made in my notoriety here. So many of the rising French generation now read English (and Chuzzlewit is now being translated daily in the *Moniteur*), that I can't go into a shop and give my card without being acknowledged in the pleasantest way possible. A curiosity-dealer brought home some little knick-knacks I had bought, the other night, and knew all about my books from beginning to end of 'em. There is much of the personal friendliness in my readers, here, that is so delightful at home; and I have been greatly surprised and pleased by the unexpected discovery." To this I may add a line from one of his letters six years later. "I see my books in French at every railway station great and small."—13th of Oct. 1862.

[78] "I forget whether" (6th of Jan. 1856) "I have already told you that I have received a proposal from a responsible bookselling house here, for a complete edition, authorized by myself, of a French translation of all my books. The terms involve questions of space and amount of matter; but I should say, at a rough calculation, that I shall get about £300 by it—perhaps £50 more." "I have arranged" (30th of Jan.) "with the French bookselling house to receive, by monthly payments of £40, the sum of £440 for the right to translate all my books: that is, what they call my Romances, and what I call my Stories. This does not include the Christmas Books, *American Notes, Pictures from Italy*, or the *Sketches*; but they are to have the right to translate them for extra payments if they choose. In consideration of this venture as to the unprotected property, I cede them the right of translating all future Romances at a thousand francs (£40) each. Considering that I get so much for what is otherwise worth nothing, and get my books before so clever and important a people, I think this is not a bad move?" The first friend with whom he advised about it, I should mention, was the famous Leipzig publisher, M. Tauchnitz, in whose judgment, as well as in his honour and good faith, he had implicit reliance, and who thought the offer fair. On the 17th of April he wrote: "On Monday I am going to dine with all my translators at Hachette's, the bookseller who has made the bargain for the complete edition, and who began this week to pay his monthly £40 for a year. I don't mean to go out any more. Please to imagine me in the midst of my French dressers." He wrote an address for the Edition in which he praised the liberality of his publishers and expressed his pride in being so presented to the French people whom he sincerely loved and honoured. Another word may be added. "It is rather appropriate that the French translation edition will pay my rent for the whole year, and travelling charges to boot."—24th of Feb. 1856.

[79] I subjoin from another of these French letters of later date a remark on *Robinson Crusoe*. "You remember my saying to you some time ago how curious I thought it that *Robinson Crusoe* should be the only instance of an universally popular book that could make no one laugh and could make no one cry. I have been reading it again just now, in the course of my numerous refreshings at those English wells, and I will venture to say that there is not in literature a more surprising instance of an utter want of tenderness and sentiment, than the death of Friday. It is as heartless as *Gil Blas*, in a very different and far more serious way. But the second part altogether will not bear enquiry. In the second part of *Don Quixote* are some of the finest things. But the second part of *Robinson Crusoe* is perfectly contemptible, in the glaring defect that it exhibits the man who was 30 years on that desert island with no visible effect made on his character by that experience. De Foe's women too—Robinson Crusoe's wife for instance—are terrible dull commonplace fellows without breeches; and I have no doubt he was a precious dry and disagreeable article himself—I mean De Foe: not Robinson. Poor dear Goldsmith (I remember as I write) derived the same impression."

[80] Here is another picture of Regiments in the Streets of which the date is the 30th of January. "It was cold this afternoon, as bright as Italy, and these Elysian Fields crowded with carriages, riders, and foot passengers. All the fountains were playing, all the Heavens shining. Just as I went out at 4 o'clock, several regiments that had passed out at the Barriere in the morning to exercise in the country, came marching back, in the straggling French manner, which is far more picturesque and real than anything you can imagine in that way. Alternately great storms of drums played, and then the most delicious and skilful bands, 'Trovatore' music, 'Barber of Seville' music, all sorts of music with well-marked melody and time. All bloused Paris (led by the Inimitable, and a poor cripple who works himself up and down all day in a big wheeled car) went at quick march down the avenue, in a sort of hilarious dance. If the colours with the golden eagle on the top had only been unfurled, we should have followed them anywhere, in any cause—much as the children follow *Punches* in the better cause of Comedy. Napoleon on the top of the Column seemed up to the whole thing, I thought."

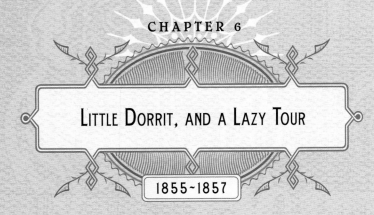

CHAPTER 6

LITTLE DORRIT, AND A LAZY TOUR

1855~1857

Between *Hard Times* and *Little Dorrit*, Dickens's principal literary work had been the contribution to *Household Words* of two tales for Christmas (1854 and 1855) which his readings afterwards made widely popular, the Story of Richard Doubledick,[81] and Boots at the Holly-Tree Inn. In the latter was related, with a charming naturalness and spirit, the elopement, to get married at Gretna Green, of two little children of the mature respective ages of eight and seven.

At Christmas 1855 came out the first number of *Little Dorrit*, and in April 1857 the last.

The book took its origin from the notion he had of a leading man for a story who should bring about all the mischief in it, lay it all on Providence, and say at every fresh calamity, "Well it's a mercy, however, nobody was to blame you know!" The title first chosen, out of many suggested, was *Nobody's Fault*; and four numbers had been written, of which the first was on the eve of appearance, before this was changed. When about to fall to work he excused himself from an engagement he should have kept because "the story is breaking out all round me, and I am going off down the railroad to humour it." The humouring was a little difficult, however; and such indications of a droop in his invention as presented themselves in portions of *Bleak House*, were noticeable again. "As to the story I am in the second number, and last night and this morning had half a mind to begin again, and work in what I have done, afterwards." It had occurred to him, that, by making the fellow-travellers at once known to each other, as the opening of the story stands, he had missed an effect. "It struck me that it would be a new thing to show people coming together, in a chance way, as fellow-travellers, and being in the same place, ignorant of one another, as happens in life; and to connect them afterwards, and to make the waiting for that connection a part of the interest." The change was not made; but the mention of it was one of several intimations to me of the altered conditions under which he was writing, and that the old, unstinted, irrepressible flow of fancy had received temporary check. In this view I have found it very interesting to compare the original notes, which as usual he prepared for each number of the tale, and which with the rest are in my possession, with those of *Chuzzlewit* or *Copperfield*; observing in the former the labour and pains, and in the latter the lightness and confidence of handling.[82] "I am just now getting to work on number three: sometimes enthusiastic, more often dull enough. There is an enormous outlay in the Father of the Marshalsea chapter, in the way of getting a great lot of matter into a small space. I am not quite resolved, but I have a great idea of overwhelming that family with wealth. Their condition would be very curious. I can make Dorrit very strong in the story, I hope." The Marshalsea part of the tale undoubtedly was excellent, and there was masterly treatment of character in the contrasts of the brothers Dorrit; but of the family generally it may be said that its least important members had most of his genius in them.

The younger of the brothers, the scapegrace son, and "Fanny dear," are perfectly real people in what makes them unattractive; but what is meant for attractiveness in the heroine becomes often tiresome by want of reality.

The first number appeared in December 1855, and on the 2nd there was an exultant note. "*Little Dorrit* has beaten even *Bleak House* out of the field. It is a most tremendous start, and I am overjoyed at it;" to which he added, writing from Paris on the 6th of the month following, "You know that they had sold 35,000 of number two on new year's day." He was still in Paris on the day of the appearance of that portion of the tale by which it will always be most vividly remembered, and thus wrote on the 30th of January 1856: "I have a grim pleasure upon me to-night in thinking that the Circumlocution Office sees the light, and in wondering what effect it will make. But my head really stings with the visions of the book, and I am going, as we

DICKENS'S CONTRIBUTION TO THE 1855 CHRISTMAS NUMBER OF *HOUSEHOLD WORDS*, "THE BOOTS" AT "THE HOLLY TREE INN":

SIR, Boots was at this identical Holly-Tree Inn (having left it several times to better himself, but always come back through one thing or another), when, one summer afternoon, the coach drives up, and out of the coach gets them two children. The Guard says to our Governor, "I don't quite make out these little passengers, but the young gentleman's words was, that they was to be brought here." The young gentleman gets out; hands his lady out; gives the Guard something for himself; says to our Governor, "We're to stop here to-night, please. Sitting-room and two bedrooms will be required. Chops and cherry-pudding for two!" and tucks her in her little sky-blue mantle, under his arm, and walks into the house much bolder than Brass.

Boots leaves me to judge what the amazement of that establishment was, when these two tiny creatures all alone by themselves was marched into the Angel—much more so when he, who had seen them without their seeing him, give the Governor his views upon the expedition they was upon. "Cobbs," says the Governor, "if this is so, I must set off myself to York, and quiet their friends' minds. In which case you must keep your eye upon 'em, and humor 'em till I come back. But before I take these measures, Cobbs, I should wish you to find from themselves whether your opinions is correct." "Sir, to you," says Cobbs, "that shall be done directly."

So Boots goes up-stairs to the Angel, and there he finds Master Harry, on a e'normous sofa—immense at any time, but looking like the Great Bed of Ware, compared with him—a-drying the eyes of Miss Norah with his pocket-hankecher. Their little legs was entirely off the ground, of course, and it really is not possible for Boots to express to me how small them children looked.

"It's Cobbs! It's Cobbs!" cries Master Harry, and comes running to him on t'other side, and catching hold of his t'other hand, and they both jump for joy.

"I see you a-getting out, sir," says Cobbs. "I thought it was you. I thought I couldn't be mistaken in your height and figure. What's the object of your journey, sir? Matrimonial?"

"We're going to be married, Cobbs, at Gretna Green," returned the boy. "We have run away on purpose. Norah has been in rather low spirits, Cobbs; but she'll be happy, now we have found you to be our friend."

"Thank you, sir, and thank *you*, miss," says Cobbs, "for your good opinion. *Did* you bring any luggage with you, sir?"

If I will believe Boots when he gives me his word and honor upon it, the lady had got a parasol, a smelling-bottle, a round and a half of cold buttered toast, eight peppermint drops, and a hair-brush—seemingly a doll's. The gentleman had got about half a dozen yards of string, a knife, three or four sheets of writing-paper, folded up surprising small, a orange, and a Chaney mug with his name upon it. [. . .]

French say, to disembarrass it by plunging out into some of the strange places I glide into of nights in these latitudes."

The Circumlocution heroes led to the Society scenes, the Hampton-court dowager-sketches, and Mr. Gowan; all parts of one satire levelled against prevailing political and social vices. Aim had been taken, in the course of it, at some living originals, disguised sufficiently from recognition to enable him to make his thrust more sure; but there was one exception self-revealed. "I had the general idea," he wrote while engaged on the sixth number, "of the Society business before the Sadleir affair, but I shaped Mr. Merdle himself out of that precious rascality. Society, the Circumlocution

First monthly part of *Little Dorrit*, illustrations by Hablot Knight Browne (Phiz), 1855

RIGHT: *Little Dorrit*,
by Fred Barnard
ca. 1894

well-constructed story, some of the most deeply considered things that occur in it have really little to do with the tale itself. The surface-painting of both Miss Wade and Tattyco-ram, to take an instance, is anything but attractive, yet there is under it a rare force of likeness in the unlikeness between the two which has much subtlety of intention; and they must both have had, as well as Mr. Gowan himself, a striking effect in the novel, if they had been made to contribute in a more essential way to its interest or development. The fail-ure nevertheless had not been for want of care and study, as well of his own design as of models by masters in his art. A happier hint of apology, for example, could hardly be given for Fielding's introduction of such an episode as the Man of the Hill between the youth and manhood of Blifil and Tom Jones, than is suggested by what Dickens wrote of the least interesting part of *Little Dorrit*. In the mere form, Fielding of course was only following the lead of Cervantes and Le Sage; but Dickens rightly judged his purpose also to have been, to supply a kind of connection between the episode and the story. "I don't see the practicability of making the History of a Self-Tormentor, with which I took great pains, a written narrative. But I do see the possibility" (he saw the other practicability before the number was published) "of making it a chapter by itself, which might enable me to dispense with the necessity of the turned commas. Do you think that would be better? I have no doubt that a great part of Fielding's reason for the introduced story, and Smollett's also, was, that it is sometimes really impossible to present, in a full book, the idea it contains (which yet it may be on all accounts desirable to present), without supposing the reader to be possessed of almost as much romantic allow-ance as would put him on a level with the writer. In Miss Wade I had an idea, which I thought a new one, of making the introduced story so fit into surroundings impossible of separation from the main story, as to make the blood of the book circulate through both. But I can only suppose, from what you say, that I have not exactly succeeded in this."

Shortly after, he was in London on business connected with the purchase of Gadshill Place, and he went over to the Borough to see what traces were left of the prison of which his first impression was taken in his boyhood, which had played so important a part in this latest novel, and every brick and stone of which he had been able to rebuild in his book by the mere vividness of his marvellous memory. "Went to the Borough yesterday morning before going to Gadshill, to see if I could find any ruins of the Marshalsea. Found a great part of the original building—now 'Marshalsea Place.' Found the rooms that have been in my mind's eye in the story."

Mention was made of this visit in the preface that appeared with the last number; and all it is necessary to add of the completed book will be, that, though in the humour and satire of its finer parts not unworthy of him, and though it had the clear design, worthy of him in an especial degree, of contrasting, both in private and in public life, and in poverty equally as in wealth, duty done and duty not done, it made no material addition to his reputation. His public, however, showed no falling-off in its enormous numbers; and what is said in one of his letters, noticeable for this touch of character, illustrates his anxiety to avoid any set-off from the disquiet that critical discourtesies might give. "I was ludicrously foiled here the other night in a resolution I have kept for twenty years not to know of any attack upon myself, by stumbling, before I could pick myself up, on a short extract in the *Globe* from *Blackwood's Magazine*, informing me that *Little Dorrit* is 'Twaddle.' I was sufficiently put out by it to be angry with myself for being such a fool, and then pleased with myself for having so long been constant to a good resolution."

There was a scene that made itself part of history not four months after his death, which, if he could have lived to hear of it, might have more than consoled him. It was the meeting of Bismarck and Jules Favre under the walls of Paris. The Prussian was waiting to open fire on the city; the French-man was engaged in the arduous task of showing the wisdom of not doing it; and "we learn," say the papers of the day, "that while the two eminent statesmen were trying to find a basis of negotiation, Von Moltke was seated in a corner reading *Little Dorrit*." Who will doubt that the chapter on HOW NOT TO DO IT was then absorbing the old soldier's attention?

Preparations for the private play had gone on incessantly up to Christmas, and, in turning the school-room into a theatre, sawing and hammering worthy of Babel continued for weeks.

Little Dorrit, Chapter 10

The general obfuscation of the Bleak House fog is developed into a more precise critique of the endless confusions of the cirumlocation office, where progress is terminally impeded by govermental red tape.

THE Circumlocution Office was (as everybody knows without being told) the most important Department under Government. No public business of any kind could possibly be done at any time without the acquiescence of the Circumlocution Office. Its finger was in the largest public pie, and in the smallest public tart. It was equally impossible to do the plainest right and to undo the plainest wrong without the express authority of the Circumlocution Office. If another Gunpowder Plot had been discovered half an hour before the lighting of the match, nobody would have been justified in saving the parliament until there had been half a score of boards, half a bushel of minutes, several sacks of official memoranda, and a family-vault full of ungrammatical correspondence, on the part of the Circumlocution Office.

This glorious establishment had been early in the field, when the one sublime principle involving the difficult art of governing a country, was first distinctly revealed to statesmen. It had been foremost to study that bright revelation and to carry its shining influence through the whole of the official proceedings. Whatever was required to be done, the Circumlocution Office was beforehand with all the public departments in the art of perceiving—HOW NOT TO DO IT.

Through this delicate perception, through the tact with which it invariably seized it, and through the genius with which it always acted on it, the Circumlocution Office had risen to overtop all the public departments; and the public condition had risen to be—what it was.

Reprinted in Philip Collins, ed. *The Critical Heritage*

E. B. Hamley's anonymous review for Blackwood's Magazine, April 1857, presented a "Remonstrance with Dickens":

ALL this humour [in *Martin Chuzzlewit*] is Pickwickian—redolent of the days of Weller and Wardle and Winkle, the golden age of Cockaigne. Such a wealth of comic power has never been displayed by any other writer. But in these post-Pickwickian works the author aspires not only to be a humourist, but an artist and a moralist; and in his later productions, which we shall talk of by-and-by, he aims at being, besides artist and moralist, politician, philosopher and ultra-philanthropist. If we direct our attention to his weakness in these latter characters, it is solely because he has for years past evinced more and more his tendency to abandon his strong point as humourist and comic writer, and to base his pretensions on grounds which we consider utterly false and unstable. For as a humourist we prefer Dickens to all living men—as artist, moralist, politician, philosopher and ultra-philanthropist, we prefer many living men, women, and children to Dickens [. . .] What can be weaker in itself, to say nothing of the total want of art in connecting it with the story, than the intended satire on the Circumlocution Office? We don't in the least wish to stand up for the Circumlocution Office—curse the Circumlocution Office, say we. We know well the amount of insolence and ignorance to be found among government officials of all departments. But the attempt to show it up in *Little Dorrit* is as inartificial as if he had cut half-a-dozen articles out of an Opposition newspaper, and stuck them in anyhow, anywhere.

FROM THE PREFACE TO *LITTLE DORRIT*, 1857:

*As well as describing his inspiring (return) visit to the Marshalsea, Dickens uses this preface to detail the social
and political abuses that motivate his critique, and to discuss the sense of a growing,
personal relationship with his readers that was so important to him:*

IF I might offer any apology for so exaggerated a fiction as the Barnacles and the Circumlocution Office, I would seek it in the common experience of an Englishman, without presuming to mention the unimportant fact of my having done that violence to good manners, in the days of a Russian war, and of a Court of Inquiry at Chelsea. If I might make so bold as to defend that extravagant conception, Mr. Merdle, I would hint that it originated after the Railroad-share epoch, in the times of a certain Irish bank, and of one or two other equally laudable enterprises. If I were to plead anything in mitigation of the preposterous fancy that a bad design will sometimes claim to be a good and an expressly religious design, it would be the curious coincidence that it has been brought to its climax in these pages, in the days of the public examination of late Directors of a Royal British Bank. But, I submit myself to suffer judgment to go by default on all these counts, if need be, and to accept the assurance (on good authority) that nothing like them was ever known in this land. Some of my readers may have an interest in being informed whether or no any portions of the Marshalsea Prison are yet standing. I did not know, myself, until the sixth of this present month, when I went to look. I found the outer front courtyard, often mentioned here, metamorphosed into a butter shop; and I then almost gave up every brick of the jail for lost. Wandering, however, down a certain adjacent 'Angel Court, leading to Bermondsey', I came to 'Marshalsea Place:' the houses in which I recognised, not only as the great block of the former prison, but as preserving the rooms that arose in my mind's-eye when I became Little Dorrit's biographer. The smallest boy I ever conversed with, carrying the largest baby I ever saw, offered a supernaturally intelligent explanation of the locality in its old uses, and was very nearly correct. How this young Newton (for such I judge him to be) came by his information, I don't know; he was a quarter of a century too young to know anything about it of himself. I pointed to the window of the room where Little Dorrit was born, and where her father lived so long, and asked him what was the name of the lodger who tenanted that apartment at present? He said, 'Tom Pythick.' I asked him who was Tom Pythick? and he said, 'Joe Pythick's uncle.'

A little further on, I found the older and smaller wall, which used to enclose the pent-up inner prison where nobody was put, except for ceremony. But, whosoever goes into Marshalsea Place, turning out of Angel Court, leading to Bermondsey, will find his feet on the very paving-stones of the extinct Marshalsea jail; will see its narrow yard to the right and to the left, very little altered if at all, except that the walls were lowered when the place got free; will look upon rooms in which the debtors lived; and will stand among the crowding ghosts of many miserable years.

In the Preface to *Bleak House* I remarked that I had never had so many readers. In the Preface to its next successor, *Little Dorrit*, I have still to repeat the same words. Deeply sensible of the affection and confidence that have grown up between us, I add to this Preface, as I added to that, May we meet again!

The priceless help of Stanfield had again been secured, and I remember finding him one day at Tavistock House in the act of upsetting some elaborate arrangements by Dickens, with a proscenium before him made up of chairs, and the scenery planned out with walking-sticks. But Dickens's art in a matter of this kind was to know how to take advice; and no suggestion came to him that he was not ready to act upon, if it presented the remotest likelihood.

As Christmas approached the house was in a state of siege. "All day long, a labourer heats size over the fire in a great

TAVISTOCK HOUSE THEATRE.

UNDER THE MANAGEMENT OF MR. CHARLES DICKENS.

On Twelfth Night, Tuesday, January 6th, 1857, AT A QUARTER BEFORE 8 O'CLOCK, *will be presented*

AN ENTIRELY NEW

ROMANTIC DRAMA, IN THREE ACTS, BY MR. WILKIE COLLINS,

CALLED

THE FROZEN DEEP.

The Machinery and Properties by MR. IRELAND, *of the Theatre Royal, Adelphi.* *The Dresses by* MESSRS. NATHAN, *of Titchbourne Street, Haymarket.* *Perruquier,* MR. WILSON, *of the Strand.*

THE PROLOGUE WILL BE DELIVERED BY MR. JOHN FORSTER.

CAPTAIN EBSWORTH, *of The Sea Mew*	MR. EDWARD PIGOTT.
CAPTAIN HELDING, *of The Wanderer*	MR. ALFRED DICKENS.
LIEUTENANT CRAYFORD	MR. MARK LEMON.
FRANK ALDERSLEY	MR. WILKIE COLLINS.
RICHARD WARDOUR	MR. CHARLES DICKENS.
LIEUTENANT STEVENTON	MR. YOUNG CHARLES.
JOHN WANT, *Ship's Cook*	MR. AUGUSTUS EGG, A.R.A.
BATESON } *Two of The Sea Mew's People*	{ MR. EDWARD HOGARTH.
DARKER }	{ MR. FREDERICK EVANS.

(OFFICERS AND CREWS OF THE SEA MEW AND WANDERER.)

MRS. STEVENTON	MISS HELEN.
ROSE EBSWORTH	MISS KATE.
LUCY CRAYFORD	MISS HOGARTH.
CLARA BURNHAM	MISS MARY.
NURSE ESTHER	MRS. WILLS.
MAID	MISS MARTHA.

THE SCENERY AND SCENIC EFFECTS OF THE FIRST ACT, BY MR. TELBIN.
THE SCENERY AND SCENIC EFFECTS OF THE SECOND AND THIRD ACTS, BY **Mr. STANFIELD, R.A.**
ASSISTED BY MR. DANSON.
THE ACT-DROP, ALSO BY **Mr. STANFIELD, R.A.**

AT THE END OF THE PLAY, HALF-AN-HOUR FOR REFRESHMENT.

To Conclude with MRS. INCHBALD'S Farce, in Two Acts, of

ANIMAL MAGNETISM.

(THE SCENE IS LAID IN SEVILLE.)

THE DOCTOR	MR. CHARLES DICKENS.
PEDRILLO	MR. MARK LEMON.
THE MARQUIS DE LA GUARDIA	MR. YOUNG CHARLES.
GREGORIO	MR. WILKIE COLLINS.
CAMILLA	MISS KATE.
JACINTHA	MISS HOGARTH.

Musical Composer and Conductor of the Orchestra—Mr. FRANCESCO BERGER, who will preside at the Piano.

CARRIAGES MAY BE ORDERED AT HALF-PAST ELEVEN.

GOD SAVE THE QUEEN!

Playbill for *The Frozen Deep*, Tavistock House, 1857

crucible. We eat it, drink it, breathe it, and smell it. Seventy paint-pots (which came in a van) adorn the stage; and thereon may be beheld, Stanny, and three Dansons (from the Surrey Zoological Gardens), all painting at once!! Meanwhile, Telbin, in a secluded bower in Brewer-street, Golden-square, plies *his* part of the little undertaking." How worthily it turned out in the end, the excellence of the performances and the delight of the audiences, became known to all London; and the pressure for admittance at last took the form of a tragi-comedy, composed of ludicrous makeshifts and gloomy disappointments, with which even Dickens's resources could not deal. "My audience is now 93," he wrote one day in despair, "and at least 10 will neither hear nor see." There was nothing for it but to increase the number of nights; and it was not until the 20th of January he described "the workmen smashing the last atoms of the theatre."

His book was finished soon after at Gadshill Place, to be presently described, which he had purchased the previous year, and taken possession of in February; subscribing himself, in the letter announcing the fact, as "the Kentish Freeholder on his native heath, his name Protection."[83] The new abode occupied him in various ways in the early part of the summer; and Hans Andersen the Dane had just arrived upon a visit to him there, when Douglas Jerrold's unexpected death befell. It was a shock to every one, and an especial grief to Dickens. Jerrold's wit, and the bright shrewd intellect that had so many triumphs,

The death of Wardour (played by Dickens) in the Tavistock House production of *The Frozen Deep. Illustrated London News*, 1857

need no celebration from me; but the keenest of satirists was one of the kindliest of men, and Dickens had a fondness for Jerrold as genuine as his admiration for him.

"I propose that there shall be a night at a theatre when the actors (with old Cooke) shall play the *Rent Day* and *Black-ey'd Susan*; another night elsewhere, with a lecture from Thackeray; a day reading by me; a night reading by me; a lecture by Russell; and a subscription performance of the *Frozen Deep*, as at Tavistock House. I don't mean to do it beggingly; but merely to announce the whole series, the day after the funeral, 'In memory of the late Mr. Douglas Jerrold,' or some such phrase. I have got hold of Arthur Smith as the best man of business I know, and go to work with him to-morrow morning—inquiries being made in the meantime as to the likeliest places to be had for these various purposes. My confident hope is that we shall get close upon two thousand pounds."

The friendly enterprise was carried to the close with a vigour, promptitude, and success, that well corresponded with this opening. In addition to the performances named, there were others in the country also organized by Dickens, in which he took active personal part; and the result did not fall short of his expectations. The sum was invested ultimately for our friend's unmarried daughter, who still receives the income from myself, the last surviving trustee.

So passed the greater part of the summer, and when the country performances were over at the end of August I had this intimation. "I have arranged with Collins that he and I will start next Monday on a ten or twelve days' expedition to out-of-the-way places, to do (in inns and coast-corners) a little tour in search of an article and in avoidance of railroads. I must get a good name for it, and I propose it in five articles, one for the beginning of every number in the October part." Next day: "Our decision is for a foray upon the fells of Cumberland; I having discovered in the books some promising moors and bleak places thereabout." Into the lake-country they went accordingly; and *The Lazy Tour of Two Idle Apprentices*, contributed to *Household Words*, was a narrative of the trip.

On their way home the friends were at Doncaster, and this was Dickens's first experience of the St. Leger and its saturnalia. The impressions received from the race-week

The Frozen Deep company, with Dickens seated in foreground

were not favourable. It was noise and turmoil all day long, and a gathering of vagabonds from all parts of the racing earth. Every bad face that had ever caught wickedness from an innocent horse had its representative in the streets; and as Dickens, like Gulliver looking down upon his fellow-men after coming from the horse-country, looked down into Doncaster High-street from his inn-window, he seemed to see everywhere a then notorious personage who had just poisoned his betting-companion. "Everywhere I see the late Mr. Palmer with his betting-book in his hand. Mr. Palmer

sits next me at the theatre; Mr. Palmer goes before me down the street; Mr. Palmer follows me into the chemist's shop where I go to buy rose water after breakfast, and says to the chemist 'Give us soom sal volatile or soom damned thing o' that soort, in wather—my head's bad!' And I look at the back of his bad head repeated in long, long lines on the race course, and in the betting stand and outside the betting rooms in the town, and I vow to God that I can see nothing in it but cruelty, covetousness, calculation, insensibility, and low wickedness."

---

[81] The framework for this sketch was a graphic description, also done by Dickens, of the celebrated Charity at Rochester founded in the sixteenth century by Richard Watts, "for six poor travellers, who, not being Rogues or Proctors, may receive gratis for one night, lodging, entertainment, and fourpence each." A quaint monument to Watts is the most prominent object on the wall of the south-west transept of the cathedral, and underneath it is now placed a brass thus inscribed: "CHARLES DICKENS. Born at Portsmouth, seventh of February 1812. Died at Gadshill Place by Rochester, ninth of June 1870. Buried in Westminster Abbey. To connect his memory with the scenes in which his earliest and his latest years were passed, and with the associations of Rochester Cathedral and its neighbourhood which extended over all his life, this Tablet, with the sanction of the Dean and Chapter, is placed by his Executors."

[82] So curious a contrast, taking *Copperfield* for the purpose, I have thought worth giving in fac-simile; and can assure the reader that the examples taken express very fairly the general character of the *Notes* to the two books respectively.

[83] In the same letter was an illustration of the ruling passion in death, which, even in so undignified a subject, might have interested Pope. "You remember little Wieland who did grotesque demons so well. Did you ever hear how he died? He lay very still in bed with the life fading out of him—suddenly sprung out of it, threw what is professionally called a flip-flap, and fell dead on the floor."

CHAPTER 7

WHAT HAPPENED AT THIS TIME

1857~1858

A**N UNSETTLED FEELING** greatly in excess of what was usual with Dickens, more or less observable since his first residence at Boulogne, became at this time almost habitual, and the satisfactions which home should have supplied, and which indeed were essential requirements of his nature, he had failed to find in his home. He had not the alternative that under this disappointment some can discover in what is called society. It did not suit him, and he set no store by it. No man was better fitted to adorn any circle he entered, but beyond that of friends and equals he rarely passed. He would take as much pains to keep out of the houses of the great as others take to get into them. Not always wisely, it may be admitted. Mere contempt for toadyism and flunkeyism was not at all times the prevailing motive with him which he supposed it to be. Beneath his horror of those vices of Englishmen in his own rank of life, there was a still stronger resentment at the social inequalities that engender them, of which he was not so conscious and to which he owned less freely.

Nothing of all this has yet presented itself to notice, except in occasional forms of restlessness and desire of change of place, which were themselves, when his books were in progress, so incident as well to the active requirements of his fancy as to call, thus far, for no other explanation. Up to the date of the completion of *Copperfield* he had felt himself to be in possession of an all-sufficient resource. Against whatever might befall he had a set-off in his imaginative creations, a compensation derived from his art that never failed him, because there he was supreme. It was the world he could bend to his will, and make subserve to all his desires.

It was during the composition of *Little Dorrit* that I think he first felt a certain strain upon his invention which brought with it other misgivings. In a modified form this was present during the latter portions of *Bleak House*, of which not a few of the defects might be traced to the acting excitements amid which it was written; but the succeeding book made it plainer to him; and it is remarkable that in the interval between them he resorted for the first and only time in his life to a practice, which he abandoned at the close of his next and last story published in the twenty-number form, of putting down written "Memoranda" of suggestions for characters or incidents by way of resource to him in his writing. Never before had his teeming fancy seemed to want such help; the need being less to contribute to its fullness than to check its overflowing; but it is another proof that he had been secretly bringing before himself, at least, the possibility that what had ever been his great support might some day desert him. It was strange that he should have had such doubt, and he would hardly have confessed it openly; but apart from that wonderful world of his books, the range of his thoughts was not always proportioned to the width and largeness of his nature.

To one very earnestly made in the early autumn of 1857, in which opportunity was taken to compare his recent rush up Carrick Fell to his rush into other difficulties, here was the reply. "Too late to say, put the curb on, and don't rush at hills—the wrong man to say it to. I have now no relief but in action. I am become incapable of rest. I am quite confident I should rust, break, and die, if I spared myself. Much better to die, doing. What I am in that way, nature made me first, and my way of life has of late, alas! confirmed. I must accept the drawback—since it is one—with the powers I have; and I must hold upon the tenure prescribed to me."

Later in the same year he thus wrote from Boulogne: "I have had dreadful thoughts of getting away somewhere altogether by myself. If I could have managed it, I think possibly I might have gone to the Pyreennees (you know what I mean that word for, so I won't re-write it) for six months! I have put the idea into the perspective of six months, but have not abandoned it. I have visions of living for half a year

RIGHT: Charles Dickens by John Henry Frederick Bacon (detail), (1865–1914)

370

or so, in all sorts of inaccessible places, and opening a new book therein. A floating idea of going up above the snow-line in Switzerland, and living in some astonishing convent, hovers about me. If *Household Words* could be got into a good train, in short, I don't know in what strange place, or at what remote elevation above the level of the sea, I might fall to work next. *Restlessness*, you will say. Whatever it is, it is always driving me, and I cannot help it. I have rested nine or ten weeks, and sometimes feel as if it had been a year—though I had the strangest nervous miseries before I stopped. If I couldn't walk fast and far, I should just explode and perish." Again, four months later he wrote: "You will hear of me in Paris, probably next Sunday, and I *may* go on to Bordeaux. Have general ideas of emigrating in the summer to the mountain-ground between France and Spain. Am altogether in a dishevelled state of mind—motes of new books in the dirty air, miseries of older growth threatening to close upon me. Why is it, that as with poor David, a sense comes always crushing on me now, when I fall into low spirits, as of one happiness I have missed in life, and one friend and companion I have never made?"

Early in 1856 (20th of January) the notion revisited him of writing a book in solitude. "Again I am beset by my former notions of a book whereof the whole story shall be

Catherine Dickens, photograph

on the top of the Great St. Bernard. As I accept and reject ideas for *Little Dorrit*, it perpetually comes back to me. Two or three years hence, perhaps you'll find me living with the Monks and the Dogs a whole winter—among the blinding snows that fall about that monastery. I have a serious idea that I shall do it, if I live." "It is much better to go on and fret, than to stop and fret. As to repose—for some men there's no such thing in this life. The foregoing has the appearance of a small sermon; but it is so often in my head in these days that it cannot help coming out. The old days—the old days! Shall I ever, I wonder, get the frame of mind back as it used to be then? Something of it perhaps—but never quite as it used to be. I find that the skeleton in my domestic closet is becoming a pretty big one."

It would be unjust and uncandid not to admit that these and other similar passages in the letters that extended over the years while he lived abroad, had served in some degree as a preparation for what came after his return to England in the following year. It came with a great shock nevertheless; because it told plainly what before had never been avowed, but only hinted at more or less obscurely. The opening reference is to the reply which had been made to a previous expression of his wish for some confidences as in the old time. I give only what is strictly necessary to account for what followed, and even this with deep reluctance. "Your letter of yesterday was so kind and hearty, and sounded so gently the many chords we have touched together, that I cannot leave it unanswered, though I have not much (to any purpose) to say. My reference to 'confidences' was merely to the relief of saying a word of what has long been pent up in my mind. Poor Catherine and I are not made for each other, and there is no help for it. It is not only that she makes me uneasy and unhappy, but that I make her so too—and much more so. She is exactly what you know, in the way of being amiable and complying; but we are strangely ill-assorted for the bond there is between us. God knows she would have been a thousand times happier if she had married another kind of man, and that her avoidance of this destiny would have been at least equally good for us both. I am often cut to the heart by thinking what a pity it is, for her own sake, that I ever fell in her way; and if I were sick or disabled to-morrow, I know how sorry she would be, and how deeply grieved myself, to think how we had lost each other. But exactly the same incompatibility would arise, the moment I was well again; and nothing on earth could make her understand me, or suit us to each other. Her temperament will not go with mine. It mattered not so much when we had only ourselves to consider, but reasons have been growing since which make it all but hopeless that we should even try to struggle on. What is now befalling me I have seen steadily coming, ever since the days you remember when Mary was born; and I know too well that you cannot, and no one can, help me. Why I have even written I hardly know; but it is a miserable sort of comfort that you should be clearly aware how matters stand. The mere mention of the fact, without any complaint or blame of any sort, is a relief to my present state of spirits—and I can get this only from you, because I can speak of it to no one else."

It will not seem to most people that there was anything here which in happier circumstances might not have been susceptible of considerate adjustment; but all the circumstances were unfavourable, and the moderate middle course which the admissions in that letter might wisely have prompted and wholly justified, was unfortunately not taken. Compare what before was said of his temperament, with what is there said by himself of its defects, and the explanation will not be difficult. Every counteracting influence against the one idea which now predominated over him had been so weakened as to be almost powerless. His elder children were no longer children; his books had lost for the time the importance they formerly had over every other consideration in his life; and he had not in himself the resource that such a man, judging him from the surface, might be expected to have had. Not his genius only, but his whole nature, was too exclusively made up of sympathy for, and with, the real in its most intense form, to be sufficiently provided against failure in the realities around him. There was for him no "city of the mind" against outward ills, for inner consolation and shelter. It was in and from the actual he still stretched forward to find the freedom and satisfactions of an ideal, and by his very attempts to escape the world he was driven back into the thick of it. But what he would have sought there, it supplies to none; and to get the infinite out of anything so finite, has broken many a stout heart.

At the close of that last letter from Gadshill (5th of September) was this question—"What do you think of my paying for this place, by reviving that old idea of some Readings from my books. I am very strongly tempted. Think of it." The reasons against it had great force, and took, in my judgment, greater from the time at which it was again proposed. The old ground of opposition remained. It was a substitution of lower for higher aims; a change to common-place from more elevated pursuits; and it had so much of the character of a public exhibition for money as to raise, in the question of respect for his calling as a writer, a question also of respect for himself as a gentleman.

An occurrence of the time hastened the decision in this case. An enterprise had been set on foot for establishment of a hospital for sick children;[84] a large old-fashioned mansion in Great Ormond-street, with spacious garden, had been fitted up with more than thirty beds; during the four or five years of its existence, outdoor and indoor relief had been afforded by it to nearly fifty thousand children, of whom thirty thousand were under five years of age; but, want of funds having threatened to arrest the merciful work, it was resolved to try a public dinner by way of charitable appeal, and for president the happy choice was made of one who had enchanted everybody with the joys and sorrows of little children. Dickens threw himself into the service heart and soul. There was a simple pathos in his address from the chair quite startling in its effect at such a meeting; and he probably never moved any audience so much as by the strong personal feeling with which he referred to the sacrifices made for the Hospital by the very poor themselves: from whom a subscription of fifty pounds, contributed in single pennies, had come to the treasurer during almost every year it had been open.

That night alone added greatly more than three thousand pounds to its funds, and Dickens put the crown to his good work by reading on its behalf, shortly afterwards, his *Christmas Carol*; when the sum realized, and the urgent demand that followed for a repetition of the pleasure given by the reading, bore down farther opposition to the project of his engaging publicly in such readings for himself.

The Child's Hospital night was the 9th of February, its Reading was appointed for the 15th of April, and, nearly a

month before, renewed efforts at remonstrance had been made. "Your view of the reading matter," Dickens replied, "I still think is unconsciously taken from your own particular point. You don't seem to me to get out of yourself in considering it. A word more upon it. You are not to think I have made up my mind. If I had, why should I not say so? I find very great difficulty in doing so because of what you urge, because I know the question to be a balance of doubts, and because I most honestly feel in my innermost heart, in this matter (as in all others for years and years), the honour of the calling by which I have always stood most conscientiously. But do you quite consider that the public exhibition of oneself takes place equally, whosoever may get the money? And have you any idea that at this moment—this very time—half the public at least supposes me to be paid? My dear F, out of the twenty or five-and-twenty letters a week that I get about Readings, twenty will ask at what price, or on what terms, it can be done. (—At this place, enter Beale. He called here yesterday morning, and then wrote to ask if I would see him to-day. I replied 'Yes,' so here he came in. With long preface called to know whether it was possible to arrange anything in the way of Readings for this autumn—say, six months. Large capital at command. Could produce partners, in such an enterprise, also with large capital. Represented such. Returns would be enormous. Would I name a sum? a minimum sum that I required to have, in any case? Would I look at it as a Fortune, and in no other point of view? I shook my head, and said, my tongue was tied on the subject for the present; I might be more communicative at another time. Exit Beale in confusion and disappointment.) I must do *something*, or I shall wear my heart away. I can see no better thing to do that is half so hopeful in itself, or half so well suited to my restless state."

What is pointed at in those last words had been taken as a ground of objection, and thus he turned it into an argument the other way. During all these months many sorrowful misunderstandings had continued in his home, and the relief sought from the misery had but the effect of making desperate any hope of a better understanding. "It becomes necessary," he wrote at the end of March, "with a view to the arrangements that would have to be begun next month if I decided on the Readings, to consider and settle the question of the Plunge. Quite dismiss from your mind any reference whatever to present circumstances at home. Nothing can put *them* right, until we are all dead and buried and risen. It is not, with me, a matter of will, or trial, or sufferance, or good humour, or making the best of it, or making the worst of it, any longer. It is all despairingly over. Have no lingering hope of, or for, me in this association. A dismal failure has to be borne, and there an end. Will you then try to think of this reading project (as I do) apart from all personal likings and dislikings, and solely with a view to its effect on that peculiar relation (personally affectionate, and like no other man's) which subsists between me and the public? I want your most careful consideration. If you would like, when you have gone over it in your mind, to discuss the matter with me and Arthur Smith (who would manage the whole of the business, which I should never touch); we will make an appointment. But I ought to add that Arthur Smith plainly says, 'Of the immense return in money, I have no doubt. Of the Dash into the new position, however, I am not so good a judge.' I enclose you a rough note of my project, as it stands in my mind."

Mr. Arthur Smith, a man possessed of many qualities that justified the confidence Dickens placed in him, might not have been a good judge of the "Dash" into the new position, but no man knew better every disadvantage incident to it, or was less likely to be disconcerted by any. His exact fitness to manage the scheme successfully, made him an unsafe counsellor respecting it. Within a week from this time the reading for the Charity was to be given. "They have let," Dickens wrote on the 9th of April, "five hundred stalls for the Hospital night; and as people come every day for more, and it is out of the question to make more, they cannot be restrained at St. Martin's Hall from taking down names for other readings." This closed the attempt at further objection. Exactly a fortnight after the reading for the children's hospital, on Thursday the 29th April, came the first public reading for his own benefit; and before the next month was over, this

launch into a new life had been followed by a change in his old home. Thenceforward he and his wife lived apart. The eldest son went with his mother, Dickens at once giving effect to her expressed wish in this respect; and the other children remained with himself, their intercourse with Mrs. Dickens being left entirely to themselves. It was thus far an arrangement of a strictly private nature, and no decent person could have had excuse for regarding it in any other light, if public attention had not been unexpectedly invited to it by a printed statement in *Household Words*. Dickens was stung into this by some miserable gossip at which in ordinary circumstances no man would more determinedly have been silent; but he had now publicly to show himself, at stated times, as a public entertainer, and this, with his name even so aspersed, he found to be impossible. All he would concede to my strenuous resistance against such a publication, was an offer to suppress it, if, upon reference to the opinion of a certain distinguished man (still living), that opinion should prove to be in agreement with mine. Unhappily it fell in with his own, and the publication went on. It was followed by another statement, a letter subscribed with his name, which got into print without his sanction; nothing publicly being known of it (I was not among those who had read it privately) until it appeared in the *New York Tribune*. It had been addressed and given to Mr. Arthur Smith as an authority for correction of false rumours and scandals, and Mr. Smith had given a copy of it, with like intention, to the *Tribune* correspondent in London. Its writer referred to it always afterwards as his "violated letter."

The course taken by the author of this book at the time of these occurrences, will not be departed from here. Such illustration of grave defects in Dickens's character as the passage in his life affords, I have not shrunk from placing side by side with such excuses in regard to it as he had unquestionable right to claim should be put forward also. How far what remained of his story took tone or colour from it, and especially from the altered career on which at the same time he entered, will thus be sufficiently explained; and with anything else the public have nothing to do.

---

[84] The Board of Health returns, showing that out of every annual thousand of deaths in London, the immense proportion of four hundred were those of children under four years old, had established the necessity for such a scheme. Of course the stress of this mortality fell on the children of the poor, "dragged up rather than brought up," as Charles Lamb expressed it, and perishing unhelped by the way.

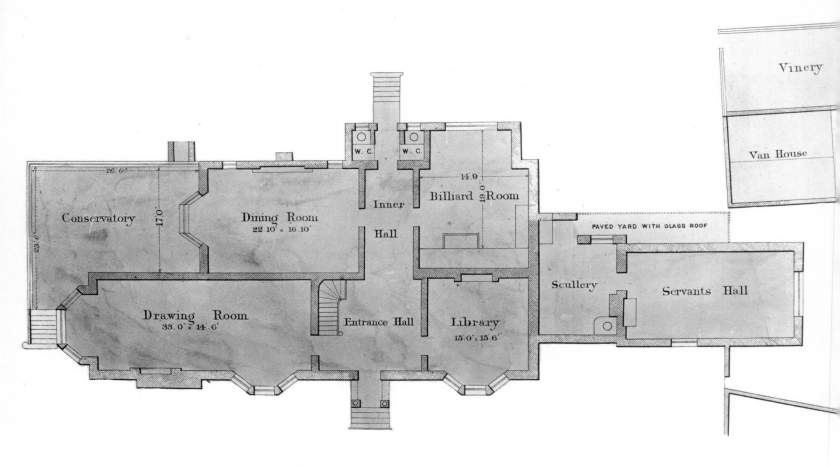

Floor plan of Gadshill

for four months in 1859; in the following year, on the sale of Tavistock House, he transferred to it his books and pictures and choicer furniture; and thenceforward, varied only by houses taken from time to time for the London season, he made it his permanent family abode. Now and then, even during those years, he would talk of selling it; and on his last return from America, when he had sent the last of his sons out into the world, he really might have sold it if he could then have found a house in London suitable to him, and such as he could purchase. But in this he failed; secretly to his own satisfaction, as I believe; and thereupon, in that last autumn of his life, he projected and carried out his most costly addition to Gadshill. Already of course more money had been spent upon it than his first intention in buying it would have justified. He had so enlarged the accommoda-

tion, improved the grounds and offices, and added to the land, that, taking also into account this final outlay, the reserved price placed upon the whole after his death more than quadrupled what he had given in 1856 for the house, shrubbery, and twenty years' lease of a meadow field. It was then purchased, and is now inhabited, by his eldest son.

Its position has been described, and one of the last-century-histories of Rochester quaintly mentions the principal interest of the locality. "Near the twenty-seventh stone from London is Gadshill, supposed to have been the scene of the robbery mentioned by Shakespeare in his play of Henry IV; there being reason to think also that it was Sir John Falstaff, of truly comic memory, who under the name of Oldcastle inhabited Cooling Castle of which the ruins are in the neighbourhood. A small distance to

"Personal," *Household Words*, 12 June 1858. Reprinted in *Dickens's Journalism*, vol. 3

*Dickens, goaded by rumors that he was having an affair with his sister-in-law, Georgina Hogarth,
as well as by the professional anxieties that Forster identifies, printed this statement in
The Times (7 June, 1858) and Household Words:*

FOR the first time in my life, and I believe for the last, I now deviate from the principle I have so observed, by presenting myself in my own Journal in my own private character, and entreating all my brethren (as they deem that they have reason to think well of me, and to know that I am a man who has ever been unaffectedly true to our common calling), to lend their aid to the dissemination of my present words. Some domestic trouble of mine, of long-standing, on which I will make no further remark than that it claims to be respected, as being of a sacredly private nature, has lately been brought to an arrangement, which involves no anger or ill-will of any kind, and the whole origin, progress, and surrounding circumstances of which have been, throughout, within the knowledge of my children. It is amicably composed, and its details have now but to be forgotten by those concerned in it.

By some means, arising out of wickedness, or out of folly, or out of inconceivable wild chance, or out of all three, this trouble has been made the occasion of misrepresentations, most grossly false, most monstrous and most cruel—involving, not only me, but innocent persons, dear to my heart, and innocent persons of whom I have no knowledge, if , indeed, they have any existence—and so widely spread, that I doubt if one reader in a thousand will peruse these lines, by whom some touch of the breath of these slanders will not have passed, like an unwholesome air.

Those who know me and my nature, need no assurance under my hand that such calumnies are as irreconcilable with me, as they are, in their frantic incoherence, with one another. But, there is a great multitude who know me through my writings, and who do not know me otherwise; and I cannot bear that one of them should be left in doubt, or hazard of doubt, through my poorly shrinking from taking the unusual means to which I now resort, of circulating the Truth.

I must solemnly declare, then – and this I do, both in my own name and in my wife's name – that all the lately whispered rumours touching the trouble at which I have glanced, are abominably false. And that whosoever repeats one of them after this denial, will lie as wilfully and foully as it is possible for any false witness to lie, before Heaven and earth.

—Charles Dickens

---

the left appears on an eminence the Hermitage the seat of the late Sir Francis Head, Bart;[86] and close to the road, on a small ascent, is a neat building lately erected by Mr. Day. In descending Strood-hill is a fine prospect of Strood, Rochester, and Chatham, which three towns form a continued street extending above two miles in length." It had been supposed[87] that "the neat building lately erected by Mr. Day" was that which the great novelist made famous; but Gadshill Place had no existence until eight years after the date of the history. The good rector who so long lived in it told me, in 1859, that it had been built eighty years before by a then well-known character in those parts, one Stevens, father-in-law of Henslow the Cambridge professor of botany. Stevens, who could only with much difficulty manage to write his name, had begun life as ostler at an inn; had become husband to the landlord's widow; then a brewer; and finally, as he subscribed himself on one occasion, "mare" of Rochester. Afterwards the house was inhabited by Mr. Lynn (from some of the members of whose family Dickens made his purchase); and, before the Rev. Mr. Hindle became its tenant, it was inhabited by a Macaroni parson named Townshend, whose horses the Prince Regent bought, throwing into the bargain a box of much desired cigars. Altogether the place had notable associations even apart from those which have connected it with the masterpieces of English humour. "THIS HOUSE, GADSHILL PLACE, stands on the summit of Shakespeare's Gadshill, ever memorable for its association with Sir John Falstaff in his noble fancy. *But, my lads, my lads, to-morrow morning, by four o'clock, early at Gadshill! there are pilgrims going to Canterbury with rich offerings, and traders riding to London with fat purses: I have vizards for you all; you have horses for yourselves.*" Illuminated by Mr. Owen Jones, and placed in a frame on the first-floor landing, these words were the greeting of the new tenant to his visitors. It was his first act of ownership.

With even such varying fortune he effected other changes.[88] The exterior remained to the last much as it was when he used as a boy to see it first; a plain, old-fashioned, two-story, brick-built country house, with a bell-turret on the roof, and over the front door a quaint neat wooden porch with pillars and seats. But, among his additions and alterations, was a new drawing-room built out from the smaller existing one, both being thrown together ultimately; two good bedrooms built on a third floor at the back; and such rearrangement of the ground floor as, besides its handsome drawing-room, and its dining-room which he hung with pictures, transformed its bedroom into a study which he lined with books and sometimes wrote in, and changed its breakfast-parlour into a retreat fitted up for smokers into which he put a small billiard-table. These several rooms opened from a hall having in it a series of Hogarth prints, until, after the artist's death, Stanfield's noble scenes were placed there, when the Hogarths were moved to his bedroom; and in this hall, during his last absence in America, a parquet floor was laid down. Nor did he omit such changes as might increase the comfort of his servants. He built entirely new offices and stables, and replaced a very old coach-house by a capital servants' hall, transforming the loft above into a commodious school-room or study for his boys. He made at the same time an excellent croquet-ground out of a waste piece of orchard.

Belonging to the house, but unfortunately placed on the other side of the high road, was a shrubbery, well wooded though in desolate condition, in which stood two magnificent cedars; and having obtained, in 1859, the consent of the local authorities for the necessary underground work, Dickens constructed a passage beneath the road [89] from his front lawn; and in the shrubbery thus rendered accessible, and which he then laid out very prettily, he placed afterwards a Swiss châlet presented to him by Mr. Fechter, which arrived from Paris in ninety-four pieces fitting like the joints of a puzzle, but which proved to be somewhat costly in setting on its legs by means of a foundation of brickwork. Once up, however, it was a great resource in the summer months, and much of Dickens's work was done there.

One or two more extracts from letters having reference to these changes may show something of the interest to him with which Gadshill thus grew under his hands. A sun-dial on his back-lawn had a bit of historic interest about it. "One of the balustrades of the destroyed old Rochester Bridge," he wrote to his daughter in June 1859, "has been (very nicely) presented to me by the contractors for the works, and has been duly stone-masoned and set up on the lawn behind the house. I have ordered a sun-dial for the top of it, and it will be a very good object indeed." That was in the autumn of 1860, when, on the sale of his London house, its contents were transferred to his country home. "I shall have an alteration or two to show you at Gadshill that greatly improve the little property; and when I get the workmen out this time, I think I'll leave off." October 1861 had now come, when the new bedrooms were built; but in the same month of 1863 he announced his transformation of the old coach-house. "I shall have a small new improvement to show you at Gads, which I think you will accept as the crowning ingenuity of the inimitable." But of course it was not over yet. "My small work and planting," he wrote in the spring of 1866, "really, truly, and positively the last, are nearly at an end in these regions, and the result will await summer inspection." No, nor even yet. He afterwards obtained, by exchange of some land with the trustees of Watts's Charity, the much coveted meadow at the back of the house of which heretofore he had the lease only; and he was then able to plant a number of young limes and

FROM LEFT TO RIGHT: Henry Fothergill Chorley, Katey Dickens, Mamie Dickens, Charles Dickens, Charles Collins, and Georgina Hogarth; on the porch at Gadshill, 1862

Dickens in his study at Gadshill

chestnuts and other quick-growing trees. He had already planted a row of limes in front. He had no idea, he would say, of planting only for the benefit of posterity, but would put into the ground what he might himself enjoy the sight and shade of. He put them in two or three clumps in the meadow, and in a belt all round.

Still there were "more last words," for the limit was only to be set by his last year of life. On abandoning his notion, after the American Readings, of exchanging Gadshill for London, a new staircase was put up from

LEFT: Swiss Chalet. A gift from actor Charles Fechter in 1864, it became Dickens's favorite place for writing during temperate months.

the hall; a parquet floor laid on the first landing; and a conservatory built, opening into both drawing-room and dining-room, "glass and iron," as he described it, "brilliant but expensive, with foundations as of an ancient Roman work of horrible solidity." This last addition had long been an object of desire with him; though he would hardly even now have given himself the indulgence but for the golden shower from America. He saw it first in a completed state on the Sunday before his death, when his younger daughter was on a visit to him. "Well, Katey," he said to her, "now you see POSITIVELY the last improvement at Gadshill;" and every one laughed at the joke against himself. The success of the new conservatory was unquestionable. It was the remark of all around him that he was certainly, from this last of his improvements, drawing more enjoyment than from any of its predecessors, when the scene for ever closed.

His mornings were reserved wholly to himself; and he would generally preface his morning work (such was his love of order in everything around him) by seeing that all was in its place in the several rooms, visiting also the dogs, stables, and kitchen garden, and closing, unless the weather was very bad indeed, with a turn or two round the meadow before settling to his desk. His dogs were a great enjoyment to him;[90] and, with his high road traversed as frequently as any in England by tramps and wayfarers of a singularly undesirable description, they were also a necessity. There were always two, of the mastiff kind, but latterly the number increased. His own favourite was Turk, a noble animal, full of affection and intelligence, whose death by a railway-accident, shortly after the Staplehurst catastrophe, caused him great grief. Turk's sole companion up to that date was Linda, puppy of a great St. Bernard brought over by Mr. Albert Smith, and grown into a superbly beautiful creature. After Turk there was an interval of an Irish dog, Sultan, given by Mr. Percy Fitzgerald; a cross between a St. Bernard and a bloodhound, built and coloured like a lioness and of splendid proportions, but of such indomitably aggressive propensities, that, after breaking his kennel-chain and nearly devouring a luckless little sister of one of the servants, he had to be killed. Dickens always protested that Sultan was a Fenian, for that no dog, not a secretly sworn member of that body, would ever have made such a point, muzzled as he was, of rushing at and bearing down with fury anything in scarlet with the remotest resemblance to a British uniform. Sultan's successor was Don, presented by Mr. Frederic Lehmann, a grand Newfoundland brought over very young, who with Linda became parent to a couple of Newfoundlands, that were still gambolling about their master, huge, though hardly out of puppydom, when they lost him. He had given to one of them the name of Bumble, from having observed, as he described it, "a peculiarly pompous and overbearing manner he had of appearing to mount guard over the yard when he was an absolute infant."

Restoration House, Rochester, 1889

Charles Dickens with, Mamie, Katey, and Georgina at Gadshill

Round Cobham, skirting the park and village and passing the Leather Bottle famous in the page of *Pickwick*, was a favourite walk with Dickens. By Rochester and the Medway, to the Chatham Lines, was another. He would turn out of Rochester High-street through The Vines (where some old buildings, from one of which called Restoration-house he took Satis-house for *Great Expectations*, had a curious attraction for him), would pass round by Fort Pitt, and coming back by Frindsbury would bring himself by some cross fields again into the high road. Or, taking the other side, he would walk through the marshes to Gravesend, return by Chalk church, and stop always to have greeting with a comical old monk who for some incomprehensible reason sits carved in stone, cross-legged with a jovial pot, over the porch of that sacred edifice.

To another drearier churchyard, itself forming part of the marshes beyond the Medway, he often took friends to show them the dozen small tombstones of various sizes adapted to the respective ages of a dozen small children of one family which he made part of his story of *Great Expectations*, though, with the reserves always necessary in copying nature not to overstep her modesty by copying too closely, he makes the number that appalled little Pip not more than half the reality.

---

[85] On New Year's Day he had written from Paris. "When in London Coutts's advised me not to sell out the money for Gadshill Place (the title of my estate sir, my place down in Kent) until the conveyance was settled and ready."

[86] Two houses now stand on what was Sir Francis Head's estate, the Great and Little Hermitage, occupied respectively by Mr. Malleson and Mr. Hulkes, who became intimate with Dickens. Perry of the *Morning Chronicle*, whose town house was in that court out of Tavistock-square of which Tavistock House formed part, had occupied the Great Hermitage previously.

[87] By the obliging correspondent who sent me this History of Rochester, 8vo. (Rochester, 1772), p. 302.

[88] "As to the carpenters," he wrote to his daughter in September 1860, "they are absolutely maddening. They are always at work yet never seem to do anything, L. was down on Friday, and said (with his eye fixed on Maidstone and rubbing his hands to conciliate his moody employer) that 'he didn't think there would be very much left to do after Saturday the 29th.' I didn't throw him out of window."

[89] A passage in his paper on Tramps embodies very amusingly experience recorded in his letters of this brick-work tunnel and the sinking of the well; but I can only borrow one sentence. "The current of my uncommercial pursuits caused me only last summer to want a little body of workmen for a certain spell of work in a pleasant part of the country; and I was at one time honoured with the attendance of as many as seven-and-twenty, who were looking at six." Bits of wonderful observation are in that paper.

[90] Dickens's interest in dogs (as in the habits and ways of all animals) was inexhaustible, and he welcomed with delight any new trait. The subjoined, told him by a lady friend, was a great acquisition. "I must close" (14th of May 1867) "with an odd story of a Newfoundland dog. An immense black good-humoured Newfoundland dog. He came from Oxford and had lived all his life at a brewery. Instructions were given with him that if he were let out every morning alone, he would immediately find out the river; regularly take a swim; and gravely come home again. This he did with the greatest punctuality, but after a little while was observed to smell of beer. She was so sure that he smelt of beer that she resolved to watch him. Accordingly, he was seen to come back from his swim, round the usual corner, and to go up a flight of steps into a beer-shop. Being instantly followed, the beer-shop-keeper is seen to take down a pot (pewter pot), and is heard to say: 'Well, old chap! Come for your beer as usual, have you?' Upon which he draws a pint and puts it down, and the dog drinks it. Being required to explain how this comes to pass, the man says, 'Yes ma'am. I know he's your dog ma'am, but I didn't when he first come. He looked in ma'am—as a Brickmaker might—and then he come in—as a Brickmaker might—and he wagged his tail at the pots, and he giv' a sniff round, and conveyed to me as he was used to beer. So I draw'd him a drop, and he drunk it up. Next morning he come agen by the clock and I drawed him a pint, and ever since he has took his pint reglar.'"

CHAPTER 9

FIRST PAID READINGS

1858~1859

DICKENS GAVE HIS PAID public Readings successively, with not long intervals, at four several dates; in 1858-9, in 1861-63, in 1866-67, and in 1868-70; the first series under Mr. Arthur Smith's management, the second under Mr. Headland's, and the third and fourth, in America as well as before and after it, under that of Mr. George Dolby, who, excepting in America, acted for the Messrs. Chappell. The references in the present chapter are to the first series only.

It began with sixteen nights at St. Martin's Hall, the first on the 29th of April, the last on the 22nd of July, 1858; and there was afterwards a provincial tour of 87 readings, beginning at Clifton on the 2nd of August, ending at Brighton on the 13th of November, and taking in Ireland and Scotland as well as the principal English cities: to which were added, in London, three Christmas readings, three in January, with two in the following month; and, in the provinces in the month of October, fourteen, beginning at Ipswich and Norwich, taking in Cambridge and Oxford, and closing with Birmingham and Cheltenham. The series had comprised altogether 125 Readings when it ended on the 27th of October, 1859; and without the touches of character and interest afforded by his letters written while thus employed, the picture of the man would not be complete.

Here was one day's work at the opening which will show something of the fatigue they involved even at their outset. "On Friday we came from Shrewsbury to Chester; saw all right for the evening; and then went to Liverpool. Came back from Liverpool and read at Chester. Left Chester at 11 at night, after the reading, and went to London. Got to Tavistock House at 5 A.M. on Saturday, left it at a quarter past 10 that morning, and came down here" (Gadshill: 15th of August 1858).

The "greatest personal affection and respect" had greeted him everywhere. Nothing could have been "more strongly marked or warmly expressed;" and the readings had "gone" quite wonderfully. What in this respect had most impressed him, at the outset of his adventures, was Exeter. "I think they were the finest audience I ever read to; I don't think I ever read in some respects so well; and I never beheld anything like the personal affection which they poured out upon me at the end. I shall always look back upon it with pleasure." He often lost his voice in these early days, having still to acquire the art of husbanding it; and in the trial to recover it would again waste its power. "I think I sang half the Irish melodies to myself as I walked about, to test it."

An audience of two thousand three hundred people (the largest he had had) greeted him at Liverpool on his way to Dublin, and, besides the tickets sold, more than two hundred pounds in money was taken at the doors. This taxed his business staff a little. "They turned away hundreds, sold all the books, rolled on the ground of my room knee-deep in checks, and made a perfect pantomime of the whole thing." (20th of August.) He had to repeat the reading thrice.

It was the first time he had seen Ireland, and Dublin greatly surprised him by appearing to be so much larger and more populous than he had supposed. He found it to have altogether an unexpectedly thriving look, being pretty nigh as big, he first thought, as Paris; of which some places in it, such as the quays on the river, reminded him. Half the first day he was there, he took to explore it; walking till tired, and then taking a car.

In respect of the number of his audience, and their reception of him, Dublin was one of his marked successes.

The last night in Dublin was an extraordinary scene. "You can hardly imagine it. All the way from the hotel to the Rotunda (a mile), I had to contend against the stream of people who were turned away. When I got there, they had broken the glass in the pay-boxes, and were offering £5 freely for a stall. Half of my platform had to be taken down, and people heaped in among the ruins. You never saw such a scene."[91]

Belfast he liked quite as much as Dublin in another way. "A fine place with a rough people; everything looking

USING ACCUMULATED EYEWITNESS ACCOUNTS, MALCOLM ANDREWS RECREATES THE EXPERIENCE OF A DICKENS READING:

'MARLEY WAS DEAD: TO BEGIN WITH . . .' The greatest storyteller alive is here, before us, telling his greatest story. At the end of the first paragraph, there are whispers that Dickens doesn't seem to have a very powerful voice— 'A bit husky and monotonous.' We have to agree. There's also the slightest hint of a lisp. And why does he always use that rising inflection at the end of each sentence? His manner is very engaging. There's nothing formal in the reading, no particular strain or effort. It's exactly as if he were telling the story for the first time, freshly, just for us. The left hand holds the book, the right hand moves continually, slightly indicating the action described. There's really nothing to distinguish the performance from a parlour reading.

But now he comes to introduce us to Scrooge, and instantly things change. Reading becomes acting, and a magnetic current runs between reader and listeners. He suddenly becomes Scrooge, and it's as if he, Dickens, has disappeared. What we see is Scrooge, and what we hear is Scrooge: the old features, the pointed nose, the shrewd grating voice. He draws his face down into his collar, like a great turtle drawing in his head, puts on a surly look and speaks in a gruff voice. Now comes Scrooge's nephew, then little lisping Bob Cratchit (we didn't know he lisped: the story didn't tell us). Each character comes alive and is utterly distinct, both from the other characters and from Dickens the reader: a blind man could see them all distinctly. He does it not just through different voices, but with different facial settings—a comical twist of the mouth to the right, a savage twist to the left, eyes rolling, eyebrows jigging up and down. He rubs and pats his hands, flourishes all his fingers, shakes them, points them. At the Cratchit dinner he stirs the gravy, mashes the potatoes, dusts the plates, tastes the punch and smacks his lips and sniffs the pudding; the very smell of the feast seems to steal around us. He can use his hands freely because he seems hardly at all to need to hold his book. He must know it off by heart. He just dives in and out of each of these characters—twenty-three different characters, each with an individual tone!

Dickens actually puzzles you with his complete abstraction from himself while he spends time dazzling you with so many different personalities. But on some occasions— usually when he says something that makes the audience laugh heartily—he lets down the curtain from his face and smiles. And the smile turns to laughter as he laughs along with his audience. At those moments we come closest to him. The smile is quite wonderful; quick, curious, and beautiful. That smile is the secret of the man's whole nature. We're soon lost in the story—or is it in the storyteller?

Malcolm Andrews, *Charles Dickens and His Performing Selves:*
Dickens and the Public Readings
(Oxford: Oxford Universtiy Press, 2006)

LEFTT: Charles Dickens, albumen print by (George) Herbert Watkins, April 29, 1858

prosperous; the railway ride from Dublin quite amazing in the order, neatness, and cleanness of all you see; every cottage looking as if it had been whitewashed the day before; and many with charming gardens, prettily kept with bright flowers." The success, too, was quite as great. "Enormous audiences. We turn away half the town.[92] I think them a better audience on the whole than Dublin; and the personal affection is something overwhelming. I wish you and the dear girls" (he is writing to his sister-in-law) "could have seen the people look at me in the street; or heard them ask me, as I hurried to the hotel after the reading last night, to 'do me the honor to shake hands Misther Dickens and God

bless you sir; not ounly for the light you've been to me this night, but for the light you've been in mee house sir (and God love your face!) this many a year!'"

At Harrogate he read twice on one day (a Saturday), and had to engage a special engine to take him back that night to York, which, having reached at one o'clock in the morning, he had to leave, because of Sunday restrictions on travel, the same morning at half-past four, to enable him to fulfil a Monday's reading at Scarborough. Such fatigues became matters of course; but their effect, not noted at the time, was grave. "At York I had a most magnificent audience, and might have filled the place for a week. . . .

Charles Dickens by William Powell Frith, 1859

I think the audience possessed of a better knowledge of character than any I have seen."

The reception that awaited him at Manchester had very special warmth in it, occasioned by an adverse tone taken in the comment of one of the Manchester daily papers on the letter which by a breach of confidence had been then recently printed. "My violated letter" Dickens always called it. "When I came to Manchester on Saturday I found seven hundred stalls taken! When I went into the room at night 2500 people had paid, and more were being turned away from every door. The welcome they gave me was astounding in its affectionate recognition of the late trouble, and fairly for once unmanned me. I never saw such a sight or heard such a sound. When they had thoroughly done it, they settled down to enjoy themselves; and certainly did enjoy themselves most heartily to the last minute." Nor, for the rest of his English tour, in any of the towns that remained, had he reason to complain of any want of hearty greeting. At Sheffield great crowds came in excess of the places. At Leeds the hall overflowed in half an hour. At Hull the vast concourse had to be addressed by Mr. Smith on the gallery stairs, and additional Readings had to be given, day and night, "for the people out of town and for the people in town."

The net profit to himself, thus far, had been upwards of three hundred pounds a week;[93] but this was nothing to the success in Scotland, where his profit in a week, with all expenses paid, was five hundred pounds. The pleasure was enhanced, too, by the presence of his two daughters, who had joined him over the Border. "I think I am better pleased with what was done in Edinburgh than with what has been done anywhere, almost. It was so completely taken by storm, and carried in spite of itself. Mary and Katey have been infinitely pleased and interested with Edinburgh. We are just going to sit down to dinner and therefore I cut my missive short. Travelling, dinner, reading, and everything else, come crowding together into this strange life."

The subjects of his readings during this first circuit were the *Carol*, the *Chimes*, the *Trial in Pickwick*, the chapters containing *Paul Dombey*, *Boots at the Holly Tree Inn*, the *Poor Traveller* (Captain Doubledick), and *Mrs. Gamp*: to which he continued to restrict himself through the supplementary nights that closed in the autumn of 1859. Of these the most successful in their uniform effect upon his audiences were undoubtedly the *Carol*, the *Pickwick* scene, *Mrs. Gamp*, and the *Dombey*—the quickness, variety, and completeness of his assumption of character, having greatest scope in these. Here, I think, more than in the pathos or graver level passages, his strength lay; but this is entitled to no weight other than as an individual opinion, and his audiences gave him many reasons for thinking differently.

This too was the year when Mr. Frith completed Dickens's portrait, and it appeared upon the walls of the Academy in the following spring. "I wish," said Edwin Landseer as he stood before it, "he looked less eager and busy, and not so much out of himself, or beyond himself. I should like to catch him asleep and quiet now and then." There is something in the objection, and he also would be envious at times of what he too surely knew could never be his lot. On the other hand who would willingly have lost the fruits of an activity on the whole so healthy and beneficent?

---

[91] "They had offered frantic prices for stalls. Eleven bank-notes were thrust into a paybox at one time for eleven stalls. Our men were flattened against walls and squeezed against beams. Ladies stood all night with their chins against my platform. Other ladies sat all night upon my steps. We turned away people enough to make immense houses for a week." Letter to his eldest daughter.

[92] "Shillings get into stalls, and half-crowns get into shillings, and stalls get nowhere, and there is immense confusion." Letter to his daughter.

[93] "That is no doubt immense, our expenses being necessarily large, and the travelling party being always five." Another source of profit was the sale of the copies of the several Readings prepared by himself. "Our people alone sell eight, ten, and twelve dozen a night." A later letter says: "The men with the reading books were sold out, for about the twentieth time, at Manchester. Eleven dozen of the *Poor Traveller*, *Boots*, and *Gamp* being sold in about ten minutes, they had no more left; and Manchester became green with the little tracts, in every bookshop, outside every omnibus, and passing along every street. The sale of them, apart from us, must be very great." "Did I tell you," he writes in another letter, "that the agents for our tickets who are also booksellers, say very generally that the readings decidedly increase the sale of the books they are taken from? We were first told of this by a Mr. Parke, a wealthy old gentleman in a very large way at Wolverhampton, who did all the business for love, and would not take a farthing. Since then, we have constantly come upon it; and M'Glashin and Gill at Dublin were very strong about it indeed."

CHAPTER 10

ALL THE YEAR ROUND AND THE UNCOMMERCIAL TRAVELLER

1859~1861

In the interval before the close of the first circuit of readings, painful personal disputes arising out of the occurrences of the previous year were settled by the discontinuance of *Household Words,* and the establishment in its place of *All the Year Round.* The disputes turned upon matters of feeling exclusively, and involved no charge on either side that would render any detailed reference here other than gravely out of place. The question into which the difference ultimately resolved itself was that of the respective rights of the parties as proprietors of *Household Words;* and this, upon a bill filed in Chancery, was settled by a winding-up order, under which the property was sold. It was bought by Dickens, who, even before the sale, exactly fulfilling a previous announcement of the proposed discontinuance of the existing periodical and establishment of another in its place, precisely similar but under a different title, had started *All the Year Round.* It was to be regretted perhaps that he should have thought it necessary to move at all, but he moved strictly within his rights.

To the publishers first associated with his great success in literature, Messrs. Chapman and Hall, he now returned for the issue of the remainder of his books; of which he always in future reserved the copyrights, making each the subject of such arrangement as for the time might seem to him desirable. In this he was met by no difficulty; and indeed it will be only proper to add, that, in any points affecting his relations with those concerned in the production of his books, though his resentments were easily and quickly roused, they were never very lasting.

At the opening of 1859, bent upon such a successor to *Household Words* as should carry on the associations connected with its name, Dickens was deep in search of a title to give expression to them. "My determination to settle the title arises out of my knowledge that I shall never be able to do anything for the work until it has a fixed name; also out of my observation that the same odd feeling affects everybody else." He had proposed to himself a title that, as in *Household Words,* might be capable of illustration by a line from Shakespeare; and alighting upon that wherein poor Henry the Sixth is fain to solace his captivity by the fancy, that, like birds encaged he might soothe himself for loss of liberty "at last by notes of household harmony," he for the time forgot that this might hardly be accepted as a happy comment on the occurrences out of which the supposed necessity had arisen of replacing the old by a new household friend. "Don't you think," he wrote on the 24th of January, "this is a good name and quotation? I have been quite delighted to get hold of it for our title.

"*Household Harmony.*

"'At last by notes of Household Harmony.'—*Shakespeare.*"

He was at first reluctant even to admit the objection when stated to him. "I am afraid we must not be too particular about the possibility of personal references and applications: otherwise it is manifest that I never can write another book. I could not invent a story of any sort, it is quite plain, incapable of being twisted into some such nonsensical shape. It would be wholly impossible to turn one through half a dozen chapters." Of course he yielded, nevertheless; and much consideration followed over sundry other titles submitted. Reviving none of those formerly rejected, here were a few of these now rejected in their turn. *The Hearth. The Forge. The Crucible. The Anvil of the Time. Charles Dickens's Own. Seasonable Leaves. Evergreen Leaves. Home. Home-Music. Change. Time and Tide. Twopence. English Bells. Weekly Bells. The Rocket. Good Humour.* Still the great want was the line adaptable from Shakespeare, which at last exultingly he sent on the 28th of January.

"I am dining early, before reading, and write literally with my mouth full. But I have just hit upon a name that I think really an admirable one—especially with the quotation *before* it, in the place where our present *H. W.* quotation stands.

"'The story of our lives, from year to year.'—Shakespeare."
"*All the Year Round*.
"A weekly journal conducted by Charles Dickens."

With the same resolution and energy other things necessary to the adventure were as promptly done. "I have taken the new office," he wrote from Tavistock House on the 21st of February; "have got workmen in; have ordered the paper; settled with the printer; and am getting an immense system of advertising ready. Blow to be struck on the 12th of March. . . . Meantime I cannot please myself with the opening of my story" (the *Tale of Two Cities*, which *All the Year Round* was to start with), "and cannot in the least settle at it or take to it."

The first number of *All the Year Round* appeared on the 30th of April, and the result of the first quarter's accounts of the sale will tell everything that needs to be said of a success that went on without intermission to the close. "A word before I go back to Gadshill," he wrote from Tavistock House in July, "which I know you will be glad to receive. So well has *All the Year Round* gone that it was yesterday able to repay me, with five per cent. interest, all the money I advanced for its establishment (paper, print &c. all paid, down to the last number), and yet to leave a good £500 balance at the banker's!"

The periodical thus established was in all respects, save one, so exactly the counterpart of what it replaced, that a mention of this point of difference is the only description of it called for. Besides his own three-volume stories of *The Tale of Two Cities* and *Great Expectations*, Dickens admitted into it other stories of the same length by writers of character and name, of which the authorship was avowed. It published tales of varied merit and success by Mr. Edmund Yates, Mr. Percy Fitzgerald, and Mr. Charles Lever. Mr. Wilkie Collins contributed to it his *Woman in White*, *No Name*, and *Moonstone*, the first of which had a pre-eminent success; Mr. Reade his *Hard Cash*; and Lord Lytton his *Strange Story*. Conferring about the latter Dickens passed a week at Knebworth, accompanied by his daughter and sister-in-law, in the summer of 1861, as soon as he had closed *Great Expectations*; and there met Mr. Arthur Helps, with whom and Lord Orford he visited the so-called "Hermit" near Stevenage, whom he described as Mr. Mopes in *Tom Tiddler's Ground*.

In *All the Year Round*, as in its predecessor, the tales for Christmas were of course continued, but with a surprisingly increased popularity; and Dickens never had such sale for any of his writings as for his Christmas pieces in the later periodical. It had reached, before he died, to nearly three hundred thousand.

His tales were not his only important work in *All the Year Round*. The detached papers written by him there had a character and completeness derived from their plan, and from the personal tone, as well as frequent individual confessions, by which their interest is enhanced, and which will always make them specially attractive. Their title expressed a personal liking. Of all the societies, charitable or self-assisting, which his tact and eloquence in the "chair" so often helped, none had interested him by the character of its service to its members, and the perfection of its management, so much as that of the Commercial Travellers. His, admiration of their schools introduced him to one who then acted as their treasurer, and whom, of all the men he had known, I think he rated highest for the union of business qualities in an incomparable measure to a nature comprehensive enough to deal with masses of men, however differing in creed or opinion, humanely and justly. He never afterwards wanted support for any good work that he did not think first of Mr. George Moore,[94] and appeal was never made to him in vain. it was another form of the same liking when he took to himself the character and title of a Traveller *Un* commercial.

Many of his papers, such as "Travelling Abroad," "City Churches," "Dullborough," "Nurses' Stories," and "Birthday Celebrations," have supplied traits, chiefly of his younger days, to portions of this memoir; and parts of his later life receive illustration from others, such as "Tramps," "Night Walks," "Shy Neighbourhoods," "The Italian Prisoner," and "Chatham Dockyard." Indeed hardly any is without its personal interest or illustration. One may learn from them, among other things, what kind of treatment he resorted to for the disorder of sleeplessness from which he had often suffered amid his late anxieties. Experimenting upon it in bed, he found to be too slow and

OVERLEAF: *Piccadilly, color lithograph by Thomas Shotter Boys, 1842*

NEW SERIES

VOL 4

JUNE

"THE·STORY·OF·OUR·LIVES·FROM·
YEAR·TO·YEAR"

All the Year Round

A
Weekly Journal

CONDUCTED BY

CHARLES DICKENS, JUN.

WITH·WHICH·IS·INCORPORATED

"HOUSEHOLD WORDS"

PART 19.

PRICE
NINEPENCE.

1870

LONDON
26 WELLINGTON ST.
STRAND.
W.C.

Nos.
79 to 82

C. WHITING,]   ADVERTISEMENTS are to be sent to ADAMS & FRANCIS, 59, Fleet Street.   [LONDON.

Cover to collected parts of Dickens's weekly journal *All the Year Round*, 1870

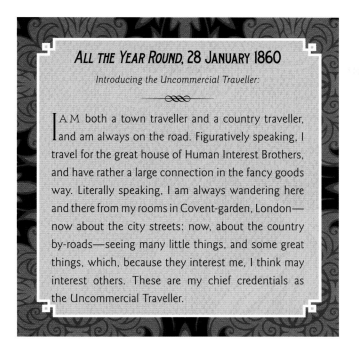

reprinted in it, on the completion of his first story, a short tale called "Hunted Down," written for a newspaper in America called the *New York Ledger*. Its subject had been taken from the life of a notorious criminal already named, and its principal claim to notice was the price paid for it. For a story not longer than half of one of the numbers of *Chuzzlewit* or *Copperfield*, he had received a thousand pounds.[95] It was one of the indications of the eager desire which his entry on the career of a public reader had aroused in America to induce him again to visit that continent; and at the very time he had this magnificent offer from the New York journal, Mr. Fields of Boston, who was then on a visit to Europe, was pressing him so much to go that his resolution was almost shaken. "I am now," he wrote to me from Gadshill on the 9th of July 1859, "getting the *Tale of Two Cities* into that state that IF I should decide to go to America late in September, I could turn to, at any time, and write on with great vigour. Mr. Fields has been down here for a day, and with the strongest intensity urges that there is no drawback, no commercial excitement or crisis, no political agitation; and that so favourable an opportunity, in all respects, might not occur again for years and years. I should be one of the most unhappy of men if I were to go, and yet I cannot help being much stirred and influenced by the golden prospect held before me."

He yielded nevertheless to other persuasion, and for that time the visit was not to be. In six months more the Civil War began, and America was closed to any such enterprise for nearly five years.

doubtful a process for him; but he very soon defeated his enemy by the brisker treatment, of getting up directly after lying down, going out, and coming home tired at sunrise. "My last special feat was turning out of bed at two, after a hard day pedestrian and otherwise, and walking thirty miles into the country to breakfast."

The Uncommercial Traveller papers, his two serial stories, and his Christmas tales, were all the contributions of any importance made by Dickens to *All the Year Round*; but he

---

[94] If space were available here, his letters would supply many proofs of his interest in Mr. George Moore's admirable projects; but I can only make exception for his characteristic allusion to an incident that tickled his fancy very much at the time. "I hope" (20th of Aug. 1863) "you have been as much amused as I am by the account of the Bishop of Carlisle at (my very particular friend's) Mr. George Moore's schools? It strikes me as the funniest piece of weakness I ever saw, his addressing those unfortunate children concerning Colenso. I cannot get over the ridiculous image I have erected in my mind, of the shovel-hat and apron holding forth, at that safe distance, to that safe audience. There is nothing so extravagant in Rabelais, or so satirically humorous in Swift or Voltaire."

[95] Eight years later he wrote "Holiday Romance" for a Child's Magazine published by Mr. Fields, and "George Silverman's Explanation"—of the same length, and for the same price. There are no other such instances, I suppose, in the history of literature.

CHAPTER 11

SECOND SERIES OF READINGS

1861~1863

At the end of the first year of residence at Gadshill it was the remark of Dickens that nothing had gratified him so much as the confidence with which his poorer neighbours treated him. He had tested generally their worth and good conduct, and they had been encouraged in illness or trouble to resort to him for help. There was pleasant indication of the feeling thus awakened, when, in the summer of 1860, his younger daughter Kate was married to Charles Alston Collins, brother of the novelist, and younger son of the painter and academician, who might have found, if spared to witness that summer-morning scene, subjects not unworthy of his delightful pencil in many a rustic group near Gadshill. All the villagers had turned out in honour of Dickens, and the carriages could hardly get to and from the little church for the succession of triumphal arches they had to pass through. It was quite unexpected by him; and when the feu de joie of the blacksmith in the lane, whose enthusiasm had smuggled a couple of small cannon into his forge, exploded upon him at the return, I doubt if the shyest of men was ever so taken aback at an ovation.

His daughter's marriage was the chief event that had crossed the even tenor of Dickens's life since his first paid readings closed; and it was followed by the sale of Tavistock House, with the resolve to make his future home at Gadshill. In the brief interval (29th of July) he wrote to me of his brother Alfred's death. "I was telegraphed for to Manchester on Friday night. Arrived there at a quarter past ten, but he had been dead three hours, poor fellow! He is to be buried at Highgate on Wednesday. I brought the poor young widow back with me yesterday." All that this death involved,[96] the troubles of his change of home, and some difficulties

in working out his story, gave him more than sufficient occupation till the following spring; and as the time arrived for the new Readings, the change was a not unwelcome one.

The first portion of this second series was planned by Mr. Arthur Smith, but he only superintended the six readings in London which opened it. These were the first at St. James's Hall (St. Martin's Hall having been burnt since the last readings there) and were given in March and April 1861. "We are all well here and flourishing," he wrote to me from Gadshill on the 28th of April. "On the 18th I finished the readings as I purposed. We had between seventy and eighty pounds *in the stalls*, which, at four shillings apiece, is something quite unprecedented in these times. . . . The result of the six was, that, after paying a large staff of men and all other charges, and Arthur Smith's ten per cent. on the receipts, and replacing everything destroyed in the fire at St. Martin's Hall (including all our tickets, country-baggage, cheque-boxes, books, and a quantity of gas-fittings and what not), I got upwards of £500. A very great result. We certainly might have gone on through the season, but I am heartily glad to be concentrated on my story."

It had been part of his plan that the Provincial Readings should not begin until a certain interval after the close of his story of *Great Expectations*. They were delayed accordingly until the 28th of October, from which date, when they opened at Norwich, they went on with the Christmas intervals to be presently named to the 30th of January 1862, when they closed at Chester. Kept within England and Scotland, they took in the border town of Berwick, and, besides the Scotch cities, comprised the contrasts and varieties of Norwich and Lancaster, Bury St. Edmunds and Cheltenham, Carlisle and Hastings, Plymouth and Birmingham, Canterbury and Torquay, Preston and Ipswich, Manchester and Brighton, Colchester and Dover, Newcastle and Chester. They were followed by ten readings at the St. James's Hall, between the 13th of March and the 27th of June 1862; and by four at Paris in January 1863, given at the Embassy in aid of the British Charitable Fund. The second series had thus in the number of the readings nearly equalled the first, when it closed at London in June 1863 with thirteen readings in the Hanover Square Rooms; and it is exclusively the subject of such illustrations or references as this chapter will supply.

On *Great Expectations*'s closing in June 1861, Bulwer Lytton, at Dickens's earnest wish, took his place in *All the Year Round* with the "Strange Story;" and he then indulged himself in idleness for a little while. "Every day for two or three hours, I practise my new readings, and (except in my office work) do nothing else. With great pains I have made a continuous narrative out of *Copperfield*, that I think will reward the exertion it is likely to cost me. Unless I am much mistaken, it will be very valuable in London. I have also done *Nicholas Nickleby* at the Yorkshire school, and hope I have got something droll out of Squeers, John Browdie, & Co. Also, the Bastille prisoner from the *Tale of Two Cities*. Also, the Dwarf from one of our Christmas numbers." Only the first two were added to the list for the present circuit.

It was in the midst of these active preparations that painful news reached him. An illness under which Mr. Arthur Smith had been some time suffering took unexpectedly a dangerous turn, and there came to be but small chance of his recovery. A distressing interview on the 28th of September gave Dickens little hope. "And yet his wakings and wanderings so perpetually turn on his arrangements for the Readings, and he is so desperately unwilling to relinquish the idea of 'going on with the business' to-morrow and to-morrow and to-morrow, that I had not the heart to press him for the papers. He told me that he believed he had by him '70 or 80 letters unanswered.' You may imagine how anxious it makes me, and at what a deadstop I stand." The poor fellow died in October; and on the day after attending the funeral, Dickens heard of the death of his brother-in-law and friend, Mr. Henry Austin, whose abilities and character he respected as much as he liked the man. He lost much in losing the judicious and safe counsel which had guided him on many public questions in which he took lively interest, and it was with a heavy heart he set out at last upon his second circuit. "With what difficulty I get myself back to the readings after all this loss and trouble, or with what unwillingness I work myself up to the mark of looking them in the face, I can hardly say. As for poor Arthur Smith at this time, it is as if my right arm were gone." That November interval was also the date of the marriage of his eldest son to the daughter of Mr. Evans, so long, in connection with Mr. Bradbury, his publisher and printer.

The start of the readings at Norwich was not good, so many changes of vexation having been incident to the opening announcements as to leave some doubt of their fulfilment. But the second night, when trial was made of the *Nickleby* scenes, "we had a splendid hall, and I think *Nickleby* will top all the readings. Somehow it seems to have got in it, by accident, exactly the qualities best suited to the purpose; and it went last night, not only with roars, but with a general hilarity and pleasure that I have never seen surpassed."[97] From this night onward, the success was uninterrupted, and here was his report to me from Brighton on the 8th of November. "We turned away half Dover and half Hastings and half Colchester; and, if you can believe such a thing, I may tell you that in round numbers we find 1000 stalls already taken here in Brighton! I left Colchester in a heavy snow-storm. To-day it is so warm here that I can hardly bear the fire, and am writing with the window open down to the ground.

The effect of the readings at Hastings and Dover really seems to have outdone the best usual impression; and at Dover they wouldn't go, but sat applauding like mad. The most delicate audience I have seen in any provincial place, is Canterbury" ("an intelligent and delightful response in them," he wrote to his daughter, "like the touch of a beautiful instrument"); "but the audience with the greatest sense of humour certainly is Dover. The people in the stalls set the example of laughing, in the most curiously unreserved way; and they laughed with such really cordial enjoyment, when Squeers read the boys' letters, that the contagion extended to me. For, one couldn't hear them without laughing too. . . . So, I am thankful to say, all goes well, and the recompense for the trouble is in every way Great."

Enthusiastic greeting awaited him in Edinburgh. "We had in the hall exactly double what we had on the first night last time. The success of *Copperfield* was perfectly unexampled. Four great rounds of applause with a burst of cheering at the end, and every point taken in the finest manner." But this was nothing to what befell on the second night, when, by some mistake of the local agents, the tickets issued were out of proportion to the space available. Writing from Glasgow next day (3rd of December) he described the scene. "Such a pouring of hundreds into a place already full to the throat, such indescribable confusion, such a rending and tearing of dresses, and yet such a scene of good humour on the whole,

DICKENS'S READINGS WERE VERY SIMPLY STAGED; HE NEEDED ONLY A READING DESK, BACKBOARD AND THE MOST SIMPLE PROPS. ANDREWS DESCRIBES THE DICKENS READING SET, AND EXPLAINS THE SEVERE PHYSICAL AND PRACTICAL DEMANDS OF ADDRESSING SUCH LARGE AUDIENCES.

'Props'

By the late 1860s Dickens had learned all his Reading by heart and his books had become props. They lay on the reading desk. Dickens glanced at them from time to time, and would flick pages over, but he was no longer reading from them. He had few other props, though one or two deserve mention.

The *Sheffield Times's* report on a Reading of 1855 mentioned his flourishing of a large paperkrnife, which he used now and again to divide the leaves of his text. This is an odd prop. It seems to have been used habitually, in the early years of the Readings, as part of Dickens's repertoire of gestures, and not just to ease the turning of pages [. . .] A somewhat sneering review of an October 1858 Reading deplored Dickens's descending to 'the most artificial conventionalities, even to the display of a monster paper-knife – we presume in case a book, which has been read a score of times and which the Reader evidently knew well nigh by heart, should require to be cut open.' Dickens persisted with the knife long after he really needed it for its proper services. It had become a theatrical accessory. In reading the 'Carol', when he came to Fezziwig's dance and described how the dancer 'appeared to wink with his legs', he gave an expressive look and a wave of the paperknife. In later years when he had dispensed with the knife, he used to perform the actions of the dance with his fingers on the Reading desk.

The knife was still in use in 1863, if the long-term memory of an eyewitness can be trusted. Writing in 1911, W. Ridley Kent recalled a performance of 'Mrs Gamp' in 1863, towards the end of which Mrs Gamp is described as sitting close to the fender and drowsily amusing herself with sliding her nose backwards and forwards along the brass top. Dickens reproduced the action by rubbing his nose to left and right along the paperknife. [. . .]

'The Platform'

Because Dickens read in halls and Corn Exchanges rather than theatres, he had to go to some lengths to enhance the visual and acoustic focus. Where there was no stage, this often entailed the making of improvised platforms, to increase his visibility throughout the hall. The auditoria at such venues were not raked, by and large, so every effort was needed to keep sight-lines clear. Ladies in the reserved stalls were respectfully requested not to wear bonnets. He wrote home from Shewsbury, during the first month of the first provincial tour in 1858, reporting his disappointment with the hall there, after his preliminary inspection: 'everything was wrong [. . .] I have left Arthur [Smith, his first tour manager] making a platform for me out of dining-tables.' Over the years the stage set developed in elaborate ways to compensate for auditoria with poor acoustics or inadequate lighting, or both. One refinement was a back-screen. He took all the components of his staging with him across the Atlantic for the American tour, where the set attracted much attention from the newspaper reporters. The back-screen was judged to be about fifteen feet long by seven feet high, and was positioned about four feet behind the desk. It was probably a folding screen, to make transportation easier. Even so, it suffered some battering in its time and at least one replacement had to be made. It was constructed as a series of wooden frames covered with canvas, and this was itself covered again with maroon cloth (or a 'brown-crimson colour') to match the Reading desk. It served two purposes. One was to act as a sounding board, the other was to throw the figure of the Reader into higher relief. An additional, mischievous suggestion was that the deep maroon backing helped to 'relieve' Dickens's 'very red face'. The more experience he had of the Readings the more adamant Dickens became about these devices.

From Malcolm Andrews,
Charles Dickens and His Performing Selves: Dickens and the Public Readings (Oxford: Oxford University Press, 2006) pp.136–138

I never saw the faintest approach to." He came home for his Christmas rest by way of Manchester, and thus spoke of the reading there on the 14th of December. "*Copperfield* in the Free Trade Hall last Saturday was really a grand scene."

He was in southern latitudes after Christmas, and on the 8th of January wrote from Torquay: "We are now in the region of small rooms, and therefore this trip will not be as profitable as the long one. I imagine the room here to be very small. Exeter I know, and that is small too. I am very much used up on the whole, for I cannot bear this moist warm climate. It would kill me very soon. And I have now got to the point of taking so much out of myself with *Copperfield* that I might as well do Richard Wardour. . . . This is a very pretty place—a compound of Hastings, Tunbridge Wells, and little bits of the hills about Naples; but I met four respirators as I came up from the station, and three pale curates without them who seemed in a bad way." They had been not bad omens, however. The success was good, at both Torquay and Exeter; and he closed the month, and this series of the country readings, at the great towns of Liverpool and Chester.

Two brief extracts from letters of the dates respectively of the 8th of April and the 28th of June will sufficiently describe the London readings. "The money returns have been quite astounding. Think of £190 a night! The effect of *Copperfield* exceeds all the expectations which its success in the country led me to form. It seems to take people entirely by surprise. If this is not new to you, I have not a word of news. The rain that raineth every day seems to have washed news away or got it under water." That was in April. In June he wrote: "I finished my readings on Friday night to an enormous hall—nearly £200. The success has been throughout complete. It seems almost suicidal to leave off with the town so full, but I don't like to depart from my public pledge. A man from Australia is in London ready to pay £10,000 for eight months there. If—" It was an If that troubled him for some time, and led to agitating discussion. The civil war having closed America, an increase made upon the just-named offer tempted him to Australia. He tried to familiarize himself with the fancy that he should thus also get new material for observation, and he went so far as to plan an Uncommercial Traveller Upside Down. It is however very doubtful if such a scheme would have been entertained for a moment, but for the unwonted difficulties of invention that were now found to beset a twenty-number story. Such a story had lately been in his mind, and he had just chosen the title for it (*Our Mutual Friend*); but still he halted and hesitated sorely. "If it was not," (he wrote on the 5th of October 1862) "for the hope of a gain that would make me more independent of the worst, I could not look the travel and absence and exertion in the face. I know perfectly well beforehand how unspeakably wretched I should be. But these renewed and larger offers tempt me."

In January 1863 he had taken his daughter and his sister-in-law to Paris, and he read twice at the Embassy in behalf of the British Charitable Fund, the success being such that he consented to read twice again.[98] He passed his birthday of that year (the 7th of the following month) at Arras.

Upon Dickens's arrival in London the second series of his readings was brought to a close; and opportunity may be taken, before describing the third, to speak of the manuscript volume found among his papers, containing Memoranda for use in his writings.

---

[96] He was now hard at work on his story; and a note written from Gadshill after the funeral shows, what so frequently was incident to his pursuits, the hard conditions under which sorrow, and its claim on his exertion, often came to him. "To-morrow I have to work against time and tide and everything else, to fill up a No. keeping open for me, and the stereotype plates of which must go to America on Friday. But indeed the enquiry into poor Alfred's affairs; the necessity of putting the widow and children somewhere; the difficulty of knowing what to do for the best; and the need I feel under of being as composed and deliberate as I can be, and yet of not shirking or putting off the occasion that there is for doing a duty; would have brought me back here to be quiet, under any circumstances."

[97] Of his former manager he writes in the same letter: "I miss him dreadfully. The sense I used to have of compactness and comfort about me while I was reading, is quite gone; and on my coming out for the ten minutes, when I used to find him always ready for me with something cheerful to say, it is forlorn. . . . Besides which, H. and all the rest of them are always somewhere, and he was always everywhere."

[98] A person present thus described (1st of February 1863) the second night to Miss Dickens. "No one can imagine the scene of last Friday night at the Embassy . . . a two hours' storm of excitement and pleasure. They actually murmured and applauded right away into their carriages and down the street."

CHAPTER 12

HINTS FOR BOOKS WRITTEN AND UNWRITTEN

1855~1865

DICKENS BEGAN THE BOOK OF MEMORANDA for possible use in his work, to which occasional reference has been made, in January 1855, six months before the first page of *Little Dorrit* was written; and I find no allusion leading me to suppose, except in one very doubtful instance, that he had made addition to its entries, or been in the habit of resorting to them, after the date of *Our Mutual Friend*. It seems to comprise that interval of ten years in his life.

It is very interesting in this book, last legacy as it is of the literary remains of such a writer, to compare the way in which fancies were worked out with their beginnings entered in its pages. Those therefore will first be taken that in some form or other appeared afterwards in his writings, with such reference to the latter as may enable the reader to make comparison for himself.

"Our House. Whatever it is, it is in a first-rate situation, and a fashionable neighbourhood. (Auctioneer called it 'a gentlemanly residence.') A series of little closets squeezed up into the corner of a dark street—but a Duke's Mansion round the corner. The whole house just large enough to hold a vile smell. The air breathed in it, at the best of times, a kind of Distillation of Mews." He made it the home of the Barnacles in *Little Dorrit*.

One of the people of the same story who becomes a prominent actor in it, Henry Gowan, a creation on which he prided himself as forcible and new, seems to have risen to his mind in this way. "I affect to believe that I would do anything myself for a ten-pound note, and that anybody else would. I affect to be always book-keeping in every man's case, and posting up a little account of good and evil with every one. Thus the greatest rascal becomes 'the dearest old fellow,' and

there is much less difference than you would be inclined to suppose between an honest man and a scoundrel. While I affect to be finding good in most men, I am in reality decrying it where it really is, and setting it up where it is not. Might not a presentation of this far from uncommon class of character, if I could put it strongly enough, be likely to lead some men to reflect, and change a little? I think it has never been done."

In *Little Dorrit* also will be found a picture which seems to live with a more touching effect in his first pleasing fancy of it. "The ferryman on a peaceful river, who has been there from youth, who lives, who grows old, who does well, who does ill, who changes, who dies—the river runs six hours up and six hours down, the current sets off that point, the same allowance must be made for the drifting of the boat, the same tune is always played by the rippling water against the prow."

He seems to have designed, for the sketches of society in the same tale, a "Full-length portrait of his lordship, surrounded by worshippers;" of which, beside that brief memorandum, only his first draft of the general outline was worked at. "Sensible men enough, agreeable men enough, independent men enough in a certain way;—but the moment they begin to circle round my lord, and to shine with a borrowed light from his lordship, heaven and earth how mean and subservient! What a competition and outbidding of each other in servility."

The last of the Memoranda hints which were used in the story whose difficulties at its opening seem first to have suggested them, ran thus: "The unwieldy ship taken in tow by the snorting little steam tug"—by which was prefigured the patriarch Casby and his agent Panks.

His first intention as to the *Tale of Two Cities* was to write it upon a plan proposed in this manuscript book. "How as to a story in two periods—with a lapse of time between, like a French Drama? Titles for such a notion. TIME! THE LEAVES OF THE FOREST. SCATTERED LEAVES. THE GREAT WHEEL. ROUND AND ROUND. OLD LEAVES. LONG AGO. FAR APART. FALLEN LEAVES. FIVE AND TWENTY YEARS. YEARS AND YEARS. ROLLING YEARS. DAY AFTER DAY. FELLED TREES. MEMORY CARTON. ROLLING STONES. TWO GENERATIONS." That special title of *Memory Carton* shows that what led to the greatest success of the book as written was always in his mind; and another of the memoranda is this rough hint of the character itself. "The drunken?—dissipated?—What?—LION—and his JACKALL and Primer, stealing down to him at unwonted hours."

The studies of Silas Wegg and his patron as they exist in *Our Mutual Friend*, are hardly such good comedy as in the form which the first notion of them seems to have intended. "Gibbon's Decline and Fall. The two characters. One reporting to the other as he reads. Both getting confused as to whether it is not all going on now." In connection with the same book, the last in that form which he lived to complete, another fancy may be copied from which, though not otherwise worked out in the tale, the relation of Lizzie Hexam to her brother was taken. "A man, and his wife—or daughter—or niece. The man, a reprobate and ruffian; the woman (or girl) with good in her, and with compunctions. He believes nothing, and defies everything; yet has suspicions always, that she is 'praying against' his evil schemes, and making them go wrong. He is very much opposed to this, and is always angrily harping on it. 'If she *must* pray, why can't she pray in their favour, instead of going against 'em? She's always ruining me—she always is—and calls that, Duty! There's a religious person! Calls it Duty to fly in my face! Calls it Duty to go sneaking against me!'"

The subjects for stories are various, and some are striking. There was one he clung to much, and thought of frequently as in a special degree available for a series of papers in his periodical; but when he came to close quarters with it the difficulties were found to be too great. "English landscape. The beautiful prospect, trim fields, clipped hedges, everything so neat and orderly—gardens, houses, roads. Where are the people who do all this? There

must be a great many of them, to do it. Where are they all? And are *they*, too, so well kept and so fair to see? Suppose the foregoing to be wrought out by an Englishman: say, from China: who knows nothing about his native country." To which may be added a fancy that savours of the same mood of discontent, political and social. "How do I know that I, a man, am to learn from insects—unless it is to learn how little my littlenesses are? All that botheration in the hive about the queen bee, may be, in little, me and the court circular."

A theme touching closely on ground that some might think dangerous, is sketched in the following fancy. "The father (married young) who, in perfect innocence, venerates his son's young wife, as the realization of his ideal of woman. (He not happy in his own choice.) The son slights her, and knows nothing of her worth. The father watches her, protects her, labours for her, endures for her,—is for ever divided between his strong natural affection for his son as his son, and his resentment against him as this young creature's husband." Here is another, less dangerous, which he took from an actual occurrence made known to him when he was at Bonchurch. "The idea of my being brought up by my mother (me the narrator), my father being dead; and growing up in this belief until I find that my father is the gentleman I have sometimes seen, and oftener heard of, who has the handsome young wife, and the dog I once took notice of when I was a little child, and who lives in the great house and drives about."

Other portions of a female group are as humorously sketched and hardly less entertaining. "The enthusiastically complimentary person, who forgets you in her own flowery prosiness: as—'I have no need to say to a person of your genius and feeling, and wide range of experience'—and then,

Charles Dickens, Photograph by J. Gurney & Son, 1867

 403

being shortsighted, puts up her glass to remember who you are."—"Two sisters" (these were real people known to him). "One going in for being generally beloved (which she is not by any means); and the other for being generally hated (which she needn't be)."—"The bequeathed maid-servant, or friend. Left as a legacy. And a devil of a legacy too."—"The woman who is never on any account to hear of anything shocking. For whom the world is to be of barley-sugar."—"The lady who lives on her enthusiasm; and hasn't a jot."—"Bright-eyed creature selling jewels. The stones and the eyes." Much significance is in the last few words. One may see to what uses Dickens would have turned them.

The female character in its relations with the opposite sex has lively illustration in the Memoranda. "The man who is governed by his wife, and is heartily despised in consequence by all other wives; who still want to govern *their* husbands, notwithstanding." An alarming family pair follows that. "The playful—and scratching—family. Father and daughter." And here is another. "The agreeable (and wicked) young-mature man, and his devoted sister." What next was set down he had himself partly seen; and, by enquiry at the hospital named, had ascertained the truth of the rest. "The two people in the Incurable Hospital.—The poor incurable girl lying on a water-bed, and the incurable man who has a strange flirtation with her; comes and makes confidences to her; snips and arranges her plants; and rehearses to her the comic songs(!) by writing which he materially helps out his living."[99]

"The people who persist in defining and analysing their (and everybody else's) moral qualities, motives and what not, at once in the narrowest spirit and the most lumbering manner;—as if one should put up an enormous scaffolding for the building of a pigstye."

"The house-full of Toadies and Humbugs. They all know and despise one another; but—partly to keep their hands in, and partly to make out their own individual cases—pretend not to detect one another."

"People realising immense sums of money, imagi-natively—speculatively—counting their chickens before hatched. Inflaming each other's imaginations about great gains of money, and entering into a sort of intangible, impossible, competition as to who is the richer."

"A thoroughly sulky character—perverting everything. Making the good, bad—and the bad, good."

"The people who lay all their sins negligences and igno-rances, on Providence."

"The man who marries his cook at last, after being so desperately knowing about the sex."

"The swell establishment, frightfully mean and miser-able in all but the 'reception rooms.' Those very showy."

First there are titles for books; and from the list subjoined were taken two for Christmas numbers and two for stories, though *Nobody's Fault* had ultimately to give way to *Little Dorrit*.

"*The Lumber Room. Somebodys Luggage. To Be Left Till Called For. Something Wanted. Extremes Meet. Nobody's Fault. The Grindstone. Rokesmith's Forge. Our Mutual Friend. The Cinder Heap. Two Generations. Broken Crockery. Dust. The Home Department. The Young Person. Now or Never. My Neigh-bours. The Children of the Fathers. No Thoroughfare.*"

The last of the Memoranda, and the last words written by Dickens in the blank paper book containing them, are these. "'Then I'll give up snuff.' Brobity.—An alarming sacrifice. Mr. Brobity's snuff-box. The Pawnbroker's account of it?" What was proposed by this must be left to conjec-ture; but "Brobity" is the name of one of the people in his unfinished story, and the suggestion may have been meant for some incident in it. If so, it is the only passage in the volume which can be in any way connected with the piece of writing on which he was last engaged. Some names were taken for it from the lists, but there is otherwise nothing to recall *Edwin Drood*.

LEFT: Charles Dickens about the age of fifty, after a photograph by Mason & Co., ca. 1862

---

[99] Following this in the "Memoranda" is an advertisement cut from *The Times*: of a kind that always expressed to Dickens a child-farming that deserved the gallows quite as much as the worst kind of starving, by way of farming, babies. The fourteen guineas a-year, "tender" age of the "dear" ones, maternal care, and no vacations or extras, to him had only one meaning.
"Education for Little Children.—Terms 14 to 18 guineas per annum; no extras or vacations. The system of education embraces the wide range of each useful and ornamental study suited to the tender age of the dear children. Maternal care and kindness may be relied on.—X., Heald's Library, Fulham-road."

CHAPTER 13

THIRD SERIES OF READINGS

1864~1867

THE SUDDEN DEATH OF THACKERAY on the Christmas eve of 1863 was a painful shock to Dickens. It would not become me to speak, when he has himself spoken, of his relations with so great a writer and so old a friend.

"I saw him first, nearly twenty-eight years ago, when he proposed to become the illustrator of my earliest book. I saw him last,[100] shortly before Christmas, at the Athenaeum Club, when he told me that he had been in bed three days . . . and that he had it in his mind to try a new remedy which he laughingly described. He was cheerful, and looked very bright. In the night of that day week, he died. The long interval between these two periods is marked in my remembrance of him by many occasions when he was extremely humorous, when he was irresistibly extravagant, when he was softened and serious, when he was charming with children."

Other griefs were with Dickens at this time, and close upon them came the too certain evidence that his own health was yielding to the overstrain which had been placed upon it by the occurrences and anxieties of the few preceding years. His mother, whose infirm health had been tending for more than two years to the close, died in September 1863; and on his own birthday in the following February he had tidings of the death of his second son Walter, on the last day of the old year in the officers' hospital at Calcutta; to which he had been sent up invalided from his station, on his way home. He was a lieutenant in the 26th Native Infantry regiment, and had been doing duty with the 42nd Highlanders. In 1853 his father had thus written to the youth's godfather, Walter Savage Landor: "Walter is a very good boy, and comes home from school with honorable commendation and a prize into the bargain. He never gets into trouble, for he is a great favourite with the whole house and one of the most amiable boys in the boy-world. He comes out on birthdays in a blaze of shirt pin." The pin was a present from Landor; to whom three years later, when the boy had obtained his cadetship through the kindness of Miss Coutts, Dickens wrote again. "Walter has done extremely well at school; has brought home a prize in triumph; and will be eligible to 'go up' for his India examination soon after next Easter. Having a direct appointment he will probably be sent out soon after he has passed, and so will fall into that strange life 'up the country' before he well knows he is alive, or what life is—which indeed seems to be rather an advanced state of knowledge." If he had lived another month he would have reached his twenty-third year, and perhaps not then the advanced state of knowledge his father speaks of. But, never forfeiting his claim to those kindly paternal words, he had the goodness and simplicity of boyhood to the last.

Dickens had at this time begun his last story in twenty numbers, and my next chapter will show through what unwonted troubles, in this and the following year, he had to fight his way. What otherwise during its progress chiefly interested him, was the enterprise of Mr. Fechter at the Lyceum, of which he had become the lessee; and Dickens was moved to this quite as much by generous sympathy with the difficulties of such a position to an artist who was not an Englishman, as by genuine admiration of Mr. Fechter's acting. He became his helper in disputes, adviser on literary points, referee in matters of management; and for some years no face was more familiar than the French comedian's at Gadshill or in the office of his journal.

The old year ended and the new one opened sadly enough. The death of Leech in November affected Dickens very much,[101] and a severe attack of illness in February put a broad mark between his past life and what remained to him of the future. The lameness now began in his left foot which never afterwards wholly left him, which was attended by great suffering, and which baffled experienced physicians. He had persisted in his ordinary exercise during heavy snow-storms, and to the last he had the fancy that his illness

RIGHT: Charles Dickens seated at desk, by J. Gurney & Son, 1867

PETER ACKROYD GIVES THIS ACCOUNT OF THE STAPLEHURST RAILWAY DISASTER OF 9 JUNE 1865, IN WHICH 10 PASSENGERS WERE KILLED AND 40 INJURED. DICKENS SUFFERED THE AFTER-EFFECTS OF THIS ACCIDENT FOR THE REST OF HIS LIFE, AND DIED FIVE YEARS TO THE DAY AFTER IT.

As was usually the case, Dickens continued to write, even while on vacation. While in France he worked on the second chapter of the sixteenth number of *Our Mutual Friend* (drawing towards the close), and brought the manuscript back to England with him in the pocket of his overcoat. With Ellen Ternan and her mother, he boarded the ferry and travelled from Boulogne to Folkestone. On this occasion a fellow-passenger noticed him and recorded the following observation: "Travelling with him was a lady not his wife, nor his sister-in-law, yet he strutted about the deck with the air of a man bristling with self-importance, every line of his face and every gesture of his limbs seemed haughtily to say—'Look at me; make the most of your chance. I am the great, the *only* Charles Dickens; whatever I may choose to do is justified by that fact.'" Dickens, Ternan, and Mrs. Ternan were booked into a first-class carriage and they took the 2:38 tidal train from Folkestone to London. Passing the town of Headcorn thirty-three minutes later they approached the viaduct over the river Beult just before Staplehurst where the accident would take place. They were travelling at a speed of fifty miles an hour on a downward gradient. At that moment repair work was being conducted on the viaduct itself (which was in fact little more than a bridge) and two of the rails had been lifted from the railbed and placed at the side of the track. The foreman in charge of the construction site had consulted the wrong time-table, and he did not expect Dickens's train for another two hours. Furthermore, and, against regulations, the flagman who was supposed to give warning to oncoming trains of any obstruction was only 550 yards from the construction site. The train conductor saw the red flag and applied his brakes, but it was too late. The train approached the broken line in the rail at a speed of between twenty and thirty miles per hour. It jumped a gap of forty-two feet, and swerved onto the bed of the river below. All of the seven first-class carriages plummeted downwards—except for one car. That car was the one occupied by Dickens and the Ternans, and it held by its couplings onto a second-class carriage. Dickens's car had come off the rail and was now hanging over the bridge at an angle. With a makeshift arrangement of planks Dickens managed to extricate the Ternans from the suspended carriage, and as he was doing this, he saw the other first-class carriages lying at the bottom of the river bed. With his familiar aplomb he went returned to the teetering carriage, and took out a travelling flask of brandy as well as his top hat. He filled his hat with water, clambered down the bank, and then began his work among the injured and the dead. He found a man with a cracked skull; he gave the man some brandy, poured a bit of water on his face, and laid him on the grass beside the stream. The man said only "I am gone," and then died. A woman with a blood-covered face was propped against a tree; Dickens gave her a little brandy from his flask, but in a moment she too was dead. The scene was covered with corpses and injured bodies. One young passenger, Mr. Dickenson, later recalled how it was the urging and assistance of Charles Dickens that ultimately helped to free him from a pile of twisted wreckage. Another passenger would later recall how Dickens, with his hat full of water, was "running about with it and doing his best to revive and comfort every poor creature he met who had sustained serious injury."

And then, as he prepared to take leave of the death scene, Dickens did a remarkable thing. Remembering that his manuscript was still in the pocket of his overcoat, he clambered back into the swaying carriage and retrieved it. He then travelled back to London with the other survivors on an emergency train. Dickens returned to Gad's Hill Place the next day, and told the landlord of the Falstaff Inn that "I never thought I should be here again." His eldest son found his father "greatly shaken, though making as light of it as possible—how greatly shaken I was able to perceive from his continually repeated injunctions to me by and by, as I was driving him in the basket-carriage, to 'go slower, Charley' until we came to foot-pace, and it was still 'go slower, Charley.'"

From Peter Ackroyd, *Dickens* (New York: Harper Collins, 1990), chapter 31

was merely local. But that this was an error is now certain; and it is more than probable that if the nervous danger and disturbance it implied had been correctly appreciated at the time, its warning might have been of priceless value to Dickens. Unhappily he never thought of husbanding his strength except for the purpose of making fresh demands upon it, and it was for this he took a brief holiday in France during the summer. "Before I went away," he wrote to his daughter, "I had certainly worked myself into a damaged state. But the moment I got away, I began, thank God, to get well. I hope to profit by this experience, and to make future dashes from my desk before I want them." At his return he was in the terrible railway accident at Staplehurst, on a day[102] which proved afterwards more fatal to him; and it was with shaken nerves but unsubdued energy he resumed the labour to be presently described.

His foot troubled him more or less throughout the autumn;[103] he was beset by nervous apprehensions which the accident had caused to himself, not lessened by his generous anxiety to assuage the severer sufferings inflicted by it on others;[104] and that he should nevertheless have

determined, on the close of his book, to undertake a series of readings involving greater strain and fatigue than any hitherto, was a startling circumstance. He had perhaps become conscious, without owning it even to himself, that for exertion of this kind the time left him was short; but, whatever pressed him on, his task of the next three years, self-imposed, was to make the most money in the shortest time without any regard to the physical labour to be undergone. The very letter announcing his new engagement shows how entirely unfit he was to enter upon it.

"For some time," he wrote at the end of February 1866, "I have been very unwell. F. B. wrote me word that with such a pulse as I described, an examination of the heart was absolutely necessary. 'Want of muscular power in the heart,' B said. 'Only remarkable irritability of the heart,' said Doctor Brinton of Brook-street, who had been called in to consultation. I was not disconcerted; for I knew well beforehand that the effect could not possibly be without the one cause at the bottom of it, of some degeneration of some function of the heart. Of course I am not so foolish as to suppose that all my work can have been

Ellen Ternan

LEFT: Dickens ministering to other casualties of the Staplehurst rail disaster

achieved without *some* penalty, and I have noticed for some time a decided change in my buoyancy and hopefulness—in other words, in my usual 'tone.' But tonics have already brought me round. So I have accepted an offer, from Chappells of Bond-street, of £50 a night for thirty nights to read 'in England, Ireland, Scotland, or Paris;' they undertaking all the business, paying all personal expenses, travelling and otherwise, of myself, John" (his office servant), "and my gasman; and making what they can of it. I begin, I believe, in Liverpool on the Thursday in Easter week, and then come to London. I am going to read at Cheltenham (on my own account) on the 23rd and 24th of this month, staying with Macready of course."

The arrangement of this series of Readings differed from those of its predecessors in relieving Dickens from every anxiety except of the reading itself; but, by such rapid and repeated change of nights at distant places as kept him almost wholly in a railway carriage when not at the reading-desk or in bed, it added enormously to the physical fatigue. He would read at St. James's Hall in London one night, and at Bradford the next. He would read in Edinburgh, go on to Glasgow and to Aberdeen, then come back to Glasgow, read again in Edinburgh, strike off to Manchester, come back to St. James's Hall once more, and begin the same round again. It was labour that must in time have broken down the strongest man, and what Dickens was when he assumed it we have seen.

He did not himself admit a shadow of misgiving. "As to the readings" (11th of March), "all I have to do is, to take in my book and read, at the appointed place and hour, and come out again. All the business of every kind, is done by Chappells. They take John and my other man, merely for my convenience. I have no more to do with any detail whatever, than you have. They transact all the business at their own cost, and on their own responsibility. I think they are disposed to do it in a very good spirit, because, whereas the original proposition was for thirty readings 'in England, Ireland, Scotland, or Paris,' they wrote out their agreement 'in London, the Provinces, or elsewhere, *as you and we may agree*.' For this they pay £1500 in three sums; £500 on beginning, £500 on the fifteenth Reading, £500 at the close. Every charge of every kind, they pay besides. I rely for mere

curiosity on *Doctor Marigold* (I am going to begin with him in Liverpool, and at St. James's Hall). I have got him up with immense pains, and should like to give you a notion what I am going to do with him."

The success everywhere went far beyond even the former successes. A single night at Manchester, when eight hundred stalls were let, two thousand five hundred and sixty-five people admitted, and the receipts amounted to more than three hundred pounds, was followed in nearly the same proportion by all the greater towns; and on the 20th of April the outlay for the entire venture was paid, leaving all that remained, to the middle of the month of June, sheer profit. "I came back last Sunday," he wrote on the 30th of May, "with my last country piece of work for this time done. Everywhere the success has been the same. St. James's Hall last night was quite a splendid spectacle. Two more Tuesdays there, and I shall retire into private life. I have only been able to get to Gadshill once since I left it, and that was the day before yesterday."

The same letter which told of his uninterrupted success to the last, told me also that he had a heavy cold upon him and was "very tired and depressed." Some weeks before the first batch of readings closed, Messrs. Chappell had already tempted him with an offer for fifty more nights to begin at Christmas, for which he meant, as he then said, to ask them seventy pounds a night. "It would be unreasonable to ask anything now on the ground of the extent of the late success, but I am bound to look to myself for the future. The Chappells are speculators, though of the worthiest and most honourable kind. They make some bad speculations, and have made a very good one in this case, and will set this against those. I told them when we agreed: 'I offer these thirty Readings to you at fifty pounds a night, because I know perfectly well beforehand that no one in your business has the least idea of their real worth, and I wish to prove it.' The sum taken is £4720." The result of the fresh negotiation, though not completed until the beginning of August, may be at once described. "Chappell instantly accepts my proposal of forty nights at sixty pounds a night, and every conceivable and inconceivable expense paid. To make an even sum, I have made it forty-two nights for £2500. So I shall now try to discover a Christmas number" (he means the subject for one), "and shall, please Heaven, be quit of the whole series of readings so as to get to work on a new story for the new series of *All the Year Round* early in the spring. The readings begin probably with the New Year." These were fair designs, but the fairest are the sport of circumstance, and though the subject for Christmas was found, the new series of *All the Year* Round never had a new story from its founder. With whatever consequence to himself, the strong tide of the Readings was to sweep on to its full. The American war had ceased, and the first renewed offers from the States had been made and rejected. Hovering over all, too, were other sterner dispositions. "I think," he wrote in September, "there is some strange influence in the atmosphere. Twice last week I was seized in a most distressing manner—apparently in the heart; but, I am persuaded, only in the nervous system."

Everything was done to make easier the labour of travel, but nothing could materially abate either the absolute physical exhaustion, or the nervous strain. "We arrived here," he wrote from Aberdeen (16th of May), "safe and sound between 3 and 4 this morning. There was a compartment for the men, and a charming room for ourselves furnished with sofas and easy chairs. We had also a pantry and washing-stand. This carriage is to go about with us." Two days later he wrote from Glasgow: "We halted at Perth yesterday, and got a lovely walk there. Until then I had been in a condition the reverse of flourishing; half strangled with my cold, and dyspeptically gloomy and dull; but, as I feel much more like myself this morning, we are going to get some fresh air aboard a steamer on the Clyde." The last letter during his country travel was from Portsmouth on the 24th of May, and contained these words: "You need have no fear about America." The readings closed in June.

The readings of the new year began with even increased enthusiasm, but not otherwise with happier omen. Here was his first outline of plan: "I start on Wednesday afternoon (the 15th of January) for Liverpool, and then go on to Chester, Derby, Leicester, and Wolverhampton. On Tuesday the 29th I read in London again, and in February I read at Manchester and then go on into Scotland." From Liverpool he wrote on the 21st: "The enthusiasm has been unbounded. On Friday night I quite astonished myself; but

I was taken so faint afterwards that they laid me on a sofa, at the hall for half an hour. I attribute it to my distressing inability to sleep at night, and to nothing worse. Everything is made as easy to me as it possibly can be. Dolby would do anything to lighten the work, and *does* everything."

On the 15th of February he wrote to his sister-in-law from Liverpool that they had had "an enormous turnaway" the previous night. "The day has been very fine, and I have turned it to the wholesomest account by walking on the sands at New Brighton all the morning. I am not quite right within, but believe it to be an effect of the railway shaking. There is no doubt of the fact that, after the Staplehurst experience, it tells more and more (railway shaking, that is) instead of, as one might have expected, less and less."

On the 4th of March he wrote from Newcastle: "The readings have made an immense effect in this place, and it is remarkable that although the people are individually rough, collectively they are an unusually tender and sympathetic audience; while their comic perception is quite up to the high London standard. I am wonderfully well, and quite fresh and strong." Three days later he was at Leeds; from which he was to work himself round through the most important neighbouring places to another reading in London, before again visiting Ireland.

This was the time of the Fenian excitements; it was with great reluctance he consented to go;[105] and he told us all at his first arrival that he should have a complete breakdown. More than 300 stalls were gone at Belfast two days before the reading, but on the afternoon of the reading in Dublin not 50 were taken. Strange to say however a great crowd pressed in at night, he had a tumultuous greeting, and on the 22nd of March I had this announcement from him: "You will be surprised to be told that we have done WONDERS! Enthusiastic crowds have filled the halls to the roof each night, and hundreds have been turned away. At Belfast the night before last we had £246 5s. In Dublin to-night everything is sold out, and people are besieging Dolby to put chairs anywhere, in doorways, on my platform, in any sort of hole or corner. In short the Readings are a perfect rage at a time when everything else is beaten down." He took the Eastern Counties at his return, and this brought the series to a close. "The reception at Cambridge was something to be proud of in such a place.

CHARLES [John Huffman] DICKENS'
The great Novelist appears in various characters, all, however, showing the same prolific "head" — Dickens, alias Pickwick, alias Copperfield, alias Sam Weller, &c., &c.

Dickens as his characters

The colleges mustered in full force, from the biggest guns to the smallest; and went beyond even Manchester in the roars of welcome and rounds of cheers. The place was crammed, and all through the reading everything was taken with the utmost heartiness of enjoyment." The temptation of offers from America had meanwhile again been presented to him so strongly, and in such unlucky connection with immediate family claims threatening excess of expenditure even beyond the income he was making, that he was fain to write to his sister-in-law: "I begin to feel myself drawn towards America as Darnay in the *Tale of Two Cities* was attracted to Paris. It is my Loadstone Rock." Too surely it was to be so; and Dickens was not to be saved from the consequence of yielding to the temptation, by any such sacrifice as had rescued Darnay.

"It is curious" (20th May) "that you should touch the American subject, because I must confess that my mind is in a most disturbed state about it. That the people there have set themselves on having the readings, there is no question. Every mail brings me proposals, and the number of Americans at St. James's Hall has been surprising. A certain Mr. Grau, who took Ristori out, and is highly responsible, wrote to me by the last mail (for the second time) saying that if I would give him a word of encouragement he would come over immediately and arrange on the boldest terms for any number I chose, and would deposit a large sum of money at Coutts's. Mr. Fields writes to me on behalf of a committee of private gentlemen at Boston who wished for the credit of getting me out, who desired to hear the readings and did not want profit, and would put down as a guarantee £10,000—also to be banked here. Every American speculator who comes to London repairs straight to Dolby, with similar proposals. And, thus excited, Chappells, the moment this last series was over, proposed to treat for America!" Upon the mere question of these various offers he had little difficulty in making up his mind. If he went at all, he would go on his own account, making no compact with any one. Whether he should go at all, was what he had to determine.

At the end of May he wrote: "Poor dear Stanfield!" (our excellent friend had passed away the week before). "I cannot think even of him, and of our great loss, for this spectre of doubt and indecision that sits at the board with me and stands at the bedside. I am in a tempest-tossed condition, and can hardly believe that I stand at bay at last on the American question. The difficulty of determining amid the variety of statements made to me is enormous, and you have no idea how heavily the anxiety of it sits upon my soul. But the prize looks so large!" One way at last seemed to open by which it was possible to get at some settled opinion. "Dolby sails for America" (2nd of July) "on Saturday the 3rd of August. It is impossible to come to any reasonable conclusion, without sending eyes and ears on the actual ground. He will take out my MS. for the *Children's Magazine*. I hope it is droll, and very child-like; though the joke is a grown-up one besides. You must try to like the pirate story, for I am very fond of it." The allusion is to his pleasant *Holiday Romance* which he had written for Mr. Fields.

Hardly had Mr. Dolby gone when there came that which should have availed to dissuade, far more than any of the arguments which continued to express my objection to the enterprise. "I am laid up," he wrote on the 6th of August, "with another attack in my foot, and was on the sofa all last night in tortures. I cannot bear to have the fomentations taken off for a moment. I was so ill with it on Sunday, and it looked so fierce, that I came up to Henry Thompson. He has gone into the case heartily, and says that there is no doubt the complaint originates in the action of the shoe, in walking, on an enlargement in the nature of a bunion."

My own part in the discussion was that of steady dissuasion throughout: though this might perhaps have been less persistent if I could have reconciled myself to the belief, which I never at any time did, that Public Readings were a worthy employment for a man of his genius. But it had by this time become clear to me that nothing could stay the enterprise. The result of Mr. Dolby's visit to America—drawn up by Dickens himself in a paper possessing still the interest of having given to the Readings when he crossed the Atlantic much of the form they then assumed[106]—reached me when I was staying at Ross; and upon it was founded my last argument against the scheme. This he received in London on the 28th of September, on which day he thus wrote to his eldest daughter: "As I telegraphed after I saw you, I am off to Ross to consult with Mr. Forster

Lord Robert Lytton, son of Edward Bulwer Lytton

and Dolby together. You shall hear, either on Monday, or by Monday's post from London, how I decide finally." The result he wrote to her three days later: "You will have had my telegram that I go to America. After a long discussion with Forster, and consideration of what is to be said on both sides, I have decided to go through with it. We have telegraphed 'Yes' to Boston." Seven days later he wrote to me: "The Scotia being full, I do not sail until lord mayor's day; for which glorious anniversary I have engaged an officer's cabin on deck in the Cuba. I am not in very brilliant spirits at the prospect before me, and am deeply sensible of your motive and reasons for the line you have taken; but I am not in the least shaken in the conviction that I could never quite have given up the idea."

The remaining time was given to preparations; on the 2nd of November there was a Farewell Banquet in the Freemasons' Hall over which Lord Lytton presided; and on the 9th Dickens sailed for Boston. Before he left he had contributed his part to the last of his Christmas Numbers; all the writings he lived to complete were done; and the interval of his voyage may be occupied by a general review of the literary labour of his life.

---

[100] There had been some estrangement between them since the autumn of 1858, hardly now worth mention even in a note. Thackeray, justly indignant at a published description of himself by the member of a club to which both he and Dickens belonged, referred it to the Committee, who decided to expel the writer. Dickens, thinking expulsion too harsh a penalty for an offence thoughtlessly given, and, as far as might be, manfully atoned for by withdrawal and regret, interposed to avert that extremity. Thackeray resented the interference, and Dickens was justly hurt by the manner in which he did so. Neither was wholly right, nor was either altogether in the wrong.

[101] Writing to me three months before, he spoke of the death of one whom he had known from his boyhood and with whom he had fought unsuccessfully for some years against the management of the Literary Fund. "Poor Dilke! I am very sorry that the capital old stout-hearted man is dead." Sorrow may also be expressed that no adequate record should remain of a career which for steadfast purpose, conscientious maintenance of opinion, and pursuit of public objects with disregard of self, was one of very high example. So averse was Mr. Dilke to every kind of display that his name appears to none of the literary investigations which were conducted by him with an acuteness wonderful as his industry, and it was in accordance with his express instructions that the literary journal which his energy and self-denial had established kept silence respecting him at his death.

[102] One day before, the 8th of June 1865, his old friend Sir Joseph Paxton had breathed his last.

[103] Here are allusions to it at that time. "I have got a boot on to-day,—made on an Otranto scale, but really not very discernible from its ordinary sized companion." After a few days' holiday: "I began to feel my foot stronger the moment I breathed the sea air. Still, during the ten days I have been away, I have never been able to wear a boot after four or five in the afternoon, but have passed all the evenings with the foot up, and nothing on it. I am burnt brown and have walked by the sea perpetually, yet I feel certain that if I wore a boot this evening, I should be taken with those torments again before the night was out."

[104] I give one such instance: "The railway people have offered, in the case of the young man whom I got out of the carriage just alive, all the expenses and a thousand pounds down. The father declines to accept the offer. It seems unlikely that the young man, whose destination is India, would ever be passed for the Army now by the Medical Board. The question is, how far will that contingency tell, under Lord Campbell's Act?"

[105] He wrote to me on the 15th of March from Dublin: "So profoundly discouraging were the accounts from here in London last Tuesday that I held several councils with Chappell about coming at all; had actually drawn up a bill announcing (indefinitely) the postponement of the readings; and had meant to give him a reading to cover the charges incurred—but yielded at last to his representations the other way. We ran through a snow storm nearly the whole way, and in Wales got snowed up, came to a stoppage, and had to dig the engine out. . . . We got to Dublin at last, found it snowing and raining, and heard that it had been snowing and raining since the first day of the year. . . . As to outward signs of trouble or preparation, they are very few. At Kingstown our boat was waited for by four armed policemen, and some stragglers in various dresses who were clearly detectives. But there was no show of soldiery. My people carry a long heavy box containing gas-fittings. This was immediately laid hold of; but one of the stragglers instantly interposed on seeing my name, and came to me in the carriage and apologised. . . . The worst looking young fellow I ever saw, turned up at Holyhead before we went to bed there, and sat glooming and glowering by the coffee-room fire while we warmed ourselves. He said he had been snowed up with us (which we didn't believe), and was horribly disconcerted by some box of his having gone to Dublin without him. We said to one another 'Fenian:' and certainly he disappeared in the morning, and let his box go where it would." What Dickens heard and saw in Dublin, during this visit, convinced him that Fenianism and disaffection had found their way into several regiments.

[106] This renders it worth preservation in a note. He called it "THE CASE IN A NUTSHELL.

"1. I think it may be taken as proved, that general enthusiasm and excitement are awakened in America on the subject of the Readings, and that the people are prepared to give me a great reception. The New York Herald, indeed, is of opinion that 'Dickens must apologise first'; and where a New York Herald is possible, anything is possible. But the prevailing tone, both of the press and of people of all conditions, is highly favourable. I have an opinion myself that the Irish element in New York is dangerous; for the reason that the Fenians would be glad to damage a conspicuous Englishman. This is merely an opinion of my own.

"2. All our original calculations were based on 100 Readings. But an unexpected result of careful enquiry on the spot, is the discovery that the month of May is generally considered (in the large cities) bad for such a purpose. Admitting that what governs an ordinary case in this wise, governs mine, this reduces the Readings to 80, and consequently at a blow makes a reduction of 20 per cent., in the means of making money within the half year—unless the objection should not apply in my exceptional instance.

"3. I dismiss the consideration that the great towns of America could not possibly be exhausted—or even visited—within 6 months, and that a large harvest would be left unreaped. Because I hold a second series of Readings in America is to be set down as out of the question: whether regarded as involving two more voyages across the Atlantic, or a vacation of five months in Canada.

"4. The narrowed calculation we have made, is this: What is the largest amount of clear profit derivable, under the most advantageous circumstances possible, as to their public reception, from 80 Readings and no more? In making this calculation, the expenses have been throughout taken on the New York scale—which is the dearest; as much as 20 per cent., has been deducted for management, including Mr. Dolby's commission; and no credit has been taken for any extra payment on reserved seats, though a good deal of money is confidently expected from this source. But on the other hand it is to be observed that four Readings (and a fraction over) are supposed to take place every week, and that the estimate of receipts is based on the assumption that the audiences are, on all occasions, as large as the rooms will reasonably hold.

"5. So considering 80 Readings, we bring out the net profit of that number, remaining to me after payment of all charges whatever, as £15,500.

"6. But it yet remains to be noted that the calculation assumes New York City, and the State of New York, to be good for a very large proportion of the 80 Readings; and that the calculation also assumes the necessary travelling not to extend beyond Boston and adjacent places, New York City and adjacent places, Philadelphia, Washington, and Baltimore. But, if the calculation should prove too sanguine on this head, and if these places should not be good for so many Readings, then it may prove impracticable to get through 80 within the time: by reason of other places that would come into the list, lying wide asunder, and necessitating long and fatiguing journeys.

"7. The loss consequent on the conversion of paper money into gold (with gold at the present ruling premium) is allowed for in the calculation. It counts seven dollars to the pound."

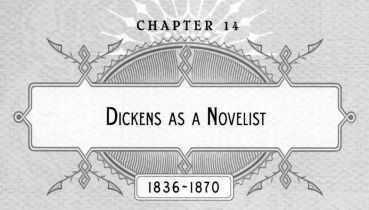

CHAPTER 14

DICKENS AS A NOVELIST

1836~1870

WHAT I HAVE TO SAY GENERALLY of Dickens's genius as a writer may be made part of the notice, which still remains to be given, of his writings from *The Tale of Two Cities* to the time at which we have arrived, leaving *Edwin Drood* for mention in its place; and this will be accompanied, as in former notices of individual stories, by illustrations drawn from his letters and life. His literary work was so intensely one with his nature that he is not separable from it, and the man and the method throw a singular light on each other. But some allusion to what has been said of these books, by writers assuming to speak with authority, will properly precede what has to be offered by me; and I shall preface this part of my task with the hint of Carlyle, that in looking at a man out of the common it is good for common men to make sure that they "see" before they attempt to "oversee" him.

Of the French writer, M. Henri Taine, it has before been remarked that his inability to appreciate humour is fatal to his pretensions as a critic of the English novel. But there is much that is noteworthy in his criticism notwithstanding, as well as remarkable in his knowledge of our language; his position entitles him to be heard without a suspicion of partizanship or intentional unfairness; whatever the value of his opinion, the elaboration of its form and expression is itself no common tribute; and what is said in it of Dickens's handling in regard to style and character, embodies temperately objections which have since been taken by some English critics without his impartiality and with less than his ability. As to style M. Taine does not find that the natural or simple prevails sufficiently. The tone is too passionate. Fondling and exaggerating thus what is occasional in the subject of his criticism, into what he has

evidently at last persuaded himself is a fixed and universal practice with Dickens, M. Taine proceeds to explain the exuberance by comparing such imagination in its vividness to that of a monomaniac. He fails altogether to apprehend that property in Humour which involves the feeling of subtlest and most affecting analogies, and from which is drawn the rare insight into sympathies between the nature of things and their attributes or opposites, in which Dickens's fancy revelled with such delight.

So far from it, the critic had satisfied himself that such a power of style must be adverse to a just delineation of character. Dickens is not calm enough, he says, to penetrate to the bottom of what he is dealing with. He takes sides with it as friend or enemy, laughs or cries over it, makes it odious or touching, repulsive or attractive, and is too vehement and not enough inquisitive to paint a likeness. His imagination is at once too vivid and not sufficiently large.

He has, however much concession in reserve, being satisfied, by his observation of England, that it is to the people for whom Dickens wrote his deficiencies in art are mainly due. The taste of his nation had prohibited him from representing character in a grand style. The English require too much morality and religion for genuine art. They made him treat love, not as holy and sublime in itself, but as subordinate to marriage; forced him to uphold society and the laws, against nature and enthusiasm; and compelled him to display, in painting such a seduction as in *Copperfield*, not the progress, ardour, and intoxication of passion, but only the misery, remorse, and despair. The result of such surface religion and morality, combined with the trading spirit, M. Taine continues, leads to so many national forms of hypocrisy, and of greed as well as worship for money, as to justify this great writer of the nation in his frequent choice of those vices for illustration in his tales.

Between the judgment thus passed by the distinguished French lecturer, and the later comment to be now given from an English critic, certainly not in arrest of that judgment, may fitly come a passage from one of Dickens's letters saying something of the limitations placed upon the artist in England. It may read like a quasi-confession of one of M. Taine's charges, though it was not written with reference to his own but to one of Scott's later novels. "Similarly"

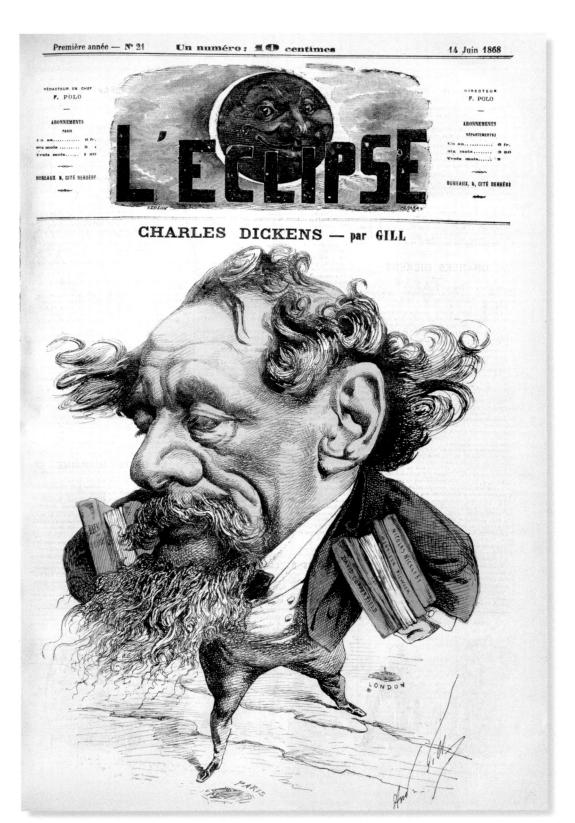

L'Eclipse caricature, 1868

(15th of August, 1856) "I have always a fine feeling of the honest state into which we have got, when some smooth gentleman says to me or to some one else when I am by, how odd it is that the hero of an English book is always uninteresting—too good—not natural, &c. I am continually hearing this of Scott from English people here, who pass their lives with Balzac and Sand."

M. Taine's criticism was written three or four years before Dickens's death, and to the same date belong some notices in England which adopted more or less the tone of depreciation; conceding the great effects achieved by the writer, but disputing the quality and value of his art. For it is incident to all such criticism of Dickens to be of necessity accompanied by the admission, that no writer has so completely impressed himself on the time in which he lived, that he has made his characters a part of literature, and that his readers are the world.

But, a little more than a year after his death, a paper was published of which the object was to reconcile such seeming inconsistency, to expound the inner meanings of "Dickens in relation to Criticism," and to show that, though he had a splendid genius and a wonderful imagination, yet the objectors were to be excused who called him only a stagy sentimentalist and a clever caricaturist. This critical essay appeared in the *Fortnightly Review* for February, 1872, with the signature of Mr. George Henry Lewes; and the pretentious airs of the performance, with its prodigious professions of candour, force upon me the painful task of stating what it really is. During Dickens's life, especially when any fresh novelist could be found available for strained comparison with him, there were plenty of attempts to write him down: but the trick of studied depreciation was never carried so far or made so odious as in this case, by intolerable assumptions of an indulgent superiority; and to repel it in such a form once for all is due to Dickens's memory.

He says that Dickens was so great in "fun" (humour he does not concede to him anywhere) that Fielding and Smollett are small in comparison, but that this would only have been a passing amusement for the world if he had not been "gifted with an imagination of marvellous

Dickens's Dream, an unfinished painting by R.W. Buss, 1875

vividness, and an emotional sympathetic nature capable of furnishing that imagination with elements of universal power."

"He was," we are told, "a seer of visions." Amid silence and darkness, we are assured, he heard voices and saw objects; of which the revived impressions to him had the vividness of sensations, and the images his mind created in explanation of them had the coercive force of realities;[107] so that what he brought into existence in this way, no matter how fantastic and unreal, was (whatever this may mean) universally intelligible. "His types established themselves in the public mind like personal experiences. Their falsity was unnoticed in the blaze of their illumination. Every humbug seemed a Pecksniff, every jovial improvident a Micawber, every stinted serving-wench a Marchioness."

His leading quality was Humour. It has no mention in either of the criticisms cited, but it was his highest faculty; and it accounts for his magnificent successes, as well as for his not infrequent failures, in characteristic delineation. He was conscious of this himself. Five years before he died, a great and generous brother artist, Lord Lytton, amid much ungrudging praise of a work he was then publishing, asked him to consider, as to one part of it, if the modesties of art were not a little overpassed. "I

cannot tell you," he replied, "how highly I prize your letter, or with what pride and pleasure it inspires me. Nor do I for a moment question its criticism (if objection so generous and easy may be called by that hard name) otherwise than on this ground—that I work slowly and with great care, and never give way to my invention recklessly, but constantly restrain it; and that I think it is my infirmity to fancy or perceive relations in things which are not apparent generally. Also, I have such an inexpressible enjoyment of what I see in a droll light, that I dare say I pet it as if it were a spoilt child. This is all I have to offer in arrest of judgment." To perceive relations in things which are not apparent generally, is one of those exquisite properties of humour by which are discovered the affinities between the high and the low, the attractive and the repulsive, the rarest things and things of every day, which bring us all upon the level of a common humanity.

THE TALE OF TWO CITIES.

Dickens's next story to *Little Dorrit* was the *Tale of Two Cities*, of which the first notion occurred to him while acting with his friends and his children in the summer of 1857 in Mr. Wilkie Collins's drama of *The Frozen Deep*. But it was only a vague fancy, and the sadness and trouble of the winter of that year were not favourable to it. Towards the close (27th) of January 1858, talking of improvements at Gadshill in which he took little interest, it was again in his thoughts. "Growing inclinations of a fitful and undefined sort are upon me sometimes to fall to work on a new book. Then I think I had better not worry my worried mind yet awhile. Then I think it would be of no use if I did, for I couldn't settle to one occupation.—And that's all!" "If I can discipline my thoughts," he wrote three days later, "into the channel of a story, I have made up my mind to get to work on one: always supposing that I find myself, on the trial, able to do well. Nothing whatever will do me the least 'good' in the way of shaking the one strong possession of change impending over us that every day makes

Dickens's personal effects: chain coin purse and gold mounted cigar case inscribed with a monogram

FROM A REVIEW OF VOL. I OF FORSTER'S *LIFE, FORTNIGHTLY REVIEW,*
FEBRUARY 1872, REPRINTED IN PHILIP COLLINS, *THE CRITICAL HERITAGE*

George Henry Lewes vividly expresses his sense of Dickens's failings:

The critic is distressed to observe the substitution of mechanisms for minds, puppets for characters. It is needless to dwell on such monstrous failures as Mantalini, Rosa Dartle, Lady Dedlock, Esther Summerson, Mr. Dick, Arthur Gride, Edith Dombey, Mr. Carker—needless, because if one studies the successful figures one finds even in them only touches of veri-similitude. When one thinks of Micawber always presenting himself in the same situation, moved with the same springs, and uttering the same sounds, always confident of something turning up, always crushed and rebounding, always making punch—and his wife always declaring she will never part from him, always referring to his talents and her family—when one thinks of the 'catchwords' personified as characters, one is reminded of the frogs whose brains have been taken out for physiological purposes, and whose actions henceforth want the distinctive peculiarity of organic action, that of fluctuating spontaneity [. . .] It is this complexity of the organism which Dickens wholly fails to conceive; his characters having noth-ing fluctuating and incalculable in them, even when they embody true observations; and very often they are so fantastic that one is at a loss to understand how he could, without hallucination, believe them to be like reality. There are dialogues bearing the traces of straining effort at effect, which in their incongruity painfully resemble the absurd and eager expositions which insane patients pour into the listener's ear when detailing their wrongs, or their schemes.

stronger; but if I could work on with some approach to steadiness, through the summer, the anxious toil of a new book would have its neck well broken before beginning to publish, next October or November.

"This is merely to certify," he wrote on the 11th of March 1859, "that I have got exactly the name for the story that is wanted; exactly what will fit the opening to a 'T.' A TALE OF TWO CITIES. Also, that I have struck out a rather original and bold idea. That is, at the end of each month to publish the monthly part in the green cover, with the two illustrations, at the old shilling. This will give *All the Year Round* always the interest and precedence of a fresh weekly portion during the month; and will give me my old standing with my old public, and the advantage (very necessary in this story) of having numbers of people who read it in no portions smaller than a monthly part. . . . My American ambassador pays a thousand pounds for the first year, for the privilege of republishing in America one day after we publish here. Not bad?" . . . He had to struggle at

the opening through a sharp attack of illness, and on the 9th of July progress was thus reported. "I have been getting on in health very slowly and through irksome botheration enough. But I think I am round the corner. This cause—and the heat—has tended to my doing no more than hold my ground, my old month's advance, with the *Tale of Two Cities.* The small portions thereof, drive me frantic; but I think the tale must have taken a strong hold. The run upon our monthly parts is surprising, and last month we sold 35,000 back numbers. A note I have had from Carlyle about it has given me especial pleasure." A letter of the following month expresses the intention he had when he began the story, and in what respect it differs as to method from all his other books. Sending in proof four numbers ahead of the current publication, he adds: "I hope you will like them. Nothing but the interest of the subject, and the pleasure of striving with the difficulty of the form of treatment,—nothing in the way of mere money, I mean,—could else repay the time and trouble of the incessant condensation."

The Footsteps Die Out For Ever:

THE supposed Evremonde descends, and the seamstress is lifted out next after him. He has not relinquished her patient hand in getting out, but still holds it as he promised. He gently places her with her back to the crashing engine that constantly whirrs up and falls, and she looks into his face and thanks him.

"But for you, dear stranger, I should not be so composed, for I am naturally a poor little thing, faint of heart; nor should I have been able to raise my thoughts to Him who was put to death, that we might have hope and comfort here to-day. I think you were sent to me by Heaven."

"Or you to me," says Sydney Carton. "Keep your eyes upon me, dear child, and mind no other object."

"I mind nothing while I hold your hand. I shall mind nothing when I let it go, if they are rapid."

"They will be rapid. Fear not!"

The two stand in the fast-thinning throng of victims, but they speak as if they were alone. Eye to eye, voice to voice, hand to hand, heart to heart, these two children of the Universal Mother, else so wide apart and differing, have come together on the dark highway, to repair home together, and to rest in her bosom.

[. . .] "Am I to kiss you now? Is the moment come?"

"Yes."

She kisses his lips; he kisses hers; they solemnly bless each other. The spare hand does not tremble as he releases it; nothing worse than a sweet, bright constancy is in the patient face. She goes next before him—is gone; the knitting-women count Twenty-Two.

"I am the Resurrection and the Life, saith the Lord: he that believeth in me, though he were dead, yet shall he live: and whosoever liveth and believeth in me shall never die."

The murmuring of many voices, the upturning of many faces, the pressing on of many footsteps in the outskirts of the crowd, so that it swells forward in a mass, like one great heave of water, all flashes away. Twenty-Three.

They said of him, about the city that night, that it was the peacefullest man's face ever beheld there. Many added that he looked sublime and prophetic.

One of the most remarkable sufferers by the same axe—a woman—had asked at the foot of the same scaffold, not long before, to be allowed to write down the thoughts that were inspiring her. If he had given any utterance to his, and they were prophetic, they would have been these:

"I see Barsad, and Cly, Defarge, The Vengeance, the Juryman, the Judge, long ranks of the new oppressors who have risen on the destruction of the old, perishing by this retributive instrument, before it shall cease out of its present use. I see a beautiful city and a brilliant people rising from this abyss, and, in their struggles to be truly free, in their triumphs and defeats, through long years to come, I see the evil of this time and of the previous time of which this is the natural birth, gradually making expiation for itself and wearing out.

"I see the lives for which I lay down my life, peaceful, useful, prosperous and happy, in that England which I shall see no more. I see Her with a child upon her bosom, who bears my name. I see her father, aged and bent, but otherwise restored, and faithful to all men in his healing office, and at peace. I see the good old man, so long their friend, in ten years' time enriching them with all he has, and passing tranquilly to his reward.

"I see that I hold a sanctuary in their hearts, and in the hearts of their descendants, generations hence. I see her, an old woman, weeping for me on the anniversary of this day. I see her and her husband, their course done, lying side by side in their last earthly bed, and I know that each was not more honoured and held sacred in the other's soul, than I was in the souls of both.

"I see that child who lay upon her bosom and who bore my name, a man winning his way up in that path of life which once was mine. I see him winning it so well, that my name is made illustrious there by the light of his. I see the blots I threw upon it, faded away. I see him, fore-most of just judges and honoured men, bringing a boy of my name, with a forehead that I know and golden hair, to this place—then fair to look upon, with not a trace of this day's disfigurement—and I hear him tell the child my story, with a tender and a faltering voice.

"It is a far, far better thing that I do, than I have ever done; it is a far, far better rest that I go to than I have ever known."

These are interesting intimations of the care with which Dickens worked; and there is no instance in his novels, excepting this, of a deliberate and planned departure from the method of treatment which had been pre-eminently the source of his popularity as a novelist. To rely less upon character than upon incident, and to resolve that his actors should be expressed by the story more than they should express themselves by dialogue, was for him a hazardous, and can hardly be called an entirely successful, experiment. With singular dramatic vivacity, much constructive art, and with descriptive passages of a high order everywhere (the dawn of the terrible outbreak in the journey of the marquis from Paris to his country seat, and the London crowd at the funeral of the spy, may be instanced for their power), there was probably never a book by a great humourist, and an artist so prolific in the conception of character, with so little humour and so few rememberable figures.

Its merits lie elsewhere. Though there are excellent traits and touches all through the revolutionary scenes, the only full-length that stands out prominently is the picture of the wasted life saved at last by heroic sacrifice. Dickens speaks of his design to make impressive the dignity of Carton's death, and in this he succeeded perhaps even beyond his expectation. Carton suffers himself to be mistaken for another, and gives his life that the girl he loves may be happy with that other; the secret being known only to a poor little girl in the tumbril that takes them to the scaffold, who at the moment has discovered it, and whom it strengthens also to die. The incident is beautifully told; and it is at least only fair to set against verdicts not very favourable as to this effort of his invention, what was said of the particular character and scene, and of the book generally, by an American critic whose literary studies had most familiarized him with the rarest forms of imaginative writing.[108] "Its pourtrayal

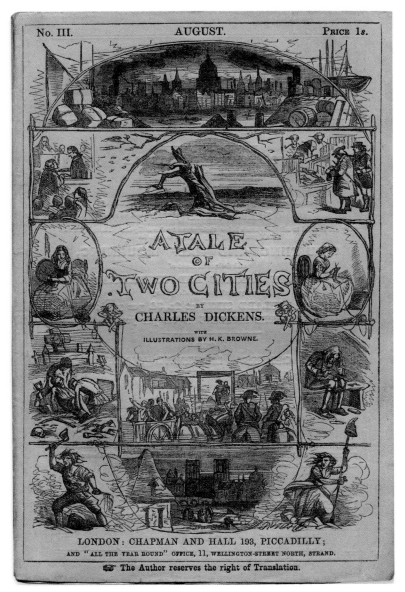

Cover to a monthly part of *A Tale of Two Cities*, with illustrations by Hablot Knight Browne (Phiz), August 1859

of the noble-natured castaway makes it almost a peerless book in modern literature, and gives it a place among the highest examples of literary art." I should myself prefer to say that its distinctive merit is less in any of its conceptions of character, even Carton's, than as a specimen of Dickens's power in imaginative story-telling. There is no piece of fiction known to me, in which the domestic life of

A TALE OF TWO CITIES, BOOK 2, CHAPTER 7

Monseigneur encounters the people of Saint Antoine:

———⚇———

IT appeared, under the circumstances, rather agreeable to him to see the common people dispersed before his horses, and often barely escaping from being run down. His man drove as if he were charging an enemy, and the furious recklessness of the man brought no check into the face, or to the lips, of the master. The complaint had sometimes made itself audible, even in that deaf city and dumb age, that, in the narrow streets without footways, the fierce patrician custom of hard driving endangered and maimed the mere vulgar in a barbarous manner. But, few cared enough for that to think of it a second time, and, in this matter, as in all others, the common wretches were left to get out of their difficulties as they could.

With a wild rattle and clatter, and an inhuman abandonment of consideration not easy to be understood in these days, the carriage dashed through streets and swept round corners, with women screaming before it, and men clutching each other and clutching children out of its way. At last, swooping at a street corner by a fountain, one of its wheels came to a sickening little jolt, and there was a loud cry from a number of voices, and the horses reared and plunged.

But for the latter inconvenience, the carriage probably would not have stopped; carriages were often known to drive on, and leave their wounded behind, and why not? But the frightened valet had got down in a hurry, and there were twenty hands at the horses' bridles.

"What has gone wrong?" said Monsieur, calmly looking out.

A tall man in a nightcap had caught up a bundle from among the feet of the horses, and had laid it on the basement of the fountain, and was down in the mud and wet, howling over it like a wild animal.

"Pardon, Monsieur the Marquis!" said a ragged and submissive man, "it is a child."

"Why does he make that abominable noise? Is it his child?"

"Excuse me, Monsieur the Marquis—it is a pity—yes."

The fountain was a little removed; for the street opened, where it was, into a space some ten or twelve yards square. As the tall man suddenly got up from the ground, and came running at the carriage, Monsieur the Marquis clapped his hand for an instant on his sword-hilt.

"Killed!" shrieked the man, in wild desperation, extending both arms at their length above his head, and staring at him. "Dead!"

The people closed round, and looked at Monsieur the Marquis. There was nothing revealed by the many eyes that looked at him but watchfulness and eagerness; there was no visible menacing or anger. Neither did the people say anything; after the first cry, they had been silent, and they remained so. The voice of the submissive man who had spoken, was flat and tame in its extreme submission. Monsieur the Marquis ran his eyes over them all, as if they had been mere rats come out of their holes.

He took out his purse.

"It is extraordinary to me," said he, "that you people cannot take care of yourselves and your children. One or the other of you is for ever in the way. How do I know what injury you have done my horses. See! Give him that."

He threw out a gold coin for the valet to pick up, and all the heads craned forward that all the eyes might look down at it as it fell. The tall man called out again with a most unearthly cry, "Dead!"

He was arrested by the quick arrival of another man, for whom the rest made way. On seeing him, the miserable creature fell upon his shoulder, sobbing and crying, and pointing to the fountain, where some women were stooping over the motionless bundle, and moving gently about it. They were as silent, however, as the men.

"I know all, I know all," said the last comer. "Be a brave man, my Gaspard! It is better for the poor little plaything to die so, than to live. It has died in a moment without pain. Could it have lived an hour as happily?"

"You are a philosopher, you there," said the Marquis, smiling. "How do they call you?"

"They call me Defarge."

"Of what trade?"

"Monsieur the Marquis, vendor of wine."

"Pick up that, philosopher and vendor of wine," said the Marquis, throwing him another gold coin, "and spend it as you will. The horses there; are they right?"

Without deigning to look at the assemblage a second time, Monsieur the Marquis leaned back in his seat, and was just being driven away with the air of a gentleman who had accidentally broke some common thing, and had paid for it, and could afford to pay for it; when his ease was suddenly disturbed by a coin flying into his carriage, and ringing on its floor.

"Hold!" said Monsieur the Marquis. "Hold the horses! Who threw that?"

He looked to the spot where Defarge the vendor of wine had stood, a moment before; but the wretched father was grovelling on his face on the pavement in that spot, and the figure that stood beside him was the figure of a dark stout woman, knitting.

"You dogs!" said the Marquis, but smoothly, and with an unchanged front, except as to the spots on his nose: "I would ride over any of you very willingly, and exterminate you from the earth. If I knew which rascal threw at the carriage, and if that brigand were sufficiently near it, he should be crushed under the wheels."

So cowed was their condition, and so long and hard their experience of what such a man could do to them, within the law and beyond it, that not a voice, or a hand, or even an eye was raised. Among the men, not one. But the woman who stood knitting looked up steadily, and looked the Marquis in the face. It was not for his dignity to notice it; his contemptuous eyes passed over her, and over all the other rats; and he leaned back in his seat again, and gave the word "Go on!"

The Stoppage at the Fountain, Hablot Knight Browne (Phiz), 1859

a few simple private people is in such a manner knitted and interwoven with the outbreak of a terrible public event, that the one seems but part of the other. When made conscious of the first sultry drops of a thunderstorm that fall upon a little group sitting in an obscure English lodging, we are witness to the actual beginning of a tempest which is preparing to sweep away everything in France. And, to the end, the book in this respect is really remarkable.

GREAT EXPECTATIONS.

The *Tale of Two Cities* was published in 1859; the series of papers collected as the *Uncommercial Traveller* were occupying Dickens in 1860; and it was while engaged in these, and throwing off in the course of them capital "samples" of fun

Sydney Carton, from *A Tale of Two Cities*

and enjoyment, he thus replied to a suggestion that he should let himself loose upon some single humorous conception, in the vein of his youthful achievements in that way. This was the germ of Pip and Magwitch, which at first he intended to make the groundwork of a tale in the old twenty-number form, but for reasons perhaps fortunate brought afterwards within the limits of a less elaborate novel.

"Last week," he wrote on the 4th of October 1860, "I got to work on the new story. I had previously very carefully considered the state and prospects of *All the Year Round*, and, the more I considered them, the less hope I saw of being able to get back, *now*, to the profit of a separate publication in the old 20 numbers." (A tale, which at the time was appearing in his serial, had disappointed expectation.) "However I worked on, knowing that what I was doing would run into another groove; and I called a council of war at the office on Tuesday. It was perfectly clear that the one thing to be done was, for me to strike in. I have therefore decided to begin the story as of the length of the *Tale of Two Cities* on the first of December—begin publishing, that is. I must make the most I can out of the book. You shall have the first two or three weekly parts to-morrow. The name is GREAT EXPECTATIONS. I think a good name?"

A few more days brought the first instalment of the tale, and explanatory mention of it. "The book will be written in the first person throughout, and during these first three weekly numbers you will find the hero to be a boy-child, like David. Then he will be an apprentice. You will not have to complain of the want of humour as in the *Tale of Two Cities*. I have made the opening, I hope, in its general effect exceedingly droll. I have put a child and a good-natured foolish man, in relations that seem to me very funny. Of course I have got in the pivot on which the story will turn too—and which indeed, as you remember, was the grotesque tragi-comic conception that first encouraged me. To be quite sure I had fallen into no unconscious repetitions, I read *David Copperfield* again the other day, and was affected by it to a degree you would hardly believe."

It may be doubted if Dickens could better have established his right to the front rank among novelists claimed for him, than by the ease and mastery with which, in these two books of *Copperfield* and *Great Expectations*, he kept perfectly distinct the two stories of a boy's childhood, both told in the form of autobiography. A subtle penetration into character marks the unlikeness in the likeness; there is enough at once of resemblance and of difference in the position and surroundings of each to account for the divergences of character that arise; both children are good-hearted, and both have the advantage of association with models of tender simplicity and oddity, perfect in their truth and quite distinct from each other; but a sudden tumble into distress steadies Peggotty's little friend, and as unexpected a stroke of good fortune turns the head of the small protege of Joe Gargery. What a deal of spoiling nevertheless, a nature that is really good at the bottom of it will stand without permanent damage, is nicely shown in Pip; and the way he reconciles his determination to act very shabbily to his early friends, with a conceited notion that he is setting them a moral example, is part of the shading of a character drawn with extraordinary skill.

Sending the chapters which open the third division of the tale, he wrote thus: "It is a pity that the third portion cannot be read all at once, because its purpose would be much more apparent; and the pity is the greater, because the general turn and tone of the working out and winding up, will be away from all such things as they conventionally go. But what must be, must be. As to the planning out from week to week, nobody can imagine what the difficulty is, without trying. But, as in all such

"After the sentence—Lucie Manette faints," illustration by Hablot Knight Browne (Phiz), 1859

Great Expectations, Chapter I

In this grave meeting, the young Pip encounters Magwitch, the convict, who will have such a profound effect on his expectations:

OURS was the marsh country, down by the river, within, as the river wound, twenty miles of the sea. My first most vivid and broad impression of the identity of things seems to me to have been gained on a memorable raw afternoon towards evening. At such a time I found out for certain that this bleak place overgrown with nettles was the churchyard; and that Philip Pirrip, late of this parish, and also Georgiana wife of the above, were dead and buried; and that Alexander, Bartholomew, Abraham, Tobias, and Roger, infant children of the aforesaid, were also dead and buried; and that the dark flat wilderness beyond the churchyard, intersected with dikes and mounds and gates, with scattered cattle feeding on it, was the marshes; and that the low leaden line beyond was the river; and that the distant savage lair from which the wind was rushing was the sea; and that the small bundle of shivers growing afraid of it all and beginning to cry, was Pip.

"Hold your noise!" cried a terrible voice, as a man started up from among the graves at the side of the church porch. "Keep still, you little devil, or I'll cut your throat!"

A fearful man, all in coarse gray, with a great iron on his leg. A man with no hat, and with broken shoes, and with an old rag tied round his head. A man who had been soaked in water, and smothered in mud, and lamed by stones, and cut by flints, and stung by nettles, and torn by briars; who limped, and shivered, and glared, and growled; and whose teeth chattered in his head as he seized me by the chin.

"Oh! Don't cut my throat, sir," I pleaded in terror. "Pray don't do it, sir."

"Tell us your name!" said the man. "Quick!"

"Pip, sir."

"Once more," said the man, staring at me. "Give it mouth!"

"Pip. Pip, sir."

"Show us where you live," said the man. "Pint out the place!"

I pointed to where our village lay, on the flat in-shore among the alder-trees and pollards, a mile or more from the church.

The man, after looking at me for a moment, turned me upside down, and emptied my pockets. There was nothing in them but a piece of bread. When the church came to itself,—for he was so sudden and strong that he made it go head over heels before me, and I saw the steeple under my feet,—when the church came to itself, I say, I was seated on a high tombstone, trembling while he ate the bread ravenously.

"You young dog," said the man, licking his lips, "what fat cheeks you ha' got."

I believe they were fat, though I was at that time undersized for my years, and not strong.

"Darn me if I couldn't eat em," said the man, with a threatening shake of his head, "and if I han't half a mind to't!"

I earnestly expressed my hope that he wouldn't, and held tighter to the tombstone on which he had put me; partly, to keep myself upon it; partly, to keep myself from crying.

"Now lookee here!" said the man. "Where's your mother?"

"There, sir!" said I.

He started, made a short run, and stopped and looked over his shoulder.

"There, sir!" I timidly explained. "Also Georgiana. That's my mother."

"Oh!" said he, coming back. "And is that your father alonger your mother?"

"Yes, sir," said I; "him too; late of this parish."

"Ha!" he muttered then, considering. "Who d'ye live with,—supposin' you're kindly let to live, which I han't made up my mind about?"

"My sister, sir,—Mrs. Joe Gargery,—wife of Joe Gargery, the blacksmith, sir."

"Blacksmith, eh?" said he. And looked down at his leg.

After darkly looking at his leg and me several times, he came closer to my tombstone, took me by both arms, and tilted me back as far as he could hold me; so that his eyes looked most powerfully down into mine, and mine looked most helplessly up into his.

"Now lookee here," he said, "the question being whether you're to be let to live. You know what a file is?"

"Yes, sir."

"And you know what wittles is?"

"Yes, sir."

After each question he tilted me over a little more, so as to give me a greater sense of helplessness and danger.

"You get me a file." He tilted me again. "And you get me wittles." He tilted me again. "You bring 'em both to me." He tilted me again. "Or I'll have your heart and liver out."

cases, when it is overcome the pleasure is proportionate. Two months more will see me through it, I trust. All the iron is in the fire, and I have 'only' to beat it out." One other letter throws light upon an objection taken not unfairly to the too great speed with which the heroine, after being married, reclaimed, and widowed, is in a page or two again made love to, and remarried by the hero. This summary proceeding was not originally intended. But, over and above its popular acceptance, the book had interested some whose opinions Dickens specially valued (Carlyle among them, I remember);[109] and upon Bulwer Lytton objecting to a close that should leave Pip a solitary man, Dickens substituted what now stands. "You will be surprised" he wrote "to hear that I have changed the end of *Great Expectations* from and after Pip's return to Joe's, and finding his little likeness there. Bulwer, who has been, as I think you know, extraordinarily taken by the book, so strongly urged it upon me, after reading the proofs, and supported his view with such good reasons, that I resolved to make the change. You shall have it when you come back to town. I have put in as pretty a little piece of writing as I could, and I have no doubt the story will be more acceptable through the alteration." This turned out to be the case; but the first ending nevertheless seems to be more consistent with the drift, as well as natural working out, of the tale, and for this reason it is preserved in a note.[110]

CHRISTMAS SKETCHES.

Between that fine novel, which was issued in three volumes in the autumn of 1861, and the completion of his next serial story, were interposed three sketches in his happiest vein at which everyone laughed and cried in the Christmas times of 1862, '3, and '4. Of the waiter in *Somebody's Luggage* Dickens has himself spoken; and if any theme is well treated, when, from the point of view taken, nothing more is left to say about it, that bit of fun is perfect. Call it exaggeration, grotesqueness, or by what hard name you will, laughter will always intercept any graver criticism. Writing from Paris of what he was himself responsible for in the articles left by Somebody with his wonderful Waiter, he said that in one of them he had made the story a camera

obscura of certain French places and styles of people; having founded it on something he had noticed in a French soldier. This was the tale of Little Bebelle, which had a small French corporal for its hero, and became highly popular. But the triumph of the Christmas achievements in these days was Mrs. Lirriper. She took her place at once among people known to everybody; and all the world talked of Major Jemmy Jackman, and his friend the poor elderly lodging-house keeper of the Strand, with her miserable cares and rivalries and worries, as if they had both been as long in London and as well known as Norfolk-street itself.

A dozen volumes could not have told more than those dozen pages did. The *Legacy* followed the *Lodgings* in 1864, and there was no falling off in the fun and laughter.

OUR MUTUAL FRIEND.

The publication of *Our Mutual Friend*, in the form of the earliest stories, extended from May 1864 to November 1865. Four years earlier he had chosen this title as a good one, and he held to it through much objection. Between that time and his actual commencement there is mention, in his letters, of the three leading notions on which he founded the story. In his water-side wanderings during his last book, the many handbills he saw posted up, with dreary description of persons drowned in the river, suggested the 'long shore men and their ghastly calling whom he sketched in Hexam and Riderhood, "I think," he had written, "a man, young and perhaps eccentric, feigning to be dead, and *being* dead to all intents and purposes external to himself, and for years retaining the singular view of life and character so imparted, would be a good leading incident for a story;" and this he partly did in Rokesmith. The benevolent old Jew whom he makes the unconscious agent of a rascal, was meant to wipe out a reproach against his Jew in *Oliver Twist* as bringing dislike upon the religion of the race he belonged to.[111]

Having got his title in '61 it was his hope to have begun in '62. "Alas!" he wrote in the April of that year, "I have hit upon nothing for a story. Again and again I have tried. But this odious little house" (he had at this time for a few weeks exchanged Gadshill for a friend's house near Kensington) "seems to have stifled and darkened my invention." It was

JOHN IRVING

JOHN IRVING DISCUSSES DICKENS'S CONTROVERSIAL REWRITING OF THE END OF GREAT EXPECTATIONS.

The hopefulness that makes everyone love *A Christmas Carol* draws fire when Dickens employs it in *Great Expectations*; when Christmas is over, Dickens's hopefulness strikes many as mere wishful thinking. Dickens's original ending for *Great Expectations*, that Pip and his impossible love, Estella, should stay apart, is thought by most modern critics to be the proper (and certainly the modern) conclusion—from which Dickens eventually shied away; for such a change of heart and mind he is accused of selling out. After an early manhood of shallow goals, Pip is meant finally to see the falseness of his values—and of Estella—and he emerges a sadder though wiser fellow. Many readers have expressed the belief that Dickens stretches credulity too far when he leads us to suppose, in his revised ending, that Estella and Pip could be happy ever after; or that anyone can. Of his new ending—where Pip and Estella are reconciled—Dickens himself remarked to a friend: "I have put in a very pretty piece of writing, and I have no doubt that the story will be more acceptable through the alteration." That Estella would make Pip—or anyone—a rotten wife is not the point. "Don't be afraid of my being a blessing to him," she slyly tells Pip, who is bemoaning her choice of a first husband. The point is, Estella and Pip are linked; fatalistically, they belong to each other, happily or unhappily. Although the suggestion that Dickens revise the original ending came from his friend Bulwer Lytton, who wished the book to close on a happier note, Edgar Johnson wisely points out that "the changed ending reflected a desperate hope that Dickens could not banish from within his own heart." That hope is not a last-minute alteration, tacked on, but simply the culmination of a hope that abides throughout the novel: that Estella might change. After all, Pip changes (he is the first major character in a Dickens novel who changes realistically, albeit slowly). The book isn't called *Great Expectations* for nothing. It is not, I think, meant to be an entirely bitter title—although I can undermine my own argument by reminding myself that we first hear that Pip is "a young fellow of great expectations" from the ominous and cynical Mr. Jaggers, that veteran hardliner who will, quite rightfully, warn Pip to "take nothing on its looks; take everything on evidence. There's no better rule." But that was never Dickens's rule. Mr. Gradgrind, from *Hard Times*, believed in nothing and possessed nothing but the facts; yet it is Mr. Sleary's advice that Dickens heeds, to "do the withe thing and the kind thing too." It is both kind and the "withe" thing that Pip and Estella end up together. [...]

The revised ending reads: "I took her hand in mind, and we went out of the ruined place; and as the morning mists had risen long ago when I first left the forge, so the evening mists were rising now, and in all the broad expanse of tranquil light they showed to me, I saw no shadow of another parting from her." A very pretty piece of writing, as Dickens noted, and eternally open—still ambiguous (Pip's hopes have been dashed before) but far more the mirror of the quality of trust in the novel as a whole. It is that hopeful ending that sings with all the rich contradiction we should love Dickens for; it both underlines and undermines everything before it. Pip is basically good, basically gullible; he starts out being human, he learns by error—and by becoming ashamed of himself—and he keeps on being human. That touching illogic seems not only generous but true. [...]

In *Great Expectations*, maybe he felt he had given Pip and Estella—and his readers—enough pain. Why not give Pip and Estella to each other at the end? Charles Dickens would never find that "one happiness I have missed in life, and the one friend and companion I never made." But to Pip he would give that pleasure; he would give Pip his Estella.

From John Irving, "The King of the Novel," *Trying to Save Piggy Sneed* (New York: Ballantine Books, 1996), pp. 363-366, 369-370

not until the autumn of the following year he saw his way to a beginning. "The Christmas number has come round again" (30th of August 1863)—"it seems only yesterday that I did the last—but I am full of notions besides for the new twenty numbers. When I can clear the Christmas stone out of the road, I think I can dash into it on the grander journey." He persevered through much difficulty; which he described six weeks later, with characteristic glance at his own ways when writing, in a letter from the office of his journal. "I came here last night, to evade my usual day in the week—in fact to shirk it—and get back to Gad's for five or six consecutive days. My reason is, that I am exceedingly anxious to begin my book. I am bent upon getting to work at it. I want to prepare it for the spring; but I am determined not to begin to publish with less than five numbers done. I see my opening perfectly, with the one main line on which the story is to turn; and if I don't strike while the iron (meaning myself) is hot, I shall drift off again, and have to go through all this uneasiness once more."

He had written, after four months, very nearly three numbers, when upon a necessary rearrangement of his chapters he had to hit upon a new subject for one of them. "While I was considering" (25th of February) "what it should be, Marcus,[112] who has done an excellent cover, came to tell me of an extraordinary trade he had found out, through one of his painting requirements. I immediately went with him to Saint Giles's to look at the place, and found—what you will see." It was the establishment of Mr. Venus, preserver of animals and birds, and articulator of human bones.

The first number was launched at last, on the first of May; and after two days he wrote: "Nothing can be better than *Our Friend*, now in his thirtieth thousand, and orders flowing in fast." But between the first and second number there was a drop of five thousand, strange to say, for the larger number was again reached, and much exceeded, before the book closed. "This leaves me" (10th of June) "going round and round like a carrier-pigeon before swooping on number seven." Thus far he had held his ground; but illness came, with some other anxieties, and on the 29th of July he wrote sadly enough. "Although I have not been wanting in industry, I have been wanting in

invention, and have fallen back with the book. Looming large before me is the Christmas work, and I can hardly hope to do it without losing a number of *Our Friend*. I have very nearly lost one already, and two would take one half of my whole advance. This week I have been very unwell; am still out of sorts; and, as I know from two days' slow experience, have a very mountain to climb before I shall see the open country of my work." The three following months brought hardly more favourable report. "I have not done my number. This death of poor Leech (I suppose) has put me out woefully. Yesterday and the day before I could do nothing; seemed for the time to have quite lost the power; and am only by slow degrees getting back into the track to-day." He rallied after this, and satisfied himself for a while; but in February 1865 that formidable illness in his foot broke out which, at certain times for the rest of his life, deprived him more or less of his inestimable solace of bodily exercise. In April and May he suffered severely; and after trying the sea went abroad for more complete change. "Work and worry, without exercise, would soon make an end of me. If I were not going away now, I should break down. No one knows as I know to-day how near to it I have been."

That was the day of his leaving for France, and the day of his return brought these few hurried words. "Saturday, tenth of June, 1865. I was in the terrific Staplehurst accident yesterday, and worked for hours among the dying and dead. I was in the carriage that did not go over, but went off the line, and hung over the bridge in an inexplicable manner. No words can describe the scene.[113] I am away to Gads." Though with characteristic energy he resisted the effects upon himself of that terrible ninth of June, they were for some time evident; and, up to the day of his death on its fatal fifth anniversary, were perhaps never wholly absent. But very few complaints fell from him. "I am curiously weak—weak as if I were recovering from a long illness." "I begin to feel it more in my head. I sleep well and eat well; but I write half a dozen notes, and turn faint and sick."

The book thus begun and continued under adverse influences, though with fancy in it, descriptive power, and characters well designed, will never rank with his higher efforts. It has some pictures of a rare veracity of soul amid

MRS. LIRRIPER'S LODGINGS, CHAPTER 1

Mrs. Lirriper's Lodgings receive Major Jemmy Jackman:

D EAR dear, thirteen years have passed though it seems but yesterday since I was sitting with my glasses on at the open front parlour window one evening in August (the parlours being then vacant) reading yesterday's paper my eyes for print being poor though still I am thankful to say a long sight at a distance, when I hear a gentleman come posting across the road and up the street in a dreadful rage talking to himself in a fury and d'ing and c'ing somebody. "By George!" says he out loud and clutching his walking-stick, "I'll go to Mrs. Lirriper's. Which is Mrs. Lirriper's?" Then looking round and seeing me he flourishes his hat right off his head as if I had been the queen and he says, "Excuse the intrusion Madam, but pray Madam can you tell me at what number in this street there resides a well-known and much-respected lady by the name of Lirriper?" A little flustered though I must say gratified I took off my glasses and courtesied and said "Sir, Mrs. Lirriper is your humble servant." "Astonishing!" says he. "A million pardons! Madam, may I ask you to have the kindness to direct one of your domestics to open the door to a gentleman in search of apartments, by the name of Jackman?" I had never heard the name but a politer gentleman I never hope to see, for says he, "Madam I am shocked at your opening the door yourself to no worthier a fellow than Jemmy Jackman. After you Madam. I never precede a lady." Then he comes into the parlours and he sniffs, and he says "Hah! These are parlours! Not musty cupboards" he says "but parlours, and no smell of coal-sacks." Now my dear it having been remarked by some inimical to the whole neighbourhood that it always smells of coal-sacks which might prove a drawback to Lodgers if encouraged, I says to the Major gently though firmly that I think he is referring to Arundel or Surrey or Howard but not Norfolk. "Madam" says he "I refer to Wozenham's lower down over the way—Madam you can form no notion what Wozenham's is—Madam it is a vast coal-sack, and Miss Wozenham has the principles and manners of a female heaver—Madam from the manner in which I have heard her mention you I know she has no appreciation of a lady, and from the manner in which she has conducted herself towards me I know she has no appreciation of a gentleman—Madam

my name is Jackman—should you require any other reference than what I have already said, I name the Bank of England—perhaps you know it!" Such was the beginning of the Major's occupying the parlours and from that hour to this the same and a most obliging Lodger and punctual in all respects except one irregular which I need not particularly specify, but made up for by his being a protection and at all times ready to fill in the papers of the Assessed Taxes and Juries and that, and once collared a young man with the drawing-room clock under his coat, and once on the parapets with his own hands and blankets put out the kitchen chimney and afterwards attending the summons made a most eloquent speech against the Parish before the magistrates and saved the engine, and ever quite the gentleman though passionate. And certainly Miss Wozenham's detaining the trunks and umbrella was not in a liberal spirit though it may have been according to her rights in law or an act I would myself have stooped to, the Major being so much the gentleman that though he is far from tall he seems almost so when he has his shirt-frill out and his frock-coat on and his hat with the curly brims, and in what service he was I cannot truly tell you my dear whether Militia or Foreign, for I never heard him even name himself as Major but always simple "Jemmy Jackman" and once soon after he came when I felt it my duty to let him know that Miss Wozenham had put it about that he was no Major and I took the liberty of adding "which you are sir" his words were "Madam at any rate I am not a Minor, and sufficient for the day is the evil thereof" which cannot be denied to be the sacred truth, nor yet his military ways of having his boots with only the dirt brushed off taken to him in the front parlour every morning on a clean plate and varnishing them himself with a little sponge and a saucer and a whistle in a whisper so sure as ever his breakfast is ended, and so neat his ways that it never soils his linen which is scrupulous though more in quality than quantity, neither that nor his mustachios which to the best of my belief are done at the same time and which are as black and shining as his boots, his head of hair being a lovely white.

the lowest forms of social degradation, placed beside others of sheer falsehood and pretence amid unimpeachable social correctness, which lifted the writer to his old place; but the judgment of it on the whole must be, that it wants freshness and natural development.

DR. MARIGOLD AND TALES FOR AMERICA.

He had scarcely closed that book in September, wearied somewhat with a labour of invention which had not been so free or self-sustaining as in the old facile and fertile days, when his customary contribution to Christmas became due from him; and his fancy, let loose in a narrower field, resumed its old luxury of enjoyment. Here are notices of it from his letters. "If people at large understand a Cheap Jack, my part of the Christmas number will do well. It is wonderfully like the real thing, of course a little refined and humoured." "I do hope that in the beginning and end of this Christmas number you will find something that will strike you as being fresh, forcible, and full of spirits." He described its mode of composition afterwards. "Tired with *Our Mutual*, I sat down to cast about for an idea, with a depressing notion that I was, for the moment, overworked. Suddenly, the little character that you will see, and all belonging to it, came flashing up in the most cheerful manner, and I had only to look on and leisurely describe it." This was *Dr. Marigold's Prescriptions*, one of the most popular of all the pieces selected for his readings, and a splendid example of his humour, pathos, and character.

There were three more Christmas pieces before he made his last visit to America: *Barbox Brothers*, *The Boy at Mugby Station*, and *No Thoroughfare*: the last a joint piece of work with Mr. Wilkie Collins, who during Dickens's absence in the States transformed it into a play for Mr. Fechter, with a view to which it had been planned originally. There were also two papers written for first publication in America, *George Silverman's Explanation*, and *Holiday Romance*, containing about the quantity of half a shilling number of his ordinary serials, and paid for at a rate unexampled in literature. They occupied him not many days in the writing, and he received a thousand pounds for them.

The year after his return, as the reader knows, saw the commencement of the work which death interrupted. The fragment will hereafter be described; and here meanwhile may close my criticism—itself a fragment left for worthier completion by a stronger hand than mine.

But at least I may hope that the ground has been cleared by it from those distinctions and comparisons never safely to be applied to an original writer, and which always more or less intercept his fair appreciation. It was long the fashion to set up wide divergences between novels of incident and manners, and novels of character; the narrower range being left to Fielding and Smollett, and the larger to Richardson; yet there are not many now who will accept such classification. Nor is there more truth in other like distinctions alleged between novelists who are assumed to be real, or ideal, in their methods of treatment. To any original novelist of the higher grade there is no meaning in these contrasted phrases. Neither mode can exist at all perfectly without the other. No matter how sensitive the mind to external impressions, or how keen the observation to whatever can be seen, without the rarer seeing of imagination nothing will be arrived at that is real in any genuine artist-sense.

The something "from above" never seems to be absent from Dickens, even at his worst. When the strain upon his invention became apparent, and he could only work freely in a more confined space than of old, it was still able to assert itself triumphantly; and his influence over his readers was continued by it to the last day of his life. Looking back over the series of his writings, the first reflection that rises to the mind of any thoughtful person, is one of thankfulness that the most popular of writers, who had carried into the lowest scenes and conditions an amount of observation, fun, and humour not approached by any of his contemporaries, should never have sullied that world-wide influence by a hint of impurity or a possibility of harm. Nor is there anything more surprising than the freshness and variety of character which those writings include, within the range of the not numerous types of character that were the limit of their author's genius.

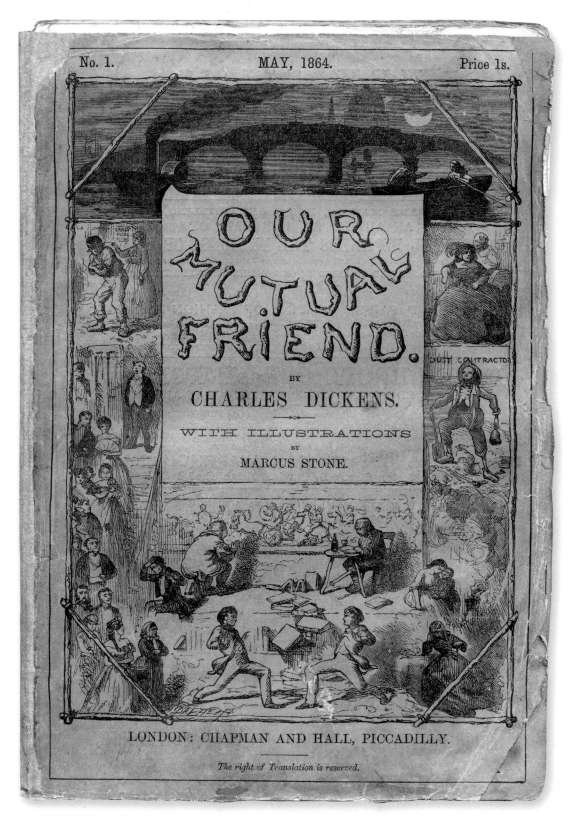

The first monthly part of *Our Mutual Friend*, with illustrations by Marcus Stone, May 1864

Our Mutual Friend, Book 1, Chapter 1

In this, another iconic opening London scene, Dickens introduces Gaffer Hexam's ghastly work, angling for corpses:

———⊶⊷⊷———

IN these times of ours, though concerning the exact year there is no need to be precise, a boat of dirty and disreputable appearance, with two figures in it, floated on the Thames, between Southwark bridge which is of iron, and London Bridge which is of stone, as an autumn evening was closing in.

The figures in this boat were those of a strong man with ragged grizzled hair and a sun-browned face, and a dark girl of nineteen or twenty, sufficiently like him to be recognizable as his daughter. The girl rowed, pulling a pair of sculls very easily; the man, with the rudder-lines slack in his hands, and his hands loose in his waistband, kept an eager look out. He had no net, hook, or line, and he could not be a fisherman; his boat had no cushion for a sitter, no paint, no inscription, no appliance beyond a rusty boathook and a coil of rope, and he could not be a waterman; his boat was too crazy and too small to take in cargo for delivery, and he could not be a lighterman or river-carrier; there was no clue to what he looked for, but he looked for something, with a most intent and searching gaze. The tide, which had turned an hour before, was running down, and his eyes watched every little race and eddy in its broad sweep, as the boat made slight headway against it, or drove stern foremost before it, according as he directed his daughter by a movement of his head. She watched his face as earnestly as he watched the river. But, in the intensity of her look there was a touch of dread or horror.

Allied to the bottom of the river rather than the surface, by reason of the slime and ooze with which it was covered, and its sodden state, this boat and the two figures in it obviously were doing something that they often did, and were seeking what they often sought. Half savage as the man showed, with no covering on his matted head, with his brown arms bare to between the elbow and the shoulder, with the loose knot of a looser kerchief lying low on his bare breast in a wilderness of beard and whisker, with

such dress as he wore seeming to be made out of the mud that begrimed his boat, still there was a business-like usage in his steady gaze. So with every lithe action of the girl, with every turn of her wrist, perhaps most of all with her look of dread or horror; they were things of usage.

'Keep her out, Lizzie. Tide runs strong here. Keep her well afore the sweep of it.'

Trusting to the girl's skill and making no use of the rudder, he eyed the coming tide with an absorbed attention. So the girl eyed him. But, it happened now, that a slant of light from the setting sun glanced into the bottom of the boat, and, touching a rotten stain there which bore some resemblance to the outline of a muffled human form, coloured it as though with diluted blood. This caught the girl's eye, and she shivered.

'What ails you?' said the man, immediately aware of it, though so intent on the advancing waters; 'I see nothing afloat.'

The red light was gone, the shudder was gone, and his gaze, which had come back to the boat for a moment, travelled away again. Wheresoever the strong tide met with an impediment, his gaze paused for an instant. At every mooring-chain and rope, at every stationery boat or barge that split the current into a broad-arrowhead, at the offsets from the piers of Southwark Bridge, at the paddles of the river steamboats as they beat the filthy water, at the floating logs of timber lashed together lying off certain wharves, his shining eyes darted a hungry look. After a darkening hour or so, suddenly the rudder-lines tightened in his hold, and he steered hard towards the Surrey shore.

Always watching his face, the girl instantly answered to the action in her sculling; presently the boat swung round, quivered as from a sudden jerk, and the upper half of the man was stretched out over the stern.

OUR MUTUAL FRIEND, BOOK 1, CHAPTER 7

Mr. Venus's Shop:

IT being one of Mr Wegg's guiding rules in life always to partake, he says he will. But, the little shop is so excessively dark, is stuck so full of black shelves and brackets and nooks and corners, that he sees Mr Venus's cup and saucer only because it is close under the candle, and does not see from what mysterious recess Mr Venus produces another for himself until it is under his nose. Concurrently, Wegg perceives a pretty little dead bird lying on the counter, with its head drooping on one side against the rim of Mr Venus's saucer, and a long stiff wire piercing its breast. As if it were Cock Robin, the hero of the ballad, and Mr Venus were the sparrow with his bow and arrow, and Mr Wegg were the fly with his little eye.

Mr Venus dives, and produces another muffin, yet untoasted; taking the arrow out of the breast of Cock Robin, he proceeds to toast it on the end of that cruel instrument. When it is brown, he dives again and produces butter, with which he completes his work.

Mr Wegg, as an artful man who is sure of his supper by-and-bye, presses muffin on his host to soothe him into a compliant state of mind, or, as one might say, to grease his works. As the muffins disappear, little by little, the black shelves and nooks and corners begin to appear, and Mr Wegg gradually acquires an imperfect notion that over against him on the chimney-piece is a Hindoo baby in a bottle, curved up with his big head tucked under him, as he would instantly throw a summersault if the bottle were large enough.

When he deems Mr Venus's wheels sufficiently lubricated, Mr Wegg approaches his object by asking, as he lightly taps his hands together, to express an undesigning frame of mind:

'And how have I been going on, this long time, Mr Venus?'

'Very bad,' says Mr Venus, uncompromisingly.

'What? Am I still at home?' asks Wegg, with an air of surprise.

'Always at home.'

This would seem to be secretly agreeable to Wegg, but he veils his feelings, and observes, 'Strange. To what do you attribute it?'

'I don't know,' replies Venus, who is a haggard melancholy man, speaking in a weak voice of querulous complaint, 'to what to attribute it, Mr Wegg. I can't work you into a miscellaneous one, no how. Do what I will, you can't be got to fit. Anybody with a passable knowledge would pick you out at a look, and say,—"No go! Don't match!"'

'Well, but hang it, Mr Venus,' Wegg expostulates with some little irritation, 'that can't be personal and peculiar in ME. It must often happen with miscellaneous ones.'

'With ribs (I grant you) always. But not else. When I prepare a miscellaneous one, I know beforehand that I can't keep to nature, and be miscellaneous with ribs, because every man has his own ribs, and no other man's will go with them; but elseways I can be miscellaneous. I have just sent home a Beauty—a perfect Beauty—to a school of art. One leg Belgian, one leg English, and the pickings of eight other people in it. Talk of not being qualified to be miscellaneous! By rights you OUGHT to be, Mr Wegg.'

Silas looks as hard at his one leg as he can in the dim light, and after a pause sulkily opines 'that it must be the fault of the other people. Or how do you mean to say it comes about?' he demands impatiently.

'I don't know how it comes about. Stand up a minute. Hold the light.' Mr Venus takes from a corner by his chair, the bones of a leg and foot, beautifully pure, and put together with exquisite neatness. These he compares with Mr Wegg's leg; that gentleman looking on, as if he were being measured for a riding-boot. 'No, I don't know how it is, but so it is. You have got a twist in that bone, to the best of my belief. I never saw the likes of you.'

Mr. Wegg having looked distrustfully at his own limb, and suspiciously at the pattern with which it has been compared, makes the point:

'I'll bet a pound that ain't an English one!'

'An easy wager, when we run so much into foreign! No, it belongs to that French gentleman.'

As he nods towards a point of darkness behind Mr. Wegg, the latter, with a slight start, looks round for 'that French gentleman,' whom he at length descries to be represented (in a very workmanlike manner) by his ribs only, standing on a shelf in another corner, like a piece of armour or a pair of stays.

'Oh!' says Mr. Wegg, with a sort of sense of being introduced; 'I dare say you were all right enough in your own country, but I hope no objections will be taken to my saying that the Frenchman was never yet born as I should wish to match.'

At this moment the greasy door is violently pushed inward, and a boy follows it, who says, after having let it slam:

'Come for the stuffed canary.'

'It's three and ninepence,' returns Venus; 'have you got the money?'

The boy produces four shillings. Mr. Venus, always in exceedingly low spirits and making whimpering sounds, peers about for the stuffed canary. On his taking the can-dle to assist his search, Mr. Wegg observes that he has a convenient little shelf near his knees, exclusively appropriated to skeleton hands, which have very much the appearance of wanting to lay hold of him. From these Mr. Venus rescues the canary in a glass case, and shows it to the boy.

'There!' he whimpers. 'There's animation! On a twig, making up his mind to hop! Take care of him; he's a lovely specimen.-And three is four.'

The boy gathers up his change and has pulled the door open by a leather strap nailed to it for the purpose, when Venus cries out:

'Stop him! Come back, you young villain! You've got a tooth among them halfpence.'

'How was I to know I'd got it? You giv it me. I don't want none of your teeth; I've got enough of my own.' So the boy pipes, as he selects it from his change, and throws it on the counter.

'Don't sauce ME, in the wicious pride of your youth,' Mr. Venus retorts pathetically.' Don't hit ME because you see I'm down. I'm low enough without that. It dropped into the till, I suppose. They drop into everything. There was two in the coffee-pot at breakfast time. Molars.'

Mr. Venus's Shop, illustration by Marcus Stone, 1865

CHARLES DICKENS'S
DRAMATIC READINGS
AS READ IN AMERICA.

DOCTOR MARIGOLD.

BOSTON:
LEE & SHEPARD, Publishers.
1876.

American edition of Dickens's reading text of *Doctor Marigold*, 1876

What kind of work it has been in his case, the attempt is made in preceding pages to show; and on the whole it can be said with some certainty that the best ideals in this sense are obtained, not by presenting with added comeliness or grace the figures which life is ever eager to present as of its best, but by connecting the singularities and eccentricities, which ordinary life is apt to reject or overlook, with the appreciation that is deepest and the laws of insight that are most universal. It is thus that all things human are happily brought within human sympathy. It was at the heart of everything Dickens wrote. It was the secret of the hope he had that his books might help to make people better; and it so guarded them from evil, that there is scarcely a page of the thousands he has written which might not be put into the hands of a little child.[114] It made him the intimate of every English household, and a familiar friend wherever the language is spoken whose stores of harmless pleasure he has so largely increased.

Engraving from *The Period: An Illustrated Review of What is Going On.*
"Our Mutual Friend," 1869

"The loss of no single man during the present generation, if we except Abraham Lincoln alone," said Mr. Horace Greeley, describing the profound and universal grief of America at his death, "has carried mourning into so many families, and been so unaffectedly lamented through all the ranks of society." "The terrible news from England," wrote Longfellow to me (Cambridge, Mass. 12th of June 1870), "fills us all with inexpressible sadness. Dickens was so full of life that it did not seem possible he could die, and yet he has gone before us, and we are sorrowing for him. . . . I never knew an author's death cause such general mourning. It is no exaggeration to say that this whole country is stricken with grief . . ." Nor was evidence then wanting, that far beyond the limits of society on that vast continent the English writer's influence had penetrated.

[107] I hope my readers will find themselves able to understand that, as well as this which follows: "What seems preposterous, impossible to us, seemed to him simple fact of observation. When he imagined a street, a house, a room, a figure, he saw it not in the vague schematic way of ordinary imagination, but in the sharp definition of actual perception, all the salient details obtruding themselves on his attention. He, seeing it thus vividly, made us also see it; and believing in its reality however fantastic, he communicated something of his belief to us. He presented it in such relief that we ceased to think of it as a picture. So definite and insistent was the image, that even while knowing it was false we could not help, for a moment, being affected, as it were, by his hallucination."

[108] Mr. Grant White, whose edition of Shakespeare has been received with much respect in England.

[109] A dear friend now gone, used laughingly to relate what outcry there used to be, on the night of the week when a number was due, for "that Pip nonsense!" and what roars of laughter followed, though at first it was entirely put aside as not on any account to have time wasted over it.

[110] There was no Chapter xx. as now; but the sentence which opens it ("For eleven years" in the original, altered to "eight years") followed the paragraph about his business partnership with Herbert, and led to Biddy's question whether he is sure he does not fret for Estella ("I am sure and certain, Biddy" as originally written, altered to "O no—I think not, Biddy"): from which point here was the close. "It was two years more, before I saw herself. I had heard of her as leading a most unhappy life, and as being separated from her husband who had used her with great cruelty, and who had become quite renowned as a compound of pride, brutality, and meanness. I had heard of the death of her husband (from an accident consequent on ill-treating a horse), and of her being married again to a Shropshire doctor, who, against his interest, had once very manfully interposed, on an occasion when he was in professional attendance on Mr. Drummle, and had witnessed some outrageous treatment of her. I had heard that the Shropshire doctor was not rich, and that they lived on her own personal fortune. I was in England again—in London, and walking along Piccadilly with little Pip—when a servant came running after me to ask would I step back to a lady in a carriage who wished to speak to me. It was a little pony carriage, which the lady was driving; and the lady and I looked sadly enough on one another. 'I am greatly changed, I know; but I thought you would like to shake hands with Estella too, Pip. Lift up that pretty child and let me kiss it!' (She supposed the child, I think, to be my child.) I was very glad afterwards to have had the interview; for, in her face and in her voice, and in her touch, she gave me the assurance, that suffering had been stronger than Miss Havisham's teaching, and had given her a heart to understand what my heart used to be."

[111] On this reproach, from a Jewish lady whom he esteemed, he had written two years before. "Fagin, in *Oliver Twist*, is a Jew, because it unfortunately was true, of the time to which that story refers, that that class of criminal almost invariably was a Jew. But surely no sensible man or woman of your persuasion can fail to observe—firstly, that all the rest of the wicked dramatis personæ are Christians; and, secondly, that he is called 'The Jew,' not because of his religion, but because of his race."

[112] Mr. Marcus Stone had, upon the separate issue of the *Tale of Two Cities*, taken the place of Mr. Hablot Browne as his illustrator. *Hard Times* and the first edition of *Great Expectations* were not illustrated; but when Pip's story appeared in one volume, Mr. Stone contributed designs for it.

[113] He thus spoke of it in his "Postscript in lieu of Preface" (dated 2nd of September 1865), which accompanied the last number of the story under notice. "On Friday the ninth of June in the present year, Mr. and Mrs. Boffin (in their manuscript dress of receiving Mr. and Mrs. Lammle at breakfast) were on the South-Eastern Railway with me, in a terribly destructive accident. When I had done what I could to help others, I climbed back into my carriage—nearly turned over a viaduct, and caught aslant upon the turn—to extricate the worthy couple. They were much soiled, but otherwise unhurt. The same happy result attended Miss Bella Wilfer on her wedding-day, and Mr. Riderhood inspecting Bradley Headstone's red neckerchief as he lay asleep. I remember with devout thankfulness that I can never be much nearer parting company with my readers for ever, than I was then, until there shall be written against my life the two words with which I have this day closed this book—THE END."

[114] I borrow this language from the Bishop of Manchester, who, on the third day after Dickens's death, in the Abbey where he was so soon to be laid, closed a plea for the toleration of differences of opinion where the foundations of religious truth are accepted, with these words. "It will not be out of harmony with the line of thought we have been pursuing—certainly it will be in keeping with the associations of this place, dear to Englishmen, not only as one of the proudest Christian temples, but as containing the memorials of so many who by their genius in arts, or arms, or statesmanship, or literature, have made England what she is—if in the simplest and briefest words I allude to that sad and unexpected death which has robbed English literature of one of its highest living ornaments, and the news of which, two mornings ago, must have made every household in England feel as though they had lost a personal friend. He has been called in one notice an apostle of the people. I suppose it is meant that he had a mission, but in a style and fashion of his own; a gospel, a cheery, joyous, gladsome message, which the people understood, and by which they could hardly help being bettered; for it was the gospel of kindliness, of brotherly love, of sympathy in the widest sense of the word. I am sure I have felt in myself the healthful spirit of his teaching. Possibly we might not have been able to subscribe to the same creed in relation to God, but I think we should have subscribed to the same creed in relation to man. He who has taught us our duty to our fellow men better than we knew it before, who knew so well to weep with them that wept, and to rejoice with them that rejoiced, who has shown forth in all his knowledge of the dark corners of the earth how much sunshine may rest upon the lowliest lot, who had such evident sympathy with suffering, and such a natural instinct of purity that there is scarcely a page of the thousands he has written which might not be put into the hands of a little child, must be regarded by those who recognise the diversity of the gifts of the spirit as a teacher sent from God. He would have been welcomed as a fellow-labourer in the common interests of humanity by Him who asked the question 'If a man love not his brother whom he hath seen, how can he love God whom he hath not seen?'"

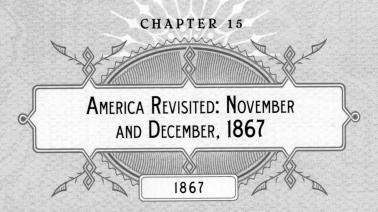

CHAPTER 15

AMERICA REVISITED: NOVEMBER AND DECEMBER, 1867

1867

IT IS THE INTENTION of this and the following chapter to narrate the incidents of the visit to America in Dickens's own language, and in that only. They will consist almost exclusively of extracts from his letters written home, to members of his family and to myself.

On the night of Tuesday the 19th of November he arrived at Boston, where he took up his residence at the Parker House hotel; and his first letter (21st) stated that the tickets for the first four Readings, all to that time issued, had been sold immediately on their becoming saleable. "An immense train of people waited in the freezing street for twelve hours, and passed into the office in their turns, as at a French theatre. The receipts already taken for these nights exceed our calculation by more than £250."

"Even in England," said one of the New York journals, "Dickens is less known than here; and of the millions here who treasure every word he has written, there are tens of thousands who would make a large sacrifice to see and hear the man who has made happy so many hours. Whatever sensitiveness there once was to adverse or sneering criticism, the lapse of a quarter of a century, and the profound significance of a great war, have modified or removed." The point was more pithily, and as truly, put by Mr. Horace Greeley in the *Tribune*. "The fame as a novelist which Mr. Dickens had already created in America, and which, at the best, has never yielded him anything particularly munificent or substantial, is become his capital stock in the present enterprise."

The first Reading was appointed for the second of December, and in the interval he saw some old friends and made some new ones.[115] Boston he was fond of comparing to Edinburgh as Edinburgh was in the days when

several dear friends of his own still lived there. Twenty-five years had changed much in the American city; some genial faces were gone, and on ground which he had left a swamp he found now the most princely streets; but there was no abatement of the old warmth of kindness, and, with every attention and consideration shown to him, there was no intrusion.

On Monday the second of December he read for the first time in Boston, his subjects being the *Carol* and the *Trial from Pickwick*; and his reception, from an audience than which perhaps none more remarkable could have been brought together, went beyond all expectations formed. "It is really impossible," he wrote to me next morning, "to exaggerate the magnificence of the reception or the effect of the reading. The whole city will talk of nothing else and hear of nothing else to-day. Every ticket for those announced here, and in New York, is sold. All are sold at the highest price, for which in our calculation we made no allowance; and it is impossible to keep out speculators who immediately sell at a premium. At the decreased rate of money even, we had above £450 English in the house last night; and the New York hall holds 500 people more. Everything looks brilliant beyond the most sanguine hopes, and I was quite as cool last night as though I were reading at Chatham." The next night he read again; and also on Thursday and Friday; on Wednesday he had rested; and on Saturday he travelled to New York.

He had written, the day before he left, that he was making a clear profit of thirteen hundred pounds English a week, even allowing seven dollars to the pound. "The work is of course rather trying too; but the sound position that everything must be subservient to it enables me to keep aloof from invitations. To-morrow," ran the close of the letter, "we move to New York. We cannot beat the speculators in our tickets. We sell no more than six to any one person for the course of four readings; but these speculators, who sell at greatly increased prices and make large profits, will employ any number of men to buy. One of the chief of them—now living in this house, in order that he may move as we move!—can put on 50 people in any place we go to; and thus he gets 300 tickets into his own hands." Almost while Dickens was writing these words an eye-witness was describing to a

Buying tickets for the Dickens readings at Steinway Hall, Boston, Massachusetts, *Harper's Weekly*, December 28, 1867

Philadelphia paper the sale of the New York tickets. The pay-place was to open at nine on a Wednesday morning, and at midnight of Tuesday a long line of speculators were assembled in *queue*; at two in the morning a few honest buyers had begun to arrive; at five there were, of all classes, two lines of not less than 800 each; at eight there were at least 5000 persons in the two lines; at nine each line was more than three-quarters of a mile in length, and neither became sensibly shorter during the whole morning. "The tickets for the course were all sold before noon. Members of families relieved each other in the *queues*; waiters flew across the streets and squares from the neighbouring restaurant, to serve parties who were taking their breakfast in the open December air; while excited men offered five and ten dollars for the mere permission to exchange places with other persons standing nearer the head of the line!"

The effect of the reading in New York corresponded with this marvellous preparation, and Dickens characterised his audience as an unexpected support to him; in its appreciation quick and unfailing, and highly demonstrative in its satisfactions. On the 11th of December he wrote to his daughter: "Amazing success. A very fine audience, far better than at Boston. *Carol* and *Trial* on first night, great: still greater, *Copperfield* and *Bob Sawyer* on second. For the tickets of the four readings of next week there were, at nine o'clock this morning, 3000 people in waiting, and they had begun to assemble in the bitter cold as early as two o'clock in the morning." To myself he wrote on the 15th, adding touches to the curious picture. "Dolby has got into trouble about the manner of issuing the tickets for next week's series. He cannot get four thousand people into a room holding only two thousand, he cannot induce people to pay at the ordinary price for themselves instead of giving thrice as much to speculators, and he is attacked in all directions . . . I don't much like my hall, for it has two large balconies far removed from the platform; but no one ever waylays me as I go into it or come out of it, and it is kept as rigidly quiet as the Francais at a rehearsal. We have not yet had in it less than £430 per night, allowing for the depreciated currency! I send £3000 to England by this packet. From all parts of the States, applications and offers continually come in. We go to Boston next Saturday for two more readings, and come back here on Christmas Day for four more. I am not yet bound to go elsewhere, except three times (each time for two nights) to Philadelphia; thinking it wisest to keep free for the largest places.

Dolby hopes you are satisfied with the figures so far; the profit each night exceeding the estimated profit by £130 odd. He is anxious I should also tell you that he is the most unpopular and best-abused man in America."

Dickens had been a week in New York before he was able to identify the great city which a lapse of twenty-five years had so prodigiously increased. "The only portion that has even now come back to me," he wrote, "is the part of Broadway in which the Carlton Hotel (long since destroyed)

used to stand. There is a very fine new park in the outskirts, and the number of grand houses and splendid equipages is quite surprising. There are hotels close here with 500 bedrooms and I don't know how many boarders; but this hotel is quite as quiet as, and not much larger than, Mivart's in Brook Street. My rooms are all en suite, and I come and go by a private door and private staircase communicating with my bed-room. The waiters are French, and one might be living in Paris.

He had got through half of his first New York readings when a winter storm came on, and from this time until very near his return the severity of the weather was exceptional even for America. When the first snow fell, the railways were closed for some days; and he described New York crowded with sleighs, and the snow piled up in enormous walls the whole length of the streets. "I turned out in a rather gorgeous sleigh yesterday with any quantity of buffalo robes, and made an imposing appearance." "If you were to behold me driving out," he wrote to his daughter, "furred up to the moustache, with an immense white red-and-yellow-striped rug for a covering, you would suppose

Fairmount Waterworks on the Schuylkill River, Philadelphia, Pa., 1853

me to be of Hungarian or Polish nationality." These protections nevertheless availed him little; and when the time came for getting back to Boston, he found himself at the close of his journey with a cold and cough that never again left him until he had quitted the country, and of which the effects became more and more disastrous. For the present there was little allusion to this, his belief at the first being strong that he should overmaster it; but it soon forced itself into all his letters.

A letter to his sister-in-law told of personal attentions awaiting him on his return to Boston by which he was greatly touched. He found his rooms garnished with flowers and holly, with real red berries, and with festoons of moss; and the homely Christmas look of the place quite affected him.

It is right to add what was said to me a few days later. "The *Tribune* is an excellent paper. Horace Greeley is editor in chief, and a considerable shareholder too. All the people connected with it whom I have seen are of the best class. It is also, a very fine property—but here the *New York Herald* beats it hollow, hollow, hollow! Another able and well edited paper is the *New York Times*. A most respectable journal too is Bryant's *Evening Post*, excellently written. There is generally a much more responsible and respectable tone than prevailed formerly, however small may be the literary merit, among papers pointed out to me as of large circulation. In much of the writing there is certainly improvement, but it might be more widely spread."

The time had now come when the course his Readings were to take independently of the two leading cities must be settled, and the general tour made out. "This will include, East here—the two or three best New England towns; South—Baltimore and Washington; West—Cincinnati, Pittsburgh, Chicago, and St. Louis; and towards Niagara—Cleveland and Buffalo. Philadelphia we are already pledged to, for six nights; and the scheme will pretty easily bring us here again twice before the farewells. I feel convinced that this is the sound policy." (It was afterwards a little modified, as will be seen, by public occurrences and his own condition of health; the West, as well as a promise to Canada, having to be abandoned; but otherwise it was carried out.)

Dickens read at Boston on the 23rd and the 24th of December, and on Christmas day travelled back to New York where he was to read on the 26th. The last words written before he left were of illness. "The low action of the heart, or whatever it is, has inconvenienced me greatly this last week. On Monday night, after the reading, I was laid upon a bed, in a very faint and shady state; and on the Tuesday I did not get up till the afternoon."

His stronger will prevailed, and he went on without stopping. On the last day of the year he announced to us that though he had been very low he was getting right again; that in a couple of days he should have accomplished a fourth of the entire Readings; and that the first month of the new year would see him through Philadelphia and Baltimore, as well as through two more nights in Boston. He also prepared his English friends for the startling intelligence they might shortly expect, of four readings coming off in a church, before an audience of two thousand people accommodated in pews, and with himself emerging from a vestry.

---

[115] Among these I think he was most delighted with the great naturalist and philosopher, Agassiz, whose death is unhappily announced while I write, and as to whom it will no longer be unbecoming to quote his allusion. "Agassiz, who married the last Mrs. Felton's sister, is not only one of the most accomplished but the most natural and jovial of men." Again he says: "I cannot tell you how pleased I was by Agassiz, a most charming fellow, or how I have regretted his seclusion for a while by reason of his mother's death." A valued correspondent, Mr. Grant Wilson, sends me a list of famous Americans who greeted Dickens at his first visit, and in the interval had passed away. "It is melancholy to contemplate the large number of American authors who had, between the first and second visits of Mr. Dickens, 'gone hence, to be no more seen.' The sturdy Cooper, the gentle Irving, his friend and kinsman Paulding, Prescott the historian and Percival the poet, the eloquent Everett, Nathaniel Hawthorne, Edgar A. Poe, N. P. Willis, the genial Halleck, and many lesser lights, including Prof. Felton and Geo. P. Morris, had died during the quarter of a century that elapsed between Dickens's visits to this country, leaving a new generation of writers to extend the hand of friendship to him on his second coming."—Let me add to this that Dickens was pleased, at this second visit, to see his old secretary who had travelled so agreeably with him through his first tour of triumph. "He would have known him anywhere."

CHAPTER 16

AMERICA REVISITED: JANUARY TO APRIL, 1868

1868

THE READING ON THE THIRD OF JANUARY closed a fourth of the entire series, and on that day Dickens wrote of the trouble brought on them by the "speculators," which to some extent had affected unfavourably the three previous nights in New York. When adventurers buy up the best places, the public resent it by refusing the worst; to prevent it by first helping themselves, being the last thing they ever think of doing. "We try to withhold the best seats from the speculators, but the unaccountable thing is that the great mass of the public buy of them (prefer it), and the rest of the public are injured if we have not got those very seats to sell them. We have now a travelling staff of six men, in spite of which Dolby, who is leaving me to-day to sell tickets in Philadelphia to-morrow morning, will no doubt get into a tempest of difficulties. You may get an idea of the staff's work, by what is in hand now. They are preparing, numbering, and stamping, 6000 tickets for Philadelphia, and 8000 tickets for Brooklyn. The moment those are done, another 8000 tickets will be wanted for Baltimore, and probably another 6000 for Washington; and all this in addition to the correspondence, advertisements, accounts, travelling, and the nightly business of the Readings four times a week. . . . I cannot get rid of this intolerable cold!"

The day after (the 4th) he went back to Boston, and next day wrote to me: "I am to read here on Monday and Tuesday, return to New York on Wednesday, and finish there (except the farewells in April) on Thursday and Friday. The New York reading of *Doctor Marigold* made really a tremendous hit. The people doubted at first, having evidently not the least idea what could be done with it, and broke out at last into a perfect chorus of delight. At the end they made

a great shout, and gave a rush towards the platform as if they were going to carry me off. It puts a strong additional arrow into my quiver. Another extraordinary success has been *Nickleby* and *Boots at the Holly Tree* (appreciated here in Boston, by the bye, even more than *Copperfield*); and think of our last New York night bringing £500 English into the house, after making more than the necessary deduction for the present price of gold!

"Well, the work is hard, the climate is hard, the life is hard: but so far the gain is enormous. My cold steadily refuses to stir an inch. It distresses me greatly at times, though it is always good enough to leave me for the needful two hours. I have tried allopathy, homoeopathy, cold things, warm things, sweet things, bitter things, stimulants, narcotics, all with the same result. Nothing will touch it."

In the same letter, light was thrown on the ecclesiastical mystery. "At Brooklyn I am going to read in Mr. Ward Beecher's chapel: the only building there available for the purpose. You must understand that Brooklyn is a kind of sleeping-place for New York, and is supposed to be a great place in the money way. We let the seats pew by pew! the pulpit is taken down for my screen and gas! and I appear out of the vestry in canonical form! These ecclesiastical entertainments come off on the evenings of the 16th, 17th, 20th, and 21st, of the present month."

His testimony as to improved social habits and ways was expressed very decidedly. "I think it reasonable to expect that as I go westward, I shall find the old manners going on before me, and may tread upon their skirts mayhap. But so far, I have had no more intrusion or boredom than I have when I lead the same life in England. I write this in an immense hotel, but I am as much at peace in my own rooms, and am left as wholly undisturbed, as if I were at the Station Hotel in York. I have now read in New York city to 40,000 people, and am quite as well known in the streets there as I am in London. People will turn back, turn again and face me, and have a look at me, or will say to one another 'Look here! Dickens coming!' But no one ever stops me or addresses me. Sitting reading in the carriage outside the New York post-office while one of the staff was stamping the letters inside, I became conscious that a few people who had been looking at the turn-out had discovered me within. On my peeping out

or they never could pet with such extraordinary pleasure as they do, the Boots' story of the elopement of the two little children. They seem to see the children; and the women set up a shrill undercurrent of half-pity and half-pleasure that is quite affecting. To-night's reading is my 26th; but as all the Philadelphia tickets for four more are sold, as well as four at Brooklyn, you must assume that I am at—say—my 35th reading. I have remitted to Coutts's in English gold £10,000 odd; and I roughly calculate that on this number Dolby will have another thousand pounds profit to pay me. These figures are of course between ourselves, at present; but are they not magnificent? The expenses, always recollect, are enormous. On the other hand we never have occasion to print a bill of any sort (bill-printing and posting are great charges at home); and have just now sold off £90 worth of bill-paper, provided beforehand, as a wholly useless incumbrance."

Baltimore and Washington were the cities in which he was now, on quitting New York, to read for the first time; and as to the latter some doubts arose. The exceptional course had been taken in regard to it, of selecting a hall with space for not more than 700 and charging everybody five dollars; to which Dickens, at first greatly opposed, had yielded upon use of the argument, "you have more people at New York, thanks to the speculators, paying more than five dollars every night." Dickens took the additional resolve so far to modify the last arrangements of his tour as to avoid the distances of Chicago, St. Louis, and Cincinnati, to content himself with smaller places and profits, and thereby to get home nearly a month earlier. He was at Philadelphia on the 23rd of January, when he announced this intention. "The worst of it is, that everybody one advises with has a monomania respecting Chicago. 'Good heavens sir,' the great Philadelphia authority said to me this morning, 'if you don't read in Chicago the people will go into fits!' Well, I answered, I would rather they went into fits than I did. But he didn't seem to see it at all."

From Baltimore he wrote to his sister-in-law on the 29th, in the hour's interval he had to spare before going back to Philadelphia. "It has been snowing hard for four and twenty hours—though this place is as far south as Valentia in Spain; and my manager, being on his way to New York,

Charles Dickens's reading desk, photograph

good-humouredly, one of them (I should say a merchant's book-keeper) stepped up to the door, took off his hat, and said in a frank way: 'Mr. Dickens, I should very much like to have the honour of shaking hands with you—and, that done, presented two others. Nothing could be more quiet or less intrusive. In the railway cars, if I see anybody who clearly wants to speak to me, I usually anticipate the wish by speaking myself. If I am standing on the brake outside (to avoid the intolerable stove), people getting down will say with a smile: 'As I am taking my departure, Mr. Dickens, and can't trouble you for more than a moment, I should like to take you by the hand sir.' And so we shake hands and go our ways. . . . Of course many of my impressions come through the readings. Thus I find the people lighter and more humorous than formerly; and there must be a great deal of innocent imagination among every class,

Impressions of Dickens's Readings by Robert Hannah, ca. 1855 (left) and ca. 1858 (right)

has a good chance of being snowed up somewhere. I go from here to Philadelphia, to read to-morrow night and Friday; come through here again on Saturday on my way back to Washington; come back here on Saturday week for two finishing nights; then go to Philadelphia for two fare-wells—and so turn my back on the southern part of the country. Our new plan will give 82 readings in all." (The real number was 76, six having been dropped on subsequent political excitements.) "Of course I afterwards discovered that we had finally settled the list on a Friday. I shall be halfway through it at Washington; of course on a Friday

also, and my birthday." To myself he wrote on the following day from Philadelphia, beginning with a thank Heaven that he had struck off Canada and the West, for he found the wear and tear "enormous."

On the fourth of February he wrote from Washington. "You may like to have a line to let you know that it is all right here, and that the croakers were simply ridiculous. I began last night. A charming audience, no dissatisfaction whatever at the raised prices, nothing missed or lost, cheers

OVERLEAF: View of Washington City, ca. 1869

 447

at the end of the *Carol*, and rounds upon rounds of applause all through. All the foremost men and their families had taken tickets for the series of four. A small place to read in. £300 in it." It will be no violation of the rule of avoiding private detail if the very interesting close of this letter is given. Its anecdote of President Lincoln was repeatedly told by Dickens after his return, and I am under no necessity to withhold from it the authority of Mr. Sumner's name. "I am going to-morrow to see the President, who has sent to me twice. I dined with Charles Sumner last Sunday, against my rule; and as I had stipulated for no party, Mr. Secretary Stanton was the only other guest, besides his own secretary. Stanton is a man with a very remarkable memory, and extraordinarily familiar with my books. . . . He and Sumner having been the first two public men at the dying President's bedside, and having remained with him until he breathed his last, we fell into a very interesting conversation after dinner, when, each of them giving his own narrative separately, the usual discrepancies about details of time were observable."

On his birthday, the seventh of February, Dickens had his interview with President Andrew Johnson. "This scrambling scribblement is resumed this morning, because I have just seen the President: who had sent to me very courteously asking me to make my own appointment. He is a man with a remarkable face, indicating courage, watchfulness, and certainly strength of purpose. It is a face of the Webster type, but without the 'bounce' of Webster's face. I would have picked him out anywhere as a character of mark. Figure, rather stoutish for an American; a trifle under the middle size; hands clasped in front of him; manner, suppressed, guarded, anxious. Each of us looked at the other very hard. . . . It was in his own cabinet that I saw him. As I came away, Thornton drove up in a sleigh—turned out for a state occasion—to deliver his credentials. There was to be a cabinet council at 12. The room was very like a London club's ante-drawing room. On the walls, two engravings only: one, of his own portrait; one, of Lincoln's."

The first reading had been four days earlier, and was described to his daughter in a letter on the 4th, with a comical incident that occurred in the course of it. "The gas was very defective indeed last night, and I began with a small speech to the effect that I must trust to the brightness of their faces for the illumination of mine. This was taken greatly. In the *Carol* a most ridiculous incident occurred. All of a sudden, I saw a dog leap out from among the seats in the centre aisle, and look very intently at me. The general attention being fixed on me, I don't think anybody saw this dog; but I felt so sure of his turning up again and barking, that I kept my eye wandering about in search of him. He was a very comic dog, and it was well for me that I was reading a comic part of the book. But when he bounced out into the centre aisle again, in an entirely new place, and (still looking intently at me) tried the effect of a bark upon my proceedings, I was seized with such a paroxysm of laughter that it communicated itself to the audience, and we roared at one another, loud and long."

What is expressed in these letters, of a still active, hopeful, enjoying, energetic spirit, able to assert itself against illness of the body and in some sort to overmaster it, was also so strongly impressed upon those who were with him, that, seeing his sufferings as they did, they yet found it difficult to understand the extent of them. The sadness thus ever underlying his triumph makes it all very tragical. "That afternoon of my birthday," he wrote from Baltimore on the 11th, "my catarrh was in such a state that Charles Sumner, coming in at five o'clock, and finding me covered with mustard poultice, and apparently voiceless, turned to Dolby and said: 'Surely, Mr. Dolby, it is impossible that he can read to-night!' Says Dolby: 'Sir, I have told Mr. Dickens so, four times to-day, and I have been very anxious. But you have no idea how he will change, when he gets to the little table.' After five minutes of the little table I was not (for the time) even hoarse. The frequent experience of this return of force when it is wanted, saves me a vast amount of anxiety; but I am not at times without the nervous dread that I may some day sink altogether."

After Baltimore he was reading again at Philadelphia, from which he wrote to his sister-in-law on the 13th as to a characteristic trait observed in both places. "Nothing will induce the people to believe in the farewells. At Baltimore on Tuesday night (a very brilliant night indeed), they asked as they came out: 'When will Mr. Dickens read here again?' 'Never.' 'Nonsense! Not come back, after such houses as these? Come. Say when he'll read again.' Just the same here. We could as soon persuade them that I am the President, as that to-morrow night I am going to read here for the last time."

On the 15th he was again at New York, in the thick of more troubles with the speculators. They involved even charges of fraud in ticket-sales at Newhaven and Providence; indignation meetings having been held by the Mayors, and unavailing attempts made by his manager to turn the wrath aside. "I expect him back here presently half bereft of his senses, and I should be wholly bereft of mine if the situation were not comical as well as disagreeable. We can sell at our own box-office to any extent; but we cannot buy back of the speculators, because we have informed the public that all the tickets are gone; and even if we made the sacrifice of buying at their price and selling at ours, we should be accused of treating with them and of making money by it." It ended in Providence by his going himself to the town and making a speech; and in Newhaven it ended by his sending back the money taken, with intimation that he would not read until there had been a new distribution of the tickets approved by all the town. Fresh disturbance broke out upon this; but he stuck to his determination to delay the reading until the heats had cooled down, and what should have been given in the middle of February he did not give until the close of March.

The Readings he had promised at the smaller outlying places by the Canadian frontier and Niagra district, including Syracuse, Rochester, and Buffalo, were appointed for that same March month which was to be the interval between the close of the ordinary readings and the farewells in the two leading cities. All that had been promised in New York were closed when he returned to Boston on the 23rd of February, ready for the increase he had promised there; but the check of a sudden political excitement came. It was the month when the vote was taken for impeachment of President Johnson. "It is well" (25th of February) "that the money has flowed in hitherto so fast, for I have a misgiving that the great excitement about the President's impeachment will damage our receipts. . . . The vote was taken at 5 last night. At 7 the three large theatres here, all in a rush of good business, were stricken with paralysis. At 8 our long line of outsiders waiting for unoccupied places, was

nowhere. To-day you hear all the people in the streets talking of only one thing. I shall suppress my next week's promised readings (by good fortune, not yet announced), and watch the course of events. Nothing in this country, as I before said, lasts long; and I think it likely that the public may be heartily tired of the President's name by the 9th of March, when I read at a considerable distance from here. So behold me with a whole week's holiday in view!"

On the 28th he wrote: "To-morrow fortnight we purpose being at the Falls of Niagara, and then we shall come back and really begin to wind up. I have got to know the *Carol* so well that I can't remember it, and occasionally go dodging about in the wildest manner, to pick up lost pieces. They took it so tremendously last night that I was stopped every five minutes. One poor young girl in mourning burst into a passion of grief about Tiny Tim, and was taken out. We had a fine house, and, in the interval while I was out, they covered the little table with flowers. The cough has taken a fresh start as if it were a novelty, and is even worse than ever to-day. There is a lull in the excitement about the President: but the articles of impeachment are to be produced this afternoon, and then it may set in again. Osgood came into camp last night from selling in remote places, and reports that at Rochester and Buffalo (both places near the frontier), tickets were bought by Canada people, who had struggled across the frozen river and clambered over all sorts of obstructions to get them. Some of those distant halls turn out to be smaller than represented; but I have no doubt—to use an American expression—that we shall 'get along.' The second half of the receipts cannot reasonably be expected to come up to the first; political circumstances, and all other surroundings, considered."

On the 13th he wrote to me from Buffalo. "We go to the Falls of Niagara to-morrow for our own pleasure; and I take all the men, as a treat. We found Rochester last Tuesday in a very curious state. Perhaps you know that the Great Falls of the Genessee River (really very fine, even so near Niagara) are at that place. In the height of a sudden thaw, an immense bank of ice above the rapids refused to yield; so that the town was threatened (for the second time in four years) with submersion. Boats were ready in the streets, all the people were up all night, and none but the children slept. In the dead of the night a thundering noise was heard, the ice gave way, the swollen river came raging and roaring down the Falls, and the town was safe. Very picturesque! but 'not very good for business,' as the manager says. Especially as the hall stands in the centre of danger, and had ten feet of water in it on the last occasion of flood. But I think we had above £200 English. On the previous night at Syracuse—a most out of the way and unintelligible-looking place, with apparently no people in it—we had £375 odd. Here, we had last night, and shall have to-night, whatever we can cram into the hall.

"'This Buffalo has become a large and important town, with numbers of German and Irish in it. But it is very curious to notice, as we touch the frontier, that the American female beauty dies out; and a woman's face clumsily compounded of German, Irish, Western America, and Canadian, not yet fused together, and not yet moulded, obtains instead. Our show of Beauty at night is, generally, remarkable; but we had not a dozen pretty women in the whole throng last night, and the faces were all blunt. I have just been walking about, and observing the same thing in the streets. . . . The winter has been so severe, that the hotel on the English side at Niagara (which has the best view of the Falls, and is for that reason very preferable) is not yet open. So we go, perforce, to the American: which telegraphs back to our telegram: 'all Mr. Dickens's requirements perfectly understood.'"

Baltimore from Federal Hill, ca. 1831

His letter was resumed at Rochester on the 18th. "After two most brilliant days at the Falls of Niagara, we got back here last night. To-morrow morning we turn out at 6 for a long railway journey back to Albany. But it is nearly all 'back' now, thank God! I don't know how long, though, before turning, we might have gone on at Buffalo. . . . We went everywhere at the Falls, and saw them in every aspect. There is a suspension bridge across, now, some two miles or more from the Horse Shoe; and another, half a mile nearer, is to be opened in July. They are very fine but very ticklish, hanging aloft there, in the continual vibration of the thundering water: nor is one greatly reassured by the printed notice that troops must not cross them at step, that bands of music must not play in crossing, and the like. I shall never forget the last aspect in which we saw Niagara yesterday. We had been everywhere, when I thought of struggling (in an open carriage) up some very difficult ground for a good distance, and getting where we could stand above the river, and see it, as it rushes forward to its tremendous leap, coming for miles and miles. All away to the horizon on our right was a wonderful confusion of bright green and white water. As we stood watching it with our faces to the top of the Falls, our backs were towards the sun. The majestic valley below the Falls, so seen through the vast cloud of spray, was made of rainbow. The high banks, the riven rocks, the forests, the bridge, the buildings, the air, the sky, were all made of

rainbow. Nothing in Turner's finest water-colour drawings, done in his greatest day, is so ethereal, so imaginative, so gorgeous in colour, as what I then beheld. I seemed to be lifted from the earth and to be looking into Heaven. What I once said to you, as I witnessed the scene five and twenty years ago, all came back at this most affecting and sublime sight. The 'muddy vesture of our clay' falls from us as we look. . . . I chartered a separate carriage for our men, so that they might see all in their own way, and at their own time.

"Last Sunday evening I left the Falls of Niagara for this and two intervening places. As there was a great thaw, and the melted snow was swelling all the rivers, the whole country for three hundred miles was flooded. On the Tuesday afternoon (I had read on the Monday) the train gave in, as under circumstances utterly hopeless, and stopped at a place called Utica; the greater part of which was under water, while the high and dry part could produce nothing particular to eat. Here, some of the wretched passengers passed the night in the train, while others stormed the hotel. I was fortunate enough to get a bed-room, and garnished it with an enormous jug of gin-punch; over which I and the manager played a double-dummy rubber. At six in the morning we

were knocked up: 'to come aboard and try it.' At half-past six we were knocked up again with the tidings 'that it was of no use coming aboard or trying it.' At eight all the bells in the town were set agoing, to summon us to 'come aboard' instantly. And so we started, through the water, at four or five miles an hour; seeing nothing but drowned farms, barns adrift like Noah's arks, deserted villages, broken bridges, and all manner of ruin. I was to read at Albany that night, and all the tickets were sold. A very active superintendent of works assured me that if I could be 'got along' he was the man to get me along: and that if I couldn't be got along, I might conclude that it couldn't possibly be fixed. He then turned on a hundred men in seven-league boots, who went ahead of the train, each armed with a long pole and pushing the blocks of ice away. Following this cavalcade, we got to land at last, and arrived in time for me to read the *Carol* and *Trial* triumphantly. My people (I had five of the staff with me) turned to at their work with a will, and did a day's labour in a couple of hours. If we had not come in as we did, I should have lost £350, and Albany would have gone distracted. You may conceive what the flood was, when I hint at the two most notable incidents of our journey:—1, We took the passengers out of two trains, who had been in the water, immovable all night and all the previous day. 2, We released a large quantity of sheep and cattle from trucks that had been in the water I don't know how long, but so long that the creatures in them had begun to eat each other, and presented a most horrible spectacle.—

Beside Springfield, he had engagements at Portland, New Bedford, and other places in Massachusetts, before the Boston farewells began; and there wanted but two days to bring him to that time, when he thus described to his daughter the labour which was to occupy them. His letter was from Portland on the 29th of March, and it will be observed that he no longer compromises or glozes over what he

Mr. Charles Dickens and his former American acquaintances "not at home," drawn by Charles Green Bush, wood engraving, 1867. Published in *Harper's Weekly*, 21 December 1867

was and had been suffering. During his terrible travel to Albany his cough had somewhat spared him, but the old illness had broken out in his foot; and, though he persisted in ascribing it to the former supposed origin ("having been lately again wet, from walking in melted snow, which I suppose to be the occasion of its swelling in the old way"), it troubled him sorely, extended now at intervals to the right foot also, and lamed him for all the time he remained in the States. "I should have written to you by the last mail, but I really was too unwell to do it. The writing day was last Friday, when I ought to have left Boston for New Bedford (55 miles) before eleven in the morning. But I was so exhausted that I could not be got up, and had to take my chance of an evening train's producing me in time to read—which it just did. With the return of snow, nine days ago, my cough became as bad as ever. I have coughed every morning from two or three till five or six, and have been absolutely sleepless. I have had no appetite besides, and no taste.[116] Last night here, I took some laudanum; and it is the only thing that has done me good, though it made me sick this morning. But the life, in this climate, is so very hard! When I did manage to get to New Bedford, I read with my utmost force and vigour. Next morning, well or ill, I must turn out at seven, to get back to Boston on my way here. I dined at Boston at three, and at five had to come on here (a hundred and thirty miles or so) for to-morrow night: there being no Sunday train. To-morrow night I read here in a very large place; and Tuesday morning at six I must again start, to get back to Boston once more. But after to-morrow night I have only the farewells, thank God! Even as it is, however, I have had to write to Dolby (who is in New York) to see my doctor there, and ask him to send me some composing medicine that I can take at night, inasmuch as without sleep I cannot get through. However sympathetic and devoted the people are about one, they CAN NOT be got to comprehend, seeing me able to do the two hours when the time comes round, that it may also involve much misery."

On the 31st he closed his letter at Boston, and he was at home when I heard of him again. "The latest intelligence, my dear old fellow, is, that I have arrived here safely, and that I am certainly better. I consider my work virtually over, now. My impression is, that the political crisis will damage the

DICKENS'S POSTSCRIPT OF 1868 TO *AMERICAN NOTES* AND *MARTIN CHUZZLEWIT*

AT a public Dinner given to me on Saturday the 18th of April, 1868, in the City of New York, by two hundred representatives of the Press of the United States of America, I made the following observations among others: 'So much of my voice has lately been heard in the land, that I might have been contented with troubling you no further from my present-standing point, were it not a duty with which I henceforth charge myself, not only here but on every suitable occasion whatsoever and wheresoever, to express my high and grateful sense of my second reception in America, and to bear my honest testimony to the national generosity and magnanimity. Also, to declare how astounded I have been by the amazing changes I have seen around me on every side,—changes moral, changes physical, changes in the amount of land subdued and peoples, changes in the rise of vast new cities, changes in the growth of older cities almost out of recognition, changes in the graces and amenities of life, changes in the Press, without whose advancement no advancement can take place anywhere. Nor am I, believe me, so arrogant as to suppose that in five-and-twenty years there have been no changes in me, an that I had nothing to learn and no extreme impressions to correct when I was here first [. . .]

farewells by about one half. I cannot yet speak by the card; but my predictions here, as to our proceedings, have thus far been invariably right. We took last night at Portland, £360 English; where a costly Italian troupe, using the same hall to-night, had not booked £14! It is the same all over the country, and the worst is not seen yet. Everything is becoming absorbed in the Presidential impeachment, helped by the next Presidential election. Connecticut is particularly excited. The night after I read at Hartford this last week, there were two political meetings in the town; meetings of two parties; and the hotel was full of speakers coming in from outlying places. So at Newhaven: the moment I had finished, carpenters came in to prepare for next night's politics. So at Buffalo. So everywhere very soon."

Dickens's last letter from America was written to his daughter Mary from Boston on the 9th of April, the day before his sixth and last farewell night. "I not only read last Friday when I was doubtful of being able to do so, but read as I never did before, and astonished the audience quite as much as myself. You never saw or heard such a scene of excitement. Longfellow and all the Cambridge men have urged me to give in. I have been very near doing so, but feel stronger to-day. I cannot tell whether the catarrh may have done me any lasting injury in the lungs or other breathing organs, until I shall have rested and got home. I hope and believe not. Did I tell you that the New York Press are going to give me a public dinner on Saturday the 18th?"

In New York, where there were five farewell nights, three thousand two hundred and ninety-eight dollars were the receipts of the last, on the 20th of April; those of the last at Boston, on the 8th, having been three thousand four hundred and fifty-six dollars. But on earlier nights in the same cities respectively, these sums also had been reached; and indeed, making allowance for an exceptional night here and there, the receipts varied so wonderfully little, that a mention of the highest average returns from other places will give no exaggerated impression of the ordinary receipts throughout. Excluding fractions of dollars, the lowest were New Bedford ($1640), Rochester ($1906), Springfield ($1970), and Providence ($2140). Albany and Worcester averaged something less than $2400; while Hartford, Buffalo, Baltimore, Syracuse, Newhaven, and Portland rose to $2600. Washington's last night was $2610, no night there having less than $2500. Philadelphia exceeded Washington by $300, and Brooklyn went ahead of Philadelphia by $200. The amount taken at the four Brooklyn readings was 11,128 dollars.

The New York public dinner was given at Delmonico's, the hosts were more than two hundred, and the chair was taken by Mr. Horace Greeley. Dickens attended with great difficulty,[117] and spoke in pain. But he used the occasion to bear his testimony to the changes of twenty-five years; the rise of vast new cities; growth in the graces and amenities of life; much improvement in the press, essential to every other advance; and changes in himself leading to opinions more deliberately formed. He promised his kindly entertainers that no copy of his *Notes*, or his *Chuzzlewit*, should in future be issued by him without accompanying mention of the changes to which he had referred that night; of the politeness, delicacy, sweet temper, hospitality, and consideration in all ways for which he had to thank them; and of his gratitude for the respect shown, during all his visit, to the privacy enforced upon him by the nature of his work and the condition of his health.

He had to leave the room before the proceedings were over. On the following Monday he read to his last American audience, telling them at the close that he hoped often to recall them, equally by his winter fire and in the green summer weather, and never as a mere public audience but as a host of personal friends. He sailed two days later in the "Russia," and reached England in the first week of May 1868.

---

[116] Here was his account of his mode of living for his last ten weeks in America. "I cannot eat (to anything like the necessary extent) and have established this system. At 7 in the morning, in bed, a tumbler of new cream and two tablespoonsful of rum. At 12, a sherry cobbler and a biscuit. At 3 (dinner time) a pint of champagne. At five minutes to 8, an egg beaten up with a glass of sherry. Between the parts, the strongest beef tea that can be made, drunk hot. At a quarter past 10, soup, and any little thing to drink that I can fancy. I do not eat more than half a pound of solid food in the whole four-and-twenty hours, if so much."

[117] Here is the newspaper account: "At about five o'clock on Saturday the hosts began to assemble, but at 5.30 news was received that the expected guest had succumbed to a painful affection of the foot. In a short time, however, another bulletin announced Mr. Dickens's intention to attend the dinner at all hazards. At a little after six, having been assisted up the stairs, he was joined by Mr. Greeley, and the hosts forming in two lines silently permitted the distinguished gentlemen to pass through. Mr. Dickens limped perceptibly; his right foot was swathed, and he leaned heavily on the arm of Mr. Greeley. He evidently suffered great pain."

CHAPTER 17

LAST READINGS

1868~1870

FAVOURABLE WEATHER HELPED HIM pleasantly home. He had profited greatly by the sea voyage, perhaps greatly more by its repose; and on the 25th of May he described himself to his Boston friends as brown beyond belief, and causing the greatest disappointment in all quarters by looking so well. "My doctor was quite broken down in spirits on seeing me for the first time last Saturday. *Good Lord! seven years younger!* said the doctor, recoiling." That he gave all the credit to "those fine days at sea," and none to the rest from such labours as he had passed through, the close of the letter too sadly showed. "We are already settling—think of this!—the details of my farewell course of readings."

Even on his way out to America that enterprise was in hand. From Halifax he had written to me. "I told the Chappells that when I got back to England, I would have a series of farewell readings in town and country; and then read No More. They at once offer in writing to pay all expenses whatever, to pay the ten per cent. for management, and to pay me, for a series of 75, six thousand pounds." The terms were raised and settled before the first Boston readings closed. The number was to be a hundred; and the payment, over and above expenses and per centage, eight thousand pounds. Such a temptation undoubtedly was great; and though it was a fatal mistake which Dickens committed in yielding to it, it was not an ignoble one. He did it under no excitement from the American gains, of which he knew nothing when he pledged himself to the enterprise. No man could care essentially less for mere money than he did. But the necessary provision for many sons was a constant anxiety; he was proud of what the Readings had done to abridge this care; and the very strain

of them under which it seems certain that his health had first given way, and which he always steadily refused to connect especially with them, had also broken the old confidence of being at all times available for his higher pursuit.

"We had great difficulty in getting our American accounts squared to the point of ascertaining what Dolby's commission amounted to in English money. After all, we were obliged to call in the aid of a money-changer, to determine what he should pay as his share of the average loss of conversion into gold. With this deduction made, I think his commission (I have not the figures at hand) was £2,888; Ticknor and Fields had a commission of £1,000, besides 5 per cent. on all Boston receipts. The expenses in America to the day of our sailing were 38,948 dollars;—roughly 39,000 dollars, or £13,000. The preliminary expenses were £614. The average price of gold was nearly 40 per cent., and yet my profit was within a hundred or so of £20,000. Supposing me to have got through the present engagement in good health, I shall have made by the Readings, *in two years*, £33,000: that is to say, £13,000 received from the Chappells, and £20,000 from America. What I had made by them before, I could only ascertain by a long examination of Coutts's books. I should say, certainly not less than £10,000: for I remember that I made half that money in the first town and country campaign with poor Arthur Smith. These figures are of course between ourselves; but don't you think them rather remarkable? The Chappell bargain began with £50 a night and everything paid; then became £60; and now rises to £80."

The last readings were appointed to begin with October; and at the request of an old friend, Chauncy Hare Townshend, who died during his absence in the States, he had accepted the trust, which occupied him some part of the summer, of examining and selecting for publication a bequest of some papers on matters of religious belief, which were issued in a small volume the following year.

He had scarcely begun these last readings than he was beset by a misgiving, that, for a success large enough to repay Messrs. Chappell's liberality, the enterprise would require a new excitement to carry him over the old ground; and it was while engaged in Manchester and Liverpool at the outset of October that this announcement came. "I have made a short reading of the murder in *Oliver Twist*. I cannot make up my mind, however, whether to do it or not. I have no doubt that I could perfectly petrify an audience by carrying out the notion I have of the way of rendering it. But whether the impression would not be so horrible as to keep them away another time, is what I cannot satisfy myself upon. What do you think?" It was impossible for me to admit that the effect to be produced was legitimate, or such as it was desirable to associate with the recollection of his readings.

Mention should not be omitted of two sorrows which affected him at this time. At the close of the month before the readings began his youngest son went forth from home to join an elder brother in Australia. "These partings are hard hard things" (26th of September), "but they are the lot of us all, and might have to be done without means or influence, and then would be far harder. God bless him!" Hardly a month later, the last of his surviving brothers, Frederick, the next to himself, died at Darlington. "He had been tended" (24th of October) "with the greatest care and affection by some local friends. It was a wasted life, but God forbid that one should be hard upon it, or upon anything in this world that is not deliberately and coldly wrong."

Before October closed the renewal of his labour had begun to tell upon him. He wrote to his sister-in-law on the 29th of sickness and sleepless nights, and of its having become necessary, when he had to read, that he should lie on the sofa all day. After arrival at Edinburgh in December he had been making a calculation that the railway travelling over such a distance involved something more than thirty thousand shocks to the nerves; but he went on to

Caricature of Charles Dickens, a sketch from memory by "Spy," 1870. Spy was the pseudonym of Sir Leslie Matthew Ward.

Christmas, alternating these far-off places with nights regularly intervening in London, without much more complaint than of an inability to sleep. Trade reverses at Glasgow had checked the success there,[118] but Edinburgh made compensation. "The affectionate regard of the people exceeds all bounds and is shown in every way. The audiences do everything but embrace me, and take as much pains with the readings as I do."

The second portion of the enterprise opened with the New Year, and the *Sikes and Nancy* scenes, everywhere his prominent subject, exacted the most terrible physical exertion from him. In January he was at Clifton, where he had given, he told his sister-in-law, "by far the best Murder yet done;" while at the same date he wrote to his daughter: "At Clifton on Monday night we had a contagion of fainting; and yet the place was not hot. I should think we had from a dozen to twenty ladies taken out stiff and rigid, at various times! It became quite ridiculous."

In the second week of February he was in London, under engagement to return to Scotland (which he had just left) after the usual weekly reading at St. James's Hall, when there was a sudden interruption. "My foot has turned lame again!" was his announcement to me on the 15th, followed next day by this letter. "Henry Thompson will not let me read to-night, and will not let me go to Scotland to-morrow. Tremendous house here, and also in Edinburgh. Here is the certificate he drew up for himself and Beard to sign. 'We the undersigned hereby certify that Mr. C. D. is suffering from inflammation of the foot (caused by over-exertion), and that we have forbidden his appearance on the platform this evening, as he must keep his room for a day or two.' I have sent up to the Great Western Hotel for apartments, and, if I can get them, shall move there this evening. Heaven knows what engagements this may involve in April! It throws us all back, and will cost me some five hundred pounds."

A few days' rest again brought so much relief, that, against the urgent entreaties of members of his family as well as other friends, he was in the railway carriage bound for Edinburgh on the morning of the 20th of February, accompanied by Mr. Chappell himself. "I came down lazily on a sofa," he wrote to me from Edinburgh next day, "hardly changing my position the whole way. The railway authorities had done all sorts of things, and I was more comfortable than on the sofa at the hotel. The foot gave me no uneasiness, and has been quiet and steady all night." He was nevertheless under the necessity, two days later, of consulting Mr. Syme; and he told his daughter that this great authority had warned him against over-fatigue in the readings, and given him some slight remedies, but otherwise reported him in "joost pairfactly splendid condition."

The whole of that March month he went on with the scenes from *Oliver Twist*. "The foot goes famously," he wrote to his daughter. "I feel the fatigue in it (four Murders in one week[119]) but not overmuch. It merely aches at night; and so does the other, sympathetically I suppose." At Hull on the 8th he heard of the death of the old and dear friend, Emerson Tennent, to whom he had inscribed his last book; and on the morning of the 12th I met him at the funeral. He had read the *Oliver Twist* scenes the night before at York; had just been able to get to the express train, after shortening the pauses in the reading, by a violent rush when it was over; and had travelled through the night. He appeared to, me "dazed" and worn. No man could well look more so than he did, that sorrowful morning.

The end was near. A public dinner, which will have mention on a later page, had been given him in Liverpool on the 10th of April, with Lord Dufferin in the chair, and a reading was due from him in Preston on the 22nd of that month. But on Sunday the 18th we had ill report of him from Chester, and on the 21st he wrote from Blackpool to his sister-in-law. "I have come to this Sea-Beach Hotel (charming) for a day's rest. I am much better than I was on Sunday; but shall want careful looking to, to get through the readings. My weakness and deadness are all on the left side; and if I don't look at anything I try to touch with my left hand, I don't know where it is. I am in (secret) consultation with Frank Beard, who says that I have given him indisputable evidences of overwork which he could wish to treat immediately; and so I have telegraphed for him. I have had a delicious walk by the sea to-day, and I sleep soundly, and have picked up amazingly in appetite. My foot is greatly better too, and I wear my own boot. To-morrow night at Warrington I shall have but 25 more nights to work through. If he can coach me up for them, I do not doubt that I shall get all right again—as I did when I became free in America."

Even to the close of that letter he had buoyed himself up with the hope that he might yet be "coached" and that the readings need not be discontinued. But Mr. Beard stopped them at once, and brought his patient to London. On Friday morning the 23rd, the same envelope brought me a note from himself to say that he was well enough, but tired; in perfectly good spirits, not at all uneasy, and writing this himself that I should have it under his own hand; with a note from his eldest son to say that his father appeared to him to be very ill, and that a consultation had been appointed with Sir Thomas Watson. The statement of that distinguished physician, sent to myself in June 1872, completes for the present the sorrowful narrative.

"It was, I think, on the 23rd of April 1869 that I was asked to see Charles Dickens, in consultation with Mr. Carr Beard. After I got home I jotted down, from their joint account, what follows.

"After unusual irritability, C. D. found himself, last Saturday or Sunday, giddy, with a tendency to go backwards, and to turn round. Afterwards, desiring to put something on a small table, he pushed it and the table forwards, undesignedly. He had some odd feeling of insecurity about his left leg, as if there was something unnatural about his heel; but he could lift, and he did not drag, his leg. Also he spoke of some strangeness of his left hand and arm; missed the spot on which he wished to lay that hand, unless he carefully looked at it; felt an unreadiness to lift his hands towards his head, especially his left hand—when, for instance, he was brushing his hair.

Poster advertising a Dickens Reading at York. It was cancelled due to the author's health.

"The state thus described showed plainly that C. D. had been on the brink of an attack of paralysis of his left side, and possibly of apoplexy. It was, no doubt, the result of extreme hurry, overwork, and excitement, incidental to his Readings.

"When I saw him he *appeared* to be well. His mind was unclouded, his pulse quiet. His heart was beating with some slight excess of the natural impulse. He told me he had of late sometimes, but rarely, lost or misused a word; that he forgot names, and numbers, but had always done that; and he promised implicit obedience to our injunctions.

"We gave him the following certificate.

"'The undersigned certify that Mr. Charles Dickens has been seriously unwell, through great exhaustion and fatigue of body and mind consequent upon his public Readings and long and frequent railway journeys. In our judgment Mr. Dickens will not be able with safety to himself to resume his Readings for several months to come.

"'Thos. Watson, M.D.'

"'F. Carr Beard.'

"However, after some weeks, he expressed a wish for my sanction to his endeavours to redeem, in a careful and moderate way, some of the reading engagements to which he had been pledged before those threatenings of brain-mischief in the North of England.

"As he had continued uniformly to seem and to feel perfectly well, I did not think myself warranted to refuse that sanction: and in writing to enforce great caution in the trials, I expressed some apprehension that he might fancy we had been too peremptory in our injunctions of mental and bodily repose in April; and I quoted the following remark, which occurs somewhere in one of Captain Cook's Voyages. 'Preventive measures are always invidious, for when most successful, the necessity for them is the least apparent.'

"I mention this to explain the letter which I send herewith, [120] and which I must beg you to return to me, as a precious remembrance of the writer with whom I had long enjoyed very friendly and much valued relations."

The twelve readings to which Sir Thomas Watson consented, with the condition that railway travel was not to accompany them, were farther to be delayed until the opening months of 1870. They were an offering from Dickens by way of small compensation to Messrs. Chappell for the breakdown of the enterprise on which they had staked so much. But here practically he finished his career as a public reader, and what remains will come with the end of what is yet to be told. One effort only intervened, by which he hoped to get happily back to his old pursuits; but to this, as to that which preceded it, sterner Fate said also No, and his Last Book, like his Last Readings, prematurely closed.

---

[118] "I think I shall be pretty correct in both places as to the run being on the Final readings. We had an immense house here" (Edinburgh, 12th of December) "last night, and a very large turnaway. But Glasgow being shady and the charges very great, it will be the most we can do, I fancy, on these first Scotch readings, to bring the Chappells safely home (as to them) without loss."

[119] I take from the letter a mention of the effect on a friend. "The night before last, unable to get in, B. had a seat behind the screen, and was nearly frightened off it, by the Murder. Every vestige of colour had left his face when I came off, and he sat staring over a glass of champagne in the wildest way."

[120] In this letter Dickens wrote: "I thank you heartily" (23rd of June, 1869) "for your great kindness and interest. It would really pain me if I thought you could seriously doubt my implicit reliance on your professional skill and advice. I feel as certain now as I felt when you came to see me on my breaking down through over fatigue, that the injunction you laid upon me to stop in my course of Readings was necessary and wise. And to its firmness I refer (humanly speaking) my speedy recovery from that moment. I would on no account have resumed, even on the turn of this year, without your sanction. Your friendly aid will never be forgotten by me; and again I thank you for it with all my heart."

CHAPTER 18

LAST BOOK

1869~1870

THE LAST BOOK UNDERTAKEN by Dickens was to be published, in illustrated monthly numbers, of the old form, but to close with the twelfth.[121] It closed, unfinished, with the sixth number, which was itself underwritten by two pages.

His first fancy for the tale was expressed in a letter in the middle of July. "What should you think of the idea of a story beginning in this way?—Two people, boy and girl, or very young, going apart from one another, pledged to be married after many years—at the end of the book. The interest to arise out of the tracing of their separate ways, and the impossibility of telling what will be done with that impending fate." This was laid aside; but it left a marked trace on the story as afterwards designed, in the position of Edwin Drood and his betrothed.

I first heard of the later design in a letter dated "Friday the 6th of August 1869," in which after speaking, with the usual unstinted praise he bestowed always on what moved him in others, of a little tale he had received for his journal,[122] he spoke of the change that had occurred to him for the new tale by himself. "I laid aside the fancy I told you of, and have a very curious and new idea for my new story. Not a communicable idea (or the interest of the book would be gone), but a very strong one, though difficult to work." The story, I learnt immediately afterward, was to be that of the murder of a nephew by his uncle; the originality of which was to consist in the review of the murderer's career by himself at the close, when its temptations were to be dwelt upon as if, not he the culprit, but some other man, were the tempted. The last chapters were to be written in the condemned cell, to which his wickedness, all elaborately elicited from him as if told of another, had brought him. Discovery by the murderer of the utter needlessness of the murder for its object, was to follow hard upon commission of the deed; but all discovery of the murderer was to be baffled till towards the close, when, by means of a gold ring which had resisted the corrosive effects of the lime into which he had thrown the body, not only the person murdered was to be identified but the locality of the crime and the man who committed it. So much was told to me before any of the book was written; and it will be recollected that the ring, taken by Drood to be given to his betrothed only if their engagement went on, was brought away with him from their last interview. Rosa was to marry Tartar, and Crisparkle the sister of Landless, who was himself, I think, to have perished in assisting Tartar finally to unmask and seize the murderer.

Nothing had been written, however, of the main parts of the design excepting what is found in the published numbers; there was no hint or preparation for the sequel in any notes of chapters in advance. "I hope his book is finished," wrote Longfellow when the news of his death was flashed to America. "It is certainly one of his most beautiful works, if not the most beautiful of all. It would be too sad to think the pen had fallen from his hand, and left it incomplete."

The last page of *Edwin Drood* was written in the Chalet in the afternoon of his last day of consciousness. His greater pains and elaboration of writing, it may be mentioned, become first very obvious in the later parts of *Martin Chuzzlewit*; but not the least remarkable feature in

"Durdles cautions Mr. Sapsea against boasting," illustration from *The Mystery of Edwin Drood*, by by Samuel Luke Fildes, engraved by Charles Roberts, 1870

EDWIN DROOD, CHAPTER 2

Edwin Drood confides in his uncle Jasper about his dissatisfaction in his arranged engagement,
not knowing that his uncle has an obsessive love for Rosa—or Pussy, as she is called here.

MR. Jasper lifts his dark eyebrows inquiringly.

'Isn't it unsatisfactory to be cut off from choice in such a matter? There, Jack! I tell you! If I could choose, I would choose Pussy from all the pretty girls in the world.'

'But you have not got to choose.'

'That's what I complain of. My dead and gone father and Pussy's dead and gone father must needs marry us together by anticipation. Why the—Devil, I was going to say, if it had been respectful to their memory—couldn't they leave us alone?'

'Tut, tut, dear boy,' Mr. Jasper remonstrates, in a tone of gentle deprecation.

'Tut, tut? Yes, Jack, it's all very well for YOU. YOU can take it easily. YOUR life is not laid down to scale, and lined and dotted out for you, like a surveyor's plan. YOU have no uncomfortable suspicion that you are forced upon anybody, nor has anybody an uncomfortable suspicion that she is forced upon you, or that you are forced upon her. YOU can choose for yourself. Life, for YOU, is a plum with the natural bloom on; it hasn't been over-carefully wiped off for YOU—'

'Don't stop, dear fellow. Go on.'

'Can I anyhow have hurt your feelings, Jack?'

'How can you have hurt my feelings?'

'Good Heaven, Jack, you look frightfully ill! There's a strange film come over your eyes.'

Mr. Jasper, with a forced smile, stretches out his right hand, as if at once to disarm apprehension and gain time to get better. After a while he says faintly:

'I have been taking opium for a pain—an agony—that sometimes overcomes me. The effects of the medicine steal over me like a blight or a cloud, and pass. You see them in the act of passing; they will be gone directly. Look away from me. They will go all the sooner.'

With a scared face the younger man complies by casting his eyes downward at the ashes on the hearth. Not relaxing his own gaze on the fire, but rather strengthening it with a fierce, firm grip upon his elbow-chair, the elder sits for a few moments rigid, and then, with thick drops standing on his forehead, and a sharp catch of his breath, becomes as he was before. On his so subsiding in his chair, his nephew gently and assiduously tends him while he quite recovers. When Jasper is restored, he lays a tender hand upon his nephew's shoulder, and, in a tone of voice less troubled than the purport of his words—indeed with something of raillery or banter in it—thus addresses him:

'There is said to be a hidden skeleton in every house; but you thought there was none in mine, dear Ned.'

all his manuscripts, is the accuracy with which the portions of each representing the several numbers are exactly adjusted to the space the printer had to fill. Whether without erasure or so interlined as to be illegible, nothing is wanting, and there is nothing in excess. So assured was the habit, that he has himself remarked upon an instance the other way, in *Our Mutual Friend*, as not having happened to him for thirty years. But *Edwin Drood* more startlingly showed him how unsettled the habit he most prized had become, in the clashing of old and new pursuits. "When I had written" (22nd of December, 1869) "and, as I thought, disposed of the first two Numbers of my story, Clowes

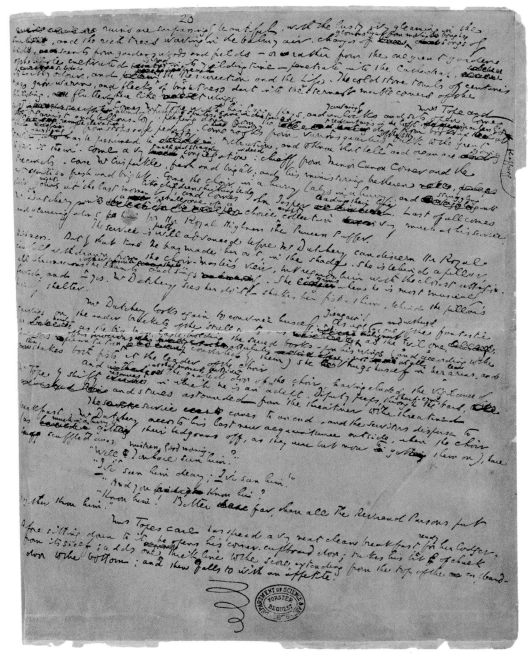

Final page of the original manuscript for *The Mystery of Edwin Drood*, written earlier on the day of
June 8, 1870, before Dickens suffered a stroke.

informed me to my horror that they were, together, *twelve printed pages too short*!!! Consequently I had to transpose a chapter from number two to number one, and remodel number two altogether! This was the more unlucky, that it came upon me at the time when I was obliged to leave the book, in order to get up the Readings" (the additional twelve for which Sir Thomas Watson's consent had been obtained), "quite gone out of my mind since I left them

PHILLIP ALLINGHAM

ALTHOUGH FORSTER CONFIDENTLY BELIEVED HE KNEW THE ENDING DICKENS INTENDED, THE JURY IS STILL OUT IN SOLVING THIS MYSTERY. SINCE DICKENS'S DEATH THERE HAS BEEN AN UNCEASING WEALTH OF THEORIES AND RESPONSES, INCLUDING A TRIAL OF JOHN JASPER (1913), IN WHICH G. K. CHESTERTON PRESIDED AS JUDGE, WITH GEORGE BERNARD SHAW AS FOREMAN OF THE JURY. PHILIP ALLINGHAM SUMMARIZES SOME EARLY DRAMATIC SOLUTIONS:

Post-modernism may have a penchant for ambiguity that often manifests itself in the indeterminate ending, which compels the reader to assume the role of author in order to bring closure to the narrative, but the cinema and the stage find such ambiguity highly unsatisfactory. Hence a number of playwrights, including Dickens's own son, Charles, determined to solve the mystery. Where they left off in the early twentieth century is the starting point for the film adaptations of *The Mystery of Edwin Drood*, some of which borrow heavily from these early dramatizations. On 4 November 1871, in Walter Stephens' dramatic adaptation of the novel for London's Surrey Theatre, John Jasper murdered his nephew and was then tracked by Datchery, who turned out to be Helena Landless in disguise. Like the brutal villain Jonas Chuzzlewit in the 1843 Dickens novel *Martin Chuzzlewit*, the more subtle Jasper poisoned himself rather than face a trial, incarceration, and capital punishment for his crime. The following year, on 22 July at the Britannia Theatre, London, in G. H. Macdermott's adaptation, the detective Datchery turned out to be Bazzard, the sardonic clerk of the lawyer, Mr. Grewgious, in disguise. While under the influence of opium, Jasper confessed having murdered his nephew—however, Edwin had survived this attempt on his life. When he miraculously returned as from the dead, Jasper suffered a heart attack, literally dying of fright. In 1880, Charles Dickens Junior, who had assumed the editorship of his father's weekly literary journal *All the Year Round*, and Joseph Hatton dramatized the novel, but their script was never produced on stage. In this version, having strangled Drood, Jasper attempts to eliminate his second rival for Rosa's affections, Neville Landless, in the same manner. With the assistance of the opium-vendor, Princess Puffer, Grewgious acquires proof against Jasper, who poisons himself just as the police arrive to apprehend him for murder and attempted-murder. Less information is available about Robert Hall's drama *Alive or Dead* (1880), performed at the Park Theatre, Camden Town, London on May 3. In 1907-8, J. Comyns Carr's four-act play based on the novel opened at His Majesty's Theatre, Cardiff, on 4 January, produced by celebrated actor-manager Sir Herbert Beerbohm Tree. There followed a series of newspaper reviews and articles based on interviews with Tree in such organs as the *Daily Telegraph* (London), the *Daily Chronicle*, and the *Morning Post*. The play enacts Carr's theory that Jasper attempted to act upon his murderous impulses while under the influence of opium, and that Drood, overhearing his uncle's ravings, was able to escape. The play ran for one month. Less is known about another dramatic adaptation in 1908, that by C. A. Clarke and S. B. Rogerson, produced at the Osborne Theatre, Manchester, in March, and reviewed by J. Cuming Walters on March 10 in the *Manchester City News*.

From Phillip Allingham, The Victorian Web
http://www.victorianweb.org/mt/adaptations/39.html

off. However, I turned to it and got it done, and both numbers are now in type. Charles Collins has designed an excellent cover." It was his wish that his son-in-law should have illustrated the story; but, this not being practicable, upon an opinion expressed by Mr. Millais which the result thoroughly justified, choice was made of Mr. S. L. Fildes.

This reference to the last effort of Dickens's genius had been written as it thus stands, when a discovery of some interest was made by the writer. Within the leaves of one of Dickens's other manuscripts were found some detached slips of his writing, on paper only half the size of that used for the tale, so cramped, interlined, and blotted as to be nearly illegible, which on close inspection proved to be a scene in which Sapsea the auctioneer is introduced as the principal figure, among a group of characters new to the story. The explanation of it perhaps is, that, having become a little nervous about the course of the tale, from a fear that he might have plunged too soon into the incidents leading on to the catastrophe, such as the Datchery assumption in the fifth number (a misgiving he had certainly expressed to his sister-in-law), it had occurred to him to open some fresh veins of

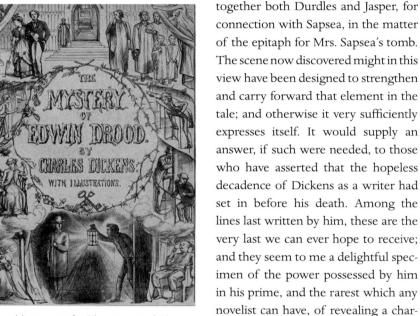
Monthly wrapper for *The Mystery of Edwin Drood*, 1870

character incidental to the interest, though not directly part of it, and so to handle them in connection with Sapsea as a little to suspend the final development even while assisting to strengthen it. Before beginning any number of a serial he used, as we have seen in former instances, to plan briefly what he intended to put into it chapter by chapter; and his first number-plan of *Drood* had the following: "Mr. Sapsea. Old Tory jackass. Connect Jasper with him. (He will want a solemn donkey by and by):" which was effected by bringing together both Durdles and Jasper, for connection with Sapsea, in the matter of the epitaph for Mrs. Sapsea's tomb. The scene now discovered might in this view have been designed to strengthen and carry forward that element in the tale; and otherwise it very sufficiently expresses itself. It would supply an answer, if such were needed, to those who have asserted that the hopeless decadence of Dickens as a writer had set in before his death. Among the lines last written by him, these are the very last we can ever hope to receive; and they seem to me a delightful specimen of the power possessed by him in his prime, and the rarest which any novelist can have, of revealing a character by a touch.

---

[121] In drawing the agreement for the publication, Mr. Ouvry had, by Dickens's wish, inserted a clause thought to be altogether needless, but found to be sadly pertinent. It was the first time such a clause had been inserted in one of his agreements. "That if the said Charles Dickens shall die during the composition of the said work of the *Mystery of Edwin Drood*, or shall otherwise become incapable of completing the said work for publication in twelve monthly numbers as agreed, it shall be referred to John Forster, Esq, one of Her Majesty's Commissioners in Lunacy, or in the case of his death, incapacity, or refusal to act, then to such person as shall be named by Her Majesty's Attorney-General for the time being, to determine the amount which shall be repaid by the said Charles Dickens, his executors or administrators, to the said Frederic Chapman as a fair compensation for so much of the said work as shall not have been completed for publication." The sum to be paid at once for 25,000 copies was £7500; publisher and author sharing equally in the profit of all sales beyond that impression; and the number reached, while the author yet lived, was 50,000. The sum paid for early sheets to America was £1000; and Baron Tauchnitz paid liberally, as he always did, for his Leipzig reprint. "All Mr. Dickens's works," M. Tauchnitz writes to me, "have been published under agreement by me. My intercourse with him lasted nearly twenty-seven years. The first of his letters dates in October 1843, and his last at the close of March 1870. Our long relations were not only never troubled by the least disagreement, but were the occasion of most hearty personal feeling; and I shall never lose the sense of his kind and friendly nature. On my asking him his terms for *Edwin Drood*, he replied 'Your terms shall be mine.'"

[122] "I have a very remarkable story indeed for you to read. It is in only two chapters. A thing never to melt into other stories in the mind, but always to keep itself apart." The story was published in the 37th number of the new series of *All the Year Round*, with the title of "An Experience." The "new series" had been started to break up the too great length of volumes in sequence, and the only change it announced was the discontinuance of Christmas Numbers. He had tired of them himself; and, observing the extent to which they were now copied in all directions (as usual with other examples set by him), he supposed them likely to become tiresome to the public.

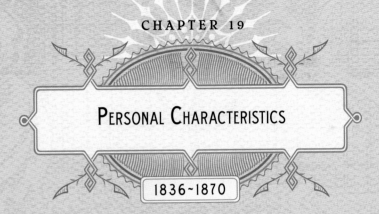

CHAPTER 19

PERSONAL CHARACTERISTICS

1836~1870

OBJECTION HAS BEEN TAKEN to this biography as likely to disappoint its readers in not making them "talk to Dickens as Boswell makes them talk to Johnson." But where will the blame lie if a man takes up *Pickwick* and is disappointed to find that he is not reading *Rasselas*? A book must be judged for what it aims to be, and not for what it cannot by possibility be. I suppose so remarkable an author as Dickens hardly ever lived who carried so little of authorship into ordinary social intercourse. Potent as the sway of his writings was over him, it expressed itself in other ways. Traces or triumphs of literary labour, displays of conversational or other personal predominance, were no part of the influence he exerted over friends. To them he was only the pleasantest of companions, with whom they forgot that he had ever written anything, and felt only the charm which a nature of such capacity for supreme enjoyment causes every one around it to enjoy.

Of course a book must stand or fall by its contents. Macaulay said very truly that the place of books in the public estimation is fixed, not by what is written about them, but by what is written in them. I offer no complaint of any remark made upon these volumes, but there have been some misapprehensions. Though Dickens bore outwardly so little of the impress of his writings, they formed the whole of that inner life which essentially constituted the man; and as in this respect he was actually, I have thought that his biography should endeavour to present him. The story of his books, therefore, at all stages of their progress, and of the hopes or designs connected with them, was my first care. With that view, and to give also to the memoir what was attainable of the value of autobiography, letters to myself, such as were never addressed to any other of his correspondents, and covering all the important incidents in the life to be retraced, were used with few exceptions exclusively; and though the exceptions are much more numerous in the present volume, this general plan has guided me to the end.

The other properties of these letters are quite subordinate to this main fact that the man who wrote them is thus perfectly seen in them. But they do not lessen the estimate of his genius. Admiration rises higher at the writer's mental forces, who, putting so much of himself into his work for the public, had still so much overflowing for such private intercourse. The sunny health of nature in them is manifest; its largeness, spontaneity, and manliness; but they have also that which highest intellects appreciate best.

There is another consideration of some importance. Sterne did not more incessantly fall back from his works upon himself than Dickens did, and undoubtedly one of the impressions left by the letters is that of the intensity and tenacity with which he recognized, realized, contemplated, cultivated, and thoroughly enjoyed, his own individuality in even its most trivial manifestations. But if any one is led to ascribe this to self-esteem, to a narrow exclusiveness, or to any other invidious form of egotism, let him correct the impression by observing how Dickens bore himself amid the universal blazing-up of America, at the beginning and at the end of his career. Of his hearty, undisguised, and unmistakeable enjoyment of his astonishing and indeed quite bewildering popularity, there can be as little doubt as that there is not a particle of vanity in it, any more than of false modesty or grimace.[123]

Other personal incidents and habits, and especially some matters of opinion of grave importance, will help to make his character better known. Much questioning followed a brief former reference to his religious belief, but, inconsistent or illogical as the conduct described may be, there is nothing to correct or to modify in my statement of it;[124] and, to what otherwise appeared to be in doubt, explicit answer will be afforded by a letter, written upon the youngest of his children leaving home in September 1868 to join his brother in Australia, than which none worthier appears in his story. "I write this note to-day because your

going away is much upon my mind, and because I want you to have a few parting words from me, to think of now and then at quiet times. I need not tell you that I love you dearly, and am very, very sorry in my heart to part with you. But this life is half made up of partings, and these pains must be borne. It is my comfort and my sincere conviction that you are going to try the life for which you are best fitted. I think its freedom and wildness more suited to you than any experiment in a study or office would have been; and without that training, you could have followed no other suitable occupation. What you have always wanted until now, has been a set, steady, constant purpose. I therefore exhort you to persevere in a thorough determination to do whatever you have to do, as well as you can do it. I was not so old as you are now, when I first had to win my food, and to do it out of this determination; and I have never slackened in it since. Never take a mean advantage of any one in any transaction, and never be hard upon people who are in your power. Try to do to others as you would have them do to you, and do not be discouraged if they fail sometimes. It is much better for you that they should fail in obeying the greatest rule laid down by Our Saviour than that you should. I put a New Testament among your books for the very same reasons, and with the very same hopes, that made me write an easy account of it for you, when you were a little child. Because it is the best book that ever was, or will be, known in the world; and because it teaches you the best lessons by which any human creature, who tries to be truthful and faithful to duty, can possibly be guided. As your brothers have gone away, one by one, I have written to each such words as I am now writing to you, and have entreated them all to guide themselves by this Book, putting aside the interpretations and inventions of Man. You will remember that you have never at home been harassed about religious observances, or mere formalities. I have always been anxious not to weary my children with such things, before they are old enough to form opinions respecting them. You will therefore understand the better that I now most solemnly impress upon you the truth and beauty of the Christian Religion, as it came from Christ Himself, and the impossibility of your going

Left: Portrait of John Forster

far wrong if you humbly but heartily respect it. Only one thing more on this head. The more we are in earnest as to feeling it, the less we are disposed to hold forth about it. Never abandon the wholesome practice of saying your own private prayers, night and morning. I have never abandoned it myself, and I know the comfort of it. I hope you will always be able to say in after life, that you had a kind father. You cannot show your affection for him so well, or make him so happy, as by doing your duty." They who most intimately knew Dickens will know best that every word there is written from his heart, and is radiant with the truth of his nature.

A dislike of all display was rooted in him; and his objection to posthumous honours, illustrated by the instructions in his will, was very strikingly expressed two years before his death, when Mr. Thomas Fairbairn asked his help to a proposed recognition of Rajah Brooke's services by a memorial in Westminster Abbey. "I am very strongly impelled" (24th of June 1868) "to comply with any request of yours. But these posthumous honours of committee, subscriptions, and Westminster Abbey are so profoundly unsatisfactory in my eyes that—plainly—I would rather have nothing to do with them in any case. My daughter and her aunt unite with me in kindest regards to Mrs. Fairbairn, and I hope you will believe in the possession of mine until I am quietly buried without any memorial but such as I have set up in my lifetime."

His aversion to every form of what is called patronage of literature[125] was part of the same feeling. A few months earlier a Manchester gentleman[126] wrote for his support to such a scheme. "I beg to be excused," was his reply, "from complying with the request you do me the honour to prefer, simply because I hold the opinion that there is a great deal too much patronage in England. The better the design, the less (as I think) should it seek such adventitious aid, and the more composedly should it rest on its own merits."

Less has been said in this work than might perhaps have been wished, of the way in which his editorship of *Household Words* and *All the Year Round* was discharged. It was distinguished above all by liberality; and a scrupulous consideration and delicacy, evinced by him to all his contributors, was part of the esteem in which he held literature itself. It was said in a newspaper after his death, evidently by one of his contributors, that he always brought the best out of a man by encouragement and appreciation; that he liked his writers to feel unfettered; and that his last reply to a proposition for a series of articles had been: "Whatever you see your way to, I will see mine to, and we know and understand each other well enough to make the best of these conditions." A few lines from another letter will show the difficulties in which he was often involved by the plan he adopted for Christmas numbers, of putting within a framework by himself a number of stories by separate writers to whom the leading notion had before been severally sent. "As yet" (25th of November 1859), "not a story has come to me in the least belonging to the idea (the simplest in the world; which I myself described in writing, in the most elaborate manner); and everyone of them turns, by a strange fatality, on a criminal trial!" It had all to be set right by him, and editorship on such terms was not a sinecure.

But periodical writing is not without its drawbacks, and its effect on Dickens, who engaged in it largely from time to time, was observable in the increased impatience of allusion to national institutions and conventional distinctions to be found in his later books. Party divisions he cared for less and less as life moved on; but the decisive, peremptory, dogmatic style, into which a habit of rapid remark on topics of the day will betray the most candid and considerate commentator, displayed its influence, perhaps not always consciously to himself, in the underlying tone of bitterness that runs through the books which followed *Copperfield*. The resentment against remediable wrongs is as praiseworthy in them as in the earlier tales; but the exposure of Chancery abuses, administrative incompetence, politico-economic shortcomings, and social flunkeyism, in *Bleak House*, *Little Dorrit*, *Hard Times*, and *Our Mutual Friend*, would not have been made less odious by the cheerier tone that had struck with much sharper effect at prison abuses, parish wrongs, Yorkshire schools, and hypocritical humbug, in *Pickwick*, *Oliver Twist*, *Nickleby*, and *Chuzzlewit*. It will be remembered of him always that he desired to set right what was wrong, that he held no abuse to be unimprovable, that he left none of the evils named exactly as he found them, and that to influences drawn from his writings were due not a few of the salutary changes which marked the age in which he lived; but anger

does not improve satire, and it gave latterly, from the causes named, too aggressive a form to what, after all, was but a very wholesome hatred of the cant that everything English is perfect, and that to call a thing *un*English is to doom it to abhorred extinction.

With the good sense that still overruled all his farthest extremes of opinion he yet never thought of parliament for himself. He could not mend matters, and for him it would have been a false position. The people of the town of Reading and others applied to him during the first half of his life, and in the last half some of the Metropolitan constituencies. To one of the latter a reply is before me in which he says: "I declare that as to all matters on the face of this teeming earth, it appears to me that the House of Commons and Parliament altogether is become just the dreariest failure and nuisance that ever bothered this much-bothered world."

Two incidents at the close of his life will show what upon these matters his latest opinions were. At the great Liverpool dinner after his country readings in 1869, over which Lord Dufferin eloquently presided, he replied to a remonstrance from Lord Houghton against his objection to entering public life,[127] that when he took literature for his profession he intended it to be his sole profession; that at that time it did not appear to him to be so well understood in England, as in some other countries, that literature was a dignified profession by which any man might stand or fall; and he resolved that in his person at least it should stand "by itself, of itself, and for itself;" a bargain which "no consideration on earth would now induce him to break." Here however he probably failed to see the entire meaning of Lord Houghton's regret, which would seem to have been meant to say, in more polite form, that to have taken some part in public affairs might have shown him the difficulty in a free state of providing remedies very swiftly for evils of long growth. A half reproach from the same quarter for alleged unkindly sentiments to the House of Lords, he repelled with vehement warmth; insisting on his great regard for individual members, and declaring that there was no man in England he respected more in his public capacity, loved more in his private capacity, or from whom he had received more remarkable proofs of his honour and love of literature, than Lord Russell.[128]

In a memoir published shortly after his death there appeared this statement. "For many years past Her Majesty the Queen has taken the liveliest interest in Mr. Dickens's literary labours, and has frequently expressed a desire for an interview with him. . . . This interview took place on the 9th of April, when he received her commands to attend her at Buckingham Palace, and was introduced by his friend Mr. Arthur Helps, the clerk of the Privy Council. . . . Since our author's decease the journal with which he was formerly connected has said: 'The Queen was ready to confer any distinction which Mr. Dickens's known views and tastes would permit him to accept, and after more than one title of honour had been declined, Her Majesty desired that he would, at least, accept a place in her Privy Council.'" As nothing is too absurd[129] for belief, it will not be superfluous to say that Dickens knew of no such desire on her Majesty's part; and though all the probabilities are on the side of his unwillingness to accept any title or place of honour, certainly none was offered to him.

It had been hoped to obtain her Majesty's name for the Jerrold performances in 1857, but, being a public effort in behalf of an individual, assent would have involved "either perpetual compliance or the giving of perpetual offence." Her Majesty however then sent, through Colonel Phipps, a request to Dickens that he would select a room in the palace, do what he would with it, and let her see the play there. "I said to Col. Phipps thereupon" (21st of June 1857) "that the idea was not quite new to me; that I did not feel easy as to the social position of my daughters, &c. at a Court under those circumstances; and that I would beg her Majesty to excuse me, if any other way of her seeing the play could be devised. To this Phipps said he had not thought of the objection, but had not the slightest doubt I was right. I then proposed that the Queen should come to the Gallery of Illustration a week before the subscription night, and should have the room entirely at her own disposal, and should invite her own company. This, with the good sense that seems to accompany her good nature on all occasions, she resolved within a few hours to do." The effect of the performance was a great gratification. "My gracious sovereign" (5th of July 1857) "was so pleased that she sent round begging me to go and see her and accept her

thanks. I replied that I was in my Farce dress, and must beg to be excused. Whereupon she sent again, saying that the dress 'could not be so ridiculous as that,' and repeating the request. I sent my duty in reply, but again hoped her Majesty would have the kindness to excuse my presenting myself in a costume and appearance that were not my own. I was mighty glad to think, when I woke this morning, that I had carried the point."

The opportunity of presenting himself in his own costume did not arrive till the year of his death, another effort meanwhile made having proved also unsuccessful. "I was put into a state of much perplexity on Sunday" (30th of March 1858). "I don't know who had spoken to my informant, but it seems that the Queen is bent upon hearing the Carol read, and has expressed her desire to bring it about without offence; hesitating about the manner of it, in consequence of my having begged to be excused from going to her when she sent for me after the Frozen Deep. I parried the thing as well as I could; but being asked to be prepared with a considerate and obliging answer, as it was known the request would be preferred, I said, 'Well! I supposed Col. Phipps would speak to me about it, and if it were he who did so, I should assure him of my desire to meet any wish of her Majesty's, and should express my hope that she would indulge me by making one of some audience or other—for I thought an audience necessary to the effect.' Thus it stands: but it bothers me." The difficulty was not surmounted, but her Majesty's continued interest in the Carol was shown by her purchase of a copy of it with Dickens's autograph at Thackeray's sale;[130] and at last there came, in the year of his death, the interview with the author whose popularity dated from her accession, whose books had entertained larger numbers of her subjects than those of any other contemporary writer, and whose genius will be counted among the glories of her reign. Accident led to it. Dickens had brought with him from America some large and striking photographs of the Battle Fields of the Civil War, which the Queen, having heard of them through Mr. Helps, expressed a wish to look at. Dickens sent them at once; and went afterwards to Buckingham Palace with Mr. Helps, at her Majesty's request, that she might see and thank him in person.

Suffice it that the Queen's kindness left a strong impression on Dickens. Upon her Majesty's regret not to have heard his Readings, Dickens intimated that they were become now a thing of the past, while he acknowledged gratefully her Majesty's compliment in regard to them. She spoke to him of the impression made upon her by his acting in the *Frozen Deep*; and on his stating, in reply to her enquiry, that the little play had not been very successful on the public stage, said this did not surprise her, since it no longer had the advantage of his performance in it. Then arose a mention of some alleged discourtesy shown to Prince Arthur in New York, and he begged her Majesty not to confound the true Americans of that city with the Fenian portion of its Irish population; on which she made the quiet comment that she was convinced the people about the Prince had made too much of the affair. He related to her the story of President Lincoln's dream on the night before his murder. She asked him to give her his writings, and could she have them that afternoon? but he begged to be allowed to send a bound copy. Her Majesty then took from a table her own book upon the Highlands, with an autograph inscription "to Charles Dickens"; and, saying that "the humblest" of writers would be ashamed to offer it to "one of the greatest" but that Mr. Helps, being asked to give it, had remarked that it would be valued most from herself, closed the interview by placing it in his hands. That the grateful impression sufficed to carry him into new ways, I had immediate proof, coupled with intimation of the still surviving strength of old memories. "As my sovereign desires" (26th of March, 1870) "that I should attend the next levee, don't faint with amazement if you see my name in that unwonted connexion. I have scrupulously kept myself free for the second of April, in case you should be accessible." The name appeared at the levee accordingly, his daughter was at the drawing-room that followed, and Lady Houghton writes to me "I never saw Mr. Dickens more agreeable than at a dinner at our house about a fortnight before his death, when he met the King of the Belgians and the Prince of Wales at the special desire of the latter." Up to nearly the hour of dinner, it was doubtful if he could go. He was suffering from the distress in his foot; and on arrival at the house, being unable to ascend the stairs, had to be assisted at once into the dining-room.

It is also very noticeable that what would have constituted the strength of Dickens if he had entered public life, the attractive as well as the commanding side of his nature, was that which kept him most within the circle of home pursuits and enjoyments. This "better part" of him had now long survived that sorrowful period of 1857-8, when, for reasons which I have not thought myself free to suppress, a vaguely disturbed feeling for the time took possession of him, and occurrences led to his adoption of other pursuits than those to which till then he had given himself exclusively. It was a sad interval in his life; but, though changes incident to the new occupation then taken up remained, and with them many adverse influences which brought his life prematurely to a close, it was, with any reference to that feeling, an interval only; and the dominant impression of the later years, as of the earlier, takes the marvellously domestic home-loving shape in which also the strength of his genius is found. It will not do to draw round any part of such a man too hard a line, and the writer must not be charged with inconsistency who says that Dickens's childish sufferings,[131] and the sense they burnt into him of the misery of loneliness and a craving for joys of home, though they led to what was weakest in him, led also to what was greatest. It was his defect as well as his merit in maturer life not to be able to live alone. When the fancies of his novels were upon him and he was under their restless influence, though he often talked of shutting himself up in out of the way solitary places, he never went anywhere unaccompanied by members of his family. His habits of daily life he carried with him wherever he went. In Albaro and Genoa, at Lausanne and Geneva, in Paris and Boulogne, his ways were as entirely those of home as in London and Broadstairs. If it is the property of a domestic nature to be personally interested in every detail, the smallest as the greatest, of the four walls within which one lives, then no man had it so essentially as Dickens. No man was so inclined naturally to derive his happiness from home concerns. Even the kind of interest in a house which is commonly confined to women, he was full of. Not to speak of changes of importance, there was not an additional hook put up wherever he inhabited, without his knowledge, or otherwise than as part of some small

RIGHT: Queen Victoria by Lady Julia Abercromby (detail), after Heinrich von Angeli, watercolor, 1883

The Charles Dickens Museum, at the site of his only surviving London
home, 48 Doughty Street, London

ingenuity of his own. Nothing was too minute for his personal superintendence. Whatever might be in hand, theatricals for the little children, entertainments for those of larger growth, cricket matches, dinners, field sports, from the first new year's eve dance in Doughty Street to the last musical party in Hyde Park Place, he was the centre and soul of it.

Of his ordinary habits of activity I have spoken, and they were doubtless carried too far. In youth it was all well, but he did not make allowance for years. This has had abundant illustration, but will admit of a few words more. To all men who do much, rule and order are essential; method in everything was Dickens's peculiarity; and

between breakfast and luncheon, with rare exceptions, was his time of work. But his daily walks were less of rule than of enjoyment and necessity. In the midst of his writing they were indispensable, and especially, as it has often been shown, at night. Mr. Sala is an authority on London streets, and, in the eloquent and generous tribute he was among the first to offer to his memory, has described himself encountering Dickens in the oddest places and most inclement weather, in Ratcliffe-highway, on Haver-stock-hill, on Camberwell-green, in Gray's-inn-lane, in the Wandsworth-road, at Hammersmith Broadway, in Norton Folgate, and at Kensal New Town.

Wherever there was "matter to be heard and learned," in back streets behind Holborn, in Borough courts and passages, in city wharfs or alleys, about the poorer lodging-houses, in prisons, workhouses, ragged-schools, police-courts, rag-shops, chandlers' shops, and all sorts of markets for the poor, he carried his keen observation and untiring study.

For several consecutive years I accompanied him every Christmas Eve to see the marketings for Christmas down the road from Aldgate to Bow; and he had a surprising fondness for wandering about in poor neighbourhoods on Christmas-day, past the areas of shabby genteel houses in Somers or Kentish Towns, and watching the dinners preparing or coming in. But the temptations of his country life led him on to excesses in walking. "Coming in just now," he wrote in his third year at Gadshill, "after twelve miles in the rain, I was so wet that I have had to change and get my feet into warm water before I could do anything."

It was from a letter of the 21st of February 1865 I first learnt that he was suffering tortures from a "frost-bitten" foot, and ten days later brought more detailed account. "I got frost-bitten by walking continually in the snow, and getting wet in the feet daily. My boots hardened and softened, hardened and softened, my left foot swelled, and I still forced the boot on; sat in it to write, half the day; walked in it through the snow, the other half; forced the boot on again next morning; sat and walked again; and being accustomed to all sorts of changes in my feet, took no heed. At length, going out as usual, I fell lame on the walk, and had to limp home dead lame, through the snow, for the last three miles—to the remarkable terror, by-the-bye, of the two big dogs." The dogs were Turk and Linda. Boisterous companions as they always were, the sudden change in him brought

Cartoon of Charles Dickens in Great Walking Match

them to a stand-still; and for the rest of the journey they crept by the side of their master as slowly as he did, never turning from him.

The saying in his letter to his youngest son that he was to do to others what he would that they should do to him, without being discouraged if they did not do it; and his saying to the Birmingham people that they were to attend to self-improvement not because it led to fortune, but because it was right; express a principle that at all times guided himself. Capable of strong attachments, he was not what is called an effusive man; but he had no half-heartedness in any of his likings. The one thing entirely hateful to him, was indifference. "I give my heart to very few people; but I would sooner love the most implacable man in the world than a careless one, who, if my place were empty to-morrow, would rub on and never miss me." There was nothing he more repeatedly told his children than that they were not to let indifference in others appear to justify it in themselves.

Of his attractive points in society and conversation I have particularized little, because in truth they were himself. Such as they were, they were never absent from him. His acute sense of enjoyment gave such relish to his social qualities that probably no man, not a great wit or a professed talker, ever left, in leaving any social gathering, a blank so impossible to fill up. In quick and varied sympathy, in ready adaptation to every whim or humour, in help to any mirth or game, he stood for a dozen men. If one may say such a thing, he seemed to be always the more himself for being somebody else, for continually putting off his personality. His versatility made him unique. What he said once of his own love of acting, applied to him equally when at his happiest among friends he loved; sketching a character, telling a story, acting a charade, taking part in a game; turning into comedy an incident of the day, describing the last good or bad thing he had seen, reproducing in quaint, tragical, or humorous form and figure, some part of the passionate life with which all his being overflowed.

Among his good things should not be omitted his telling of a ghost story. He had something of a hankering after them, as the readers of his briefer pieces will know; and such was his interest generally in things supernatural that, but for the strong restraining power of his common sense, he might have fallen into the follies of spiritualism. As it was, the fanciful side of his nature stopped short at such pardonable superstitions as those of dreams, and lucky days, or other marvels of natural coincidence; and no man was readier to apply sharp tests to a ghost story or a haunted house, though there was just so much tendency to believe in

any such, "well-authenticated," as made perfect his manner of telling one.

Another kind of dream has had previous record, with no superstition to build itself upon but the loving devotion to one tender memory. With longer or shorter intervals this was with him all his days. Never from his waking thoughts was the recollection altogether absent; and though the dream would leave him for a time, it unfailingly came back. It was the feeling of his life that always had a mastery over him. What he said on the sixth anniversary of the death of his sister-in-law, that friend of his youth whom he had made his ideal of all moral excellence, he might have said as truly after twenty-six years more. In the very year before he died, the influence was potently upon him. "She is so much in my thoughts at all times, especially when I am successful, and have greatly prospered in anything, that the recollection of her is an essential part of my being,

Dickens took pleasure in reporting the The Great International Walking Match in great detail. Here, the participants sign their agreement with the "articles" or rules.

THE GREAT INTERNATIONAL WALKING-MATCH
OF FEBRUARY 29, 1868.

THE origin of this highly exciting and important event cannot be better stated than in the articles of agreement subscribed by the parties.

THE ARTICLES

Articles of Agreement entered into at Baltimore, in the United States of America, this Third day of February in the year of our Lord one thousand eight hundred and sixty-eight, between GEORGE DOLBY, British Subject, *alias* the Man of Ross, and JAMES RIPLEY OSGOOD, American Citizen, *alias* the Boston Bantam. Whereas, some Bounce having arisen between the above men in reference to feats of pedestrianism and agility, they have agreed to settle their differences and prove who is the better man, by means of a walking-match for two hats a side and the glory of their respective countries; and whereas they agree that the said match shall come off, whatsoever the weather, on the Mill Dam road outside Boston on Saturday, the Twenty-ninth day of this present month; and whereas they agree that the personal attendants on themselves during the whole walk, and also the umpires and starters and declarers of victory in the match shall be JAMES T. FIELDS of Boston, known in sporting circles as Massachusetts Jemmy, and CHARLES DICKENS of Falstaff's Gad's Hill, whose surprising performances (without the least variation) on that truly national instrument, the American Catarrh, have won for him the well-merited title of The Gad's Hill Gasper.

Now, these are to be the articles of the match:—

1. The men are to be started, on the day appointed, by Massachusetts Jemmy and The Gasper.
2. Jemmy and The Gasper are, on some previous day, to walk out at the rate of not less than four miles an hour by the Gasper's watch, for one hour and a half. At the expiration of that one hour and a half, they are to carefully note the place at which they halt. On the match's coming off, they are to station themselves in the middle of the road, at that precise point, and the men (keeping clear of them and of each other) are to turn round them, right shoulder inward, and walk back to the starting-point. The man declared by them to pass the starting-point first is to be the victor and the winner of the match.
3. No jostling or fouling allowed.
4. All cautions or orders issued to the men by the umpires, starters, and declarers of victory, to be considered final and admitting of no appeal.

5. A sporting narrative of the match to be written by The Gasper within one week after its coming off, and the same to be duly printed (at the expense of the subscribers to these articles) on a broadside. The said broadside to be framed and glazed, and one copy of the same to be carefully preserved by each of the subscribers to these articles.
6. The men to show on the evening of the day of walking, at six o'clock precisely, at the Parker House, Boston, when and where a dinner will be given them by The Gasper. The Gasper to occupy the chair, faced by Massachusetts Jemmy. The latter promptly and formally to invite, as soon as may be after the date of these presents, the following Guests to honor the said dinner with their presence: that is to say:— Mistress Annie Fields, Mr. Charles Eliot Norton and Mrs. Norton, Professor James Russell Lowell and Mrs. Lowell and Miss Lowell, Doctor Oliver Wendell Holmes and Mrs. Holmes, Mr. Howard Malcom Ticknor and Mrs. Ticknor, Mr. Aldrich and Mrs. Aldrich, Mr. Schlesinger, and an obscure poet named Longfellow (if discoverable) and Miss Longfellow.

Now, Lastly. In token of their accepting the trusts and offices by these articles conferred upon them, these articles are solemnly and formally signed by Massachusetts Jemmy and by the Gad's Hill Gasper, as well as by the men themselves.

Signed by the Man of Ross, otherwise   *George Dolby*

Signed by the Boston Bantam, otherwise   *James R. Osgood*

Signed by Massachusetts Jemmy, otherwise   *James T. Fields*

Signed by The Gad's Hill Gasper, otherwise   *Charles Dickens*

Witness to the signatures.   *W. S. Anthony*

THE SPORTING NARRATIVE

THE MEN.

THE Boston Bantam (*alias* Bright Chanticleer) is a young bird, though too old to be caught with chaff. He comes of a thorough game breed and has a clear though modest crow. He pulls down the scale at ten stone and a half and add a pound or two. His previous performances in the Pedestrian line have not been numerous. He once achieved a neat little match against time in two left boots at Philadelphia; but this must be considered as a pedestrian eccentricity, and cannot be accepted by the rigid chronicler as high art. The old mower with the scythe and hour-glass has not yet laid his mawley heavily on the Bantam's frontispiece, but he has had a grip at the Bantam's top feathers, and in plucking out a handful was very near making him like the great Napoleon Bonaparte (with the exception of the victualling-department), when the ancient one found himself too much occupied to carry out the idea, and gave it up. The Man of Ross (*alias* old Alick Pope, *alias* Allourpraiseswhyshouldlords, &c.) is a thought and a half too fleshy, and, if he accidentally sat down upon his baby, would do it to the tune of fourteen stone. This popular Codger is of the rubicund and jovial sort, and has long been known as a piscatorial pedestrian ... his

THE RACE.

In the teeth of an intensely cold and bitter wind before which the snow flew fast and furious across the road from right to left, The Bantam slightly led. But The Man responded to the challenge and soon breasted him. For the first three miles, each led by a yard or so alternately; but the walking was very even. On four miles being called by The Gasper, the men were side by side; and then ensued one of the best periods of the race, the same splitting pace being held by both, through a heavy snow-wreath and up a dragging hill. At this point it was anybody's game, a dollar on Rossius and two half-dollars on the member of the feathery tribe. When five miles were called, the men were still shoulder to shoulder. At about six miles, the Gasper put on a tremendous spirt to leave the men behind and establish himself as the turning-point at the entrance of the village. He afterwards declared that he received a mental knock-downer, on taking his station and facing about, to find Bright Chanticleer close in upon him, and Rossius steaming up like a Locomotive. The Bantam rounded first; Rossius rounded wide; and from that moment the Bantam steadily shot ahead. Though both were breathed at the turn, the Bantam quickly got his

and is as inseparable from my existence as the beating of my heart is." Through later troubled years, whatever was worthiest in him found in this an ark of safety; and it was the nobler part of his being which had thus become also the essential. It gave to success what success by itself had no power to give; and nothing could consist with it, for any length of time, that was not of good report and pure. What more could I say that was not better said from the pulpit of the Abbey where he rests?

"He whom we mourn was the friend of mankind, a philanthropist in the true sense; the friend of youth, the friend of the poor, the enemy of every form of meanness and oppression. I am not going to attempt to draw a portrait of him. Men of genius are different from what we suppose them to be. They have greater pleasures and greater pains, greater affections and greater temptations, than the generality of mankind, and they can never be altogether understood by their fellow men. . . . But we feel that a light has gone out, that the world is darker to us, when they depart. There are so very few of them that we cannot afford to lose them one by one, and we look vainly round for others who may supply their places. He whose loss we now mourn occupied a greater space than any other writer in the minds of Englishmen during the last thirty-three years. We read him, talked about him, acted him; we laughed with him; we were roused by him to a consciousness of the misery of others, and to a pathetic interest in human life. Works of fiction, indirectly, are great instructors of this world; and we can hardly exaggerate the debt of gratitude which is due to a writer who has led us to sympathize with these good, true, sincere, honest English characters of ordinary life, and to laugh at the egotism, the hypocrisy, the false respectability of religious professors and others. To another great humourist who lies in this Church the words have been applied that his death eclipsed the gaiety of nations. But of him who has been recently taken I would rather say, in humbler language, that no one was ever so much beloved or so much mourned."

---

[123] Mr. Grant Wilson has sent me an extract from a letter by Fitz-Greene Halleck (author of one of the most delightful poems ever written about Burns) which exactly expresses Dickens as he was, not only in 1842, but, as far as the sense of authorship went, all his life. It was addressed to Mrs. Rush of Philadelphia, and is dated the 8th of March, 1842. "You ask me about Mr. Boz. I am quite delighted with him. He is a thorough good fellow, with nothing of the author about him but the reputation, and goes through his task as Lion with exemplary grace, patience, and good nature. He has the brilliant face of a man of genius. . . . His writings you know. I wish you had listened to his eloquence at the dinner here. It was the only real specimen of eloquence I have ever witnessed. Its charm was not in its words, but in the manner of saying them."

[124] In a volume called *Home and Abroad*, by Mr. David Macrae, is printed a correspondence with Dickens on matters alluded to in the text, held in 1861, which will be found to confirm all that is here said.

[125] I may quote here from a letter (Newcastle-on-Tyne, 5th Sept. 1858) sent me by the editor of the Northern Express. "The view you take of the literary character in the abstract, or of what it might and ought to be, expresses what I have striven for all through my literary life—never to allow it to be patronized, or tolerated, or treated like a good or a bad child. I am always animated by the hope of leaving it a little better understood by the thoughtless than I found it."—To James B. Manson, Esq.

[126] Henry Ryder-Taylor, Esq. Ph.D. 8th Sept. 1868.

[127] On this remonstrance and Dickens's reply *The Times* had a leading article of which the closing sentences find fitting place in his biography. "If there be anything in Lord Russell's theory that Life Peerages are wanted specially to represent those forms of national eminence which cannot otherwise find fitting representation, it might be urged, for the reasons we have before mentioned, that a Life Peerage is due to the most truly national representative of one important department of modern English literature. Something may no doubt be said in favour of this view, but we are inclined to doubt if Mr. Dickens himself would gain anything by a Life Peerage. Mr. Dickens is pre-eminently a writer of the people and for the people. To our thinking, he is far better suited for the part of the 'Great Commoner' of English fiction than for even a Life Peerage. To turn Charles Dickens into Lord Dickens would be much the same mistake in literature that it was in politics to turn William Pitt into Lord Chatham."

[128] One of the many repetitions of the same opinion in his letters may be given. "Lord John's note" (September 1853) "confirms me in an old impression that he is worth a score of official men; and has more generosity in his little finger than a Government usually has in its whole corporation." In another of his public allusions, Dickens described him as a statesman of whom opponents and friends alike felt sure that he would rise to the level of every occasion, however exalted; and compared him to the seal of Solomon in the old Arabian story inclosing in a not very large casket the soul of a giant.

[129] In a memoir by Dr. Shelton McKenzie which has had circulation in America, there is given the following statement, taken doubtless from publications at the time, of which it will be strictly accurate to say, that, excepting the part of its closing averment which describes Dickens sending a copy of his works to her Majesty by her own desire, there is in it not a single word of truth. "Early in 1870 the Queen presented a copy of her book upon the Highlands to Mr. Dickens, with the modest autographic inscription, 'from the humblest to the most distinguished author of England.' This was meant to be complimentary, and was accepted as such by Mr. Dickens, who acknowledged it in a manly, courteous letter. Soon after, Queen Victoria wrote to him, requesting that he would do her the favour of paying her a visit at Windsor. He accepted, and passed a day, very pleasantly, in his Sovereign's society. It is said that they were mutually pleased, that Mr. Dickens caught the royal lady's particular humour, that they chatted together in a very friendly manner, that the Queen was never tired of asking questions about certain characters in his books, that they had almost a tete-a-tete luncheon, and that, ere he departed, the Queen pressed him to accept a baronetcy (a title which descends to the eldest son), and that, on his declining, she said, 'At least, Mr. Dickens, let me have the gratification of making you one of my Privy Council.' This, which gives the personal title of 'Right Honourable,' he also declined—nor, indeed, did Charles Dickens require a title to give him celebrity. The Queen and the author parted, well pleased with each other. The newspapers reported that a peerage had been offered and declined—but even newspapers are not invariably correct. Mr. Dickens presented his Royal Mistress with a handsome set of all his works, and, on the very morning of his death, a letter reached Gad's Hill, written by Mr. Arthur Helps, by her desire, acknowledging the present, and describing the exact position the books occupied at Balmoral—so placed that she could see them before her when occupying the usual seat in her sitting-room. When this letter arrived, Mr. Dickens was still alive, but wholly unconscious. What to him, at that time, was the courtesy of an earthly sovereign?" I repeat that the only morsel of truth in all this rigmarole is that the books were sent by Dickens, and acknowledged by Mr. Helps at the Queen's desire. The letter did not arrive on the day of his death, the 9th of June, but was dated from Balmoral on that day.

[130] The book was thus entered in the catalogue. "DICKENS (C.), A CHRISTMAS CAROL, in prose, 1843; Presentation Copy, inscribed 'W. M. Thackeray, from Charles Dickens (whom he made very happy once a long way from home).'" Some pleasant verses by his friend had affected him much while abroad. I quote the *Life of Dickens* published by Mr. Hotten. "Her Majesty expressed the strongest desire to possess this presentation copy, and sent an unlimited commission to buy it. The original published price of the book was 5s. It became Her Majesty's property for £25 10s., and was at once taken to the palace."

[131] An entry, under the date of July 1833, from a printed but unpublished Diary by Mr. Payne Collier, appeared lately in the Athenaeum, having reference to Dickens at the time when he first obtained employment as a reporter, and connecting itself with what my opening volume had related of those childish sufferings. "Soon afterwards I observed a great difference in C. D.'s dress, for he had bought a new hat and a very handsome blue cloak, which he threw over his shoulder a l' Espagnole. . . . We walked together through Hungerford Market, where we followed a coal-heaver, who carried his little rosy but grimy child looking over his shoulder; and C. D. bought a halfpenny-worth of cherries, and as we went along he gave them one by one to the little fellow without the knowledge of the father. . . . He informed me as we walked through it that he knew Hungerford Market well. . . . He did not affect to conceal the difficulties he and his family had had to contend against."

CHAPTER 20

THE END

1869~1870

THE SUMMER AND AUTUMN of 1869 were passed quietly at Gadshill. He received there, in June, the American friends to whom he had been most indebted for unwearying domestic kindness at his most trying time in the States. In August, he was at the dinner of the International boat-race; and, in a speech that might have gone far to reconcile the victors to changing places with the vanquished, gave the healths of the Harvard and the Oxford crews. He went to Birmingham, in September, to fulfil a promise that he would open the session of the Institute; and there, after telling his audience that his invention, such as it was, never would have served him as it had done, but for the habit of commonplace, patient, drudging attention, he declared his political creed to be infinitesimal faith in the people governing and illimitable faith in the People governed. In such engagements as these, with nothing of the kind of strain he had most to dread, there was hardly more movement or change than was necessary to his enjoyment of rest.

He had been able to show Mr. Fields something of the interest of London as well as of his Kentish home. He went over its "general post-office" with him, took him among its cheap theatres and poor lodging-houses, and piloted him by night through its most notorious thieves' quarter. Its localities that are pleasantest to a lover of books, such as Johnson's Bolt-court and Goldsmith's Temple-chambers, he explored with him; and, at his visitor's special request, mounted a staircase he had not ascended for more than thirty years, to show the chambers in Furnival's Inn where the first page of *Pickwick* was written.

Before beginning his novel he had written his last paper for his weekly publication. It was a notice of my *Life*

of *Landor*, and contained some interesting recollections of that remarkable man. His memory at this time dwelt much, as was only natural, with past pleasant time, as he saw familiar faces leaving us or likely to leave. My mind still constantly misgives me concerning Macready. Curiously, I don't think he has been ever, for ten minutes together, out of my thoughts.

He finished his first number of *Edwin Drood* in the third week of October, and on the 26th read it at my house with great spirit. A few nights before we had seen together at the Olympic a little drama taken from his *Copperfield*, which he sat out with more than patience, even with something of enjoyment. He was at Gadshill till the close of the year; coming up for a few special occasions, such as Procter's

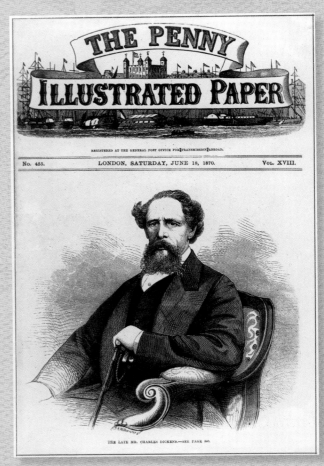

"The Late Mr. Charles Dickens" front page portrait, *The Penny Illustrated Paper*, London, Saturday, June 18, 1870

Dickens "Exhausted Montage" by Harry Furniss, 1910

ROTUNDA, DUBLIN.

Messrs. CHAPPELL & CO. beg to announce that
they have made arrangements with

MR. CHARLES DICKENS

FOR THREE

FAREWELL READINGS,

THE LAST THAT WILL EVER
TAKE PLACE IN DUBLIN,

AS FOLLOWS:

On MONDAY, JANUARY 11, 1869,

On TUESDAY, JANUARY 12,
AND

On WEDNESDAY, JANUARY 13,

THE LAST READING IN DUBLIN.

Announcement for
Dickens's Farewell
Readings at the
Rotunda, Dublin,
January 11, 12, and
13, 1869

eighty-second birthday; and at my house on new-year's eve he read to us, again aloud, a fresh number of his book. Yet these very last days of December had not been without a reminder of the grave warnings of April. The pains in somewhat modified form had returned in both his left hand and his left foot a few days before we met; and they were troubling him still on that day. His only allusion to an effect from his illness was his mention of a now invincible dislike which he had to railway travel. This had decided him to take a London house for the twelve last readings in the early months of 1870, and he had become Mr. Milner-Gibson's tenant at 5, Hyde Park Place.

St. James's Hall was to be the scene of these Readings, and they were to occupy the interval from the 11th of January to the 15th of March; two being given in each week to the close of January, and the remaining eight on each of the eight Tuesdays following. Nothing was said of any kind of apprehension as the time approached; but, with a curious absence of the sense of danger, there was certainly both distrust and fear. Sufficient precaution was supposed to have been taken[132] by arrangement for the presence, at each reading, of his friend and medical attendant, Mr. Carr

Beard; but this resolved itself, not into any measure of safety, the case admitting of none short of stopping the reading altogether, but simply into ascertainment of the exact amount of strain and pressure, which, with every fresh exertion, he was placing on those vessels of the brain where the Preston trouble too surely had revealed that danger lay. No supposed force in reserve, no dominant strength of will, can turn aside the penalties sternly exacted for disregard of such laws of life as were here plainly overlooked; and though no one may say that it was not already too late for any but the fatal issue, there will be no presumption in believing that life might yet have been for some time prolonged if these readings could have been stopped.

"I am a little shaken," he wrote on the 9th of January, "by my journey to Birmingham to give away the Institution's prizes on Twelfth Night, but I am in good heart; and, notwithstanding Lowe's worrying scheme for collecting a year's taxes in a lump, which they tell me is damaging books, pictures, music, and theatres beyond precedent, our 'let' at St. James's Hall is enormous." He opened with *Copperfield* and the *Pickwick Trial*; and I may briefly mention, from the notes taken by Mr. Beard and placed at my disposal, at what cost of exertion to himself he gratified the crowded audiences that then and to the close made these evenings memorable. His ordinary pulse on the first night was at 72; but never on any subsequent night was lower than 82, and had risen on the later nights to more than 100. After *Copperfield* on the first night it went up to 96, and after *Marigold* on the second to 99; but on the first night of the *Sikes and Nancy* scenes (Friday the 21st of January) it went from 80 to 112, and on the second night (the 1st of February) to 118. From this, through the six remaining nights, it never was lower than 110 after the first piece read; and after the third and fourth readings of the *Oliver Twist* scenes it rose, from 90 to 124 on the 15th of February, and from 94 to 120 on the 8th of March; on the former occasion, after twenty minutes' rest, falling to 98, and on the latter, after fifteen minutes' rest, falling to 82. His ordinary pulse on entering the room, during these last six nights, was more than once over 100, and never lower than 84; from which it rose, after *Nickleby* on the 22nd of February, to 112. On the 8th of February, when he read *Dombey*, it had risen from 91 to 114; on the 1st of March, after *Copperfield*, it rose from 100 to 124; and when he entered the room on the last night it was at 108, having risen only two beats more when the reading was done. The pieces on this occasion were the *Christmas Carol*, followed by the *Pickwick Trial*; and probably in all his life he never read so well. On his return from the States, where he had to address his effects to audiences composed of immense numbers of people, a certain loss of refinement had been observable; but the old delicacy was now again delightfully manifest, and a subdued tone, as well in the humorous as the serious portions, gave something to all the reading as of a quiet sadness of farewell. The charm of this was at its height when he shut the volume of *Pickwick* and spoke in his own person. He said that for fifteen years he had been reading his own books to audiences whose sensitive and kindly recognition of them had given him instruction and enjoyment in his art such as few men could have had; but that he nevertheless thought it well now to retire upon older associations, and in future to devote himself exclusively to the calling which had first made him known. "In but two short weeks from this time I hope that you may enter, in your own homes, on a new series of readings at which my assistance will be indispensable; but from these garish lights I vanish now for evermore,

with a heartfelt, grateful, respectful, affectionate farewell." The brief hush of silence as he moved from the platform; and the prolonged tumult of sound that followed suddenly, stayed him, and again for another moment brought him back; will not be forgotten by any present.

Little remains to be told that has not in it almost unmixed pain and sorrow. Hardly a day passed, while the readings went on or after they closed, unvisited by some effect or other of the disastrous excitement shown by the notes of Mr. Beard. On the 23rd of January, when for the last time he met Carlyle, he came to us with his left hand in a sling; on the 7th of February, when he passed with us his last birthday, and on the 25th, when he read the third number of his novel, the hand was still swollen and painful; and on the 21st of March, when he read admirably his fourth number, he told us that as he came along, walking up the length of Oxford-street, the same incident had recurred as on the day of a former dinner with us, and he had not been able to read, all the way, more than the right-hand half of the names over the shops.

His last public appearances were in April. On the 5th he took the chair for the Newsvendors, whom he helped with a genial address in which even his apology for little speaking overflowed with irrepressible humour. He would try, he said, like Falstaff, "but with a modification almost as large as himself" less to speak himself than to be the cause of speaking in others.

On the 30th of the same month he returned thanks for "Literature" at the Royal Academy dinner, and I may preface my allusion to what he then said with what he had written to me the day before. Three days earlier Daniel Maclise had passed away. "Like you at Ely, so I at Higham, had the shock of first reading at a railway station of the death of our old dear friend and companion. What the shock would be, you know too well. It has been only after great difficulty, and after hardening and steeling myself to the subject by at once thinking of it and avoiding it in a strange way, that I have been able to get any command over it or over myself. If I feel at the time that I can be sure of the necessary composure, I shall make a little reference to it at the Academy to-morrow. I suppose you won't be there."[133] The reference made was most touching and manly. He told those who listened that since he first entered the public lists, a very young man

indeed, it had been his constant fortune to number among his nearest and dearest friends members of that Academy who had been its pride; and who had now, one by one, so dropped from his side that he was grown to believe, with the Spanish monk of whom Wilkie spoke, that the only realities around him were the pictures which he loved, and all the moving life but a shadow and a dream. "For many years I was one of the two most intimate friends and most constant companions of Mr. Maclise, to whose death the Prince of Wales has made allusion, and the President has referred with the eloquence of genuine feeling. Of his genius in his chosen art, I will venture to say nothing here; but of his fertility of mind and wealth of intellect I may confidently assert that they would have made him, if he had been so minded, at least as great a writer as he was a painter. The gentlest and most modest of men, the freshest as to his generous appreciation of young aspirants and the frankest and largest hearted as to his peers, incapable of a sordid or ignoble thought, gallantly sustaining the true dignity of his vocation, without one grain of self-ambition, wholesomely natural at the last as at the first, 'in wit a man, simplicity a child,'—no artist of whatsoever denomination, I make bold to say, ever went to his rest leaving a golden memory more pure from dross, or having devoted himself with a truer chivalry to the art-goddess whom he worshipped." These were the last public words of Dickens, and he could not have spoken any worthier.

Left: Daniel Maclise (1806–1870), oil on panel, by Edward Matthew Ward (detail), 1846

Dickens reading Sikes and Nancy, March 16, 1870

Upon his appearance at the dinner of the Academy had followed some invitations he was led to accept; greatly to his own regret, he told me on the night (7th of May) when he read to us the fifth number of *Edwin Drood*; for he was now very eager to get back to the quiet of Gadshill. He dined with Mr. Motley, then American minister; had met Mr. Disraeli at a dinner at Lord Stanhope's; had breakfasted with Mr. Gladstone; and on the 17th was to attend the Queen's ball with his daughter. But she had to go there without him; for on the 16th I had intimation of a sudden disablement. "I am sorry to report, that, in the old preposterous endeavour to dine at preposterous hours and preposterous places, I have been pulled up by a sharp attack in my foot. And serve me right. I hope to get the better of it soon, but I fear I must not think of dining with you on Friday. I have cancelled everything in the dining way for this week, and that is a very small precaution after the horrible pain I have had and the remedies I have taken." He had to excuse himself also from the General Theatrical Fund dinner, where the Prince of Wales was to preside; but at another dinner a week later, where the King of the Belgians and the Prince were to be present, so much pressure was put upon him that he went, still suffering as he was, to dine with Lord Houghton.

We met for the last time on Sunday the 22nd of May, when I dined with him in Hyde Park Place. The death of Mr. Lemon, of which he heard that day, had led his thoughts to the crowd of friendly companions in letters and art who had so fallen from the ranks since we played Ben Jonson together that we were left almost alone.

A matter discussed that day with Mr. Ouvry was briefly resumed in a note of the 29th of May, the last I ever received from him; which followed me to Exeter, and closed thus. "You and I can speak of it at Gads by and by. Foot no worse. But no better." The old trouble was upon him when we parted, and this must have been nearly the last note written before he quitted London. He was at Gadshill on the 30th of May; and I heard no more until the

telegram reached me at Launceston on the night of the 9th of June, which told me that the "by and by" was not to come in this world.

The few days at Gadshill had been given wholly to work on his novel. He had been easier in his foot and hand; and, though he was suffering severely from the local hemorrhage before named, he made no complaint of illness. But there was observed in him a very unusual appearance of fatigue. "He seemed very weary." He was out with his dogs for the last time on Monday the 6th of June, when he walked with his letters into Rochester. On Tuesday the 7th, after his daughter Mary had left on a visit to her sister Kate, not finding himself equal to much fatigue, he drove to Cobhamwood with his sister-in-law, there dismissed the carriage, and walked round the park and back. He returned in time to put up in his new conservatory some Chinese lanterns sent from London that afternoon; and, the whole of the evening, he sat with Miss Hogarth in the dining-room that he might see their effect when lighted. More than once he then expressed his satisfaction at having finally abandoned all intention of exchanging Gadshill for London; and this he had done more impressively some days before. While he lived, he said, he should like his name to be more and more associated with the place; and he had a notion that when he died he should like to lie in the little graveyard belonging to the Cathedral at the foot of the Castle wall.

On the 8th of June he passed all the day writing in the Chalet. He came over for luncheon; and, much against his usual custom, returned to his desk. He was late in leaving the Chalet; but before dinner, which was ordered at six o'clock with the intention of walking afterwards in the lanes, he wrote some letters, among them one to his friend Mr. Charles Kent appointing to see him in London next day; and dinner was begun before Miss Hogarth saw, with alarm, a singular expression of trouble and pain in his face. "For an hour," he then told her, "he had been very

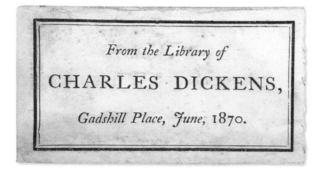

Dickens's Bookplate

ill;" but he wished dinner to go on. These were the only really coherent words uttered by him. They were followed by some, that fell from him disconnectedly, of quite other matters; of an approaching sale at a neighbour's house, of whether Macready's son was with his father at Cheltenham, and of his own intention to go immediately to London; but at these latter he had risen, and his sister-in-law's help alone prevented him from falling where he stood. Her effort then was to get him on the sofa, but after a slight struggle he sank heavily on his left side. "On the ground" were the last words he spoke. It was now a little over ten minutes past six o'clock. His two daughters came that night with Mr. Beard, who had also been telegraphed for, and whom they met at the station. His eldest son arrived early next morning, and

was joined in the evening (too late) by his younger son from Cambridge. All possible medical aid had been summoned. The surgeon of the neighbourhood was there from the first, and a physician from London was in attendance as well as Mr. Beard. But all human help was unavailing. There was effusion on the brain; and though stertorous breathing continued all night, and until ten minutes past six o'clock on the evening of Thursday the 9th of June, there had never been a gleam of hope during the twenty-four hours. He had lived four months beyond his 58th year.

The excitement and sorrow at his death are within the memory of all. Before the news of it even reached

Dickens's grave, Westminster Abbey

The Grave of Charles Dickens, Westminster Abbey, watercolor by Sir Samuel Luke Fildes (1844-1927), 1873

the remoter parts of England, it had been flashed across Europe; was known in the distant continents of India, Australia, and America; and not in English-speaking communities only, but in every country of the civilised earth, had awakened grief and sympathy. In his own land it was as if a personal bereavement had befallen every one. Her Majesty the Queen telegraphed from Balmoral "her deepest regret at the sad news of Charles Dickens's death;" and this was the sentiment alike of all classes of her people. There was not an English journal that did not give it touching and noble utterance; and the *Times* took the lead in suggesting[134] that the only fit resting-place for the remains of a man so dear to England was the Abbey in which the most illustrious Englishmen are laid.

With the expression thus given to a general wish, the Dean of Westminster lost no time in showing ready compliance; and on the morning of the day when it appeared was in communication with the family and representatives. The public homage of a burial in the Abbey had to be reconciled with his own instructions to be privately buried without previous announcement of time or place, and without monument or memorial. He would himself have preferred to lie in the small graveyard under Rochester Castle wall, or in the little churches of Cobham or Shorne; but all these were found to be closed; and the desire of the Dean and Chapter of Rochester to lay him in their Cathedral had been entertained, when the Dean of Westminster's request, and the considerate kindness of his generous assurance that there should be only such ceremonial as would strictly obey all injunctions of privacy, made it a grateful duty to accept

The Empty Chair, illustration of Dickens's study at Gadshill by Sir Samuel Luke Fildes. Made in tribute after the author's death.

that offer. The spot already had been chosen by the Dean; and before mid-day on the following morning, Tuesday the 14th of June, with knowledge of those only who took part in the burial, all was done. The solemnity had not lost by the simplicity. Nothing so grand or so touching could have accompanied it, as the stillness and the silence of the vast Cathedral. Then, later in the day and all the following day, came unbidden mourners in such crowds, that the Dean had to request permission to keep open the grave until Thursday; but after it was closed they did not cease to come, and "all day long," Doctor Stanley wrote on the 17th, "there was a constant pressure to the spot, and many flowers were strewn upon it by unknown hands, many tears shed from unknown eyes." He alluded to this in the impressive funeral discourse delivered by him in the Abbey on the morning of Sunday the 19th, pointing to the fresh flowers that then had been newly thrown (as they still are thrown, in this fourth year after the death), and saying that "the spot would thenceforward be a sacred one with both the New World and the Old, as that of the representative of the literature, not of this island only, but of all who speak our English tongue." The stone placed upon it is inscribed

Charles Dickens. Born February the Seventh 1812. Died June the Ninth 1870.

The highest associations of both the arts he loved surround him where he lies. Next to him is RICHARD CUMBERLAND. Mrs. PRITCHARD'S monument looks down upon him, and immediately behind is DAVID GARRICK'S. Nor is the actor's delightful art more worthily represented than the nobler genius of the author. Facing the grave, and on its left and right, are the monuments of CHAUCER, SHAKESPEARE, and DRYDEN, the three immortals who did most to create and settle the language to which CHARLES DICKENS has given another undying name.

Finis.

---

[132] I desire to guard myself against any possible supposition that I think these Readings might have been stopped by the exercise of medical authority. I am convinced of the contrary. Dickens had pledged himself to them; and the fact that others' interests were engaged rather than his own supplied him with an overpowering motive for being determinedly set on going through with them. At the sorrowful time in the preceding year, when, yielding to the stern sentence passed by Sir Thomas Watson, he had dismissed finally the staff employed on his country readings, he had thus written to me. "I do believe" (3rd of May 1869) "that such people as the Chappells are very rarely to be found in human affairs. To say nothing of their noble and munificent manner of sweeping away into space all the charges incurred uselessly, and all the immense inconvenience and profitless work thrown upon their establishment, comes a note this morning from the senior partner, to the effect that they feel that my overwork has been 'indirectly caused by them, and by my great and kind exertions to make their venture successful to the extreme.' There is something so delicate and fine in this, that I feel it deeply." That feeling led to his resolve to make the additional exertion of these twelve last readings, and nothing would have turned him from it as long as he could stand at the desk.

[133] I preserve also the closing words of the letter. "It is very strange—you remember I suppose?—that the last time we spoke of him together, you said that we should one day hear that the wayward life into which he had fallen was over, and there an end of our knowledge of it." The waywardness, which was merely the having latterly withdrawn himself too much from old friendly intercourse, had its real origin in disappointments connected with the public work on which he was engaged in those later years, and to which he sacrificed every private interest of his own. His was only the common fate of Englishmen, so engaged, who do this; and when the real story of the "Fresco-painting for the Houses of Parliament" comes to be written, it will be another chapter added to our national misadventures and reproaches in everything connected with Art and its hapless cultivators.

[134] It is a duty to quote these eloquent words. "Statesmen, men of science, philanthropists, the acknowledged benefactors of their race, might pass away, and yet not leave the void which will be caused by the death of Dickens. They may have earned the esteem of mankind; their days may have been passed in power, honour, and prosperity; they may have been surrounded by troops of friends; but, however pre-eminent in station, ability, or public services, they will not have been, like our great and genial novelist, the intimate of every household. Indeed, such a position is attained not even by one man in an age. It needs an extraordinary combination of intellectual and moral qualities . . . before the world will thus consent to enthrone a man as their unassailable and enduring favourite. This is the position which Mr. Dickens has occupied with the English and also with the American public for the third of a century. . . . Westminster Abbey is the peculiar resting-place of English literary genius; and among those whose sacred dust lies there, or whose names are recorded on the walls, very few are more worthy than Charles Dickens of such a home. Fewer still, we believe, will be regarded with more honour as time passes and his greatness grows upon us."

"The Empty Chair," surrounded by Dickens's characters

APPENDIX I:
THE WRITINGS OF CHARLES DICKENS

1835

Sketches by Boz. Illustrative of Every-day Life and Every-day People. (The detached papers collected under this title were in course of publication during this year, in the pages of the *Monthly Magazine* and the columns of the *Morning* and the *Evening Chronicle*.)

1836

Sketches by Boz. Illustrative of Every-day Life and Every-day People. Two volumes: Illustrations by George Cruikshank. (Preface dated from Furnival's Inn, February 1836.) John Macrone.

The Posthumous Papers of the Pickwick Club. Edited by Boz. With Illustrations by R. Seymour and Phiz (Hablot Browne). (Nine numbers published monthly from April to December.) Chapman and Hall.

Sunday Under Three Heads. As it is; as Sabbath Bills would make it; as it might be made. By Timothy Sparks. Illustrated by H. K. B. (Hablot Browne). Dedicated (June 1836) to the Bishop of London. Chapman & Hall.

The Strange Gentleman. A Comic Burletta, in two acts. By "Boz." (Performed at the St. James's Theatre, 29th of September 1836, and published with the imprint of 1837.) Chapman & Hall.

The Village Coquettes. A Comic Opera, in two acts. By Charles Dickens. The Music by John Hullah. (Dedication to Mr. Braham is dated from *Furnival's Inn*, 15th of December 1836.) Richard Bentley.

Sketches by Boz. Illustrated by George Cruikshank. Second Series. One volume. (Preface dated from *Furnival's Inn*, 17th of December 1836.) John Macrone.

1837

The Posthumous Papers of the Pickwick Club. Edited by Boz. (Eleven numbers, the last being a double number, published monthly from January to November. Issued complete in the latter month, with Dedication to Mr. Serjeant Talfourd dated from Doughty-street, 27th of September, as The Posthumous Papers of the Pickwick Club. By Charles Dickens.) Chapman & Hall.

Oliver Twist; or the Parish Boy's Progress. Begun in *Bentley's Miscellany* for January, and continued throughout the year. Richard Bentley.

1838

Oliver Twist. By Charles Dickens, Author of the *Pickwick Papers*. With Illustrations by George Cruikshank. Three volumes. (Had appeared in monthly portions, in the numbers of *Bentley's Miscellany* for 1837 and 1838, with the title of *Oliver Twist; or the Parish Boy's Progress*. By Boz. Illustrated by George Cruikshank. The Third Edition, with Preface dated Devonshire-terrace, March 1841, published by Messrs. Chapman & Hall.) Richard Bentley.

Memoirs of Joseph Grimaldi. Edited by "Boz." Illustrated by George Cruikshank. Two volumes. (For Dickens's small share in the composition of this work, his preface to which is dated from Doughty-street, February 1838) Richard Bentley.

Sketches of Young Gentlemen. Illustrated by Phiz. Chapman & Hall.

Life and Adventures of Nicholas Nickleby. By Charles Dickens. With Illustrations by Phiz (Hablot Browne). (Nine numbers published monthly from April to December.) Chapman & Hall.

1839

Life and Adventures of Nicholas Nickleby. (Eleven numbers, the last being a double number, published monthly from January to October. Issued complete in the latter month, with dedication to William Charles Macready.) Chapman & Hall.

Sketches by Boz. Illustrative of Every-day Life and Every-day People. With forty Illustrations by George Cruikshank. (The first complete edition, issued in monthly parts uniform with *Pickwick* and *Nickleby*, from November 1837 to June 1839, with preface dated 15th of May 1839.) Chapman & Hall.

1840

Sketches of Young Couples; with an urgent Remonstrance to the Gentlemen of England, being Bachelors or Widowers, at the present alarming crisis. By the Author of *Sketches of Young Gentlemen.* Illustrated by Phiz. Chapman & Hall.

1840~1841

Master Humphrey's Clock. By Charles Dickens. With Illustrations by George Cattermole and Hablot Browne. Three volumes. In addition to occasional detached papers and a series of sketches entitled MR. WELLER'S WATCH, occupying altogether about 90 pages of the first volume, 4 pages of the second, and 5 pages of the third, which have not yet appeared in any other collected form, this serial comprised the stories of *The Old Curiosity Shop* and *Barnaby Rudge*; each ultimately sold separately in a single volume, from which the pages of the *Clock* were detached. Chapman and Hall.

I. *Old Curiosity Shop* (1840)
Began at p. 37 of vol. i.; resumed at intervals up to the appearance of the ninth chapter; from the ninth chapter at p. 133, continued without interruption to the close of the volume (then issued with dedication to Samuel Rogers and preface from Devonshire-terrace, dated September 1840); resumed in the second volume, and carried on to the close of the tale at p. 223.

II. *Barnaby Rudge* (1841)
Introduced by brief paper from *Master Humphrey* (pp. 224–8), and carried to end of Chapter XII. in the closing 78 pages of volume ii., which was issued with a preface dated in March 1841. Chapter XIII. began the third volume, and the story closed with its 82nd chapter at p. 420; a closing paper from Master Humphrey (pp. 421–426) then winding up the Clock, of which the concluding volume was published with a preface dated November 1841.

1841

The Pic-Nic Papers by Various Hands. Edited by Charles Dickens. With Illustrations by George Cruikshank, Phiz, &c. Three volumes. (To this Book, edited for the benefit of Mrs. Macrone, widow of his old publisher, Dickens contributed a preface and the opening story, the *Lamplighter.*) Henry Colburn.

1842

American Notes for General Circulation. By Charles Dickens. Two volumes. Chapman and Hall.

1843

The Life and Adventures of Martin Chuzzlewit. With Illustrations by Hablot Browne. (Begun in January, and, up to the close of the year, twelve monthly numbers published). Chapman & Hall.

A Christmas Carol in Prose. Being a Ghost Story of Christmas. By Charles Dickens. With Illustrations by John Leech. (Preface dated December 1843.) Chapman & Hall.

1844

The Life and Adventures of Martin Chuzzlewit. With Illustrations by Hablot Browne. (Eight monthly numbers issued; the last being a double number, between January and July; in which latter month the completed work was published, with dedication to Miss Burdett Coutts, and Preface dated 25th of June.) Chapman & Hall.

Evenings of a Working Man. By John Overs. With a Preface relative to the Author, by Charles Dickens. (Dedication to Doctor Elliotson, and Preface dated in June.) T. C. Newby.

The Chimes: a Goblin Story of some Bells that Rang an Old Year out and a New Year in. By Charles Dickens. With Illustrations by Maclise R.A., Stanfield R.A., Richard Doyle, and John Leech. Chapman & Hall.

1845

The Cricket on the Hearth. A Fairy Tale of Home. By Charles Dickens. With Illustrations by Maclise R.A., Stanfield R.A., Edwin Landseer

R.A., Richard Doyle, and John Leech. (Dedication to Lord Jeffrey dated in December 1845.) Bradbury & Evans (for the Author).

1846

Pictures from Italy. By Charles Dickens. (Published originally in the *Daily News* from January to March 1846, with the title of "Travelling Letters written on the Road.") Bradbury & Evans (for the Author).

Dealings with the Firm of Dombey and Son, Wholesale, Retail, and For Exportation. By Charles Dickens. With Illustrations by Hablot Browne. (Three monthly numbers published, from October to the close of the year.) Bradbury & Evans. (During this year Messrs. Bradbury & Evans published "for the Author," in numbers uniform with the other serials, and afterwards in a single volume, *The Adventures of Oliver Twist, or the Parish Boy's Progress.* By Charles Dickens. With 24 Illustrations by George Cruikshank. A new Edition, revised and corrected.).

The Battle of Life. A Love Story. By Charles Dickens. Illustrated by Maclise R.A., Stanfield R.A., Richard Doyle, and John Leech. (Dedicated to his "English Friends in Switzerland.") Bradbury & Evans (for the Author).

1847

Dealings with the Firm of Dombey and Son. (Twelve numbers published monthly during the year.) Bradbury & Evans.

First Cheap Issue of the Works of Charles Dickens. An Edition, printed in double columns, and issued in weekly three-halfpenny numbers. The first number, being the first of *Pickwick,* was issued in April 1847; and the volume containing that book, with preface dated September 1847, was published in October. New prefaces were for the most part prefixed to each story, and each volume had a frontispiece. The first series (issued by Messrs. Chapman and Hall, and closing in September 1852) comprised *Pickwick, Nickleby, Curiosity Shop, Barnaby Rudge, Chuzzlewit, Oliver Twist, American Notes, Sketches by Boz,* and *Christmas Books.* The second (issued by Messrs. Bradbury & Evans, and closing in 1861) contained *Dombey and Son, David Copperfield, Bleak House,* and *Little Dorrit.* The third, issued by Messrs. Chapman & Hall, has since included

Great Expectations (1863), *Tale of Two Cities* (1864), *Hard Times* and *Pictures from Italy* (1865), *Uncommercial Traveller* (1865), and *Our Mutual Friend* (1867). Among the Illustrators employed for the Frontispieces were Leslie R.A., Webster R.A., Stanfield R.A., George Cattermole, George Cruikshank, Frank Stone A.R.A., John Leech, Marcus Stone, and Hablot Browne.

1848

Dealings with the Firm of Dombey & Son: Wholesale, Retail and for Exportation. (Five numbers issued monthly, the last being a double number, from January to April; in which latter month the complete work was published with dedication to Lady Normanby and preface dated Devonshire-terrace, 24th of March.) Bradbury & Evans.

The Haunted Man and the Ghost's Bargain. A Fancy for Christmas Time. By Charles Dickens. Illustrated by Stanfield R.A., John Tenniel, Frank Stone A.R.A., and John Leech. Bradbury & Evans

1849

The Personal History of David Copperfield. By Charles Dickens. With Illustrations by Hablot Browne. (Eight parts issued monthly from May to December.) Bradbury & Evans.

1850

The Personal History of David Copperfield. By Charles Dickens. Illustrated by Hablot Browne. (Twelve numbers issued monthly, the last being a double number, from January to November; in which latter month the completed work was published, with inscription to Mr. and Mrs. Watson of Rockingham, and preface dated October.) Bradbury & Evans.

Household Words. On Saturday the 30th of March in this year the weekly serial of *Household Words* was begun, and was carried on uninterruptedly to the 28th of May 1859, when, its place having been meanwhile taken by the serial in the same form still existing, *Household Words* was discontinued.

Christmas Number of *Household Words. Christmas.* To this Dickens contributed *A Christmas Tree.*

1851

Christmas Number of *Household Words. What Christmas Is.* To this Dickens contributed *What Christmas Is as We Grow Older.*

1852

Bleak House. By Charles Dickens. With Illustrations by Hablot Browne. (Ten numbers, issued monthly, from March to December.) Bradbury & Evans.

Christmas Number of *Household Words. Stories for Christmas.* To this Dickens contributed *The Poor Relation's Story,* and *The Child's Story.*

1853

Bleak House. By Charles Dickens. Illustrated by Hablot Browne. (Ten numbers issued monthly, the last being a double number, from January to September, in which latter month, with dedication to his "Companions in the Guild of Literature and Art," and preface dated in August, the completed book was published.) Bradbury & Evans.

A Child's History of England. By Charles Dickens. Three vols. With frontispieces from designs by F. W. Topham. Reprinted from *Household Words,* where it appeared between the dates of the 25th of January 1851 and the 10th of December 1853. (It was published first in a complete form with dedication to his own children in 1854.) Bradbury & Evans.

Christmas Number of *Household Words. Christmas Stories.* To this Dickens contributed *The School Boy's Story,* and *Nobody's Story.*

1854

Hard Times. For These Times. By Charles Dickens. (This tale appeared in weekly portions in *Household Words,* between the dates of the 1st of April and the 12th of August 1854; in which latter month it was published complete, with inscription to Thomas Carlyle.) Bradbury & Evans.

Christmas Number of *Household Words. The Seven Poor Travellers.* To this Dickens contributed three chapters. I. *In the City of Rochester;* II. *The Story of Richard Doubledick;* III. *The Road.*

1855

Little Dorrit. By Charles Dickens. Illustrated by Hablot Browne. The first number published in December. Bradbury & Evans.

Christmas Number of *Household Words. The Holly-Tree.* To this Dickens contributed three branches. I. *Myself;* II. *The Boots;* III. *The Bill.*

1856

Little Dorrit. By Charles Dickens. Illustrated by Hablot Browne. (Twelve numbers issued monthly, between January and December.) Bradbury & Evans.

Christmas Number of *Household Words.* THE WRECK OF THE GOLDEN MARY. To this Dickens contributed the leading chapter: THE WRECK.

1857

Little Dorrit. By Charles Dickens. Illustrated by Hablot Browne. (Seven numbers issued monthly, the last being a double number, from January to June, in which latter month the tale was published complete, with preface, and dedication to Clarkson Stanfield.) Bradbury & Evans.

The Lazy Tour of Two Idle Apprentices, in *Household Words* for October. To the first part of these papers Dickens contributed all up to the top of the second column of page 316; to the second part, all up to the white line in the second column of page 340; to the third part, all except the reflections of Mr. Idle (363–5); and the whole of the fourth part. All the rest was by Mr. Wilkie Collins.

Christmas Number of *Household Words. The Perils of Certain English Prisoners.* To this Dickens contributed the chapters entitled *The Island of Silver-Store,* and *The Rafts on the River.*
The First Library Edition of the Works of Charles Dickens. The first volume, with dedication to John Forster, was issued in December 1857, and the volumes appeared monthly up to the 24th, issued in November 1859. The later books and writings have been added in subsequent volumes, and an addition has also been issued with the illustrations. To the second volume of the *Old Curiosity Shop,* as issued in this edition, were added 31 *"Reprinted Pieces"* taken from

Dickens's papers in *Household Words*; which have since appeared also in other collected editions. Chapman & Hall.

Authorized French Translation of the Works of Dickens. Translations of Dickens exist in every European language; but the only version of his writings in a foreign tongue authorized by him, or for which he received anything, was undertaken in Paris. Nickleby was the first story published, and to it was prefixed an address from Dickens to the French public dated from Tavistock-house the 17th January 1857. Hachette.

1858

Christmas Number of *Household Words*. A House to Let. To this Dickens contributed the chapter entitled *Going into Society*.

1859

All the Year Round, the weekly serial which took the place of *Household Words*. Began on the 30th of April in this year, went on uninterruptedly until Dickens's death, and is continued under the management of his son.

A Tale of Two Cities. By Charles Dickens. Illustrated by Hablot Browne. This tale was printed in weekly portions in *All the Year Round*, between the dates of the 30th of April and the 26th of November 1859; appearing also concurrently in monthly numbers with illustrations, from June to December; when it was published complete with dedication to Lord John Russell.

Christmas Number of *All the Year Round*. THE HAUNTED HOUSE. To which Dickens contributed two chapters. I. THE MORTALS IN THE HOUSE. II. THE GHOST IN MASTER B'S ROOM.

1860

HUNTED DOWN. A Story in two Portions. (Written for an American newspaper, and reprinted in the numbers of *All the Year Round* for the 4th and the 11th of August.)

THE UNCOMMERCIAL TRAVELER. By Charles Dickens. (Seventeen papers, which had appeared under this title between the dates of 28th of January and 13th of October 1860 in *All the Year Round*,

were published at the close of the year, in a volume, with preface dated December. A later impression was issued in 1868, as a volume of what was called the Charles Dickens Edition; when eleven fresh papers, written in the interval, were added; and promise was given, in a preface dated December 1868, of the Uncommercial Traveller's intention "to take to the road again before another winter sets in." Between that date and the autumn of 1869, when the last of his detached papers were written, *All the Year Round* published seven "New Uncommercial Samples" which have not yet been collected. Their title's were, i. Aboard ship (which opened, on the 5th of December 1868, the New Series of *All the Year Round*); ii. A Small Star in the East; iii. A Little Dinner in an Hour; iv. Mr. Barlow; v. On an Amateur Beat; vi. A Fly-Leaf in a Life; vii. A Plea for Total Abstinence. The date of the last was the 5th of June 1869; and on the 24th of July appeared his last piece of writing for the serial he had so long conducted, a paper entitled *Landor's Life*.)

Christmas Number of *All the Year Round*. A Message from the Sea. To which Dickens contributed nearly all the first, and the whole of the second and the last chapter: *The Village*, *The Money*, and *The Restitution*; the two intervening chapters, though also with insertions from his hand, not being his.

Great Expectations. By Charles Dickens. Begun in *All the Year Round* on the 1st of December, and continued weekly to the close of that year.

1861

Great Expectations. By Charles Dickens. Resumed on the 5th of January and issued in weekly portions, closing on the 3rd of August, when the complete story was published in three volumes and inscribed to Chauncy Hare Townshend. In the following year it was published in a single volume, illustrated by Mr. Marcus Stone. Chapman & Hall. (the words there used "on *Great Expectations* closing in June 1861" refer to the time when the Writing of it was closed: it did not close in the Publication until August, as above stated).

Christmas Number of *All the Year Round*. Tom Tiddler's Ground. To which Dickens contributed three of the seven chapters. I. *Picking Up Soot and Cinders*; II. *Picking Up Miss Kimmeens*; III. *Picking Up the Tinker*.

1862

Christmas Number of *All the Year Round. Somebody's Luggage.* To which Dickens contributed four chapters. I. *His Leaving It Till Called For*; II. *His Boots*; III. *His Brown-Paper Parcel*; IV. *His Wonderful End.* To the chapter of *His Umbrella* he also contributed a portion. iii. 351; 370.

1863

Christmas Number of *All the Year Round. Mrs. Lirriper's Lodgings.* To which Dickens contributed the first and the last chapter. I. *How Mrs. Lirriper Carried on the Business*; II. *How the Parlours Added a Few Words.*

1864

Our Mutual Friend. By Charles Dickens. With Illustrations by Marcus Stone. Eight numbers issued monthly between May and December. Chapman & Hall.

Christmas Number of *All the Year Round. Mrs. Lirriper's Legacy.* To which Dickens contributed the first and the last chapter. I. *Mrs. Lirriper Relates How She Went On, and Went Over*; II. *Mrs. Lirriper Relates How Jemmy Topped Up.*

1865

Our Mutual Friend. By Charles Dickens. With Illustrations by Marcus Stone. In Two Volumes. (Two more numbers issued in January and February, when the first volume was published, with dedication to Sir James Emerson Tennent. The remaining ten numbers, the last being a double number, were issued between March and November, when the complete work was published in two volumes.) Chapman & Hall. *Christmas Number* of *All the Year Round. Doctor Marigold's Prescriptions.* To this Dickens contributed three portions. I. *To Be Taken Immediately.* II. *To Be Taken for Life*; III. The portion with the title of *To Be Taken with a Grain of Salt*, describing a Trial for Murder, was also his.

1866

Christmas Number of *All the Year Round. Mugby Junction.* To this Dickens contributed four papers. I. *Barbox Brothers*; II. *Barbox Brothers and Co.* III. *Main Line—the Boy at Mugby.* IV. *No. 1 Branch Line—the Signal-Man.*

1867

The Charles Dickens Edition. This collected edition, which had originated with the American publishing firm of Ticknor and Fields, was issued here between the dates of 1868 and 1870, with dedication to John Forster, beginning with Pickwick in May 1868, and closing with the Child's History in July 1870. The *Reprinted Pieces* were with the volume of *American Notes*, and the *Pictures from Italy* closed the volume containing *Hard Times*. Chapman & Hall.

Christmas Number of *All the Year Round. No Thorourghfare.* To this Dickens contributed, with Mr. Wilkie Collins, in nearly equal portions. With the new series of *All the Year Round*, which began on the 5th of December 1868, Dickens discontinued the issue of Christmas Numbers.

1868

A Holiday Romance. George Silverman's Explanation. Written respectively for a *Child's Magazine*, and for the *Atlantic Monthly*, published in America by Messrs. Ticknor and Fields. Republished in *All the Year Round* on the 25th of January and the 1st and 8th of February 1868.

1870

The Mystery of Edwn Drood. By Charles Dickens, with twelve illustrations by S. L. Fildes. (Meant to have comprised twelve monthly numbers, but prematurely closed by the writer's death in June.) Issued in six monthly numbers, between April and September. Chapman & Hall.

APPENDIX II:
THE WILL OF CHARLES DICKENS

"I, Charles Dickens, of Gadshill Place, Higham in the county of Kent, hereby revoke all my former Wills and Codicils and declare this to be my last Will and Testament. I give the sum of £1000 free of legacy duty to Miss Ellen Lawless Ternan, late of Houghton Place, Ampthill Square, in the county of Middlesex. I Give the sum of £19 19 0 to my faithful servant Mrs. Anne Cornelius. I Give the sum of £19 19 0 to the daughter and only child of the said Mrs. Anne Cornelius. I Give the sum of £19 19 0 to each and every domestic servant, male and female, who shall be in my employment at the time of my decease, and shall have been in my employment for a not less period of time than one year. I Give the sum of £1000 free of legacy duty to my daughter Mary Dickens. I also give to my said daughter an annuity of £300 a year, during her life, if she shall so long continue unmarried; such annuity to be considered as accruing from day to day, but to be payable half yearly, the first of such half-yearly payments to be made at the expiration of six months next after my decease. If my said daughter Mary shall marry, such annuity shall cease; and in that case, but in that case only, my said daughter shall share with my other children in the provision hereinafter made for them. I Give to my dear sister-in-law Georgina Hogarth the sum of £8000 free of legacy duty. I also give to the said Georgina Hogarth all my personal jewellery not hereinafter mentioned, and all the little familiar objects from my writing-table and my room, and she will know what to do with those things. I Also Give to the said Georgina Hogarth all my private papers whatsoever and wheresoever, and I leave her my grateful blessing as the best and truest friend man ever had. I Give to my eldest son Charles my library of printed books, and my engravings and prints; and I also give to my son Charles the silver salver presented to me at Birmingham, and the silver cup presented to me at Edinburgh, and my shirt studs, shirt pins, and sleeve buttons. And I Bequeath unto my said son Charles and my son Henry Fielding Dickens, the sum of £8000 upon trust to invest the same, and from time to time to vary the investments thereof, and to pay the annual income thereof to my wife during her life, and after her decease the said sum of £8000 and the investments thereof shall be in trust for my children (but subject as to my daughter Mary to the proviso hereinbefore contained) who being a son or sons shall have attained or shall attain the age of twenty-one years or being a daughter or daughters shall have attained or shall attain that age

Georgina Hogarth

or be previously married, in equal shares if more than one. I Give my watch (the gold repeater presented to me at Coventry), and I give the chains and seals and all appendages I have worn with it, to my dear and trusty friend John Forster, of Palace Gate House, Kensington, in the county of Middlesex aforesaid; and I also give to the said John Forster such manuscripts of my published works as may be in my possession at the time of my decease. And I

RIGHT: Henry Fielding Dickens and Francis Jeffrey Dickens, photograph, late 1850s

496

Devise and Bequeath all my real and personal estate (except such as is vested in me as a trustee or mortgagee) unto the said Georgina Hogarth and the said John Forster, their heirs, executors, administrators, and assigns respectively, upon trust that they the said Georgina Hogarth and John Forster, or the survivor of them or the executors or administrators of such survivor, do and shall, at their, his, or her uncontrolled and irresponsible direction, either proceed to an immediate sale or conversion into money of the said real and personal estate (including my copyrights), or defer and postpone any sale or conversion into money, till such time or times as they, he, or she shall think fit, and in the meantime may manage and let the said real and personal estate (including my copyrights), in such manner in all respects as I myself could do, if I were living and acting therein; it being my intention that the trustees or trustee for the time being of this my Will shall have the fullest power over the said real and personal estate which I can give to them, him, or her. And I Declare that, until the said real and personal estate shall be sold and converted into money, the rents and annual income thereof respectively shall be paid and applied to the person or persons in the manner and for the purposes to whom and for which the annual income of the monies to arise from the sale or conversion thereof into money would be payable or applicable under this my Will in case the same were sold or converted into money. And I Declare that my real estate shall for the purposes of this my Will be considered as converted into personalty upon my decease. And I Declare that the said trustees or trustee for the time being, do and shall, with and out of the monies which shall come to their, his, or her hands, under or by virtue of this my Will and the trusts thereof, pay my just debts, funeral and testamentary expenses, and legacies. And I Declare that the said trust funds or so much thereof as shall remain after answering the purposes aforesaid, and the annual income thereof, shall be in trust for all my children (but subject as to my daughter Mary to the proviso hereinbefore contained), who being a son or sons shall have attained or shall attain the age of twenty-one years, and being a daughter or daughters shall have attained or shall attain that age or be previously married, in equal shares if more than one. Provided Always, that, as regards my copyrights and the produce and profits thereof, my said daughter Mary, notwithstanding the proviso hereinbefore contained with reference to her, shall share with my other children therein whether she be married or not. And I Devise the estates vested in me at my decease as a trustee or mortgagee unto the use of the said Georgina Hogarth and John Forster, their heirs and assigns, upon the trusts and subject to the equities affecting the same respectively. And I Appoint the said Georgina Hogarth and John Forster executrix and executor of this my Will, and Guradians of the persons of my children during their respective minorities. And Lastly, as I have now set down the form of words which my legal advisers assure me are necessary to the plain objects of this my Will, I solemnly enjoin my dear children always to remember how much they owe to the said Georgina Hogarth, and never to be wanting in a grateful and affectionate attachment to her, for they know well that she has been, through all the stages of their growth and progress, their ever useful self-denying and devoted friend. And I Desire here simply to record the fact that my wife, since our separation by consent, has been in the receipt from me of an annual income of £600, while all the great charges of a numerous and expensive family have devolved wholly upon myself. I emphatically direct that I be buried in an inexpensive, unostentatious, and strictly private manner; that no public announcement be made of the time or place of my burial; that at the utmost not more than three plain mourning coaches be employed; and that those who attend my funeral wear no scarf, cloak, black bow, long hat-band, or other such revolting absurdity. I Direct that my name be inscribed in plain English letters on my tomb, without the addition of 'Mr.' or 'Esquire.' I conjure my friends on no account to make me the subject of any monument, memorial, or testimonial whatever. I rest my claims to the remembrance of my country upon my published works, and to the remembrance of my friends upon their experience of me in addition thereto. I commit my soul to the mercy of God through our Lord and Saviour Jesus Christ, and I exhort my dear children humbly to try to guide themselves by the teaching of the New Testament in its broad spirit, and to put no faith in any man's narrow construction of its letter here or there. In Witness whereof I the said Charles Dickens, the testator, have to this my last Will and Testament set my hand this 12th day of May in the year of our Lord, 1869.

"Signed published and declared by the above-named Charles Dickens the testator as and for his last Will and Testament in the presence of us (present together at the same time) who in his presence at his request and in the presence of each other have hereunto subscribed our names as witnesses.

—*Charles Dickens.*

"G. Holsworth," 26 Wellington Street, Strand.
"Henry Walker," 26 Wellington Street, Strand.

"I, Charles Dickens of Gadshill Place near Rochester in the county of Kent Esquire declare this to be a Codicil to my last Will and Testament which Will bears date the 12th day of May 1869. I Give to my son Charles Dickens the younger all my share and interest in the weekly journal called 'All the Year Round,' which is now conducted under Articles of Partnership made between me and William Henry Wills and the said Charles Dickens the younger, and all my share and interest in the stereotypes stock and other effects belonging to the said partnership, he defraying my share of all debts and liabilities of the said partnership which may be outstanding at the time of my decease, and in all other respects I confirm my said Will. In Witness whereof I have hereunto set my hand the 2nd day of June in the year of our Lord, 1870.

"Signed and declared by the said Charles Dickens, the testator as and for a Codicil to his Will in the presence of us present at the same time who at his request in his presence and in the presence of each other hereunto subscribe our names as witnesses.

—*Charles Dickens.*

"G. Holsworth," 26 Wellington Street, Strand.
"Henry Walker," 26 Wellington Street, Strand.

The real and personal estate—taking the property bequeathed by the last codicil at a valuation of something less than two years' purchase; and of course before payment of the legacies, the (inconsiderable) debts, and the testamentary and other expenses,—amounted, as nearly as may be calculated, to £93,000.

J. F. Palace Gate House, Kensington, 22nd of January, 1874

TEXT CREDITS

p. 39: Slater, Michael, *Charles Dickens* (New Haven and London: Yale University Press, 2009), pp. 619–621. Used by permission of Yale University Press.

p. 66: Arnold, Gaynor, *Girl in a Blue Dress* (Birmingham: Tindal Street Press, 2008), p. 105. Used by permission of the author, Gaynor Arnold, and Tindal Street Press.

p. 78: Whitman, Walt, "Boz and Democracy," *Brother Jonathan*, repr. in *The Collected Writings of Walt Whitman: The Journalism,* ed. by Herbert Bergman, Vol. 1 (New York: Peter Lang, 1998), pp. 35–38

p. 99: Cruse, Amy, *The Victorians and Their Books* (London: George Allen and Unwin, 1935), pp. 171–172. Used by permission of Harper Collins Publishers Ltd.

p. 119: Hayward, Jennifer, *Consuming Pleasures: Active Audiences and Serial Fictions from Dickens to Soap Opera* (Kentucky: University Press of Kentucky, 1997), pp. 21, 45–46. Reprinted with the permission of the author, Jennifer Hayward.

p. 148: Patten, Robert, "Copyright," *The Oxford Reader's Companion to Dickens*, ed. by Paul Schlicke (Oxford: Oxford University Press, 2000), pp. 123–124. Used by permission of Oxford University Press.

p. 193: Davis, Paul, *The Lives and Times of Ebenezer Scrooge* (New Haven: Yale University Press, 1990), pp. 4–5. Courtesy of Yale University Press.

p. 204: Hawksley, Lucinda, *Katey: The Life and Loves of Dickens's Artist Daughter* (London: Doubleday, 2006), pp. 37–39. Reprinted with the permission of the author, Lucinda Hawksley.

p. 214: Newsom, Robert, "Roman Catholic Church," *The Oxford Reader's Companion to Dickens*, ed. by Paul Schlicke (Oxford: Oxford University Press, 2000), pp. 510–11. Used by permission of Oxford University Press.

p. 268: Lester, Valerie Browne, *Phiz: The Man Who Drew Dickens* (London: Chatto and Windus, 2004), pp. 129–30. Used by permission of The Random House Group Ltd.

p. 292: Patten, Robert L, 'Publishing in Parts', in *Palgrave Advances in Charles Dickens Studies*, ed. Robert L. Patten and John Bowen (Basingstoke: Palgrave, 2005), pp. 11–12, 19, 32–33. Reproduced with permission of Palgrave Macmillan.

p. 389: Andrews, Malcolm, *Charles Dickens and His Performing Selves: Dickens and the Public Readings* (Oxford: Oxford University Press, 2006). Used by permission of Oxford University Press.

p. 400: Andrews, Malcolm, *Charles Dickens and His Performing Selves: Dickens and the Public Readings* (Oxford: Oxford University Press, 2006), pp. 136–38. Used by permission of Oxford University Press.

p. 408: Ackroyd, Peter, *Dickens* (New York: Harper Collins, 1990), chapter 31. Used by permission of the author, Peter Ackroyd, and The Random House Group Ltd.

p. 430: Irving, John "The King of the Novel," *Trying to Save Piggy Sneed* (New York: Ballantine Books, 1996), pp. 363–66, 369–70. Reprinted with the permission of the author, John Irving.

p. 465: Allingham, Philip, 'Some Early Dramatic Solutions to Dickens's Unfinished Mystery' The Victorian Web, http://victorian.lang.nagoya-u.ac.jp/victorianweb/mt/adaptations/39.html Reprinted with the permission of the author, Philip Allingham and The Victorian Web.

EXCERPTED WORKS BY CHARLES DICKENS

A Christmas Carol and Other Christmas Writings
A Tale of Two Cities
American Notes
Bleak House
David Copperfield
Dombey and Son
Great Expectations
Hard Times
Little Dorrit
Martin Chuzzlewit
Master Humphrey's Clock, 3 volumes
Nicholas Nickleby
Oliver Twist
Our Mutual Friend
Pictures from Italy
Sketches by Boz
The Battle of Life
The Christmas Stories, ed. by Ruth Glancy
The Mystery of Edwin Drood
The Old Curiosity Shop
The Pickwick Papers

PERIODICALS AND NEWSPAPERS:

All The Year Round
The Daily News
Household Words
The Times

ADDITIONAL SOURCES

Collins, Philip, ed., *Dickens: The Critical Heritage* (London: Routledge and Kegan Paul, 1971)

Collins, Phillip, *Dickens and Crime* (London: Macmillan, 1962)

Nayder, Lillian, *Unequal Partners: Charles Dickens, Wilkie Collins, and Victorian Authorship* (London and Ithaca: Cornell University Press, 2002)

Slater, Michael, ed., *The Dent Uniform Edition of Dickens's Journalism* (London: Dent, 1998)

Storey, G., K. Tillotson and others (eds), *The Letters of Charles Dickens*, 12 vols (Oxford: Clarendon, 1965–2002)

ART CREDITS

THE CHARLES DICKENS MUSEUM, LONDON

The Charles Dickens Museum in London is the world's most important collection of material relating to the great Victorian novelist and social commentator. The only surviving London home of Dickens (from 1837 until 1839) was opened as a Museum in 1925 and is still welcoming visitors from all over the world in an authentic and inspiring surrounding.

Images are reproduced by courtesy of the Charles Dickens Museum, London, except for the following.

THE BRIDGEMAN ART LIBRARY

Guildhall Library, City of London/The Bridgeman Art Library: pp. 31, 394–395
Private Collection/The Bridgeman Art Library: pp. 46–47, 99, 323
Yale Center for British Art, Paul Mellon Collection, USA/ The Bridgeman Art Library: p. 51
Private Collection/Barbara Singer/The Bridgeman Art Library: p. 83 right:
Private Collection/Ken Welsh/The Bridgeman Art Library: p. 87
Private Collection/The Stapleton Collection/The Bridgeman Art Library: pp. 106, 361
Private Collection/Photo © Bonhams, London, UK/The Bridgeman Art Library: pp. 126–127
Photo © Liszt Collection/The Bridgeman Art Library: pp. 288, 322
Private Collection/© Look and Learn/The Bridgeman Art Library: p. 313 left & right
Private Collection/Archives Charmet/The Bridgeman Art Library: p. 315
Eastgate Museum, Rochester, Kent, U.K./The Bridgeman Art Library: p. 371
The Bridgeman Art Library: p. 474

CORBIS

© Lebrecht Authors/Lebrecht Music & Arts/Corbis: pp. 85, 97, 182
© Fine Art Photographic Library/Corbis: p. 111
© Bettmann/Corbis: pp. 114, 115, 150–151, 340
© Historical Picture Archive/Corbis: pp. 220–221, 246

© Burstein Collection/Corbis: p. 285
© Leonard de Selva/Corbis: p. 417
© Lebrecht Music & Arts/Corbis: p. 427

GETTY IMAGES

Photo by Science & Society Picture Library/SSPL/Getty Images: p. 200
The Bridgeman Art Library/Getty Images: p. 225

THE IMAGE WORKS

© Mary Evans Picture Library/The Image Works: pp. 71, 137
© ArenaPal/Topham/The Image Works: p. 76
© Corporation of London/HIP/The Image Works: p. 185

LIBRARY OF CONGRESS PRINTS AND PHOTOGRAPHS

DIVISION: pp. 83 left, 144–145, 156–157, 168–169, 171, 238–239, 245, 252, 261, 314, 341, 343, 407, 443, 448–449, 452–453, 454, 458, 462

MARY EVANS PICTURE LIBRARY

Mary Evans Picture Library: Front cover (detail) and pp. 2, 62, 102, 193 right, 355
IBL Bildbyra/Mary Evans Picture Library: p. 73
Mary Evans Picture Library/Arthur Rackham: p. 193 left
© Illustrated London News Ltd/Mary Evans Picture Library: p. 368
Mary Evans Picture Library/Francis Frith: pp. 384–385

NATIONAL PORTRAIT GALLERY, LONDON

Tate 2011; on loan to the National Portrait Gallery, London: pp. 20, 177
© National Portrait Gallery, London: pp. 174, 277 left, 305, 308, 349, 388, 473, 482

NORTH WIND PICTURE ARCHIVES: p. 426

V&A IMAGES/VICTORIA AND ALBERT MUSEUM

V&A Images/Victoria and Albert Museum: pp. 14, 464, 486
Given by D. R. Crawfurth Smith. V&A Images/Victoria and Albert Museum: p. 61
Bequeathed by John Forster. V&A Images/Victoria and Albert Museum: p. 232

INDEX

ABOUT THE AUTHOR

JOHN FORSTER (1812–1876), author, biographer, and critic, is perhaps best known for his biography of his close friend and advisee, Charles Dickens. The first written, it continues to be the basis for much of what we know about Dickens. Forster rose to literary prominence in the 1830s, joining the circles of notable artists as a critic of drama and literature, and Forster first met Dickens in 1837, after he favorably reviewed the novelist's *Sketches by Boz*. Forster quickly became Dickens's trusted confidant and literary advisor: he first read most of the material that became *American Notes* (1842) in Dickens's colorful letters to him, and Forster saw the manuscripts of nearly all of Dickens's novels before they were published in his appointed role as Dickens's literary executor. In fact, Dickens modeled the character John Podsnap (*Our Mutual Friend*) on Forster, and the residence of lawyer Tulkinghorn in *Bleak House* is understood to be derived from Forster's home.

His other works include *Lives of the Statesmen of the Commonwealth* (1836–1839), *Treatise on the Popular Progress in English History* (1840), *Arrest of Five Members* (1860), *Debates on the Grand Remonstrance* (1860), *Sir John Eliot, A Biography* (1864), and the first volume of *The Life of Swift* (1875). During his career, Forster served as the editor for the *Foreign Quarterly Review*, *The Daily News*, and *The Examiner* (1847–56).

ABOUT THE CONTRIBUTORS

DR. HOLLY FURNEAUX is a lecturer in Victorian Studies at the University of Leicester. She is author of *Queer Dickens: Erotics, Families, Masculinities* (Oxford University Press, 2009), and co-editor, with Professor Sally Ledger, of *Dickens in Context* (Cambridge University Press, 2011). She has also co-edited special editions of the journals *19: Interdisciplinary Studies in the Long Nineteenth Century* and *Critical Survey,* and has written a number of articles and book chapters on Dickens and his contemporaries. Her current book project looks at male tenderness in wartime from the Crimea to the First World War.

JANE SMILEY is the author of numerous novels for adults and young adults, including *The Age of Grief, The Greenlanders, A Thousand Acres* (which won the Pulitzer Prize) *Moo, Horse Heaven,* and most recently *Private Life*. She has written many essays for such magazines as *Vogue, The New Yorker, Practical Horseman, Harper's, The New York Times Magazine, Allure,* and *The Nation,* and her subjects range from farming and horse training to child-rearing, literature, impulse buying, getting dressed, Barbie, and marriage. She is also the author of the non-fiction books *A Year at the Races, Thirteen Ways of Looking at the Novel,* and from Penguin Lives Series, a biography of Charles Dickens. In 2001, she was inducted into the American Academy of Arts and Letters and in 2006, she received the PEN USA Lifetime Achievement Award for Literature.